Belize, Guatemala & Southern Mexico

Peter Hutchison and Claire Boobbyer

The monuments themselves stand in the depths of a tropical forest, silent and solemn, strange in design, excellent in sculpture, rich in ornament... their uses and purposes and whole history so entirely unknown, with hieroglyphics explaining all but being perfectly unintelligible. Often the imagination was pained in gazing at them.

John Lloyd Stephens, Incidents of Travel In Central America, Chiapas and Yucatan (1841)

Highlights...
1 Oaxaca City ▸▸ p84.
2 San Cristóbal de las Casas ▸▸ p124.
3 Palenque ▸▸ p145.
4 Chichén Itzá ▸▸ p176.
5 Tulum and the Riviera Maya ▸▸ p195.
6 Northern cayes ▸▸ p229.
7 Antigua ▸▸ p278.
8 Lake Atitlán ▸▸ p308.
9 Chichicastenango ▸▸ p314.
10 Tikal ▸▸ p369.
Gulf of Mexico
Caribbean Sea
Pacific Ocean
Gulf of Tehuantepec
Gulf of Honduras
MEXICO
BELIZE
GUATEMALA
HONDURAS
YUCATAN
QUINTANA ROO
CAMPECHE
TABASCO
VERACRUZ
CHIAPAS
OAXACA
Progreso
Mérida
Hoctún
Tizimín
Cancún
Valladolid
Chichén Itzá
Cobá
Tulum
Isla Cozumel
Felipe Carrillo Puerto
Campeche
Champotón
Ciudad del Carmen
Escárcega
Candelaria
Chetumal
Orange Walk
Belize City
BELMOPAN
Dangriga
Placencia
Tikal
El Petén
Flores
Livingston
Río Dulce
Lago de Izabal
Copán
Veracruz
San Andrés Tuxtla
Cosamaloapan
Coatzacoalcos
Tuxtepec
Cuichapa
Villahermosa
Tenosique
Palenque
Isthmus of Tehuantepec
Monte Albán
Oaxaca
Palomares
Juchitán de Zarazoga
Tehuantepec
Arriaga
Tonalá
Tuxtla Gutiérrez
San Cristóbal de las Casas
Comitán
Huatulco
Pijijiapan
Tapachula
Quetzaltenango
Sierra de los Cuchumatanes
Chichicastenango
Lake Atitlán
GUATEMALA CITY
Antigua
Escuintla
N
100 km

Introduction

For 3000 years, great civilizations have fought to dominate southern Mexico, Belize and Guatemala, and it is not difficult to understand why. Blessed with a tropical climate, abundant wildlife and a varied landscape of mountains, rainforest and coast, this is a region whose natural appeal is instant and inspiring. The human story is no less compelling. Across the region, monumental ruins are the custodians of the Classic Maya world, gradually revealing secrets that have been hidden for generations. Early colonial churches and palaces stand testament to the conquering power and Christian zeal of the Spanish era. And the modern world leaves its footprint, too, as it struggles to balance cultural and environmental conservation with the pressures of business and tourism. The intermingling of these influences is what makes the region so beguiling – and overwhelming. Delve into the past at Tikal, Palenque or Lamanai. Buy technicolour fabrics in Chichicastenango or San Cristóbal. Seek high adventure on a volcano trek, explore submarine delights on a scuba dive or just fly 'n' flop on beautiful beaches. And wherever you go, don't miss the chance to experience a local fiesta, which turns even the remotest village into a hypnotic whirlwind of colour and noise.

Contents

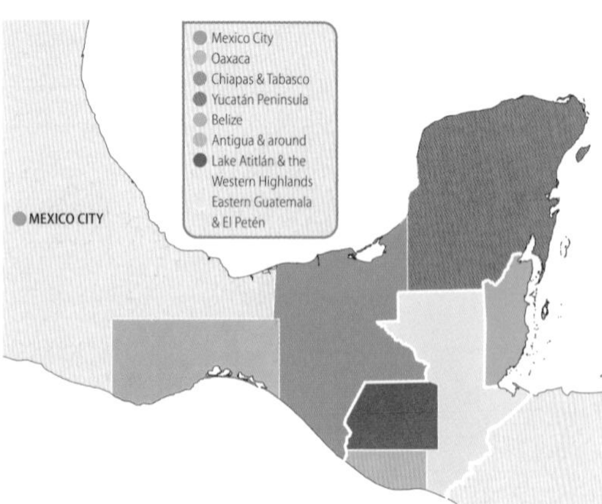
Mexico City
Oaxaca
Chiapas & Tabasco
Yucatán Peninsula
Belize
Antigua & around
Lake Atitlán & the Western Highlands
Eastern Guatemala & El Petén
MEXICO CITY

Yucatán Peninsula 158

Belize 214

Antigua & around 274

Lake Atitlán & the Western Highlands 304

Eastern Guatemala & El Petén 342

About the guide

Until recently, backpacking was the preserve of the impecunious student, stretching their pesos/baht/rupees as far as possible, sleeping in cockroach-infested, cell-like rooms and risking food poisoning by eating at the cheapest market stalls they could find. Today's backpackers, however, are different. They still have the same adventurous spirit but they probably don't have endless months to swan around the globe; they're interested in the people, culture, wildlife and history of a region and they're willing to splash out occasionally to ensure that their trip is truly memorable.

Footprint's Backpacker guides are designed precisely for this new breed of traveller. We've selected the best sights, sleeping options, restaurants and a range of adventure activities so that you can have the experience of a lifetime. With over 80 years experience of writing about Latin America, we hope that you find this guide easy to use, enjoyable to read and good to look at.

Essentials, the first chapter, deals with practicalities: introducing the region and suggesting where and when to go, what to do and how to get around; we give the lowdown on visas, money, health and transport, and provide overviews of history, culture and wildlife. The rest of the guide is divided into area-based chapters, colour-coded for convenience, with an extra chapter on **Mexico City** for those visitors that use this city as their gateway to the region. At the start of each chapter, a highlights map gives an instant overview of the area and its attractions. Follow the cross references to the district that interests you to find a more detailed map, together with a snapshot of the area, showing the amount of time you will need, how to get there and move around, and what to expect in terms of weather, accommodation and restaurants. **Special features** include expert tips, inspiring travellers' tales, suggestions for busting your budget and ideas for going that little bit further.

We use a range of symbols throughout the guide to indicate the following information:
Sleeping
Eating
Entertainment
Festivals
Shopping
Activities and tours
Transport
Directory

Please note that hotel and restaurant codes, pages 25 and 27, should only be used as a guide to the prices and facilities offered by the establishment. It is at the discretion of the owners to vary them from time to time.

Footprint feedback We try as hard as we can to make each Footprint guide as up to date as possible but, of course, things always change. If you want to let us know about your experiences – good, bad or ugly – then don't delay, go to www.footprintbooks.com and send in your comments.

Essentials

Guatemalan women in the Western Highlands

Where to go

If time is limited, by the far the best option is to get an open-jaw flight where you fly into one city and out of another. The cheapest points of entry are usually Mexico City or Cancún but Guatemala City and Belize City are good alternatives if you want to concentrate on those countries.

One week

A one-week trip will require careful planning and prioritizing. Either take internal flights, if you want to cover a lot of ground, or limit yourself to just one country or area to keep travel time to a minimum. Flying into Belize, head straight for **San Ignacio** to explore the caves and forest, with a possible side trip to **Tikal** in Guatemala, before relaxing on **Caye Caulker**. In Guatemala, your first stop must be **Antigua**, followed by a couple of days at **Lake Atitlán** before heading to **Chichicastenango** to stock up on souvenirs. A trip to **Todo Santos** or a flight to **Tikal** will easily fill the rest of the week. Deciding on a Mexico itinerary is harder, due to its size. A smart choice, with convenient flights, would be to enter at **Cancún** to explore the Yucatán region by bus or car, including the key Maya sites at **Chichén Itzá**, or even **Palenque**, before returning to the coast around **Tulum** for a couple of days on the beach.

Two weeks

Building on the one week options, you have the chance to cross a border or two. If you fly into **Mexico City**, you should spend a couple of days in the capital, before heading south by air or bus to the lovely city of **Oaxaca**. From here, surf bums will make straight for the **Pacific Coast**; alternatively head east to the Maya heartland around **San Cristóbal de las Casas**. From there you can easily cross south into the Guatemalan highlands or stay in Mexico to visit **Palenque** and the Yucatán Peninsula. Flying into Guatemala City, you can explore the mountains beyond **Antigua** at leisure, before heading north to **Tikal** or east across the Honduras border to visit the Maya ruins at **Copán**. Cross into Belize for some jungle adventures around **San Ignacio** or snorkelling and diving around the **cayes** and the **Blue Hole**, before flying out of Belize City. From Cancún, you could extend the one week itinerary to include more of the **Riviera Maya** and the Yucatán and still have time to cross into Belize and onto Flores, Santa Elena and **Tikal**.

One month

A month is long enough to explore the entire Maya Route – you could even do it in three weeks at a push. Start from **Cancún**, head across to **Palenque**, stopping to explore **Chichén Itzá**, **Uxmal** and the **Puuc Route** on the way. From Palenque drop down to **San Cristóbal de las Casas** and then over the border to **Lake Atitlán** and **Antigua**. Head north to **Tikal**, then east into Belize taking in **Xunantunich** and **Lamanai**, before making your way back to Mexico via Chetumal. You'd have to be really keen on the Maya world to take in all that sightseeing, so mix it up with a spot of adventure along the way. A more balanced itinerary might start from **Mexico City**, heading south to **Oaxaca** and east to **San Cristóbal**, with a side trip to **Palenque**. Continue to **Antigua** for a short Spanish course, before heading across to **Belize** for a few days diving or jungle exploration. Then head north via **Tikal**, to the Yucatán, for either more ruins or to chill on the beaches, before flying out of Cancún.

(Clockwise from top left) Temple of the Inscriptions, Palenque, Mexico; Zunil, Guatemala; Caye Caulker, Belize; Volcán San Pedro, Guatemala.

When to go

The best time to visit this area is between **October** and **April**, although there are slight regional variations. The **rainy season** works its way up from the south beginning in May and running through until August, September and even October. This is also **hurricane season** along the Caribbean (check for hurricanes at www.huracan.com). Despite the high profile of Hurricane Mitch and a few lesser-known local hurricanes and tropical storms, landfall is relatively rare. You also shouldn't be put off by the term 'rainy season', if this is your only opportunity for travel as, in most places and in most years, heavy rain falls for just an hour or two each day.

The most important regional celebrations are **Semana Santa** (Easter), the **Day of the Dead** (2 November) and **Christmas**. Beyond that each country celebrates wildly on **Independence Day**: 15 September in Guatemala, 21 September in Belize and 16 September in Mexico. Other fiestas are held throughout the year. **August** is vacation time for Mexicans and Central Americans so accommodation is scarce especially in the smaller resorts.

Sports and activities

Two varied coastlines and a host of different landscapes and climates makes this region perfectly suited to outdoor adventures. Facilities for adventure tourism tend to develop in correlation with general tourist services so always make sure the infrastructure and equipment is adequate before signing up for a potential dangerous activity. Also check the experience and qualifications of operators and guides. In Belize, tour organizers must be approved by the Tour Guide Association and should have a licence to prove it. In Mexico, **AMTAVE** (Associación Mexicana de Turismo de Aventura y Ecoturismo; www.amtave.org) regulates many specialist agencies for sea kayaking, rafting, climbing and other adventure sports and is making steady progress in promoting and protecting ecotourism alongside such pursuits (see page 16). Also check out the website, http://gorp.away.com/index.html

Archaeology

In a region with such a rich cultural heritage, archaeology is a big attraction. Where possible, try to use operators that use locals to help with the expeditions, so there is some economic benefit to the local community.

★ **Head for**
Cahal Pech ›› *p249* **El Pilar** ›› *p249* **Xunantunich** ›› *p250* **Caracol** ›› *p253* **Piedras Negras** ›› *p374*

ⓘ **Archaeology Department**, Belize University, Belmopan, T822-2106. Recommended tour operators are **Maya Expeditions**, 15 Calle "A", 14-07, Zona 10, Guatemala City, T2363-4955, www.mayaexpeditions.com and **Explorations**, 27655 Kent Road, Bonita Springs, Florida, FL 34135, T1-941 992 9660; both use archaeologists and Maya specialists as guides.

Canyoning and caving

Belize has some of the longest caving systems in the world. The main attractions are the natural crystal formations and the artefacts and paintings left in caves used by the Maya. In the Yucatán, water-filled caves and caverns known as cenotes offer the chance for swimming and cave diving.

Specialist experience is required to explore many caves and caverns in the region, although there are some notable exceptions in western Belize. In all countries, government permission is required to enter unexplored systems.

★ **Head for**
Valladolid (for cenote swimming) ›› *p178* **Tulum** (for cenote diving) ›› *p208* **San Ignacio** ›› *p249* **Caves Branch Jungle Lodge** ›› *p265* **Lanquín** ›› *p361* **Finca Ixobel** ›› *p374*

Cycling/mountain biking

Cycling is an excellent way to experience the region, although cyclists face heavy traffic in and around towns, poor road surfaces in remote areas and a lack of specialized spare parts, particularly for mountain bikes. That said, mountain biking is an increasingly popular activity in Guatemala, with tracks and paths across the country and numerous operators offering guided bike tours. Those in Antigua often sell cycling gear.

Diving and snorkelling

Belize and Mexico offer some of the best diving in the world. Belize is top for safety and opportunity, although it tends to be more expensive than elsewhere in the region. The largest barrier reef in the Western Hemisphere is located offshore here, with beautiful coral formations, including the world-famous Blue Hole. The Mexican state of Quintana Roo,

Top tips

How big is your flipper?

Diving is popular in Belize and the Yucatán due to the warm water and accessible reefs. However, there are decreasing numbers of small fish – an essential part of the coral lifecycle – and, in Belize, the coral around the most popular cayes is dying, probably as a result of tourism pressures. Do your bit to avoid further damage.

- ✔ Practise your snorkelling technique at the beach or in a swimming pool before you venture out to the reef.
- ✔ Encourage the boat owners who are taking you to the reef not to damage the coral in any way (ie by dropping the anchor on it).
- ✔ When diving on the reef, control your initial descent, so that you don't whack into the reef below.
- ✖ Don't touch the reef, either with your body or with your fins, tanks and tubes. Even the gentle brush of a flipper can remove the protective covering from a coral colony, causing its death.
- ✖ Don't remove anything from the reef, however small or pretty, unless it's a piece of rubbish, in which case pick it up and dispose of it suitably on land.
- ✖ Old wrecks and other underwater treasures are protected by law and must not be removed.
- ✔ Support local organizations, working to the protect the reef.

meanwhile, has warm water reefs close to the shore and visibility of over 30m.

Popular alternatives to sea diving include the water-filled cenotes around Tulum or high-altitude diving in Lake Atitlán.

★ **Head for**

Cozumel ▸▸ *p193* **Isla Mujeres** ▸▸ *p190* **Tulum** (for cenote diving) ▸▸ *p208* **Lighthouse Reef** ▸▸ *p231* **Turneffe Islands** ▸▸ *p232* **Panajachel** (for Lake Atitlán) ▸▸ *p322*

Budget buster

Sport fishing

On the 'flats' or further out in the deep sea, Belize offers some great fishing with snook, tarpon, permit and bonefish all up for grabs. Prices from US$150-US$400 a day.

Belize River Lodge, PO Box 459, Belize City, T225-2002, www.belizeriverlodge.com, is located on the river near the capital and offers combined fishing and accommodation packages for serious anglers.
Seasports Belize, 83 North Front Street, Belize City, T223-5505, www.seasportsbelize.com, offers 5-6 hrs deep sea, reef and flats fishing, as well as other watersports.

Fishing

This is a popular sport in all three countries. The Pacific coast of Guatemala is world renowned for deep-sea fishing Nov-Jun. Sport fishing for sailfish, marlin, wahoo, barracuda and tuna is also very popular along the Caribbean coast in Mexico and Belize, Mar-Jun, with bonefish, the most exciting fish for light tackle, found in great abundance on the flats. There's also river fishing for catfish, tarpon and snook. Costs, however, can be prohibitive, running to several hundred dollars for the day; see Budget buster, above. Note too that there are restrictions on the fishing or sale of lobster, shrimp and conch at certain times of year.

Head for
Huatulco » *p115* **Placencia** » *p271* **Belize City** » *above* **Northern Cayes** » *p229* **Turneffe Islands** » *p232* **Iztapa** (near Monterrico) » *p299*

ⓘ www.fishinginternational.com

Rafting and canoeing

The rivers of the region offer everything from sedate floats to Grade V rapids. The

Bone fishing on the flats, Belize

5 Best

Adventures

Diving or snorkelling in the cenotes around Tulum ›› *p208*
Diving the Blue Hole on Lighthouse Reef ›› *p231*
Hiking through the jungle to Actun Tunichil Muknal Cave ›› *p249*
Climbing Volcán Pacaya ›› *p285*
Rafting the Río Usumacinta to Piedras Negras ›› *p374*

season for whitewater rafting is generally Jul-Sep, when rivers are fuller, but Jan and Feb may be preferred as the climate is cooler. Kayaking and canoeing are popular in western Belize and are a great way of exploring the area's river systems.

★ **Head for**
Huatulco ›› *p116* **San Cristóbal de las Casas** ›› *p138* **San Ignacio** ›› *p256* **Río Usumacinta** ›› *p374*

Trekking and climbing

There are over 30 volcanoes in Guatemala, many of which can be climbed Oct-May. Although there are few technical routes, crampons, ice-axe and occasionally rope are required for safe ascents. Walking park of the way around Lake Atitlán is also popular. One of the attractions of remote trekking is to visit indigenous communities. However, you should be sensitive to the local reaction to tourist intrusion. Seek advice before trekking in Chiapas due, to the presence of rebel groups and the military that goes with them.

★ **Head for**
Victoria Peak ›› *262* **Antigua** (for volcanoes Pacaya, Agua and Fuego) ›› *p285* **Lake Atitlán north shore** ›› *p314* **Sierra Cuchumatanes** ›› *p325* **Volcán Santa María** ›› *p337*

ⓘ **Club Alpino Mexicano**, Córdoba 234, Col Roma (Metro Hospital General), Mexico City, T55-5574 9683, is very helpful and arranges (free) mountain hiking at weekends, also runs ice-climbing courses. The **Instituto**

Climbing Volcán Pacaya, Guatemala

How big is your footprint?

Ecotourism has expanded greatly in the region in recent years. Conservation is a particularly high priority in Belize, where tourism is a key foreign currency earner in the national economy and the fastest growing industry (see also p54).

Useful contacts
Associación Mexicana de Turismo de Aventura y Ecoturismo (AMTAVE), www.amtave.org, promotes and protects ecotourism alongside adventure activities. **Bioplanet@**, T55-5661 6156, www.bioplaneta.com, promotes cultural heritage and ecotourism. The **Belize Enterprise for Sustained Technology** (BEST), PO Box 35, Forest Drive, Belmopan, T802-3043, is a non-profit organization committed to the sustainable development of Belize's disadvantaged communities. **Belize Ecotourism Association**, T722-2119, promotes cultural heritage and ecotourism. Useful international contacts include **Tourism Concern**, www.tourismconcern.org.uk; the **Eco-Tourism Society** http://ecotourism.org, and **Conservation International**, www.ecotour.org.

- ✔ Choose a destination, tour operator or hotel with a proven ethical and environmental commitment; if in doubt ask.
- ✔ Spend money on locally produced (rather than imported) goods and services and use common sense when bargaining.
- ✔ Stay in local, rather than foreign-owned, accommodation; the economic benefits for host communities are far greater.
- ✔ Use water and electricity carefully; travellers may receive preferential supply while local communities are overlooked.
- ✔ Learn about local etiquette and culture; consider local norms of behaviour and dress appropriately.
- ✔ Protect wildlife and other natural resources.
- ✔ Always ask before taking photographs or videos of people.
- ✖ Don't give money or sweets to children – it encourages begging – instead give to a recognized project, charity or school.

Geográfico Militar in each country sells topographical maps. The authorities responsible for national parks and other protected areas are also useful sources of trekking information: **Instituto Nacional de Ecología**, www.ine.gob.mex, in Mexico; **CONAP**, http://conap.online.fr, in Guatemala; for Belize, see p54 . For volcano climbing agencies around Guatemala City and Antigua, see p299.

Watersports

The Pacific coast of Mexico is renowned for surfing. Sailing, sea kayaking and windsurfing are offered in tourist centres along the Caribbean coast of Mexico and Belize.

★ **Head for**
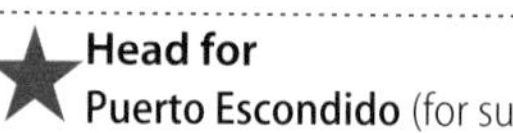
Puerto Escondido (for surfing) ⏩ *p114* **Huatulco** ⏩ *p115* **Cancún** ⏩ *p206* **Caye Caulker** ⏩ *p237* **Placencia** ⏩ *p270*

Taking a tour

Numerous operators offer organized trips to this region, ranging from a whistle-stop tour of the highlights to specialist trips that focus on a specific destination or activity. The advantage of travelling with a reputable operator is that your transport, accommodation and activities are all arranged for you in advance – particularly valuable if you only have limited time in the region or you don't speak Spanish. By travelling independently, however, you can be much more flexible and spontaneous about where you go and what you do. You will be able to explore less visited areas, practise your Spanish and you will save money, if you budget carefully. A list of specialist tour operators can be found in Essentials A-Z, page 42. See also How big is your footprint?, page 16.

Getting there and flying around

Arriving by air

The majority of international flights to this region arrive at Mexico City (MEX, page 59), Cancún (CUN, page 189), Guatemala City (GUA, page 283) or Belize City (BZE, page 219), with the first two receiving by far the most flights. One way and return tickets are available to all these destinations. Also enquire about 'Open Jaws' (flying into one point and returning from another). Some airlines are flexible on the age limit for student/youth and discount fares, others are more strict. Do not assume student tickets are the cheapest; though they are often very flexible. Check whether you are entitled to any refund or re-issued ticket if you lose, or have stolen, a discounted air ticket. Some airlines require the repurchase of a ticket before you can apply for a refund, which will not be given until after the validity of the original ticket has expired. Airpasses for Mexico are often bought in conjunction with international flights so ask when booking if you plan to use internal flights, see page 21.

Flights from Europe

Most European airlines have a regular weekly service to **Mexico City** throughout the year, making it a useful entry/exit point, with the widest range of options and prices. Direct flights are available from London and Manchester with **British Airways**; from Amsterdam with **KLM**; from Frankfurt with **Lufthansa** and **AeroMéxico**; from Barcelona with **Iberia**; from Madrid with **Iberia** and **AeroMéxico**; from Paris with **Air France** and **AeroMéxico**. Most connecting flights in

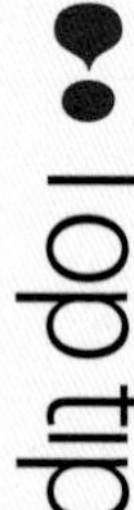

Transport

General

✔ If you're determined to cover a lot of ground in a short space of time, take an internal flight. Don't underestimate distances, especially in Mexico.

✔ For international journeys make sure you have small denominations of local currency or US dollars for border taxes.

✖ Travelling overnight in Chiapas, whether by bus or car, is dangerous and not recommended.

✖ Hitchhiking is relatively easily but not necessarily safe. Exercise caution.

Bus

✔ Once you know your travel plans, book tickets in advance, especially if you're travelling in the Yucatán Peninsula or during Christmas and the school holidays.

✔ Remember to take a jacket, jumper or blanket to counteract the intense air-conditioning on Mexican buses.

✔ In remote areas, lifts in the back of a pick-up are usually available, when bus services are few and far between.

Car

✔ If you're in a group or can afford it, renting a car for a few days in Mexico and Belize is definitely worthwhile. However, theirs is little point renting a car in Guatemala.

✔ At some tourist resorts, Cancún for example, you can pick up a VW Beetle convertible for US$25 per day.

✖ In general, hire cars are not permitted across international borders. Only one car rental company in Belize (Crystal – see p227) will release registration papers to enable cars to enter Guatemala or Mexico.

✖ Never take hitchhikers across an international border.

✖ Never leave a car unattended except in a locked garage or guarded parking space. Street children will generally protect your car fiercely in exchange for a tip. Lock the clutch or accelerator to the steering wheel with a heavy, obvious chain or lock.

✖ Don't wash the car: smart cars attract thieves.

✖ In the case of an accident do not abandon your vehicle. Call your insurance company immediately and do not leave the country without first filing a claim. Always carry with you, your policy identification card and the names of the company's adjusters.

Europe are through Madrid or Gatwick. Fares vary from airline to airline and according to time of year; between February and June they can be very low, commensurate with some fares to the USA. Check with a flight agency for the best deals.

There has also been an increase in the number of scheduled flights to **Cancún** as a gateway to the Yucatán, Belize and Guatemala. **British Airways** operates a daily flight from

London Gatwick, via Dallas Fort Worth; there are also flights from Amsterdam with **Martinair**; Frankfurt with **LTU** and **Condor**; Munich with **LTU** and **Condor**; Madrid with **AeroMéxico** and **Avianca**; Milan with **Lauda Air** and Paris with **American Airlines**.

With the exception of flights from neighbouring countries, all international services to **Belize** go via the USA (see below). Note that flights from European destinations to Miami or Houston do not connect with onward flights to Belize, so you have to stay overnight.

There are no direct flights to **Guatemala City** from the UK. However, **Air France** flies daily direct from Paris and **Iberia** flies from Madrid via Miami. Long-haul operators from Europe often take passengers across the Atlantic, normally to Miami, and then use **Taca**, for example, to link to Guatemala City.

Flights from the USA and Canada

Flights from the USA are plentiful and can be surprisingly cheap, if you get a special offer with an international carrier. A variety of airlines fly to **Mexico City** from all over the country, including **American Airlines**, **AeroMéxico**, **Delta**, **Continental**, **United**, **Northwest**, **Taesa** and **Americawest**; the main through points are Miami, Dallas/Fort Worth, Los Angeles and San Francisco. From Canada, there are flights from Montreal and Sault Ste Matie with **Mexicana**; from Toronto with **Mexicana** and **United**; and from Vancouver with **Japan Airlines**.

There are flights to **Cancún** from Albany, Atlanta, Baltimore, Buffalo (NY), Charlotte (NC), Chicago, Dallas/Fort Worth, Detroit, Houston, Indianapolis, Las Vegas, Los Angeles, Memphis, Miami, New Orleans, New York, Philadelphia, Phoenix, Pittsburgh, St Louis, San Francisco, Seattle/Tacoma and Washington DC; also from Montreal and Vancouver with **Mexicana**.

There are regular flights to **Belize** from Baltimore, Charlotte (North Carolina), Dallas/Fort Worth, Hartford, Houston, Miami, Minneapolis, New Orleans, New York and Washington DC, with **American Airlines**, **Continental**, **Grupo Taca** and **US Airways**.

There are flights to **Guatemala City** from Atlanta with **American** and **Delta**; from Chicago with **American**; from Houston with **Continental**; from Los Angeles with **United** and from Miami with **American** and **Grupo Taca**. From Canada, connections are made through San Salvador (El Salvador), Los Angeles or Miami.

Flights from Australia and New Zealand

Most flights are with **United** via Los Angeles and cost around AUS$2,500.

Discount flight agents

In the UK

Journey Latin America, 12-13 Heathfield Terr, London, W4 4JE, T020-8747 8315; 12 St Ann's Square, Manchester, M2 7HW, T0161-832 1441, www.journeylatinamerica.co.uk

South American Experience, 47 Causton St, London, SW1P 4AT, T020-7976 5511, www.southamericanexperience.co.uk

STA Travel, 6 Wrights Lane, London, W8 6TA, T0870-1606599, www.statravel.co.uk, with branches throughout the world. Specialists in low-cost student/youth flights and tours, also good for student IDs.

Trailfinders, 194 Kensington High St, London, W8 7RG, T0207- 938 3939, www.trailfinders.com

North America

Air Brokers International, 323 Geary St, Suite 411, San Francisco, CA94102, T01-800-883-3273, www.airbrokers.com

Discount Airfares Worldwide On-Line, www.etn.nl/discount.htm Discount agent links.

Exito Latin American Travel Specialists, 108 Rutgers St, Fort Collins, CO 80525, T1-800-655-4053; worldwide T970-482-3019, www.exito-travel.com

STA Travel, T1-800-781-4040, www.statravel.com Branches throughout

Over the border

An overland departure tax of US$37.50 is charged on leaving Belize. An unofficial tourist tax is usually charged in both directions at Guatemala land borders; bribery is rife so always ask for a receipt. *Customs and duty free ▸▸ p30. Visas and immigration ▸▸ p44.*

USA-Mexico Travelling overland from the US, the main border crossings are at Tijuana, Mexicali, Nogales, Ciudad Juárez, Piedras Negras, Nuevo Laredo and Matamoros. Note that you need private vehicle insurance and an import permit to bring a car into Mexico.

Mexico-Guatemala The principal border town is Tapachula, with a crossing over the Talismán Bridge (see p336) or at Ciudad Hidalgo (see p288). More interesting routes are via Ciudad Cuauhtémoc (see p130) or southeast from Palenque via Tenosique (see p147) or Frontera Echeverria (see p149) to Santa Elena/Flores.

Mexico-Belize The main border crossing is Chetumal/Santa Elena (see p198). There's a modern immigration terminal here and formalities are usually swift. A less widely used crossing, for non-vehicular travellers, is at La Unión/Blue Creek (not recommended unless you like a challenge). There are immigration facilities here but officials are only used to dealing with Mexicans and Belizeans, so delays are likely.

Belize-Guatemala The most commonly used crossing is between Benque Viejo del Carmen and El Petén (see p251), where the immigration office has recently been remodelled, reducing waiting times. Boat services link Punta Gorda and Puerto Barrios (see p264).

Belize-Honduras There is a boat service from Placencia, via Mango Creek, to Puerto Cortés (see p273). Obtain all necessary exit stamps and visas before sailing.

Guatemala-Honduras Links with Honduras are possible on the Caribbean near Corinto (see p350); for the ruins at Copán the best crossing is El Florido (see p347).

the US and Canada.
Travel CUTS, 187 College St, Toronto, ON, M5T 1P7, T1-866- 246-9762, www.travelcuts.com Student discount fares.

Australia and New Zealand

Flight Centre, 82 Elizabeth St, Sydney, T133-133, www.flightcentre.com.au; 205 Queen St, Auckland, T0800-243544, www.flightcentre.co.nz. With branches in other towns and cities.
STA Travel, 260 Hoddle St, Abbotsford VIC 3067, toll free on T1300-733035, www.statravel.com.au. In NZ: Level 8, 229 Queen St, Auckland, www.statravel.co.nz, T0508-782-872. Also in major towns and

university campuses.

Travel.com.au, 76-80 Clarence St, Sydney, T02-9249-6000, www.travel.com.au

Trailfinders, 8 Spring St, Sydney, NSW 2000, www.trailfinders.com.au, T1300-780212.

... and leaving again

When you buy your ticket, always check whether departure tax is included in the price. International departure tax is US$40 in **Mexico**, payable in dollars or pesos, US$30 in **Guatemala**, payable in dollars or quetzales, and US$35 in **Belize** (including PACT conservation tax; see page 54). The PACT tax, BZ$7.50, is payable by all foreign visitors on departure from the country. However, it must be paid only once every 30 days, so if you go to Tikal for a short trip from Belize, for example, keep your receipt in order not to pay again at the airport when you fly home.

Regional flights

Mexico Most medium sized towns are served with internal flights. **Mexicana**, www.mexicana.com, and **Aero California** provide airpasses, covering much of the country, valid for 3-90 days; eligible only to those arriving on transatlantic flights. These must be bought in advance and fares range from US$50 to US$400 per coupon. Sales tax is payable on domestic plane tickets bought in Mexico, 15%. Direct flights to **Flores/Santa Elena** (for Tikal) are available from Cancún, with **Grupo Taca**, see below. To avoid overcharging, the government has taken control of **taxi** services from airports to cities. Only those with government licences are allowed to carry passengers from the airport. No further tipping is then required, except when the driver provides some extra service for you.

From Belize City There are daily flights to **Flores** (Guatemala) with **Maya Island Air**, 6 Fort St, PO Box 458, Belize City, T233-1140, www.mayaislandair.com, and **Tropic Air**, Albert Street, Belize City T224-5671, www.tropicair.com, as well as regular flights to domestic destinations: Corozal, Big Creek, San Ignacio, Placencia, Dangriga, Punta Gorda and the cayes. In addition to the international airport, a municipal airstrip handles local flights, with services about US$15 cheaper each way. Charters are also available to airstrips where there are no scheduled flights, such as Gallon Jug or Central Farm near San Ignacio.

From Guatemala City There is 17% tax on all international tickets sold in Guatemala. Domestic departure tax is Q5/US$0.65. **Grupo Taca** (includes Aviateca, Lacsa, Nica and Inter), at the airport and at Hotel Intercontinental, Zona 10, Guatemala City, T5331-8222, T2470-8222, www.taca.com, www.grupotaca.com, has flights to **Cancún** and **Belize**, as well as domestic flights to **Flores**. **Tikal Jets**, 11 Av 7-15, Zona 13, Guatemala City, T2361-0042-44, www.tikaljets.com, flies to **Flores**, **Belize City**, **Mexico City** and **Cancún**. **Mexicana** flies to **Mexico City**.

Getting around by land and sea

Mexico

Bus The Mexican bus system is extensive but can be both complicated and confusing, with companies operating out of numerous different terminals in each town. (www.magic-bus.com is a very useful source of information). Services, ranging from second-class to first-class (tickets 10% more) and luxury (more again), are generally well organized, clean and prompt. Luxury and some first class services have reclining seats,

Travellers' tale

All aboard the chicken bus

If you haven't heard the sound of the bus *ayudante* shouting 'Guate, Guate Guate' in a full pitch crescendo perforating your ear drum, as part of an entire choral work of bus destinations yelled at full volume, competing with baskets of squawking chickens, and tearful children buried in colourful bundles on the backs of their mothers, while perching half a buttock on a seat designed for two, but bummed up with five, trying to balance your bag, *chocobanano*, water bottle, and wadge of quetzal notes, as well as avoiding being knocked out by a flying pom pom from a Maya headdress and the straps of a 101 small rucksacks, while trying to tune out from the Latin singers crooning from the crackling radio, and paying a respectful nod to the plastic Christ figure swinging acrobatically from the rear mirror as you lurch round a bend and lose your 3 square inch 'space' on the chicken bus... then, you have not experienced Guatemala.

Guatemala's chicken buses were built for school kids in America. The seats and the spaces between them were designed for the legs and bums of little 'uns. Despite these considerable design constraints, about a hundred or so bodies are squeezed on for every journey and if you obeyed the *ayudante* each time he shouted: 'Señores, más atrás por favor' (move back, please), you'd be bundled up on the overhead racks.

Once your journey begins, it will soon become apparent that the driver is aiming to graduate with honours from the Guatemalan School of Kamikaze Bus Tactics. Journeys that should take 50 minutes start nudging at the half-hour barrier and you're likely to spot the skeletal remains of another bus down a ravine. These routes include Santa Cruz del Quiché to Chichicastenango, Sacapulas to Santa Cruz del Quiché and between Los Encuentros and the capital on the Pan-American Highway.

Buses pull up as if they were making a pit stop on a Formula One racing track, so be ready for your knees to be shunted into the metal seat in front of you – a fleece acting as knee pads may soften the blow. The exchange of people and goods happens at lightning speed: bags are thrown up or down, and passengers are either helped up the high step into the back of the bus or hurried in at the front. Dawdlers are not welcome.

Once you've squeezed into your tiny space, check out the interior design: rows of naked seated women with pointed Madonna-like breasts decorate many a front windscreen. There may also be huge stickers of the Virgin Mary on the ceiling or even a giant pair of Salvador Dalí lips, which glow red each time the brake light goes on. *Claire Boobbyer*

toilets, drinks and videos. Second class services are more basic and stop at more intermediate destinations. Useful companies for southern Mexico are **ADO GL** (T01-800 702 8000,

Guatemalan 'chicken' bus

www.adogl.com.mx), **Cristóbal Colón** (T01-800 702 8000, www.cristobalcolon.com.mx), **Grupo Estrella** (T01-800 507 5500, www.estrellablanca.com.mx) and **Primera Plus** (www.primeraplus.com.mx). Tickets should be booked in advance for longer journeys and during busy periods.

Car Car hire is expensive, from US$400 a week for a basic model with 15% sales tax added; double the price if you want to drop the car off at a different destination at the end of your trip. It can be cheaper to arrange hire in the US or Europe, but rentals booked abroad cannot be guaranteed. Make sure the deal gives you unlimited mileage. The age limit is normally at least 25, and a deposit is required, normally set against a credit card. Renting a vehicle without a credit card is nearly impossible.

Petrol stations are run by PEMEX so fuel costs the same throughout the country: roughly US$0.55 a litre. All *gasolina* is unleaded. Toll roads (*cuota*) charge about one peso per kilometre. Some tolls can be avoided, but this may involve unpaved roads, which should not be attempted in the wet. The toll-free roads (*carreteras libres*) are normally perfectly acceptable and more interesting, as they travel through small towns and countryside. A helpline for road accidents is available by phoning 02 and asking the operator to connect you to Mexico City T55-5684 9715 or 5684 9761.

To bring your own car into Mexico you will need private vehicle insurance, an import permit, a certificate of ownership, a registration card and a driver's licence. This is not a practical option unless you are travelling the length of Mexico from the USA.

Belize

Boat Several **boats** ferry passengers to the most popular cayes of Caye Caulker and Ambergris Caye, with regular daily services from the Marine Terminal by the swing bridge in Belize City and from Corozal. Further south, boat transport is available from Dangriga and Placencia to nearby cayes and to Puerto Cortés, Honduras. There are also boats from Punta Gorda to Puerto Barrios and Lívingston, Guatemala.

Bus US-style school buses are used for public transport but distances are short enough to be bearable. Schedules are generally regular and reliable but you should buy tickets in advance. Most buses have no luggage compartments so large bags are stacked at the back; get a seat at the back to keep an eye on your gear. Trucks can carry passengers to many isolated destinations, when there are no bus services.

Car Car hire is expensive in Belize: expect to pay between US$65 for a Suzuki Samuri and US$125 for an Isuzu Trooper per day. Valid International Driving Licences are accepted in place of Belize driving permits. Third-party insurance is mandatory and can be purchased at any border (Bz$25 a week, Bz$50 a month for both cars and motorbikes), with cover of up to Bz$20,000 from the **Insurance Corporation of Belize**, 7 Daly Street, Belize City, T224-5328.

Cautious driving is advised as road conditions, although improving, are totally unpredictable, especially in the Mountain Pine Ridge area where good maps are essential. Emory King's annually updated *Drivers' Guide to Belize* is helpful when driving to remote areas. Fuel costs about Bz$6.58 (regular) or Bz$6.87 (super) for a US gallon but can be more in remote areas. Unleaded petrol is now available.

Guatemala

Bus Guatemala has an extensive network of bus routes. The notorious 'chicken' buses are mostly in a poor state and overloaded (see page 22) but faster and more reliable Pullman services operate on some routes. Many long-distance buses leave very early in the morning. Correct fares should be posted, however bus drivers often charge tourists more; ask the locals, then tender the exact fare. Most buses will take bicycles on the roof for two-thirds of the passenger fare. On several popular tourist routes, for example Antigua-Panajachel, there are **minibus shuttles**, which are comfortable, convenient and recommended by INGUAT.

Sleeping

Mexico

The price of mid-range hotels and *hospedajes* is very reasonable by US and European standards, with rooms normally charged at a flat rate. Single rooms are around 80% the price of a double, so sharing works out cheaper and a room with three or more beds is often very economical even in the mid-price range. In all establishments, always check the room before paying. *Casas de huéspedes* are usually the cheapest places to stay and are often dirty with poor plumbing. A hotel (or *hospedaje*) tax, ranging between 1% and 4%, according to the state, is generally levied only when a formal bill is issued.

During peak season (Nov-Apr) accommodation is often fully booked and the week after Semana Santa (Easter) is normally a holiday, so prices remain high. Discounts on hotel prices can often be arranged in the low season (May-Oct), but this is more difficult in the Yucatán.

Motels and auto-hotels (with curtains over the garage and red and green lights above the door) are not usually places where guests stay the whole night, although they may be acceptable if you wish to avoid sleeping in your car. Most campsites are called 'Trailer Parks', although tents are usually allowed.

Belize

Accommodation throughout the country varies greatly. For the budget traveller there are options in most towns of interest, although prices are higher than in neighbouring countries. Mid-range accommodation tends to be clean but simple and prices rise steeply with every service option added. Top-of-the-range places offer better deals when booked in advance and frequently offer all-inclusive packages, with transport and activities. The area around San Ignacio has several secluded forest hideaways of varying price and, to the south, there are

A bed for the night

This guide focuses on the best accommodation in the mid-range category (A-D). Bottom-end budget accommodation (E-F) is only included if it represents excellent value for money or is the only option in a certain area. 'Budget buster' boxes highlight more expensive options (LL-L) that offer a really unique or special experience.

LL (over US$150) to A (US$46-65) Hotels in these categories can be found in most of the large cities but especially where there is a strong concentration of tourists or business travellers. They should offer extensive leisure and business facilities (including email), plus restaurants and bars. Credit cards are usually accepted and dollars cash changed typically at poor rates.

B (US$31-45) Hotels in this category should provide more than the standard facilities and a fair degree of comfort. Many include a good breakfast and offer extras such as a TV, minibar, air conditioning and a swimming pool. They may also provide tourist information and airport pick-ups. Most accept credit cards.

C (US$21-30) and D (US$12-20) Hotels in these categories range from very comfortable to functional and there are some real bargains to be had. You should expect your own bathroom, constant hot water, a towel, soap and toilet paper. There is sometimes a restaurant and a communal sitting area. Hotels used to catering for foreign tourists and backpackers often have luggage storage, money exchange and kitchen facilities.

E (US$7-11) and F (under US$6) Hotels in these categories are often extremely simple with bedside or ceiling fans, shared bathrooms and little in the way of furniture.

5 Best

Alternative places to stay

Na Bolom, San Cristóbal de las Casas ▸▸ *p133*
Genesis Retreat, Ek-Balam ▸▸ *p182*
Lamanai Outpost Lodge, Orange Walk ▸▸ *p245*
Ek Tun, San Ignacio ▸▸ *p254*
San Marcos La Laguna, Lake Atitlán ▸▸ *p317*

options for staying in Maya communities that maintain the cultural identity of the region. All hotels are subject to 7% government hotel tax (room rate only). Camping is gaining in popularity, with private facilities to be found in most tourist areas, offering a variety of amenities. Camping on the beaches, in forest reserves or in other public places is not allowed.

Guatemala

The tourist institute INGUAT publishes a list of maximum prices for single, double and triple occupancy of hundreds of hotels throughout the country in all price ranges. It will deal with complaints about overcharging, if you can produce bills or other proof. Room rates should be posted in all registered hotels but ask if taxes (*impuestos*) are included when you are given the room rate. Busiest seasons are Easter, December and the European summer holiday (July-August). Most low-budget hotels do not supply toilet paper, soap or towels. There are no official campsites .

Eating and drinking

Mexico

For most Mexicans, food is an integral part of their national identity. However, there are so many regional specialities all over the country that it is difficult to use such a simple term as 'Mexican cooking'. The use of chilli as the principal seasoning means that Mexican food is usually perceived as spicy or hot but the use of maize as the key element in many dishes is even more characteristic. It has, after all, been the staple crop in Central America for centuries. Various shapes and sizes of corn *tortillas* are served, with a variety of fillings, as *antojitos* (light snacks that may be eaten by themselves or as a starter), usually garnished with a hot sauce.

Eat *chapulines*

Drink Corona

Restaurant price codes

The following price codes are used for restaurants and other eateries in this guide. Prices refer to the cost of a meal for one person, with a drink.

- over US$15
- US$8-15
- under US$8

Some of the most common are *quesadillas, sopes, tostadas, tlacoyos* and *gorditas*. Other dishes, such as *mole* (chicken or turkey prepared in a chilli-based sauce) or *pozole* (a pot-au-feu with a base of maize and stock) are closer to indigenous traditions. Oaxaca state has a particularly varied and distinctive cuisine (see page 87).

An egg-based breakfast is followed by a heavy lunch between 1400 and 1500 and a light supper between 1800 and 2000. Meals in modest establishments cost US$1.50-2 for breakfast, US$2-3 for set lunch (US$3-5.50 for a special *comida corrida*) and US$5-8 for dinner (generally no set menu). À la carte meals at modest establishments cost about US$7; a very good meal can be had for US$11 at a middle-level establishment.

The beer is good: brands include Dos Equis-XX, Montejo, Corona, Sol, Superior and Negra Modelo, a dark beer. Some beer is drunk with lime juice and a salt-rimmed glass, or *michelada* with chilli sauce (both available in Oaxaca). Local wine is cheap and improving in quality. The native drinks are *pulque*, the fermented juice of the agave plant (those unaccustomed to it should not over-indulge), *tequila*, made mostly in Jalisco, and *mezcal* from Oaxaca; also distilled from agave plants. *Mezcal* usually has a *gusano de maguey* (worm) in the bottle, considered to be a particular delicacy. Tequila and *mezcal* rarely have an alcoholic content above 40-43%; Herradura, Sauza and Cuervo tequilas are recommended.

Belize

Dishes here suffer from a preponderance of rice'n'beans – a cheap staple to which you add chicken, fish, beef and so on. Douse liberally with a splash of Marie Sharp's hot pepper sauce to liven up the dish. Belize has some of the best burritos in Central America but you have to seek them out, hidden away in stalls at the markets. Along the coastal region and on the cayes seafood is abundant, fresh and cheap, but try not to buy lobster between 15 February and 14 June (out of season) as stocks are low. Presentation varies and vegetables are not always served with a meat course. Better restaurants offer a greater variety and a break from the standards, often including a selection of Mexican dishes; there are also many Chinese restaurants, not always good and sometimes overpriced. Belikin beer is the local brew,

Cooking *antojitos* in Guatemala

average cost US$1.75 a bottle. Many brands of local rum are also available. Wines and liqueurs are made from local fruit, including *nanche*, made from *crabou* fruit and very sweet, as is cashew wine. All imported food and drink is expensive.

Guatemala

Tortillas, *tamales*, *tostadas*, etc are found everywhere. *Tacos* are less spicy than in Mexico. *Chiles rellenos*, chillies stuffed with meat and vegetables, are a speciality in Guatemala and may be *picante* (spicy) or *no picante*. *Churrasco*, charcoal-grilled steak, is often accompanied by *chirmol*, a sauce of tomato, onion and mint. *Guacamole* is also excellent. Local dishes include *pepián* (thick meat stew with vegetables) in Antigua; *patín* (tomato-based sauce served with *pescaditos*, small fish from Lake Atitlán wrapped in leaves) and *cecina* (beef marinated in lemon and bitter orange) from the same region. *Fiambre* is widely prepared for families and friends who gather on All Saints' Day (1 November). It consists of all kinds of meat, fish, chicken, vegetables, eggs or cheese served as a salad with rice, beans and other side dishes. Desserts include *mole* (plantain and chocolate), *torrejas* (sweet bread soaked in egg and *panela* or honey), *borracho* (cake soaked in rum) and *buñuelos* (similar to profiteroles) served with hot cinnamon syrup. For breakfast try *mosh* (oats cooked with milk and cinnamon), fried plantain with cream, black beans in various forms.

Local beers are good (Monte Carlo, Cabra, Gallo and Moza, a dark beer); bottled, carbonated soft drinks (*gaseosas*) are safest. Milk should be pasteurized. Freshly made *refrescos* and ice creams are delicious made of many varieties of local fruits; *licuados* are fruit juices with milk or water, but hygiene varies, so take care. Water should be filtered or bottled.

Shopping

Visiting a market in Guatemala or southern Mexico is always a memorable experience, not just for the amazing colours, sounds and smells but also for the bartering – a rite of passage for visitors to the region. Bartering is the norm in this area and, if you get good at it, you'll pick up some great bargains. That said, don't get so obsessed with haggling that you end up nit-picking over five cents; most vendors expect to receive about half their original asking price. Belize lacks the ethnic souvenirs of neighbouring Guatemala and Mexico but authentic purchases might include one of Marie Sharp's spicy sauces, a funky Belikan beer T-shirt or a CD of the infectious *punta* rock beat of Andy Palacio. Belize postage stamps are attractive and much in demand; a trip to the Philatelic Bureau in Belize City may provide you with your most treasured souvenir.

Unmissable markets

Mexican crafts

The crafts (*artesanía*) in Mexico are an amalgam of ancient and modern design, influenced by the traditional popular art forms of indigenous communities the length and breadth of the country. Colonial towns such as Oaxaca (see Buying Oaxacan crafts, page 100) and San Cristóbal de las Casas (page 137) are convenient market centres for buying a superb range of products from the surrounding region. The range of **textiles** is particularly wide. These can be spun in cotton, wool or synthetic fibres on the traditional *telar de cintura*, 'waist loom', or the *telar de pie*, a pedal-operated loom introduced by the Spanish. Look out for *sarapes* (a type of long poncho) and *rebozos* (fine cotton dresses) in Oaxaca state, especially in Santa Ana and Teotitlán del Valle. The best *huipiles* (traditional blouses without sleeves) are made and sold around San Cristóbal de las Casas, Tuxtla Gutiérrez and on the Tehuantepec isthmus, and the famous *guayabera* shirt is sold in Mérida. Woven *morrales* (shoulder bags) are found throughout the region, while wall-hangings, rugs and bedspreads are a speciality of Oaxaca. Buy **hammocks** (see page 184) and *henequen* (sisal) bags in the Yucatán, along with **Panama hats** from Becal. **Ceramics** are generally crafted out of baked clay or plaster and are polished or glazed or polychrome. Black and green-glazed pottery is produced in villages around Oaxaca city along with small animals, called *alebrijes*. Ceramic dolls are made on the Isthmus of Tehuantepec. Lacquer-ware, known as *maque* or *laca*, is a more regionalized craft found in Chiapas, particularly around Chiapa de Corzo. Mexican silver from Taxco is sold as **jewellery** all over the country, often combined with semi-precious stones such as onyx, obsidian, amethyst and turquoise, particularly in Oaxaca. **Masks**, depicting animals such as eagles, jaguars, goats, monkeys and coyotes, are used in ceremonies and rituals but are also sold in craft shops. From late October, you'll also find **papier mâche** crafts, associated with the Day of the Dead celebrations, particularly images of skeletons (*calaveras*).

Guatemalan crafts

Guatemala's markets and shops are overflowing with the best traditional crafts in the region. Perhaps the most visible are the brightly coloured **textiles**, produced throughout the Highlands. These are normally cheapest if bought in the town of origin; try to avoid middlemen and buy direct from the weaver. There are great textiles for sale at markets in San Francisco El Alto, Panajachel, Santiago Atitlán, Antigua and, most famously, at Chichicastenango, where the dizzying array of crafts and intense atmosphere make for a unmissable experience. **Pottery** and glassware are found all over the Highlands, with recycled glass for sale in Quetzaltenango. Gorgeous heavy blankets are sold in Momostenango. **Masks**, used in festive dancing, can be bought from markets, shops or direct from mask factories (*morerías*). For **leather** goods go to Antigua, Chinaulta, near Huehuetenango and Cobán. **Silverwork** is sold in villages in Alta Verapaz, while **wooden objects**, such as bowls, sculptures and salad spoons, are mainly found in the Petén. Guatemalan **coffee** is highly recommended, although the best is exported and the coffee sold locally is not vacuum-packed.

Accident & emergency

Contact the relevant emergency service and your embassy (p32). Make sure you obtain police /medical reports in order to file insurance claims.

Emergency services

Mexico T060
Belize Ambulance T90, Fire T90, Police T911
Guatemala Ambulance T128/123, Fire T122/123, Police T120/110.

Children

Travelling with children may bring you into closer contact with Latin American families. Officials tend to be more amenable where children are concerned and even thieves and pickpockets seem to have traditional respect for families.

If you're covering large distances, consider taking an internal flight. All airlines charge a reduced price for children under 12 and less for children under two but double check the child's baggage allowance – some are as low as 7 kg. On long-distance buses children generally pay half or reduced fares. For shorter trips it is cheaper, if less comfortable, to seat small children on your knee. In hotels and on sightseeing tours, always bargain for a family rate – often children can go free, although this means they are not always covered by the operator's travel insurance. Always carry a copy of your child's birth certificate and passport-size photos, and remember to pack enough toys, books and food for long journeys. For an overview of travelling with children look at www.babygoes2.com.

Customs & duty free

Mexico

The list of permitted items is extensive and generally allows for all items that could reasonably be for personal use, although large quantities of any item may attract suspicion. Adults entering Mexico are allowed to bring in up to 3 litres of wine, beer or spirits; 20 packs of cigarettes or 25 cigars or 200 g of tobacco, and medicines for personal use. Goods imported into Mexico with a value of more than US$1,000 (or computer equipment, with a value of more than US$4,000) have to be handled by an officially appointed agent.

Belize

Clothing and articles for personal use can be imported duty free, although laptop computers, video cameras, cellular phones, CD players and radios may be stamped on your passport to ensure they leave with you. Other import allowances are: 200 cigarettes or ½ lb of tobacco; one litre of alcohol; one bottle of perfume and an unspecified amount of non-Belizean currency. No fruit or vegetables may be brought into Belize; searches are infrequent, but thorough.

Guatemala

The following items may be brought into the country duty free: personal effects and articles for your own use, 2 bottles of spirits and 80 cigarettes or 100 g of tobacco. Temporary visitors can take in any amount in quetzales or foreign currencies; they may not, however, take out more than they brought in. The local equivalent of US$100 per person may be reconverted into US dollars on

Don't forget your toothbrush...

- Take as little as possible. Clothes that are quick and easy to wash and dry are a good idea. Loose-fitting clothes are more comfortable in hot climates and can be layered if it gets cooler.
- You can easily, and cheaply, buy things en route, but five musts are: good walking shoes, a sun hat, sunglasses, flip-flops and a sarong.
- Don't load yourself down with toiletries. They're heavy and can be bought everywhere. Items like contact lens solutions and tampons may be harder to find, so stock up in major cities.
- Keep a stash of toilet paper and tissues on your person.
- Other useful items are a Swiss Army knife (with corkscrew), a money belt, a headtorch/flashlight, the smallest alarm clock you can find, a padlock, dental floss and a basic medical kit.
- Pack photocopies of essential documents like passport, visas and travellers' cheque receipts just in case you lose the originals.
- Photographers should take all the film that they will require for the trip, ideally in a bag that is both water and dust proof.

departure at the airport, provided a ticket for immediate departure is shown.

Disabled

As in most Latin American countries, facilities for disabled travellers are severely lacking in this region. Most airports, as well as hotels and restaurants in major resorts, will have wheelchair ramps and adapted toilets but outside these areas wheelchair access is very limited, while facilities for the visually or hearing impaired are practically non-existent, even at major sights. Some travel companies specialize in tailormade holidays for individuals with a variety of disabilities. For general information, consult the Global Access-Disabled Travel Network website, www.geocities.com/Paris/1502.

Useful organizations

Directions Unlimited,123 Green Lane, Bedford Hills, NY 10507, T1-800-533-5343, T914-241 1700. A tour operator specializing in tours for disabled US travellers.

Disability Action Group, 2 Annadale Ave, Belfast BT7 3JH, T01232-491011. Information about access for British disabled travellers.

Disabled Persons' Assembly, PO Box 27-524, , Wellington 6035, New Zealand, T04-801-9100, gen@dpa.org.nz. Has lists of tour operators and travel agencies catering for the disabled.

Drugs

Mexico

Possession of even a small amount of illegal drugs is punishable by a minimum prison sentence of 10 years. Foreigners may be searched for drugs at state borders in Mexico, so carry copies of all medical prescriptions and a notice of any medical condition that needs a hypodermic syringe or emergency treatment. Keep medicines in the original container. If searched, cooperate with narcotics officers (who wear black and yellow, and have an identity number on a large fob attached to the belt); do not intrude, but watch the proceedings closely. Zipolite, on the Pacific Coast, has a bad reputation for drugs and drug-related crime, although it's cleaned up its act in recent years. Avoid deserted beaches on either coast, which may be used as drug-landing points.

Belize

Despite the apparent availability of illegal drugs, the penalties for possession of marijuana are six months in prison or a minimum US$3,000 fine.

Guatemala

Possession of illegal drugs will land you in prison for a minimum of 5 years. San Pedro on Lake Atitlán has a reputation as a drug haven but police presence has increased there in recent years.

Electricity

Mexico 125 volts AC. Some hotels have universal plugs.
Belize 110/220 volts single phase, 60 cycles for domestic supply. Some hotels use 12 volt generators.
Guatemala Generally 110 volts AC, 60 cycles. Electricity is generally reliable in the towns but can be a problem in remoter areas like Petén.

Embassies and consulates

Mexican

Australia, 14 Perth Av, Yarralumia, 2600 ACT, Canberra, T6273-3963, www.embassyofmexicoinaustralia.org
Belize, 18 North Park St, Belize City, T223-0193, www.sre.gob.mx/belice/
Canada, 45 O´Connor St, Suite 1000, K1P 1A4, Ottawa, Ont, T613-233-8988, www.embamexcan.com
Ireland, 43 Ailesbury Road, Ballsbridge 4, Dublin, T260-0699, www.sre.gob.mx/irlanda
New Zealand, 111-115 Customhouse Quay, 8th floor, Wellington, T472-5555, www.mexico.org.nz
South Africa, 1 Hatfield Sq, 3rd Floor, 1101 Burnett St, Hatfield 0083 Pretoria, PO Box 9077, 0001, T12-362-2822, www.sre.gob.mx/sudafrica.
UK, 42 Hertford St, Mayfair, London, W1Y 7JR, T7499-8586, www.embamex.co.uk
USA, 1911 Pennsylvania Av, NW, 20006 Washington DC, T728-1600, www.sre.gob.mx/eua

Belizean

For the latest information, refer to www.belize.gov.bz and click on diplomat link.
Canada (changes frequently), 1800 McGill College, Suite 2480, Montreal, Quebec H3A 3J6, T514-288-1687, F514-288-4998.
European Communities, Blvd Brand Whitlock 136, 1200 Brussels, Belgium, T/F+32-2-7326246, embelize@skynet.be
Guatemala and Central America, Edificio El Reformador 8th Floor, Suite 803, Av Reforma 1-50 Zone 9, Guatemala City, T334-5531, F334-5536.
Mexico, Nader 34, Cancún, Quintana Roo, T998-887 8631.
UK, High Commission, 22 Harcourt House, 19 Cavendish Square, London, W1G 0PL, T/F020-74914139.
USA, 2535 Massachusetts Av, NW Washington DC 20008, T/F202-332-6888.

Guatemalan

Australia and **New Zealand**, see Japan.
Belize, No 8 'A' St, Belize City, T2-33314, embbelice1@minex.gob.gt
Canada, 130 Albert St, Suite 1010, Ottawa, Ontario, KIP 5G4, T613-2337237, embcanada@minex.gob.gt
Honduras, C Arturo López Redezno 2421, Colonia Las Minitas, Tegucigalpa, T231-1543, embhonduras@minex.gob.gt
Japan, No 38 Kowa Bldg, Room 905, Nishi-Azabu, Minato-Ku, Tokyo 106, T3-38001830, embjapon@minex.gob.gt (also covers Australia, Bangladesh, India, Iraq, Philippines and Thailand).
Mexico, Av Explanada No 1025, Lomas de Chapultepec, 11000 México DF, T55-5540 7520.
UK, 13 Fawcett St, London SW10 9HN, T020-7351 3042

USA, 2220 R St NW, Washington DC, 20008, T202-745-4952, www.guatemala-embassy.org

Gay and lesbian

Many Latin American countries are not particularly liberal in their attitude to gays and lesbians. Even in cities, people are fairly conservative; they are likely to be even less open-minded in provincial towns and rural areas. Having said that, you'll find a gay scene, with bars and clubs, in most of the bigger cities and resorts. The Zona Rosa in Mexico City has a number of gay venues.

Health

See your GP or travel clinic at least six weeks before departure for general advice on travel risks and vaccinations. Try ringing a specialist travel clinic if your own doctor is unfamiliar with health in the region. Make sure you have sufficient medical travel insurance, get a dental check, know your own blood group and if you suffer a long-term condition such as diabetes or epilepsy, obtain a Medic Alert bracelet/ necklace (www.medicalalert.co.uk).

Vaccinations

There are no mandatory inoculations required to enter the region unless you are coming from a country where yellow fever is a problem. It is, however, advisable to vaccinate against hepatitis, typhoid, paratyphoid and poliomyelitis. Malaria prophylaxis is also strongly recommended. In 2004, the Mexican Secretariat of Health reported 64 cases of measles in the Federal District and the states of Mexico, Hidalgo, Campeche and Coahuila. Travellers who have never had measles should ideally be vaccinated with the MMR vaccine.

Health risks

There is some risk of malaria in the low-lying tropical zones of all three countries, especially in Eastern Guatemala. Also seek advice about dengue fever and protect yourself against mosquito bites; using insect repellent is the best prevention for both diseases. The most common ailment for visitors to Mexico is severe diarrhoea, known as 'Montezuma's Revenge'; locals recommend *Imecol* as treatment; if this doesn't work seek medical advice. Be wary of drinking water, milk, uncooked vegetables and peeled fruits throughout the region, especially in Guatemala, where carelessness on this point is likely to lead to amoebic dysentery. Cholera has been reported since 1991 in Guatemala and is also on the rise in Mexico. You should be particularly careful buying uncooked food in market *comedores* where hygiene may be doubtful. Insect bites should be scrutinized carefully to rule out the possibility of Chagas disease, leishmaniasis or botfly larvae. You may also pick up parasites if you swim in lakes and rivers. Hepatitis is a problem in Mexico; if you have not been vaccinated, gamma globulin is available at better pharmacies/chemists. HIV has increased in Belize over the past few years, transmitted by both sexual contact and blood transfusions; always practise safe sex. There may be a yellow fever risk in remote tropical areas of Guatemala.

Medical services

Social Security hospitals in Mexico are restricted to members, but will take visitors in emergencies; they are more up to date than the **Centros de Salud** and **Hospitales Civiles**, which are very cheap and open to everyone.

Medical services in Belize have improved in recent years with the completion of the **Karl Heusner Memorial Hospital** in Belize City, though many Belizeans still seek medical care for serious ailments in Guatemala City, where there are three good hospitals (see p303), but you must have full medical insurance or sufficient funds to pay for treatment.

Most small towns in Guatemala have clinics. Public hospitals are seriously underfunded; they may give you an examination for a nominal fee, but drugs are expensive.

Further information

www.btha.org British Travel Health Association.
www.cdc.gov US government site that gives excellent advice on travel health and details of disease outbreaks.
www.fco.gov.uk British Foreign and Commonwealth Office travel site has useful information on each country, people, climate and a list of UK embassies/consulates.
www.fitfortravel.scot.nhs.uk A-Z of vaccine/health advice for each country.
www.travelscreening.co.uk Travel Screening Services gives vaccine and travel health advice, email/SMS text vaccine reminders and screens returned travellers for tropical diseases.

Insurance

Always take out comprehensive insurance before you travel, including full medical cover and extra cover for any activities (hiking, rafting, diving, riding etc) that you may undertake. Check exactly what's being offered, the maximum cover for each element and also the excess you will have to pay in the case of a claim. Keep details of your policy and the insurance company's telephone number with you at all times and get a police report for any lost or stolen items.

Internet

Internet cafés are found in almost every town and tourist destination in Mexico and Guatemala, with more springing up daily. Internet cafés are less common in Belize due to the relatively high cost of telephone calls, although there are plenty in San Ignacio, Ambergris Caye and Caye Caulker. Rates vary from US$1-2 per hour in Mexico, US$2 and upwards in Belize, US$1-5 in Guatemala.

Regional websites

www.mundomaya.com Excellent site devoted to Maya culture.
www.visitcentroamerica.com A pool of Central American resources.
www.planeta.com A phenomenal resource for everything from ecotourism and language schools to cybercafés.
www.latinnews.com Up-to-date site with political comment.

Language

The official language of Mexico and Guatemala is Spanish. English is spoken at the best hotels and is increasingly common throughout Mexico, but there are few people who speak English outside the main tourist areas. Adding to the challenges of communication are many indigenous languages. English is the official language of Belize but half the population speak Creole or Spanish, particularly in border areas. A pocket dictionary and phrase book together with some initial study or a beginner's Spanish course before you leave are strongly recommended. Guatemala, and especially Antigua, is one of the biggest centres for learning Spanish in Latin America, see p302.

Amerispan, PO Box 58129, Philadelphia, PA 19103, USA, T1-800-879 6640 (USA & Canada), T215-751 1100 (worldwide), www.amerispan.com, offers language courses in Mexico, Guatemala and throughout Latin America.

Media

Latin America has more local and community radio stations than practically anywhere else in the world. A shortwave radio will allow you to absorb local culture, as well as pick up BBC World Service (www.bbc.co.uk /worldservice/) or the Voice of America (www.voa.gov).

Mexico

The influential daily newspapers are *Excelsior*, *Novedades*, *El Día*, *Uno Más Uno*, *El Universal*, *El Heraldo*, *La Jornada* (www.jornada.unam.mx, more to the left), *La Prensa* (tabloid, with the largest circulation) and *El Nacional* (mouthpiece of the government). *The News*, an English-language daily, is currently not available. The New York edition of the *Financial Times* and other British and European papers are available at Mexico City airport and a few other newsagents in the capital. *The Miami Herald* is stocked by most newspaper stalls. Current affairs, feature articles and advice on travel are also available online at www.mexicanwave.com and www.mexperience.com.

Belize

There are no daily newspapers in Belize. The following Sunday papers are generally available from Friday morning: the *Belize Times*, the *Guardian*, the *Reporter*, and *Amandala*. Good coverage of Ambergris Caye is provided by the *San Pedro Sun*, and *Placencia Breeze* covers Placencia. Small district newspapers are published sporadically. Local news is also covered by www.belizereport.com and www.belizenews.com, with links to the local newspapers.

Belize First!, www.belizefirst.com, a quarterly magazine published in the USA (Equator Travel Publications Inc, 287 Beaverdam Road, Candler, NC 28715, USA, F828-6671717), has articles on travel, life, news and history in Belize (US$29 a year in Belize, USA, Canada, Mexico, US$49 elsewhere).

Check out radio station **Love FM** (95.1FM; p225) and www.belizeweb.com for Belizean internet radio. www.belizenet.com, www.belize.net and www.belize.com are good search engines with general information. The government site, www.belize.gov.bz, is packed with official information. Other useful sites are given throughout the text.

Guatemala

The main newspaper is *Prensa Libre* (www.prensalibre.com); *Siglo Veintiuno* (www.sigloxxi.com) is also worth a look. Mega popular is *Nuestro Diario*, a tabloid with more pics than copy. The *Guatemala Post* (www.guatemalapost.com) is published in English. The *Revue* (www.revuemag.com), produced monthly in Antigua, carries articles, advertisements, lodgings, tours and excursions for Antigua, Pana, Xela, Río Dulce and Guatemala City. Also has coverage of El Salvador, Honduras and Belize. Other websites to consult include www.terra.com.gt, the Guatemala search engine at www.spanishconnection.com and www.guatemalaweb.com.

Money

Take US dollars in cash and traveller's cheques (TCs). Banks and *casas de cambio* in the region are increasingly able to change Euros but the US dollar is still the most readily accepted and exchanged. To exchange TCs, you may be asked to show your passport and even proof of purchase (keep it separate from your traveller's cheques). Also take a Visa credit card and a Plus or Cirrus debit card for ATM (*cajero automático*) withdrawals in Mexico and Guatemala. The rates of exchange on ATM withdrawals are the best available, although your bank or building society will charge a handling fee. Credit card transactions are normally at an officially recognized rate of exchange but are often subject to sales tax and a handling fee of up to 5%. For lost or stolen cards, call Visa T1-800-999-0115; MasterCard T1-800-999-1480; American Express T1-800-999-0245.

Whenever possible, change money at a bank or *casa de cambio* rather than from money changers on the street. Try to change any local currency before you leave the country or at the border.

Cost of travelling

A realistic, sustainable budget would be US$30-US$45 per day; rising considerably if you want to stay in good hotels, eat in the best restaurants or take part in lots of extra activities. In Mexico, expect to pay from US$20 for a decent room, US$10 for basic meals and around US$5 per hour for bus travel. Guatemala is generally cheaper than Mexico, while Belize tends to be the most expensive of the three. Beware tourist rates in the most popular areas of all three countries. There are bargains to be found throughout the region but also some opportunities to splash your cash – don't miss them.

Mexico

The monetary unit is the Mexican peso, represented by '$', making the potential of confusion great, especially in popular tourist places where prices are higher and often quoted in US$. In Feb 2005 the conversion rate was US$1=11 pesos. US$ are easily changed in all cities and towns and can often be used as an alternative currency in tourist areas. US$ traveller's cheques from any well-known bank are also widely accepted, especially AmEx and Visa. *Casas de cambio* are generally quicker than banks and stay open later; fees are not charged but their rates may not be as good. MasterCard, Visa and AmEx credit cards are widely accepted for payment of goods and services (6% tax often charged), for ATM cash withdrawals (widespread even in small towns) and for obtaining cash over the counter from banks.

Belize

The monetary unit is the Belizean dollar ($), stabilized at around US$1=BZ$2. Currency notes issued by the Central Bank are in denominations of BZ$100, 50, 20, 10, 5 and 2, along with coinage of BZ$2, BZ$1 and 50, 25, 10, 5 and 1 cents. US dollars are accepted everywhere and prices tend to be given in US$ for anything over BZ$100; make sure it is clear from the start whether you are being charged in US or Belizean dollars.

The government has recently restricted the exchange of foreign currency to government-licensed *casas de cambio*, but these only operate in major towns. You can still find some illegal money changers at the borders but the exchange rate is not as high as before and there is a risk of being arrested and fined. ATMs (no foreign debit cards) are available in Belize City but are not widespread in the rest of the country. All banks in Belize City have facilities to arrange cash advance on Visa.

Guatemala

The unit is the quetzal (GTQ), divided into 100 centavos. The conversion rate in Feb 2005 was US$1=GTQ7.70. There are coins of Q1, 50 centavos, 25 centavos, 10 centavos, 5 centavos and 1 centavo. The paper currency is for 50 centavos and Q1, 5, 10, 20, 50 and 100.

The majority of banks in cities and towns have ATMs that accept Visa/Plus credit and debit cards. MasterCard is only generally accepted at **G&T Continental** (where there is a daily withdrawal limit of US$65) and at **Credomatic/Banco de América Central**, which are few and far between. All banks will change US$ cash into quetzales, the majority will also change US$ traveller's cheques, although AmEx TCs are less easy to change outside the main cities and Thomas Cook TCs are not accepted. Most banks will accept Visa for a cash advance but usually charge up to 2% per transaction and give a less favourable rate of exchange. The majority of hotels, restaurants etc charge for use of credit cards – about US$3. Check before you sign. Neither MasterCard nor AmEx are widely accepted.

Opening hours

Mexico

Banks are open 0900-1330 Mon-Fri, some main branches are also open 0900-1230 Sat. Businesses are usually open 0900-1300 and 1400-1800. However, hours vary considerably according to climate and custom.

Belize

Shops are open 0800-1200, 1300-1600 Mon-Sat and Fri 1900-2100, with a half day from 1200 on Wed. Small shops may also open most late afternoons and evenings and on Sun 0800-1000. Government and commercial office hours are 0800-1200 and 1300-1600 Mon-Fri.

Guatemala

Business offices are open 0800-1200, 1400-1800 Mon-Fri. Shops are open 0900-1300 and 1500-1900, often mornings only on Sat. Banks in Guatemala City are open 0900-1500, with some open to 2000, while in the main tourist towns, some banks are open 7 days a week.

Police and the law

The best advice is to have as little to do with the police in this region as possible. In remote areas, drugs may be planted in your vehicle or problems may occur. An exception to this rule are the Tourist Police, who provide assistance in some of the big cities and resorts. Carry some form of identification with you at all times; if you cannot produce it when stopped by the police, you may be jailed. If you are stopped and fined, take the policeman's identity number and insist on going to the precinct station to make sure the fine is genuine. If you are imprisoned, contact your embassy or consulate for advice. Note that in the event of a vehicle accident in which anyone is injured, all drivers are automatically detained until blame has been established – usually no less than two weeks. Never offer nor accept drinks, cigarettes, gifts or money and, under no circumstances, try to bribe an official to do something illegal.

Post

The poste restante service is known as *lista de correos* and is available at most major post offices. Check under both your surname and your first name when collecting mail and be prepared to show your passport.

Mexico

International service has improved and bright red mailboxes are reliable for letters, although delivery times to/from the interior may well be longer than those from Mexico City. Parcel counters often close earlier than other sections of the post office in Mexico. Airmail under 20g is MEX$8.50 to USA and Central America; MEX$10.50 to Europe, and MEX$11.50 to Australia. Rates tend to rise in line with the peso's devaluation against the dollar.

Belize

Airmail to Europe takes 8 days and costs US$0.38 for a letter, US$0.20 for a postcard. A letter to USA costs US$0.30 and a postcard costs US$0.15. A letter to Australia costs US$0.50 and a postcard costs US$0.30, and takes 2-3 weeks. Parcels cost US$3.50 per ½ kg to Europe, US$0.38 per ½ kg to USA. Surface mail is not reliable.

Guatemala

Airmail to Europe takes 10-14 days. Letters cost US$0.52 for the first 20 g and between US$5.85 for 100 g to US$48 for a maximum weight of 2 kg. Airmail letters to the US and Canada cost US$0.39 for the first 20 g. Airmail parcel service to US is reliable (four to 14 days) and costs US$3.76 for 100 g up to US$31.90 for 2 kg. Parcels over 2 kg may only be sent abroad from Guatemala City, Correos y Telégrafos, 7 Avenida y 12 Calle, Zona 1.

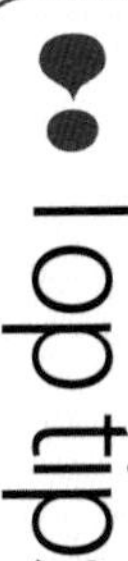

Travel safe

- Keep valuables out of sight.
- Keep all documents and money secure.
- Split up your main cash supply and hide it in different places.
- Lock your luggage together at bus or train stations.
- At night, take a taxi between transport terminals and your hotel. Use the hotel safe deposit box and keep an inventory of what you have deposited.
- Look out for tricks, used to distract your attention and steal your belongings.
- Notify the police of any losses and get a written report for insurance claims.
- Avoid hiking alone in remote areas.
- Avoid travelling at night.
- Avoid all political demonstrations.
- Don't fight back – it is better to hand over your valuables rather than risk injury.

See under Panajachel and Chichicastenango for alternative services.

Public holidays

Mexico

1 Jan New Year; **5 Feb** Constitution Day; **21 Mar** Birthday of Benito Juárez; **Maundy Thu**; **Good Fri**; **Easter Sat**; **1 May** Labour Day; **5 May** Battle of Puebla; **1 Sep** El Informe (Presidential Message); **16 Sep** Independence Day; **12 Oct** Día de la Raza (Discovery of America); **20 Nov** Día de la Revolución; **25 Dec** Christmas Day.

The Mexican calendar of religious fiestas lists over 5,000 each year. The most widely celebrated are: **6 Jan** Santos Reyes (Three Kings); **10 May** Día de las Madres (Mothers' Day); **1-2 Nov** Día de los Muertos (All Souls' Day); **12 Dec** La Virgen de Guadalupe (Our Lady of Guadalupe).

Belize

1 Jan New Year's Day; **9 Mar** Baron Bliss Day; **Good Fri; Easter Sat; Easter Mon**; **1 May** Labour Day; **24 May** Commonwealth Day; **10 Sep** St George's Caye Day; **21 Sep** Belize Independence Day; **11 Oct** Pan-American Day; **25 Dec** Christmas Day; **26 Dec** Boxing Day.

Guatemala

1 Jan New Year's Day; **Maundy Thu**; **Good Fri**; **Easter Sat**; **1 May** Labour Day; **30 Jun**; **15 Aug** (Guatemala City only); **15 Sep** Independence Day; **12 Oct** Discovery of America (businesses stay open); **20 Oct** Revolution Day; **1 Nov** All Saint's' Day. **24 Dec** Christmas Eve (from noon); **25 Dec** Christmas Day; **31 Dec** (from noon).

Safety

Most visits to the region are trouble-free, but you should always take precautions to safeguard yourself and your belongings. Be particularly alert in Mexico City (p79), Belize City (p221) and Guatemala City (p283), especially on public transport, in some taxis and when handling money in a public place. In Mexico, take care travelling in Oaxaca and Chiapas, especially after dark and in remote areas. In Belize, crimes against travellers are harshly punished and special tourist police have been introduced but precautions are still advised. Violent crime against tourists is becoming more common in Guatemala: take shuttles rather than public buses between Guatemala City and Antigua and seek local advice before climbing the volcanoes around Antigua and Lake Atitlán. Bus hijacks have been reported on the road between Tikal and Flores (although this situation has improved) and between Flores and the Belizean border. Visitors are strongly advised to seek up-to-date advice from **INGUAT**, hotels and other travellers. See also Drugs, p31 and Police and the law, p38.

Student travellers

If you are in full-time education you will be entitled to an **International Student Identity Card** (ISIC), which is distributed by student travel offices and travel agencies in 70 countries. The ISIC gives you special prices on transport and access to a variety of other concessions and services, including an emergency helpline (T+44-20-8762-8110). Discounts are often extended to teachers, who are entitled to an **International Teacher Identity Card** (ITIC). Both are available from www.isic.org.

Telephone

Mexico

Country code +52

Mexican phone numbers consist of 7 digits (or 8 in Mexico City). To make a local call, dial the 7-digit number only. To make a long-distance call within Mexico, dial 01 then the 2- or 3-digit area code, then the 7 digit number. If calling Mexico from abroad, dial the international access code (00 from the UK), followed by the Mexico country code (52), then the area code and the number. All Mexican telephone numbers given in this guide include the 2- or 3- digit area code.

Most public phones (marked **Ladatel** or Telmex) only take pre-paid phone cards (*tarjetas telefónicas*), costing 30, 50 or 100 pesos from shops and news kiosks everywhere. You can use public phones to call collect (reverse-charge) although this can be ridiculously expensive; phone the operator and say you want to *llamar por cobrar*. Some silver phones, for local and direct long-distance calls, take coins. Other public phones take foreign credit cards (Visa, MasterCard, but not AmEx). AT&T's US Direct service is available from public phones; if you have an AT&T phone card, dial **01, otherwise dial T412-553-7458, ext 359. Commercially run *casetas*, or phone booths, where you pay after phoning are available nationwide but charge up to twice as much as private phones.

For international calls, the best-value option is a pre-paid card from **Ekofon** (www.ekofon.com), available at various airport and other outlets. Ekofon provides a pre-chargeable account service, which can be opened and recharged online.

Belize

Country code +501

The much maligned Belizean telephone system is steadily modernizing but if the number you are calling is not working contact the operator (114) for help. All phone numbers are now 7 digits and area codes have been scrapped. Direct dialling is available between the major towns and

Phone facts

	Mexico	Belize	Guatemala
Country code	+52	+501	+502
IDD access code	00	00	00
Operator	020	114/110	171
International operator	090	115	171
Directory enquiries	040	113	124

to Mexico and USA. Local calls cost US$0.25 for 3 mins, plus US$0.12 for each extra minute within the city or US$0.15-0.55 depending on the zone. International calls are much cheaper from Belize than from neighbouring countries: US$3 per minute to Europe; US$1.60 to North, South and Central America.

Payphones and card phones are fairly commonplace in Belize City and other major tourist areas. Otherwise, all towns have a telephone office and most villages will allow visitors to use the community phone. Mobile phones are used in the most remote areas.

Guatemala

Country code +502

All phone numbers are 7 digits; there are no area codes. There are two main service providers – **Telgua** and **Telefónica**. Telgua phone booths are ubiquitous. They use cards sold in values of Q20, Q30 and Q50. Telefónica sell cards with access codes for up to Q45, which can be used from any private or public Telefónica phone. The price of a local call is US$0.05 per min; a national call costs US$0.77 per min. Most businesses offering a phone call service charge a minimum of US$0.13 for a local call, so it's cheaper to buy a phone card. International calls can be made from Telgua phone booths, but it is cheaper to find an internet café or shop which tend to offer better rates; in Antigua some companies offer calls through the internet at US$0.26 per minute to Europe. Operator-assisted calls are more expensive. For calling card and credit card call options you need a fixed line in a hotel or private house; dial 9999 plus the following three-digit numbers: Sprint USA, 195; MCI USA, 189; AT&T USA, 190; Canada, 198; UK (BT), 044. Collect calls may be made from public Telgua phones by dialling T147-120.

Time

Southern Mexico, Belize and Guatemala are all 6 hrs behind GMT, equivalent to US Central Standard Time. Mexico operates daylight saving from the first Sun in Apr to last Sun in Oct, when it is only 5 hrs behind GMT and therefore 1 hr ahead of Belize and Guatemala.

Tipping

You should normally tip 10% in better restaurants but check whether a service charge has already been added to the bill. Porters are tipped US$0.25 per bag (more if heavy), or US$2 in Belize. Taxi drivers are not usually tipped in Mexico or Guatemala, unless they provide an exceptional service. In Belize taxi drivers may be tipped US$1-10, depending on the length of the transfer, number of stops and whether 'touring' took place.

Tourist information

Contact details for tourist offices and other information resources are given in 'Ins and outs' throughout the text. The internet is an invaluable source of information, with countless websites dedicated to each country.

South American Explorers, Head Office in the USA at 126 Indian Creek Rd, Ithaca, NY 14850, USA T607-277-0488, www.samexplo.org Despite the name, this organization covers the whole of Latin America. Members receive help with travel planning as well as informed access on books and maps to the region.

Mexico

The **Mexican tourist board** has an office in the UK at 41 Trinity Sq, London, EC3N 1DJ, T020-7488 9392; in the USA, at 21 East 63rd St, 2nd floor, New York, NY10021, T1-800 44 MEXICO (toll free), and in Canada, at 2 Bloor St West, Suite 1502, Toronto, ON M4W 3E2, T416-925 0704. Once in Mexico, there are offices in all major towns and tourist areas; call T01-800-446-3942 for information. The Mexico Tourist Board website, www.visitmexico.com, is a multilingual, comprehensive site with information on the entire country. Also look at www.sectur.gob.mx, from the Tourism Secretariat, with less glossy links but equally comprehensive information.

Belize

Belize Tourist Board, New Central Bank Building, Level 2, Gabourel Lane, PO Box 325, T223-1913, www.travelbelize.org. A freephone information service is provided from the USA and Canada, T1-800 624 0686. In the Cayes, Placencia and the developed sections of Cayo, there is a steady supply of information available but, elsewhere, information may be less reliable. Tourist guides are checked and validated in popular areas (always make sure you have an official guide, particularly in Belize City) but off the main routes the guide system is more ad hoc. Maps of the country are limited, and topographical maps have not been readily available for several years. The best available maps are from ITMB.

Guatemala

Instituto Guatemalteco de Turismo (INGUAT), 7 Av, 1-17, Zona 4, Centro Cívico, Guatemala City, T2421-2800, T1-801-INGUAT-1, www.inguat.gob.gt Staff at INGUAT can offer travel and safety advice and provide bus timetables, hotel lists and road maps. Some maps include Belize as Guatemalan territory and roads marked in El Petén are often inaccurate. Information is available by phone from the USA, T202-518 5514. In the UK, background information on Guatemala and the Maya can be found at the **Guatemalan Maya Centre**, 94A Wandsworth Bridge Rd, London SW6 2TF, T/F020-7371 5291, www.maya.org.uk

Tour operators

In the UK

Bridge the World, 45-47 Chalk Farm Rd, Camden Town, London, NW1 8AJ, T0870 814 4400, www.bridgetheworld.com
Condor Journeys and Adventures, 2 Ferry Bank, Colintraive, Argyll, PA22 3AR, T01700-841 318, www.condorjourneys-adventures.com
Exodus Travels, T020-8675-5550, www.exodus.co.uk.
Explore, 1 Frederick St, Aldershot, Hants, GU11 1LQ, T01252 760 100 www.explore.co.uk
Galapagos Classic Cruises, 6 Keyes Rd, London, NW2 3XA, T020 8933 0613, www.galapagoscruises.co.uk
Journey Latin America, 12-13 Heathfield Terr, Chiswick, London, W4 4JE, T020-8747 8315; also Manchester, T0161-832 1441, www.journeylatinamerica.co.uk, tours@journeylatinamerica.co.uk
Last Frontiers, Fleet Marston Farm, Aylesbury, Buckinghamshire, HP18 0QT, T01296 653000, www.lastfrontiers.com
Select Latin America (incorporating Galapagos Adventure Tours), 79 Maltings Place, 169 Tower Bridge Rd, London SE1 3LJ, T020-7407 1478, www.selectlatinamerica.com. Quality tailor-made holidays and small group tours.
South American Experience, 47 Causton St, London, SW1P 4AT T020 7976 5511, www.southamericanexperience.co.uk
Trips Worldwide, 14 Frederick Place, Clifton, Bristol, BS8 1AS, T0117-311 4400, www.tripsworldwide.co.uk
Tucan Travel, 316 Uxbridge Road, London, W3 9RE, T020-8896-1600, www.tucantravel.com, uk@tucantravel.com

In North America

Exito Latin American Travel Specialists, 108 Rutgers St, Fort Collins, CO 80525, T970-482-3019, toll free on T1-800-655-4053, www.exito-travel.com
GAP Adventures, 355 Eglinton Av East, Toronto, Ontario, M4P 1M5, T1-800-465-5600, www.gap.ca
LADATCO tours, 2200 S Dixie Highway, Suite 704, Coconut Grove, FL 33133, T1-800-327-6162, www.ladatco.com
Mila Tours, 100 S Greenleaf Av, Gurnee, Il

60031, T1-800-367-7378, www.milatours.com

Quasar Nautica, 7855 NW 12th St, Suite 221, Miami, Florida 33126, T800 884 2105 (USA), T305-599 9008 (international), www.quasarexpeditions.com

S and S tours, 3366 E Trevino Dr, Sierra Vista, AZ 85650, T800-499-5685, www.ss-tours.com

Visas and immigration

Mexico

US citizens need only show an original birth certificate and photo ID to enter Mexico. A passport is required for citizens of Western European countries, Canada, Australia, New Zealand, Hungary, Iceland, Japan, Singapore, South Korea, Argentina, Bermuda, Chile, Costa Rica, Uruguay, Venezuela and Israel.

When arriving in Mexico by air, make sure you fill in the immigration document before joining the queue to have your passport checked. Once proof of nationality has been verified, you receive a Mexican Tourist Card (FM-T), issued for up to 180 days, which is returned to immigration officials when you depart the country. Citizens of other countries need to obtain a visa before travelling, multiple entry is not allowed, and visas must be renewed before re-entry. Business visitors and technical personnel should also apply for the requisite visa and permit. At the border crossings with Belize and Guatemala, you may be refused entry into Mexico if you have less than US$200 (or US$350 for each month of intended stay, up to a maximum of 180 days). If a person under 18 is travelling alone or with one parent, both parents' consent is required, certified by a notary or authorized by a consulate; exact details available from any Mexican Consulate.

Belize

All nationalities need passports, as well as sufficient funds and, officially, an onward ticket, although this is rarely requested for stays of 30 days or less. Visas are not usually required by (among others) nationals from countries within the EU, Australia and New Zealand, most Caribbean states, Mexico, USA and Canada. Other nationalities should consult the Belize consulate. Free transit visas (for 24 hours) are available at borders. It is possible that a visa may not be required if you have an onward ticket, but check all details at a consulate (eg in Chetumal) before arriving at the border. Those going to other countries after leaving Belize should get any necessary visas in their home country. Visitors are initially granted 30 days' stay in Belize; this may be extended every 30 days for US$12.50 for up to six months at the **Immigration Office**, Government Complex, Mahogany Street, Belize City, T222-4620 (to the west of the city) or at the **General Office of the Immigration and Nationality Dept** in Belmopan, Bliss Parade, opposite the market, T822-2423. At the end of six months, visitors must leave the country for at least 24 hours.

For details of PACT exit tax, see p21 and p54.

Guatemala

Citizens of (among others) all Western European countries, the USA, Canada, Mexico, all Central American countries, Australia and New Zealand only require a valid passport. The majority of visitors will receive a stamp in their passport on arrival, granting them 90 days in the country. Other nationalities require tourist cards (US$10), which can be bought at the border or visas (US$25), which may require reference to immigration authorities in Guatemala (3-4 weeks). After 90 days (or on expiry) all visitors must renew their passport stamps or visas at the immigration office at **Dirección General de Migración**, 7 Avenida, 1-17, Zona 4, Guatemala City, 2nd floor of the blue and white INGUAT building, T2361-8476 /78/79, Mon-Fri 0800-1600, but until 1230 for payments. This office will extend visas and passport stamps only once for a further period of time, depending on the original time awarded. The process is meant to take two full working days, but up to a week is possible. Flouting these rules will incur a US$1.30 fine per day of overstaying. These rules have been introduced to discourage people from leaving the country for 72 hours every six months and then returning.

A sprint through history

Pre-history Humans arrive in the Americas crossing the Bering Strait approximately 15,000 years ago. Hunter gatherers begin to settle in the most fertile lands as early as 2000 BC.

Mesoamerican culture, as shared by numerous interdependent civilizations from northern Mexico south to Honduras and El Salvador, can be divided into three periods: the Pre-classic (1500 BC-AD 300), the Classic (AD 300-900) and the Post-classic (AD 900 until the Spanish conquest). Common features are an agriculture based on maize, beans and squash; an enormous pantheon, dominated by the god of rain and the feathered serpent-hero; blood offerings and sacrifice to the gods; pyramid-building; ritualistic ball games; trade in feathers, jade and other valuable objects; hieroglyphic writing; astronomy, and an elaborate calendar. Along with the Aztecs, the most famous Mesoamerican civilization are the Maya (p49), who are a continuous presence in the region from 1500 BC but reach their apotheosis at the height of the Classic period.

Pre-classic The **Olmecs** flourish in the Mexican Gulf Coast region 1400-400 BC, with a large ceremonial centre at La Venta; all later Mesoamerican civilizations have their roots in Olmec culture. Their immediate successors are the **Zapotecs** in the 1st millennium BC at Monte Albán in the Valley of Oaxaca, and the **Izapa** on the Pacific between Mexico and Guatemala.

Classic The great city state of **Teotihuacán** dominates the central highlands of Mexico (AD 300-700), spreading its influence south through Oaxaca, the Gulf coast and the Maya area. Its apotheosis coincides with the Classic Maya period. The **Mixtecs** (AD 800-1200) infiltrate Zapotec territory in western Oaxaca, successfully withstanding Aztec invasion.

Post-classic The militaristic **Toltecs** (AD 1000-1300) from northern Mexico invade central and southern city states, influencing culture and architecture as far afield as the Yucatán and southern Guatemala. They are succeeded by the **Aztecs** (AD 1150-1519), based at Tenochtitlán in the Valley of Mexico, who conquer vast swathes of Mexico and exact heavy tribute from subjected peoples.

1519-1521 Hernán Cortés lands at Cozumel, off the Yucatán coast and advances west towards the Aztec capital, Tenochtitlán. He defeats the Aztecs and conquers Mexico, initiating 300 years of Spanish rule. The Spanish take over land from the Aztec overlords, putting indigenous peoples to work and developing the system of haciendas that sits at the core of Mexican land ownership and use.

1523-1525 Pedro de Alvarado conquers Chiapas en route to Guatemala. He finds fading Maya civilizations and warring tribes, which his men have little trouble in crushing. Land is divided into large estates (*encomiendas*), indigenous people are made to work as slaves and pay tribute to their new owners.

1530-1565 The Yucatán is subjugated by Francisco de Montejo, and then by his son and nephew, with the founding of the fortified towns of Campeche in 1541 and Mérida in 1542. In 1562 Fray Diego de Landa orders the burning of Maya codices and idols at Maní but later records many aspects of Maya life and custom in his book, *Relación de las Cosas de Yucatán.*

1640-1798 English settlers arrive in Belize with black slaves from Jamaica. The British Government secures logging rights through treaties with Spain. A naval victory by the British at St George's Caye eventually secures Belize for Britain.

1697 Fall of the last independent Maya city state to the *conquistadores* at Tayasal on Lake Petén Itzá in Guatemala.

1808-1822 Napoleon invades Spain usurping the power of King Ferdinand VII and opening the way for independence movements in the New World. On 16 September 1810 a curate from Dolores, Miguel Hidalgo, launches a popular revolt against Spanish rule in Mexico. Hidalgo is executed the following year but rebellion continues until 1821 when both Guatemala and Mexico achieve independence. Each claims sovereignty over Belize, but these claims are rejected by Britain. In 1822 Agustín de Iturbide declares himself Emperor of Mexico.

1822-39 Iturbide is overthrown within a year and Mexico becomes a Republic. In 1823 Central American provinces including Guatemala, but not Belize, meet to establish a federation, the Provincias Unidas del Centro de América. Reforms in education, finance, religion and justice systems improve life for *criollos* and *mestizos* but not for indigenous peoples. The federation's power eventually declines and Guatemala declares its independence in 1839.

1840-1847 A Maya revolt against the *encomienda* system, known as the War of the Caste, almost succeeds in driving the Spanish out of the Yucatán.

1857-63 A period of reform in Mexico ('La Reforma') is led by the popular Zapotec lawyer, Benito Juárez, who becomes president in 1861. Liberal modernizing policies include popular education, freedom of the press and of speech and a separation of church and state. The resulting civil strife from opponents wrecks the economy and Juárez suspends payment of foreign debt.

1862-71 Great Britain declares Belize a colony, renaming it British Honduras. Nine years later it becomes a Crown Colony under the Governor of Jamaica.

1863-7 England, France and Spain invade Mexico to reclaim their debt. The French occupy Mexico City and invite Maximilian of Hapsburg to be Emperor. Juárez leads guerrilla warfare against the invaders, French troops withdraw and the Republic is restored. The stranded Emperor is executed in 1867.

1870s A Liberal revolt is launched in Guatemala. The anti-clerical Justo Rufino is elected president in 1873. He aims to reinstate the federation, set up a modern state separate from the church and introduce universal education.

1876-1910 General Porfirio Díaz seizes power in Mexico and rules as president for 35 years. Political opposition, free press and free elections are banned. Peasants have their land stolen and their personal liberties curtailed; many are sold into forced labour on tobacco plantations. Discontent leads to strikes.

1897 September Revolution in Guatemala, prompted by an extravagant government building spree combined with plummeting coffee prices affecting farmers in the western part of the country.

1898-1920 Guatemalan Dictator Manuel Estrada Cabrera opens up Guatemala to foreign investment. The US-owned United Fruit Company becomes the country's largest landowner, employer and exporter. Cabrera is toppled in 1920.

1910-1920 Francisco Madero leads the Mexican Revolution, supported by disaffected peasants and the progressive middle class. Madero becomes president in 1911 and begins a programme of reform but is assassinated by the military in 1913. Nearly two million die in the years that follow as governments oscillate between right-wing interests and radical leaders, such as Emiliano Zapata, who demand greater land reform. The Mexican Constitution is passed in 1917.

1919 The beginning of the Independence movement in Belize (British Honduras).

1929 The Partido Nacional Revolucionario is formed in Mexico (later renamed the Partido Revolucionario Institucional or PRI) and rules for over 70 years.

1930s Belize City is hit by fierce hurricanes that compound its economic problems.

1931-44 Jorge Ubico rules Guatemala as a dictator. He introduces a secret police, bans communist movements and persecutes intellectuals. Maya are forced to work for their landlords for free for half the year. The military government that replaces Ubico is overthrown on 20 October 1944 in the October Revolution.

1945-54 Liberal Juan José Arévalo establishes Guatemala's national security and health systems and introduces rights for the Maya. He survives over 20 attempted coups. His successor, Jacobo Arbenz Guzmán, continues to implement liberal policies and land reform. His policies are supported by the Communist party, which provokes a US-backed military coup. Arbenz is forced to resign in 1954.

1960-1996 Guatemalan Civil War. The assassination of Guatemalan President Carlos Castillo Armas in 1957 provokes a wave of violence. The army and its right-wing supporters suppress left-wing efforts to restore liberal policies. Tens of thousands are killed and disappear in the following three decades, with the worst atrocities taking place in the 1970s and '80s. The US withdraws its support for the government, due to human rights abuses.

1964-1979	Self-government is instituted in British Honduras. George Price of the People's United Party (PUP) becomes Prime Minister. In 1973 British Honduras reverts to the name of Belize. From 1975 onwards, successive UN Resolutions endorse Belize's right to self-determination, independence and territorial integrity.
1968	In Mexico the PRI administration, under Díaz Ordaz, has virtual monopoly over all political activity and has repressed free speech. These policies, in addition to over-spending in the build up to the Olympic Games provoke a student protest in Tlatelolco, which ends in a massacre by the military.
1976	A devastating earthquake in Guatemala kills 27,000 people and leaves more than a million homeless.
1980s	The Guatemalan military unleash a huge offensive against the guerillas, who unite as URNG in response. Around 11,000 people are killed in the massive counter-insurgency campaign.
1981	Belize becomes independent on 21 September, following a United Nations declaration and holds its first general elections in 1984. Guatemala refuses to recognize the independent state.
1985	Presidential elections in Guatemala are won by a civilian, Vinicio Cerezo Arévalo of the Christian Democrat party (DC), the first democratically elected president since 1966. He opens the door for discussions with the URNG.
1985	A major earthquake in Mexico City kills more than 4,000 people; many buildings are destroyed and thousands of people are left homeless. Mexico spirals into economic depression, with political dissent from both left and right.
1990s	Belize is admitted into the Organization of American States (OAS). Guatemala recognizes the right of the Belizean people to self-determination. British troops withdraw in 1994.
1992	Rigoberta Menchú is awarded the Nobel Peace prize in recognition of her efforts to bring peace to Guatemala.
1993	Mexican parliament ratifies the North American Free Trade Agreement (NAFTA) with the US and Canada. Five Central American states, including Guatemala, sign the Central American Integration Treaty Protocol.
1994	The Guatemalan government and the URNG sign agreements on human rights (1994), resettlement (1994) and indigenous rights (1995).
1994	The Ejército Zapatista de Liberación Nacional (EZLN) initiate an armed guerrilla uprising in Chiapas. They oppose NAFTA and seek better conditions for the poor, indigenous population.
1996	A peace treaty is signed in Guatemala, ending 36 years of armed conflict. Guerrilla troops are demobilized but difficulties with human rights remain.

1998 Hurricane Mitch misses Belize but causes devastation in Honduras and parts of Guatemala. However, Belize fails to escape Hurricane Iris in 2001.

1999 Guatemala holds its first peacetime elections. Victorious right-wing president Alfonso Portillo of the FRG (Frente Republicano Guatemalteco) promises to clean up the judicial system, crack down on crime, tax the rich and respect human rights. Former president Efraín Ríos Montt who held office during the worst atrocities of the civil war, becomes head of Congress.

2000 Presidential elections bring to an end 71 years of PRI rule in Mexico when President Vicente Fox (PAN - Partido de Acción Nacional) takes office on 1 December. Fox sets out to tackle government corruption, drug-trafficking, crime and poverty, and the economic conditions driving migration to the US.

2003-2005 Regional integrations continue to develop with signature of the Central American Free Trade Agreement in 2004. CAFTA sits within the larger Plan Puebla which aims to create an economic corridor stretching from Puebla, east of Mexico City, south to Panama.

2004 Guatemalan voters elect Oscar Berger president as leader of the newly formed Gran Alianza Nacional (GANA). Berger promises to work towards a more just country. Peace accords are to be overseen by Nobel peace prize winner Rigoberta Menchú.

The Maya

Thought to have evolved in the Pacific Highlands of Guatemala between 1500 BC and AD 100, the Maya civilization entered its Classic period in AD 300, when it flourished in Guatemala, El Salvador, Belize, Honduras and southern Mexico. Unlike other pre-Colombian civilizations, the Maya did not develop a large, centralized empire, instead they formed independent and antagonistic city states. Recent research has revealed that these cities, far from being the peaceful ceremonial centres as was once imagined, were warring adversaries, constantly striving to capture victims for sacrifice. Furthermore, much of the cultural activity and religious worship involved blood-letting by even the highest members of society, in which stingray spines or a rope studded with thorns was pulled through the penis, tongue, ear or elbow. Society was controlled by a theocratic minority of priests and nobles, headed by a near-divine king. Status was indicated by the wearing of jewellery (especially jade) and the consumption of highly prized cocoa beans, which were also used as currency.

Alongside their preoccupation with blood, the great centres were noted for wonderful architecture and sculpture, painted ceramics and impressive advances in mathematics. They achieved paper codices and developed glyphic writing, which also appears on stone monuments. To support urban populations now believed to number tens of thousands, an agricultural system was developed of raised fields, fertilized by fish and vegetable matter from surrounding canals. The Maya traded over wide areas, although they had not invented the wheel and had no beasts of burden. The height of the Classic period lasted until AD 900-1000, after which the Maya came under the influence of the Toltecs. In the following centuries, the power of the great Maya centres collapsed, possibly due to land exhaustion, invasion from the Central Highlands, or a peasant revolt against the conspicuous consumption of the Maya's ever-expanding elite.

5 Best

Maya sites

Palenque ›› *p145*
Uxmal ›› *p174*
Chichén Itzá ›› *p176*
Lamanai ›› *p242*
Tikal ›› *p369*

Astronomy and time

Astronomy and time were fundamental to all aspects of Maya belief and culture. Despite the absence of any technical equipment for measuring distances, angles or time, Maya astronomy was extraordinarily advanced and accurate. Observatories, such as those at Uaxactún and Tikal, were used to plot and predict the movements of the sun, moon, Venus and other planets, and to time important events. The Mesoamerican calendar, refined with extraordinary sophistication by the Maya, was a combination of a 260-day almanac year (called a *tzolkín*) and the 365-day solar year. The two calendars only corresponded once every 52 years in a cycle called the Calendar Round. In order to give the Calendar Round a context within a larger timescale, a start date for both years was devised by the Classic Maya, equivalent to 3114 BC. Dates measured from this point are called Long Count dates and required a refinement of the solar calendar to a cycle of 360 days, known as a *tun*. The Maya calendar was a nearer approximation to sidereal time than either the Julian or the Gregorian calendars of Europe; inaccurate by only 0.000069 of a day in any year. It used zero centuries in advance of the Old World and conceived a Great Cycle of more than 1,800 million days (13 *baktúns*). The first Great Cycle is due to end on 23 December 2012.

Art and architecture

The architectural achievements of the Maya were exemplified in the superb temples, palaces and pyramids of their urban capitals. Maya tools and weapons were flint and hard

Chac masks at Chicanná, Yucatán

Carved Maya figure, Chiapas

obsidian and fire-hardened wood, and yet with these they hewed out and transported great monoliths over miles of difficult country, and carved them with intricate glyphs and figures. Maya art is highly mathematical: each column, figure, face, animal, frieze, stairway and temple expresses a date or a time relationship. When, for example, an ornament on the ramp of the Hieroglyphic Stairway at Copán was repeated some 15 times, it was to express that number of elapsed 'leap' years, with the 75 steps representing the number of elapsed intercalary (leap) days. Major buildings were also aligned to celestial bodies or events, such as eclipses.

Writing

Modern perception of the Maya has come from a greater understanding of the Maya's hieroglyphic writing, which tells many secrets of their society. The Maya used as many as 800 different glyphs representing either a phonetic sound or a whole word. These were written onto paper codices or intricately carved onto stone monuments or ceramics. The codices were almost all destroyed by Spanish friars during early attempts to Christianize the region in the 16th century but a book written at the time by one of the friars, Fray Diego de Landa, later helped decipher the Maya alphabet and calendar. Another breakthrough came in the 1960s, when Russian epigraphers proved that inscriptions found on Maya temples and stelae told of rulers, accessions, conquests and deaths, as well as representing calendar dates. Further insights into Maya culture and belief have come from *Popol Vuh*, the story of Maya creation as written by Ki'che' Maya in Guatemala in the 16th century. Although many centuries separate the writing of *Popol Vuh* from the Classic Period, elements of the story correspond with inscriptions found on Classic Maya ceramics.

Modern Maya

Today, descendants of the Maya still occupy Chiapas, the Yucatán peninsula and Guatemala, as well as parts of Belize. Half of the population of Guatemala are purely indigenous and, although many have opted for a more modern lifestyle, there are still a significant number who speak Maya languages and live by traditional methods and beliefs. They have proved themselves to be a resilient and adaptable people and as a result, the Maya and their culture have endured.

Traditional costume, Chichicastenango

Religious elder, Chajul

The Maya were able to adopt the new faith brought by Spanish friars in the 16th century and by missionaries in the 19th century, while still worshipping their own gods. Today they profess Christianity laced with a more ancient nature worship. Maya beliefs are centred around the earth and the sun and their sacred powers and energies. Physical and spiritual health are considered as one and shamans practise healing using traditional medicines combined with magic and ritual. Saint worship is an essential element of much Maya religious practice; some of the most fascinating rituals revolve around the cult of Maximón in Guatemala, page 312. Religious festivals are also the time to appreciate traditional music and dance. Dances are often accompanied by the marimba, an instrument like a xylophone, and usually feature special costumes and masks.

Weaving is an important aspect of indigenous cultural tradition and few indigenous costumes are as dramatic and colourful as that of the Maya. In recent times (especially in Chiapas), traditional costume has become emblematic of renewed Maya pride and self confidence. Different designs and aspects of dress can denote different ethnic groups and status. Maya women traditionally wear bright *huípiles* and wraparound skirts, along with sashes, headdresses or shoulder capes. Traditional dress is less common among Maya men, although the citizens of Todos Santos (page 326) are a notable exception. Yarn is spun by hand and coloured using natural and synthetic dyes before being woven on the 'back-strap' loom. The fabric is then embroidered with colourful symbols, flowers, animals and other motifs, which may have cultural or magic significance.

The region today

The history of Belize, Guatemala and southern Mexico is rooted in the Maya world, when the region was a loose affiliation of city states that competed for dominance. This common foundation transcends many of the contemporary differences that come with nationality, passports and international borders.

Regional integration is now working towards formalizing the countries' links in economic terms. When warring factions in Guatemala signed peace agreements in 1996, it removed the last barrier to regional cooperation within Central America. The next step is the Central America Free Trade Agreement linking Central America to Mexico and the North American Free Trade Agreement (NAFTA). For some, the removal of quotas and barriers is a victory for free trade; for others it is another route to the exploitation of people, nature and resources that will only benefit multinational businesses. Certainly, Mexico's membership of NAFTA has set in motion a domino effect of economic migration: as Mexicans have moved north to the United States, so Guatemalans have moved north to southern Mexico.

Meanwhile, Guatemala must endure the slow and painful process of reconciliation as its horrific history of human rights abuses is revealed, and in Mexico, President Fox must tackle the continuing problem of land reform and indigenous rights. The arrival of 200,000 Zapatista supporters in the Zócalo in Mexico City in March 2001 showed the strength of feeling these issues engender in Mexico. The plight of Mexico's poor also gained an international forum, when the 2002 World Trade Organisation talks at Cancún were hijacked by small producers and anti-globalization protestors.

For the visitor, travel in the region has become significantly smoother as borders become easier to cross, making it possible to visit the entire Maya world in one trip if you have the time. When properly managed, income earned from tourism can also benefit poor local communities and environmental projects (see How big is your footprint? page 16), although changing fashions in travel lead many to question the sustainability of the industry.

Destinations for wildlife-spotting

The sea around **Caye Caulker**, Belize, or **Isla Mujeres**, Mexico, for coral, marine life and whale sharks ›› *p190 and p230*
Crooked Tree Wildlife Sanctuary, Belize, for birds ›› *p241*
Gales Point, Belize, for manatee ›› *p258*
Tikal, Guatemala, for monkeys, toucans, white-nosed coati ›› *p369*
El Zotz, Guatemala, for bats ›› *p373*

Nature and wildlife

Central America is the meeting place of two of the world's major biological regions – the Nearctic to the north and the Neotropical to the south. It has a remarkable geological and climatic complexity and consequently an enormous range of habitats: rainforests, dry forests, cloud forests, mangroves and stretches of wetlands. Mexico alone has over 430 mammal species, more than 960 different birds, around 720 reptiles and almost 300 amphibians and far more insects than you want to know about. The majority of tour operators listed in this guide will offer nature-oriented tours and there are several national parks, *biotopos* or protected areas throughout the region, each with its own highlights.

Landscape and climate

The Sierra Madre del Sur mountains, which stretch through Oaxaca, mark the zone where North America ends and Central America begins. At their eastern end is the narrow Isthmus of Tehuantepec; to the north, the Gulf Coast is a swampy plain, dotted with lagoons and rivers which drain the large volume of water that flows off the Chiapas highlands. The Yucatán peninsula consists of a low, flat plateau, covered with tropical savannah with a dry, desert-like region at its tip. Between the foothills of the highlands and the Caribbean coast is an area of tropical rainforest, although much of this is being cut down for agricultural purposes. South of the main forest, the highlands stretch from western Chiapas through Guatemala to the Maya Mountains of Belize. A chain of 33 volcanoes, many of them still active, run through Guatemala, the highest of which is 4,220 m. The Guatemalan Pacific Coast is a humid coastal plain with black volcanic sand, while Belize's Caribbean shoreline has white coral sand. Offshore lies the second largest barrier reef in the world.

The rainy season runs from May to November, with the heaviest rainfall in southern Belize – a massive 4 m annually. During the rainy season, days are often sunny with brief torrential downpours, but it is generally more overcast and humid. The hottest time of year is April/May just before the rains. Hurricane season is at its peak towards November/December. Altitude has a big effect on temperature with the highlands enjoying temperate days and cool or cold nights. The lowlands can get uncomfortably hot and humid, especially in the tropical forests. The coasts and islands are moderated by sea breezes.

Mammals

Primates are among the most easily sighted mammals in the region. **Howler monkeys** are noticeable for the huge row they make, especially around dawn or dusk. The **spider monkey** is more agile and slender and uses its prehensile tail to swing around the canopy. The smaller, white-throated **capuchins** are also commonly seen, moving around in noisy groups. The most frequently spotted carnivore is the **white-nosed coati**, a member of the racoon family, with a long snout and ringed tail. Members of the cat family are rarely seen, those in the area

Conservation in Belize

Belize is at the forefront of nature conservation in the region, with nature reserves supported by a combination of private and public organizations. A Wildlife Protection Act was introduced in 1982 which forbids the sale, exchange or dealings in wildlife, or parts thereof, for profit. The import, export, hunting or collection of wildlife is not allowed without a permit. Also prohibited is the removal or export of black coral, picking orchids, exporting turtle or turtle products and spear fishing. On 1 June 1996 a National Protected Areas Trust Fund (**PACT**; www.pactbelize.org) was established to provide finance for the "protection, conservation and enhancement of the natural and cultural treasures of Belize". Funds for PACT come from a conservation fee paid by all foreign visitors on departure by air, land and sea (see p21), and from 20% of revenues derived from entrance fees to protected areas and passenger fees on cruise ships.

Useful contacts include the **Belize Audubon Society** (PO Box 1001, 12 Fort Street, Belize City, T223-5004, www.belizeaudubon.org); the **Programme for Belize** (PO Box 749, 1 Eyre Street, Belize City, T227-5616, www.pfbelize.org), which cover most of the protected areas of interest and support Belize's strong conservation focus. See also p16.

include the **bobcat** (in Mexico only), **jaguar**, **puma**, **ocelot** and **margay**. The largest land mammal in the region is **Baird's tapir**, weighing up to 300 kg, but it is a forest species and very secretive. More likely to be seen are **peccaries**, medium-sized pig-like animals that are active both day and night. The **white-tailed deer** can often be spotted at dawn or dusk in drier, woodland patches. The smaller **red brocket** is a rainforest deer and more elusive. Rodent species you might see include the forest-dwelling **agouti**, which looks rather like a long-legged guinea pig. Considerably larger is the nocturnal **paca** (**gibnut** in Belize), another forest species. Many species of **bat** are found throughout the region.

Birds

Toucans and the smaller **toucanets** are widespread throughout the tropical areas of the region and easy to spot. Other popular sightings include the **hummingbird**, frequently drawn to sugar-feeders, and the **scarlet macaw**. The resplendent **quetzal**, the national symbol of Guatemala, is brilliant emerald green, with males having a bright scarlet breast and belly and long green tail streamers. The **harpy eagle** is extremely rare with sightings a possibility in rainforest region of northern Guatemala, Belize and southern Mexico. Other rare birds include the threatened **horned guam**, found only in high cloud forests. Along the coasts are masses of different seabirds, including **pelicans**, **boobies** and the magnificent **frigate bird**. In the coastal wetlands of the Yucután **pink flamingoes** can be spotted.

Reptiles and amphibians

Mexico has more reptiles than any other country in the world. Snakes are rarely sighted, but If you are lucky you could see a **boa constrictor** curled up digesting its latest meal. In contrast, **lizards** are everywhere, from small geckos walking up walls in your hotel room to the large **iguanas** sunbathing in the tree tops. The **American crocodile** and **spectacled caiman** are both found throughout the area, with the latter being seen quite frequently. **Morlet's crocodile** is found only in Mexico, Belize and Guatemala. You'll also be able to see nesting **turtles** along the Pacific coastal beaches of Guatemala and Mexico. You'll certainly hear frogs and toads, even if you do not see them. However, the brightly coloured **poison-dart frogs** and some of the **tree frogs** are well worth searching out. Look for them in damp places, under logs and moist leaf litter, in rock crevices and by ponds and streams, many will be more active at night.

Insects and spiders

There are uncounted different species of insect in the area. Probably, most desirable for ecotourists are the **butterflies**, though some of the **beetles**, such as the jewel **scarabs**, are also pretty spectacular. If you are fascinated by spiders, look out for **tarantulas**, there are many different species.

Marine wildlife

The **whale shark** makes a seasonal migration through the coastal waters of Belize and Honduras between March and May. Less natural shark encounters can be had off **Caye Caulker**, Belize, and **Isla Mujeres**, on the Yucatán, Mexico, where hand-feeding brings in **sting rays** and **nurse sharks** for close but safe encounters. Marine mammals that can be sighted include **whales**, **dolphins** and **manatees**.

Toucan, white-tailed deer, manatee

Mexico City

Independence Monument, Paseo de la Reforma

Introduction

One of the largest cities in the world, the Ciudad de México, Distrito Federal, or DF as it is often called, can be overwhelming on first acquaintance and you'll need some time to do it justice, especially the Centro Histórico. Monumental architecture, magnificent church interiors, museums and vibrant pulsating murals full of the optimism of the post-Revolution period, invite you to savour the delights (and unfortunately, the pollution) of this vast metropolis.

Explore the former heart of the Aztec world, or be serenaded by *mariachis* in Plaza Garibaldi. Stroll along the impressive Paseo de la Reforma and dine in the chic restaurants of Polanco. Soak up the atmosphere in Chapultepec Park, before swotting up on some essential history at the anthropology museum. When the pace becomes too much, head to Coyoacán for lunch and visit the house where Frida Kahlo lived, or wander around the floating gardens of Xochimilco.

More than just a gateway to Central America, the city provides an intense introduction to *Mexicanidad* – or national identity. Colourful, bawdy, vibrant, gaudy, cultured, noisy, sometimes dangerous and always fascinating – it is a celebration of chaotic humanity, good and bad.

Ratings

Landscape
★

Chillin'
★

Activities
★★★★

Culture
★★★★★

Costs
$$$

Ins and outs » p76

Getting there

Air Aeropuerto Internacional Benito Juárez (T55-5571 3600), Mexico City's only passenger airport, is 13 km east of the city centre. It has one terminal, divided into sections, each designated by a letter (A-F). A-C for national arrivals, D for departures, E for international check-in, F for international arrivals. There are airport information kiosks at A, D, E and F. There is a hotel desk before passing through customs. The tourist office at A has phones for calling hotels, no charge, helpful, but Spanish only. The travel agency at east exit will book hotels or confirm flights for a fee of 5 pesos. Banks and *casas de cambio* between them provide a 24-hr service.

Fixed-price taxis are 88 pesos (US$8.50) to the Centre/Zócalo; buy tickets from booths at exit of A, E and F. To reserve a taxi call T55-5571 9344, daily 0800-0200. A cheaper alternative if you don't have much luggage is to cross the Blvd Puerto Aéreo to the Metro Terminal Aérea and either flag down an ordinary taxi from outside the **Ramada** hotel (not recommended if travelling alone), or take a metro into the centre, US$0.15. There are no direct buses to/from the centre. *For details of flights to and from Mexico City » p17.*

Bus There are four long-distance bus terminals: North, South, East and West, divided, more or less, according to the regions of Mexico they serve. All bus terminals operate taxis with a voucher system; pay at the booth in advance. The terminals are connected by metro, but this is not a good option at rush hour, or if carrying too much luggage. Terminals have left luggage, toilets, pay phones, post and fax facilities and cafeterias.

Getting around

It is best to base yourself in the Centro Histórico, from where you can walk, or take the metro, to most major sights. The **metro** is the most straightforward, cheap and efficient way of getting around, see map, page 77. It also avoids the pollution and congestion of the streets. **Buses** are frequent and good for getting down the main arteries. Fixed-rate *sitio* **taxis** have an orange stripe and operate from taxi ranks or can be booked in advance. Ordinary taxis are green and white VW Beetles (but due to change to white with a broad red band); they run by the meter and are cheaper, but are not as safe. *Colectivo* taxis (minibuses) run on fixed routes. Driving is not recommended.

View north along Avenida Lázaro Cárdenas

Tourist information

Information is available at the **Secretaría de Turismo** ⓘ *Masaryk 172, 5th floor, Polanco* (bus No 32) or the government-operated **tourist information centres** throughout the city. The **main office** ⓘ *Nuevo León 56, 9th floor, 06100, T55-5553 1260, www.mexicocity.gob.mx*, is helpful and has a good website. **Tourist assistance** (T55-5250 0123), provides information and maps, and can help with hotel bookings. There are **information bureaux** outside Insurgentes metro station and another on Juárez, near Paseo de la Reforma, closed Sun; or you can call **tourist information** (T55-5525 9380, 0800-2000), which has a bilingual operator. See also www.mexicocity.com.mx. Note that most museums and galleries are closed on Monday and that many are free to students and teachers with ID.

Maps Free city maps are available from tourist information booths – there's one on the northwest corner of the Zócalo. An A to Z, US$14, is available from *Guía Roji*. Specialized maps can be bought from the **Instituto Nacional de Estadística Geografía e Informática (INEGI)** ⓘ *Metro Insurgentes, Mon-Fri 0800-2000, Sat 0800-1600*. **La Rosa de los Vientos**, Higuera, Coyoacán, in the south of the city, sells maps to all parts of the country.

History

When Hernán Cortés and his Spanish soldiers arrived in Tenochtitlán in 1519, they found a highly developed city, built across several islands, linked by a sophisticated system of causeways. The Aztecs had settled here in the mid-1300s after finding the sign they had been searching for: an eagle perched on a nopal cactus, eating a snake. The arrival of Cortés coincided with the predicted return of the Aztec god, Quetzalcoatl, the Plumed Serpent, from the east. Cortés exploited this superstition and within three years of arriving in Mexico, had taken over the city and murdered the Aztec king, Moctezuma. Following the Aztec defeat, the Spanish began the construction of the capital of New Spain; many Aztec buildings were destroyed, and the lake was drained, filled and built over. Rapid industrialization in the 20th century led to a massive influx of people looking for work. Sheer numbers created pressure on services and shanty towns sprung up around the city. The momentum was set for a city infrastructure that struggles to cope with a population that now numbers 20 million, and is still growing by some 1,000 immigrants a day.

Zócalo

Mexico City is vast, but many of the interesting sites are within a relatively small area. The heart of the city is the Zócalo, the main square in the Centro Histórico, surrounded by colonial streets. Just west of the Zócalo are the gardens of the Alameda. From here, the grand boulevard of Paseo de la Reforma heads southwest to Chapultepec Park, 'the lungs of the city'. The city's main thoroughfare, Avenida Insurgentes, bisects Reforma about halfway between the Alameda and Chapultepec Park, sweeping past the Basílica de Guadalupe in the north, and heading south towards the beautiful bohemian suburbs of San Angel and Coyoacán.

Getting there International and domestic flights. Good long distance buses.
Getting around Metro, bus, taxi or on foot.
Time required 2 days at the start or end of your trip.
Weather Temperate all year, but chilly at night in winter.
Sleeping Great range from luxurious to cheap and cheerful.
Eating Plenty of choice and international cuisine.
Activities and tours Football, hiking, shopping and sightseeing.
★ **Don't miss...** soaking up some history at the Anthropology Museum. » *p67*

Centro Histórico » *pp70-79*

Still largely colonial and surrounded by the city's oldest streets, the historic centre is elegant and chic heading west down Calles 5 de Mayo, Tacuba and Madero, and somewhat less upmarket towards the east and southeast, down Calles Corregidora and Venustiano Carranza. Both areas are fascinating to explore; the boutiques and restaurants of the former are replaced by the street vendors and chaotic stalls exuding exotic smells of the latter.

Zócalo

The great main square, or Plaza Mayor, the heart of the Aztec city Tenochtitlán, is always alive with people and often vivid with official ceremonies or political demonstrations. The huge flag in the centre of the square is raised at 0600, and taken down, with great pomp and ceremony, at 1800 each day. On the north side, sits the enormous **cathedral** and to the east is the **Palacio Nacional,** housing the Presidential offices and the city's administration. Opposite this are the **Portales de los Mercaderes**, or Arcades of the Merchants, where small shops and businesses have traded since their construction in 1524. North of them, opposite the cathedral, is the **Monte de Piedad** (National Pawnshop) ⓘ *Mon-Fri 0830-1800, Sat 0830-1300*, established in the 18th century. Prices are government controlled; auctions are held each Friday at 1000.

Cathedral

ⓘ *Daily 0700-0100, free, guided visits to the bell tower, US$1.*

This is the largest and oldest cathedral in Latin America. It was first built in 1525, just two years after the Conquest, using stones taken from the Aztec Templo Mayor. The Santa María de Guadalupe is the largest bell in Latin America, weighing a massive 13 tonnes. Like many of the city's heavy colonial buildings, the cathedral is sinking into the soft lakebed below and a lengthy programme of work is underway to build new foundations. The tilt is quite obvious. The most attractive feature is the enormous gilt Retablo de los Reyes behind the main altar, built between 1718-1737, depicting European monarchs. The cathedral is flanked by the beautiful **Sagrario Metropolitano** church (1769), with a fine churrigueresque façade and gilt interior.

Palacio Nacional

ⓘ *T55-9158 1259, Tue-Sun 0930-1900, free.*

The National Palace takes up the whole of the eastern side of the Zócalo. Built on the site of the Palace of Moctezuma at the time of the Conquest, it has been rebuilt and added to many times over the centuries. Over the central door hangs the Liberty Bell, rung at 2300 on 15 September by the President to commemorate Independence from Spain. A series of fine Diego Rivera murals decorate the staircase and the first floor.

Templo Mayor

ⓘ *Seminario 4 y Guatemala, entrance in the northeast corner of the Zócalo, T55-5542 4784, Tue-Sun until 1630, museum and temple US$3.50; guided tours in Spanish Tue-Fri 0930-1630, Sat 0930-1130, audio guides in English, US$0.85.*

To the side of the cathedral are the Aztec ruins of the Templo Mayor, the most important excavated pre-Hispanic site in the city. Thought to be built on the exact spot where the symbolic eagle was found perched on a cactus eating a snake, it was the spiritual and ceremonial centre of Tenochtitlán and the Aztec world. The Aztecs would build a new temple every 52 years at the completion of their calendar cycle – seven temples have been identified piled on top of each other. The fascinating museum houses a reconstruction of how Tenochtitlán would have looked at the height of its power, as well as sculptures found in the main pyramid. Look out for the huge, circular monolith representing the dismembered body of Coyolxauhqui, who was killed by her brother Huitzilopochtli, the Aztec tutelary god.

North of the Zócalo

On Calle Justo Sierra, north of the cathedral, is the former **Colegio San Ildefonso** ⓘ *T55-5702 2594, www.sanildefonso.org.mx, Tue-Sun 1000-1800, US$3.50, Tue free*, home to some interesting murals. Built in 1749 in splendid baroque as a Jesuit school, the complex has been magnificently restored and converted into one of the city's most important exhibition spaces. Don't miss the Orozco murals *The Trench*, and the satirical *The Aristocrats*.

Three blocks north of the Zócalo, the **Secretaría de Educación Pública** ⓘ *Argentina 28, daily 1000-1730, free*, was built in 1922. It contains over 200 frescoes by a number of painters and includes some of Diego Rivera's masterpieces, painted between 1923 and 1928, illustrating the lives and sufferings of the common people, as well as satirizing the rich.

Two blocks north of the cathedral is the small, intimate **Plaza Santo Domingo**, surrounded by fine colonial buildings. The Antigua Aduana (former customs house) is on the east side; the Portales de Santo Domingo, on the west, where public scribes and owners of small hand-operated printing presses still carry out their business; the church of Santo Domingo, 1737, in Mexican baroque, on the north side; and the old Edificio de la Inquisición, where the tribunals of the Inquisition were held, at the northeast corner.

La Merced

Dating back over 400 years, the **Mercado Merced** ⓘ *Rosario Puerto 4, several blocks southeast of the Zócalo, metro Merced, daily 0700-1900*, said to be the largest market in all the Americas, spills out over several blocks in a riot of commercial activity, colour and exotic smells. It sells everything from fresh market produce to shoes and cheap nylon clothes.

Wander south of the Zócalo and east along Calle República de El Salvador past tiny alley ways crammed with stalls and bustling with street vendors, all of which end at the market itself.

Zócalo to La Alameda

Avenida Madero leads from the Zócalo west to the Alameda and holds a number of interesting buildings. The beautifully restored, 18th-century **Palacio de Iturbide** ⓘ *Av Madero 17, metro Bellas Artes, Tue-Sun 0900-1800, free*, is among the most elegant baroque buildings in the city. Built between 1779-1784, it was once the home of Emperor Agustín de Iturbide (1821-1823), a royalist general, who changed sides during the struggle for Independence. It is now owned by the Mexican bank, Banamex.

Towards the Alameda, the 16th-century **Casa de los Azulejos** (House of Tiles) ⓘ *Madero 4, T55-5512 1331, daily 0700-0100, free*, is brilliantly faced with blue and white 18th-century Puebla tiles. Occupied by the Zapatista army during the Revolution, it is now home to Sanborn's Restaurant. The central courtyard is graced by Moorish arches and stone pillars; while the staircase walls are covered with an Orozco fresco.

Opposite the Casa de los Azulejos is the **Church of San Francisco**, founded in 1525 by the 'Apostles of Mexico', the first 12 Franciscans to reach the country. By far the most important church in colonial days, mass here was attended by the Viceroys themselves, including Hernán Cortés, whose body rested here for some time.

Further north, near the post office, the **Museo Nacional de Arte** ⓘ *Tacuba 8, T55-5512 9908, Tue-Sun 1030-1730, US$3, free Sun*, was built in 1904 and designed by the Italian architect Silvio Contri. The building has magnificent staircases made by the Florentine firm Pignone. Stunningly refurbished in 2003, the museum houses more than 100 paintings by José María Velasco, as well as a large collection of Mexican art dating from the 16th century.

La Alameda and around

Alameda Central

The Alameda park has had many roles in its long history – from Aztec market, to execution area for the Spanish Inquisition, to temporary camp for US soldiers in the late 1840s. The 19th century was its heyday as all social classes mingled for their Sunday stroll. Today the park has temporary stalls and is well lit at night. Badly affected by the 1985 earthquake, the surrounding area is being transformed by new building work. Within the gardens of the Alameda Central is the great glass tower of the **Torre Latinoamericana** ⓘ *daily 0930-2230, US$4.50 to go up*, which has a viewing platform with telescopes on the 44th floor, although the daytime view is often obscured by smog.

Palacio de Bellas Artes

ⓘ *Plaza de la Constitución, metro Zócalo. Daily 0930-1900, free. Performances by the Ballet Folklórico de México, Sun 0930 and 2030, Wed 2030 (T55-5521 9251 or www.balletamalia.com for details); book in advance.* A large, flamboyant art deco building, home to the Ballet Folklórico de Mexico. The building has sunk 4 m since it was built, and has frescoes by Rivera, Orozco, Tamayo and Siqueiros, including Rivera's superb *Man at the Crossroads*, a second version of the mural destroyed by the New York Rockefeller Center in 1934, because of its anti-capitalist slant. Perhaps the most remarkable thing about the theatre is its glass curtain designed by Tiffany – which can only be seen during performances.

Museo Mural Diego Rivera

ⓘ *north side of the Jardín de la Solidaridad at the west end of the Alameda Central, Tue-Sun 1000-1800, US$1.50, free for students with ISIC card.*

A highly recommended museum, purpose-built to house Diego Rivera's huge (15 m by 4.8 m) and fascinating mural, the *Sueño de una Tarde Dominical en la Alameda Central*, which was removed from the earthquake-damaged Hotel del Prado on Avenida Juárez in 1985. One of Rivera's finest works, it presents a pageant of Mexican history from the Conquest up to the 1940s with portraits of national and foreign figures, heroes and villains, as well as his wife, Frida Kahlo.

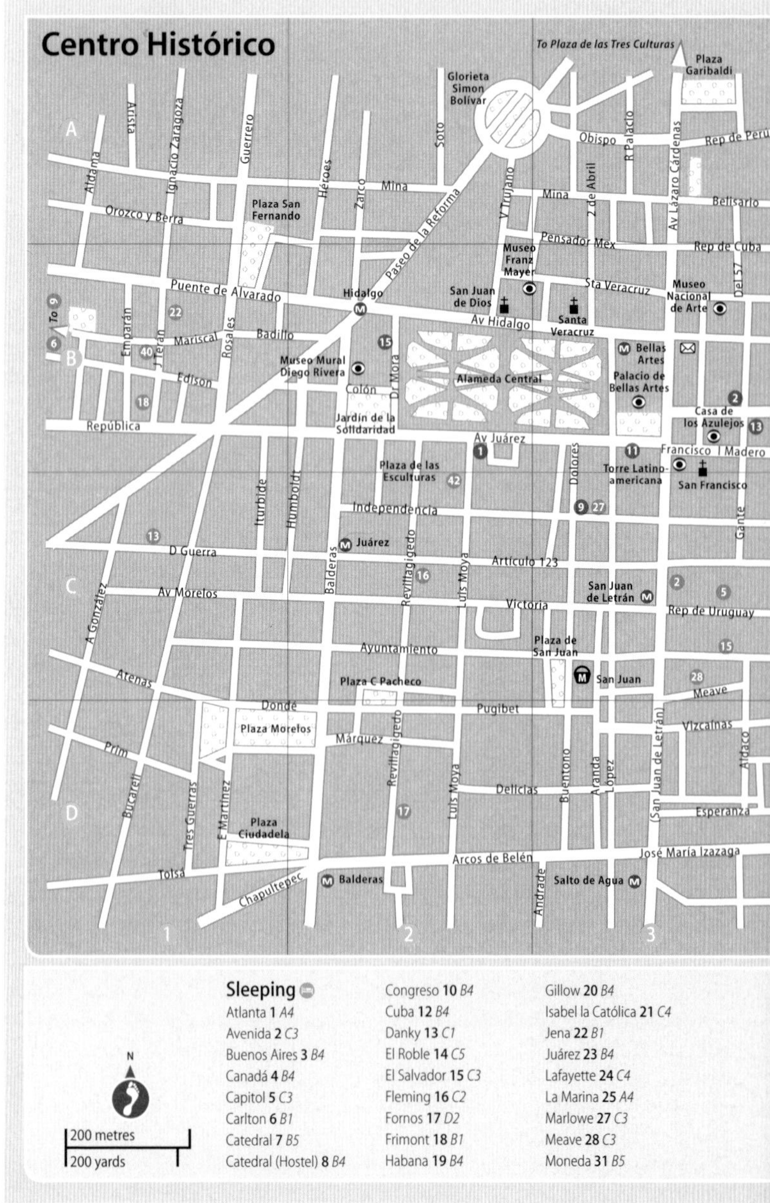

Museo Franz Mayer

On the northern side of the Alameda, the **Museo Franz Mayer** ⓘ *Hidalgo 45, T5518-2265, Tue-Sun 1000-1700, US$3 (US$0.50 cloister only), Tue free*, in the former Hospital de San Juan de Dios, was built in the 17th century. Exquisitely restored, it houses a library and an important decorative arts collection of ceramics, glass, silver, timepieces, furniture and textiles, as well as Mexican and European paintings from the 16th to 20th centuries. Its cloister is an oasis of peace in the heart of the city.

Monte Carlo **32** *C4*
República **37** *B4*
Rioja **39** *B4*
Royalty **40** *B1*
San Antonio **41** *B4*
San Francisco **42** *C2*
Texas **9** *B1*
Tuxpan **44** *A4*
Washington **45** *B4*
Zamora **46** *B4*

Eating

Bamerette **1** *B2*
Bar la Opera **2** B3
Café El Popular **3** *B4*
Café La Blanca **4** *B4*
Café Tacuba **5** *B4*
La Casa de las Sirenas **7** *B5*
Mr Lee **9** *C3*
Nadja **10** *D4*
Sanborn's **11** *B3*
Sushi Roll **13** *B3*
Trevi **15** *B2*

Background

Murals de Los Tres Grandes

Muralism in Mexico is dominated by 'Los Tres Grandes' – Diego Rivera, José Clemente Orozco and David Alfaro Siqueiros. Out of the turmoil of the 1910 Revolution emerged a need for a visual expression of Mexican identity (*Mexicanidad*) and unity. In 1921 Orozco and Siqueiros were commissioned by the Minister of Education to create a visual analogue on a massive scale that would spread awareness of Mexican history and encourage social change. Driven by left-wing ideas, and influenced by frescoes they had seen in Italy, they painted scenes of pre-Columbian society, modern agriculture and medicine, and a didactic Mexican history showing the benefits of technology. The 'movement' fell apart almost from its inception. There were riots objecting to the communist content of murals and a long ideological and artistic disagreement between Siqueiros and Rivera. Yet, despite the failings of the 'movement' many outstanding murals continued to be painted into the early 1970s.

The main mural sites in Mexico City include the Palacio Nacional, Palacio de Bellas Artes, Museo Mural Diego Rivera, Colegio San Ildefonso, Secretaría de Educación Pública (pictured), Museo Nacional de Historia and the Ciudad Universitaria.

Plaza Garibaldi

About four blocks north of the post office off Eje Central Lázaro Cárdenas is Plaza Garibaldi, a must one evening, ideally on a Friday or Saturday, when up to 200 *mariachis* in their traditional costume of huge sombrero, tight silver-embroidered trousers, pistol and *sarape*, will play your favourite Mexican serenade for between US$5 and US$10. The whole square throbs with life and the packed bars are cheerful.

West of La Alameda

Paseo de la Reforma and Zona Rosa

The wide and handsome tree-lined **Paseo de la Reforma** is the city's main boulevard, which continues southwest from the Alameda to the Bosque de Chapultepec. Laid out during the 1860s, it is lined with fine mansions, banks, luxury hotels and chic boutiques. Along it are monuments to Columbus, Cuauhtémoc – the last Aztec King – and, at the intersection of Tiber/Florencia, a 45-m marble column supporting a golden angel representing Independence. This is a favourite spot for national celebrations and political demonstrations.

The famous **Zona Rosa** (Pink Zone) lies to the south of Reforma, west of Avenida Insurgentes, and is a pleasant area in which to stroll, shop and dine.

Bosque de Chapultepec

ⓘ *Metro to Chapultepec station for first section. Tue-Sun until 1600, free.*

This beautiful green space covering 1,600 hectares offers plenty to see. Sundays are the most animated days, but expect to queue at some sights. The park is divided into three sections; most of the interesting sites and museums are in the first section, described below.

Entering the park from the eastern gate, you pass the large, six-columned **Monumento a los Niños Héroes**, commemorating the young soldiers who defended the castle of Chapultepec against the 1847 American occupation. Behind the monument is Chapultepec Hill, with its imposing castle affording great views over the Valley of Mexico; it now houses the **Museo Nacional de Historia** ⓘ *Tue-Sun 0900-1615, US$4*. Further down Avenida Reforma is the **Museo de Arte Moderno** ⓘ *Tue-Sun 1000-1800, US$1*, where Orozco, Siqueiros and Rivera are well represented in the excellent collection of modern Mexican art. Further still, en route to the Anthropological Museum (see below), the **Museo Rufino Tamayo** ⓘ *Tue-Sun 1000-1800, US$2*, has a fine collection of works by this Modernist painter as well as his private collection of 20th-century art.

Behind the Museo de Anthropology lies the upmarket area known as **Polanco**. This is one of the chicest neighbourhoods in the city, with exclusive private residences, commercial art galleries, fashion stores and expensive restaurants.

Museo Nacional de Antropología

ⓘ *Av Paseo de la Reforma y Calzada Gandhi, Chapultepec Park, nearest metro station Chapultepec/Auditorio, or any colectivo along Reforma marked 'Auditorio', T55-5553 6381, Tue-Sun 0900-1900, US$3.50 except Sun (free, very crowded, arrive early). Guided tours in English or Spanish free for a minimum of 5 people, specify the parts you want to see.*

Without a doubt, this is one of the world's most important anthropology museums and provides a meaningful context to many ancient sights in Central America. The museum is famous not only for its vast collection of pre-Hispanic artefacts, but also for the originality of its design – the building is a work of art in itself, designed by architect Pedro Ramírez Vásquez in 1964. The exhibits are very well organized, with each room dedicated to a major Mesoamerican culture. For those travelling on to southern Mexico, Guatemala or Belize, the Oaxaca and Maya sections will be of particular interest. Because of the enormous amount to see, focus on a few highlights and allow plenty of time; floorplans are available.

Preclásico The first cultures of the Valley of México, spanning 2300 BC-AD 100. Note the miniature female figurines, dating from 1700-1300 BC, and the lovely acrobat figure, found in the grave of a shaman suggesting the existence of mysterious religious rites.

Teotihuacán This room contains some of the most important objects found at the first great city of the Valley of Mexico, page 79. The craftsmanship is notably more sophisticated. The stunning turquoise, obsidian and shell-covered stone burial mask as well as the complex and coloured incense pot representing the god Xochipilli stand out among other exquisite pieces. Note also the massive full-scale reconstruction of part of the Temple of Quetzalcoatl.

Toltec Pieces from several Toltec cities, most notably Xochitécatl and Tula, from AD 750-1200. From Tula come the "Atlantitos" – stone sculptures of warriors with their arms raised – as does the beautiful Chac Mool, a reclining figure with an abdominal cavity in which sacrificial offerings were placed. From Xochicalco near Cuernavaca come the weighty stone columns; note the intricately carved column depicting Tlaloc, god of water, with his characteristically long tongue.

Piedra del Sol (1479) in the Museo Nacional de Antropologia

Mexica The Aztec room is the highlight of the museum, with its stunning artefacts from perhaps the most bewitching of pre-Hispanic cultures. At the entrance is the Ocelotl-Cuauhxicalli, a jaguar baring its teeth with a hollow in its back for the placing of sacrificial human hearts. The huge statue of Coatlicue, goddess of the earth, shows her wearing a necklace of hands and hearts and a skirt of serpents under which her eagle claw feet protrude. The centrepiece is the Piedra del Sol, popularly (though not accurately) known as the Aztec calendar, the epitome of the cosmological and mathematical knowledge of the people of pre-Hispanic America. This vision of the Aztec universe was found by early colonists, reburied, then rediscovered in 1790. At the centre is the sun god, Tonatiuh, with his tongue shaped like a sacrificial knife.

Oaxaca Dedicated to Zapotec and Mixtec cultures from the Oaxaca Valley. Look out for the Zapotec jade bat god and jaguar motif pottery; as well as the rare Mixtec musical instruments, including a flute made from a human femur.

Golfo de México Covering the modern-day regions of Tuxtla, Veracruz and Tabasco, this room is dedicated to the Olmec civilization, a sophisticated culture that preceded Teotihuacán. The colossal heads are the highlight, noted for their mysteriously African features. But also look out for the handsome sculpture of the *hombre barbado*, or the wrestler, a wonderfully evocative piece.

Maya The influence of the Maya culture, at its apogee between AD 300-900, spread as far as modern-day Costa Rica. The undisputed highlight of this room is the sunken reproduction of the tomb of the Temple of the Inscriptions at Palenque that includes the spectacular jade death mask of the prince Pakal.

Norte/Occidente Less sophisticated and primarily agricultural, the cultures of the North and West have bequeathed a less impressive historical legacy, although this room has an interesting reconstruction of adobe houses from Paquimé in Chihuahua, as well as some pottery from Chicomoztoc, the desert site from which some claim the Aztecs originated.

Beyond the city centre

San Angel

ⓘ *Bus from Chapultepec Park or metro line 3 to Miguel Angel de Quevedo.*
San Angel, 13 km southwest of the centre, has narrow, cobbled streets, attractive colonial-era mansions, huge trees, and the charm of an era now largely past. Many visitors come for the **Bazar del Sábado** (Sat 0900-1400), a splendid folk art and curiosity market, and to see the tile-covered domes of the **Iglesia del Carmen**, now the **Museo del Carmen** ⓘ *Tue-Sun 1000-1645, $3, free Sun*, which houses colonial furniture and art, and has several mummified bodies displayed in the crypt. Also interesting are the **Museo Estudio Diego Rivera** ⓘ *Av Altavista y Calle Diego Rivera, Tue-Sun 1000-1800, free Sun*, where Rivera and Frida Kahlo lived and worked; and the **Museo de Arte Carrillo Gil** ⓘ *Av Revolución 1608, 1000-1800, US$3*, which has excellent temporary exhibits and a permanent collection from the 1930s to the 1960s, including murals by *Los Tres Grandes* (page 66) and works by Rodin, Picasso and Klee.

Coyoacán

ⓘ *Nearest metro stations are Viveros, Miguel Angel de Quevedo or General Anaya – note that these are more convenient than Coyoacán station. From General Anaya there is a pleasant walk along Héroes del 47, across División del Norte and down Hidalgo to the square. Alternatively, take the metro to Coyoacán, followed by a colectivo towards Villa Coapa.*
This charming neighbourhood south of the historic centre is where Hernán Cortés had his headquarters during the battle for Tenochtitlán. It is also one of the most culturally dynamic and best-preserved parts of the city, with scores of fine old buildings, pavement cafés, bookshops and cultural centres that come alive at weekends. Two of the area's best-known former residents, Frida Kahlo and León Trotsky, have left fascinating museums. The **Museo Frida Kahlo** ⓘ *Calles Allende and Londres 247, northeast of Plaza Hidalgo, Tue-Sun 1000-1800; US$3*, has two rooms preserved as lived in by Kahlo and husband Diego Rivera, while the rest contain Kahlo's collection of traditional costumes and folk art, as well as her wheelchair and several paintings. In the same direction is **La Casa de Trotsky** ⓘ *Calle Río Churubusco 410, between Calles Gómez Farías and Morelos, Tue-Sun 1000-1700, US$3*, where the Russian revolutionary was murdered in his study in 1940. In the sombre house you can see the bullet holes of a previous attempt on his life and in the garden is the tomb where his ashes are laid.

Just south of Coyoacán, to the east side of Avenida Insurgentes, is the world-famous **Ciudad Universitaria** or UNAM (Universidad Nacional Autónoma de México), the biggest university in Latin America, with impressive architecture, sculptures and exhibits, page 78.

Xochimilco

ⓘ *28 km southeast of the city centre. Metro to Tasqueña, then tren ligero (about 20 mins). Get off at the last stop.*
Xochimilco ('the place where flowers grow') is an extraordinary network of canals and islands. It is based on the 'floating gardens', formed by mud and reeds, used by the Aztecs to make the lake fertile. Today it is famous for its lively Saturday market and for its carnivalesque atmosphere on Sundays, when colourful punt-like boats laden with hundreds of daytrippers from the capital jostle along the waterways. Go during the week for a more peaceful trip along the canals.

North of the city centre

Heading north from Centro Histórico (Metro line 3 to Tlatelolco), is the **Plaza de las Tres Culturas**, which retains elements of Aztec, colonial and modern architecture and holds great symbolism for Mexicans. It was here, in 1521, that the last battle of the Conquest of

 Mexico took place, and in 1968 it was the site of a massacre in which a large number of students were killed in clashes with the police. The remains of the main Aztec market are open to the public (0800-1800, free).

Further north, you can make your own pilgrimage to Mexico's most important shrine at the **Basílica de Guadalupe** ⓘ *US$3, buses marked 'La Villa' go close to the site, or Metro to La Villa (line 6)*. Built on the site of an earlier temple, the basílica celebrates two apparitions of the Virgin back in 1531 and draws up to 50,000 people on 12 December, her feast day. A trip to the Basílica is easily combined with a visit to the pyramids at Teotihuacán, page 79.

Sleeping

Prices of the more expensive hotels do not normally include breakfast or 15% tax; service is sometimes included but always check in advance. Reductions are often available. There are hotel reservation services at the airport and bus stations. **Corresponsales de Hoteles**, Blvd Centro 224-4, T55-5360 3356, can make reservations for more upmarket hotels.

Zócalo *p61, map p64*

B **Catedral**, Donceles 95, T55-5518 5232, www.hotelcatedral.com.mx, behind cathedral. Clean, spacious, good service.

B **Gillow**, 5 de Mayo e Isabel la Católica 17, T55-5518 1440. Central, large, clean, best rooms on 6th floor, many services, attractive, hospitable, good value, mediocre restaurant.

C **Canadá**, Av 5 de Mayo 47, T55-5518 2106. Smart place with bath, hot water, TV, a little overpriced but friendly and helpful.

C-D **San Antonio**, 2nd Callejón, 5 de Mayo 29, T55-5512 1625. Clean, pleasant, popular, friendly, TV in room. Get a receipt if paying in advance.

D **El Roble**, Uruguay y Pino Suárez, 2 blocks south of the Zócalo. Bath, TV, restaurant closes early.

D **Hostel Catedral**, Guatemala 4, T55-5518 1726, www.hostelcatedral.com New hostel just behind the cathedral, 209 beds (private rooms and dorms), kitchen restaurant, laundry, internet, secure storage, travel agency, great roof terrace and happy to accommodate late arrivals.

D **Juárez**, up a quiet alley off 5 de Mayo 17, 1-min walk from Zócalo, T55-5512 6929. Ask for room with window, safe, clean, marble bathrooms, phone, radio, TV. Will hold bags, book in advance as often full. Great location near the Zócalo.

D **Monte Carlo**, Uruguay 69, T55-5518 1418 (where DH Lawrence famously stayed). Elegant, clean, friendly owner, also suites, with bath, hot water, good about storing luggage, safe car park US$3.45, rooms in front noisy, disco 2230-0300 Wed-Sat. Refuses to take bookings without payment in advance.

D **Washington**, Av 5 de Mayo 54, T55-5512 3502. Clean, small rooms, cable TV. Credit cards accepted.

D-E **Hostal Moneda**, Moneda 8, 1 block east of the cathedral, T55-5522 5821, www.hostalmoneda.com.mx Clean, friendly, safe and very good location. Great meeting place. Rooftop terrace for great inclusive breakfasts with a beautiful view of the cathedral. Internet, tours.

D-E **Rioja**, Av 5 de Mayo 45, next door to **Canadá**, T55-5521 8333. Shared or private baths, reliable hot water, clean, popular, luggage store, well placed and recently remodelled. Watch your gear.

D-E **Zamora**, 5 de Mayo 50, T55-5512 1832. Generally ok, but the bathrooms are a bit tired. Big rooms work out very cheap for more than 2.

North of the Zócalo *p62, map p64*

E **Tuxpan**, Colombia 11, near Brasil, T55-5526 1118. In the heart of a street market so a lively spot, but modern, clean, TV, hot showers and each room has a mirror on the ceiling!

Zócalo to La Alameda *p63, map p64*

The best of the cheaper hotels are between the Zócalo and the Alameda.

C Buenos Aires, Av 5 de Mayo, T55-5518 2104. Safe, friendly, TV, stores luggage, hot water.
C Capitol, Uruguay 12, T55-5518 1750. Attractive lobby, recently remodelled, TV, bath, clean, friendly, don't miss the restaurant in the building: El Malecón.
C Congreso, Allende 18, T55-5510 4446. With bath, hot water, good, central, clean, quiet, TV, garage.
C Habana, República de Cuba 77 (near Metro Allende), T55-5518 1589. Spacious rooms, huge beds, renovated, very clean, phone, TV, friendly and helpful staff. Can be noisy, but good location, good choice if you're looking to avoid the crowds. Highly recommended.
D Atlanta, corner of Blvd Domínguez and Allende, T55-5518 1200. Good, clean, quiet if you ask for a room away from street, friendly, luggage store.
D Avenida, Lázaro Cárdenas 38 (Metro San Juan de Letrán), T55-5518 1007. With bath, central, friendly, will store luggage, good value, cheapest hotel that can be booked at airport. Recommended.
D El Salvador, República del Salvador 16, T55-5521 1247, near Zócalo. Modern, clean, laundry, safe, parking, good value.
D Lafayette, Motolinía 40 and 16 de Septiembre, T55-5521 9640. With bath and TV, good, clean, quiet (pedestrian precinct), but check rooms, there's a variety of sizes.
D La Marina, Allende 30 y Blvd Domínguez, T55-5518 2445. Clean, comfortable, safe, friendly, TV, hot water, will store luggage. Recommended.
D República, Cuba 57, T55-5512 9517. Wonderful old building, rooms a bit tired, but charming in a run-down way. With bath, hot water, rooms upstairs quieter. Recommended.
D-E Cuba, Cuba 69, T55-5518 1380. With bath, TV, good beds but some sheets too small.
D-E Isabel la Católica, Isabel la Católica 63, T55-5518 1213. Pleasant, popular, clean, helpful, safe, roof terrace, large shabby rooms with bath and hot water (some without windows), central, a bit noisy, restaurant, luggage held, cheaper rooms with shared bathroom. Recommended.

La Alameda *p63, map p64*

A San Francisco, Luis Moya 11, T55-5521 8960, www.sanfrancisco.com.mx, just off Alameda. Great views, friendly, excellent value, takes credit cards, good set meals.
B Fleming, Revillagigedo 35, T55-5510 4530, hotelfleming@prodigy.net.mx Good value, clean, central, restaurant, taxi service for guests.
C Marlowe, Independencia 17, T55-5521 9540. Clean, modern, finished to a high standard, safe parking, lift, restaurant good but service is slow (tourist office at airport refers many travellers here).
D Danky, Donato Guerra 10, T55-5546 9960/61. With bath, central, hot water, phone, clean, easy parking. Recommended.
D-E Fornos, Revillagigedo 92, near Metro Balderas, 10 mins' walk to Alameda. Extremely clean, bathroom, TV, radio, restaurant, large indoor car park, friendly staff, Dutch-speaking Spanish owner, very good value.
E Meave, Meave 6, esq Lázaro Cárdenas, T55-5521 6712. Bath, TV, clean, quiet, very friendly, ground-floor rooms rented by hour, but very discreet.

West of La Alameda *p66, map p64*

A fairly run-down part of town, but close to the working heart of the city.
A Jena, Jesús Terán 12, T55-5566 0277. New, central. Recommended (but not the travel agency on the premises).
C Texas, Ignacio Mariscal 129, T55-5564 4626. With bath, clean, hot water, small rooms, good breakfasts.
D Royalty, Jesús Terán 21, opposite Hotel Jena. With bath, TV, clean, very quiet, near Metro Hidalgo.
D-E Frimont, Jesús Terán 35, T55-5705 4169. Clean and central, with good views from rooms up on the 5th floor. Good, cheap restaurant.

E **Carlton**, Ignacio Mariscal 32-bis, T55-5566 2911. Getting rough around the edges, small rooms but some with fine views, rooms at front noisy, good restaurant. Recommended.

Paseo de la Reforma/Zona Rosa *p66*

A **Viena**, Marsella 28 (close to Juárez market and Metro Cuauhtémoc), T55-5566 0700. Quiet, with Swiss decor, garage and dining room.
B **Prim**, Versalles 46, T55-5592 4600, www.hotelprim.com.mx Clean and good in all respects.
C **Casa González**, Lerma y Sena 69 (near British Embassy), T55-5514 3302. Full board available, shower, clean, quiet and friendly, English spoken, no credit cards.
C **Uxmal**, Madrid 13, quite close to Zona Rosa. Clean rooms, same owner as more expensive **Madrid** next door (**AL**). With access to their better facilities.
D-E **Mansión Havre**, Havre 40, T55-5533 1271, mansionhavre@hotmail.com Good hostel with dorms, kitchen, small balcony.
E **Hostel Home**, Tabasco 303, Col Roma, T55-5511 1683, www.hostelhome.com.mx Great little hostel with the cleanliness and services you expect (kitchen, friendly staff, dormitory accommodation) in a quiet part of town.

Eating

The number and variety of eating places is vast; this is only a small selection.

Zócalo *p61, map p64*

¥¥¥ **Centro Catalán**, Bolívar 31, open 1100-1700 only. Excellent paella and other Spanish cuisine (2nd floor).
¥¥¥ **La Casa de las Sirenas**, Tacuba y Seminario, behind the cathedral. Mexican menu, fantastic selection of tequilas. Excellent food and service.
¥¥¥ **Mesón del Castellano**, Bolívar y Uruguay, T55-5518 6080. Good atmosphere, plentiful and not too dear, excellent steaks. Daytime only.
¥¥ **Centro Castellano**, Uruguay. Excellent value, try the steaks.
¥ **El Reloj**, 5 de Febrero 50. Good *comida* and *à la carte*.
¥ **Mariscos**, República de Uruguay, opposite No 28. Bustling lunch stop, good seafood meals and fish soup.
¥ **Nadja**, Mesones 65, near Pino Suárez. Typical food, set menu for US$1.30, large portions, friendly.
¥ **Pancho** Uruguay 84. Recommended for its breakfasts, cheap meals and service.
¥ **Restaurante Vegetariano**, Filomeno Mata 13, open until 2000, Sun 0900-1900. Good and cheap *menú del día*.

North of the Zócalo *p62, map p64*

¥¥¥ **Hostería Santo Domingo**, 70 Belisario Domínguez, 2 blocks west of Plaza Santo Domingo, T55-5510 1612. Oldest restaurant in town with former diners creating a who's who of Mexican history. Good food and service and excellent live music.
¥ **Comida Económica Verónica**, República de Cuba, 2 doors from **Hotel Habana** (No 77). For tasty breakfasts and set *comida corrida*, very hot *chilaquiles*, good value, delightful staff. Closed Sun.

Zócalo to La Alameda *p63, map p64*

¥¥¥ **Café Tacuba**, Tacuba 28, very old restaurant with stunning tiles, not touristy, Mexican food, live music and mariachis. Politician, Danilo Fabio Altamirano, was assassinated here in 1936.
¥¥¥ **Bar La Opera**, 5 de Mayo near Bellas Artes, T55-5512 8959, Mon-Sat 1300-2400, Sun 1300-1800. Elegant bar, open since 1870. Relaxing atmosphere, Mexican appetizers and entrées and expensive drinks. The bullet hole in the ceiling was allegedly left by Pancho Villa.
¥¥¥ **Sanborn's Casa de los Azulejos**, Av Madero 17. **Sanborn's** has 36 locations in Mexico, with soda fountain, drugstore, restaurant, international magazines, handicrafts, chocolates, etc. This is the most famous branch in the 16th-century 'house of tiles'. Beautiful high-ceilinged

room, with Orozco mural on staircase.
ŸŸ **El Patio del Gaucho**, Uruguay. Moderate prices, attentive, good *asado*.
ŸŸ-Ÿ **Café El Popular**, 5 de Mayo 52, on corner of alley to **Hotel Juárez**. Cheap, rushed, open 24 hrs, good meeting place.

West of La Alameda *p66, map p*

Ÿ **El Sol**, Gómez Farías 67, Col San Rafael. Frequented by journalists, superb Mexican cuisine and *comida corrida*.

Paseo de la Reforma/Zona Rosa *p66*

ŸŸŸ **Cardenal**, Palma 23. Food, service and music, all outstanding, 1930s ambience.
ŸŸŸ **Carousel Internacional**, Hamburgo and Niza. Very popular drinking-hole for smartly-dressed Mexicans, resident *mariachi*, food not gourmet but fun.
ŸŸŸ **Karl**, Amberes near junction with Londres. Excellent vegetarian buffet.
ŸŸ La Puerta del Angel, Varsovia y Londres. Local food and American cuts, very good.
Ÿ **El Huequito**, Bolívar 58. Casual, friendly, cheap meals for US$2.
Ÿ **Yug**, Varsovia 3. Vegetarian, 4-course set lunch US$3.50. Health food shop.

Bosque de Chapultepec and Polanco *p67*

ŸŸŸ **Cambalache**, Arquimedes north of Presidente Masaryk. Argentine steakhouse, wide selection of wines, cosy atmosphere.
ŸŸŸ **Charlotte´s**, Lope de Vega 341, north of Horacio. English and international cuisine, stunningly inventive.
ŸŸŸ **Fisher's**, Taine 311, Polanco. Superb seafood, not expensive for the quality and presentation. No reservations accepted.
ŸŸŸ **La Parrilla Suiza**, Arquimedes y Presidente Masaryk. For grilled meats, *alambres*, *sopa de tortilla* and other meat-and-cheese dishes, very popular, especially 1400-1600, service fair.
ŸŸ **Chilango's**, Molière between Ejército Nacional and Homero. Good value and service, MTV videos. Recommended
ŸŸ **Embers**, Séneca y Ejército Nacional. 43 types of hamburger, good French fries.

San Angel *p69*

ŸŸŸ **San Angel Inn**, Diego Rivera 50, T55-5616 2222, www.sanangelinn.com Mon-Sat 1230-0030, Sun 1300-2130. Top-quality dining in the former Carmelite monastery. If you can't afford a meal, it's worth going for a drink.

Coyoacán *p69*

ŸŸŸ **El Jolgorio**, tucked away on Higuera, opposite the post office. Excellent lunch menu, reasonable set meal prices, good salads and vegetarian dishes.
ŸŸŸ **Mesón Antiguo Santa Catarina**, delightful restaurant in the square of the same name. Good Mexican cuisine at reasonable prices, splendid atmosphere, especially for breakfast or supper.
ŸŸŸ-ŸŸ **Hacienda de Cortés**, Fernández Leal 74, T55-5659 3741, www.hacienda decortes.com.mx. Large shaded outdoor dining area, excellent breakfast, good value *comida corrida* US$5, try the *sábana de res con chilaquiles verdes*.
ŸŸ-Ÿ **La Guadalupana**, Higuera and Caballocalco, a few steps behind the church of San Juan Bautista, T55-5554 6253, Mon-Sat 0900-2300. One of the best-known *cantinas* in Mexico, dating from 1932, fantastic food, a great atmosphere and no apologies for the passionate interest in bull fighting.
ŸŸ-Ÿ **El Morral**, Allende 2. Set lunch, good Mexican food, handmade tortillas, price doubles at weekends, no credit cards, palatial lavatories.
Ÿ **Mercado**, between Malintzin and Xicoténcatl, opposite Jardín del Carmen. Exquisite *quesadillas* at Local 31; outside try the seafood at *El Jardín del Pulpo*.
Ÿ **Rams**, Hidalgo, almost opposite Museo Nacional de las Culturas Populares. Excellent fish, great value *comida corrida*.

Entertainment

For all cultural events, check *Tiempo Libre*, every Thu from news-stands, US$1, or monthly programmes available from Bellas Artes bookshop.

Bars and clubs

Nightlife in Mexico City is as lively and varied as everything else the city has to offer. From gentle supper clubs with floorshows to loud, brash nightclubs, and from piano bars to *antros* (or disco-bars) and traditional Mexican music bars – all tastes are catered for. Popular districts include Zona Rosa, Polanco, San Angel and Coyoacán. Clubbing starts late with most just getting going by midnight. Prices of drinks and admission vary enormously depending on the area. Many bars and nightclubs close on Sun. Remember that, because of the high altitude, 1 alcoholic drink in Mexico City can have the effect of 2 at lower altitudes.

Cinemas

A number of cinemas show films in the original language with Spanish subtitles; check *Tiempo Libre* magazine for details. Most cinemas, except **Cineteca Nacional**, offer reduced prices on Wed. **Cine Diana**, Av Reforma, at the end where Parque Chapultepec starts. **Cine Electra**, Río Guadalquivir (near El Angel). **Cine Latino**, Av Reforma between the statue of Cuauhtémoc and El Angel. **Cine Palacio Chino**, in the Chinese *barrio* south of Av Juárez (also interesting for restaurants). **Cine Versalles**, Versalles (side street off Av Reforma, near statue of Cuauhtémoc). **Cinematógrafo del Chopo**, Dr Atl, non-commercial films daily 1700 and 1930. **Cineteca Nacional**, Metro Coyoacán (excellent film bookshop and library).

Theatres

Palacio de Bellas Artes (for Ballet Folklórico, opera and classical concerts, p 63). **Teatro la Blanquita**, Av Lázaro Cárdenas Sur near Plaza Garibaldi. Variety show nightly with singers, dancers, comedians, magicians and ventriloquists. **Teatro de la Ciudad**, Donceles 36, T55-5510 2197, Ballet Folklórico Nacional Aztlán, US$3- US$15 for tickets, very good shows Sun and Wed.

Auditorio Nacional, Paseo de la Reforma, Chapultepec, is where major concerts and spectaculars are often staged. The **Central Nacional de las Artes**, on the edge of the Delegación Coyoacán, at the southeast corner of Churubusco and Tlalpan (Metro General Anaya), is a huge complex of futuristic buildings dedicated to the training and display of the performing and visual arts.

Festivals and events

15 Sep, **Independence** celebration, the President gives the *Grito*, 'Viva México', from the Palacio Nacional on the Zócalo at 2300 and rings the Liberty Bell (now, sadly, electronic!). This is followed by fireworks. Just as much fun, and probably safer, is the *Grito* that takes place at the same time in the Plaza in Coyoacán.
16 Sep, military and regional **Independence parades** in the Zócalo and around, 0900-1400, great atmosphere.
12 Dec, **Guadalupana** at the Basílica de Guadalupe, definitely worth a visit.

Shopping

Art and handicrafts

There is an annual **national craft fair** in Mexico City, first week in Dec.
Fonart, Av Patriotismo 594 (Metro Mixcoac), T55-5598 1666; also at Av Juárez 89 (Metro Hidalgo). Fondo Nacional para el Fomento de las Artesanías, is a state organization founded to rescue and promote the traditional crafts of Mexico. Competitive prices, superb quality.
La Carreta, underneath Sanborn's, San Angel, dozens of stalls selling Mexican crafts and *artesanías*. See also Markets.

Books

Many good bookshops in the city centre, especially along Juárez, Madero and Donceles, also along MA de Quevedo (Coyoacán/San Angel – Metro MA de Quevedo). **American Bookstore**, Madero 25, has large stocks of Penguins and

Pelicans. **Sanborn's** chain sells English-language magazines and some best-selling paperbacks in English. **Casa Libros**, Monte Athos 355, Lomas, has 2nd-hand books in English, all proceeds to the American Benevolent Society, gifts of books welcome. **La Torre de Papel**, Filomeno Mata 6-A, Club de Periodistas, sells newspapers from all over Mexico and US. **El Agora**, Insurgentes and **El Parnaso**, on the square in Coyoacán, specialize in art and have a good selection in English.

Markets

As at all markets, be particularly vigilant about pickpockets.

Buena Vista craft market, Aldama 187 y Degollado (Metro Guerrero), excellent quality (Mon-Sat 0900-1800, Sun 0900-1400). **Mercado La Lagunilla** near Glorieta Cuitláhuac (*colectivo* from Metro Hidalgo), a flea market with some antiques and collectable bargains (daily, but Sun best day). Good atmosphere. **Mercado Insurgentes**, Londres, Zona Rosa, good for silver, but other things are expensive, stallholders pester visitors. **San Angel Bazar del Sábado**, expensive but good, leather belts, crafts and silver; Sat only from 1100. **Mercado Jamaica**, Metro Jamaica, line 4, huge variety of fruits and veg, also flowers, pottery and birds. **Mercado Merced** (p 62), Metro Merced, vast typical local market, good atmosphere. **Mercado San Juan**, Ayuntamiento and Arandas, near Metro Salto del Agua, good prices for handicrafts, especially leather goods and silver; Mon-Sat 0900-1900, Sun 0900-1600 (don't go before 1000). **Plaza Ciudadela** market (Mercado Central de Artesanías, weekdays 1100-1800, Sun 1100-1400), beside Balderas 95 between Ayuntamiento y Plaza Morelos, government-sponsored, fixed prices, good selection, reasonable and uncrowded. **Mercado Sonora**, secret potions and remedies, animals and *artesanías*. **Tianguis del Chopo**, Aldama, No 211, between Sol and Luna, Sat 1000-1600, clothes, records, frequented by hippies, punks, rockers and police.

Activities and tours

Football

Estadio Azteca Sun midday. To get there take metro to Taxqueña terminus, then tram en route to Xochimilco to Estadio station; about 75 mins from Zócalo.

Hiking

Club de Exploraciones de México, Juan A Mateos 146, Col Obrero (Metro Chabacano), T55-5578 5730, Wed or Fri 1930-2400. Walks in and around the city.

Horse races

Hipódromo de las Américas, west of Blvd Avila Camacho, off Av Conscriptos. Beautiful track with lagoons, flamingoes, and plenty of atmosphere. Incorporates exhibition and convention centre.

Tour operators

Al Aire Libre, Centro Comercial Interlomas, Local 2122, Lomas Anáhuac Huixquilucan, T55-5291 9217. Rafting, climbing, caving, ballooning, parapenting.

Ecogrupos de México, Centro Comercial Plaza Inn, Insurgentes Sur 197-1251, T55-5661 9121. Nature tours.

Grey Line Tours, Londres 166, T55-5208 1163. Reasonably priced tours, car hire, produces *This is Mexico* book (free).

Hivisa Viajes, Río Támesis 5, Col Cuauhtémoc, T55-5703 0911, sheratondfmex@webtelmex.net.mx Reliable, good for flights.

Humboldt Tours, José María Velasco 34, San José Insurgentes, T55-5660 9152. One of Mexico's leading tour operators.

Intercontinental Adventures, Homero 526-801, Col Polanco, T55-5225 4400. Historical tours, rafting and sea kayaking.

Mundo Joven Travel Shop, Guatemala 4, Col Centro, T55-5518 1755, www.mundojoven.com, issues ISIC card, agents for International Youth Hostel Federation.

Protures Viajes, Av Baja California 46, Col Roma Sur, T55-5264-4497, www.proturs-.com.mx Recommended for flights.

Transport

Air

For airport information, see p59. For details of flights, see p17.

Airline offices Many offices are on Paseo de la Reforma or Hamburgo. **Aero California**, Reforma 332, T55-5207 1392. **Air Canada**, Hamburgo 108, p5, T55-5511 2004. **Aeromar**, Sevilla 4, T55-5133 1111.

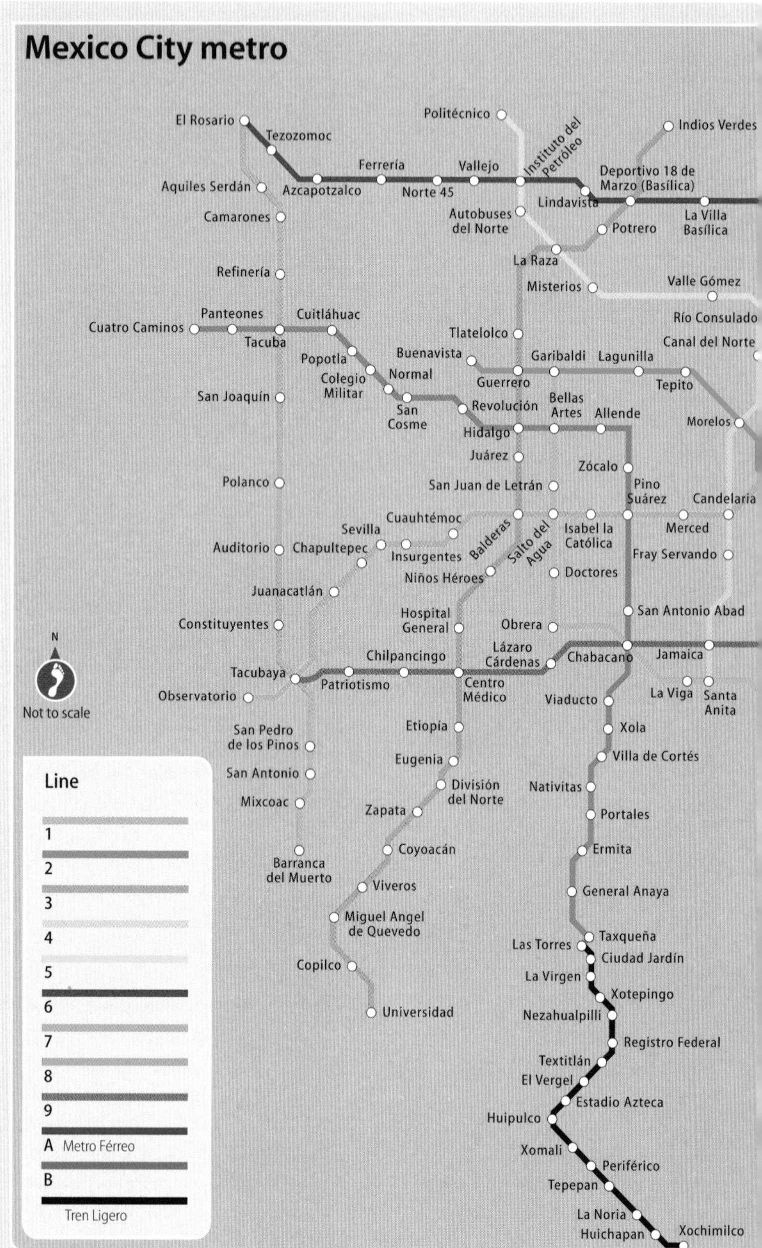

AeroMéxico, Insurgentes Sur 724, T55-5133 4010. **Air France**, Edgar Allan Poe 90, T55-5627 6000, airport T55-5571 6150. **American Airlines**, Reforma 314, T55-5208 6396. **Avianca**, Reforma 195, T55-5566 8588. **British Airways**, Jaime Balmes 8, Los Morales, T55-5387 0310. **Canadian Airlines**, Reforma 390, T55-5207 6611. **Continental**, Andrés Bello 45, T55-5546 9503. **Delta**, Reforma 381, T55-5525 4840. **Iberia**, Reforma 24, T55-5566 4011. **KLM**, Paseo de las Palmas 735, T55-5202 4444. **Lufthansa**, Paseo de las Palmas 239, T55-5202 8866. **Mexicana**, Xola 535, Col del Valle, T55-5660 4433. **Northwest Airlines**, Reforma y Amberes 312, T55-5511 3579, Reforma 300, T55-5525 7090. **Taca**, Morelos 108, Col Juárez, T55-5546 8807. **United Airlines**, Leibnitz 100, T55-5250 1657.

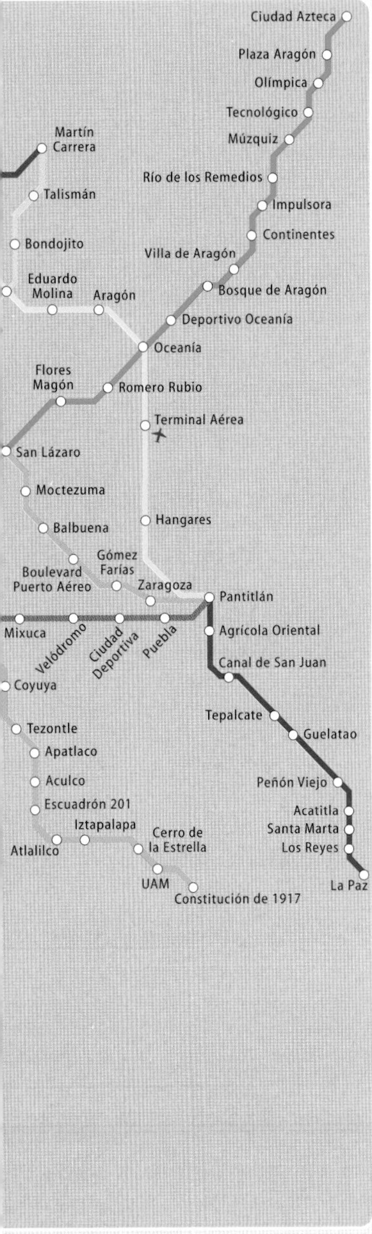

Bus

Local Buses with odd numbers run north–south, even numbers run east–west. Fares cost US$0.20, exact change only. A useful route is No 76 from Uruguay (about the level of the Juárez Monument at Parque Alameda) along Paseo de la Reforma. A *Peribus* service goes round the entire Anillo Periférico. Trolley buses charge US$0.15.

Long distance For transport to/from terminals, see p59. Advance booking is highly recommended for all trips, especially during Holy Week or Christmas. Buses to southern Mexico depart from **Terminal del Sur**, corner of Tlalpan 2205, Metro Taxqueña; buses to the south and east, including Oaxaca, the Yucatán and Guatemala, depart from **Terminal Oriente** (TAPO) Calzada Ignacio Zaragoza, Metro San Lázaro. Companies include **Cristóbal Colón**, Blvd Ignacio Zaragoza 200, T55-5542 7263 to 66, from TAPO; **ADO**, Buenavista 9 (T55-5592 3600 or 55-5542 7192 at terminal). **Estrella de Oro**, Calzada de Tlalpan 2205 (T55-5549 8520 to 29).

Car hire

Auto Rent, Reforma Nte 604; quick service at Av Chapultepec 168, T55-5533 5335 (55-5762 9892 airport). **Avis**, Medellín 14. **Budget Rent Auto**, Reforma 60. **Hertz**, Revillagigedo 2. **VW**, Av Chapultepec 284-6. **National Car Rental**, Insurgentes Sur

1883. **Odin**, Balderas 24-A. **Pamara**, Hamburgo 135, T55-5525 5572.

Metro *map p77*

Beware of pickpocketing. Trains are fast, frequent and clean but crowded during rush hour; there are separate areas for women and children at some stations, 1800-2100. 2 pieces of medium-sized luggage only. Tickets cost 2 pesos, buy several at a time to avoid queuing. Lines 1, 2, 3 and A run Mon-Fri 0500-0030, Sat 0600-0130, and Sun 0700-0030; the other lines open 1 hr later on weekdays. Lost property is held at Chabacano (lines 2, 8 and 9), Mon-Fri only. Metro information and maps are available from Insurgentes on the Pink line 1; most interchange stations also have information kiosks.

Taxi

For information or complaints, T55-5605 5520, and quote the taxi's ID number. Ordinary VW taxis can be flagged down anywhere but are not recommended for lone travellers. **Sitio taxis** (fixed ranks) are a much safer option as they can be booked in advance, T55-5571 9344, or taken from a taxi rank outside a hotel; they charge US$4.60 for up to 4 km, rising to US$22 for up to 22 km. **Colectivos** (often called *peseros*) run on fixed routes, often between metro stations and other known landmarks; the destination and route is displayed on the windscreen; fares are US$0.20 up to 5 km, US$0.25 up to 10 km and US$0.35 after.

Directory

Banks and currency exchange

ATMs are widespread. Credit cards are accepted in many hotels, restaurants and shops, but check for surcharges. There are several *casas de cambio* on Reforma and Madero in the centre. Major banks include **Banco Nacional de México** (Banamex), **Banco Internacional**, **Banco de Comercio** (Bancomer, Visa agent) and **Banca Serfín**. Hours are generally Mon-Fri 0930-1700, Sat 0900-1300. **American Express**, Reforma 234 y Havre, T55-5533 0380, Mon-Fri 0900-1800, Sat 0900-1300, slow but helpful.

Cultural centres

Amistad Británico-Mexicana, Benjamin Franklin Library, Londres 116, T55-5286 0017, www.amistadbm.org.mx. **Anglo-Mexican Cultural Institute**, Maestro Antonio Caso 127, T55-5566 6144. **British Council**, Lope de Vega 316, Polanco, T55-5263 1900. **Centro Cultural Universitario**, UNAM, www.unam.mx, has theatres, cinemas and concert halls. Its **Centro de Enseñanza para Extranjeros** offers excellent classes in Spanish language and Mexican culture, US$200 for 6 weeks; a student card from here allows free entry to museums and half price on many buses.

Embassies and consulates

Australia, Rubén Darío 55, Col Polanco, T55-5531 5225. **Belize**, Bernardo de Gálvez 215, Lomas Virreyes, T55-5520 1346, Mon-Fri 0900-1300. **Canada**, Schiller 529 (corner Tres Picos), near Anthropology Museum, T55-5724 7900, www.canada.org.mx **Guatemala**, Explanada 1025, Lomas de Chapultepec, CP11000, T55-5540 7520, Mon-Fri 0900-1300. **Ireland**, Sylvia Moronadi, San Jerónimo 790a, Metro Miguel Angel, T55-5595 3333, Mon-Fri

Going further

Teotihuacán

Located 49 km north of Mexico City, the ancient city of Teotihuacán is one of the most visited archaeological sites in Mexico. Dating back to 300 BC, it is a remarkable relic of an ancient civilization. There are three main areas: the **Ciudadela**, the **Pyramid of the Sun** (the third largest pyramid in the world) and the **Pyramid of the Moon**. The site is connected by the **Avenue of the Dead**, (the 'Calle de los Muertos'), which runs almost due north for nearly 4 km and is surrounded by temples and palaces. The **Palace of the Jaguars** and the **Palace of the Quetzal-butterfly** have well-preserved murals; the citadel and **Temple of Quetzalcóatl** have some bold sculptures. At the spring equinox, 21 March, the sun is perfectly aligned with the west face of the Pyramid of the Sun. Be prepared for lots of walking and don't forget that at altitude, it can become exhausting. Take plenty of water. If possible, try to arrive early as it gets crowded when the tour companies arrive around 1100.

Getting there Buses leave the Terminal del Norte (Metro Autobuses del Norte) every 30 mins until 1800, US$2 one way, 1 hr. 'Pirámides' buses are white with a yellow stripe – check that your bus goes to the site entrance, not just to the nearby town of San Juan Teotihuacán. Mexbus, T55-5514 2233 or T01800- 523-9412 (toll free), www.mexbus.net, provides day trips, including a stop at the Basílica de Guadalupe (p70), with pick-up and return from central hotels, English-speaking guide and lunch for US$18.

0900-1700. **New Zealand**, JL Lagrange 103, 10th floor, Polanco, T55-5281 5486. UK, Río Lerma 71, T55-5242 8500 (Apdo 96 bis, México 5), Mon, Thu 0900-1400, 1500-1800, Tue, Wed, Fri 0900-1500. **USA**, Reforma 305, Col Cuauhtémoc, T55-5211 0042, Mon-Fri 0830-1730.

Internet

Internet cafés are abundant, usually open Mon-Sat 1000-2200. Rates US$2-3 per hr.

Medical services

Ambulance T060 or T080. **American British Cowdray Hospital (ABC)**, Observatorio past Calle Sur 136, T55-5277 5000 (emergency T55-5515 8359); **Hospital de Jesús Nazareno**, 20 de Noviembre 82. **Hospital Santa Elena**, Querétaro 58, Col Roma, T55-5574 7711. **Vaccination centre** Benjamín Hill 14, Metro Juanacatlán (line 1). Mon-Fri 0830-1430, 1530-2030, Sat 0830-1430. **Dr César Calva Pellicer** (speaks English), Copenhague 24, 3rd floor, T55-5514 2529.

Post

Correo Central Tacuba y Lázaro Cárdenas, opposite Palacio de Bellas Artes, Mon-Fri 0800-2400, Sat 0800-2000, Sun 0900-1600. Mail kept for 10 days at Poste Restante, closed Sat and Sun. Also branches at the airport and bus stations.

Safety

As with any big city, take precautions, especially on public transport or in crowded areas such as markets. If robbed or attacked, complaints can be made at Tourist Information Centres or to the Tourist Police, in blue uniforms, who are usually very friendly. For problems such as theft, fraud or abuse of power by officials, call **Protectur**, T55-5516 0490.

Oaxaca

Gold Zapotec mask from Tomb 7, Monte Albán

Don't miss...
1 Santo Domingo, Oaxaca City ▸▸ p86.
2 Mercado de Abastos, Oaxaca City ▸▸ p99.
3 Monte Albán ▸▸ p89.
4 Puerto Escondido & the Pacific coast ▸▸ p104.
5 Tehuantepec ▸▸ p109.
p84
p104
MEXICO
OAXACA
Pacific Ocean
Golfo de Tehuantepec
Laguna Superior
Laguna Inferior
Laguna Mar Muerto
Sierra Juárez
Sierra Madre del Sur
Presa B Juárez
Río Nanchital
Oaxaca
Huitzo
Guelache
El Punto
Oacaotepec
Santa María Peñoles
Santiago Tlazoyaltepec
Monte Albán
Cuilapan de Guerrero
Zaachila
El Tule
Teotitlán del Valle
Tlacolula
Yagul
Mitla
San Bartolo Coyotepec
San Pablo Villa de Mitla
Zimatlán
Santiago Matatlán
San Lorenzo Albarradas
San Baltazar Guelavila
Ocotlan de Morelos
Santa Gertrudis
Santa María Ayoquesco
La Pe
San Pedro Totolapan
Mano de León
Las Margaritas
Ejutla
Solá de Vega
Yogana
San Nicolás
San Vicente Coatlán
Juchatengo
Guixe
Río Anona
Monjas
Xitla
Miahuatlán
San Esteban Amatlán
Santa María Zoquitlán
Río Mijangos
San José Lachiguire
Quioquitani
Santa María Ozolotepec
La Ciénega
San Pablo Coatlán
San Gabriel Mixtepec
Santa Catarina Loxicha
San Miguel Suchixtepec
San Mateo Piñas
Puerto Escondido
Santo Domingo Morelos
San Bernadino
Candelaría Loxicha
San Isidro Apanga
Santa María Huatulco
Pechutla
Figueroa
Huatulco
Lagarto
Zipolite
Mazunte
Puerto Angel
Bajos de Coyula
Bajos del Arenal
Xadani
Morro Ayuta
Santiago Astata
Zaachilac
Santa Clarac
Morro Mazatlán
Salina Cruz
Rincón Moreno
Tehuantepec
Jalapa
Guiengola
San Pedro Huilotepec
San Mateo del Mar
Juchitán de Zarazoga
Magdalena Tlacotepec
Benito Juárez
Ixaltepec
Union Hidalgo
Niltepec
Santo Domingo
San Miguel Chimalapa
San Francisco Ixhuatan
San Pedro Tepanatepec
Chahuites
Trejo
Pueblo Viejo
Arriaga
La Gloria
Paredón
Chachimbo
Puerto Arista
Santa Isabel
Tierra Libertad
Boca del C
Jayacatlán
Santa Ana Yareni
Atepec
San Pedro Yaneri
San Miguel Talea
Tecohuilco
Ixtlan de Juárez
Guelatao de Juárez
Santiago Zoochila
Totontepec
Yaganiza
Mixistlán
San Pedro y San Ayutla
Santo Domingo Tepuxtepec
Santiago Zacatepec
Santa María Asunción Cacalotepec
Santo Domingo Narro
San José de Gracia
Santa Ana Tavela
Nejapa de Madero
El Camarón
El Coyul
San Carlos Yautepec
Santa María Ecatepec
Santo Domingo Chontecomatlón
Topiltepec
San José Chiltepec
San Miguel Ecatepec
Santiago Choapan
Santiago Jalahuy
Santiago Yaveo
Chinantequilla
Matamoros
San Juan Cotzoncón
Juan Otzolotepec
Jaltepec de Candayoc
El Coyalito
San Lucas Mazatlán
San Lucas Camotlán
Santo Quivicuzas
Guigovelaga
Agua Zarca
Lachidola
Tehuantepec
Guadalupe
Santa María
Santa María Guienagati
Almoloya
Matias Romero
Guichicoqui
Palomares
La Mixtequita
Donaji
Sarabiá
Cuauhtémoc
Boca del Monte
San María Chimalapa
Carranza
Suchilapan
Poblado Dos
RM Vidal
Aquiles Sérdan
135
178
131
190
185
200
N
20 km
20 miles

Introduction

The state of Oaxaca is rugged and remote, until you come to the lively, colourful and cosmopolitan city of Oaxaca, where very pleasant evenings can be spent at the terrace restaurants watching the world go by. Days are filled visiting the magnificent Santo Domingo church and museum and exploring the archaeological hilltop site of Monte Albán, with its gory engravings, or taking in a performance of the colourful Guelaguetza. Within easy reach of the city are several archaeological sites and villages where the descendants of those who built these wonderful pyramids create some of Mexico's most beautiful and varied handicrafts.

On the Pacific Coast, the resorts of Huatulco and Puerto Escondido offer all the usual beach-holiday activities, including surfing, water-skiing, parascending and scuba diving. If you want to avoid the crowds, there are many beautiful offbeat beaches away from the major resorts, but beware of strong undertows and rips. Further round the coast, on the Isthmus, allow some time to explore the friendly town of Tehuantepec, where you can admire the Zapotec dress and the white churches of the early colonial period which dot the landscape.

Ratings

Culture
★★★★★

Landscape
★★★★

Chillin'
★★★★

Activities
★★★★

Wildlife
★★★★

Costs
$$$$

Oaxaca City and around

Oaxaca, the cosmopolitan capital of the State of Oaxaca, lies 465 km from Mexico City. Declared a UNESCO World Heritage Site in 1987, it is one of Mexico's most beautiful cities. It is relatively compact and best explored on foot; at every turn breezy patios and majestic stone buildings reveal Oaxaca's importance during the colonial period, while markets, local crafts, traditional folk dances and ebullient feast days point to its indigenous roots. Highlights include the animated Zócalo, the sublime Santo Domingo church and museum, the hypnotic Mercado Abasto and mystical Monte Albán archaeological site overlooking the town.

The Central Valleys of the State of Oaxaca, which surround the capital, make a fine destination for day trips or overnight visits. The area features awe-inspiring archaeology (Mitla and Yagul are the best known), plus authentic native towns and villages. There is also good walking with impressive views and interesting mineral deposits at Hierve El Agua.

Getting there Frequent daily bus services and flights from Mexico City.

Getting around Good bus network, plenty of taxis or organized tours.

Time required 1 week.

Weather Very pleasant, eternal spring.

Sleeping From converted monasteries to bohemian hotels and artistic adobe posadas.

Eating Varied regional cuisine, specialities include *mole* and bitter chocolate.

Activities and tours Eco-tourism projects, cycling, hiking.

★ **Don't miss...** Santo Domingo ▸▸*86*

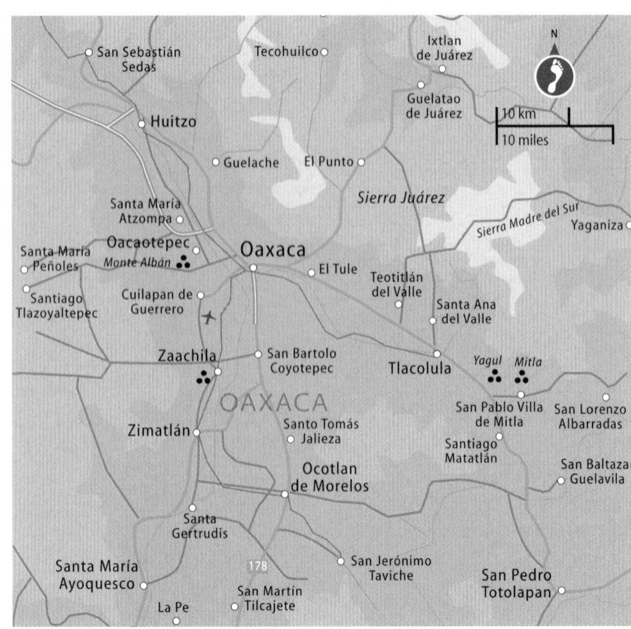

Ins and outs

Getting there Aeropuerto Xoxocotlán (OAX), is 9 km south of the city. **Transportación Terrestre Aeropuerto** ⓘ *Alameda de León No 1-G, opposite the cathedral in the Zócalo, T951-514 4350, office Mon-Sat 0900-1400, 1700-2000*, runs airport taxis (*colectivos*) to and from hotels in the city centre (US$2.30 per person). Other *colectivos* from Bustamante (3rd block from the Zócalo) charge US$0.50 to the airport

The first-class **bus** terminal is northeast of the Zócalo on Calzada Niños Héroes (some second-class buses also leave from here). The second-class terminal is west of the Zócalo on Calzada Valerio Trujano, near the Central de Abastos market. **Autobuses Unidos** (AU) have their own terminal northwest of the Zócalo at Prolongación Madero.

Getting around Local town minibuses mostly charge US$0.20. For the first-class bus terminal, buses marked 'VW' leave from Avenida Juárez; for the second-class terminal, buses are marked 'Central'. Most of the important sites are in or near the city centre and can be reached on foot.

Tourist information Sedetur ⓘ *Independencia 607, T951-516 0123, daily 0800-2000, www.oaxaca.gob.mx* has maps, postcards and information. A second **tourist office** ⓘ *Murgia 206, T951-516-0984*, has opened and is friendly and very helpful; ask here about the **Tourist Yú'ù** hostel programme in local communities (see page 94). **Instituto Nacional de Estadística, Geografía e Informática (INEGI)** ⓘ *Independencia 805*, for topographic maps and information about the state. Tourist publications include *Oaxaca Times*, monthly in English, www.oaxacatimes.com; *Oaxaca*, monthly in Spanish, English and French; *Comunicación*, in Spanish, with a few articles translated into English and French. *Guía Cultural*, published monthly by the Instituto Oaxaqueño de las Culturas, has a complete listing of musical events, exhibitions, conferences and libraries.

Safety Oaxaca is generally a safe city, however, sensible precautions are advised. Pickpockets are active in the markets, bus stations and wherever there are crowds. Women should be aware of so-called 'Zócalo boys' or *gavacheros*, local young men who hang around the Zócalo picking up foreign women and seeking favours. Oaxaca has a brand-new force of tourist police, some of whom speak English.

Sights » *pp93-103*

The major sights are concentrated around the Zócalo or along Macedonio Alcalá, a cobbled pedestrian mall that joins the Zócalo with the church of Santo Domingo. Avenida Independencia is the main street running east-west; the most photogenic part of the old city lies to the north; a commercial area, housing the cheaper hotels, lies to the south. Independencia is also a dividing line for the north-south streets, which change names here.

Zócalo and around

The **Zócalo** is the heart of town. Oaxacan life ebbs and flows through its leafy central park, along its serene arcades and beneath shady porticos lined with open-air cafés and restaurants. Circling the ornate centrepiece bandstand, men have their shoes shined, while munching on deep fried grasshoppers and, in the shade of giant laurel trees, vendors sell *pulsadores* to prevent the loss of the soul. Relaxing on park benches, *Oaxaqueños*, both young and old, deep in conversation, slurp a *café de olla* or a take a gulp of *mezcal* with a lick of salt. The square has a perpetual carnival atmosphere with colourful helium balloons bobbing over romantic fountains, pearly pink candyfloss and live music. Political demonstrations are often held opposite the graceful arcades of the **Palacio de Gobierno** (closed to the public in 2004), which occupies the south side of the Zócalo and contains two beautiful murals painted by Arturo García Bustos in 1980. The 17th-century **cathedral** has a fine baroque façade and, inside, an antique pipe organ. In front, scattered among the laurels and shocking-pink bougainvillea, a myriad of stalls sell everything from cloth dyed with purple snails to fruit-flavoured sherbets. In the evening, music and dance events provide great free entertainment.

The **Teatro Macedonio Alcalá**, 5 de Mayo y Independencia, is an elegant theatre from Porfirio Díaz's times. It has a Louis XV-style entrance and white marble staircase; regular performances are held here (although it was closed for restoration in 2004 for an unspecified time).

The **Museo de Arte Contemporáneo** ⓘ *Macedonio Alcalá 202, T951-514 2228, Wed-Mon 1030-2000, US$1*, is housed in a late 17th-century building with a stone façade, also known as the House of Cortés. There are 14 exhibit rooms, with a permanent exhibition of Oaxacan artists, including Rufino Tamayo, Francisco Gutierrez and Rodolfo Nieto. International exhibits have featured modern art, ranging from sculptures by Francisco Zuñiga to traditional African sculptures and pop art. There is also a library and café.

Further west, the **Museo de Arte Prehispánico Rufino Tamayo** ⓘ *Morelos 503, Mon, Wed-Sat 1000-1400, 1600-1900, Sun 1000-1500, US$3*, has an outstanding display of pre-Columbian artefacts dating from 1250 BC to AD 1100, donated by the Oaxacan painter Rufino Tamayo in 1974. Information is in Spanish only and is not comprehensive.

Santo Domingo and around

Four blocks from the square, along Calle Macedonio Alcalá, is Oaxaca's unmissable sight, the Franciscan church of **Santo Domingo**. The church is considered one of the best examples of baroque style in Mexico. When Aldous Huxley visited in 1933, he declared the church was "one of the most extravagantly beautiful churches in the world." Elaborately carved by the Dominicans in 1608, the church underwent extensive refurbishments in the 1950s, which have revealed stunning ceilings and walls, 30-feet thick, ablaze with gold leaf. The church is dominated by a three-storey gilded altar and polychrome bas relief, which reveals the family tree of Santo Domingo de Guzmán, the founder of the order.

The façade of Santo Domingo

Background

Hitting the sauce

The food of the state of Oaxaca is a fine representation of the complexity and variety of its cultures. The region's cuisine ranges from sublime to highly unusual.

A stroll through any of Oaxaca's markets will quickly bring you into contact with vendors selling *chapulines*. These small grasshopper-like creatures are fried, turning them bright red, and then served with lime. Another interesting ingredient in the diet is *gusanito*, a small red worm that is used to make a special sauce or ground with salt to accompany mezcal.

There are local curiosities for vegetarians as well. Flor de *calabaza*, squash flowers, are used in soup, in *empanadas*, or as a garnish. Soup is also prepared from *nopales*, the young leaves of the prickly-pear cactus.

The most typical regional snacks are *tlayudas*, huge crispy tortillas, covered with a variety of toppings (beef, sausage, beans or cheese) and grilled over the coals. Oaxacan string cheese, known as *quesillo*, is also famous, as is the area's excellent chocolate, made from ground cacao beans, almond, sugar and cinnamon, best enjoyed as a hot beverage. A slightly fermented drink made from corn flour is known as *atole*.

Another popular drink, for which the Oaxaca region is renowned, is *mezcal*. This highly alcoholic drink is prepared from the heart of the *agave espadin* and baked in dry ovens, which give the drink its characteristic smoky flavour. It is traditionally drunk straight, accompanied only by lime wedges dipped in *sal de guisano* – salt into which a special bright red worm has been ground.

Barbacoa is a pork, lamb or beef dish combining several different types of chillies and special condiments such as avocado leaves. The colour of the resulting sauce is a very deep red, reminiscent of another platter appropriately called *mancha manteles* (tablecloth stain).

The essence of Oaxacan cooking, however, and the recipes for which the state is most famous, are its many *moles*, which come in all colours of the rainbow. They are served as sauces accompanying beef, chicken, turkey or pork. The most complex by far is *mole negro* (black), combining at least 17 different ingredients including cocoa beans and sesame seeds. *Mole colorado* (red), or just *coloradito*, is quite spicy; *almendrado* (also red) is milder and slightly sweet; *mole verde* (green) is a bit tangy, while *mole amarillo* (yellow) rounds out Oaxaca's culinary chromatic spectrum.

For those interested in learning to cook Oaxacan cuisine, Susan Trilling, T951-518 7726, www.seasonsofmyheart.com is recommended.

Housed in the former convent adjoining the church, the **Centro Cultural Santo Domingo** ⓘ *Macedonia Alcalá and Gurrión, T951-516 2991, 1000-2000, closed Mon, US$3.80,* use of video US$3.50, no flash photographs allowed, includes the Museo de las Culturas de Oaxaca, a botanical garden, library, newspaper archives and bookstore. Construction of the convent started in 1575 and Dominican friars occupied the convent from 1608 to 1812. After the expulsion of the church, it was occupied by the Mexican army between 1812 and 1972, before housing the regional museum. Between 1994 and 1998, the convent was beautifully restored, using only original materials and techniques. The **Museo de las Culturas de Oaxaca**, referred to as 'the Louvre of Oaxaca', is a superb museum that requires at least four hours to visit. Exhibits displayed in 14 galleries are beautifully displayed, with detailed explanations in Spanish (audio visual tours available in English US$5). The history of Oaxaca from pre-Hispanic times to the contemporary period is presented through an archaeology collection and includes spectacular riches found in Tomb 7 of Monte Albán, uncovered in 1932 by archaeologist Juan Valenzuela. The museum also features different aspects of Oaxacan culture such as crafts, cooking and traditional medicine, as well as temporary exhibits showing the work of contemporary Mexican artists. The **Biblioteca Francisco Burgoa** (admission included), houses a collection of 24,000 ancient volumes dating from 1484. There are temporary exhibits and the library is open for research.

Also in the Centro Cultural is the interesting **Jardín Etnobotánico** ⓘ *T951-516 7615, free, guided tours (one hour) in Spanish at 1300 and 1800, in English Tue, Thu, Sat at 1100 and 1600, sign up in advance*. This garden aims to preserve different species of plants that are native to southern Mexico and that continue to play a role in the lives of different ethnic groups in Oaxaca: you can learn about the different species of *agaves* used to make mezcal, pulque and tequila; the trees used to make crafts; the *grana cochinilla*, an insect that lives in certain cacti and is used to dye cloth; the plants used in folk medicine; and many more.

Opposite Santo Domingo, an 18th-century colonial home houses the **Instituto de Artes Gráficas de Oaxaca** (IAGO) ⓘ *Macedonio Alcalá 507, T951-516 4750, daily 0900-2000, closed Tue, free (donation appreciated)*, which presents an interesting graphic arts collection donated by Oaxacan artist Francisco Toledo. There is also a very good reference library and beautiful courtyards filled with flowers.

The **Museo Casa de Juárez** ⓘ *García Vigil 609, T951-516 1860, 1000-1900, Sun 1000-1700, closed Mon, US$3*, is located in the former home of Benito Juárez, who lived here from the age of 12. The museum provides an atmospheric homage to Mexico's most revered president with an engaging display of Juárez's possessions, historical documents and some bookbinding tools. The house of the Maza family, for whom Benito Juárez worked and whose daughter he married, still stands at Independencia 1306 and is marked by a plaque.

Worth a visit are the **Arcos de Xochimilco** on García Vigil, which begins at Cosijopi, eight blocks north of the Zócalo, a picturesque area of cobbled passageways draped in jacaranda, closet-sized taco cafés, romantic fountains, gigantic cacti and ornate street lanterns. Callejón Hidalgo is one of the area's most beguiling streets.

West of the centre

The massive 17th-century **Basílica de La Soledad** (between Morelos and Independencia, west of Unión) has fine colonial ironwork and sculpture, including an exquisite Virgen de la Soledad. Its interior is predominantly fawn and gold, with plaques on the walls painted like cross-sections of polished stone. The fine façade is made up of stone of different colours; it is considered the best example of carved stonework in the city. Built on the site of the hermitage to San Sebastián, begun in 1582, it was consecrated in 1690 and the convent was finished in 1697.

There is a grand view from **Cerro de Fortín**, the hill to the northwest of the centre, here is the Guelaguetza amphitheatre; a monument to Juárez stands on a hillside below. Atop the hill are an observatory and **planetarium** ⓘ *shows Mon-Sat 1230 and 1900, Sun*

1230, 1800 and 1900, US$20, students US$1; best to take a taxi (about US$3.50) since the walk is dark and deserted. It is a pleasant walk from town to the hill as far as the planetarium and antennas, but muggings have been reported.

Monte Albán » pp93-103

ⓘ *10 km west of Oaxaca, T951-516 1215. Daily 0800-1800, US$3.80; video cameras US$3. Official guides US$12 per hr, check their credentials. Several buses depart from Hotel Trébol, 1 block south of Zócalo, 0930, 1030, returning 1330, 1400, US$1.30; to allow more time at the ruins (3 hrs recommended), take the tourist bus to Monte Albán, then walk the 4 km downhill to Colonia Monte Albán and get a city bus back from there. There is a museum, visitor's centre and restaurant at the site. Recommended reading includes the Bloomgarden Easy Guide to Monte Albán or Easy Guide to Oaxaca, available in major hotels or from the bookshop at Guerrero 108.*

Built on a flattened hilltop 400 m above the Oaxaca Valley, Monte Albán, the ancient capital of the Zapotecs, was declared a UNESCO World Heritage Site in 1987. Rising majestically above the Oaxaca valley, the ruins are a legacy of sophisticated architecture and fascinating iconography, with temples, tombs, plazas and ball court, revealing the enigmatic and compelling Zapotec culture at its apogee.

The Main Plaza The purpose of the Main Plaza has yet to be agreed. It was thought to have been a marketplace or ceremonial centre, but the restricted access to the site and absence of religious iconography contradict these interpretations. In addition, the imagery at Monte Albán is militaristic, with allusions to tortured captives and captured settlements.

Aligned on a north-south axis, the impressive structures at either end of the Main Plaza are believed to have been a palace (North Platform) and a temple (South Platform). There are 14 other structures around the plaza, including a ball court and an arrow-shaped building in front of the South Platform, which is aligned with the cardinal points and is thought to have been used for astronomy. One structure, known as Edificio de los Danzantes (Dancers), has bas reliefs, glyphs and calendar signs (probably 5th century BC).

The confederacy During the period AD 450-600, Monte Albán comprised 14 districts beyond the confines of the Main Plaza. It has been proposed that each of the 14 structures

The great plaza, Monte Albán

 located within the Main Plaza corresponded with one of the districts outside, each pertaining to a distinct ethnic group or polity. The site may therefore have been a pan-regional

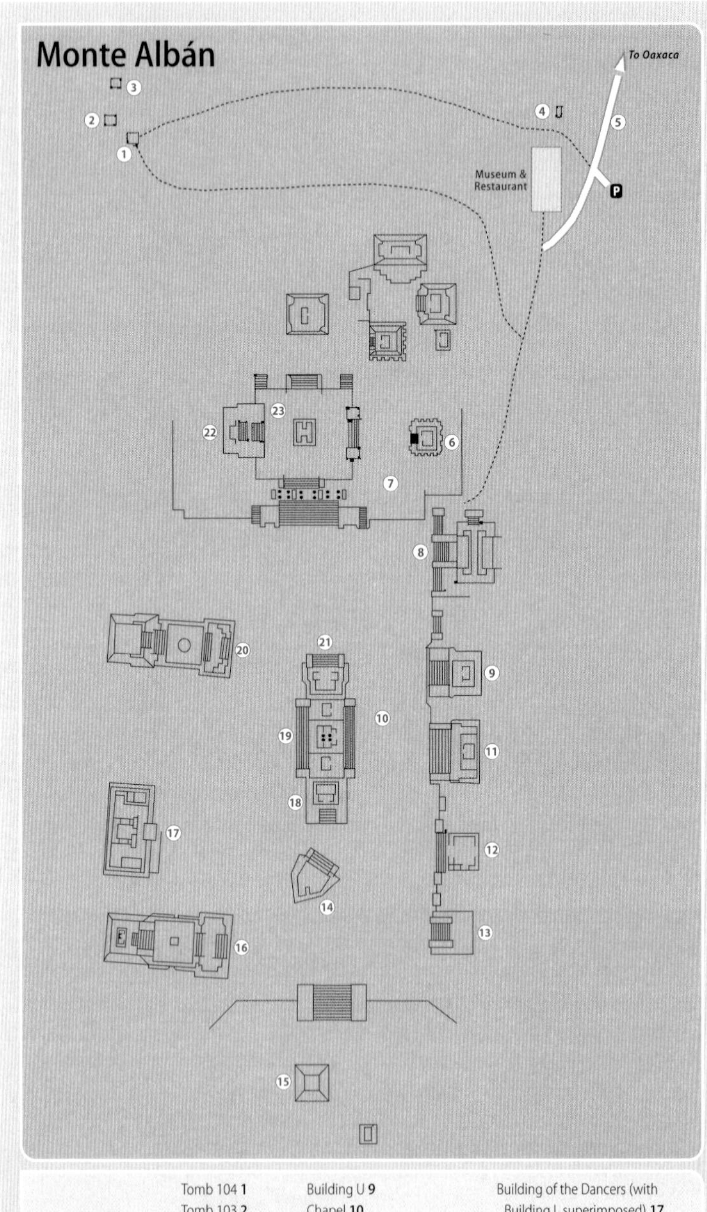

confederacy, which would have had political, economic and ideological control over the surrounding communities. The neutrality of Monte Albán's position, its absence of religious iconography and the presence of Danzantes sculptures all support this theory.

In all, about 310 stone slabs depicting captives, some of whom are sexually mutilated with streams of blood (flowers) flowing from the mutilated parts, have been found. Some of these captives are identified by name glyphs, which imply hostilities against a settlement and the capture of its warriors. It is likely that the rulers of Monte Albán sought to bring into the confederacy as many polities as possible in order to extract tribute and to protect itself from the expanding power of Teotihuacán (see page 79).

The collapse Monte Albán reached its maximum size around AD 600, with a population estimated at between 15,000-30,000. Shortly after that date, the political institution collapsed, the Main Plaza was abandoned and the majority of the people moved nearer to the valley floor. This abandonment coincides with the decline of Teotihuacán, and suggests that the removal of the Teotihuacán threat made the confederacy redundant. The site remained culturally and historically significant and was subsequently used by Mixtecs, who buried their leaders in elaborate tombs here.

Route to Mitla » pp93-103

It is 42 km from Oaxaca to Mitla, on a poor paved road (Route 190), with many potholes and occasional flooding. On the way you pass **El Tule**, 12 km east of Oaxaca, which has, what is reputed to be, the world's largest tree in the churchyard, estimated at 2,000 years old. The savino is 40 m high, measures 42 m circumference at its base, weighs an estimated 550 tonnes and is fed water by an elaborate pipe system. Continuing east along Route 190, 5 km from El Tule is **Tlacochahuaya**, with a 16th-century **church** and vivid indigenous murals; visit the cloisters at the back and see the decorated organ upstairs.

Another 5 km further, a paved road leads off Route 190 to **Teotitlán del Valle**, where wall hangings and *tapetes* (rugs) are woven, and which is now becoming rather touristy. There is an artisans' market near the church and a **Museo Comunitario** ⓘ *Mon-Sat 1000-1800, US$0.50.* The best prices for weavings are to be had at the stores along the road as you come into town, but they may be even cheaper in Oaxaca where competition is stronger. From the town of Teotitlán del Valle you can walk up to nearby hills across the river or hike north to the town of Benito Juárez on the edge of the **Sierra Juárez**, a region of beautiful landscapes and great biological diversity. The region is starting to develop ecotourism with community participation; permits are required to camp on community land.

Further along Ruta 190 is **Tlacolula**, which has an interesting Sunday market and where the townspeople are renowned for their mezcal preparation. The most important attraction, however, is the renowned **Capilla del Santo Cristo** in the church. The chapel is similar in style to Santo Domingo in Oaxaca, with intricate white and gold stucco, lots of mirrors, silver altar rails and sculptures of martyrs in gruesome detail. Two beheaded saints guard the door to the main nave. Quality weavings can be found at the peaceful village of **Santa Ana del Valle**, 3 km from Tlacolula. There is a small museum showing ancient textile techniques; ask any villager for the keyholder.

Yagul

ⓘ *T951-516 0123. Daily 0800-1700. US$2.70. Tours in English Tue, US$15, from Oaxaca agencies. Bus from Oaxaca to the paved turn-off to Yagul (5 mins after Tlacolula terminal). It is 1 km uphill from the bus stop to the site. Return the same way or walk 3 km west to Tlacolula along Route 190.*

 Yagul, meaning "arbol/palo seco" (old tree/stick), is an outstandingly picturesque archaeological site, with a majestic acropolis that overlooks the Oaxaca valley. Serene, ghostly and absorbing, it is often described as the most moving of Oaxaca's ruins. Yagul was a large Zapotec and later Mixtec religious centre that flourished following the decline of Monte Albán and that was enjoying a renaissance just prior to the arrival of the Spanish. The labyrinthine structures at Yagul bear striking similarities to those of Monte Albán and its Palace of Six Patios also resembles the Hall of Columns at Mitla. Yagul receives most attention from historians and archaeologists for its ball court set in a landscape punctuated by candelabra cactus and *agave*. The ball court is said to be the second largest discovered in Mesoamerica; it is also in the best condition discovered to date. If you take the path from behind the ruins, the last part is steep, there are fine tombs and a superb view.

Mitla

ⓘ *42 km southeast of Oaxaca, T951-568 0316. Daily 0800-1700, US$2.70, use of video US$3, literature sold at entrance. Turn left off Ruta 190, 5 km after Yagul, and continue for 4km.*
Mitla is an unmissable day excursion from Oaxaca by car or bus. Meaning 'place of the dead', Mitla is remarkable for its ornate stonework and mosaics, known as '*grecas*', which are considered peerless by many archaeologists. Inhabited in the Classic period (AD 100-65), Mitla reached its zenith in the Post-classic period (AD 750-1521) and was still inhabited when the Spanish arrived; many of Mitla's temples were destroyed and the stonework was used to build the 17th-century church of **San Pablo Mitla**. There are five structural groups, including the ruins of four great palaces amid a clutch of minor ones. The principal palace was the **Hall of the Columns**; in the depths of which is 'La Columna de la Muerte' (Column of Death). Previously, people were permitted to embrace the column; the space they were unable to reach with their fingers revealed how many years they had left to live (rather unfortunate for people with long arms). The magnificent bas reliefs in the **Hall of Mosaics** are not to be missed. In the north and east complexes there are lavish tombs where Zapotec priests and kings were buried. Some of the archaeology, outside the fenced-in site, can be seen within the present-day town.

Hierve el Agua

From Mitla take a bus to **San Lorenzo Albarradas** (one hour, US$1). From there it is 3 km to the village of Hierve el Agua (57 km from Oaxaca). Due to the concentration of minerals, a pre-Hispanic irrigation system and various waterfalls are now petrified over a cliff, forming an enormous stalactite. You can swim in the mineral pools in the dry season.

South of Oaxaca » pp93-103

Cuilapan de Guerrero and around

In Cuilapan, 12 km southwest of Oaxaca, there is a vast, unfinished 16th-century **convent** ⓘ *daily 0900-1700, US$2.20*, now in ruins, with a famous nave and columns, and an 'open chapel', whose roof collapsed in an earthquake. The last Zapotec princess, Donaji, daughter of the last ruler Cosijoeza, married a Mixtec prince at Tilantengo and was buried at Cuilapan. On the grave is an inscription with their Christian names, Mariana Cortez and Diego Aguilar.

Zaachila ⓘ *5 km beyond Cuilapan, daily 0800-1700, US$2.20*, was the last capital of the Zapotec empire. There are partially excavated ruins, with two Mixtec tombs; the outer chamber has owls in stucco work and there are carved human figures with skulls for heads inside. Today the town still maintains some of its ancestral traditions in local cooking. It also produces black pottery and has a market every Thursday. Take bus to Zaachila (US$0.60), which leaves every 30 minutes from Oaxaca's second-class bus station.

Necropolis, Mitla

Craft villages

Along Route 175 to Pochutla are several towns that specialize in the production of different crafts. **San Bartolo Coyotepec**, 12 km southeast of Oaxaca, is known for its black pottery. Doña Rosa de Nieto accidentally discovered the technique for the black-glazed ceramics in the 1930s and her family continues the tradition, as do many other potters in town. **San Martín Tilcajete**, 21 km from Oaxaca, 1 km west of the main road, is the centre of *alebrije* production. These are animals carved from copal wood, painted in bright colours, often looking supernatural. **Santo Tomás Jalieza** is the centre for cotton and wool textiles, made using backstrap looms and natural dyes in the surrounding villages. Market day is Friday.

Sleeping

Oaxaca *p84, map p97*

There are over 160 hotels in Oaxaca in all price categories. If you wish to stay at a particular hotel, however, reservations are recommended during peak holiday periods (Holy Week, Jul-Aug, Christmas and New Year).

There are many cheap hotels in the block formed by the streets Mina, Zaragoza, Díaz Ordaz and JP García; also on Trujano 4 blocks from the Zócalo (areas not safe at night).

A **Gala**, Bustamante 103 y Guerrero, southeast corner of Zócalo, T951-514 2251. Also suites, cable TV, colonial era, smallish rooms, very nice (no elevator).

A **Parador Santo Domingo de Guzmán**, Alcalá 804, T/F951-514 2171. An all-suite hotel with secure car parking, pool, cable TV. Suites have bedroom, sitting room and kitchen, daily maid included. Recommended.

A-B **Casa María B&B**, Belisario Domínguez 205, T951-515 1202, www.oaxacalive.com/maria.htm Private house with large wooden garage doors.

A-B **Casa Conzatti**, Gómez Farias 218, near the 1st-class bus station, same owners as Casa Maria (above), caters only to travellers. Bungalows and private rooms, friendly and helpful, breakfast included.

B **Las Rosas**, Trujano 112. Old charm, nice patio, clean, excellent, quiet, friendly, good view from roof.

B **Mesón del Rey**, Trujano 212, T951-516 0033, 1 block from Zócalo. Clean, modern, fan, quiet except for street-facing rooms, good value, restaurant.

B **Monte Albán**, Alameda de León 1, T951-516 2777. Friendly, colonial style, opposite cathedral, daily folk dance performances (see Entertainment p96).

B **Parador San Andrés**, Hidalgo 405, 2 blocks from the Zócalo, T/F951-514 1011, sanders@prodigy.net.mx Comfortable, colonial style, nice courtyard, new in 1999, very pleasant.

B **Posada Catarina**, Aldama 325, T951-516 4270. Modern colonial, comfortable, parking. Good value.

B-C **Antonio's**, Independencia 601, T951-516 7227, 1 block from Zócalo. Colonial patio, hot water, spotless, good restaurant, closed in evening.

C **Posada del Centro**, Independencia 403, T/F951-516 1874, posadabb@prodigy.net.mx Modern colonial, nice, spotless, cheaper with shared bath, internet service.

C **Posada Don Matías**, Aldama 316, T/F951-501 0084. New, homely, beautiful patio, tastefully decorated, clean. Recommended.

C **Principal**, 5 de Mayo 208, 2 blocks from the Zócalo, T/F951-516 2535. Colonial house, very clean, private shower, morning coffee and cookies included. English spoken, very friendly, rooms overlooking street are a bit noisy but still heavily booked.

D **Casa Arnel**, Aldama 404, Col Jalatlaco (several blocks east of Zócalo), T/F951-515 2856, casarnel.com.mx Homely, pleasant patio, good for meeting people, internet access, postal services, parking in next block, organizes good tours. Not very central. Reconfirm reservations.

D **Palmar**, JP García 504 y Mina, T951-516 4335. Cheaper without bath, convenient, friendly, family run, hot water in morning, safe motorcycle parking.

D-E **Central**, 20 de Noviembre 104, 1 block from the Zócalo, T951-514 9425. With bath, hot water, good value but very noisy, fills up early.

E **Don Mario**, Cosijopi 219 and Rufino Tamayo, T951-514 2012. Great budget choice, in a lovely area. Famed as the house where Rudolfo Tamayo was born. Sunny, colonial home with welcoming, family feel. Attractive patio, adobe walls, spiral staircases. Bedrooms, basic but spotless and airy with fan, some with private bathrooms and access to patio with views across the city. Internet, information on local tours and small handicraft shop.

E-F **Luz de Luna**, Juárez 101, T951-516 9576, www.geocities.com/luznuyoo New and funky, kitchen, courtyard, dorm rooms, live music on occasion, hammocks and tents on terrace cheaper.

F **Magic Hostel**, Fiallo 305, T951-516 7667. Popular and full of tourists, friendly, kitchen and laundry facilities, stores luggage, internet access, purified water, good place to meet travellers, breakfast.

Route to Mitla *p91*

Fpp **Tourist Yú'ù**, T951-516 4828. Tourist accommodation is provided by local communities in 13 towns throughout the Central Valleys around Oaxaca, including . Hierve el Agua, T951-516 0123, and Tlacolula (check availability in tourist office first). Each house has 6 beds, equipped kitchen, bathroom with hot water. Camping is also available US$2.70.

Eating

Oaxaca *p84, map p97*

Most restaurants on the main square cater for tourists, and are therefore pricey (efficiency and standards depend a bit on how busy they are, but generally they are good). There are also lots of good places along Macedonio Alcalá. Some of the most authentic Oaxacan food is found in the *comedores populares* in the markets.

††† **Café Bar Tapas & Pisto**, Macedonio Alcalá 403, upstairs. Artfully renovated colonial house, excellent view from top terrace, more pricey but worth visiting just for the bathroom.

††† **Flor de Oaxaca**, Armenta y López 311. Pricey but excellent meals and delicious hot chocolate.

ΨΨΨ-ΨΨ **Asador Vasco**, above **Bar Jardín**. Live Mexican music in the evening, good food and service.

ΨΨΨ-ΨΨ **Hostería de Alcalá**, Macedonio Alcalá 307. Excellent food and quiet atmosphere in colonial courtyard, good service, expensive.

ΨΨ **Arte y Tradición**, García Vigil 406. Craft centre with courtyard café, excellent service and food, Mon-Sat 1100-2200.

ΨΨ **Bar Jardín**, west side of the Zócalo. A nice place to sit and watch all the activity in the Zócalo.

ΨΨ **Café Fuente y Señor de Salud**, Juárez, just north of Morelos. Pleasant, reasonable vegetarian food.

ΨΨ **Catedral Restaurant Bar**, corner of García Vigil and Morelos, 1 block from cathedral. Good for international and local specialities, steaks, good *tamales*, classical music, excellent buffet for US$7.

ΨΨ **Coronita**, Díaz Ordaz 208 below **Hotel Valle de Oaxaca**. Tasty lunches, traditional Oaxacan dishes.

ΨΨ **El Muelle**, Nicolás del Puerto 207, behind the Mercado Merced. Great seafood dishes and tacos and *tostados*.

ΨΨ **El Naranjo**, Trujano 203, 1 block from the Zócalo. One of the most popular restaurants in Oaxaca in a restored 17th-century house. Inspired regional dishes with organic ingredients, served in the courtyard. Menu features 7 different *moles*, plus recommended rolled tortillas with *picadillo oaxaqueño* and *sopa de nuez y chipotle* (pecan and chile soup).

ΨΨ **Gaia**, Labastida 115. Organic meals, energizing juices and tarot card reading.

ΨΨ **La Crepe**, Macedonio Alcalá 307. Lovely 1st-floor location with some tables overlooking the street. Good fresh salads, crêpes and cheap breakfast combos.

ΨΨ **Los Olivos**, Calzada Madero. Good vegetarian menu and buffet.

ΨΨ **Luna y Sol Café**, Tinoco y Palacios 205. Good Mexican cuisine, tasty coffee and good Mexican atmosphere with live street music.

ΨΨ **María Bonita**, Macedonio Alcalá 706B. Just north of the Iglesia de Santo Domingo. Snug, family-run restaurant with cobbled floors and rustic tables. Extensive menu of Oaxacan cuisine. Charming and enthusiastic staff. The *comida corrida* set menus are great value.

ΨΨ **Portal de la Soledad**, north side of the Zócalo. Fine dining on the plaza with exciting adaptions of regional food.

ΨΨ-Ψ **Café Alex**, Díaz Ordaz 218 y Trujano. 3 blocks west of the Zócalo. Large and tasty breakfasts. Quirky decoration, popular with locals, lively atmosphere.

ΨΨ-Ψ **Café Amarantos** and **Mario's Terranova Restaurant**, Hidalgo, northeast corner of Zócalo. Excellent food, friendly and efficient service, pricey.

ΨΨ-Ψ **El Bicho Pobre II**, Calzada de la República. 10-minute walk from the Zócalo. Hugely popular. Large, open plan dining room. The speciality is *botano surtido*, a platter of regional delicacies.

ΨΨ-Ψ **El Decano**, 5 de Mayo 210 and Murguia, 0800-2400. Serves *comida corrida* 1400-1500, Mexican dishes, good value. Also a good night spot.

ΨΨ-Ψ **Flor de Loto**, Morelos 509, next to Museo Rufino Tamayo. Good value, clean, vegetarian and Mexican, *Supesteka* is delicious, also breakfast.

ΨΨ-Ψ **Manantial Vegetariano**, Macedonio Alcalá 407, close to Santo Domingo cathedral. Excellent cheap vegetarian meals, buffet US$4.50, pleasant patio. Live music at weekends. Recommended.

ΨΨ-Ψ **Pizza Nostrana**, corner of Allende close to Santo Domingo church, 1300-2300. Delicious Italian cuisine, specializing in vegetarian dishes.

Ψ **La Verde Antequera**, Matamoros 3 blocks north of Zócalo. Good daily lunch specials, best *comida corrida* in town.

Cafés, bakeries and snacks

The most popular place to eat *tlayudas* (oversized tortillas) and other local snacks in the evening is from stalls and restaurants along Aldama, between Cabrera and 20 de Noviembre.

Café y Arte Geono, Macedonio Alcalá 412. Nice garden, good coffee and cakes.

Budget busters

LL **Camino Real**, 5 de Mayo 300, Centro Histórico, T951-516 0611 In the heart of the historic centre, the former convent of Santa Catalina has been converted into the internationally renowned Camino Real. An ethereal ambience clings to hushed, leafy patios with ornate fountains, while the carved stone arcades are decorated with tapestries and frescoes. Rich fabrics lend a luxurious quality to each tranquil room with views onto the street or the languid gardens and swimming pool. Impeccable service extends to the restaurant El Refectorio.

L **Casa Oaxaca**, Calle García Vigil 407, 4 blocks from the Zócalo, T951-516 9923, www.casa-oaxaca.com This distinctive hotel blends clean minimalist décor, artful design and an elegant ambience. The enigmatic appeal of the restored colonial house has made it a favourite among the Oaxacan artistic community. The emphasis is on intimacy and character, so some facilities are lacking, including a/c and TV. International figures such as Gabriel García Marquez have dined in the restaurant (TTT), where chef and manager Alejandro has established a cult following. The stylish and serene patio with live music in the evenings is the perfect backdrop to Alejandro's philosophy that food is art. Fresh organic ingredients and perfectly executed international and *Oaxaqueña* specialties, combine with impeccable service and a monumental wine list to provide an excellent value fine-dining experience.

El Rincón del Libro, Jardín de la Soledad 1, on Independencia and Meir y Teran. Terrace, internet, gift shop. The plaza outside is good for ice cream (try tequila flavoured).

Hermanas Jiménez, Mercado de Abastos. Recommended for a local bread called *pan de yema*, made with egg yolk.

La Brew Coffee and Wafflehouse, García Vigil 409B, 4 blocks from the Zócalo. Great breakfast, plus fruit waffles, brownies, muffins, cookies, breads and bagels. Donations help the city's stray dogs.

Entertainment

Oaxaca *p84, map p97*

Bars and clubs

Candela, Murguía 413 y Pino Suárez. Salsa, merengue, live music from 2200, restaurant, popular, cover US$5.

Casa de Mezcal, in front of the Benito Juarez market. Popular drinking hole.

La Tentación, Murguía, between Macedonio Alcalá and García Vigil. Salsa, merengue, live music starting 2230, open late, friendly atmosphere, cover US$4.

NRG, Calzada Porfirio Díaz 102. Wed-Sat 2230-0230, disco club, cover US$5, current hotspot.

Folk dancing

There are Guelaguetza-style shows at the following hotels: **Camino Real**, see p96, Fri 1930, US$30 includes buffet dinner; **Casa de Cantera**, Murguía 102, T951-514 9522. US$12, US$22 includes buffet dinner; **Monte Albán**, see Sleeping, nightly at 2030, US$8.50, photography permitted. Book if you can; shows are cancelled if fewer than 10 in audience.

Festivals and events

Oaxaca *p84, map p97*

Jul The most important festival is the **Guelaguetza**, also called Los Lunes del

Cerro, when a festive atmosphere permeates the city for over 2 weeks at the end of **Jul** (see p98).

Oct El Señor del Rayo, is a 9-day event in the 3rd week of the month, including excellent fireworks.

2 Nov Day of the Dead, is a mixture of festivity and solemn commemoration, best appreciated at the Panteón General (main cemetery). Ask before taking photographs. In recent years Oaxaca has hosted a rugby 'tournament of death' to

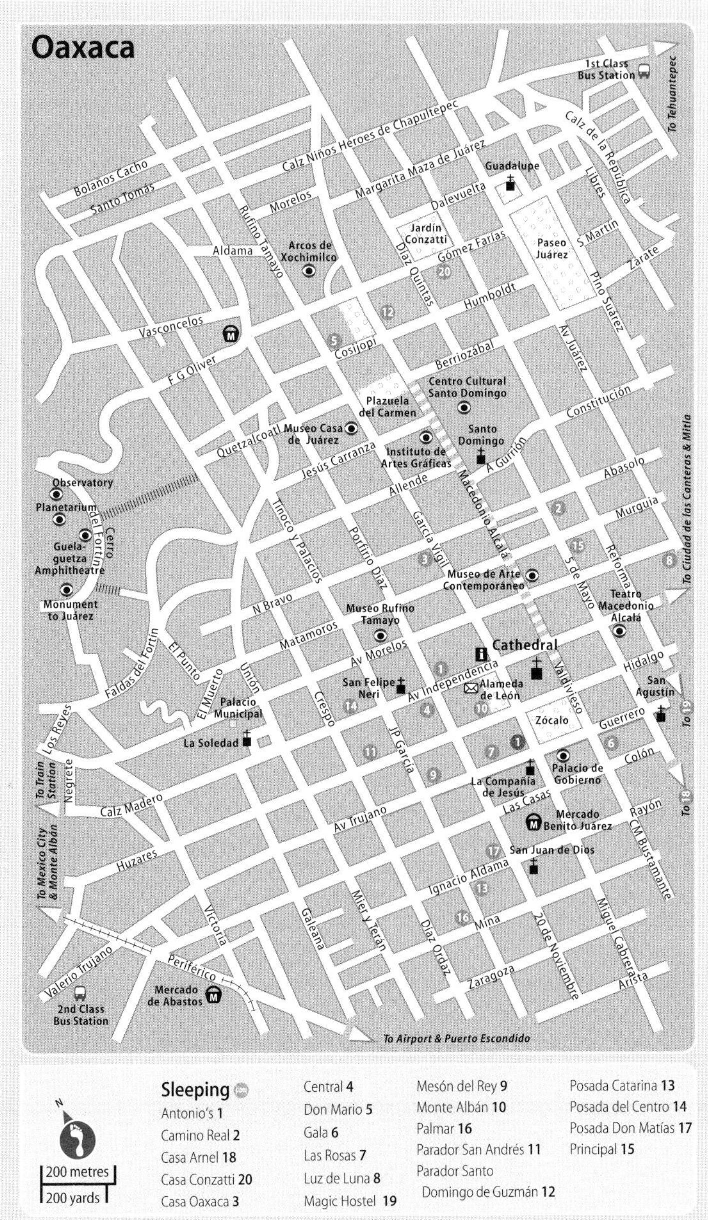

Background

Guelaguetza or Lunes del Cerro

This impressive annual celebration is brings together all the colour and variety of Oaxaca's many different cultural groups. For those with an interest in native costumes, music and dance, it should not be missed.

The word Guelaguetza means something like 'reciprocity' in Zapotec, and suggests the exchange of gifts or favours. The contemporary event is a well-organized large-scale folklore festival, held on and around the last two Mondays in July, known as Los Lunes del Cerro.

On the Saturday evening before Los Lunes del Cerro, participants parade down Macedonio Alcalá, from Santo Domingo to the Zócalo; this is a good opportunity to see their splendid costumes close up. The most elaborate costumes are those of the women from the Isthmus of Tehuantepec, who have stiffly starched lace *resplandores* (halos) on their heads. On Sunday the 'Diosa Centeotl' (goddess of the new corn) is elected to preside over the week's festivities. The main dance show is held on the Monday at the Guelaguetza stadium on the slopes of Cerro del Fortín, with the city below as a spectacular backdrop. Among the favourite dances are Flor de Piña, danced by women from the Tuxtepec area with a pineapple on their shoulder, and Danza de la Pluma, performed by men from the central valleys using enormous feather head-dresses. At the end of each performance, gifts are thrown from the stage to the audience – watch out for pineapples!

On Monday night, following the Guelaguetza, the Donají legend is presented in an elaborate torchlight performance at the same stadium starting around 2000. Donají was a Zapotec princess who fell in love with a Mixtec prince, Nucano, and eventually gave her life for her people.

In addition to the main event, there are scores of other happenings in Oaxaca at this time of year, ranging from professional cycling races to classical music concerts, a Feria del Mezcal, and several smaller celebrations in nearby villages. Many events are free and a complete programme is available from Sedetur, see page 85. Details of performances and tickets are available from the Oaxaca State Tourism Department, Murguía 206, Centro Histórico, Oaxaca, T951-514 8501, www.guelaguetza-oax.com.

coincide with the festival. For information, www.planeta.com

8-18 Dec Fine processions are centred around the **Basílica de la Soledad** and throughout the city to celebrate the patroness of Oaxaca.

23 Dec, **Noche de Rábanos**, a unique contest of figures carved out of radishes takes place outside Palacio de Gobierno. Many groups participate, stands made of flowers and corn stalks have been added in recent years to this old tradition.

Dec During the 9 days before Christmas, the **Novenas** are held, groups of people go asking for shelter, *posada*, as Joseph and Mary did. This is done in the centre as well as neighbourhoods like San Felipe (5 km north) and Xoxo, to the south. The *posadas* culminate on **24 Dec** with a parade of floats, which converge at the cathedral at 2300 (best seen from balcony of the restaurants around the Zócalo; go for supper and get a window table).

Route to Mitla *p91*

In **Teotitlán del Valle** the Fiesta de las Cruces is celebrated on **3 May**, when people climb to a cross on a beautiful summit above town (across the river). Since 1999 a Fiesta Antigua Zapoteca is celebrated in **Jul**, to coincide with the Guelaguetza in Oaxaca. The feast of Virgen de la Natividad is on **8 Sep**. **Tlacolula** celebrates its fiesta on 9 Oct. There are also 3-day fiestas in **Santa Ana del Valle** at the end of **Jan** and during 2nd week of **Aug**.

Shopping

Oaxaca *p84, map p97*

Crafts

See also Markets, below, and Top tips, p100.

Alfarería Jiménez, Zaragoza 402, fine cream and purple-black pottery (Zapotec and Mixtec designs).

Aripo, García Vigil 809, T951-516 9211. Government run, cheaper and better than most, service good. Very good small market nearby on junction of García Vigil and Jesús Carranza, for beautiful coloured belts and clothes.

Arte y Tradición, García Vigil 406, superior craft shops, offer excellent selection of quality rugs at good prices.

El Palacio de las Gemas, Alcalá 100 block, is recommended for gemstones, good selection at reasonable prices.

La Mano Mágica, Alcalá 203, for the highest quality rug collection.

Lo Mexicano, García Vigil, at end furthest from centre, excellent selection of high-quality crafts at reasonable prices.

Mujeres Artesanas de las Regiones de Oaxaca, 5 de Mayo 204, T951-516 0670, daily 0900-2000, a regional association of Oaxacan craftswomen with a sales and exhibition store.

Productos Típicos de Oaxaca, Belisario Domínguez 602, cheapest and largest selection of pottery plus a variety of fabrics and sandals (city bus near *ADO* depot goes there).

Sedetur (see Tourist offices, p85) runs a shop selling crafts, and profits go to the artisans, good prices, recommended.

Yalalag, 5 de Mayo y Murguía. Good selection of jewellery, rugs and pottery, somewhat overpriced.

Bookshops

Good bookshops selling English-language books and magazines include **Amate**, Alcalá 307, **Librería Universitaria**, Guerrero 104 and **Proveedora Escolar**, Independencia 1001 y Reforma.

Markets

The city has four main markets, all of which are worth a visit; polite bargaining is the rule everywhere.

Mercado de Abastos, also known as the

Alebrijes

Top tips

Buying Oaxacan crafts

The colourful markets and varied crafts of Oaxaca are among the foremost attractions of the region. Crafts are sold both in villages where they are produced and at the shops and markets in Oaxaca city (see Shopping, page 28). There are endless shopping temptations, such as green and black pottery, baskets and bags made from cane and rushes, embroidered shirts, skirts, painted wooden animals called *alebrijes*, hammocks, tooled leather goods, woven wall hangings and rugs.

Terracota ceramics, Santa María Atzompa

- When buying a handwoven rug, make sure you know whether you are getting all wool or a mixture and check the quality: a well-made rug will not ripple when unfolded on the floor.
- Make the most of the bus ride from Oaxaca to Teotitlán del Valle to make contact with the locals and pick up some advice on the best weavings to be found in the village.
- Check out the green glazed and terracotta ceramics being made and sold at Santa María Atzompa, 8 km northwest of Oaxaca, at the foot of Monte Albán.
- Pickpockets are common in Tlacolula: be especially careful at the Sunday market and in the scrum to board the bus.

Central de Abastos, near the second-class bus station. The largest: a cacophony of sights, sounds and aromas, busiest on Sat and not to be missed. Prices here are lower than in the smaller markets. Try the grasshopper-like critters called *chapulines*.

Mercado Artesanal, Zaragoza and JP García. A good selection of crafts intended for the tourist trade.

Mercado 20 de Noviembre, Aldama on the corner of 20 de Noviembre. Clean stalls selling prepared foods, cheese and baked goods, and *mole*.

Mercado Benito Juárez, next door to 20 de Noviembre. Larger, with a selection of household goods, fruits, vegetables, crafts and regional products, such as *quesillo* (string cheese), bread and chocolate.

Activities and tours

Oaxaca *p84, map p97*

Oaxaca is a growing hotbed of ecotourism, with many options for tours.

Cycling

Bicicletas Bravo, García Vigil 409C, T951-516 0953, www.bikeoaxaca.com New aluminium-frame bikes, front suspension, US$10 for 24-hr rental. Will also provide photocopied sections of topographic maps upon request. Great multi-level itineraries. Wonderful way to see surrounding countryside. Minimum 2 people, US$28 each, make reservations at least 1 day before. Recommended.

Horse riding

La Golondrina, Borde del Río Atoyac 800, San Jacinto Amilpas, 5 km northwest of Oaxaca de Juarez, T951-452 7570, thoroughbred Andalucían horses.

Public baths

Temazcal, Reforma 402, T951-516 1165, Indigenous ancient ceremonial steam bath with herbs, also offers massages and aromatherapy US$50.

Tour operators

Most operators offer tours of the city and trips to **Monte Albán**. Tours to **El Tule**, **Mitla** and another village on this route tend to be rather rushed (1000-1300, US$7.50, not including entry fees). There are also weekly tours to Coyotepec, Jalietza and Ocotlán (Fri); to Cuilapan and Zaachila (Thu); to Tlacolula, Mitla and El Tule (Sun) to coincide with local markets. Regular day tours cost US$11-13 per person; special tours on demand about US$22 per hr for 4 passengers.
Eugenio Cruz Castaneda, T951-513 4790. Excellent guided trips to Monte Albán, other archaeological sites and can customized itineraries throughout Oaxaca State – prices dependent on numbers.
Expediciones Sierra Norte, García Vigil 406, T951-514 8271, www.sierranorte.org.mx Hiking and mountain-bike tours in the Sierra Juárez, north of Benito Juárez. Tours depart daily from office at 0930, call day before for reservations.
La Brujita Tours, García Vigil 409B, T951-548 7334, labrujita_oax@yahoo.com Flamboyant and friendly Susan McGlynn organizes personalized tours that take you to the heart of Oaxacan markets, home-cooked meals with local families and to visit local artisans at work in their shops. She can be found at **La Brew** Coffee and Wafflehouse (see above).
Judith Reyes at Arte y Tradición, García Vigil 406. Good tours to outlying villages in her VW van, US$8 per hr.
Tierra Dentro, Reforma 528B, Centro, T951-514 9284, www.tierradentro.com One of the leading adventure tour operators.
Tierraventura, Boca del Monte 110, T/F951-514 3043, tierraventura@yahoo.com Tours to the highlands (Sierra Juárez, Sierra Mixteca, Hierve el Agua) and coast, US$20-30 per day.

Transport

Oaxaca *p84, map p97*

Air

Aeropuerto Xoxocotlán has flights to/from **Mexico City** with AeroMéxico, Mexicana, Aerocaribe and Aviacsa, several daily, US$180 single, discounts for advance booking. To **Puerto Escondido** and **Huatulco**, Aerocaribe, departs 1030 and 1705, US$120 single (US$85 advance booking) for either destination. Also to **Puerto Escondido**, Aerotucán, daily US$120, and Aerovega, US$96. To **Tuxtla Gutiérrez**, Aerocaribe, departs 1210 and 1440, Aviacsa, departs 1235, US$146 single. To **Tapachula**, Taesa, departs 1005, US$100. To **Cd Ixtepec** (Tehuantepec Isthmus), Aerocaribe, departs 0840, US$85 single. For other destinations, change in Mexico City.

Airline offices Aerocaribe, Fiallo 102 y Av Independencia, T951-516 0266. AeroMéxico, Av Hidalgo 513 Centro, T951-516 3229. Aviacsa, Pino Suárez 604, T951-518 4566. Aerotaxi (Turoca), Calz Porfirio Díaz 104, Col Reforma, T951-515 7270. AeroTucán, Alcalá 201, T951-501 0532. AeroVega, Hotel Monte Albán, Alameda de León 1, T951-516 2777. Mexicana, Fiallo 102 y Av Independencia, T951-516 8414.

Bus

Beware of thieves at all bus terminals, but especially on arrival of *plus* services. For services to Monte Albán, Mitla and intervening villages, see pp89-92.

For long-distance travel, book in advance. Tickets for 1st-class buses are sold at the **Ticket Bus Office**, 20 de Noviembre 103, T951-515 1214, Mon-Sat 0800-2200, Sun 0900-1600. Tickets for **ADO**, **Cristóbal Colón**, **AU**, **Sur** and **Cuenca** can also be purchased at Periférico 152, T951-516 3222, by the pedestrian crosswalk across from the Mercado de Abastos.

1st-class terminal (**ADO**) (for **ADO**, **Cristóbal Colón**, **Sur** and **Cuenca** and many 2nd class buses) northeast of Zócalo on Calzada Niños Héroes de Chapultepec (no luggage office, taxi from centre US$3). 1st-class terminal is the only one for **Villahermosa** and the **Yucatán**. The 2nd-class terminal, west of Zócalo on Calzada Valerio Trujano (left-luggage office, open until 2100). The **Autobuses Unidos** (AU) terminal (2nd class, 2 levels of service, modern buses but without a/c) is at Santa Rosa, near Teatro Alvaro Carillo. To **Mexico City**, day and night buses, US$21-48. To **Mérida**, Cristóbal Colón, Sun at 0900, 16½ hrs.

To Chiapas All routes to Chiapas from Oaxaca are via Tehuantepec. To **Tuxtla Gutiérrez** and **San Cristóbal de las Casas**, luxury service, **Cristóbal Colón Plus**, departs 2000, US$26.40, 10½ hrs (Tuxtla), US$27, 12½ hrs (San Cristóbal); 1st class, **Cristóbal Colón**, departs 1930 (both) and 2215 (Tuxtla only), US$20.30 (Tuxtla), US$23.50 (San Cristóbal). To **Tapachula**, 1st class, **Cristóbal Colón**, US$24, 11 hrs, book well in advance as buses often come almost full from Mexico City. To **Tehuantepec**, scenic, 1st class, **Cristóbal Colón**, 13 daily, US$9.60, 5½ hrs.

To the Pacific Coast 1st-class services to the Pacific Coast go via Tehuantepec, a long detour, 2nd-class services more convenient for all coastal destinations. To **Pochutla**, 1st class, **Cristóbal Colón**, via Isthmus, 4 daily, US$14.70, 11 hrs; 2nd class, direct, very scenic, **Oaxaca-Pacífico** and **Estrella del Valle**, comfortable buses but no a/c, depart 0945, 1415 and 2230, US$6.75. **Auto Express de Turismo**, also runs a fast, new shuttle service of comfortable vans to **Pochutla**, depart 0700, 1100, 1500, 1700 and 2130, US$12; worth booking ahead at **Oficina Matriz**, La Noria 101, T514-7077 and **Suc Maihuatlán**, 3 de Octubre 114, T951-572 0380. To **Puerto Angel**, departs 2315, arrives 0600. To **Puerto Escondido**, 1st class, **Cristóbal Colón**, via Isthmus, departs 0100, 0930 and 2400, US$14.80, 12 hrs; 2nd class, **Oaxaca-Pacífico** and **Estrella del Valle**, via Pochutla as above, 7 hrs, US$7.60; also **Estrella Roja**, superior service departs 2245, US$8.70, regular service 4 daily, US$7.60; **Tran-Sol** via **Sola de Vega** (US$2.70), departs 0600, 1300 and 2200, 7 hrs, US$7.60. To **Huatulco**, 1st class, **Cristóbal Colón**, via Isthmus, 4 daily, US$14.60, 9½ hrs; 2nd class, **Oaxaca-Pacífico**, via Pochutla, departs 2200, 7 hrs, or take a bus to Pochutla, as above, and change.

Car

Book **hire cars** in advance, a week before if possible. **Arrendadora Express**, 20 de Noviembre 204A, T/F951-516 6776, cars motorcycles and bicycles; **Hertz**, La Bastida 115, T951-516 2434; **TTN**, 5 de Mayo 217-7 y Murguía, T516-2577. Safe **car park** at Estacionamiento La Brisa, Av Zaragoza y Cabrera, US$3.50 per night, closed Sun.

Taxi

Taxis charge about US$10 per hr for touring and excursions outside the city. *Colectivos* depart from Bustamante 3rd block from the Zócalo.

Monte Albán *p89*

Autobuses Turísticos depart from **Hotel Rivera del Angel**, Mina 518 near Díaz Ordaz (bus tickets available from hotel lobby), every ½ hr from 0830 to 1530 (schedule may vary with season), fare US$2.40 return, last bus back to Oaxaca at 1800; ticket allows for just 2 hrs at the site, allowing only just enough time to visit ruins before returning (you can return on another tour on 1 ticket for an extra US$1 but you may not get a seat).

Route to Mitla *p*

Bus/colectivo

Buses to Mitla and en route destinations leave from Oaxaca 2nd-class bus station. Alternatively, you can take a *colectivo* (US$1.50 to Mitla) from beside the Mercado de Abastos on Mercaderes.

To **Mitla**, every 10 mins, 0600-1900, US$1, 40 mins. The ruins are 10 mins' walk across the village from the bus stop on the main road (2 blocks from the square). To **El Tulé**, every 30 mins, US$0.35, buy ticket on the bus, sit on the left to see the Tule tree; there are also onward buses from El Tule to **Mitla**, US$0.45. *Colectivos* to **Tlacochahuaya**, US$0.35; to **Teotitlán del Valle**, every hr 0700-2100, US$0.45; to **Tlacolula**, every 10 mins, daily 0600-1900, US$1.10. The bus station in **Tlacolula** is just off the main highway, several blocks from the centre; onward buses leave for **Santa Ana de Valle** every 30 mins. 2nd-class buses from Oaxaca pass through **Hierve El Agua** twice daily, departing 0810 and 1400, returning around noon and early the following day.

Taxi

US$10 each to **Mitla** for 4 sharing, with time to take photographs at Tule and Mitla and to buy souvenirs, or US$10 per hr for touring as you please. Taxis stop by the church in **Tlacolula**, except on Sun when they gather on a street behind the church; ask for directions.

South of Oaxaca *p92*

To **Cuilapan de Guerrero**, from the Oaxaca bus station on Calle Bustamante, near Arista, US$0.50.

Directory

Oaxaca *p84, map p97*

Banks Bancomer, on García Vigil, 1 block from Zócalo, Visa ATM. **Banco Santander Mexicano**, Independencia 605, TCs changed Mon-Fri 0900-1330. **Amex** office **Viajes Micsa**, Valdivieso 2, T951-516 2700, just off Zócalo. **Escotiabank**, Periférico near Mercado de Abastos, best rates. **Dentist** Dra Marta Fernández del Campo, Armenta y López 215, English speaking, very friendly, recommended. **Doctor** Dr Víctor Tenorio, Clínica del Carmen, Abasolo 215, T951-516 2612, close to centre (very good English). **Embassies and consulates** Canada, Pino Suárez 700 local 11B. **USA** (Consular Agency), Alcalá 407-20, Plaza Santo Domingo, T951-514 3054, conagent@prodigy.net.mx **Immigration** Pensamientos 104, Col Reforma, Mon-Fri 0900-1400, 2nd floor. **Internet** Many cyber cafés and in the post office, Mon-Fri 0800-1900, with fairly good set-ups, charging US$1 per hr. **Laundry** Lavandería Azteca, Hidalgo 404 between Díaz Ordaz y J P García, Mon-Sat 0830-2000, quick service, delivers to nearby hotels, 3½ kg US$3.80. **Luggage storage** Servicio Turístico de Guarda Equipaje y Paquetería, Av Tinoco y Palacios 312, Centro, T951-516 0432, open 24 hrs. **Pharmacy** 20 de Noviembre and Ignacio Aldama, open till 2300. **Post office**, Alameda de León, Independencia y 20 de Noviembre. **DHL**, Amado Nervo 104D and Héroes de Chapultepec, Mon-Fri 0900-1800, Sat 0900-1400, no credit card payments. **Tourist police** On Zócalo near cathedral, friendly and helpful **Centro de Protección al Turista**, T951-516 7280.

Pacific Coast

Oaxaca's Pacific coast, stretching from Guerrero in the west to Chiapas in the east, includes truly spectacular shoreline and provides the opportunity for seaside recreation. Many beaches remain entirely virgin (accessible only on foot or by sea), while others are being developed for various tastes and to varying degrees; a very few have been burnt out by overcrowding, pollution, drugs or crime. Palapas, thatched roof shacks, are found all along the coast, serving as simple restaurants and places to stay. Huatulco is the best-known international resort on the Oaxaca coast, but other popular areas include Puerto Escondido and Puerto Angel. The Sierra Madre del Sur lies between the coast and Oaxaca's Central Valleys.

Getting there Daily bus services and flights from Mexico City and Oaxaca.
Getting around Good bus network and plenty of taxis.
Time required 1 week, spending a few days travelling between coastal towns and resorts.
Weather Hot and dry.
Sleeping Good range for all budgets, from beach hammocks to glitzy Moorish-style hotels.
Eating Fresh fish by the sea.
Activities and tours Surfing, waterskiing, fishing, rafting and scuba diving.
★ **Don't miss...** The undeveloped beaches at Zipolite and Mazunte.
▸▸ *p106*

Puerto Escondido ▸▸ *p110-119*

With stunningly beautiful beaches, world-class surfing, and a relaxed alternative lifestyle, Puerto Escondido has been transformed from a sleepy fishing village into one of the most popular destinations in southern Mexico. A diverse crop of hotels, restaurants and cultural centres cater for surfers, yoga gurus and independent travellers. December-January are the most crowded months, while May-June are the quietest (and hottest) months. Daily rituals revolve around the beach, contemplating glorious sunsets, reading in hammocks and enjoying chocolate bread and cappuccino breakfasts in rustic *palapas*. At night, eclectic restaurants cater for all budgets, serving fresh feasts of shrimp and seared tuna to the sound of chilled out music or the waves.

Ins and outs

Getting there The **airport** (PXM) is 10 minutes' drive west of town and has daily flights to/from Mexico City and Oaxaca. *Colectivo* from airport, US$2.80 per person, T954-582 0030. If travelling by bus or car from Oaxaca, remember that all routes must cross the steep Sierra Madre mountain range and are subject to landslides, especially during the rainy periods. Enquire locally as to current conditions. ▸▸ *p116*

Tourist information The **Sedetur** ⓘ *Av Juárez, T954-582 0175, Mon-Sat*, is at the entrance to Playa Bacocho. There is also a **Sedetur** information kiosk ⓘ *at the west end of El Adoquín, ginainpuerto@yahoo.com*, run by Gina Machorro, a very helpful, friendly person who is knowledgeable about the town and the region. She speaks English, Spanish and French.

Puerto Escondido

Safety Even with the vast improvements in security, safety is still an issue in and around Puerto Escondido. Never walk on any beach at night, alone or in groups. The ocean currents at Zicatela can be treacherous and although there are life guards now paid by the Government, there are easier ways to meet them than getting drowned. A useful organization for those in trouble is the **International Friends of Puerto Escondido** ⓘ *ifope2002@yahoo.com*, contact Minne at the **Mayflower Hostal** on Andador Libertad.

Beaches

Experienced surfers make the pilgrimage to **Playa Zicatela**, the apogee of the Mexico surfing scene. **Playa Principal**, abutting El Adoquín pedestrian mall, has the calmest water but is not very clean. A few fishermen still bring in the catch of the day here. **Playa Manzanillo** and **Puerto Angelito** share the Bahía Puerto Angelito, an easy 15-minute walk away; they are pretty with reasonably safe swimming but a rather commercial atmosphere. To the west of the main bay, past a lovely headland (currently being built up with condominiums) and a lighthouse, are a series of picturesque bays and beaches. Further west again is **Playa Carrizalillo**, with swimming and more gentle surfing than Zicatela. **Playa Bacocho** is a long beautiful stretch of less developed beach, where the ocean is too dangerous for swimming.

Puerto Angel and around » p110-119

Puerto Angel

Sixty-six kilometres east of Puerto Escondido and 240 km south of Oaxaca is **San Pedro Pochutla**, a hot and busy supply town and the gateway to Puerto Angel, 20 minutes south. From Pochutla, a pretty road winds through hilly forest country before dropping to the sea. Until the 1960s Puerto Angel was a busy port from which coffee and timber were shipped to Asia; with the fall in coffee prices, the local population turned to selling turtle skins until 1990, when this activity was banned in Mexico. Tourism and fishing are now the main economic activities here. There is a fiesta on 1 June to celebrate the **Día de la Marina** and another on 1 October, the **Fiesta de San Angel**.

The town lies above a beautiful flask-shaped bay; unfortunately the turquoise water is polluted, but there are hopes for improvement if a planned sewage system is installed. The beach right in town is an ideal spot to watch the activity of the small dock. A short walk away, either along the road or on a concrete path built on the rocks (not safe at night), is **Playa del Panteón**, a small beach in a lovely setting, but crowded with restaurants (touts await visitors on arrival) and many bathers in season.

There are cleaner and more tranquil beaches east of town. Walk for about 20 minutes to reach **Estacahuite**, about 1 km from town. It has simple cabañas and good snorkelling (gear rental from hut selling drinks and snacks) but beware of strong waves, currents and sharp coral that can cut you. A little further on is **La Boquilla**, off a signed track on the road to Pochutla, which has comfortable Canadian-run bungalows.

Zipolite and San Agustinillo

Four kilometres west of Puerto Angel is Zipolite, one of the few nude beaches in Mexico and once an inspirationally beautiful spot that still attracted many independent travellers. Sadly, a few years ago, it became a veritable Paradise Lost, notorious for drugs, crime and violence, including murder. Things seem to be cleaning up a little now and visitor interest is recovering. The beach here is very steeply shelved and there are dangerous undercurrents, especially near the rocks at the east end.

Baby Turtles, Mazunte

Another 3 km west lies **San Agustinillo**, a long, pretty beach, with an extraordinary cave in the cliffs. The western end is quite built up with private homes but has the safest swimming; surfing is best near the centre. Nude bathing is prohibited.

Mazunte

One kilometre further west is Mazunte, perhaps the least developed major beach in the area but rapidly changing, so responsible tourism is especially important here. The beach is on federal land and drug laws are strictly enforced here; nude bathing is prohibited, the safest swimming is at either end of the bay. A trail leads from the west end of the beach to **Punta Cometa**, a spit of land with lovely views of the thundering breakers below, a popular spot to view the sunset, well worth the 30-minute walk.

At the east end of Mazunte is the **Centro Mexicano de la Tortuga** ⓘ *guided tours in Spanish and English, Tue-Sat 1000-1630, Sun 1000-1430, US$2, children under 12 US$1, crowded with tour buses from Huatulco 1100-1300 during high season, interested researchers may contact the director at cmtvasco@angel.umar.mx*, a government institute that studies sea turtles and works to conserve these frequently endangered species, as well as to educate visitors and the local population. There are interesting viewing tanks to observe many species of turtles underwater.

Huatulco » p110-119

East of Pochutla (50 km, one hour) on the coast road is Huatulco, a meticulously engineered and environmentally aware resort complex surrounded by 34,000 ha of forest reserve and nine splendid bays (where pirate ships used to shelter). It offers golf, swimming pools, international and Mexican cuisine, nightlife, beaches, watersports, excursions into the forest and exploration of archaeological sites. The product is a safe, clean, efficient international vacation resort in a lovely setting with a mild Mexican flavour.

Huatulco's coastline extends for almost 30 km between the Río Copalita to the east and the Río Coyula to the west. Hills covered in deciduous forest – very green during the rainy season (June-September), yellow and parched in the dry – sweep down to the sea, where nine turquoise bays with 36 golden beaches line the shore; some bays have road access while others can only be reached by sea.

The area encompasses several interconnected towns and developments. **Tangolunda** (meaning beautiful woman in Zapotec), on the bay of the same name and also known as the Zona Hotelera, is set aside for large luxury hotels and resorts; it also has the golf course and the most expensive restaurants, souvenir shops and nightlife. **Chahué**, on the next bay west, where development only began in 1999, has a town park with spa and beach club, a marina and a few hotels. Further west (6 km from Tangolunda) is **Santa Cruz Huatulco**, once an ancient Zapotec settlement and Mexico's most important Pacific port during the 16th century (later abandoned). It has the marina as well as facilities for visiting yachts, upscale hotels, restaurants, shops and a few luxury homes. There's an attractive open-air chapel by the beach here, Capilla de la Santa Cruz and a well-groomed park nearby. **La Crucecita**, located 2 km inland, is the functional hub of the Huatulco complex, with housing for the area's employees, bus stations, banks, a small market, ordinary shops, bars, plus the more economical hotels and restaurants. It also doubles as a Mexican town, which the tourists can visit, more cosmetic by the manicured Plaza Principal, less so towards the highway. The old-looking but brand-new Templo de Guadalupe church stands on a small hill next to the plaza. **Santa María Huatulco**, in the mountains 25 km further inland, is a pre-existing town where the municipal offices are located; there is good walking in the area but little else of interest for the visitor.

La Crucecita, Huatulco

Ins and outs

Getting there and around Aeropuerto Bahías de Huatulco (HUX) ⓘ *17 km northwest of Huatulco along Route 200, T958-581 9099*, has daily flights to/from Mexico City and Oaxaca. A van service runs from the airport to hotels T958-581 9014, US$27. The same journey by taxi takes 20 minutes and costs US$12. Taxis, second-class buses and *colectivos* run throughout the Huatulco bay area. Huatulco's high seasons include Holy Week, July-August and November-March, with regular charter flights from the USA and Canada during the latter months; prices can as much as double during these periods. » p117

Tourist information Sedetur ⓘ *Blvd Benito Juárez, Tangolunda, T/F958-581 0176, sedetur6@oaxaca.gob.mx* is near the golf course, helpful and informative. An auxiliary information booth in La Crucecita is a handy alternative source of information. Two useful websites are *hotels.baysofhuatulco.com.mx* and *www.baysofhuatulco.com.mx*

Sierra Madre del Sur

In the Huatulco area the Sierra Madre del Sur mountains drop from the highest point in the state of Oaxaca (3,750 m) right down to the sea. There are ample opportunities for day-hiking in the forested hills. The forest is deciduous, so the experience is very different in the rainy season, when it is green, and in the dry season when the area is brown and even some cacti change from green to violet. There are also a number of **coffee plantations** that can be visited. Huatulco travel agencies arrange full-day plantation tours that include a traditional meal at the farm and bathing in fresh water springs or waterfalls.

The **Río Copalita** to the north and east of Huatulco is quite scenic, with waterfalls and rapids; walking here can be combined with a visit to the **Punta Celeste** Zapotec archaeological site.

Isthmus of Tehuantepec » p110-119

Only about 210 km separate the Atlantic and the Pacific at the hot, once heavily jungled Isthmus of Tehuantepec, where the land does not rise more than 250 m. This narrowest point of Mexico is also the geographic boundary between North and Central America.

The Isthmus has a strong cultural character all of its own. The people are *mestizo* and descendants of several different indigenous groups, but Zapotecs predominate. Once a matriarchal society, Zapotec women continue to play an important role in local affairs. Their typical dress is intricate and beautiful, and they are high-pressure saleswomen.

Ins and outs

Getting there and around **Tehuantepec** lies at the junction of Route 190, which connects the city with Oaxaca, 257 km away, and the Carretera Transístmica (185), which runs north–south across the isthmus between Salina Cruz and Coatzacoalcos. The bus station is on the outskirts of town; taxi to Zócalo, US$1, *moto-carro* US$0.50 or 15 minutes' walk (walking not recommended at night). The regional airport at **Ciudad Ixtepec**, 29 km north of Tehuantepec, has flights to Oaxaca and Mexico City. » *p118*

Tourist information There are two tourist offices in Tehuantepec, **SEDETUR** ⓘ *Carretera Transístmica 7, 2nd floor, opposite the petrol station, T971-715 1236*, the regional office for the Isthmus and the **Regiduría de Turismo** in the Palacio de Gobierno.

Climate The climate throughout the area can be oppressively hot and humid, hence the region's cultural events usually take place late in the evening. Winds are very strong around on and near the Isthmus, due to the intermingling of Pacific and Caribbean weather systems.

Tehuantepec and around

Santo Domingo Tehuantepec, 257 km from Oaxaca, is a colourful town that conserves the region's indigenous flavour. Robust Zapotec matrons in bright dresses stand in the back of motorized tricycles known as *moto-carros*. Life moves slowly, centered on the plaza, which has arcades on one side, and an adjacent market – the best place to admire the Zapotec dress. In the plaza is a statue of Máximo Ramón Ortiz (1816-1855) composer of the *zandunga* music of the Isthmus, which is still very popular. Due to the importance of Tehuantepec during the early colonial period, many churches were built here; their attractive white forms with coloured trim still dot the landscape. The **Casa de la Cultura** is housed in the 16th-century Dominican ex-convent Rey Cosijopi. The building is quite run down, but original frescoes can still be seen on some walls. There is a library and some simple exhibits of regional archaeology, history and costumes.

To the northwest of town, off the road to Oaxaca, are the unrestored ruins of the **Guiengola**, known as the 'Mexican Machu Picchu', because of its lonely location on a mountain. It was the last stronghold of the Zapotecs (*guiengola* is the Zapotec word for fortress) and was never conquered; Alvarado and his forces marched past it in 1522. It has walls up to 3 m high, running, it is said, for 40 km, plus the remains of two pyramids and a ball court.

Juchitán de Zaragoza

Some 27 km from Tehuantepec is the larger and more modern city of Juchitán de Zaragoza, an important commercial and cultural centre on the Isthmus. It has a nice plaza next to impressive colonial municipal buildings and many churches. Many Zapotec women here still wear traditional costumes. The **tourist office** is at the Palacio de Gobierno. The **Mercado Central 5 de Septiembre** is the largest market on the Isthmus; traditional barter still takes place here. The meat and produce section is dirty, but the crafts section on the second floor is well worth a visit; this is the best place to see the elaborate embroidered Zapotec dresses which sell for up to US$600.

Sleeping

Puerto Escondido *p104*

Puerto Escondido has more than 100 hotels in all categories, mostly along the beaches. High season is Easter week, the last 2 weeks of Jul, all of Aug and Nov-Feb; discounts of 10-30% may be obtained at other times. Hotels right on El Adoquín may be noisy because of discos.

A **Paraíso Escondido**, Unión 10, Centro, T954-582 0444. Away from beach, a/c, pool, colonial style, restaurant open in high season.

B **Casa Blanca**, Av Pérez Gasga 905 (Adoquín), T954-582 0168. A/c in some rooms, fan, hot water, clean, well furnished, balconies and a pool.

D **Castillo de Reyes**, Av Pérez Gasga 210, T954-582 0442. Small, unpretentious and friendly. No frills but clean, airy and quiet rooms with decent bathrooms, piping hot water and firm beds. Some are air conditioned, all have fans. Staff are extremely helpful. Many long-term and repeat guests.

D **Liza's**, off Carretera Costera, Playa Marinero. Fan, very clean, safe deposit. Highly recommended.

D **Mayflower**, Andador Libertad, T954-582 1755, on pedestrian walkway perpendicular to El Adoquín. With bath, fan, kitchen facilities, pool table (F per person in dormitory), friendly, good value, showers and luggage storage for non-guests. English and German spoken. Recommended.

E **Ribera del Mar**, Felipe Merklin 205, T/F954-582 0436, behind Iglesia de la Soledad. Fan, hot water, clean, quiet, laundry facilities, some rooms with great views of the sea. Good value.

Puerto Angel *p106*

B-C **Soraya de Puerto Angel**, José Vasconcelos s/n, T958-584 3009. Beautiful views, clean, spacious terraces, a/c, good parking.

C **Cañón De Vata**, Playa del Panteón, T958-584 3137, posadacanon @yahoo.com Lovely garden setting, gets very booked up, good restaurant. Recommended.

C **Villa Florencia**, Av Principal Virgilio Uribe across from town beach, T/F958-584 3044. A/c, no hot water, cheaper with fan, clean, comfortable, friendly, Italian-Mexican run, restaurant, bar, library with terrace.

D **Casa de Huéspedes Gundi y Tomás**, central and up the hill opposite old military base, T958-584 3068, www.puertoangel-hotel.com Shared bath, clean, good value, popular, stores luggage, money exchange, breakfast and snacks served (cook prepares dinner every day for guests, but expensive).

D **Casas Penélopes**, on road to Zipolite and Mazunte. Friendly, beautiful location. Highly recommended.

D **Puesta del Sol**, on road to Playa del Panteón, T958-584 3096. Fan, cheaper with shared bath, clean, restaurant, very friendly, English and German spoken.

Zipolite and San Agustinillo *p106*

The shore at Zipolite is lined with *palapas* offering cheap meals, accommodation (beds from US$3.50 per night, hammocks from US$2.50, shared bath, basic facilities) and informal discos at night. At San Agustinillo there are simple cabañas E and restaurants.

B-C **Solstice**, Calle del Amor 94, Zipolite, www.solstice-mexico.com, 4 cabañas for up to 4 people around a palm-shaded courtyard (also dorms, E). Prices include breakfast. Quiet spot, with yoga classes (US$5 per hr).

Mazunte *p107*

Palapas offer accommodation along the middle of the beach.

B **Posada Alta Mira**, T/F958-584 3104, www.labuenavista.com On a wooded hillside overlooking the west end of the beach. 10 lovely cabañas, spacious, clean, comfortable, spectacular views, no

Budget buster

L-AL **Aldea del Bazar**, Benito Juárez 7, Puerto Escondido, T582-0508. A veritable Sultan's palace, the Moorish theme of the Aldea del Bazar extends to the staff, kitted out in Middle Eastern garb. While the well-furnished rooms are comfortable and spacious – many with twin and double beds and a sitting room, making it a very good choice for families – it's the range of facilities including an expansive lush garden with lolling palms, a beautiful pool and a restaurant serving highly rated cuisine, that makes this hotel so appealing.

LL **Quinta Real**, Blvd Benito Juárez 2, Tangolunda, T581-0428, www.hotelesboutique.com/quintareal Exclusive resort, perched overlooking the bays and golf club, with beach club, pool, excellent restaurant and bar. Recommended.

electricity yet. Restaurant serves the best food in Mazunte.
B-D **Balamjuyuc**, next to **Posada Alta Mira.**, balamjuyuc@hotmail.com Simpler but in the same splendid setting, breakfast and drinks served.
E **Ziga**, at the east end near the **Centro Mexicano de la Tortuga**. Semi-private bath, fan, mosquito net, clean, friendly, family run, nice views, good value. Recommended.

Huatulco *p107*

Discounts of up to 50% can be expected in the low season.
A-C **Misión de los Arcos**, Gardenia 902 y Tamarindo, La Crucecita, T/F958-587 0165, www.misiondelosarcos.com A/c, comfortable, elegant suites, cheaper with fan, well-equipped gym, good value.
B **Busanvi I**, Carrizal 601, La Crucecita, T958-587 0056. A/c and fan, hot water, apartments with kitchenette, pool.
C-D **Posada del Carmen**, Palo Verde 307, La Crucecita, T958-587 0593. Nice rooms, cold water, cheaper with 1 double bed.

Tehuantepec *p109*

C **Guiexhoba**, on road to Oaxaca, T971-715 0416. A/c, mini-fridge, pool, restaurant, parking.
D-E **Oasis**, Melchor Ocampo 8, T971-715 0008, 1 block from plaza. Good atmosphere, with bath and a/c, cheaper with fan, simple, safe parking, owner is helpful, good information on local history and traditions.
E **Casa de Huéspedes Istmo**, Hidalgo 31, T971-715 0019, 1½ blocks from the main plaza. Quiet, basic, with lovely patio.

Juchitán and around *p109*

B **Santo Domingo**, Carretera Transístmica, Juchitán, T971-711 1959. A/c, restaurant, pool.
C-D **Don Alex Lena Real**, 16 de Septiembre 48, Juchitán, T971-711 1064. Modern comfortable rooms, a/c, clean. Cheaper in older wing and with fan, restaurant.

Eating

Puerto Escondido *p104*

The market on 8th Nte and 3rd Pte is the place to find good and economical eating. Clean with varied typical menus, *comida corrida* from US$2.50.
TTT-TT **Hotel Santa Fé**, Playa Marinero. Excellent vegetarian, but expensive.
TTT-TT **La Galería**, in **Hotel Arcoiris**, Italian, good pizzas but pricey.
TT **Cabo Blanco**, C del Moro, Zicatela. A Puerto institution. Popular, relaxed, serves excellent grilled fish and seafood, with a range of inspired sauces, including Thai curries. Inventive,

vegetarian food usually features on the menu. After dinner, the restaurant turns to a lively beach bar with a true Zicatela vibe. Music on Thu and Sat in high season.

¶¶ **Super Café Puro**, off top flight of stairs of walkway that starts at the tourist information kiosk. Good for breakfast, pleasant terrace, Mexican, family run.

¶¶-¶ **Cappuccino**, Pérez Gasga Good coffee, fruit salads, some dishes pricey.

¶¶-¶ **El Cafecito**, C del Moro, Zicatela. Coffee shop serves superlative breakfasts – chocolate bread is particularly recommended – and robust coffee. The more cosmopolitan restaurant has blissful sea view dining and a totally tropical ambience with wicker chairs and relaxed music. Fresh fish includes seared tuna steaks and excellent value shrimp platters.

¶ **Beniditos**, Av Pérez Gasga. *The* place for pizza, good value.

Cafés, bakeries and heladerías

Carmen's Bakery, on a path to the beach from main road, Zicatela. Great pastries baked on the premises, also 2nd-hand books and magazines.

Gelatería Giardino, Av Pérez Gasga 609, just east of El Adoquín. Excellent Italian ice cream and fruit ices, made on the premises, also cappuccino coffee. Highly recommended (closed May-Jun).

Un Tigre Azul, Av Pérez Gasga on El Adoquín, upper floor. Bar, coffee and snacks, nice views and internet.

Puerto Angel *p106*

There are several fish restaurants along the main street and two cheap popular restaurants by the fishing harbour.

¶¶-¶ **Villa Florencia**, Av Principal Virgilio Uribe across from town beach, T/F958-584 3044. Excellent hotel restaurant serving good Italian and Mexican dishes, charming place.

¶¶ **Beto's** by turn-off for Playa del Panteón. Good fish (fresh tuna), cheap beer, views.

¶ **Cangrejo**, by Naval Base gate. Popular bar, good breakfasts and excellent tacos.

Mazunte *p107*

The best food and view is at the **Posada Alta Mira**, see Sleeping. There are many other simple (but not necessarily cheap) restaurants including:

¶¶-¶ **La Dolce Vita**, on main road at west end. Good Italian pizza and homemade pasta, pricey.

¶ **El Paso**, on main road west of the bridge. Inexpensive and friendly.

Huatulco *p107*

Restaurants on the beach, out of town, tend to be the cheapest. There are luxury restaurants at the Tangolunda hotels. In La Crucecita, prices get cheaper as you get away from the plaza; there are several restaurants along Gardenia.

¶¶¶ **Il Giardio del Papa**, Flamboyán 204, La Crucecita. Italian, chef was once the Pope's cook, expensive.

¶¶¶ **Las Cúpulas**, Hotel Quinta Real, Blvd Benito Juárez 2, Tangolunda. Fine dining with panoramic view of the harbour, also popular breakfast venue. Recommended.

¶¶¶-¶ **Oasis Café**, Flamboyán 211 y Bugambilia, by main plaza, La Crucecita. Varied menu, grill, seafood, Oaxacan food, good value. Recommended.

¶¶ **Café Dublin**, Carrizal 504, La Crucecita. Irish pub, popular, good hamburgers, upstairs café, popular expat hangout.

¶¶ **Don Porfirio**, Blvd Benito Juárez, Tangolunda. Fish and seafood specialities, also steak.

¶¶ **La Crema**, Carrizal and Flamboyán, La Crucecita. Popular bar restaurant, pizzas, bar food, games. Recommended.

¶¶-¶ **Los Portales**, Bugambilia 603, Plaza Principal, La Crucecita. Breakfast, tacos and other snacks, open late.

¶ **Mandinga**, Flamboyán 101, La Crucecita. Chicken and seafood, some seriously cheap dishes.

¶ **Mercado 3 Mayo**, Guamuchil, La Crucecita. Market *fondas* serving typical dishes at very cheap prices, good value.

Tehuantepec *p109*

ŸŸŸ-Ÿ **Restaurant Scaru**, Leona Vicario 4. Good food, fish and seafood specialities, upscale, nice courtyard and mural.

ŸŸ **Mariscos Angel**, 5 de Mayo No 1, by entrance from Salina Cruz. Seafood. Cheap food on top floor of market, here you can get the local speciality, pork or chicken, stuffed with potatoes, but beware of hygiene. The local *quesadillas* made of maize and cheese are delicious; sold at bus stops.

ŸŸ-Ÿ **Café Colonial**, Juana C Romero 66. Good *comida corrida* and à la carte, a variety of Mexican dishes, clean, friendly.

Juchitán and around *p109*

ŸŸŸ-Ÿ **Casa Grande**, Juárez 125, on the main square, Juchitán. In a beautifully restored colonial house, good food, live music.

ŸŸ **Los Chapulines**, 5 de Septiembre and Morelos, Juchitán. Regional and international food, *comida corrida* and à la carte, a/c.

ŸŸ **La Manzana**, Nicolás Bravo 10, Cd Ixtepec. Seafood and international cooking.

Entertainment

Puerto Escondido *p104*

Bars and clubs

It is not advisable to stay at bars and discos past 0300.

Barfly, El Adoquín pedestrian mall, Av. Perez Gasga. Good music, regular screenings of films and videos.

El Son y la Rumba, Marina Nacional 15. Rooftop bar with live salsa and rumba at night. Restaurant serves *comida corrida* during the day.

Los 3 Diablos, Av Pérez Gasga 604. New lively bar, pool table, nice friendly staff.

Tequila Sunrise, Av Marina Nacional, just west of El Adoquín. Open-air disco, varied music, international crowd.

Wipeout, El Adoquín pedestrian mall, Av. Perez Gasga. Rock and techno music.

Zipolite and San Agustinillo *p106*

Livélula, Zipolite. A quiet little bar, with ping-pong, table football, hammocks and plenty of time to relax. Open 0800-0200, Wed, Sat.

Huatulco *p107*

Folklore shows

Several luxury hotels put on shows for guests:

Barcelo Huatulco, Paseo Benito Juárez, Huatulco, reservations T958-581 0055. Mariachis and folk dancing, with Mexican buffet.

Noches Oaxaqueñas, Blvd Benito Juárez, Tangolunda, reservations T958-581 0001. La Guelaguetza folklore show.

Clubs

Magic Tropic, Anador Huatulco, Santa Cruz. Latin dancing.

La Papaya, Benito Juárez, Manzana 3, Lote 1, Bahía de Chahué, T958-583 4911, US$5 cover. Popular, European-style disco, big screen, human fish tank.

Festivals and events

Puerto Escondido *p104*

Mar long board surf tournament.

Aug Master World Surf Championship

Nov Festivities are held throughout the month, including **Festival Costeño de la Danza**, with colourful, lively folk dances. Also a surfing tournament.

Huatulco *p107*

Apr **Fiesta del Mar** in the 1st week.

May religious **Fiesta de la Santa Cruz** on the 3rd; international sail-fishing tournament during the 1st week.

12 Dec **Fiesta de la Virgen**.

Tehuantepec *p109*

Many important and colourful celebrations take place in Tehuantepec, for which the women don their elaborate embroidered dresses and lace halos, known as *resplandores*. **Fiestas Patronales** are held in honour of the patron saint of each neighbourhood: in the San José barrio the fiestas for **St John the Baptist** are held in the week leading up to **24 Jun**; in the centre of Tehuantepec the fiestas of **Santo Domingo** are held during the **1st week of Aug**, and so on. Another type of celebration are *velas*, formal dances requiring for which the attendees wear traditional dress and offer gifts of fruits and flowers: **Vela Zandunga**, **19 May**; **Velas de Agosto**, held throughout the Isthmus, **mid-Aug**; **Vela Tehuantepec**, **26 Dec**.

Juchitán and around *p109*

Velas, see above, are held throughout the year, the most important are in **May** in honour of **San Vicente Ferrer**.

Shopping

Puerto Escondido *p104*

Crafts and souvenirs

Available from shops all along **El Adoquín**, stalls on the main street, east of El Adoquín and on **Andador Libertad**, a walkway going uphill from about the middle of El Adoquín. Shop around, vendors on the beach are likely to ask for higher prices and you may find better value in shops north of the highway.

Oasis, Adoquín, opposite the tourist kiosk, fine accessories and gifts.

Papi's souvenir shop has a small selection of foreign books for sale or trade.

Mazunte *p107*

Cosméticos Naturales de Mazunte, west end of Mazunte village. Cosmetics made with natural ingredients. Especially recommended is the natural mosquito repellent.

Huatulco *p107*

Mercado de Artesanías de Santa Cruz, Blvd Santa Cruz y Mitla, Santa Cruz. Variety of regional crafts.

Museo de Artesanías Oaxaqueñas, Flamboyán 216, Plaza Principal, La Crucecita. Exhibits and sells Mexican crafts.

Activities and tours

Puerto Escondido *p104*

Diving

The coastline offers good opportunities for snorkelling and scuba diving; snorkelling from the beach is easiest at Puerto Angelito.

Aventura Submarina, Av Pérez Gasga, at west end of El Adoquín, T/F954-582 2353. Tours and diving lessons with Jorge Pérez Bravo. You are likely to see turtles and dolphins on the way to the snorkelling and diving sites. Snorkelling, 3 hrs, US$22. Diving lessons, US$55 for 1 tank; if qualified, US$38 for 1 tank, US$55 for 2.

Fishing

Boats can be hired for fishing at Playa Principal or through travel agencies for approximately US$27 per hr for up to 4 passengers.

Horse riding

T954-582 1950. Meet at point of Zicoleta, 3 hrs minimum, US$10 per hr.

Kayaking

New to Puerto Escondido, US$6 per hr, enquire at **Las Hamacas** at Matialtepec Lagoon. Recommended.

Pelota Mixteca

A modern version of an ancient Mixtec ball game is played on Sat and Sun in **Bajos de Chila**, 15 mins from Puerto Escondido, on the road to Acapulco. In a 9-m 35-m court, teams of 5-7 players propel a rubber ball weighing almost 1 kg, using elaborately decorated leather mitts that weigh between 3½ kg and 6 kg. A game can take up to 4 hrs.

Surfing

Playa Zicatela is a surfer's haven, but dangerous for the novice. Surfing gear and clothing is best bought from shops in Zicatela. Surf hire and lessons are available from **Central Surf** on Col Centro, El Adoquin, Av. Pérez Gazga,

T958-582 0568, and if you don't stand up, the lesson is free!

Tour operators

Ana's Ecotours (contact Ana Márquez at **Tigre Azul**, Av Pérez Gasga). Ana is a certified, recommended guide, speaks English and is very knowledgeable about the region and especially its birds. Tours to all the natural attractions in the area and cultural tours of her native Mixtec community, day trip, US$32 per person.
Gina Machorro (speaks English and French), offers a 2-hr walking tour of Puerto Escondido's local culture and history, US$16 per person (Wed and Sat only during the winter). Contact through the tourist information kiosk.
Margarito takes visitors to the Manialtepec lagoon for US$16 per person. Hard to find but he normally walks the beach near **Cafecito**.
Michael Malone, a Canadian ornithologist, is another recommended guide who is in Puerto Escondido Nov-Mar (ask at tourism information kiosk).

Puerto Angel *p106*

Azul Profundo, next door to **Cordelia's** on Playa del Panteón, T958-584 3109. Scuba diving with experienced instructors, up-to-date equipment, PADI available. Also runs snorkelling trips to beaches along the coast. English spoken.

Huatulco *p107*

Birdwatching

Aventura Huatulco, T958-589 3907 (mob), US$25, 3-hr trips, 0600-0900.

Boat trips

Full-day boat tours to see the different bays are offered by travel agencies for US$17-27 per person, with stops for swimming, snorkelling and a meal; there are catamarans, sail boats, yachts and small launches. Trips can also be arranged at the Santa Cruz marina directly with the boatsmen, they often only speak Spanish.

Cycling

Bike rentals in La Crucecita from restaurants near the plaza, US$1.65 per hr. Rentals and cycling tours from **Motor Tours, Eco Aventuras, Adventuras Huatulco** and other agencies (see Tour operators, below). Also scooter and off-road motorbikes for rent, Blvd Santa Cruz, local 1, T958-583 4766. Need credit card and licence.

Diving and snorkelling

Good snorkelling areas on reefs by the beach at **La Entrega** (Bahía Santa Cruz), **Riscalillo** (Bahía Cachacual) and **San Agustín** (Bahía San Agustín). The islands of **Cacaluta** (Bahía Cacaluta) and **La Montosa** (Bahía Tangolunda) are also surrounded by reefs with several species of coral, many different organisms can be seen here in relatively shallow water. Snorkel and fins at Santa Cruz marina, US$5 or through agencies.

There are good scuba diving opportunities and the cliffs that separate the different bays continue underwater for an average of 30 m.
Action Sports Marina, Barcelo Huatulco, Paseo Benito Juárez, Huatulco. Diving lessons and tours.
Buceo Sotavento, Punta Tangolunda, local 2, T581-0051. Diving lessons, tours.
Hurricane Divers Playa Santa Cruz, Manzana 19, Lote 8, T958-587 1107, www.hurricanedivers.com, lessons at about US$82, diving tour if you have your certificate, US$65.

Fishing

Launches and yachts for deep-sea fishing charge US$100 per hr, minimal rental 3 hrs. **Coorporativo Tangolunda**, T958-587 0081, Bahía Santa Cruz, cheaper option.

Golf

The Tangolunda golf course offers 18-hole, par-72 golf with nice views of the surroundings. Reservations T958-581 0037, green fee US$65, clubs and carts are extra.

Health spa

Xquenda Huatulco Spa, Vialidad Lambda s/n, Bahía Chahué, T958-583 4448, www.huatulcospa.com, massage, beauty salon, gym, 25m pool, temazcal treatments.

Horse riding

Rancho Caballo de Mar, on the shores of the Río Copalita, east of Huatulco and south of Route 200, T958-587 0530, offers riding tours along the river, on forested trails and on the beaches of Bahía de Conejos, US$25 for 3 hrs.

Rafting

Several companies run tours down the Copalita and Zimatán rivers, ranging from a float down the river to challenging class 4-5 rapids. Half-day, US$33-40, full-day US$65-76 per person. Note that Feb-May there may not be enough water.
Providers include:
Aventuras Piraguas, Plaza Oaxaca Local 19, on Flamboyán across from the plaza, La Crucecita, T/F958-587 1333, canoe trips and rafting in up to class 5 rapids.
Copalita River Tours, Gardenia and Palo Verde (**Posada Michelle** lobby), La Crucecita, T/F958-587 0535, kayak and rafting tours.

Sailing

Luna Azul, day and evening sailing trips and private charter, contact Jack Hennessey, T958-587 0945, or drop in at the **Hotel Posada Chahue**, Calle Mixie L.75 Sector R Bahia de Chahue, www.lunaazul.netfirms.com

Tour operators

Full-day tours to coffee plantations, US$44 per person. Day trips to Puerto Angel, Mazunte and Puerto Escondido, US$20.
Bahías Plus, Carrizal 704, La Crucecita, T/F958-587 0811, and at Hotel Binniguenda, Santa Cruz, T/F587-0216, airline reservations, tours, helpful, American Express reps on 2nd floor of La Crucecita office.
Eco Aventuras, La Crucecita, T958-587 0669, adventure tours, cycling, rock climbing, kayaking, birdwatching.
Motor Tours, T958-587 1818, at **Hotel Castillo Huatulco**, Santa Cruz, T958-583 0400, local and regional tours, motorcycles and all-terrain quad bikes (*cuatrimotos*).
Paraíso Huatulco, at **Hotel Flamboyán**, La Crucecita, T958-587 0181, and at **Barcelo Resort**, Tangolunda, T958-581 0218 ext 788, paraiso@huatulco.net.mx, local and regional tours, diving, fishing, quad bikes.

Watersports

Wind surfing, sailing, wave running and waterskiing equipment can be rented at the major hotels and beach clubs.
Action Sports Marina, Barcelo Huatulco, Paseo Benito Juárez, Huatulco, T958-581 0055, ext 842, diving lessons and tours, watersports.
Zax Aventura Extrema, Av Bahía San Augustín, Manzana 17, Lote 24, Coxula, T958-583 4426. Offers tubing.

Transport

Puerto Escondido *p104*

Air

With **Aerocaribe**, T954-582 2023, daily from **Mexico City** at 1140, to Mexico City at 1300, 1 hr, US$87; daily from **Oaxaca** at 0955 and 1640, to Oaxaca at 1045 and 1820, 30 mins, US$70. With **Aerovega** (T/F582-0151) daily from Oaxaca at 0700, to Oaxaca at 0900, US$100. Also with **Aerotucán**, T954-582 1725, daily from Oaxaca, US$110.

Car

Car hire Budget, Av Juárez at the entrance to Bacocho, T954-582 0312.

Bus

Local To **Pochutla**, from corner Carretera Costera and Av Oaxaca, every 20 mins, 0500-1900, 1½ hrs, US$1.60. For **Puerto Angel**, **Zipolite** and other beaches: transfer in Pochutla to pick-up or *colectivo* taxi (see below).

Long distance To **Acapulco**: Estrella Blanca, a/c, semi-direct service every couple of hrs from 0400, 7½ hrs, US$18.50; regular service, hrly 0500-1730, 9 hrs, US$14. To **Mexico City**: Estrella Blanca, 1st class at 1830, 1930 and 2030 to the Southern Terminal, US$40, 12 hrs via Acapulco, to travel during the day go to Acapulco and transfer there; Oaxaca-Pacífico/Estrella del Valle, 1st class, at 1745, US$33, 14 hrs via Oaxaca, arrives at Fletes y Pasajes terminal near TAPO (east terminal). To **Oaxaca**: for safety, travel during daytime only and take direct services that run better vehicles and do not pick up passengers along the way; Oaxaca-Pacífico/Estrella del Valle, Av Hidalgo 400 near Av Oaxaca, direct service at 0815, 1245, 2215, US$8.50, 7½ hrs, 1st class at 2230, US$10.50. Cristóbal Colón, 1a Nte 207, 3 daily via Tehuantepec, US$16.50, 12 hrs (1st-class service, takes the Isthmus route). To **Huatulco**: via Pochutla at 0730, 1130, 1530, 1900 and 0040, 2¼ hrs, US$5.20, 2nd class 1800, 2½ hrs, US$3.80. To **Tapachula**: Cristóbal Colón, 2000, 14-15 hrs, US$27. To **Tuxtla Gutiérrez** and **San Cristóbal de las Casas**: Cristóbal Colón, 0845 and 2130, Tuxtla US$4, 12 hrs, San Cristóbal, US$29, 14 hrs. To **Zihuatanejo**: Estrella Blanca, 1 direct bus daily.

Pochutla *p106*

Bus

To **Acapulco**: Estrella Blanca, 0630, 1000, 1545, 1915, 2200, 8½ hrs, US$21. To **Huatulco** (La Crucecita): small buses from lane near Oaxaca-Pacífico terminal, every 15 mins 0500-2000, 1 hr, US$1. To **Mexico City**: Estrella Blanca, 1st class, via Acapulco, 1500, 1900, US$37, 12-13 hrs; Oaxaca-Pacífico, via Oaxaca, 1800 and 1900, 13 hrs, US$24. To **Oaxaca**: Oaxaca-Pacífico/Estrella del Valle, direct service 0945, 1415, 2300, 6 hrs, US$7. 2nd-class service, 14 daily, 9 hrs, US$6.20; with Cristóbal Colón via the Isthmus, at 1445 and 1930, US$14.70. To **Puerto Escondido**: small buses from side street near church, every 20 mins 0500-1900, 1½ hrs, US$1.30; also with through buses coming from Oaxaca. To **San Cristóbal de las Casas**, twice daily, US$26, 13 hrs. To **Tapachula**: Cristóbal Colón, 2100, 12 hrs, US$24. To **Tuxtla Gutiérrez**: Cristóbal Colón, 0945 and 2230, 10 hrs, US$19.

Taxi and colectivo

For Puerto Angel, Zipolite and other beaches, pick-up trucks with benches in the back and shared taxis (*colectivos*) do round trips on the coastal road; they also offer a private service (*carreras*); in Pochutla, wait at marked bus stops on the main road. To **Puerto Angel**, truck US$0.40, *colectivo* US$0.70 per person, taxi US$4. To **Zipolite**, truck US$0.45, *colectivo* US$1, taxi US$6. To **Mazunte**, truck US$0.50, *colectivo* US$1, taxi US$6. Beware of overcharging and unscrupulous drivers. To **Puerto Escondido**, *colectivo* US$3, taxi US$20. To **Huatulco**, *colectivo* US$1.50, taxi US$10.

Huatulco *p107*

Air

All international flights are charters and run in winter only. From **Mexico City**, Mexicana, arrives 1005 and 1335 daily, departs from Huatulco 1150 and 1520; discounts for advanced purchase. From **Oaxaca**, Aerocaribe, arrives 0700 and 1705 daily, departs from Huatulco 0750 and 1755.

Airline offices Aerocaribe, Hotel Castillo Huatulco, Santa Cruz, T958-587 1220. Mexicana, Hotel Castillo Huatulco, Santa Cruz, T587-0223.

Bus

Local 2nd-class buses to **Pochutla** (for **Puerto Angel**, **Mazunte**, **Puerto Escondido** and **Zipolite**) depart from Blvd Chahué and Riscalillo, La Crucecita, every 15 mins 0500-2000, US$1.20, 1 hr. *Colectivo* taxis run from Tangolunda and Crucecita (main plaza), US$0.40.

Long distance **Acapulco**: with Estrella Blanca, 1st class, 4 daily, 9 hrs,

US$23; 2nd class, 3 daily, 11 hrs, US$17. **Mexico City**: with **Cristóbal Colón**, 1st class, 4 daily (arriving at various terminals), 14 hrs, US$44, via Isthmus and Oaxaca: with **Estrella Blanca**, 1st class, at 1800, 13 hrs, US$44, via Acapulco. **Oaxaca**: 1st class with **Cristóbal Colón**, Gardenia corner Ocotillo, La Crucecita, 2 daily, US$18, via Isthmus 8 hrs, luxury **Plus** service at 2100, US$22. 2nd class with **Oaxaca-Pacífico**, Calle Jazmín, La Crucecita, 1 daily, 7 hrs, US$9, via Pochutla. **Puerto Escondido**: with **Cristóbal Colón**, 1st class, 7 daily, US$5, 2 hrs; with **Estrella Blanca**, Gardenia corner Palma Real, La Crucecita, 1st class, 4 daily, 2½ hrs, US$5.30, 2nd class, 3 daily, US$3.90. **Salina Cruz**: with **Cristóbal Colón**, 1st class, 8 daily continuing to Tehuantepec and Juchitán, 2½ hrs, US$6.50; **Plus** service, 2 daily, US$6.50; with **Estrella Blanca**, 3 daily, 2½ hrs, US$5.80. **Tapachula**: with **Cristóbal Colón**, 1st class, at 2215, 10 hrs, US$26. **Tuxtla Gutiérrez**: with **Cristóbal Colón**, 1st class, 2045 and 2345, 8 hrs, US$20.

Tehuantepec *p108*

Air

Airport at Cd Ixtepec has flights to **Mexico City**, **Aeromar**, 2 daily Mon-Fri, 1 daily Sat-Sun, US$168-257. To **Oaxaca**, with **Aerocaribe**, daily 0935, US$8.

Bus

Regional **Istmeños** buses leave from the highway (Carretera Cristóbal Colón), by the river, at the end of 5 de Mayo: to **Juchitán**, every 10 mins, 0500-2400, US$0.80, 1 hr.

The bus station on the outskirts of town is used by **Cristóbal Colón**, **ADO**, **AU** and **Sur**. To **Cancún**: **ADO** at 1430, US$68. To **Coatzacoalcos**: **ADO** and **Sur**, 1st class 5 daily, 6 hrs, US$13; 2nd class every 30 mins, US$10. To **Oaxaca**, **Pochutla**,and **Puerto Escondido**: **Cristóbal Colón**, 1st class 4 daily, US$7.50 (Huatulco), US$10 (Pochutla), US$14 (Puerto Escondido); to **Huatulco** 2nd class, 0600, 1330, US$6. To **Mexico City**: **Cristóbal Colón**, *plus* service, 2030, US$42; 1st class, 2000, 2145, US$48. To **San Cristóbal de la Casas**: **Cristóbal Colón**, 0030 and 1400, 6½ hrs, US$16. To **Tonalá** and **Tapachula**: **Cristóbal Colón**, 2 nightly, US$9 (Tonalá), US$19 (Tapachula). To **Tuxtepec**: **AU** via Sayula, 1040, 2140, US$14, 6 hrs (Tuxtepec). To **Tuxtla Gutiérrez**: **Cristóbal Colón**, 0030, 1400, 2200, 4½ hrs, US$13. To **Villahermosa**: **Cristóbal Colón** 1st class, US$17, 8 hrs, 2nd class US$14.

Juchitán and around *p109*

Bus

To **Tehuantepec** (US$0.80) every 15 mins with **Istmeños**, 0500-2400, from Prolongación 16 de Septiembre. Joint bus station for **Cristóbal Colón**, **ADO**, **Sur** and **AU** also here, just south of the highway. To **Huatulco**: **ADO** 0600, US$8.60; **Cristóbal Colón**, 5 daily, US$9; **Sur**, 3 daily, US$5.55. To **Mexico City**: **ADO** luxury, at 2145, US$72, **ADO** 1st class, 1900 and 2100, US$52; **AU** 6 daily US$42. To **Oaxaca**: **ADO** luxury, 3 daily, US$16; 1st class: **ADO** 3 daily, **Cristóbal Colón** 7 daily, 6 hrs, US$13. To **Pochutla** and **Puerto Escondido**: **Cristóbal Colón**, 4 daily, US$14 (Puerto), US$12 (Pochutla); **Sur**, 2330, US$12 (Puerto), US$9 (Pochutla). To **San Cristóbal de las Casas**: **Cristóbal Colón**, 3 daily, US$16. To **Tapachula**: **ADO** at 0230, US$23; **Cristóbal Colón**, 2 nightly, US$19; **Sur** 0230 and 1600, US$16. To **Tuxtepec**: **AU** at 1115, US$13. To **Tuxtla Gutiérrez**: **Cristóbal Colón**, 5 daily, US$14. To **Veracruz**: **ADO** 0055 and 2130, US$215; **AU** 1115, US$24.

Directory

Puerto Escondido *p104*

Banks Plenty of banks with ATMs around town. **Doctors** Dr Francisco Serrano Severiano, 1a Nte y 2a Pte, opposite Bancomer, speaks English, 0900-1300, 1700-2000. **Hospitals and clinics** Clínica de Especialidades del Puerto, Av Oaxaca. **Internet** Lots of

Travellers' tales

Day of the Dead

San Juan Guelache was out in the sticks beyond Oaxaca city and lit by a luminous full moon. As soon as we got off the bus, we were surrounded by a crowd of costumed and masked revellers of all ages, accompanied by a noisy band. Tiny children wore the masks of old wizened grandmothers and had adopted the stoop to match; by comparison our last-minute skeletal face painting was not up to scratch. The crowd made its way through village, stopping at certain houses where masked performers enacted the death of a local and the battle between a devil and a bishop for his or her soul. The houses all had an altar, covered with bright orange flowers and decorated with candles, crucifixes and a photo of the deceased. This was Hallowe'en trick or treating on a grand scale; laden with dollops of Catholicism and indigenous spirituality. Each performance was followed by manic dancing and cacophonous music; then it was off to the next house. We departed San Juan as we had arrived: in a flurry of music, shouting and demented masked figures, waving in the moonlight. *John Hendry-Taylor*

internet cafés about town, all charge $2 per hr. **Laundry** Lavandería at east end of El Adoquín, US$1 per kg or US$3.25 per load, self-service, Mon-Sat 0900-2100. **Pharmacies** Farmacia La Moderna, Av Pérez Gasga 203, T954-582 0214, has a physician in house, open 24 hrs. **Post office** 7a Nte by Av Oaxaca, good telegraph service to wire money (need transfer number from sender), Western Union office next door.

Pochutla *p106*
Banks Several on the main street. **Hospital** Public hospital just south of town. **Internet** Email in a couple of places on Lázaro Cárdenas.

Puerto Angel *p106*
Banks Cash and TCs changed at Hotel Soraya; otherwise use banks in Pochutla. **Internet** Caseta Puerto Angel, C José Vasconcelos 3, T584-3038.

Huatulco *p107*
Banks HSBC, Bugambilia y Sabalí, La Crucecita, cash and TCs, ATM. **Internet** Informática Mare, Guanacastle 203, 2nd floor, near market, US$3 per hr. **Laundry** Lavandería Abril, Gardenia 1403 y Pochote, La Crucecita, US$0.75 per kg. **Post office** Blvd Chahué, La Crucecita. **Hospitals and clinics** Especialidades Médicas Santa Cruz, Flamboyán, La Crucecita, private, English spoken.

Tehuantepec *p109*
Banks HSBC, Juana C Romero, 0800-1700. Bancomer, 5 de Mayo. All change cash and TCs.

Juchitán and around *p109*
Banks HSBC, 16 de Septiembre y Alvaro Obregón, Mon-Fri 0800-1900, Sat 0900-1400. **Internet** Servitel, Efraín Gómez y 16 de Septiembre, US$4.35 per hr.

Chiapas & Tabasco

Zinacantán

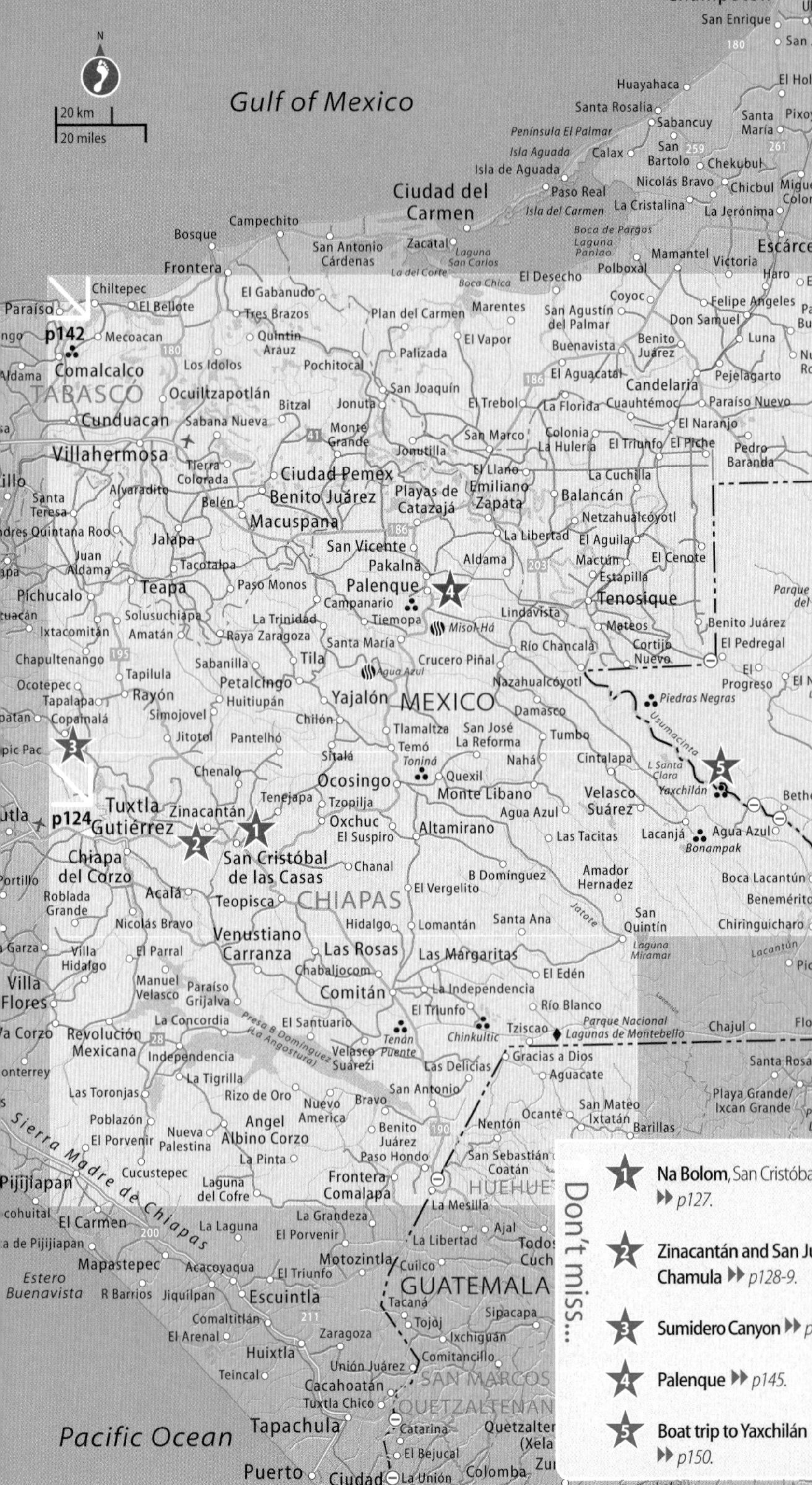

Gulf of Mexico
Pacific Ocean
20 km
20 miles
MEXICO
GUATEMALA
TABASCO
CHIAPAS
p142
p124
Villahermosa
Ciudad del Carmen
Palenque
Tuxtla Gutiérrez
San Cristóbal de las Casas
Zinacantán
Ocosingo
Comitán
Tapachula
Tenosique
Frontera
Comalcalco
Yaxchilán
Bonampak
Toniná
Misol-Há
Agua Azul
Piedras Negras
Usumacinta
Sierra Madre de Chiapas
Parque Nacional Lagunas de Montebello
Champotón
Escárcega
Don't miss...
1 Na Bolom, San Cristóbal ▸▸ p127.
2 Zinacantán and San Ju[an] Chamula ▸▸ p128-9.
3 Sumidero Canyon ▸▸ p1
4 Palenque ▸▸ p145.
5 Boat trip to Yaxchilán ▸▸ p150.

Introduction

Although in some ways Chiapas has fallen victim to the progress bug, it nevertheless seems impervious to the intrusion of outsiders, most of whom are eager to experience a step back in time, or perhaps a time warp. Woven through the pine forests cloaked in mist are ancestral traditions, potent mysticism and bloody revolution. The Lost World atmosphere is sustained by the state's indigenous inhabitants and their villages. Many visitors will know of the dreadful treatment they have suffered over centuries, the fundamental cause of the rebellion on 1 January 1994, which led to the occupation of San Cristóbal de las Casas by revolutionaries. What the visitor is unprepared for is the great dignity demonstrated by these people, who cling to ancient traditions in dress, crafts, food, religious practice, festivals and especially language. This is the land of the Classic Maya, whose descendants still inhabit the highland villages today. Most travellers base themselves in the Colonial-indigenous town of San Cristóbal de las Casas, from where they can explore jungle waterfalls, a dramatic canyon, multi-coloured lakes, and the ruins at Palenque, whose jungle setting is probably the most atmospheric and beautiful of all the Maya sites. Chiapas is also a good entry point for Guatemala.

Ratings

Landscape
★★★★

Culture
★★★★

Chillin'
★★★★

Activities
★★★★

Wildlife
★★★★

Costs
$$$

San Cristóbal de las Casas and around

One of Mexico's most beautiful towns, San Cristóbal de las Casas is stunningly located in the fertile Jovel Valley, with the mountains of Huitepec to the west and Tzontehuitz to the east. The city was laid out in the colonial period with 21 indigenous barrios on the perimeter; these were later integrated into the mestizo city that existed by the 18th century. The indigenous population is today an important part of San Cristóbal's atmosphere, with many local handicrafts on sale in the town's two markets. The centre is rich in architectural variety, with excellent examples of baroque, Neo-classical and plateresque, a Mexican style characterized by the intricate moulding of façades, resembling the work of silversmiths. Around San Cristóbal in the beautiful Chiapas highlands are indigenous Maya villages whose inhabitants preserve their traditional customs, costumes and beliefs.

Getting there Daily bus services from Oaxaca.
Getting around Good transport between cities, less reliable between villages. Check political conditions.
Time required 1 week.
Weather Mild due to the altitude.
Sleeping Good variety of accommodation for all budgets in San Cristóbal.
Eating Cheap, international variety, wholesome and healthy.
Activities and tours Horse riding, visiting waterfalls, canyons and indigenous villages.
★ **Don't miss**...Chamula and Zinacantán » *p128-129.*

Ins and outs

Getting there and around San Cristóbal's **airport** (SZT) is about 15 km from town, with limited services in small planes to Tuxtla Gutiérrez and Mexico City and charter flights to Bonampak and Yaxchilán. However, you're far more likely to arrive and leave by **bus**. There is a first-class terminal that serves destinations all over Mexico, and two second-class terminals for local buses to destinations within Chiapas and to the Guatemalan border. Tuxtla Gutiérrez is

Background

Revolutionary hero

The charismatic guerrilla leader, Emiliano Zapata (1879-1919), has become the most famous and potent symbol of the Mexican Revolution. Impatient for the implementation of land reforms promised by newly-elected president, Francisco I Madero, Zapata's guerrillas took control of Morelos state, in the south of the country, and began the process themselves. Zapata's 'Plan of Ayala' called for the expropriation of and redistribution of hacienda lands to the rural poor. Zapata was ambushed and murdered by rival revolutionary leader, Venustiano Carranza, two years after his land reform plan has been enshrined in the revolutionary constitution of 1917. Successive Mexican governments failed to realise Zapata's dream, but his name has lived on as a symbol of social justice, most notably in the formation of the Zapatista National Liberal Front (EZLN) who led an uprising in Chiapas in 1994. Despite talks with the government and an agreed ceasefire in 1995, the 'Zapatistas' continue to fight for their cause and the land they occupy is heavily patrolled by government forces.

an alternative transport hub for travellers to Chiapas, with bus connections throughout southern Mexico. Taxis are available in San Cristóbal and to the nearby villages; the cheaper *colectivos* run on fixed routes only. It is always advisable to check on political conditions in Chiapas state before travelling in the area. » *p139.*

Climate Due to its altitude, San Cristóbal has a mild climate compared to the hotter Chiapas towns such as Palenque and Tuxtla. During June, July and August, it is warm and sunny in the morning, while in the afternoon it tends to rain, with a sharp drop in temperature. Warm, waterproof clothes are needed, although the heavy rains conveniently stop in the evening.

Tourist information The **tourist office** ⓘ *Hidalgo 1, at the government offices, T967-678 6570, Mon-Sat 0800-2000, Sun 0900-1400*, is very helpful with all types of information and provides good maps; usually someone there speaks English. The **municipal office** ⓘ *Palacio Municipal, on the main plaza, T967-678 0665*, has a good free map of the town and surroundings. Ask here for accommodation in private houses and for information on ecotours to the Huitepec nature reserve. A new tourist trolley, **El Coleta** ⓘ *Mercado de Dulces y Artesanías, Av Insurgentes 24, hourly 1000-1300 and 1600-1900*, gives a one-hour city tour visiting the main sights. Good for orientation.

Sights » *p132-141.*

The main square, **Plaza 31 de Marzo**, has a gazebo built during the era of Porfirio Díaz. In front of the plaza is the Neo-classical **Palacio Municipal**, built in 1885. Close by is the 16th-century **Catedral de San Cristóbal**, painted in ochre, brown and white, with a baroque pulpit added in the 17th century. Adjacent is the church of **San Nicolás**, which houses the historical archives of the diocese. The building dates from 1613, and is thought to be the only church in Mexico to preserve its indigenous architectural design.

Background

Chiapanecos

The Chiapas government estimates that nearly one million indigenous people live in the state, descendants of the great Maya civilization of AD 250-900. However, the indigenous Chiapanecos of today are not a monolith people: they are spread out across the state and have distinct languages, dress, customs and forms of tribal government.

The **Tzotziles** and **Tzeltales** total about 626,000 and live mainly on the plateau and highlands around San Cristóbal de las Casas. The **Choles** number 110,000 and live in the towns of Tila, Tumbalá, Salto de Agua, Sabanilla and Yajalón in northwestern Chiapas. The 87,000 **Zoques** live near the volatile Chichonal volcano. The 66,000 **Tojolabales** live in Margaritas, Comitán, La Independencia, La Trinitaria and part of Altamirano. On the high mountains and slopes of the Sierra Madre are the 23,000 **Mames** and the 12,000 **Mochós** and **Kakchikeles**. The **Lacandones**, named after the rainforest they occupy in eastern Chiapas, number only 500 today. Along the border with Guatemala are 21,500 **Chujes**, **Kanjobales** and **Jacaltecos**, although that number includes some refugees remaining from the Guatemalan Civil War.

A minority of the indigenous population speaks Spanish, particularly in the Sierra Madre region and among the Zoques. Although many indigenous Chiapanecos no longer wear their *típica* clothing, they still celebrate their unique festivals and venerate their ancestors as they have for centuries. Customary positions of authority, along with stewardships and standard bearers, have been phased out of tribal governance, but medicine men continue to practise.

Chiapas is one of the poorest states in Mexico and shares many of the same problems as neighbouring Guatemala. Many Chiapanecos now live in the large cities, working as domestic servants, labourers or street pedlars; some even work for the government. Those who remain in the countryside are, for the most part, poor. Subsistence has been a way of life for centuries, illiteracy and infant mortality are high, particularly among those who have retained their languages and traditions.

The scarcity of land for the indigenous population has been a political issue for many decades but only reached the world's attention with the Zapatista uprising of January 1994.

Just off the plaza, at the beginning of Insurgentes, is the former **Casa de la Sirena**, now the **Hotel Santa Clara**. Built at the end of the 16th century, this is a rare example of colonial residential architecture in the plateresque style. The interior has the four Classic corridors of renaissance construction.

Heading off the plaza in the opposite direction, going north up 20 de Noviembre, you reach the **Church and Ex-Convento de Santo Domingo**. By far the most dramatic building in the city, it features an elaborate baroque façade in moulded mortar, especially beautiful

Baroque façade of Santo Domingo

when viewed in the late afternoon sun. The church's altarpieces are covered in gold leaf and the pulpit is intricately carved in a style peculiar to Mexico, known as churrigueresque, even more elaborate than the baroque style of Europe. Outside the church is the main handicraft market, with dozens of stalls selling traditional textiles, handmade dolls and jewellery. The **Museo de Los Altos** ⓘ *Calzada Lázaro Cárdenas, next to Santo Domingo church, Tue-Sun 1000-1700, US$3, free on Sun and bank holidays*, is an anthropological museum which contains a history of San Cristóbal, with an emphasis on the plight of the indigenous people, and a good selection of locally produced textiles. There is a small library at the back.

To the south of the centre, the **Templo del Carmen** ⓘ *Crescencio Rosas y Alvaro Obregón*, has a unique archery tower in the Moorish style. Opposite is the **Casa de la Cultura** ⓘ *Tue-Sun 0900-1700, free*, which has a range of activities on offer, including concerts, films, lectures and art exhibitions. Other cultural centres worth looking up include: **Taller de Artes y Oficios Kun Kun** ⓘ *Real de Mexicanos 21, T967-678 1417*, which exhibits hand-woven woollen textiles and ceramics, and the **Museo de Sergio Castro** ⓘ *Guadalupe Victoria 47 (6 blocks from plaza), T967-678 4289, 1800-2000*, which gives lectures and slide shows about customs and problems of the indigenous population. The **Centro de Desarrollo de la Medicina Maya** ⓘ *Salomón González Blanco, T967-678 5438, Mon-Fri 0900-1800, Sat and Sun 1000-1600, US$2*, has a herb garden with displays on the use of medicinal plants by the Maya.

West of the Templo del Carmen, up a strenuous flight of steps, is the **Templo del Cerrito**, a small church with fine views of the city and the surrounding mountains. At the other end of the city, to the east, the **Templo de Guadalupe** is a little church on a hill, used by the indigenous people of the barrio de Guadalupe. There are 21 such indigenous neighbourhoods around the city, each characterized by the unique dress of the local people and by the handicrafts produced by them. Guadalupe is the barrio of candle makers, saddle makers, and wooden toy makers. The other barrios, such as Mexicanos, the oldest in the city, are further afield and not recommended for unguided visits. The cultural centre **Na Bolom** (see below) is very helpful for information on all aspects of indigenous culture.

Na Bolom Museum and Cultural Centre

ⓘ *Vicente Guerrero 33, CP 29220, T967-678 1418, www.nabolom.org, guided tours Tue-Sun, 1130 in Spanish, 1630 in English, US$4.20 including video, 1½ hrs, US$3.20 without a guide (you cannot see the museum on your own); library opens Mon-Fri 0930-1330, 1630-1900.*

 Situated in a Neo-classical mansion dating from 1891, Na Bolom was founded in 1951 by the Danish archaeologist Frans Blom and his wife, the Swiss photographer Gertrudis Duby. After the death of Frans Blom in 1963, Na Bolom became a study centre for the universities of Harvard and Stanford, while Gertrudis Duby continued campaigning for the conservation of the Lacandón area, a jungle containing at least 20% of Mexico's biodiversity and inhabited by indigenous communities. She died in 1993, aged 92, after which the centre has continued to function as a non-profit-making organization dedicated to conserving the Chiapan environment and helping the Lacandón people; it is staffed entirely by volunteers. The photographic archives in the museum contain a detailed visual history covering the last 50 years of the Maya people with beautifully displayed artefacts, pictures and information about their present way of life. There are five galleries with collections of pre-Columbian Maya art and colonial religious paintings. There is also a good library. A shop sells products made by the indigenous people helped by the centre. Na Bolom also has 12 rooms to rent (see Sleeping, page 132) and runs good tours to local villages (see Activities and tours, page 138).

Around San Cristóbal

From San Cristóbal, you can visit a number of Tzotzil and Tzetzal villages. While this is a popular excursion, especially when led by a guide, some visitors may feel uncomfortable at the idea of observing the villagers as if they were in a zoo. Moreover, travellers are strongly warned not to wander around on their own, especially in the hills surrounding the town, as they could risk assault.

Zinacantán

Before the arrival of the Aztecs, Zinacantán (meaning 'place of the bats') was an important commercial centre and considered the capital of the Tzotziles. The Zinacantán men wear pink/red jackets with embroidery and tassels, the women vivid pale blue shawls and navy skirts. At midday every day the women prepare a communal meal, which the men eat in shifts. The main gathering place is around the **church** ⓘ *US$0.40 for entering, official ticket from tourist office next door; photography inside is strictly prohibited*, whose roof was destroyed by fire. Annual festival days here are 6 January, 19-22 January, 8-10 August.

There are two **museums** in the village but both have been closed in recent times because the community felt that they only benefited those most involved in them. Check

San Juan Chamula

Top tips

Visiting the villages

✓ Always seek full advice on the situation before you travel outside San Cristóbal de las Casas to visit the surrounding villages.
✓ You are recommended to call at Na Bolom (see above) before visiting the villages, to get information on their cultures and seek advice on the reception you are likely to get.
✓ Ask permission before taking photographs. Some indigenous peoples believe that the camera steals their souls and to photograph their church is therefore to steal the soul of God. It may also be seen as invasive and profiteering.
✗ Under no circumstances take photos of church interiors or religious festivals.
✗ Do not walk alone in the hills around the villages; robberies and assaults have occurred on the routes between Chamula, San Cristóbal and Zinacantán. Heed the warning signs in Chamula.
✗ Do not wear shorts or revealing clothes when visiting the villages. Locals are sensitive to proper dress and manners.
✗ Be prepared for the large number of children either begging or offering to look after private vehicles; persistent begging should be countered with courteous, firm replies.
✗ Much of the population does not speak Spanish.

whether they have reopened before planning a visit. **Ik'al Ojov** ⓘ *off Calle 5 de Febrero, 5 blocks down Av Cristóbal Colón from San Lorenzo church, and 1 block to the left; donation requested*, includes two traditional *palapas* or huts and has a small collection of regional costumes. It occasionally holds shows and hosts an annual festival on 17 February. The second museum is the **Museo Comunitario Autzetik ta jteklum** ⓘ *1 block from San Lorenzo church*, run by the women of Zinacantán, which has exhibits on local culture.

Above the municipal building on the right is **Antonia's House** ⓘ *Isabel la Católica 7*, a small crafts shop where Antonia and her family demonstrate back-strap weaving, the making of tortillas and many other aspects of life in the village. She usually has some *posh* (the local alcoholic drink) on the go – it's strong stuff, and the red variant will set your throat on fire. Antonia is very easy going and may not charge for a sample of *posh*, however bear in mind that she makes her living from the shop, so buy something or leave a contribution.

Tzotzil Maya weaver, Chamula

San Juan Chamula

In this Tzotzil village 10 km northwest of San Cristóbal the men wear grey, black or light pink tunics, while the women wear bright blouses with colourful braid and navy or blue shawls. The brightly painted **church** ⓘ *a permit (US$1) is needed from the village tourist office and photographing inside the church is absolutely forbidden*, has no pews but families kneel on the floor, chanting, with rows of lit candles, each representing a member of their family.

The religion of the village is centred on 'talking stones' and three idols as well as certain Christian saints. Pagan rituals are held in small huts at the end of August. The Lent festival ends with celebrants running through blazing harvest chaff. This happens just after Easter prayers are held, before the sowing season starts.

There are many handicraft stalls on the small hill southwest of the village. This has a good viewpoint of the village and valley. Take the road from the southwest corner of the square, turn left towards the ruined church then up a flight of steps on the left. Take great care when visiting this village; some readers found an unreceptive attitude toward tourists.

Tenejapa

This friendly Tzeltal village lies 28 km northeast of San Cristóbal. Few tourists make it to Tenejapa but its Thursday morning market is worth a visit. Fruit and vegetables are traditionally sold, but there are also growing number of other stalls. Excellent woven items can be purchased from the weavers' cooperative near the church and there's a fine collection of old textiles in the adjoining museum. The cooperative can arrange weaving classes. Many Tenejapan men wear local costume; ask permission before taking photos and expect to pay.

Las Grutas de San Cristóbal

ⓘ *poorly signed 10 km southeast of San Cristóbal, US$0.30.* The caves contain huge stalagmites and are 2,445 m deep but only lit for 750 m. Refreshments are available. Horses can be hired at Las Grutas for US$13 for a five-hour ride (guide extra) on beautiful trails in the surrounding forest. Some of these are best followed on foot. Yellow diamonds on trees and stones mark the way to beautiful meadows. Stay on the trail to minimize erosion. Las Grutas are reached by **Autotransportes de Pasaje** '31 de Marzo' *colectivos* every 15 minutes (0600-1900, US$0.60) from Avenida Benito Juárez 37B, across the Pan-American Highway just south of

Ciudad Cuauhtémoc-La Mesilla

From Comitán Ruta 190 winds down to the Mexican border at **Ciudad Cuauhtémoc**, a small cluster of buildings; the bus station is opposite immigration. It is 4 km to Guatemala immigration at **La Mesilla**; take a taxi, US$1.65, or *colectivo*, minimum 3 people. Beyond La Mesilla, a beautiful stretch of road leads 85 km to Huehuetenango. This route is far more interesting than the one through Tapachula (page 336). There are a couple of *pensiones* by the Guatemalan border, including **F Hotel Mily's,** 10 rooms, hot water.

Leaving Mexico Guatemalan immigration is open 0700-1900. You may be able to pass through out of hours for a surcharge. A tourist card for Guatemala can be obtained at the border. Crossing by private vehicle is reportedly straightforward. Buses run from La Mesilla to Huehuetenango and Guatemala City.

Leaving Guatemala Mexican tourist cards and visas are available at the border or from Farmacia El Cid in Huehuetenango. It is forbidden to bring fruit and vegetables into Mexico. Drivers will have their vehicle fumigated at the Mexican border (US$7.25, get receipt). Proceed 4 km to Migración, Mon-Fri 0800-1600, Sat-Sun 0900-1400, to obtain tourist card or visa, or have existing visa checked. Then go to Banjército to obtain the necessary papers and windscreen sticker or, if re-entering Mexico, to have existing papers checked.

Exchange You can change money in Banrural in La Mesilla, or haggle in the street but rates are not usually favourable at the border in either currency.

the **Cristóbal Colón** bus terminal (or take a *camioneta* from Pan-American opposite San Diego church 500 m east of Cristóbal Colón). *Colectivos* are marked 'San Cristóbal, Teopisca, Ciudad Militar, Villa Las Rosas', or ask for minibus to 'Rancho Nuevo'. To the bus stop take 'San Diego' *colectivo* 1 block east of Zócalo to the end of Benito Juárez. When you get to Las Grutas, ask the driver to drop you at Km 94; the caves are poorly signed.

Comitán and around

South of San Cristóbal paved Route 190 heads 170 km to the Guatemalan border via **Comitán de Domínguez**, a lively, attractive town with a large, shady plaza and a **tourist office** ⓘ *Mon-Fri 1000-1400, 1700-2000*. Six kilometres south of Comitán take a right turn for the Maya ruins of **Tenán Puente** (5 km), situated in a forest; there is a shortcut on foot. In 1996 the tomb of a Maya nobleman (AD 1000) was discovered here. The buildings at Tenán are more restored than those at Chinkultic (below).

A road branches off the Pan-American Highway, 16 km further on, to a very beautiful region of vari-coloured lakes and caves, the **Lagunas de Montebello** (a national park). Off this road lie the ruins of **Chinkultic** ⓘ *closes at 1600, US$3, colectivo from Comitán US$1*, with temples, ball court, carved stone stelae and a cenote (good swimming) in beautiful surroundings. Ask at **Posada Las Orquídeas** (better known as **Doña María's**), Km 31, for directions and watch out for the very small sign and gate, which will lead you about 3 km along a dirt road to the ruins; don't attempt any short cuts.

Combi vans and buses from Comitán to the Lagunas de Montebello travel via the **Lagunas de Siete Colores**, so called because oxides give the water a variety of colours. A recommended alternative route, for those with their own transport, is the dirt road via La Independencia, Buena Vista, La Patria and El Triunfo (beautiful views), which eventually joins the Montebello road west of the Chinkultic ruins.

Tuxtla Gutiérrez and around » p132-141.

The capital of Chiapas, Tuxtla Gutiérrez is a busy, shabby city, best known for its superb zoo. For limited information, visit the **tourist office** ⓘ *Belisario Domínguez 950, Plaza Instituciones, T961-602 5127, www.turismochiapas.gob.mx, Mon-Fri 0900-2100, Sat 0900-2000, Sun 0900-1500*. There is also an office in the **ADO** bus terminal on Calle 2 Poniente Norte and Avenida 2 Norte Poniente.

Zoológico Miguel Álvarez del Toro (ZOOMAT)

ⓘ *3 km south of town, up a long hill. Tue-Sun 0830-1730; in Spanish only, donations box in front of the educational centre on the right as you enter. Colectivos to 'Zoológico' and 'Cerro Hueco' from Mercado every 20 mins; buses US$0.20; taxis US$2.50-3.*

The zoo was founded by Dr Miguel Alvarez del Toro, who died in 1996. His philosophy was to provide a free zoo for the children and indigenous people of the area. The zoo is very large and many of the animals are in open areas, with plenty of room to run about. Monkeys are not in cages, but in trees pruned back so they cannot jump out of the enclosure. Some birds wander along the paths among the visitors. The zoo makes for a pleasant and educational afternoon. Recommended. Take mosquito repellent. When returning, take the bus from the same side you were dropped off as it goes up the hill to the end of the line where it fills up for the return journey.

Sumidero Canyon

ⓘ *10 km from Tuxtla Gutíerrez, www.sumidero.com. Daily 0600-1800*

From Tuxtla Gutíerrez, a short drive through spectacular scenery leads to the rim of the 1,000-m deep Sumidero canyon, now a national park rich in flora and fauna. Indian warriors,

Sumidero Canyon

unable to endure the Spanish conquest, hurled themselves into the canyon rather than submit. Myriad trails wind through lush vegetation with orchids, cascading waterfalls, and crystalline rivers. Frolicking monkeys and cavorting birdlife provide the more guaranteed wildlife spotting opportunities. The promise of jaguars and pumas is usually unfulfilled. As well as hiking, swimming and lazing in hammocks, there are also many other adventure activities in the park including kayaking (US$5 per hour) and bike rides (US$3.50, 3 km route). The animal hospital is particularly popular with children.

Chiapa del Corzo

Some 15 km beyond the national park, this colonial town is mainly visited as the embarkation point for boat trips to the canyon, but it's worth allowing a couple of hours to explore the centre, which was a Pre-classic and Proto-classic Maya site and shares features with early Maya sites in Guatemala. The ruins can be found behind the Nestlé plant, and there are also some unrestored mounds on private property. Other sights of interest include the fine 16th-century mudéjar fountain and the 16th-century church of Santo Domingo whose engraved altar is of solid silver.

Sleeping

San Cristóbal *p124, map p134*

Look on the bulletin board outside the tourist office for guesthouses advertising cheap bed and breakfast.

A **Casa Mexicana**, 28 de Agosto 1, T967-678 0698. 2 blocks from cathedral, owned by local artist Kiki Suárez, who also owns **La Paloma restaurant**. Exuberant surroundings with tropical greenhouse, sculptures, stained glass windows, patio. Rooms comfortable and well equipped, cable TV, spacious bathrooms. Services include a boutique, massage and conference room. Service can be brusque.

A **Mansión de Los Angeles**, Francisco I Madero 17, T967-678 1173. 5 mins from the Zócalo, stylish hotel in a beautiful 17th-century building, good facilities, tasteful colonial-style décor and faultless service. All rooms have cable TV, telephone and safes. The lovely courtyard restaurant, El Patio, serves extensive buffets and à la carte dishes.

B **Posada El Paraíso**, Av 5 de Febrero 19, T967-678 0085, www.hotelposadaparaiso.com 1 block from cathedral, one of the most charming hotels in town. Impeccable décor throughout, pristine

bedrooms with high ceilings and exposed beams, brick bathrooms, comfortable beds, patio lounge area. Excellent restaurant serves pricey but faultless food.
B **Na Bolom**, Vicente Guerrero 33. 12-room guesthouse in the former home of Franz and Gertrude Blum, now an unmissable cultural centre. Spacious rooms with private bathroom and fireplace, free access to the museum and library. Meals are served at 1900 each evening (US$6) at the long dining table where many famous people, including Frida Kahlo, Diego Rivera and François Mitterand, have dined. Highly recommended for those interested in indigenous cultures of Chiapas.
B **Santa Clara**, Insurgentes 1, on plaza, T967-678 1140. This colonial-style hotel has spotless, comfortable rooms, although some can be rather noisy. There is also a good restaurant and a swimming pool with pool bar. Highly recommended.
C **Palacio de Moctezuma**, Juárez 16, T967-678 0352. Colonial style, good Mexican food. Rooms downstairs sometimes damp – 1st floor much better. Highly recommended.
C **Real del Valle**, Av Real de Guadalupe 14, next to plaza, T967-678 0680, hrvalle@mundomaya.com.mx With breakfast, very clean, friendly, avoid noisy room next to kitchen, hot water, laundry, credit cards accepted, parking. Well maintained and good value.
C-D **El Cerrillo**, Belisario Domínguez 27, T967-678 1283. Lovely rooftop patio, single rooms available or cheaper per person dormitory. Recommended.
D **Posada Los Morales**, Ignacio Allende 17, T967-678 1472. Cottages with open fires (wood US$0.80), kitchen (no pots or pans) and hot showers, beautiful gardens overlook city, parking possible (some cottages are very basic, with no water), beautiful bar/restaurant with live music. Owner is a collector and exporter of rustic-style Mexican furniture.
D **Posada Vallarta**, Hermanos Pineda, near **Cristóbal Colón** bus terminal. Cheaper if you pay for several nights in advance, clean, quiet, hot water, car parking. Recommended.
E **Posada Margarita**, Real de Guadalupe 34, T967-678 0957. Private room without bath, spotless, washing and toilets, friendly, hot water, popular with backpackers, attractive restaurant (not cheap), wholefood.
E-F **Casa di Gladys** (Privates Gästelhaüs Casa Degli Ospiti), Cintalapa 6, between Av Diego Dugelay and Huixtla, T673-9396, casagladys@hotmail.com Cheaper in the dormitory, patio, hot showers, clean bathrooms, comfortable, breakfast available. 5-min walk from the Zócalo, internet access. Recommended although popularity is starting to affect standards. Laundry facilities, horse riding trips, luggage store.

Tuxtla Gutiérrez *p131*

There is plenty of budget accommodation near the 1st-class **ADO** terminal, along Av 2 Nte Ote, beyond the plaza.
B-C **Palace Inn**, Blvd Belisario Domínguez, 4 km from centre, T961-615 0574. Generally recommended, lovely garden, pool, noisy videobar.
C **Regional San Marcos**, 1 Sur y 2 Ote Sur 176, T961-613 1940, sanmarcos@chiapas.net Cheaper without TV, close to Zócalo, bath, fan or a/c, clean.
D **Estrella**, 2 Ote Nte 322, opposite **Cristóbal Colón** bus station, T961-612 3827. With bath, friendly, clean, quiet, comfy, a bit run down but safe, free drinking water. Recommended.
D **Plaza Chiapas**, Av 2 Nte Ote y 2 Ote Nte, T961-613 8365. Clean, with fan and hot shower, most rooms have balconies, good value, good restaurant, enclosed car park. Recommended.

Eating

San Cristóbal *p124, map p134*

There are several cheap, local places on Madero east of Plaza 31 de Marzo.

El Teatro, by Teatro Municipal on 16 de Septiembre. Good quality French food.

El Puente, Real de Guadalupe 55, cultural centre restaurant with good food and a great atmosphere.

La Margarita, Real de Guadalupe 34. Open 0700. Live music in the evenings, flamenco, rumba and salsa, good tacos.

La Paloma, Hidalgo 3, a few doors from Zócalo. Sophisticated restaurant, with an eclectic menu. There is also a laid-back bar with comfy wicker chairs and jazz (every night from 2130) with a searing *cucharacha*, or cappuccino and cake.

París-México, Madero 20. Reminiscent of a 1950s French brasserie, the ambience

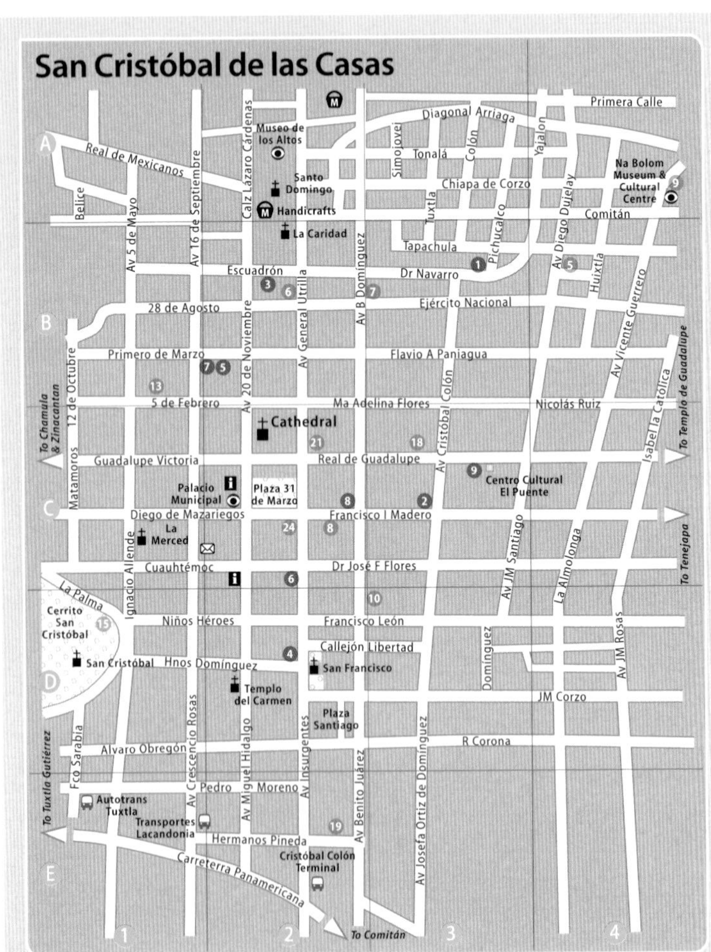

N

100 metres

100 yards

Sleeping

Casa di Gladys 5 *B4*
Casa Mexicana 6 *B2*
El Cerillo 7 *B3*
Mansión de los Angeles 8 *C2*
Na Bolom 9 *A4*
Palacio de Moctezuma 10 *D3*
Posada El Paraíso 13 *B1*
Posada Los Morales 15 *D1*
Posada Margarita 18 *C3*
Posada Vallarta 19 *E2*
Real del Valle 21 *C2*
Santa Clara 24 *C2*

Eating

El Fogón de Jovel 7 *B2*
El Gato Gordo 2 *C3*
El Puente 9 *C3*
El Teatro 5 *B2*
La Casa del Pan 1 *B3*
Las Estrellas 3 *B2*
Madre Tierra 4 *D2*
Paris-Mexico 8 *C2*
Tuluc 6 *C2*

is pure Mexican. Feisty margaritas, *sopa azteca* and fish *à la Villacruzana* team up with french onion soup, coq au vin, and crêpes with chocolate (US$3.50-US$4). Decent pasta and pizza dishes ordered à la carte can work out rather pricey.

ŸŸ **Tuluc**, Insurgentes 5. Good value especially breakfasts, fresh *tamales* every morning, near plaza, popular, classical music, art for sale and toys on display.

ŸŸ-Ÿ **El Fogón de Jovel**, Av 16 Septiembre No 11, opposite the Jade Museum. Well known for its brand of Chiapaneca "típica". Colonial house, decorated with a bizarre combination of regional handicrafts and international flags, open fires and live marimba. Rather overpriced main dishes vary in quality.

ŸŸ-Ÿ **Madre Tierra**, Insurgentes 19 (opposite Iglesia de San Francisco). Restaurant and bakery with acaded courtyard and snug interior, with candles, intimate alcoves, bookcases and an arty vibe. Main dishes can be rather bland, light snacks include pizzas, spinach *empanadas*, and quiche. The bakery sells bagels, cinnamon rolls and croissants.

Ÿ **Craft market** The cheapest places for lunch in San Cristóbal are the stalls in the craft market on Insurgentes. They do set meals for US$1.20, usually beef or chicken. Numerous stalls nearby sell punch, often made with *posh*, the alcoholic brew made in Chamula.

Ÿ **El Gato Gordo**, Madero and Colón. Cheap set breakfast, crêpes, *tortas*, vegetarian.

Ÿ **La Casa del Pan**, on B Domínguez and Dr Navarro 10. Fantastic bakery, with a sunny, calm café-restaurant and welcoming staff. Great breakfasts including wholemeal breads, fruit platters, hot cakes and omelettes. Good value *comida corrida*, recommended. There is often live music in the evenings and other cultural activities.

Ÿ **Las Estrellas**, Escuadrón 201. Good cheap food, including vegetarian, good brown bread, try the *caldo Tlalpeño*, nice atmosphere, Mexican/Dutch owned, very friendly and cheap. Recommended.

Ÿ **Naturalísimo**, 20 de Noviembre 4. Delicious food in a lovely courtyard setting. Great breakfasts include a help-yourself fruit bar. The main reason to visit however is for the *comida corrida* served from 1200-1800 daily: 3 courses including soup, salad, *jugo* and *plato fuerte* for US$4.90.

Cafés and juice stalls

Café San Cristóbal, Cuauhtémoc. Good coffee sold in bulk too, chess hangout.

El Manantial, 1 de Marzo 11. Good *licuados* and juices.

La Fe Café, Diego Mazarriegos and 12 de Octobre. T967-678 9978. Cappuccinos and a sawdust floor, express home delivery 1600-2230.

La Selva Café, Crescencio Rosas and Cuauhtémoc. Sleekly run continental-style coffee shop, owned by a coffee growers' collective. More than 30 types of organic coffee, plus hot chocolate and cakes; healthier options include salads and wholemeal baguettes. Light and airy art gallery setting, lively in the evenings with a youthful, bohemian crowd.

Santa Fe Cafetería, 20 Noviembre, 12-B. Good cappuccino, tasty toasted baguettes and chocolate cake, picturesque courtyard.

Tuxtla Gutiérrez *p131*

ŸŸ **Parrilla La Cabaña**, 2 Ote Nte 250. Excellent tacos, very clean.

ŸŸ-Ÿ **Las Pichanchas**. Av Central Ote 857. Set in lovely *casona* house with a pretty courtyard, this is one of the best restaurants in Tuxtla, if a little touristy.. Highly rated regional cooking, including *tamales* and *juacané* (chicken breast stuffed with beans and covered in Hierba Santa sauce). Traditional dancing performances and marimba music 1400-1700 and 2000-2300.

ŸŸ-Ÿ **Nah Yaxal**, 6 Pte Nte, just off Av Central Pte. Vegetarian, studenty, popular.

Ÿ **La Parcela**, 2 Ote Sur, near **Hotel Plaza Chiapas**. Good, cheap, good breakfasts. Recommended.

Cafés and ice-cream parlours

Bing, 1 Sur Pte 1480. Excellent ice-cream.
Café Avenida, Av Central just past Aerocaribe office. Good coffee shop, popular with locals.

Chiapa de Corzo *p132*

Good fish restaurants by the river.
¥¥¥-¥¥ **Jardín Turístico** on main plaza, open until 2000. *Plato jardín* is a selection of different regional dishes.
¥¥-¥ **Verónica**, along the pier. Good food, cheap, slow service. Try the local non-alcoholic drink *pozole*, made from corn with *cacoa* and *pinole*. Best version is *pozole negro*, with a distinctive chocolate flavour; choose carefully as purified water is not guaranteed.

Entertainment

San Cristóbal *p124, map p134*

Bars and clubs

Bar Makia, Hidalgo, just off plaza, above a shop. Fri and Sat from 2200 until very late.
Blue Bar, Av Crescencio Rosas 2, live music after 2300, salsa, rock, reggae, pool table, good atmosphere.
Cocodrilo, Insurgentes 1, T967-678 0871. Cappuccinos, cocktails, beer and live music nightly: reggae, *trova*, flamenco and rumba.
La Llorona Kafe-Pub, 1 de Marzo 14 Bis, la_llorona2001@hotmail.com Happy hour from 1800-2000. Wed-Mon 1600 until late. Comfortable atmosphere to read, hang out, down some beers, and then chill in the hammocks by a cosy fireplace. Sandwiches and burgers.
Las Velas, Madero, ½ block from plaza. Reggae, Honduran music, sometimes live, happy hour 2000-2200, open till dawn.
Revolución, 20 de Noviembre and 1 De Marzo. Café, bar with internet upstairs, happy hour 1500-1700, live soul, blues and rock music at 2000.

Cinema

Cine Santa Clara, Av 16 de Septiembre, Mexican and alternative films, international film festival 2nd half Feb.
Centro Cultural El Puente (see Cultural centres, p141), Real de Guadalupe 55. Videos, usually about local issues, every day except Sun, 3 good films in original version, US$1.25. Film schedules are posted around town.
Santa Clara, Insurgentes 1, daily schedule posted outside.
Teatro Daniel Zebadúa, 20 de Noviembre and 1 de Marzo, film festivals each month, films at 1800 and 2100 US$2 (US$1.50 students).

Festivals and events

San Cristóbal *p124, map p134*

In early **Nov** the Maya-Zoque Festival lasts 4 days, promoting the different Maya and Zoque cultures in the Chiapas region, with dancing and celebrations in the main plaza. There is a popular spring festival on **Easter Sun** and the week after. La Fiesta de Guadalupe is celebrated on **12 Dec**.

Chiapa de Corzo *p132*

The fiestas here are outstanding; they reach their climax on **20-23 Jan**, in honour of San Sebastián, with a pageant on the river. But there are daylight fiestas, Los Parachicos, on **15, 17 and 20 Jan**, and the Chunta Fiestas, at night, **9-23 Jan**. The musical parade is on **19 Jan**. There is another fiesta in early **Feb** and San Marcos festival on **25 Apr**, with various *espectáculos*.

Shopping

San Cristóbal *p124, map p134*

Pasaje Mazariegos (in the block bounded by Real de Guadalupe, Av B Domínguez, Madero and Plaza 31 de Marzo) has luxury clothes and bookshops, restaurants and travel agents.

Books

Bookshops selling titles in English: **La Pared**, Av Miguel Hidalgo 2, T967-678

6367, lapared9@yahoo.com, opposite the government tourist office; and **Soluna**, Real de Guadalupe 13B.

Crafts

There are many shops on Av Real de Guadalupe for amber and jade plus other *artesanías*. There's also an amber museum in Plaza Sivan shop, Utrilla 10, T967-678 3507. For local goods try **Miscelánea Betty**, Utrilla 45, good value. **Casa de Artesanías**, Niños Héroes and Hidalgo. Top-quality handicrafts. The shop is also a museum.
Casa Utrilla, Utrilla 33, houses the SODAM (Mutual Aid Society) shop, a cooperative of indigenous craftspeople selling beautiful wooden dolls and toys. Sales go towards training for the Chamula people, with a workshop at Yaalboc.
Jolom Mayaetik, 28 de Agosto on the corner of Av 5 de Mayo, works with both 'new' and traditional designs.
La Casa del Jade, Av 16 de Septiembre 16. Top quality jade, also a museum with replicas of jade relics and the Tomb of Pakal (Maya King of Palenque).
La Casona, corner of 16 de Septiembre and 5 de Febrero. Cute shop full of quality Mexican crafts; hand-painted jewellery boxes and picture frames, beautiful water pitchers and matching glasses.
Mujeres por la Dignidad, on Belisario Domínguez 8, is a cooperative with a few hundred members from San Andrés, San Juan Chamula and Chenalho. They're happy to take special orders in addition to selling more regular items.
Sna Jolobil, Ex-Convento de Santo Domingo, part of the building has been converted into a cooperative selling handicrafts from many local villages especially textiles (best quality and expensive); also concerts by local groups.
Taller Lenateros, Flavio A Paniagua 54, T967-678 5174, conjuros@sancristobal.com.mx. A paper-making workshop run primarily by a Maya group. Paper and prints from natural materials and profits help support around 30 Maya families. Demonstrations and workshops US$6.50 per day.

Markets

The **craft market** at Parque Fray Bartolomé de las Casas has stands offering an assortment of local sweets such as *cocada*, balls of sweetened and caramelized shredded coconut, as well as small, perfectly shaped animal figurines made from sweetened hard-boiled egg yolks. The municipal market north of Santo Domingo is worth seeing as well.

Colourful weavings for sale, Zinacantán

Activities and tours

San Cristóbal *p124, map p134*

Cycling

Los Pingüinos, Av Ecuador, T967-678 0202, 0915-1430, 1600-1900, rents mountain bikes for US$3 per hr or US$9 per day, US$12 for 24 hrs. Guided biking tours from US$8 to US$14, beautiful countryside and knowledgeable guides, highly recommended.

Horse riding

Horses can be hired from **Casa de Huéspedes Margarita**, prices US$16-20 for horse and guide, to Chamula, 5 hrs, US$9, reserve the day before. Also from **Sr José Hernández**, Calle Elías and Calle 10 (1 block from Av Huixtla and Chiapa de Corzo, not far from Na Bolom), US$10 for half a day, plus guide US$11.50; Real de Guadalupe 51A, to Chamula US$6.50, also to Rancho Nuevo and San José; **Francisco Ochón**, T967-678 5911, goes to Chamula, US$6.50. **Viajes Chincultik** (see Tour operators, below) offer horse riding tours to San Juan Chamula, US$11.

Rafting

Explora-Ecoturismo y Aventura, T967-678 4295, www.prodigyweb.net.mx/explora Eco-sensitive company with good recommendations offer rafting, caving, sea kayaking, river trips and multi-day camping expeditions. Price for a 6-day river and camping trip US$520.

Tour operators

There are many agencies to choose from. Tours are also offered from the Na Bolom museum (see above). As a rough guide to prices: to **San Juan Chamula** and **Zinacantán**, US$10; **horse riding** to San Juan Chamula, US$12; **Sumidero Canyon**, US$2; **Lagunas de Montebello** and Amatenango del Valle, US$26; **Palenque**, Aqua Azul and Misol-Há, US$37; **Toniná**, US$26. There's also a 3-day **jungle trip** option taking in Agua Azul, Misol-Há, the ruins at Bonampak, Cedro River Falls, Yaxchilán and Palenque ruins, with camping in the jungle, US$175. Although longer tours, such as to **Bonampak** and **Yaxchilán** can be booked by tour operators in San Cristóbal (eg **Yaxchilán Tours**, Guadalupe 26D), they are much cheaper if booked in Palenque; take care to check what is included in cheaper packages.

Héctor Mejía, T967-678 0545, walking tour (Tue and Thu, 0900, from outside Santo Domingo, US$11, 4 hrs) around cottage industries, eg candymaker, dollmaker, toymaker.

Mercedes Hernández Gómez, tours of local villages, starting at 0900 from kiosk on the Plaza 31 de Mayo (arrive early), returns about 1500, US$12 per person. Mercedes, who is training as a shaman, speaks English, is informative, but eccentric; she has been known to expel people from tours if she gets a bad vibe.

Na Bolom, Vicente Guerrero 33, CP 29220, T967-678 1418, www.nabolom.org Tours Tue-Sun to San Juan Chamula and San Lorenzo Zinacantán; US$12 per person, good guides, thorough explanations, respectful to indigenous locals.

Raúl and Alejandro, T967-678 3741, chamul@hotmail.com Offer tours to San Juan Chamula and Zinacantán, departing from the cathedral at 0930 and returning at 1400, in blue VW minibus, US$11, in English, Spanish and Italian. Friendly, very good and highly recommended.

Santa Ana Tours, Madero, ½ block from plaza, T967-678 0422. Recommended for local and international flight bookings.

Viajes Chincultik, Real de Guadalupe 34, T/F967-678 0957, agchincultik@hotmail.com Runs group tours to the Lagunas de Montebello (US$25), to the Sumidero Canyon (US$22), Palenque, Toniná and camping trips to Laguna Miramar; also to Yaxchilán, Bonampak, and Tikal in Guatemala.

Viajes Navarra, Real de Guadalupe 15D, T967-678 1143, tours include Tenam Puente ruins and Sumidero Canyon.
Viajes Pakal, Cuauhtémoc 6A, T967-678 2818, pakal@mundomaya.com.mx Reliable agency running culturally friendly tours, several branches in other cities. Good for flight bookings, with notice.

Tuxtla Gutiérrez *p131*

Tour operators

Carolina Tours, Sr José Narváez Valencia (manager), Av Central Pte 1138, T961-612 4281; reliable, recommended; also coffee shop at Av Central Pte 230.
Viajes Kali, Av Central Ote 507 esq 4 Ote, T/F961-611 3175, heugenia@chis1.telmex.net.mx Tours to Sumidero Canyon with multilingual guides, also books national flights.
Viajes Miramar, in Posada del Rey, Calle 1 Ote Nte 310, T961-612 3983, viajesmiramar@ infosel.net.mx Good, efficient service, books national flights.

Transport

San Cristóbal *p124, map p134*

Air

Aerocaribe flies to/from **Tuxtla Gutiérrez**. Charter flights available with Aerochiapas to **Lacanjá**, **Bonampak** and **Yaxchilán** on the Río Usumacinta, 7 hrs in all (US$100 per person if plane is full, more if not). Aeromar, takes small planes to **Mexico City**, US$230 return.

Airline offices Aviacsa, in Xanav agency, Pasaje Mazariegos, local 2, Real de Guadalupe, T967-678 4441, although they do not fly from San Cristóbal.

Bus

Local If you're not on a tour, you can get to outlying villages by bus or by communal VW from the market (both very packed). The buses leave very early and often don't return until the next day, so you have to stay overnight. VW to **Zinacantán**, US$0.75, 30 mins, sometimes with frequent roadside stops at local shrines; taxi US$4. VW to **Chamula**, every 20 mins, last departure 1700, last return1900, US$0.70 per person. Also minibuses to **Tuxtla Gutiérrez** from in front of 1st-class bus station, when full, US$2

Long distance Buy tickets as far in advance as possible at the ticket office, corner of Real de Guadalupe and Belisario Domínguez, T967-678 8503. During Christmas and Holy Week buses are sometimes fully booked for 10 days or more; ticket prices may also increase at this time. The 1st-class bus terminal serves all destinations in the country. There are 2 other 2nd-class terminals across the road, for Chiapas only.

From the 1st-class terminal, on Insurgentes: **Campeche**: 0930, *servicio plus*, 2100, US$25. **Cancún**: several daily, 17 hrs, US$42-51. **Cárdenas**: ADO US$17. **Chetumal**: 1430, 11 hrs, US$29. **Cd Cuauhtémoc**, several daily, 3 hrs, US$6.50. **Comitán**, 7 per day, 1½ hrs, US$3.60. **Mérida**: 0930, 1730, 13 hrs, US$34. **Mexico City**: 1350, 1530 and 1800, 18 hrs, US$50. **Oaxaca**: 2 with Cristóbal Colón at 1700 and 2000, US$28, 1 with Maya de Oro at 2200, US$35. **Palenque**: 10 daily, 5½ hrs, US$8. **Playa del Carmen**: US$42. **Pochutla**: 1815 and 2100, 13 hrs, US$26. **Puerto Escondido**: with Cristóbal Colón, 1st class, 0745, 1815 and 2100, US$27. **Tapachula**: 5 a day, 9 hrs, US$14.30. **Tuxtla Gutiérrez**: 12 a day, US$3.60 (US$6 with UNO luxury 1st class – with seats that are practically beds, at 1800 and 1445). **Tulum**: US$40. **Veracruz**: 1840, US$35. **Villahermosa**: 1125, 1830, 7 hrs, US$13.

Lacandonia 2nd-class bus to **Palenque** from 2nd-class bus station, also on Allende, 7 a day between 0100 and 2015, 4-5 hrs, US$9 (via Agua Azul, US$6); Cristóbal Colón, 1st-class, up to 4 times daily (including at least 1 *servicio plus*) US$10, bookings 5 days in advance; Maya de Oro, from Cristóbal Colón terminal, 3 times daily, a/c, videos, non-stop; Rodolfo Figueroa, 5 times a day, US$4.50, a/c. (On reaching Ocosingo it is not uncommon to be told the bus is going no further; your onward fare to Palenque will be refunded but you will have to make your own way.) Autotransportes Tuxtla, F Sarabia, between Carretera Panamericana and Alvaro Obregón, 2nd class to Palenque, reserved seats, US$5.

International Buses from Cristóbal Colón, south end of Av Insurgentes, direct to the Guatemalan border at **Cd Cuahtémoc** (p130), 170km, several daily from 0700, 3 hrs (leave bus at border, not its final destination). 1 ADO bus a day to the border at 1900, book in advance. Altos to **Cd Cuauhtémoc**, 3 a day, US$5. 2nd class to border with Autotransportes Tuxtla, US$2.75, but note that the 1430 bus arrives too late for onward transport.

Viajes Chincultik (see Tour operators above) run a shuttle to the Guatemalan border and beyond on Tue and Fri: **La Mesilla**, US$20; **Quetzaltenango**, US$40; **Panajachel** and **Lake Atitlán**, US$50, and **Antigua**, US$60.

Car hire

Budget, Mazariegos 36, T967-678 1871, in Hotel Mansión del Valle.

Taxi

US$1.60 anywhere in town, US$4 to **Chamula**. *Colectivo* US$0.70.

Comitán and around *p131*

Bus

From Comitán, Cristóbal Colón (terminal near the Pan-American Highway) runs to **San Cristóbal de las Casas**, frequent until 1930, 2 hrs, US3.60, and to the border at **Cd Cuauhtémoc** (p130), US$2.75; note that these buses are *de paso* from San Cristóbal so no advance booking is possible in Comitán. Autotransportes Tuxtla (on the highway at approximately Av 2 Sur) also has regular services to the border, 1½ hrs. Pick-ups charge US$1.55 per person from Comitán to the border; beware of short-changing. Combi vans or buses marked 'Tziscao' or 'Lagos' run to the **Lagunas de Montebello**, hourly from Av 2 Poniente Sur y Calle 3 Sur Poniente, 1 hr, US$1.30. Minibuses run from the Cristóbal Colón terminal to **Tuxtla Gutiérrez**. Cristóbal Colón also has 1st-class buses to **Mexico City**, 0900, 1100 and 1600, departing the border 2½ hrs earlier, US$40.75; to **Oaxaca**, 0700 and 1900, US$33; to **Tuxtla Gutiérrez**, 0600 and 1600, US$8; to **Tapachula** (via Arriaga), 1200 and 2000, US$20.

Entering Mexico from Guatemala at Cd Cuauhtémoc, there are at least 8 buses to **Comitán** 0800-1930 (2nd-class buses during the evening) and direct buses to **San Cristóbal de las Casas**, US$3.50. There are also minibuses to **Comitán**, US$1.55, which connect with combis to **San Cristóbal**, 1 hr, US$2.50 at Comitán's Autotransportes Tuxtla terminal.

Tuxtla Gutiérrez *p131*

Air

Terán airport is a military airport converted for civilian use. Taxi to Terán US$3. Flights to **Hualtulco**, **Mérida**, **Oaxaca**, **Palenque**, **San Cristóbal de las Casas**, **Tapachula**, **Veracruz**, **Villahermosa**.

Airline offices Aviacsa, Av Central Pte 1144, T961-612 6880, 40 mins.

Bus

Cristóbal Colón 1st-class bus terminal is at Av 2 Nte Pte 268 (opposite UNO and Maya de Oro). Left luggage at Maya de Oro bus station, opposite the ADO (San Cristóbal) terminal, US$0.50 a bag.

Cancún: 1230, US$42. **Chetumal**: 1430, US$44. **Chiapa de Corzo**: from Calle 3 Ote Sur, frequent, US$0.50. **Comitán**: 0500 then each hr to 1900 and 1 at 2300, Altos, US$5.80. **Mérida**: change at Villahermosa if no direct service at 1530 (Altos), US$26. **Mexico City**: 4 a day, 16 hrs, US$64, 1st class, US$42, 2nd class. **Oaxaca**: 1130, 1915, 10 hrs, US$24 1st class, US$18 2nd class. **Palenque**: Altos, 6 a day, 0500-2300, 7 hrs, US$9.40, other buses pass through Palenque. **Pochutla**: at

0935 and 2015, 10 hrs, US$24. **San Cristóbal de las Casas**: frequent 0500-2300, 2 hrs, US$3.60 (2nd class US$3), superb mountain journey. **Tonalá**: 1615, US$13. **Tulum**: 1230, US$51. **Veracruz**: 1930, US$34. **Villahermosa**: at 1500, 2300, 8½ hrs, US$10.30.

Taxis

Easy to flag down anywhere. US$2 within the centre, US$2.50-3 to the zoo, US$5 to Chiapa de Corzo (for Sumidero Canyon).

Chiapa de Corzo *p132*
Buses to **Tuxtla Gutiérrez**, US$0.50, frequent; also several a day (1 hr) to **San Cristóbal de las Casas**, US$3.50. Cristóbal Colón to **Mexico City**, 1815, US$36.50.

Directory

San Cristóbal *p124, map p134*
Banks Banks are usually open for exchange 0900-1600. Bancomer, Plaza 31 de Marzo 10, charges commission, cash advance on Visa, American Express or Citicorp TCs, good rates and service. Banamex, Real de Guadalupe y Portal Oriental, changes cheques without commission, 0900-1300. Banca Serfín on the Zócalo, changes Euro, Amex, MasterCard, TCs. Quetzales can be obtained for pesos or dollars in the *cambio* but better rates at the border. **Doctors** Servicio Médico Bilingüe, Av Benito Juárez 60, T967-678 0793, Dr Renato Zarate Castañeda speaks English, is highly recommended and if necessary can be reached at home, T967-678 2998. **Hospitals and clinics** Red Cross, Calle Prolongación Ignacio Allende, T967-678 0772. Recommended. **Immigration** On Carretera Panamericana and Diagonal Centenario, opposite Hotel Bonampak, 30-min walk from Zócalo. **Internet** Many internet cafés, US$0.50 per hr; service is generally good. **Language schools** Centro Cultural El Puente, Real de Guadalupe 55, Caja Postal 29230, T/F967- 6783723, T967-678 4157, spanish@mundomaya. com.mx (Spanish programme), US$6-8 per hr, homestay from US$180 per week, registration fee US$100. Mixed reports. Check the notice board for events; a good place to meet other travellers. Instituto Jovel, María Adelina Flores 21, Apdo Postal 62, T/F678-4069, jovel@sancristobal. podernet.com.mx Group or 1-to-1 classes, homestays arranged, said to be the best school in San Cristóbal. Very good reports from students. **Laundry** Superklin, Crescencio Rosas 48, T967-678 3275, US$1.30 per kg. **Pharmacies** Farmacia Bios, corner of Cuauhtémoc and Hidalgo. **Post office** Cuauhtémoc 13, between Rosas and Hidalgo, Mon-Fri 0800-1900, Sat 0900-1300. **Telephone** Computel, Insurgentes 64B, fax, guards luggage; Telmex, Niños Héroes and Hidalgo; La Pared, Av Miguel Hidalgo 2, long-distance calling service, cheap rates. Phone and fax services available at the tourist office in the Plaza. International calls from 2nd-class bus station.

Tuxtla Gutiérrez *p131*
Banks Bancomer, Av Central Pte y 2 Pte Nte, for Visa and TCs, 0900-1500. HSBC, Mon-Sat 0800, good rates and service. For cheques and cash: 1 Sur Pte 350, near Zócalo. **Immigration**, 1 Ote Nte. **Internet** Free at library of Universidad Autónoma de Chiapas, Route 190, 6 km from centre. Compucentro, 1 Nte Pte 675, upstairs. US$1 per hr. Various others cost about US$1/hr. **Post office** On main square. **Telephone** International phone calls can be made from 1 Nte, 2 Ote, directly behind post office, 0800-1500, 1700-2100 (1700-2000 Sun).

Northern Chiapas and Tabasco

From San Cristóbal, Route 199 heads 210 km north to the ancient Maya city of Palenque. With its beautiful jungle setting and imposing architecture, it is arguably one of the most impressive ruins in southern Mexico. The modern town of Palenque, a few kilometres to the east, is a good base from which to visit the surrounding area, including the spectacular waterfalls of Agua Azul. For those heading to Guatemala, the temples of Bonampak and Yaxchilán make a worthy detour and provide a remarkable insight into the rituals of blood-letting and sacrifice practised by the Maya.

Getting there Daily bus services from to Palenque and Villahermosa.
Getting around Good tours and buses.
Time required 5 days.
Weather Hot and humid.
Sleeping A good variety for all budgets.
Eating Buoyant atmosphere and lots of backpacker hangouts.
Activities and tours Horse riding, visiting waterfalls and canyons.
★ Don't miss...Palenque ▸▸*p145*.

North of Palenque, the state of Tabasco is famous for its oil, and its notoriously hot and humid climate. The highlight for most visitors is the Parque Nacional La Venta, which preserves the remains the once powerful Olmec civilization.

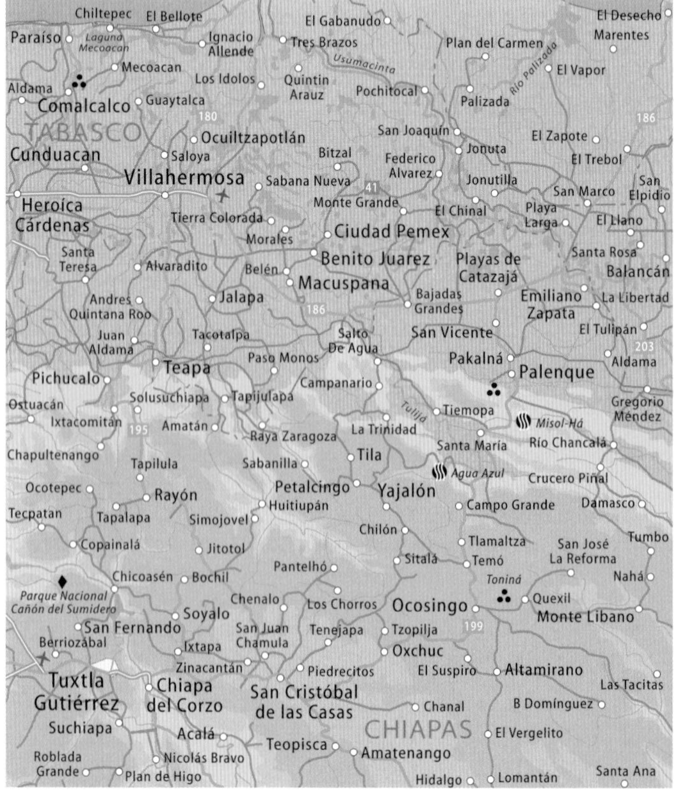

San Cristóbal to Palenque » pp152-157.

Those travelling from San Cristóbal to Palenque by car will have fine views by day but should avoid night-time journeys because of the risk of armed robberies. There are also occasional military checks on this route; if stopped at night in a private car, switch off engine and lights, and switch on the inside light. Always have your passport handy.

Toniná

ⓘ *12 km east of Ocosingo, 0900-1600, US$1.30. From San Cristóbal, tour US$15, taxi US$6; from Ocosingo, colectivos from the market (15 mins) US$1. Drinks are available at the site; also toilets and parking.*

The Maya ruins at Toniná are easily reached on a beautiful bus ride from San Cristóbal de las Casas and are well worth a visit. They are located 12 km from **Ocosingo**, which was one of the centres of fighting in the EZLN uprising in January 1994. On the way to the ruins you will pass a huge new army base, built to 'pacify' the local population. Not surprisingly resentment against the government and military is still strong in the area. You can walk to Toniná from Ocosingo, start in front of the church on the plaza and follow the signs, or take the 0900 bus from the market to the jungle and get off where the road forks (ask). You end up in the middle of one of the last Classic Maya sites, with the palace high on a hill to your left.

The temples are in the Palenque style with internal sanctuaries in the back room, but influences from many different Maya styles of various periods have been found. The huge pyramid complex, seven stone platforms making a man-made hill, is 10 m higher than the Temple of the Sun at Teotihuacán and is the tallest pyramidal structure in the Maya world. Stelae and wall panels are in very diverse forms and show styles and subjects unknown at any other Maya site. A beautiful stucco mural was discovered in December 1990. Ask the guardian to show you the second unrestored ball court and the sculpture kept at his house. There is also a small **museum**.

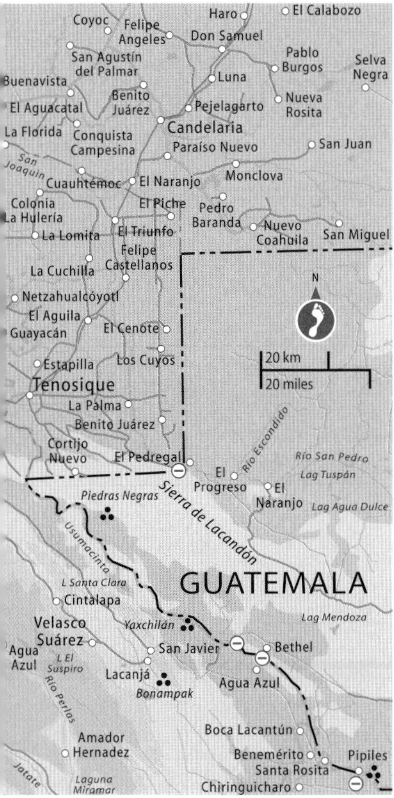

Agua Azul

ⓘ *US$1, US$3 for cars. Entry price is included in day trips from Palenque, which allow you to spend at least 3 hrs at Agua Azul. Travel agencies and many of the hotels, offer tours, around US$11, including a visit to the waterfall at Misol-Há (see below). Posada Charito in Palenque does the trip for US$7.*

The series of jungle waterfalls and rapids at Agua Azul lie about half way between Ocosingo and Palenque and run for 7 km. They are breathtakingly beautiful with superb views and secluded areas for picnics. They are easily visited on a day trip from Palenque. Swimming is good, in clear blue water during good weather, in muddy brown water during bad (but still refreshing

Agua Azul

Misol-Há

if very hot, which it usually is). Swimmers should stick to the roped areas where everyone else can see them; the various graves on the steep path alongside the rapids testify to the dangers of swimming in those areas. One of the falls, 'The Liquidizer', is an area of dramatic white water that is extremely dangerous; on no account should you enter this stretch of water; many drownings have occurred. There are several *palapas* for hammocks, and space for free camping.

To get off the tourist path, ask around for Gerónimo, who has a solid grasp of the area and its surrounding trails. He can take you either on foot or on horseback through thick and lush forest to a series of five waterfalls that are known locally as Bolon Ahao or 'Waterfalls of the King Jaguar'. This is not a well-travelled path so it is advisable to wear long trousers, take plenty of water, some food and insect repellent. The hike takes approximately four hours round trip and costs US$5 per person; or US$3 per hour on horseback.

Misol-Há

Eight kilometres from Agua Azul, **Misol-Há** is a stunning waterfall usually visited first on day trips from Palenque. A narrow path winds around behind the falls, allowing you to stand behind the immense curtain of water without getting your camera wet. Swimming is possible in the large pool at the bottom of the tumbling cascade, but it is usually better to wait until you get to Agua Azul for a good swim.

Palenque town

This is a friendly, colourful little town whose sole reason to exist is to accommodate the tourists heading for the famous archaeological site nearby. There is plenty of accommodation for every budget, with dozens of cheap *posadas* around the centre, and a new tourist barrio, **La Cañada**, with more expensive hotels, restaurants and bars. Souvenirs are available at lower prices than elsewhere on the Ruta Maya, making Palenque a convenient place to stop off en route to or from the southerly Chiapan towns of San Cristóbal and Tuxtla Gutiérrez. The **Fiesta de Santo Domingo** is held in the first week of August.

The **tourist office** ⓘ *daily 0800-2000*, is on Juárez, a block below the plaza and next to the Artesanía market. The staff are very helpful and provide good free map of Palenque and the ruins. There's another **city tourism office** ⓘ *Independencia, daily 0800-1500, 1600-2000, www.palenque.com.mx*, in the Palacio Municipal. A **tourist police office** ⓘ *Av Reforma and Francisco Javier, T916-345 0788, T916-348 3406, Mon-Sat 0900-1500, 1600-2100*, works in conjunction with the tourist office.

Palenque

ⓘ *Carretera Zona Arqueológica, T916-348 3406, www.palenque.com.mx. Daily 0800-1700. US$4; guides US$35 for up to 2 hrs, but check their credentials. From Palenque town, take a colectivo; return colectivos to Palenque town leave from outside the main entrance, US$0.80, every 15 mins. Free parking. There is a museum, restaurant and gift shop on the way back towards the town.*

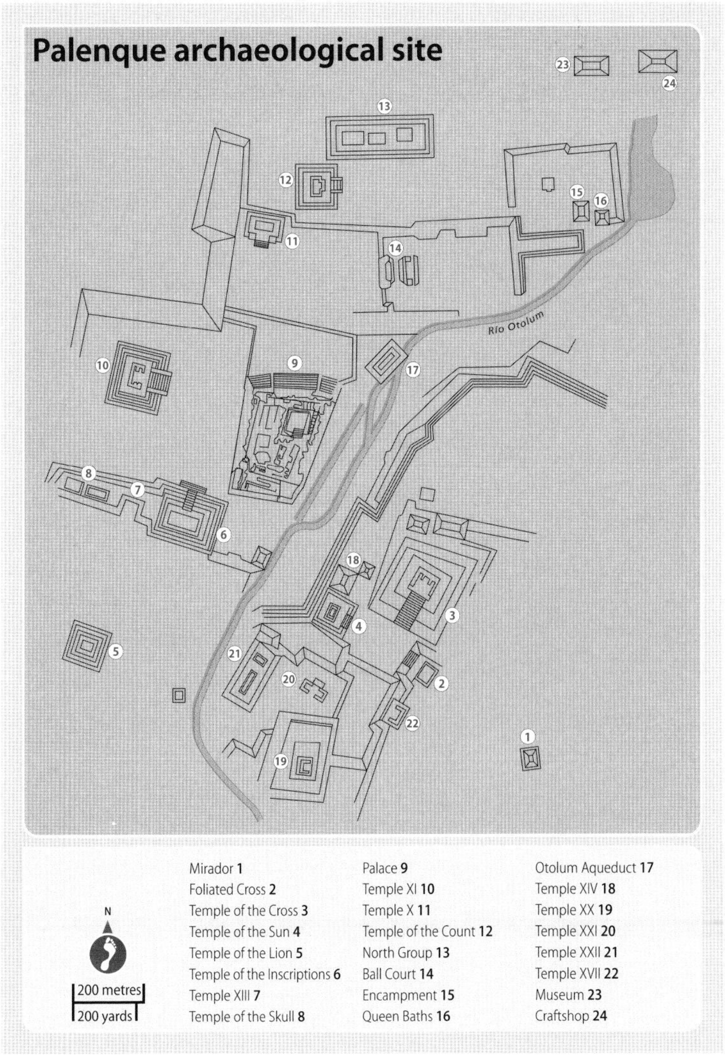

Palenque archaeological site

Río Otolum

Mirador **1**
Foliated Cross **2**
Temple of the Cross **3**
Temple of the Sun **4**
Temple of the Lion **5**
Temple of the Inscriptions **6**
Temple XIII **7**
Temple of the Skull **8**
Palace **9**
Temple XI **10**
Temple X **11**
Temple of the Count **12**
North Group **13**
Ball Court **14**
Encampment **15**
Queen Baths **16**
Otolum Aqueduct **17**
Temple XIV **18**
Temple XX **19**
Temple XXI **20**
Temple XXII **21**
Temple XVII **22**
Museum **23**
Craftshop **24**

Temple of the Sun, Palenque

Built at the height of the Classic period and surrounded by jungle, Palenque is one of the most beautiful and unique of all the Maya ruins in Mexico. First occupied by the Maya around 100 BC, it grew from a small agricultural village to one of the most important cities in the pre-Hispanic world. It flourished between AD 600-800 under the Maya leader, Lord Pacal, who reigned for 68 years and was the founder of the first ruling dynasty of Palenque. During his reign, Palenque became the regional capital and many of the buildings and plazas were constructed, including Pacal's own tomb, the Temple of the Inscriptions.

The corbelled vaults, the arrangement of its buildings, the impression of lightness created by walls broken by pillars and open spaces make Palenque-style architecture unique. It is thought some of the structures, including the Palace, the Temple of the Inscriptions and the Group of the Cross, were built to house the many extraordinary sculptures and texts that refer to historical individuals and events and to the mythological beings who endorsed the 'divine right' of the rulers. The city was eventually abandoned in the 10th century.

Exploring the site

The ruins are surrounded by jungle, so take plenty of insect repellent (especially from May to November) and arrive early to avoid the worst of the heat and humidity. Leave valuables at home as there have been reports of criminals hiding in the jungle.

The Palace The Palace and Temple XI are located in the centre of the site. The Palace stands on an artificial platform over 100 m long and 9 m high. The top of the tower is level with Pacal's mortuary temple and, on the winter solstice, the sun viewed from here sets directly above his crypt. Set into the walls of the tower are large windows where Maya astronomers could observe and chart the movement of the planets. From the time of Pacal, the Palace was later developed by many kings into a maze of rooms, corridors and courtyards.

The Temple of the Inscriptions The Temple of the Inscriptions, along with Temple XII and Temple XIII, lies to the south of the Palace group of buildings and is one of the rare Maya pyramids to have had a burial chamber incorporated at the time of its construction. The building was erected to cover the crypt in which Lord Pacal was buried. Discovered in 1952 by Alberto Ruz-Lhuillier, the burial chamber measured 7 m long, 7 m high and 3.75 m across, an incredible achievement considering the weight of the huge pyramid pressing down upon it. Inside the tomb Pacal's bones were discovered adorned with jade jewellery alongside three tablets containing the longest inscription of any Maya monument. According to the inscriptions, Pacal was born in AD 603 and died in AD 684. Other glyphs tell of Pacal's ancestors, astronomical events and an astonishing projection into the distant future (AD 4772). One of the last inscriptions reveals that, 132 days after Pacal's death, his son, Chan Bahlum, ascended to power as the new ruler of Palenque.

The **sarcophagus lid**, or coffin, is carved out of a solid piece of rock, with a carved slab covering it. The central image is that of Lord Pacal falling back into the fleshless jaws of the earth monster who will transport him to Xibalba, the realm of the dead. A long inscription runs around the edge of the lid, which includes a number of dates and personal names that records a dynastic sequence covering almost the whole of the seventh and eight centuries.

The Group of the Cross To the extreme southeast of the centre of the site lie Temple XIV and the buildings known as the *Grupo de la Cruz*, including the **Temple of the Sun**, with its beautiful relief carvings. In each of the temples a huge stone tablet with bas-relief was discovered, depicting Chan Bahlum, the new ruler, receiving the regalia of office from his father, Pacal, now in the underworld. Human and mythological time come together in the inscriptions of these temples linking the Mayan gods to celestial bodies and extraordinary astrological phenomena. When Chan Bahlum died in 702 after ruling for 18 years, his younger brother and heir erected a fourth shrine to record the apotheosis of the departed king (Temple XIV). On these reliefs, Chan Bahlum emerges triumphantly from the underworld and dances towards his mother, Lady Ahpo-Hel.

El Naranjo-La Palma

It is possible to get from Palenque to Flores in Guatemala via Tenosique and **La Palma**, from where you can take a boat along the Río San Pedro and across the border to **El Naranjo** and then continue by rough road to Flores. It is a beautiful boat trip (4-5 hrs), through mangroves with flocks of white herons and the occasional alligator. There are basic restaurants and accommodation at both borders, the best option is C **Posada San Pedro** in Naranjo, T7926-2083, which has simple cabañas with mosquito nets and restaurant.

Leaving Mexico There is a stop at the border post two hours into the journey to sign out of Mexico. If planning to return to Mexico, ensure you get an exit stamp here. When you re-enter you will then have to pay US$18 for a visa. Pick up your tourist card and a slip of paper, take this to any bank, pay US$18 and the slip is stamped. Not doing this can lead to problems when you try to leave Mexico again. There are no officials on arrival at the jetty in El Naranjo; immigration is a short way uphill on the right (entry US$5 in quetzales or dollars, beware extra unofficial charges); bus tickets to Flores are sold here. You can wait in a restaurant till the 0100 bus departs, but electricity is turned off at 2200.

Leaving Guatemala Mexican tourist cards can be obtained at the border. At the time of writing, only two-week permits were being issued but it is possible to extend them in Mexico City or Oaxaca. Boats from El Naranjo to La Palma leave at 0600 and 1300. The 1300 boat will often get you to La Palma just in time to miss the last bus to Tenosique, so be prepared to stay the night.

Exchange You can change money at the grocery store opposite immigration in El Naranjo, which will give you a better US$/Q rate than the Mexican side of the border. Or in Tenosique at the clothing shop in front of the market, Ortiz y Alvarez at Calle 28, good rates for dollars to quetzales, poor for dollars to pesos.

Bonampak, Yaxchilán and around » pp152-157.

From Palenque a paved road runs southeast, parallel to the Río Uscumacinta and the Guatemalan border, providing access to the Classic Maya sites of Bonampak and Yaxchilán and to areas of remote Lacondón rainforest; it is best to visit in May – the driest month

At **Lacanjá** (9 km from Bonampak) there is a community of Lacandones. Local guides can be hired for hikes in the jungle and to the ruins of Bonampak, US$6.50-9; the walk through the jungle is beautiful and crosses several streams. Lucas Chambor at the **Casa de Cultura** is a good source of advice. Another walk is to the **Cascadas de Moctuniha** (one hour each way, US$6.50 with guide). There have been some reports of hostility towards tourists here; for more details ask at **Na-Bolom** in San Cristóbal de las Casas.

There are two border crossings into Guatemala close to Yaxchilán and Bonampak. From **Frontera Echeverría** (aka Puerto Corozal), you can catch a launch upstream to Bethel or, southeast of Yaxchilán, you can catch a boat from **Benemérito**, along the Río Salinas to Sayaxché.

Bonampak

ⓘ 148 km from Palenque, turn off at San Javier (12 km). Tue-Sun 1000-1700. Officially free. Ecological restrictions mean that you must leave you car several km from the gate and catch a bus to the site, US$7.

Bonampak, originally under the political domination of Yaxchilán, was built in the Late Classic period on the Río Lacanjá. It is famous for its murals, dated at AD 800, which relate the story of a battle and its bloody aftermath with the sacrificial torture and execution of prisoners. The murals at Bonampak are very realistic with vivid use of colour. They describe the rituals surrounding the presentation at court of the future ruler. The participants were mainly elite, including the royal family, and a strict hierarchy was observed in which eminent lords were attended by minor nobility.

Stucco carving of a human profile, Bonampak

Room 1 presents a simple act in which a porter introduces the young prince to an assembly of lords, while the king watches from his throne. Below them, Lords are represented dressing in sumptuous clothing and jewellery, musicians appear playing instruments and they all line up for a procession. The headdresses alone are bedazzling and the great diversity in the attire of the participants illustrates the wide spectrum of social functions fulfilled by those attending the ceremony.

Room 2 depicts a ferocious battle proclaiming the right of the heir to accede to the throne while emphasizing the need to take captives to be sacrificed in honour of the king-to-be. The ruler, Chaan-Muan, shines heroically in the midst of battle. The local warriors pull the hair of the opposition, whose identity is not known. Many captives are taken. In the ensuing scene, the full horror of the fate of those captured by the Maya is illustrated. On a stepped structure, the ruler Chaan-Muan oversees the torture and mutilation of the captives taken in the recent battle. The gods demand sacrifice, which is provided by the rulers in an extravaganza of bloodletting.

Room 3 shows the events which consolidate the claim to the throne by the son of the ruler. The scenes present celebrations of the sacrifices in an exuberant public display of music and dance. The background is a pyramid; ten elegantly dressed lords dance on different levels, colourful 'dance-wings' sprouting from their hips. The dominant dancer on the uppermost level is believed to be the ruler, Chaan-Muan.

Frontera Echeverría (also known as Frontera Corozal)

The short boat ride across the Río Usumacinta between **Frontera Echeverría** in Mexico and **Bethel** in Guatemala is the most straightforward border for those who want travel between Palenque and El Petén, via the ruins of Bonampak and Yaxchilan (see p148). A dirt road leads up 18 km to the Frontier Highway (35 km to the San Javier junction for Lacanjá and Bonampak). There is a posada in Bethel **D Posada Maya Bethel**, T5801-1799 (community phone), about 1 km outside village, built in the plaza of a Maya site overlooking the river. It runs tours to Bonampak, Yaxchilan and Piedras Negras.

Leaving Mexico There are direct buses from Palenque to Frontera Echeverría, often known as Frontera Corozal. From Echeverría it's a 5-min boat ride to La Técnica, US$0.70, then 20 mins by bus to Bethel for Guatemalan immigration. Alternatively launches go direct from Echeverría to Bethel, 35 mins, US$7. From here a regular bus service goes to Santa Elena, 5 hrs.

Leaving Guatemala There are buses from Santa Elena via La Libertad to Bethel, where you must visit Guatemalan immigration, before continuing to La Técnica, the lancha point for the boat ride to Frontera Echeverría/Corozal. From the border it is four hours by bus to Palenque, or a 1 hr boat ride to the Yaxchilan ruins.

Benemérito-Pipiles

South of Frontera Echeverría, **Benemérito** is a sprawling frontier town at the end of a dirt road. Boats travel from here to **Sayaxché** in Guatemala but this is an arduous route that can tack up to 2 days. Take a hammock, mosquito net, food and insect repellent; the only accommodation between Palenque and Sayaxché are a few rooms in Benemérito.

Leaving Mexico Mexican immigration is 3 km from Benemérito just past Río Lacantún. Buses from Palenque or Fronter Echeverría will stop and wait at immigration for you to sign out of Mexico. From Benemérito, take a boat to Sayaxché, 4-8 hrs, US$8-10, stopping at the military checkpoint of Pipiles for Guatemalan immigration. From Sayaxché there are buses daily to Flores (60 km).

Leaving Guatemala Take a bus to Sayaxché and then a boat downstream to Pipiles (exit stamps must be given here – if you need a Mexican tourist card it's advisable to get it in advance to avoid paying bribes at the border) and on to Benemérito for Mexican immigration. From Benemérito there are regular buses to Palenque (7-12 hours); to Yaxchilán there are boats from Benemérito, or take the bus to Fronter Echeverría (see above); it's a shorter boat ride from there.

Exchange Dollars cannot be exchanged at this border; make sure you have local currency.

The rituals portrayed on the walls of Structure 1 at Bonampak are thought to have been performed between 790 and 792, a time when the collapse of the Classic Maya was beginning to be felt. The extravagant use of enormous amounts of fine cloth, expensive jaguar pelts, jade beads and pectorals, elegant costumes, headdresses made from rare feathers, and spondylus shells was not enough to reverse the decline of the civilization that had produced magnificent works in art, architecture, jewellery, mathematics, astronomy and glyphic writing: within a hundred years, the jungle was to claim it for its own.

Yaxchilán

ⓘ *0900-1600. Admission US$3.50 per person. 173 km from Palenque via Carretera 307 to Frontera Echeverría, then 1 hr boat trip; motorboat US$67 for up to 4, US$92 for more than 5. Try to be there before 0900 to meet other travellers wanting to share.*

Southeast from Palenque, Yaxchilán, reached by car and boat, is one of the least accessible but most rewarding of the Maya centres, built along a terrace and hills above the Río Usumacinta. The boat trip from Echeverría is a beautiful ride, and the site is breathtaking, as much for its location amid luxuriant vegetation, saturated with the sounds of birds, insects and howler monkeys, as for its exquisite inscriptions. The custodian of the ruins is very helpful but camping is restricted to the INAH site on the Usumacinta.

One of the great structures of the Classic Maya period, between AD 350 and 810, Yaxchilán developed from a small agricultural village to become one of the most outstanding Maya centres in the region. With the rise of Cráneo-Mahkina II to the throne in 526 AD, Yaxchilán became the regional capital, but it was under the reign of Escudo Jaguar I, who ascended the throne in 681 AD, that Yaxchilán's power extended throughout the region. The temples are ornately decorated with stucco and stone and the stone lintels are carved with scenes of ceremonies and conquests.

Tabasco state » pp152-157.

Until recently, Tabasco was considered an oil state that held little appeal for visitors but oil wealth has brought Villahermosa, the state capital, a certain self-assurance and vibrancy, and the parks, nature reserves and rivers in the south and east are beginning to attract visitors. Most importantly, these lands once gave rise to the first great civilization of Mesoamerica, the Olmec, whose influence was felt though vast zones of Mexico and further afield. The new **Institute of Tourism** ⓘ *Av de los Ríos y C 13, Villahermosa, T993-316 3633, intuit@tnet.net.mx, daily 0800-2000, English spoken*, is good for maps and advice on excursions throughout Tabasco state.

Villahermosa and around

Capital of Tabasco state, hot and humid Villahermosa is a busy, prosperous and attractive city on the Río Grijalva. The **Centro de Investigaciones de las Culturas Olmecas** (CICOM) is set in a new modern complex with a large public library, expensive restaurant, airline offices and souvenir shops, a few minutes' walk south, out of town along the river bank. The **Museo Regional de Antropología Carlos Pellicer** ⓘ *Tue-Sun 0900-1900, US$1*, on three floors, has well-laid out displays of Maya and Olmec artefacts. Two other museums worth visiting are the **Museo de Cultura Popular** ⓘ *Zaragoza 810, Tue-Sun 0900-2000, free* and the **Museo de Historia de Tabasco** ⓘ *Av 27 de Febrero esq Juárez, Tue-Sun 0900-2000, Sun 1000-1700, US$0.50.* **Mercado Pino Suárez** ⓘ *on the corner of Pino Suárez and Bastar Zozaya* offers a sensory overload as every nook and cranny is taken up with a variety of goods; everything from barbecued *pejelagarto* to cowboy hats, colourful handmade fabrics, spices and dangling naked chickens en route to the kettle.

Located next door to the airport, east of the city, **Parque Yumká** ⓘ *T993-356 0107, daily 0900-1600, US$2, most tour agencies offer trips for about US$8*, is a safari park containing 108 ha of Tabasco's three major habitats – jungle, savannah and lagoon, with walking, trolley and boat tours of each habitat. The ecological park promotes the diversity of the region's flora and fauna but there are also animals from Asia and Africa.

Northwest of Villahermosa are the ruins of the Maya city of **Comalcalco** ⓘ *www.comalcalco.gob.mx, daily 0900-1600, US$3, 1 hr bus journey from Villahermosa, then 3 km to the ruins or taxi to the park entrance, then 1 km to the ruins.* These are unique in Mexico because the palaces and pyramids are built of long and narrow bricks, like ancient Roman bricks, and not of stone. From Comalcalco you can go to **Paraíso** near the coast, which has an interesting covered market with good cocoa, and frequent buses to the beach, 8 km away.

Parque Nacional de La Venta

ⓘ *Blvd Adolfo Ruiz Cortines, almost opposite the old airport entrance west of downtown, T993-314 1652. Tue-Sun 0800-1600; it takes up to 2 hrs to do the park justice. US$2; excellent Spanish- and English-speaking guides US$6.65 for 1 hr 10 mins. Taxis charge US$1.50 to the park.*

In 1925 an expedition of archaeologists discovered huge sculptured human and animal figures, urns and altars in almost impenetrable forest at **La Venta**, 120 km west of Villahermosa, once the centre of the ancient Olmec culture that flourished from 1150 to 150 BC. In the 1950s the monuments were threatened with destruction by the discovery of oil nearby, so the poet Carlos Pellicer had them hauled all the way to a woodland area, with scattered lakes, near Villahermosa, now designated as the Parque Nacional de La Venta (also called the Museo Nacional de la Venta). The park has various small clearings, where the 33 exhibits are displayed, including huge Olmec heads, one of them weighing 20 tonnes . The figures have suffered a certain amount of damage from being exposed to the elements but to see them here, in natural surroundings, is an experience not to be missed. There is also a zoo in the park, with creatures from the Tabasco jungle: monkeys, alligators, deer, wild pigs and birds. Outside the park, on the lakeside, is an observation tower, **Mirador de las Aguilas**, with excellent views but lots of stairs.

Olmec head, La Venta

Sleeping

Toniná *p143*

C **Rancho Esmeralda**, 10 mins' walk from Toniná. Owned by an American couple, cabañas, good meals, homemade bread, horse riding, US$20 per person for a few hrs.

Palenque town *p145, map p152*

It is convenient to stay at hotels near the Pemex service station, as they are also nearer the ruins and the bus stations. Prices treble around fiesta time.

B-C **Kashlan**, 5 de Mayo 105, T916-345 0297. With bath, fan or a/c, hot water, quiet, clean, will store luggage, mosquito nets, helpful owner Ada Luz Navarro, tours to Agua Azul and Misol-Há falls, US$13 per person, laundry opposite, restaurant with vegetarian food in same building, bus and boat tours to Flores in Guatemala offered, internet US$1.50 per hr. Recommended.

C **La Cañada**, Merle Green 13, T916-345 0102. Very rustic but very clean, with fan, good value, lovely garden, expensive restaurant, the owner, Sr Morales, is an expert on the ruins.

D **Posada Shalom**, Av Juárez 156, T916-345 0944. New, friendly, clean, noisy, stores luggage. Recommended.

D-E **Ed and Margaritas**, El Panchan, 7 km from Palenque town, on the road to ruins, edcabanas@yahoo.com This is by far the plushest of the El Panchan accommodation options (see Top tips, p153). Comfortable private thatched-roof cabins, with private bath, sundecks and hot water. A colourful mix of people, evening entertainment, interesting conversation, and more than a whiff of spirituality makes this a perfect place for immersing in the mystique of Palenque.

D-E **Xajlel Jade**, Hidalgo 61, T916-345 0463. Clean, comfortable rooms in quiet street, family-run, hot water. Recommended.

D-E **Yun-Kax**, Av Corregidora 87 (behind Santo Domingo), T916-345 0146. Quiet, clean, big rooms, hot water. Recommended.

E **Avenida**, Juárez 216, T916-345 0116. The Avenida offers spacious, clean rooms

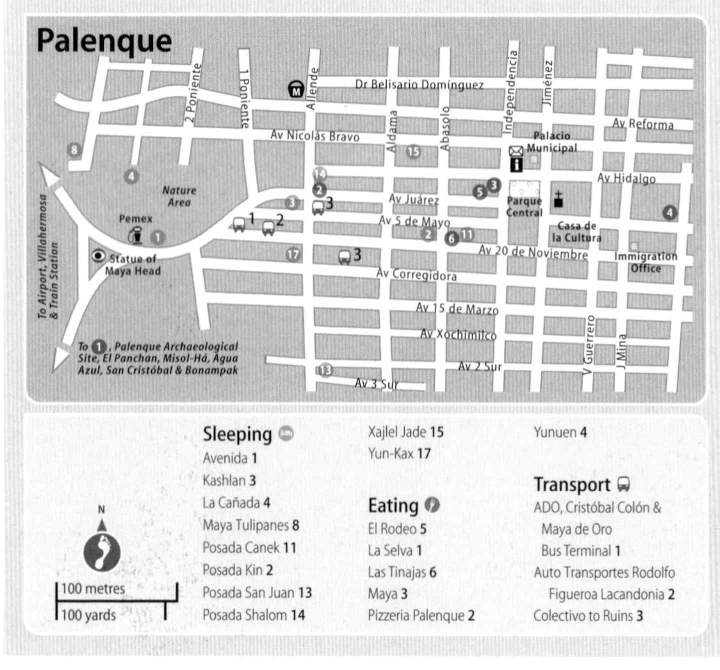

Top tips

El Panchan

For a true Palenque experience spend some time at the heady jungle retreat of El Panchan, 7 km from Palenque town, on the road to ruins. Weaved into a true Robinson Crusoe setting, El Panchan - Maya for 'heaven on earth' - is host to a fascinating mix of very different philosophies, foods and intellectual interests. Don Moisés, founder of Panchan, first came to Palenque as an archaeologist and was one of the first guides to the ruins. He bought a plot of land, which is now divided into lots for a variety of businesses owned by his children. It is about 10° cooler here than in Palenque due to the dense foliage and the laidback atmosphere is the total antithesis of the town's functional frenzy. Stay at **Ed and Margarita's** (see p152), have lunch or dinner at **Don Mucho** (see p154) or just chill out to the off-beat music and entertainment.

with a fan and private bathroom – although there is no hot water. Ask for one of the rooms that have a private balcony. There is also parking provided. It is advisable to ask for the government accommodation list as prices are not displayed in the rooms.

E **Posada Kin**, Abasolo s/n, 20 de Noviembre y 5 de Mayo T916-345 1714, very near Zócalo. Clean and large doubles with bathroom, fan, tours available, safe and luggage store. Recommended.

E **Posada Canek**, 20 de Noviembre. Popular choice. Each clean room at this friendly and helpful posada has a fan and a toilet, more expensive rooms also have a private bathroom. Dormitory accommodation near the reception is not recommended due to the noise. Rooms tend to fill up very quickly during the peak season, so arrive before the 10.00 check-out time. Prices are per person.

E **Posada San Juan** T916-345 0616, (from ADO bus terminal, go up the hill and take the 1st right, it's on the 4th block on the left). A good low end choice, rooms without a bathroom are the cheapest options. Rooms are clean and quiet with firm beds, and each has a secure lock. There is a nice courtyard for relaxing and safe parking available.

Villahermosa *p150*

The price difference between a reasonable and a basic hotel can be negligible, so you might as well go for the former. Try to book hotel rooms in advance, especially during the holiday season (May onwards). Hotels tend to be full Mon-Thu – arrive before nightfall if you can.

AL **Cencali**, Juárez y Paseo Tabasco, T315-1999, www.cencali.com.mx 5 min walk from the centre, this plush hotel has carpeted rooms, soothing décor and all mod cons. Tranquil and efficient. The restaurant is highly recommended.

B **Provincia Express**, Lerdo 303, T993-314 5376. This recently refurbished and upgraded hotel is a good mid-range base. Each room is clean, comfortable and modern, equipped with TV and a/c.

D **Oriente**, Madero 425, T993-312 0121. Clean, hot shower, fan, good restaurant. Recommended.

Eating

Palenque town *p145, map p152*

The classier restaurants are in the barrio La Cañada, behind the Maya head as you enter town. See also El Panchan, below.

𝐓𝐓𝐓 **La Selva**, Km 0.5 on Hidalgo (road to ruins). Excellent, smart dress preferred, live music at weekends, recommended.

ꔠ **Casa Grande**, upstairs on plaza. Good value, set menu and happy hour, good for people watching.

ꔠ **Don Mucho**, El Panchan, Carretera Zona Arqueológica KM 4.5, Apartado Postal 55, T916-341 4846. The Italian-Mexican menu varies from pasta with pesto to fajitas, club sandwiches, and authentic wood oven pizzas drizzled with olive oil (after 1800 only). The breakfast deals are the best in town with a chocolate and banana shake making a suitable initiation. In the evening there is plenty of amateur performances to accompany the gastro delights from fire dancers, to circus performers and many an aspiring raconteur (see also Top tips, p153).

ꔠ **El Rodeo**, Juárez 116, near plaza. Does good breakfasts and meat dishes, popular with travellers. Recommended.

ꔠ **Las Tinajas**, 20 de Noviembre 41 y Abasolo. Very popular with budget travellers due to its mega portions and now occupying larger premises, with outdoor seating. A broad menu features *pollo pibil*, huge steaks, enchiladas, quesadillas, salads, pasta and club sandwiches. Left-over take-away boxes are the norm. Breakfast deals are excellent value, if you can face a five-egg omelette.

ꔠ **Pizzería Palenque**, Juárez 168 and Allende, T916-345 0332. Small street-side pizzeria in the centre of town. Despite stark lighting and a fair coating of traffic fumes, it's worth a visit for thin crust pizzas laden with inventive toppings. Swift, smiley service and good prices.

ꔠ-ꔠ **Restaurante Maya**, Hidalgo and Independencia. Very popular, fills up by 1900, set-menu lunches and à-la-carte dinner, mainly Mexican.

ꔠ-ꔠ **Yunuen**, at Hotel Vaca Vieja. Generous portions at reasonable prices, good steaks, popular with local ranchers.

Villahermosa *p150*

ꔠ **Hotel Madan**, Madero 408, has a restaurant serving good breakfast and inexpensive fish dishes. This is a pleasant and quiet place to escape from the heat, with a/c and newspapers.

ꔠ-ꔠ **Aquarius**, Javier Mina 309, near Av Méndez. Vegetarian food, juice bar and health food store.

ꔠ-ꔠ **Café El Portal**, Independencia 301, delicious typical food of the region including *empanadas* stuffed with *pejelargarto*, a vicious-looking freshwater fish. Friendly service, arty atmosphere.

ꔠ-ꔠ **El Torito Valenzuela**, next to Hotel Madero. Mexican specialities, excellent and inexpensive. Highly recommended.

ꔠ **Zona Luz**, Aldama 615. Typical Mexican/Tabasqueña food. Cheap, quaint, airy with a charming colonial feel.

Cafés

Café La Cabaña, Juárez 303-A, opposite Museo de Historia de Tabasco. Town elders gather at the outdoor tables to debate the day's issues over hot cups of cappuccino. Very entertaining to watch. No meals.

El Café de la Calle Juárez, Juárez 513, indoor/outdoor café. Great for breakfast, good coffee, a new menu every month. Outdoor tables.

Shopping

Palenque town *p145, map p152*

Av Juárez is lined with souvenir shops selling hammocks, blankets, Maya figurines and hats. Sales staff are less pushy than in towns in the Yucatán Peninsula; bargain for the best prices.

Activities and tours

Palenque town *p145, map p152*

Horse riding

Tours can be booked at the Clínica Dental Zepeda, Juárez s/n – the dentist owns the horses. Also through Cabañas de Safari in Palenque archaeological zone Km 1, T916-345 0026. Gaspar Alvaro also rents horses. He can be located at his house on the road to the ruins, directly in front of Mayabel. Gaspar will take you on a 3-hr ride through rainforested trails in the surrounding area of the ruins. Good chance of seeing monkeys and toucans.

US$15 for 3 hrs. Tell him specifically that you want to go through the rainforest and not on the road.

Microlight

For the upwardly mobile. **Fernando Maza**'s house is next door to Gaspar's (see above). He operates a powered hang glider; for US$35 he will take you for a 10-min flight over Palenque ruins.

Tour operators and guides

All the travel agencies in Palenque do a cheap tour to both **Misol-Há** and **Agua Azul**, about US$8 per person. Most tours allow about ½ hr at Misol-Há and 3-4 hrs at Agua Azul; bring a swimsuit and plenty of drinking water. There are also 1-day trips to **Bonampak** and **Yaxchilán**, US$38 per person, including transport, breakfast and lunch. It's tough going for 13 hrs, but worth it. A 2-day road and river trip to Bonampak and Yaxchilán costs US$55 per person, all inclusive; slightly cheaper with Colectivos Chambala at Hidalgo y Allende.

Alonso Méndez is a well-versed guide with extensive knowledge of flora, fauna, medicinal uses of plants and an intimate knowledge of the Palenque ruins. A respected authority on Chiapan ethnobotany, Alonso has a gift of academic and spiritual understanding of the rainforest. He speaks English, Spanish and Tzeltzal and can be found at his home in the Panchan camping site, ask around. Full-day hiking trips US$50 for a group of 6-8 people. Highly recommended.

Inter Travel, Juárez 48, T916-345 1566, domestic and international flight arrangements, hotel reservations, a new tour to Lagunas Catazajá (27 km from Palenque). Includes a 3-hr motorboat ride and a visit to a bird sanctuary, US$45 per person, min 4 people.

José Luis Zúñiga Mendoza, T916-341 14736, tentzun@hotmail.com José has excellent knowledge of the Palenque area and in addition to guided trips around the ruins offers jungle walks and stays with local communities.

Na Chan Kan, Hidalgo y Jiménez, T916-345 0263, www.palenquemx.com/viajesnachan Offers a wide selection of packages ranging from tours to Agua Azul and the Yaxchilán and Bonampak ruins to transportation to Guatemala.

Shivalva (Marco A Morales), Merle Green 1, La Cañada, T916-345 0411, tours of Palenque, Yaxchilán, Bonampak, Tikal, Guatemala City, Belize, Copán.

Viajes Mayasol, Juárez 148, T916-345 0911, vmisolhachiapas@hotmail.com Adventure tours to Chacamax River, all-day trek, rafting, lunch US$58.

Yax-Há, Av Juárez 123, T916-345 0798. English spoken. Recommended.

Villahermosa *p150*

Tour operators

Turismo Nieves, Sarlat 202, T993-314 1888, www.turismonieves.com.mx Offers guided trips to ruins of Comalcalco, Cocona, and transportation to Parque Yumká. English speaking, very friendly, recommended.

Transport

Agua Azul *p144*

Several buses from Palenque daily (direction San Cristóbal de las Casas or Ocosingo), to the crossroads leading to the waterfall, US$3.35, 2nd class, 1½ hrs; tickets from Transportes Figueroa in Palenque. From the crossroads walk 4 km downhill to the falls or hitch a ride on a minibus for US$1. On your return, catch a ride to Palenque on tour buses that have extra space, US$4, from the Agua Azul parking lot 1500-1800. Otherwise Transportes Maya buses from the junction 1400-1600. Note that not all buses between San Cristóbal de las Casas and Palenque will stop at the Agua Azul junction; on some services you must change at Temo, north of Ocosingo.

Colectivos from Hidalgo y Allende, Palenque, for Agua Azul and Misol-Há, 2 a day, US$9; *colectivos* can also be organized between Misol-Há and Agua

Azul, in either direction. Taxi from Palenque US$45

Palenque town *p145, map p152*

Air

Aerocaribe flies daily during the high season to Palenque from **Cancún** via Flores, Guatemala; check with travel agents. Also flights from **Huatulco**, **Mérida**, **Oaxaca** and **Tuxtla Gutiérrez**.

Bus

Local Micro buses run back and forth along the main street, passing the bus station, to and from the ruins, every 10 mins, US$0.80. For buses to Agua Azul and Misol-Há, see above. All bus companies have terminals close at west end of Av Juárez, 20 de Noviembre.

Long distance There are 3 bus terminals, 2 smaller 2nd-class ones serving destinations in Chiapas state, and the 1st class **ADO/Cristóbal Colón** terminal, with buses to Chiapan destinations as well as longer journeys. **Cancún**: 1st class, 2000, 13 hrs, US$37; 2nd class, 2345, US$26. **Campeche**: 1st class, US$21, 0800 and 2100, 5 hrs, US$16 (**ADO**); 2nd class, 2345, US$10. **Mérida**: 1st class, 0800, 2100, 8 hrs, US$25. **Mexico City**: 1st class, 1800, 2000, 16 hrs, US$51, also **Alto** at 2130, US$41. **Oaxaca**: 1st class, 1730, 15 hrs, US$38 (ADO). **San Cristóbal**: 1st-class, 8 daily between 0500 and 2200, 5½ hrs, US$8 (also 1st-class service from **Lacandonia** terminal, 2 doors down, 8 a day, US$11); 2nd class, 3 a day from 0730, US$5.50; from the **Lacandonia** terminal, next door to **Express Plus**, 0530, 0645, 0845, US$5. **Tulum**: 1st class, 2000, 11 hrs, US$32. **Tuxtla Gutiérrez**: 1st class, 0930, 1200, 1830, 6 hrs, US$9.40; 2nd class, 3 a day from 0730, US$7. **Villahermosa**: 2nd class, 6 per day from 0500, US$6.50. For buses to Bonampak, Yaxchilán and Guatemala, see below.

Taxi

Taxis charge a flat rate of US$1 within the town, US$4 to **El Panchan** and **Mayabel** camping areas, US$5 to **Palenque ruins**, US$45 to **Agua Azul,** with 2 hrs at the falls, US$65 to both **Misol Há** and Agua Azul, US$20 per person for the return trip to **Bonampak**.

Colectivos to the ruins run from either Allende between Hidalgo and Juárez, or from Allende between 20 de Noviembre and Corregidora, every 15 mins starting at 0600 (last one passes **El Panchan** at 1830), US$0.70. They drop you at the ticket office from where it is a further 1 km uphill to the ruins.

Bonampak and Yaxchilán *p148*

Air

Flights from **Palenque** to Bonampak and Yaxchilán, in light plane for 5, about US$600 per plane, to both places, whole trip 6 hrs. Prices set, list available. **Viajes Misol-Há**, Juárez 48 at Aldama, T916-345 0911, run charter flights to Bonampak and Yaxchilán for US$150 per person return, minimum 4 passengers. **ATC Travel Agency**, agents for **Aviacsa**, at Av Juárez and Allende, Mon-Sat 0800-1800, to Bonampak; book at airport.

Bus

From Palenque to **Frontera Echeverría** (for connections to Yaxchilán or Guatemala, p149), bus departs 1000, 4 hrs, US$5.50, or frequent minibuses, US$4.50. Register at the immigration office in Echeverría if you are continuing on to Guatemala. Buses run by **Autotransportes Comitán Lagos de Montebello** (Manuel Velasco 48, 2 blocks west of plaza) from Palenque to **Benemérito**, 0300, 0430, 0630, 0900 and 2000, pass the turn-off to Bonampak at **San Javier**, US$5.50; check details in advance. Also from Chancalá bus terminal in Palenque every 3 hrs or so, from 0730, to **San Javier**, 3 hrs; *colectivos* US$4. From San Javier, a jungle trail leads to **Bonampak**, easy to follow but several hrs' walk with nowhere to stay en route. In the other direction, the last *colectivo* fro m Echeverría to **Palenque** passes San Javier at 1500.

Boat

Yaxchilán is reached by a lovely 1-hr boat journey from Echeverría. There is no problem finding a boat for the round trip (US$67 for up to 4 people, US$92 for more than 5, max 10 people, cost includes boatman staying overnight), but try to be there before 0900.

Villahermosa *p150*

Air

Airport Carlos R Pérez (VSA), 18 km from town. Flights to **Cancún**, **Mérida**, **Mexico City**, **Oaxaca**, **Tuxtla Gutiérrez** and **Veracruz**. VW bus to town US$3 each, taxi US$9.50 for 2.

Bus

Local To **Comalco** ruins, ADO, 1230 and 1800, US$2.50, or **Souvellera**, US$2, from Av Universidad and Ruiz Cortines, 5 blocks north of Central Camionera. To **Parque Nacional La Venta**, 'Circuito No 1' from outside second-class bus terminal, or 'Fraccionamiento Carrizal' from Parque Juárez to Parque Tomás Garrido.

Long distance 1st class, ADO terminal on Javier Mina between Méndez and Lino Merino, 12 blocks north of centre, taxi US$1.30, left luggage, 0700-2300.

Several 1st-class buses to **Mexico City**, 12 hrs, US$40, direct bus 1815 (Cristóbal Colón) or 1650 (ADO) then frequent through the night, expect long waits; buses to Mexico City are often booked up well in advance. **Cancún**: 3 a day, 12 hrs, US$49-63; **Chetumal**: 10 a day, 10 hrs, US$16; **Campeche**: 6 hrs, US$16.50, reservation required; **Mérida**: many daily, 8-10 hrs, US$19.50; **Oaxaca**: Cristóbal Colón from ADO terminal at 1930 and 2130, 1st class, US$27.50; **Palenque**: 8 a day from ADO terminal, 2½ hrs, US$2.50 to US$4.60; **San Andrés Tuxtla**: 6 hrs, US$12.50; **San Cristóbal de las Casas**: every couple of hrs, 6 hrs, US$9; also 2nd-class bus with 1 change at Tuxtla, leaves 0800, arrives 2100, fine scenery but treacherous road; **Veracruz**: many a day with ADO, 7 hrs, US$36 Primera Plus; **Xalapa**: with ADO, 3 a day, 10 hrs.

Car

Hertz car rental is available from the airport. Agrisa, M Ocampo esq Paseo Tabasco y Malecón, T993-312 9184, good prices, eg US$40 per day including taxes and insurance, but it is expensive to return the car to another city.

Directory

Palenque town *p145, map p152*

Banks Exchange rate only comes through at 1000, then banks open until 1200. Bancomer, good TC rates. Yax-Há Cambio on Juárez, daily 0700-2000, changes US$ cash and TCs. Next door at No 28, is Banamex, Mon-Fri 0930-1400, slow. Restaurante El Rodeo also changes TCs at bank rate. At weekends TCs can be changed at many travel agencies and other shops on Av Juárez; also, the owner at Farmacia Central will change US$ at a reasonable rate. ATMs at Bancomer and Banamex, but with long queues. **Internet** Several internet cafés along Juárez with good service and prices ranging from US$1-1.50 per hr. **Laundry** Opposite Hotel Kashlan, US$2 per 3 kg, 0800-1930. **Post office** Independencia, next to Palacio Municipal, helpful, Mon-Fri 0900-1300. **Telephone** Long-distance telephones at ADO bus terminal, cheaper than many other telephone offices; at Mercería bookshop in Aldama near Juárez, and a shop by Hotel Palenque in the Zócalo.

Villahermosa *p150*

Banks HSBC, Suárez and Lerdo, changes TCs at good rates. American Express, Turismo Nieves, Sarlat 202, T993-314 1818. **Internet** C@fe internet, Aldama 404-C, lobby of the Hotel Howard Johnson. US$1.50 per hr. Many others scattered around town. **Post office** On Ignacio in the centre. DHL, parcel courier service, Paseo Tabasco.

Yucatán Peninsula

Chac Mool

Don't miss...
1 Campeche ▸▸ p164.
2 Dzibilchaltún ▸▸ p173.
3 Uxmal ▸▸ p174.
4 Chichén Itza ▸▸ p176.
p170
p188
p162
Caribbean Sea
Gulf of Mexico
MEXICO
YUCATAN
QUINTANA ROO
CAMPECHE
50 km
50 miles
N
Península Río Lagartos
Las Coloradas
Río Lagartos
El Cuyo
Isla Holbox
Laguna Yalahán
Povenir
Isla Contoy
Chiquilá
Isla Mujeres
Puerto Juárez
Punta Sam
Cancún
Hidalgo
San Felipe
Loché
Moctezuma
S Arturo
Yalsihón
Panabá
Quintina
Guadalupe
Tizimín
Sucila
Leona Vicario
Vallarta
Puerto Morelos
San Crisanto
Santa Clara
Dzidzantún
Cansahcab
Yucalpetén
Progreso
Chuburna
Sinanché
Sisal
Dzibilchaltún
Motul
Izamal
Cenotillo
Espita
San Andrés
Ek-Balam
Xcan
Nuevo Xcan
Hal-Al
Mérida
Hoctún
Kantunil
Tinúm
Temozon
Bella Flor
Celestún
Umán
Sanahcat
Pisté
Valladolid
Playa del Carmen
Xcaret
San Miguel de Cozumel
San Rafael
Tedzidz
Yaxcopoli
Telchaquillo
Mayapán
Chichén Itzá
Uayma
Tekóm
Chunchucmil
Maxcanú
Tekit
Sotuta
Ticimul
Cobá
Akumal
Pamul
Isla Cozumel
La Costa
Muná
Mama
Yaxcabá
Tixcacalcupul
Playa San Francisco
Halacho
Becal
Chumayel
L Cobá
Xcacel
Ticul
Maní
Chamul
Xel-Ha
El Caracol
Calkiní
Teabo
Tepich
Yalchén
Punta Celarain
Chunhuas
Uxmal
Kabah
Oxkutzcab
Tulum
Labná
Tihosucol
San Ramón
Jaina
Savil
Tekax
Dzotzil
Pomuch
Xlapak
Chacmultún
Peto
Culumpich
Chunyaxché
Tenabo
Chunyaxnic
Boca Paila
Tinún
Nocacab
Catmis
Chumpón
Santa Rosa
Cenote Azul
Emiliano Zapata
Dziuché
Puente Allen
Campeche
Becanchén
Vigia Chico
Lerma
Hunto-Chac
Yaxley
Señor
Jose Maria Morelos
Nohalal
Felipe Carrillo Puerto
Chinal
Cayal
X-Pichil
Hopelchén
Put
Seyba Playa
San Isidro
Polyuc
Betania
Edzná
Iturbide
Xnoh-Cruz
Mulul
Sian Ka'an Biosphere Reserve
Punta Herrero
Vila Madero
Gavilanes
Uhmay
Haltunchén
La Joya
Lubna
Dzibalchén
El Ramonal
Champotón
Arellano
Chunchintok
Ramón Corona
Pres Juárez
Petcacab
San Isidro Poniente
Va Guadalupe
Kancabchén
San Enrique
Canán
Tampalam
Ucum
Carrillo Puerto
Pustunich
Limones
Huayahaca
Río Verde
Lázaro Cárdenas
Placer
Los Lirios
El Holay
Cafetal
El Uvero
Santa Rosalia
Yohatún
Bel-Ha
Cayo Norte
Península El Palmar
Santa María
Pixoyal
Payo Obispo
Judas Taden
Buenavista
Río Indio
Calax
Flores Magón
Puerto Bravo
San Román
Paso Real
Bahía de Chetumal
Majahual
Ciudad del Carmen
Chekubul
Nuevo Becar
Laguna Guerrero
Cayo Centro
La Cristalina
Centenario
Constitución
Santa Elena
Escárcega
El Rosario
Xulhá
Chetumal
Campechito
Atasta
Zacatal
Laguna de Terminos
Mamantel
Victoria
Dzinapara
Becán
Francisco Villa
Casas
Chicanná
Xpujil
Corozal Bay
Cayo Lobos
Tres Brazos
El Desecho
Haro
La Tuxpeña
Hormiguero
Río Bec
Kohunlich
Palmar
Corozal
Sarteneja
Santa Rosa
Plan del Carmen
Don Samuel
A Obregón
Progresso
Shipstern Nature Reserve
Luna
Selva Negra
Narciso Mendoza
Pochitocal
El Vapor
Buenavista
Bonfil
San Estevan
COROZAL

Introduction

The Yucatán Peninsula, which includes the states of Campeche, Yucatán and Quintana Roo, is sold to tourists as the land of Maya archaeology and Caribbean beach resorts. There's no denying that the warm turquoise sea and fine white-sand beaches of the 'Riviera Maya' are second to none. And it certainly would be a crime not to tread the beaten path to the sensational ruins at Chichén Itzá, Uxmal and Tulum. But it also pays to explore beyond the main routes to visit some of the lesser known Maya sites such as Cobá, Edzná or Dzibilchaltún, or the imposing Franciscan monastery and huge pyramid at Izamal. There are flamingo feeding grounds at Celestún and Río Lagartos and over 500 other species of bird in the region, many of which are protected in the Sian Ka'an Biosphere Reserve, which covers 4,500 sq km of tropical forest, savanna and coastline. Ever since Jacques Cousteau filmed the Palancar Reef in the 1960s, divers have swarmed to the clear waters of Cozumel, the 'Island of the Swallows', to wonder at the many species of underwater life. Also popular and specialized is diving in the many cenotes (limestone sink holes) that punctuate the peninsula, including the famous Nohooch Nah Chich, part of the world's largest underground cave system.

Ratings

Culture
★★★★

Landscape
★★★

Chillin'
★★★★★

Activities
★★★★★

Wildlife
★★★★

Costs
$$$$

Campeche

The State of Campeche is well worth exploring with plentiful colonial architecture and several fortified convents in the villages surrounding Mérida and many archaeological sites demonstrating influences of Chenes or Río Bec architecture – distinctive styles unique to the Maya of this region where ornamentation dominates over functionality. Campeche city itself was fortified to protect its citizens from pirate attacks and is now a UNESCO cultural heritage site. The exhibits at several museums reflect the seafaring nature of the area and the civilization that occupied these lands before the Conquest. Eat snapper in Campeche and buy a soft but robust Panama hat in Becal.

Getting there Frequent long-distance buses, also flights from Mexico City.

Getting around Plenty of buses and tours. Car hire is a good option for southern Campeche.

Time required 1 week.

Weather Hot and dry.

Sleeping Good range, but tends to be overpriced.

Eating Excellent fish and seafood.

Activities and tours Archaeological tours.

★ **Don't miss**...Eating fresh snapper at one of Campeche's many restaurants » *p167*.

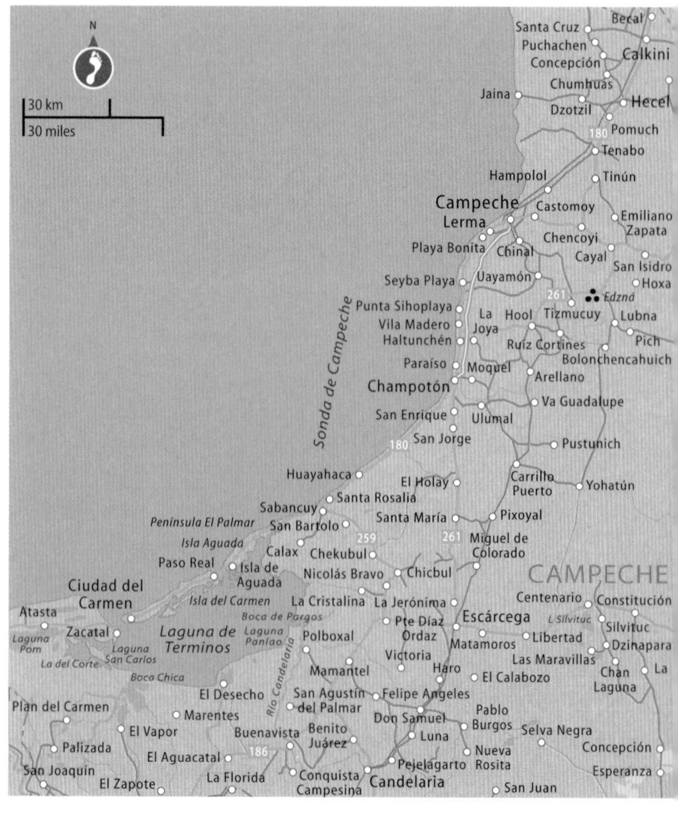

Southern Campeche p167-169

From the neighbouring state of Tabasco, the inland Highway 186 runs fast and smooth in a sweeping curve 115 km east to the Palenque turn-off at **Playas del Catazajá**, before continuing via two toll bridges (US$4.25) to **Emiliano Zapata** and **Francisco Escárcega**. Here, you can turn north on Highway 261 towards Campeche city or continue east on Highway 186 towards Chetumal, via a number of intriguing Maya sites.

The architectural style of these sites is known as 'Río Bec' and is characterized by heavy masonry towers simulating pyramids and temples, usually found rising in pairs at the ends of elongated buildings. Although the style takes its name from the ruins of **Río Bec**, there are better examples of it at Xpujil, Becán and Chicanná, around the tiny village of **Xpujil**. This village is also the place to arrange guided tours to more remote ruins, such as Calakmul.

Calakmul

ⓘ *Route 186 to Conhuás (Km 95), then south for 60 km; only accessible by car. Daily 0800-1700. US$3.* Some 300 km southeast of Campeche town, the ruins of Calakmul are thought to be one of the largest archaeological sites in Mesoamerica, and certainly the biggest Maya city, with around 10,000 buildings, many of them still unexplored. Evidence suggests that Calakmul was started in 300 BC and continually added to until AD 800. The site is centred upon the **Gran Plaza**, overlooked by a pyramid whose base covers five acres. One of the buildings around the Gran Plaza is believed to have been designed for astronomical observation, due to its curious shape and location. The largest structure is the **Gran Acrópolis**, divided into two sections: **Plaza Norte**, with the ball court, was used for ceremonies, while **Plaza Sur** was used for public activities.

Xpujil

ⓘ *Route 186 to Xpujil. Daily 0800-1700. US$2.50, US$3 to use a video camera.*

The main building at Xpujil, meaning 'cat tail', features an unusual set of three towers, with rounded corners and steps that are so steep they are unscalable. The façade features the open jaws of an enormous reptile in profile on either side of the main entrance, possibly representing Itzamná, the Maya god of creation. Xpujil's main period of activity was AD 500-750; it began to go into decline around 1100. Major excavation was carried out in 1993 but many unexcavated buildings remain. Xpujil can be very peaceful and quiet in the early mornings, compared with the throng of tourist activity at the more accessible sites.

Becán

ⓘ *7 km west of Xpujil. Daily 0800-1700. US$3. Round trip by taxi from Xpujil, including stop at Chicanná, US$10.*

Becán

Becán is another important Río Bec site. Its most outstanding feature is a moat, now dry, surrounding the entire city, which is considered one of the oldest defence systems in Mesoamerica. Seven entrance gates cross the moat to the city. The buildings on the site are a strange combination of decorative towers, fake temples (built just for effect), shrines and palaces. The main structure features twin towers, typical of the Río Bec style, set on a pyramid-shaped base that supports a cluster of buildings.

Chicanná

ⓘ *12 km west of Xpujil. Daily 0800-1700, US$2.50. Round trip by taxi, US$10 (see Becán above).* Chicanná was discovered in 1966 and takes its name from Structure II, which has a dramatic entrance in the shape of a monster's mouth, with fangs jutting out over the lintel and more fangs lining the access stairway: *chi* – mouth, *can* – serpent, and *ná* – house. Due to its dimensions and location, Chicanná was probably a small residential centre for the rulers of Becán. It was occupied during the late Pre-classic period (300 BC-AD 250) but some evidence of activity dates to the Post-classic era (AD 1100). Typical of the Río Bec style are numerous representations of the Maya god Itzamná, or Earth Mother.

Hormiguero

ⓘ *20 km southwest of Xpujil junction, entry US$1.50, round trip by taxi from Xpujil, US$20.* Hormiguero, meaning anthill in Spanish, is the site of one of the most important buildings in the Río Bec region. Elaborate carvings on the façade show an excellent example of the serpent's-mouth entrance, with huge fangs and a gigantic eye.

Campeche » pp167-169

From Villahermosa, Highway 180 follows the coast through **Ciudad del Carmen**, before converging with Highway 261 at **Champotón**. The attractive colonial city of **Campeche** is 66 km further north. The highway enters the city as Avenida Resurgimiento, passing either side of the huge **Monumento al Resurgimiento**, a stone torso holding the Torch of Democracy.

History

The Spaniards, under Francisco Hernández de Córdoba, first disembarked on Mexican soil at the trading village of Ah Kim Pech to replenish their water supply in 1517, but it was not until

1541, after a number of failed Spanish attempts at settlement that Francisco de Montejo finally founded the city of Campeche. The city became the most important port on the Yucatán Peninsula and prospered through international trade. Buccaneers raided the port in 1663, wiping out the city and slaughtering its inhabitants. Five years later the Crown began to fortify the site, creating the first walled Spanish colonial settlement. Formidable bulwarks, 3 m thick and 'a ship's height', and eight bastions (*baluartes*) were built.

After Mexican Independence, the city declined into an obscure fishing and logging town. It was only with the arrival of a road from the 'mainland' in the 1950s, followed by the oil boom of the 1970s that it begin to see many visitors, attracted by its historical monuments and relaxed atmosphere (campechano has come to mean an easy-going, pleasant person). At the end of the 20th century, the city was declared a UNESCO Cultural Heritage Site.

Ins and outs

Getting there and around If time is limited, take an overnight bus from Villahermosa to Chetumal via Escárcega, as the journey is not very interesting (unless you want to see the Maya ruins off this road, see page 163). A full circuit of the city walls is a long walk but buses marked 'Circuito Baluartes' provide a regular service around the perimeter. » *p169.*

Tourist information The **state tourist office** ⓘ *T981-816 7364, www.campeche.gob.mx, 0800-2100*, is on the Malecón in front of the Palacio de Gobierno (walk down Calle 61 towards the sea). There is another smaller **tourist office** ⓘ *Baluarte Santa Rosa, Calle 14, 0800-2000.* The Centro Histórico tour on the **tourist tram** ⓘ *daily 0900-1300, 1700-2000, 45 mins, English and Spanish spoken*, runs from the main plaza.

Sights

Clean streets of brightly painted houses give Campeche a relaxed Caribbean feel. The Malecón, destroyed by a hurricane in 1996, has since been rebuilt and is now a beautiful promenade where people stroll, cycle and relax. Of the original 17th-century fortifications, seven bulwarks (*baluartes*) and a fort remain; most points of interest are within this area.

The heart of the city is the **Zócalo** and the austere Franciscan **cathedral** (1540-1705) with its elaborately carved façade. It contains the 'Santo Entierro' (Holy Burial), a sculpture of Christ on a mahogany sarcophagus with a silver trim. Right in front of the Zócalo is the **Baluarte de la Soledad**, the central bulwark of the city walls, which now houses the **Museo de la Escultura Maya** ⓘ *Tue-Sat 0900-1400, 1600-2000, Sun 0900-1300, US$1*, containing Maya stelae and sculpture. From here you can start the Circuito Baluartes walking tour. Heading south, you reach the **Puerta del Mar**, formerly the gateway to the city by sea. Next is a pair of modern buildings, the Palacio de Gobierno and the flying-saucer like Congreso.

Heading west, you come to the **Templo de San José**, on Calle 10, an impressive baroque church with a beautifully tiled façade. Back on the Circuito, is the Baluarte de Santa Rosa, now the home of the tourist information office, and the Baluarte de San Juan. One block northwest of here is the **Museo Regional de Campeche** ⓘ *Casa Teniente del Rey, Calle 59 between 14 and 16, Tue-Sat 0800-1400, 1700-2000, Sun 0900-1300, US$3*, which charts a history of the state since Maya times, with interesting displays.

The Circuito continues past the Baluarte de San Francisco, and the market, just outside the line of the city walls. To the northwest, the Baluarte de Santiago houses the **Jardín Botánico Xmuch'Haltun** ⓘ *Mon-Sat 0900-1300, 1800-2000; Sun 0900-1300, free*, a small, but perfectly formed collection of tropical plants and flowers. A 20-minute walk along Avenida Miguel Alemán from Baluarte de Santiago is the 16th century **Iglesia de San Francisco**, with wooden altars painted in vermilion and white. Nearby are the **Portales de San Francisco**, the beautifully restored former entrance to the city.

Campeche

The **Fuerte de San Miguel**, on the Malecón 4 km southwest, is the most atmospheric of the forts; it houses the **Museo Arqueológico** ⓘ *Tue-Sat 0900-2000, Sun 0900-1300, US$1*, with a well-documented display of pre-Columbian exhibits including jade masks and black funeral pottery from Calakmul and recent finds from Jaina.

Around Campeche

A number of Maya remains are scattered throughout the rainforest and scrub to the east of Campeche; little excavation work has been done and most receive few visitors. Getting to them by bus is possible, but return trips can be tricky. The alternatives are to take a tour or to rent a vehicle (preferably with high clearance). Whichever way you travel, carry plenty of water.

Edzná

ⓘ *5 mins' walk from Highway 261, 61 km from Campeche via Cayal and Highway 261 or 50 km via China and Poxyaxum. Tue-Sun 0800-1700. US$3.50. Local guides available. Tourist bus, US$10, or bus towards Pich (Sat, Sun only, 1-hr trip; it may be hours late; return 0930, 1230, 1300).*
The closest site to Campeche is Edzná ('House of Grimaces'), gracefully situated in a tranquil valley surrounded by thick vegetation. Edzná was a huge ceremonial centre, occupied from about 600 BC to AD 200, built in the simple Chenes style mixed with Puuc, Classical and other influences. The centrepiece is the magnificent, 30 m-tall **Temple of the Five Storeys**, a stepped pyramid with four levels of living quarters for the priests and a shrine and altar at the top. Opposite is the **Paal U'na**, Temple of the Moon. Some of the site's stelae remain in position (two large stone faces with grotesquely squinting eyes are covered by a thatched shelter); others can be seen in museums in Campeche. Edzná is especially worth a visit in July (exact date varies), when a Maya rainfall ceremony to Chac is held.

Becal

North of Campeche, on the Yucatán border, Becal is the centre for the weaving of Panama hats, known as *jipis* (pronounced 'hippies'). The hats are honoured by a hefty sculpture of three concrete *sombreros* in the plaza and at the **Feria del Jipi** on 20 May. *Jipis* are finely and tightly woven so that they retain their shape even when crushed into your luggage (within reason). Many of the town's families have workshops in cool underground caves to keep the shredded leaves of the *jipijapa* palm moist and pliable. Most vendors will give visitors a tour of their workshop, but be prepared for a zealous sales pitch. Prices tend to be better in the **Centro Artesanal, Artesanías de Becaleña** at 210 Calle 30, than in the shops near the plaza.

Panama hats

Sleeping

Southern Campeche *p163*

C **Calakmul**, 800 m from bus stop, Xpujil, T/F983-832 9162. Modern fixtures, good restaurant, quiet, safe, clean. Tours.

D **Mirador**, just beyond Calakmul hotel, Xpujil. Cabañas with restaurant, slightly run down. Tours arranged.

Campeche *p164, map p168*

A **Baluartes**, Av 16 de Septiembre 128, T981-816 3911. One of the city's best mid-range options, a modern complex with bright, functional rooms with TV, a/c and bathroom. Small pool, laundry, restaurant and rooftop bar, with glittering night-time views. Staff are very obliging.

C **América**, Calle 10 No 252, T981-816 4588. Hot water, friendly, clean, fans but hot, safe parking, with night watchman.

C **Regis**, Calle 12 No 148, between 55 y 57, T981-816 3175. Nice central setting among colonial columns, good service.

D **La Posada Del Angel**, Calle 10 No 307, T981- 816 7718 (on the side of the cathedral). A/c, attractive, some rooms without windows, clean. Recommended.

D-F **Hostal Campeche**, Calle 57 and Calle 10, T981-811 6500, www.hostal campeche.com. Dormitory rooms with lockers, or private rooms. Laundry, internet, bike hire, kitchen, book swap. Price includes breakfast. Local tours.

Eating

Campeche *p164, map p168*

Campeche is known for its seafood, especially *camarones* (large shrimps), *esmedregal* (black snapper) and *pan de cazón* (baby hammerhead shark between corn tortillas with black beans). Food stands in the market serve *tortas*, tortillas, *panuchos* and *tamales* but hygiene standards vary widely; barbecued venison is also a marketplace speciality. Fruit is cheap and plentiful, but peel it yourself.

₸₸₸-₸ **La Parroquia**, Calle 55 No 8. Open 24 hrs, good atmosphere, friendly and clean.

₸₸ **La Perla**, Calle 10 between 57 and 59, off plaza. Good fish, venison, squid. Busy and popular, local haunt, erratic service.

₸₸ **La Pigua**, Av Miguel Alemán, opposite Cine Estela. Seafood restaurant with tranquil garden. Many famous visitors. Emphasis is on freshness and quality rather than presentation. Renowned for its fabulous, good value, jumbo shrimps.

₸₸ **Los Portales**, Calle 10 No 86. Authentic local atmosphere, try the *sopa de lima*, 1900-midnight.

₸₸-₸ **Marganza**, Calle 8. Good breakfast and other meals, excellent service.

₸₸-₸ **Restaurant del Parque**, on the plaza. Good, cheap seafood.

₸ **Lonchería Guayín**, Calle 53 between 16 and 14. Cheap *comida corrida*, good *licuados*, also here is Miguel Angel, spiritualist and feng shui consultant.

Festivals and events

Campeche *p164, map p168*
Good **Carnival** in **Feb/Mar**. **7 Aug** is a state holiday. **Feria de San Román**, 2nd fortnight of **Sep**. **Fiesta de San Francisco**, **4-13 Oct**.

Shopping

Campeche *p164, map p168*

Crafts

Panama hats are cheaper in Becal (p166) but other handicrafts are generally cheaper here than in Mérida. There are souvenir shops along Calle 8. Many high-quality craft items are available from the Exposición in the Baluarte San Pedro.
Artesanía Típica Naval, Calle 8 No 259. Exotic bottled fruit, *nance* and *marañón*.
Casa de Artesanía, Calle 10. Good-quality handicrafts displayed on Maya dummies, with a mock-up hammock- making cave.
El Coral, Calle 8 No 255. Maya figurines.

The **market**, from which most local buses depart, is beside Alameda Park at the south end of Calle 57. Plenty of bargains here. Try the ice cream, preferably from a shop.

Activities and tours

Southern Campeche
Tours to remote Maya sites in the area can be arranged through hotels in Xpujil

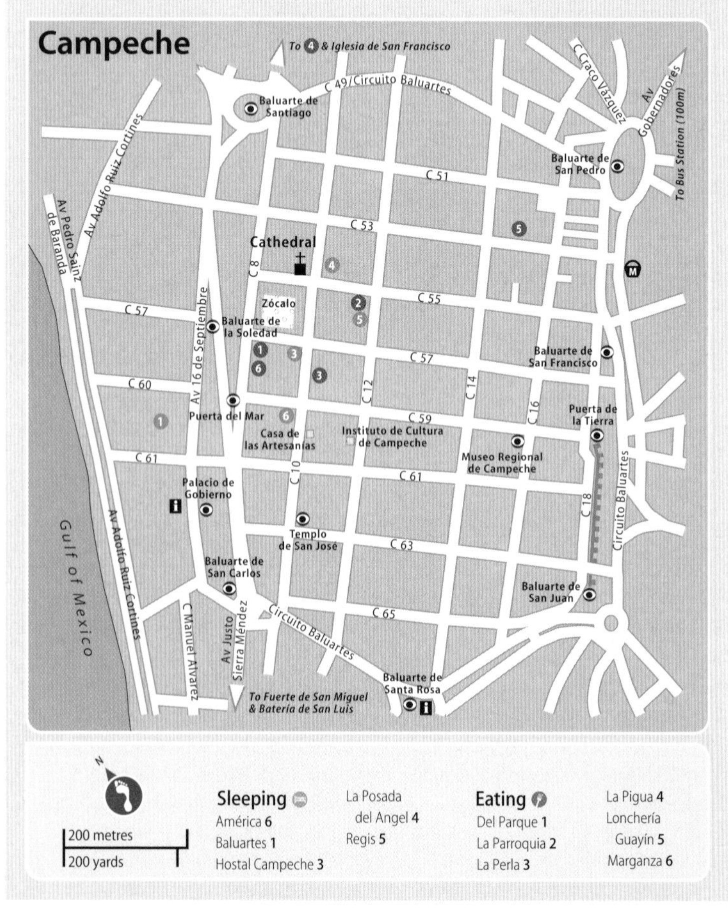

(see Sleeping, above), US$20-30 per person for the whole day.

Campeche *p164, map p168*

Tour operators

Picazh Servicios Turísticos, Calle 16 No 348 between 357 and 359, T981-816 4426, run transport to Edzná ruins, with or without guide, US$20. Recommended.
Viajes Chicanná, Av Augustín Melgar, Centro Comercial Triángulo del Sol, Local 12, T981-811 3503. Flight bookings.
Viajes del Golfo, Calle 10 No 250 D, T981-816 4044. Tours to Edzná and Calakmul.
Viajes Programados, Calle 59, Edificio Belmar, offers daily 2-hr tours to Edzná at 1000, US$20; tours from **Hotel Baluartes**.

Transport

Southern Campeche *p163*
2nd-class buses stop on the highway in the centre of Xpujil, some 800 m east of the 2 hotels. To **Chetumal**, 8 daily, 2 hrs, US$5. To **Escárcega**, 4 daily, 1030-1500, 3 hrs, US$6; change here for frequent buses to **Palenque** or **Campeche**. 1st-class buses do not stop at Xpujil.

Campeche *p164, map p168*

Air

Modern, efficient airport (CPE) on Porfirio, 10 km northeast. **Aero México** direct daily to **Mexico City**, T981-816 5678.

Bus

Local Tourist buses run to **Edzná** from Puerta de la Tierra, in front of the market, 0900 and 1400, US$20 return. To **Pich** (via Edzná) from Campeche marketplace, 0700, 1000 and 1030. To **Calakmul**, from Baluarte de San Pedro, weekends at 1700.

Long distance The main bus station is to the northeast on Av Gobernadores. The **ADO** terminal is next door; more expensive, but greater comfort and speed. The following information is for 2nd-class buses unless otherwise stated.

To **Cancún**, 2300, 2330, US$25; to **Chetumal**, 1200, US$19; to **Cd del Carmen**, 9 a day from 0745, US$10, plus **Cristóbal Colón**, 2210, US$7.50; to **Mérida**, 11 a day, 0545-1930, 2½ hrs, US$10, plus **Maya de Oro**, 0400, US$12, and **Cristóbal Colón**, 2030, US$8; to **Mexico City**, 1600, US$85; to **Oaxaca**, 2155, 2400, US$60; to **Palenque**, 1st class with **ADO**, 3 a day from 0030, 5-7 hrs, US$19; to **San Cristóbal de las Casas**, **Maya de Oro**, 2400, 14 hrs, US$36, or **Cristóbal Colón**, 2210, US$28; to **Veracruz**, 1st class, 1030, 1300 and 2100, 14 hrs, US$54; to **Villahermosa**, 5 a day from 0900, 6½ hrs, US$21.

Car

Next to Hotel del Mar, Av Ruiz Cortines 51, T816-2233. **Hertz** and **Autorent** car rentals at airport.

Directory

Campeche *p164, map p168*
Banks Banamex, Calle 10 No 15. American Express, T981-811 1010, Calle 59, Edificio Belmar, oficina 5, helpful for lost cheques, etc. **Hospitals and clinics** Red Cross, T815-2378, emergency T981-815 2411. **Immigration** The **Oficina de Migración** at the Palacio Federal will extend Mexican visas. **Internet** Cybercafé Campeche, Calle 61 between Calle 10 and 12, 0900-1300, US$1.50 per hr. **Laundry** Calle 55 between 12 and 14, US$0.60 per kg. **Post office** Av 16 de Septiembre (Malecón) y Calle 53 in Edificio Federal, Mon-Fri 0800-2000, Sat 0900-1300 for *Lista de Correos*, registered mail, money orders and stamps. **Telephone** Telmex, Calle 8 between Calle 51 y 53, free; Calle 51 No 45, between 12 and 14. **Intertel**, long-distance phones and fax, Calle 57 No 1 between 10 and 12.

Yucatán

At the north end of the peninsula, Yucatán state covers an inverted triangle of land that is strewn with fascinating archaeological sites. Chichén Itzá and Uxmal are the best known, but try not to miss some of the lesser sites, including Kabah and Labná. Yucatán was also a centre of early evangelism by the conquering Spanish, who re-used material from pre-Columbian structures to create their own Christian and colonial architecture, as seen at Izamal and at Dzibilchaltún. The state capital is the bustling city of Mérida, where you can buy hammocks and other crafts, but the friendly town of Valladolid is an excellent alternative base. The region's cenotes (deep pools or sinkholes created by the disintegration of the limestone above an underground river) were sacred to the Maya who threw precious jewels, silverware and even humans into their depths; many are perfect for swimming, snorkelling and diving.

Getting there Frequent long-distance bus services.
Getting around Plentiful buses and tours. Car hire is also a good option.
Time required 1 week.
Weather Hot and dry, with heavy rain possible Jul and Aug.
Sleeping Good range across all budgets.
Eating Mérida has plenty of gastro diversity.
Activities and tours Cycling, boat trips to observe pelicans, egrets and flamingoes.
★ **Don't miss...** Uxmal » *p174*

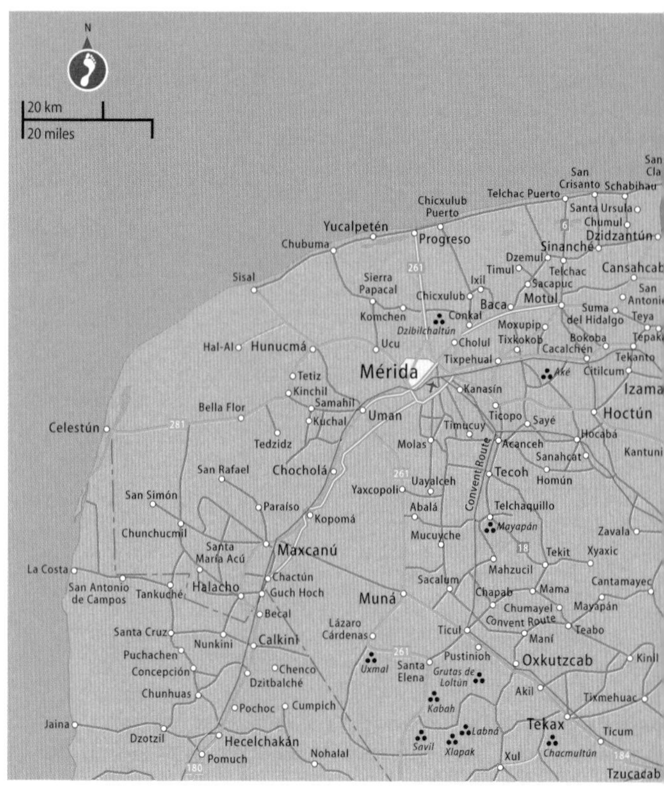

Mérida » pp179-187.

The capital of Yucatán state and its colonial heart, Mérida is a busy, tightly packed city, full of colonial buildings in varying states of repair. There is continual activity in the centre, with a huge influx of visitors during the high season mingling with busy Meridanos going about their daily business. Although the city has been developed for tourism, it nevertheless retains plenty of local flavour.

Ins and outs

Getting there Aeropuerto Rejón (MID) is 8 km from the centre of town and has a tourist office with a hotel list and car hire but no left-luggage facilities. Bus 79, marked 'Aviación', runs between the airport and calles 67, 69 and 60, roughly every 20 minutes, US$0.35. Taxis cost US$8, payable by a voucher available from the airport (don't pay the driver direct), or there are *colectivos* for US$2.50. All **buses** to/from outside Yucatán state, plus all buses to/from Chichén Itzá, arrive at the 1st-class **CAME** terminal on Calle 70 No 555 between Calle 69 y 71, a few blocks from the centre; taxi US$3.50. Buses to/from all other local destinations use the **ADO** bus terminal around the corner on Calle 69. » *p186.*

Getting around You can see most of Mérida on foot; most of the tourist sites are near to the main plaza. VW Beetle taxis are expensive, due to their scarcity; fares start at US$3 for a short journey. *Colectivo* buses are difficult to locate but you can flag them down anywhere; they appear on the bigger roads and terminate at the market, US$0.25.

Tourist information The main **tourist office** ⓘ *Calle 60 y Calle 57 (just off Parque Hidalgo), daily 0800-2000*, inside the Teatro Peón Contreras, is very helpful, often staffed by enthusiastic trainees. There are other tourist offices at the airport and in the main plaza. Mérida is a safe city, with its own **tourist police** force, recognizable by their brown and white uniforms, T999-925 2555.

History

Mérida was originally a large Maya city called Tihoo, which was conquered on 6 January 1542 by Francisco de Montejo. He dismantled the pyramids of the Maya and used the stone for the foundations of the cathedral. For the next 300 years, Mérida remained under direct Spanish control, unlike the rest of Mexico, which was governed from Mexico City. During the Caste Wars of 1847-55, Mérida held out against the indigenous forces, who had defeated the Mexican army in every other city in the Yucatán Peninsula except Campeche. Reinforcements from the centre allowed the Meridanos to defend their city but the price was to relinquish control of the region to Mexico City.

Sights

Casa de Montejo

The city revolves around the large, shady Zócalo, site of the **San Ildefonso cathedral**, built by Montejo from 1556 to 1559. It is the oldest cathedral in Latin America and has an impressive baroque façade. Inside is the 'Cristo de las Ampollas' (Christ of the Blisters), a statue carved from a tree that was hit by lightning and burned for a whole night, without showing any damage at all. The statue was placed in the church at Ichmul, which subsequently burned to the ground but, again, the statue only suffered slight charring.

Close to the cathedral on the same side of the plaza is the **Museo Macay** ⓘ *Calle 60, daily 1000-1730, US$2,* which has a permanent exhibition of Yucatecan art and temporary exhibits by local artists. The **Palacio de Gobierno**, built 1892, is on the plaza's north side and houses a collection of enormous murals by Fernando Castro Pacheco, depicting the struggle of the Maya to integrate with the Spanish. **Casa de Montejo**, on the south side of the plaza, was built by the city's founder; it is now a branch of Banamex. Two blocks west, the Casa de la Cultura houses the **Museo de la Canción Yucateca** ⓘ *Calle 63 between 64 and 66, Tue-Sat 0900-2000, free*, an exhibition of Yucatecan music.

North of the main plaza, along Calle 60, is **Parque Hidalgo**, a charming tree-filled square, which borders the 17th-century **Iglesia de Jesús**. Nearby, **Pinacoteca Juan Gamboa Guzmán**, ⓘ *Calle 59 between Calle 58 and 60, Tue-Sat 0800-2000, Sun 0800-1400, US$1*, shows old and contemporary painting and sculpture. A little further along Calle 60 is the **Teatro Peón Contreras**, with a neoclassical façade, marble staircase and Italian frescoes.

A few blocks east of Parque Hidalgo is the **Museo de Arte Popular** ⓘ *Calle 59 esquina 50, Barrio de la Mejorada, Tue-Sat 0900-2000, Sun 0800-1400, free*, which has a permanent exhibition of Maya art, handicrafts and clothing, with a good souvenir shop attached. Just to the north at Calle 59 between 48 and 50 is **La Mejorada**, one of several 16th- and 17th-century churches dotted about the city.

Attempts to create a sophisticated Champs Elysées-style boulevard north of the city centre at **Paseo Montejo** rather jars with Mérida's status as an colonial city, however, the **Museo de Antropología e Historia** ⓘ *Paseo de Montejo 485, Tue-Sun 0800-2000, US$2*, housed in the beautiful neoclassical Palacio Cantón is worth a visit. It has an excellent collection of original Maya artefacts from various sites in the state, including jade jewellery, dredged from cenotes, and some cosmetically deformed skulls.

Around Mérida » *p179-187.*

Celestún

A small, dusty fishing resort much frequented in summer by Mexicans, Celestún stands on the spit of land separating the Río Esperanza estuary from the ocean. Surrounding the town is the **Celestún Biosphere Reserve** ⓘ *Visitors' centre below the bridge, 1 km along the Mérida road, entry US$3.50, boat trips, 1½ hrs, US$35 for 6-8 people*, created to protect the thousands of migratory waterfowl who inhabit the lagoons; fish, crabs and shrimp also spawn here, and kingfishers, black hawks, wood storks and crocodiles may sometimes be glimpsed. In the winter months, the reserve hosts the largest flamingo colony in North America, consisting of around 20,000 birds; in the summer, most of the flamingoes leave for their nesting grounds in the Río Lagartos area (page 179).

Dzibilchaltún

ⓘ *15 km north of Mérida towards Progreso. Daily 0800-1700, US$4.50. Site map available at museum. From Mérida, regular VW combis (direction Chablekal) daily 0500-1900, and 5 daily buses (marked 'Tour/Ruta Polígono') Mon-Fri, all from Parque San Juan, corner of Calle 62 y 67A. Return bus every hour, US$0.60.*

The intrusion of European architecture is nowhere more startling than at this site near Mérida. According to carbon dating, this unique Maya city was founded as early as 1000 BC. The site is in two halves, connected by a *sacbé* (white road), with the **Templo de Las Siete Muñecas** (Seven Dolls) at the east end. At the west end is the ceremonial centre with temples, houses and a large plaza in which a late 16th-century open **chapel**, simple and austere sticks out like a sore thumb. The evangelizing friars clearly hijacked a pre-Conquest sacred area in order to erect a symbol of the invading religion. At the edge of the site is **Cenote Xlaca**, containing very clear water that is 44 m deep and full of fascinating fish (take mask and snorkel for swimming). An interesting nature trail starts halfway between the temple and the cenote, rejoining the *sacbé* halfway along.

Izamal

The friendly little town of Izamal lies 68 km east of Mérida. Once a major Classic Maya religious site, Izamal became one of the centres of the Spanish attempt to Christianize the Maya. The entire colonial centre is painted a rich yellow ochre, giving it the nickname of the 'golden city'.

Fray Diego de Landa, the historian of the Spanish conquest of Mérida (of whom there is a statue in the town), founded the huge **convent** and **church**, which now face the main **Plaza de la Constitución**. The church, constructed on top of a Maya pyramid, was begun in 1549 and has the second largest atrium in the world. Some of the stones that surround this magnificent space are embellished with Maya carvings. There is also a throne built for the Pope's visit in 1993. The image of the Inmaculada Virgen de la Concepción in the church was made the 'Reina de Yucatán' in 1949, and the patron saint of the state in 1970.

Flamingo

Iglesia de Izamal y Convento de San Antonio

In all, 20 Maya structures have been identified in Izamal, several on Calle 27. The most prominent are the ruins of a great mausoleum known as the **Kinich-Kakmo pyramid** ⓘ *0800-1700, free*, which is visible from the convent across a second square. Kinich-Kakmo is 195 m long, 173 m wide and 36 m high, making it the fifth highest pyramid in Mexico. From the top there is an excellent view of the town and surrounding *henequén* and citrus plantations.

From Izamal you can go by bus to **Cenotillo**, where there are several fine cenotes within easy walking distance of the town (avoid the one *in* town), especially **Ucil**, excellent for swimming, and **La Unión**.

Convent Route

This driving route from Mérida takes in numerous Maya villages and ruins, colonial churches, cathedrals, convents and cenotes. It is best to be on the road by 0800 with a full tank. The route follows Ruta 18 (take the Periférico out of Mérida towards Kanasín) as far as **Tekit**, a large village containing the church of San Antonio de Padua, with many ornate statues of saints, and then continues on minor roads to Teabo and **Maní**, where there's a large Franciscan church, convent and museum. This is where the Franciscan friar, Fray Diego de Landa, ordered important Maya documents and artefacts to be burned in 1562. On realising his great error, he set about trying to record all that had been destroyed, including 27 scrolls, 5,000 idols, 13 altars and 127 vases. The resulting text, *Relation of Things in Yucatán*, is still available today. To return to Mérida from here, head for Ticul (page 174) to the west, then follow the main road via Muná.

Other highlights along the Convent Route include **Acanceh**, where you will see the unusual combination of a Grand Pyramid, a colonial church and a modern church, all on the same small plaza, and the peaceful, late-Maya ruins of **Mayapán** ⓘ *Ruta 18, 2 km beyond Telchaquillo, daily 0800-1700, US$4.35, buses from Mérida every 30 mins, US$1*, a large walled city with 4,000 mounds, that once formed a triple alliance with Uxmal and Chichén Itzá. The village of **Mama** has the oldest church on the route, famous for its ornate altar and bell-domed roof. Nearby is **Chumayel**, where *Chilam Balam* ('Spokesman of the Jaguar') Maya manuscripts were found. These were written after the Spanish Conquest and record past and current events in order to divine the future.

Uxmal and the Puuc Route » pp179-187.

The characteristic features of Maya cities in the Puuc region are the quadrangular layout of the buildings, which are set on raised platforms, and an artificially created underground water-storage system. Uxmal and the four lesser sites (Kabah, Sayil, Xlapak and Labná) can be visited in a day, either by car or on the 'Ruta Puuc' bus (page 186), but if you want to spend longer seeing these sites, it is best to stay overnight in **Ticul**. This is a small, pleasant village, 80 km south of Mérida, known for its *huípiles* – the embroidered white dresses worn by the older Maya women. You can buy them in tourist shops in Mérida, but the prices and quality of the ones in Ticul will be much better. Ticul and the other towns in this area are notable for their large Franciscan churches from the late 16th and 17th centuries.

Uxmal

ⓘ *74 km from Mérida on highway 261, via Yaxcopoil and Muná. Daily 0800-1800, US$8, parking US$1. Son et Lumière show (in Spanish) 2000 daily in summer, 1900 in winter, US$3.*

Built during the Classic Period, Uxmal is the most famous site in the Puuc region. Visitors enter the site near the the **Pyramid of the Sorcerer**, an unusual oval-shaped pyramid set on a large rectangular base. The pyramid is 30 m tall, with two temples at the top. Behind it, the so-called **Nunnery** is set around a large courtyard, with some fine masks of Chaac, the rain

Nunnery, Uxmal

god, on the corners of the buildings. The east building has decorations depicting double-headed serpents, while the façade of the west building features some plumed serpents in relief, in excellent condition.

South of here, the **House of the Governor** is 100 m long, and is considered one of the most outstanding buildings in all of Mesoamerica. Two arched passages divide the building into three distinct sections. Above the central entrance is an elaborate trapezoidal motif, with a string of masks, depicting Chaac, interwoven into a flowing, undulating serpent-like shape extending to the façade's two corners. The stately two-headed jaguar throne in front of the structure suggests a royal or administrative function. The **House of the Turtles** has simpler decorations of carved turtles on the upper cornice, above a short row of tightly packed columns, which resemble the Maya *palapas*, made of sticks with a thatched roof, still used today. The **House of the Doves** is the oldest and most damaged of the buildings at Uxmal but the remains are still impressive: a long, low platform of wide columns topped by clusters of roof combs, whose similarity to dovecotes gave the building its name.

Kabah

ⓘ *Highway 261, south of Sta Elena. Daily 0800-1700. US$2.40.*

The Classic Puuc ruins of Kabah straddle the main road, 37 km southeast of Uxmal. On one side is the fascinating **Palace of Masks** (or *Codz-Poop*), whose façade bears the image of Chac, mesmerically repeated 260 times, the number of days in the Almanac Year. Each mask is made up of 30 units of mosaic stone. Even the central chamber is entered via a huge Chac mask whose curling snout forms the doorstep. On the other side of this wall, beneath the figure of the ruler, Kabal, are impressive carvings on the door arches, which depict a man about to be killed, pleading for mercy, and two men duelling. Across the road the outstanding feature is a reconstructed arch marking the start of the *sacbé* (sacred road), which leads all the way to Uxmal.

Sayil, Xlapak and Labná

South of Kabah, turn off highway 261 to reach **Sayil** ⓘ *5 km east of the junction, daily 0800-1700, US$3*, meaning 'The Place of the Ants'. The site dates from AD 800-1000 and incorporates an interesting palace, which in its day included 90 bathrooms for 350 people. It has a simple, elegant colonnade, reminiscent of the architecture of ancient Greece. The central motif on the upper part of the façade is a broad mask with huge fangs, flanked by two serpents surrounding the grotesque figure of a descending deity. From the upper level of the palace you can see a tiny ruin of the Nine Masks on the side of a mountain.

Some 13 km beyond Sayil, on the same road are the ruins of **Xlapak**, consisting of 14 mounds and three partially restored pyramids. A little further on is **Labná**, which has a monumental arch connecting two groups of buildings (now in ruins), an architectural concept unique to this region. The two façades on either side of the arch differ greatly in their decoration; the one at the entrance is beautifully adorned with delicate latticework and stone carving imitating the wood or palm-frond roofs of Maya huts.

Grutas de Loltún

ⓘ *South of Ticul, Tue-Sun 0930, 1100, 1230 and 1400, US$3 with obligatory guide, 1 hr 20 mins, recommended, taxi, US$10 from Ticul (or on a tour from Mérida).*

The caverns and pre-Columbian vestiges in this cave system supposedly extend for 8 km. In one of the cavities, the 'Huechi' excavations revealed animal remains, including mammoth and bison, providing evidence of climate and environmental change in the region. Relief carvings, petroglyphs and murals show the evolution of the Maya culture. One bas relief (600 BC-AD 150) known as the 'Loltun warrior', found at the Nahkab entrance, demonstrates striking similarities with Olmec culture.

Chichén Itzá » pp179-187.

ⓘ *Daily 0800-1700; check opening times of the various buildings; best to arrive before 1030; Sun very crowded. US$10, multiple entry on day of issue. Guided tours US$4-6 per person for 1½-hrs (persistent and too fast). Son et lumière in English 2000, US$5; not as good as at Uxmal. Tourist centre with car park (US$1.50), toilets, museum, restaurant, left luggage and bookshop ('Panorama' is the best guidbook). The site is hot so take a hat, sun cream and plenty of water.*

Route 180 runs southeast from Mérida for 120 km to Chichén Itzá where the scrub forest has been cleared from over 5 sq km of ruins. Chichén Itzá means 'Mouth of the well of the water-sorcerer' and is one of the most spectacular of Maya sites. It takes at least a day to see the many pyramids, temples, ball courts and palaces, all of them adorned with astonishing sculptures. The city was built by the Maya in Late Classic times (AD 600-900), but was more or less abandoned by the end of the 10th century. It was re-established in the 11th-12th centuries, but debate surrounds by whom. Some of the architecture indicates that the later inhabitants were heavily influenced by the Toltecs of Central Mexico. Interesting birdlife and iguanas can be seen around the ruins.

Exploring the site

Toltec influence can be seen in the major buildings in the north half of the site. Dominating them is **El Castillo**, a giant stepped pyramid, decorated at its summit by the symbol of Quetzalcoatl/Kukulcán. On the morning and afternoon of the spring (21 March) and autumn (21 September) equinoxes the alignment of the sun's shadow casts a serpentine image on the steps of El Castillo, however, it is very crowded on these occasions and you'll be lucky to see any of the action. The balustrade of the 91 stairs up each of the four sides is decorated at its base by the head of a plumed, open-mouthed serpent. There is also an interior ascent of 61 steep and narrow steps (not for the claustrophobic) as high as seven tiers of the pyramid to a chamber, where the red-painted jaguar that probably served as the throne of the high priest burns bright, its eyes of jade, its fangs of flint.

To the northwest of El Castillo is a **ball court** with grandstand and towering walls, each set with a projecting ring of stone high up. At eye-level is a relief showing the decapitation of either the winning or losing captain (experts argue whether sacrifice was an honour or the punishment for defeat). To the east of El Castillo is the **Temple of the Warriors** with its famous statue of the reclining Chacmool, the Maya fertility god.

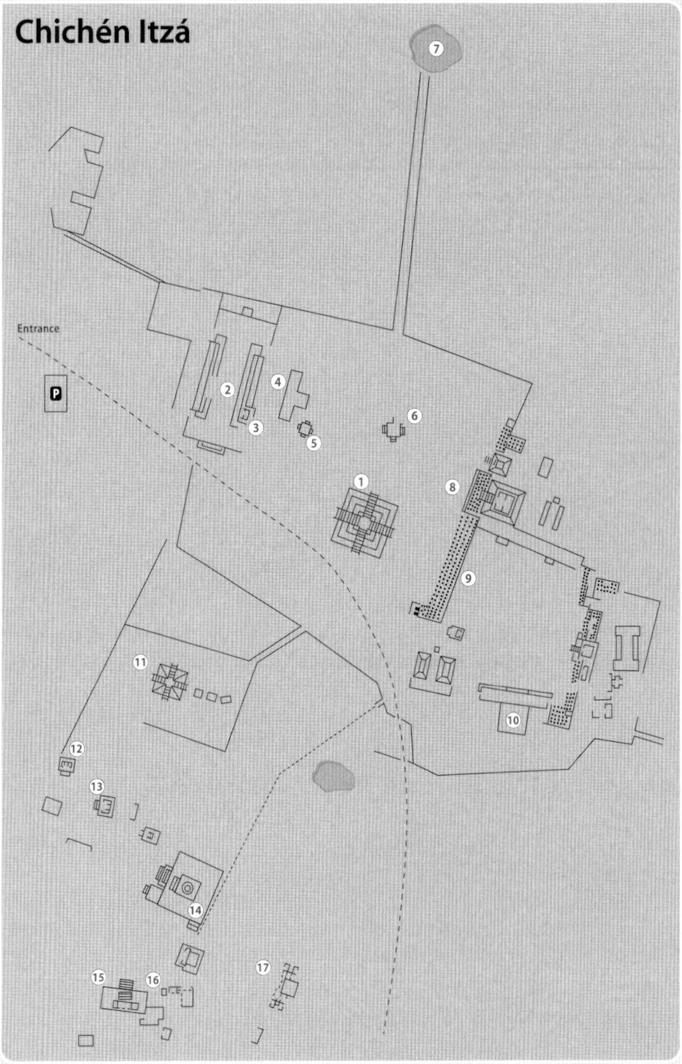
Chichén Itzá
Entrance
P
1
2
3
4
5
6
7
8
9
10
11
12
13
14
15
16
17

N
100 metres
100 yards

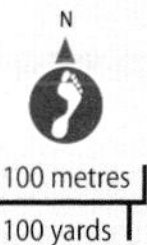

Castillo **1**
Ball Court **2**
Temple of the Jaguar **3**
Platform of the Skulls (Tzompantli) **4**
Platform of Eagles **5**
Platform of Venus **6**
Well of Sacrifice **7**
Temple of the Warriors & Chacmool Temple **8**
Group of a Thousand Columns **9**
Market **10**
Tomb of the High Priest **11**
House of the Deer **12**
Red House **13**
El Caracol (Observatory) **14**
Nunnery **15**
'Church' **16**
Akabdzilo **17**

El Castillo and El Caracol, Chichén Itzá

At a right angle to northern face of El Castillo runs the *sacbé* (sacred way) to the **Cenote Sagrado** (Well of Sacrifice), into which were thrown valuable propitiatory objects of all kinds, as well as animal and human sacrifices. Thousands of objects have been recovered from the well, including beads, pottery, copper, gold, polished jade, lumps of *copal* resin, small bells, statuettes of rubber and wood, and a quantity of animal and human bones.

Old Chichén, where the Maya buildings of the earlier city are found, lies about 500 m by path from the main clearing. The famous **El Caracol**, or Observatory, is included in this group, as is the **Casa de las Monjas**, or Nunnery. A footpath to the right of Las Monjas leads to the **Templo de los Tres Dinteles** (the Three Lintels; 30 minutes' walk).

Valladolid and around » pp179-187.

Roughly halfway between Mérida and Cancún, Valladolid is a relaxed, colourful little town, with some fine colonial architecture. There is a slightly medieval feel to the city, with some of the streets tapering off into mud tracks. Valladolid's location and its friendly inhabitants (known as Vallisoletanos) make it an ideal place to settle for a few days, while exploring the ruins of Chichén Itzá, Cobá and Tulum, the fishing village of Río Lagartos and the three beautiful cenotes in the area. With excellent value hotels and a welcoming low-key ambience, it is a much more endearing base than Mérida.

Sights and cenotes

The heart of the town is the leafy central plaza, where elderly Vallisoletanos take siestas beneath the trees and young couples share ice-cream and dance to the brass bands which often play from 2000. The Franciscan **cathedral** dominates the scene, honey gold in the late afternoon light. The town's **tourist office** ⓘ *southeast corner of the plaza*, is not very helpful but hands out a useful map. Much more information is available from **Antonio 'Negro' Aguilar** ⓘ *Calle 44 No 195*. Something of a local celebrity, he was a baseball champion in the 1950s and '60s, playing for the Leones de Yucatán and the Washington Senators. A small town **museum** ⓘ *Calle 41, free*, housed in Santa Ana church, shows the history of rural Yucatán and has some exhibits from recent excavations at the ruins of Ek-Balam.

Cenote Zací ⓘ *Calle 36 between Calle 37 and 39, daily 0800-1800, US$2, children US$1*, right in town, is an artificially lit cenote where you can swim. It has a thatched-roof restaurant and lighted promenades. Seven kilometres from Valladolid at **Dzitnup** is the beautiful **Cenote X-Kekén** ⓘ *daily 0800-1800, US$1.20*. It is stunningly lit with electric lights, the only natural light source being a tiny hole in the cavernous ceiling dripping with stalactites. Swimming is excellent here: the water is cool and refreshing – although reported to be a little dirty – and harmless bats zip around overhead. Exploratory walks can also be made through the many tunnels leading off the cenote, for which you will need a torch. *Colectivos* leave hourly from in front of **Hotel María Guadalupe**, US$1, they return until 1800, after which you will have to get a taxi back to Valladolid, US$4.

Ek-Balam

ⓘ *25 km north of Valladolid, daily 0800-1700, US$2. Minivans from Valladolid run by Antonio Aguilar.* In a beautiful setting, surrounded by traditional Maya villages, are the ruins of Ek-Balam, meaning Black Jaguar. Occupied from 300 BC, this site formed the epicentre of the Tah kingdom that dominated eastern Yucatán state during the Late Classic period, reaching its zenith around 600-1200 AD.

A series of temples, sacrificial altars and residential buildings are grouped around a central plaza, elaborately finished with carved sculptures or polychrome stucco. The most impressive is the **Acropolis**, the largest standing pyramid in the Yucatán after the Kinich Kak Moo pyramid at Izamal. It is decorated with richly carved stucco, including a monstrous mask with protruding fangs on the main façade and winged idols believed to be angels – imagery that is unique to Ek-Balam. The site's most important discovery was the tomb of the ruler Ukit Kan Lel Tok, which contained rich artefacts, including jewellery and weapons, and the only emblematic glyph found to date in the north of Yucatán state.

Río Lagartos

Río Lagartos is an attractive fishing village on the north coast of Yucatán, whose main attraction is the massive biosphere reserve that protects thousands of pink flamingoes, as well as 250 other species of bird. Boat trips to see the flamingoes can be arranged with boatmen at the harbour but make sure they take you to the larger colony near **Las Coloradas** (15 km), recognizable by a large salt mound on the horizon. Also check that the flamingoes are actually there; they usually nest during May and June and stay until August (although salt mining is disturbing their habitat). ▲▸▸ *p185*.

Sleeping

Mérida *p171, map p181*

The prices of hotels are not determined by their location. You can easily find a budget hotel near the plaza, next door to a 5-star luxury establishment. If booking into a central hotel, always try to get a room away from the street, as noise begins as early as 0500.

A **Colonial**, Calle 62 No 476, corner of Calle 57, T999-923 6444, www.hotelcolonial.com.mx Great location 2 blocks from the plaza. Small but comfortable rooms with TV and a/c. Very friendly and efficient, good buffet meals, including a highly recommended breakfast.

A **Gran Hotel**, Parque Hidalgo, Calle 60 No 496, T999-923 6963. A/c, TV, hot water, phone, clean, helpful, owner speaks English. Could do with a lick of paint but has a great atmosphere. Popular with film stars and politicians, including Fidel Castro. Only rooms on the north and west sides have external windows. Pizza/pasta restaurant, free parking.

A **Medio Mundo**, Calle 55, No 533 between 64 and 66, T/F999-924 5472, www.hotelmediomundo.com Renovated old home with 10 charming high-ceiling rooms, garden patio and swimming pool.

B-C **Dolores Alba**, Calle 63 No 464 between 52 and 54, T999-928 5650. Rooms with bath and fan, some with a/c,

Budget buster

LL Hacienda Xcanatun, Km 12, Carretera Mérida-Progreso, T/F999-941 0273, www.xcanatun.com Some 8 km north of Mérida, this is, without doubt, the most lavish option in the area. A palpable sense of history and grandeur pervades each room of the 18th-century hacienda, lovingly restored by Jorge Luz Buenfil. His father was Alberto Luz-Lullier, the esteemed archaeologist who discovered Pakal's tomb in Palenque. The hacienda is equipped with all the modern conveniences in addition to a holistic spa, 2 swimming pools and garden retreat. The superlative restaurant, Casa de Piedra 'Xcantaun' (†††, T999-941 0213) is popular, so book ahead.

quiet, friendly, good breakfast US$4.50, pool, safe parking. No credit cards.

B-C **Posada Toledo**, Calle 58 No 487 esq 57, T999-923 1690, hptoledo@pibil.finred.com.mx Good value, central, a/c extra, charming old house with lots of plants, cheap breakfast, book exchange.

C **Casa San Juan**, Calle 62 No 545A between 69 and 71, T999-986 2937, www.casasanjuan.com Colourful colonial B&B. 7 spacious rooms, with high ceilings and patio garden where breakfast is served. A new extension has 2 light modern rooms with kitchenettes, great value for longer stays. Reservations and payment in advance; no refunds.

C-E **Trinidad**, Calle 62 No 464 esq 55, T999-923 2033, www.hoteltrinidad.com Old house, dorm rooms cheaper, hot water, clean bathrooms, tranquil, courtyard, lovely garden, sun roof. Continental breakfast included. 20% discount with coupon off the website.

D **Casa Becil**, Calle 67 No 550-C, between 66 and 68, T999-924 6764. Convenient for bus station, fan, bath, hot water, clean, safe, popular, English-speaking, quiet, friendly. Rooms on 1st floor light and breezy.

D **Casa Bowen**, corner of Calle 66, No 521-B, near ADO bus station, T999-928 6109. Restored colonial house (better inside than out), often full at weekends, rooms on the main street noisy, bath, hot water but irregular, changes dollars, stores luggage, clean, some rooms with kitchen (no utensils).

D **La Paz**, Calle 62 between 65 and 67, T999-923 9446. Tall, eccentric rooms in old colonial house, some noise in the morning from nearby bus station.

D **Mucuy**, Calle 57 No 481, between 56 and 58, T999-928 5193. Good rooms, , with shower, washing facilities and fridge. 1st-floor rooms are very hot, nice gardens.

D-F **Nómadas Youth Hostal**, Calle 62 No 433, end of Calle 51, 5 blocks north of plaza, T999-924 5223, nomadashostel@hotmail.com Private rooms, dorms and camping, hot water, kitchen, clean, friendly, English-speaking, very helpful, good value, great place to meet other travellers. Free salsa classes.

E **Margarita**, Calle 66 No 506 and 63, T999-923 7236. With shower, clean, good, rooms a bit dark, noisy, cheaper rooms for 5 (3 beds) downstairs near desk, friendly, excellent value.

E **San José**, west of plaza on Calle 63 No 503, T999-928 6657. Bath, hot water, basic, clean, friendly, rooms on top floor are baked by the sun, one of the cheapest, popular with locals, will store luggage, cheap meals, local speciality *poc chuc*.

Uxmal and the Puuc Route *p174*

There is no village at Uxmal, just 3 pricey hotels. For cheaper accommodation, go to Ticul, 28 km away.

A **Club Méditerranée Villa Arqueológica**, Uxmal, T997-928 0644. The best and cheapest of the hotels at the site. Beautiful, close to ruins, good restaurant, excellent service, swimming pool.

D-E **Sierra Sosa**, Calle 26, near Zócalo, Ticul, T997-972 0008. Cheap cell-like rooms, friendly, clean and helpful.

E **San Miguel**, Calle 28, near the market, Ticul, T997-972 0382. Quiet, good value, with parking.

Valladolid *p178*

B **Mesón del Marqués**, north side of Plaza Principal, T985-859 1985. 16th-century mansion oozing character and charm. Restaurant and lobby decorated with gothic chandeliers, Mexican paintings and candles. Arcaded patio with fountain and pool area. Rooms vary so ask to see several; all have TV, a/c and phone. Romantic restaurant.

C **María de la Luz**, Calle 42 No 193-C, Plaza Principal, T985-856 1181. Friendly,

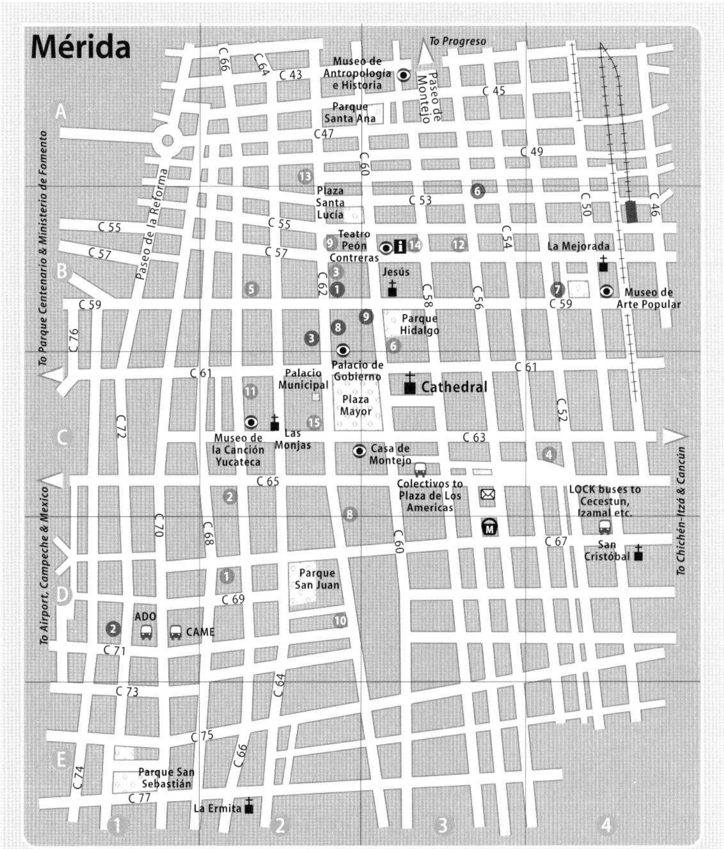

Mérida

Sleeping

Casa Becil **1** *D2*
Casa Bowen **2** *C2*
Casa San Juan **10** *D2*
Colonial **3** *B2*
Dolores Alba **4** *C4*
Gobernador **5** *B2*
Gran **6** *B3*
La Paz **8** *C2*
Margarita **11** *C2*
Mucuy **12** *B3*
Nomadas Youth Hostel **13** *A2*
Posada Toledo **14** *B3*
San José **15** *C2*
Trinidad **9** *B2*

Eating

Amaro **1** *B2*
Café Petropolis **2** *D1*
Café Restaurante Express **9** *B3*
El Trapiche **3** *B2*
La Prosperidad **6** *B3*
Los Almendros **7** *B4*
Pane y Vino **8** *B2*

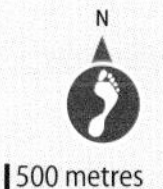

unassuming hotel. Rooms vary, some are dark and musty, but all have cable TV, noisy a/c, fans and decent bathrooms. Small pool area and good restaurant. Buffet breakfast, US$4.50.
C **San Clemente**, Calle 42 No 206, T985-856 2208. Adjacent to the cathedral just off the plaza. Peaceful colonial building with plenty of character, lovely patio and swimming pool. Spacious, clean rooms with cable TV, a/c and fan. Friendly and helpful.
D **María Guadalupe**, Calle 44 No 198, T985-856 2068. Quiet, clean, good value, hot water, fan, washing facilities.
E **Antonio 'Negro' Aguilar**, reservations from Calle 44 No 195, T985-856 2125. Best budget deal in town for 2 or more. Clean, spacious rooms on a quiet street, with garden and volleyball/ basketball court. The rooms are at Calle 41 No 225, before the **Maya Hotel**, but you need to book them at Aguilar's shop.

Ek-Balam *p179*
C-E **Genesis Retreat**, a few mins from the ruins. Ecological retreat. Basic but comfortable screened cabañas, plus 'eco showers', a garden bathtub, coffee shop and bio filtered swimming pool. Lovely gardens to observe wildlife. Maya language classes. Mountain bikes for hire. Restaurant serves wholesome regional dishes, snacks and ice-cream.

Eating

Mérida *p171, map p 181*
There are taco stands, pizzerias and sandwich places in Pasaje Picheta, off the plaza. Branches of **Jugos California** sell fruit salads and juices.
‼‼-‼ **Bologna**, Calle 21 No 117a, Col Itzimná. Great pizza (oven imported from Italy!) and handmade pasta, lovely plaza with hanging pots, live music Fri and Sat.
‼ **Café Continental**, Calle 60 between 55 and 53. Buffet breakfast, 0630-1400, nice setting, classical music.
‼ **Eric's**, Calle 62 between plaza and Calle 57. Huge sandwiches filled with roast chicken or pork, cheap set breakfast.
‼ **La Pérgola** (both drive-in and tables), at corner Calle 56 and 43. Good veal dishes. Warmly recommended. Also in Col Alemán at Calle 24 No 289A.
‼ **La Prosperidad**, Calle 53 y 56. Good Yucatecan food, live entertainment.
‼ **Los Almendros**, Calle 50A No 493 esq 59, in high-vaulted, whitewashed thatched barn. Excellent Yucatán specialities.
‼ **Mr Banderas**, Calle 61 on north side of plaza, T930-9256. Great 1st-floor location overlooking the plaza. Food can be somewhat hit and miss, but for a drink and snack this is a good spot.
‼ **Pane y Vino**, Calle 62, between 59 and 61, T928-6228. Authentic Italian restaurant with superb pasta dishes.
‼ **Pizza Bella** on the main plaza. Good meeting spot, excellent cappuccino.
‼-! **Amaro**, Calle 59 No 507 between 60 and 62, near the plaza. An oasis of tranquillity. Somewhat overpriced but romantic candlelit setting with live music from 2100. Vegetarian dishes, pasta, salads and pizzas. Very popular.
‼-! **Café Restaurante Express**, on Calle 60, at Parque Hidalgo. Traditional coffee house where locals meet, nice atmosphere, good food, including breakfast and *comida corrida*.
‼-! **La Via Olympo**, on main plaza opposite cathedral. Good-value Mexican and Yucatecan dishes, good service and outdoor seating.
! **El Trapiche**, near **Eric's** on Calle 62. Excellent pizzas and freshly made juices.

Cafés and ice cream parlours

Café Petropolis, Calle 70 opposite CAME terminal. Family run and sometimes staffed entirely by children, who do a very good job, turkey a speciality, excellent quality, good *horchata* and herb teas.
El Colón Sorbetes y Dulces Finos, Calle 62 near Colón, 13 blocks from centre. Serving ice-cream since 1907, loads of flavours (explanations in English), plus great sorbets and *meringue*.

Celestún *p172*

Many beachside restaurants along Calle 12, but be careful of food from the cheaper ones and from food stalls along Calle 11 beside the bus station.

‡‡ **Chivirico**, Calle 12, across the road from **Playita**. Decent fish, shrimp and other marine offerings.

‡‡ **El Lobo**, Calle 10 and 13, on the corner of the main square. Best spot for breakfast, with fruit salads, yoghurt, pancakes, etc. Good pizza in the evenings.

‡‡ **La Playita**, Calle 12. Recommended for fried fish and seafood cocktails.

Valladolid *p178*

There's a nice café on the corner of Calle 40 and 39, off the plaza.

‡‡ **La Sirenita**, Calle 34N, between 29 and 31, T985-856 1655, a few blocks east of main square. Highly recommended for seafood, popular and friendly, only open till 1800, closed Sun.

‡‡ **Plaza Maya**, Calle 41 No 235, a few blocks east of main square. Good *comida corrida*, step up from the rest below.

‡ **Cocinas Familiares**, northeast corner of Plaza Principal, next to **Mesón del Marqués**. Yucatecan food and pizzas.

Entertainment

Mérida *p171, map p181*

See the free listings magazine *Yucatán Today,* available at hotels and the tourist office, for other evening activities.

Bars and clubs

There are several good bars on the north side of the plaza, beer is moderate at US$1.20, although food can be expensive. There are a number of live music venues around Parque Santa Lucía, a couple of blocks from the main plaza.

El Establo, Calle 60, towards the main plaza, upstairs from the street. Daily 2100-0230. Live local bands, plus occasional Cuban cabaret entertainers. Free entry, drinks from US$2.

El Trovador Bohemio, Parque Santa Lucía. Folk trios in a tiny '50s Las Vegas- style setting, cover charge US$1, beer US$2.

El Tucho, Calle 60, near University. A restaurant, open till 2100 only, with live music, often guest performers from Cuba.

Cinema

There is a cinema showing subtitled films in English on Parque Hidalgo; also try **Cine Plaza Internacional**, Calle 58 between 59 and 57.

Cinepolis, Plaza de las Américas, north of the city. 14-screen multiplex. *Colectivos* and buses from Calle 65 between 58 and 60.

Teatro Mérida, Calle 62 between 59 and 61. European, Mexican and independent movies as well as theatre productions.

Theatre

Teatro Peón Contreras, Calle 60 with 57. Ballet and theatre performances at 2100, US$4. The University also puts on many theatre and dance productions.

Valladolid *p178*

Bars and clubs

El Zaguán, Calle 41 and 41A, 2 blocks west of the plaza. One of the few places serving alcohol without a meal, plant-filled courtyard, music, open till 0300.

Festivals and events

Mérida *p171, map p181*

Every **Sun** the central streets are closed off to traffic, for live music and parades.

6 Jan Mérida celebrates its birthday.

Carnival takes place the week before **Ash Wed** (best on Sat), with floats, dancers in regional costume, music and dancing around the plaza and children dressed in animal suits.

Río Lagartos *p179*

17 Jul Big local **fiesta**, with music, food and dancing in the plaza.

12 Dec Virgen de Guadalupe. The whole village converges on the chapel built in 1976 on the site of a vision of the Virgin Mary by a local non-believer, who

Top tips

Know your hammock

Different materials are available for hammocks: **Sisal** is very strong, light, hard-wearing but rather scratchy and uncomfortable; it can be identified by its distinctive smell. **Cotton** is soft, flexible, comfortable, not as hard-wearing but good for four to five years of everyday use with care. It is not possible to weave cotton and sisal together, although you may be told otherwise. **Cotton/silk** mixtures are offered, but will probably be made with artificial silk. **Nylon** is very strong and light but hot in hot weather and cold in cold weather. For a selection of recommended outlets, see Shopping, p184.

⊗ Never buy your first hammock from a street vendor and never accept a packaged hammock without checking the size and quality.
✔ The surest way to judge a good hammock is by weight: 1,500 g (3.3 lb) is a fine item, under 1 kg (2.2 lb) is junk (advises Alan Handleman, a US expert).
✔ Look for a hammock woven from lots of fine and thin strands of material; the more strands there are, the more comfortable the hammock will be. The best are the so-called 3-ply, but they are difficult to find. There are three sizes: single (sometimes called *doble*), matrimonial and family (buy a matrimonial at least for comfort). If judging by end-strings, 50 would be sufficient for a child, 150 would suit a medium-sized adult, 250 a couple.
✔ Prices vary considerably so shop around. Always bargain hard, the salesmen are pushy, but they expect to receive about half their original asking price.
✔ Huge, excellent quality hammocks are sold in Chichén Itzá by Mario Díaz (a most interesting character), at his house 500 m up the road forking to the left at the centre of the village.

suddenly died, along with his dog, shortly after the vision.

Shopping

Mérida *p171, map p181*

Crafts and souvenirs

Souvenir shops are dotted in the streets around the plaza. They all specialize in hammocks (see p184 and below) but also sell silver jewellery from Taxco, Panama hats, *guayabera* shirts, *huaraches* (sandals with car-tyre soles), baskets and Maya figurines. Always bargain hard.

There are several good silver and antiques shops on Calle 60 between 51 and 53. Calle 62, between Calle 57 y 61, is lined with *guayabera* shops, all of a similar price and quality. Embroidered *huipil* blouses cost about US$25. There's also a good, cheap *guayabera* shop on northwest corner of Parque San Juan, with prices half those of the souvenir shops in the centre. Clothes shopping is good along Calle 65 and in the **García Rejón Bazaar**, Calle 65 y 60. Good leather *huaraches* sandals, robust and comfortable, from the market, US$10. Excellent cowboy boots for men and women, maximum size 10, can be bought around the market for US$46.

Top tips

Cycle Yucatán

Hire a bike in Valladolid from Antonio Aguilar, who owns a sporting goods store at Calle 41 No 225, between calles 48 and 50, and explore the surrounding flat countryside on two wheels. You can cycle to the cenote at Dzitnup in 25 minutes (Antonio will explain the best route before you set off). Or stick your bike on the roof of a *colectivo* leaving for Temozón from outside the Hotel María Guadalupe, and ask to be dropped off at the turning for Ek-Balam. From there, it's a 12 km cycle ride to the ruins.

Bacho Arte Mexicano, Calle 60 No 466 between Calle 53 and 55. Silver, jewellery and ornaments.
El Becaliño, Calle 65 No 483, esq 56A, opposite post office. Good Panama hats.
Mercado de Artesanías, on Calle 67 between 56 and 58. The main handicraft market. Lovely crafts but high prices and pushy salespeople. Good postcards. There is a smaller handicraft market on Calle 62, 1 block from the plaza.
Miniaturas, Calle 59 No 507A, near plaza. Traditional folk art, Day of the Dead miniatures, wrestling masks.
Paty, Calle 64 No 549 between Calle 67 and 69. Stocks reputable 'Kary' brand *guayaberas* and hammocks.

Hammocks

The following outlets are recommended; but shop around for prices and quality: **El Aguacate**, Calle 58 No 604, corner of Calle 73, good hammocks and helpful, no hard sell, but bargaining possible if buying several items, another branch on Calle 62 opposite El Trapiche; **El Campesino**, in the market, Eustaquio Canul Cahum and family will let you watch the weaving; **El Hamaquero**, Calle 58 No 572, between 69 and 71, popular, but beware the very hard sell; **Jorge Razu**, Calle 56 No 516B between 63A and 63, very convincing salesman, accepts TCs at good rates, recommended; **Tita**, Calle 59 between Calle 60 and 62, sisal hammocks only, enthusiastic hard sell, good selection, demonstrations.

Activities and tours

Mérida *p171, map p181*

Guides

Miguel Angel Vergara, Centro de Estudios Maya Haltun-Ha, T999-927 1172, PO Box 97148. Recommended for guided tours to Chichén Itzá, US$37 per group of any size; many languages available.
Wilbert Torres Campos, T999-922 3553 or through the **Sindicato de Guías de Yucatán**, T924-8656. An excellent guide with well over 20 years' experience. Especially knowledgeable on Maya sites. Transport arranged.

Tour operators

Carmen Travel Services, Hotel María del Carmen, Calle 63 No 550 y Calle 68, T999-923 9133, 3 other branches.
Mayaland Tours, in Hotel Casa del Balam, T999-926 3851, and at Fiesta Americana, T999-925 0622. Will reserve rooms in their hotel at Chichén Itzá.
Yucatán Trails, Calle 62 No 482 between 57 and 59, T999-928 2582, yucatantrails@hotmail.com Tours to all the popular local destinations.

Río Lagartos *p179*

Boat trips

Early morning boat trips to see the flamingoes, US$35 for 8-9 seater, 2½-4 hrs, cheaper in 5 seater, fix the price before embarking.

Transport

Mérida *p171, map p181*

Air

Aeropuerto Rejón has lots of flights to **Mexico City** daily, 1¾ hrs. Other internal flights to **Cancún**, **Chetumal**, **Huatulco**, **Oaxaca**, **Palenque**, **Tuxtla Gutiérrez**, **Veracruz** and **Villahermosa**.

Airline offices AeroCaribe, Paseo Montejo 500B, T999-928 6790. **Aerolíneas Aztecas**, T01-800-229-8322. **AeroMéxico**, Av Colón 451 and Montejo, T999-920 1260. **Aviacsa**, T999-926 9087. **Aviateca**, T999-926 9087. **Mexicana**, Calle 58 No 500 esq 61, T999-924 6633, and Paseo Montejo 493.

Bus

Schedules often change. Get up-to-date information at www.yucatantoday.com /transportation/eng-bus-lines.htm

Long distance All depart from CAME terminal, Calle 70 No 555, unless otherwise stated. To **Mexico City**, 24-28 hrs, about 6 rest stops, US$78 (**ADO**, 5 a day); direct **Pullman** bus 1400 and 1700. To **Campeche**, 2nd-class ADO Terminal, via **Uxmal**, **ATS**, 6 a day 0630-1900, 2½ hrs, US$5.50; 1st-class (not via Uxmal), ADO, 8 daily, 2½ hrs, US$9. To **Cancún**, **Autobuses de Oriente**, every hr 0600-2400; 2nd class, US$12; 1st class, US$16; *plus*, US$20, 4½ hrs; for **Isla Mujeres**, ask the driver to drop you at Puerto Juárez. Buses to and from Cancún stop at Calle 50, between Calle 65 and 67. To **Chetumal**, 0730, 1300, 1800 and 2300, 7 hrs, US$18. To **Emiliano Zapata**, 5 buses a day, US$23. To **Palenque**, from ADO terminal, 0830 or 2200, US$25, also 2330, US$22, 8 hrs; **Cristóbal Colón** luxury service US$28; alternatively take bus to either Playas de Catazajá or Emiliano Zapata and change. To **San Cristóbal de las Casas**, 0700 or 1915, US$31, **Autotransportes del Sureste de Yucatán**; also **Cristóbal Colón**, 1915 and 2345. To **Tulum**, 2nd class, several daily, 6 hrs, US$12. To **Tuxtla Gutiérrez**, **Autotransportes del Sureste de Yucatán**, 1st class daily 1330, via Villahermosa and Campeche, arrives 0630 next day, US$35; also **Cristóbal Colón**, US$30. To **Valladolid**, 1st express, US$8; 2nd class, 9 daily, US$6.

Local Buses to **Celestún** depart every 1-2 hrs from Calle 71, between 64 and 66, 2nd class, frequent departures, 2 hrs, US$3.50 and from Calle 67 between 50 and 52. To **Telchaquillo** (for Mayapan), every 30 mins from Calle 50 y 67 behind the municipal market, US$1, 1 hr. To **Chichén Itzá**, ADO 2nd class, 2½ hrs, US$4, from 0500, bus station on Calle 71 between 64 and 66. 1st-class bus, US$5.80. To **Uzmal**, from terminal on Calle 69 between 68 and 70, 6 daily, US$1.80 (see also below). To **Izamal**, from Calle 50 between Calle 65 and 67, 2nd class, every 45 mins, 1½ hrs, US$1.50, through lovely countryside.

Car

Car hire firms charge around US$40-45 a day although bargains can be found in low season. Most agencies have an office at the airport. **Alamo**, at the airport, T999-946 1623; **Executive**, Calle 60, down from Gran Hotel, good value; **Hertz**, Calle 55 No 479, esq 54, T999-924 2834.

Taxi

24-hr radio taxis on Parque Hidalgo, T999-928 5328, are cheaper than the VWs that you flag down. In both types, fix the fare before the journey; there are set prices depending on the distance.

Uxmal and the Puuc Route *p174*

Bus

The **Ruta Puuc** bus to Uxmal, Kabah, Sayil, Xlapak and Labná departs from the 1st-class bus station in Mérida, Mon-Sat, 0800, US$7, entry to sites not included. This is a good whistle-stop tour, but does not give you much time at the ruins. Public buses to **Uxmal** (see Mérida transport, above), return to **Mérida** every

2 hrs; alternatively go to the main road and catch a *colectivo* to **Muná**, US$0.50, for frequent connections to Mérida.

Izamal *p173*

Bus

Bus station is on Calle 32 behind government offices, with left luggage facility. 2nd class to **Mérida**, every 45 mins, 1½ hrs, US$1.50. To **Valladolid** (96 km), 6 daily, about 2 hrs, US$2.30-3.

Chichén Itzá *p176*

Bus

Buses drop off and pick up passengers at the top of the coach park opposite entrance to the *artesanía* market. To/from **Mérida**, with ADO (see above). Note that Mon morning 2nd-class buses from Mérida may be full with workers returning to Cancún. Return tickets from the gift shop near entrance; last departure from Chichén Itzá, 1700. To/from **Valladolid**, buses hourly, 45 mins, US$2, (0715 bus reaches the ruins at 0800 when they open); return by standing on the main road at Pisté, 1 km from the entrance and flagging down any bus going straight through, US$1.50. *Colectivos* from the ruins to Valladolid, US$2.30. Also buses to/from **Cancún** and **Puerto Juárez**, many daily, 0430-2300, US$8. To **Tulum**, 1330 and 1445, 4 hrs, very crowded; also from Pisté, 1300, US$4.

Valladolid *p178*

Bus

The main bus terminal is on Calle 37 and Calle 54. To **Cancún**, Express Oriente, 9 a day, 3 hrs, US$6; Avante, 3 a day, US$8. To **Chichén Itzá**, 10 a day, 45 mins, US$2. To **Izamal**, 2 a day, 2 hrs, US$3.80. To **Mérida**, via Chichén Itzá, 9 a day, US$7-8. To **Playa del Carmen**, 9 a day, 4 hrs, US$8. To **Tizimín**, 10 a day, 2 hrs, US$2 (single or return); from here, bus or taxi (US$25) to **Río Lagartos**. To **Tulum**, 1400 and 1550, 1½ hrs, US$4.

Directory

Mérida *p171, map p181*

Banks Banamex, at Calle 56 and 59 (Mon-Fri 0900-1300, 1600-1700), ATM, quick service, good rates. Many banks on Calle 65, off the plaza. **Embassies and consulates** Belize (also British Vice Consul), Major A Dutton, Calle 58-53 No 450, T999-928 6152, 0900-1600. Canada, Av Colón, 309-D, T925-6419. **Hospitals** Red Cross, T999-924 9813. Centro Médico de las Américas (CMA), Calle 54 No 365 between 33A and Av Pérez Ponce. T999-926 2619, emergencies T999-927 3199. **Internet** Multitude of internet cafés, charging US$1-1.50. **Language schools** Instituto de Español, Calle 29, Col México, T999-927 1683. Modern Spanish Institute, Calle 29 No 128, between 26 and 28, Col México, T999-927 1683, www.modernspanish.com. **Laundry** Lavandería La Fe, Calle 61 No 518, between Calle 62 and 64. US$3.30 for 3 kg. **Post office** Calle 65 and 56. Accepts unsealed parcels for surface mail to US, airmail to Europe, US$15 for 5 kg. Also branches at airport (for quick delivery) or on Calle 58. DHL, Av Colón good service.

Valladolid *p178*

Banks Bancomer on east side of square, changes TCs 0900-1330. Banco del Sureste has a branch in the shopping centre on Calle 39, 5 blocks west from the plaza. Mon-Fri 0900-2100, Sat and Sun 0900-1400, 1700-1930. **Internet** Many internet cafés throughout town. **Laundry** Teresita, Calle 33 between 40 and 42, US$6 for 5½ kg. **Post office** East side of plaza, 0800-1500. **Telephone** Telmex, Calle 42, north of square; expensive; Computel at bus station and next to Hotel San Clemente.

Quintana Roo

The state of Quintana Roo is the largest tourist area in Mexico, encompassing the international resorts of Cancún, Isla Mujeres and Cozumel and the 100-km corridor south to Tulum. This coast is also the main area for diving and watersports in the Yucatán. Some dive sites have been spoiled by overexploitation but, further from the shore, there is still much reef life to enjoy. Diving is also possible in underwater caves or cenotes. If Cancún is your port of entry to the region, make the most of its beautiful beaches, tours and restaurants before moving on to more inspiring destinations, such as the Maya ruins of Tulum or Cobá or the wilderness reserve of Sian Ka'an. In the far south, Chetumal is the stepping-off point for travel to Belize and Guatemala.

Getting there Frequent buses to Cancún. Flights to Cancún and Cozumel.

Getting around Good local and long-distance buses along the coast.

Time required Up to 2 weeks to include some beach time.

Weather Hot and dry.

Sleeping All-inclusive beach resorts and laidback cabañas.

Eating International – more Mexican-themed than authentic.

Activities and tours Diving, watersports.

★ **Don't miss...** the ancient Maya cities of Tulum and Cobá ▸▸ *pp 195 and 196*

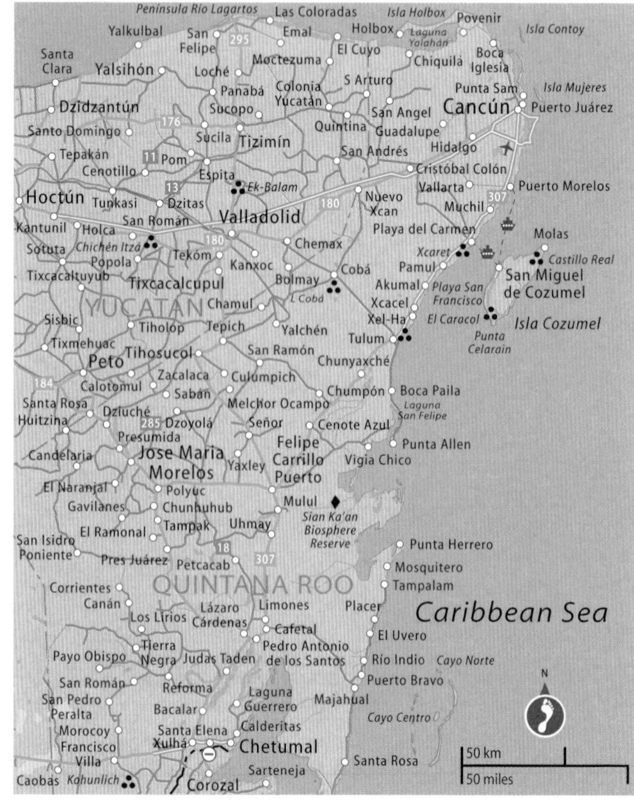

Cancún pp198-213

Before Cancún was 'discovered' by the Mexican tourist board in 1970, it was an inaccessible strip of barren land with stunning beaches; the only road went straight past to Puerto Juárez for the ferry to Isla Mujeres, which had been a national tourist destination since the 1950s. Massive international investment and government sponsorship, however, saw the luxury resort of Cancún completed within 25 years and it is now Mexico's premier tourist destination.

The 25-km **Hotel Zone**, set on a narrow strip of land in the shape of a number seven alongside the coast, is an ultra-modern American-style boulevard, with five-star hotels, high-tech nightclubs, high-class shopping malls and fastfood chains. Every hotel has its own strip of white-sand beach; the beaches are supposedly public but locals complain of being refused entry.

Cancún city (or **Downtown**, as it is known locally) lies just inland and is a world apart from the Hotel Zone. It evolved from temporary shacks housing the thousands of builders working on the development, and is now a massive city with very little character. The main road through the city is Avenida Tulum, where the handicraft market, the main shops, banks and the municipal tourist office are all located. There are also restaurants here but the better ones are along Avenida Yaxchilán, which is also the main centre for nightlife.

Ins and outs

Getting there Cancún International Airport (CUN) is 16 km south of Downtown. There are two terminals, Main and South (or 'FBO' building), connected by white shuttle minibuses. The airport has expensive shops, restaurants, a tourist information kiosk, hotel reservation agencies (no rooms under US$45) and a *casa de cambio* with poor rates. A *colectivo* taxi to either the Hotel Zone or Downtown costs US$9; pay at the kiosk outside the airport. Buses run to/from Downtown every 30 minutes, via Avenida Tulum, where there are bus stops marked 'Aeropuerto', US$0.50. For flight information p17 and 21.

Cancún **bus** terminal, at the junction of Avenidas Tulum and Uxmal, is the hub for routes west to Mérida and south to Tulum and Chetumal. It is small, well organized and handy for the cheaper hostels, open 24 hrs, left luggage US$0.55 per hr. In the peak, winter season, buses tend to fill up very quickly and prices increase by 50%. There is also a bus terminal at **Puerto Juárez**, the dock for ferries to Isla Mujeres (see page 190) but services from here are less frequent. p208

Getting around Ruta 1 buses run 24 hours from Downtown to the Hotel Zone via Avenida Tulum, US$0.60; Ruta 2 runs from Downtown to the Hotel Zone, 0500-0330, via Avenida Cobá and the bus terminal, US$0.60. Buses to Puerto Juárez, US$0.55, leave from outside **Cinema Royal**, opposite the bus terminal. Taxis are abundant; flat rate for the centre is US$1-1.50; Hotel Zone from centre US$3; Puerto Juárez US$3 (but beware overcharging). Many taxis stop at **El Crucero**, the junction of Avenida Tulum and Avenida López Portillo, but there are often queues.

Cancún

 Tourist information The **tourist office** ⓘ *Av Tulum 26, www.qroo.gob.mx*, is not very helpful (typically for Quintana Roo state); most tourists seem to get palmed off with a glossy pocket guide to Cancún full of adverts for expensive restaurants. A better bet is the new and well-equipped **conventions and visitor bureau** ⓘ *corner of Av Cobá and Av Bonampak, T998-884 6531*, where the staff are helpful and friendly, with information on new attractions, hotels and excursions.

Isla Mujeres » pp198-213

The name Isla Mujeres refers to the large number of clay female idols found by the Spaniards on the island in 1518. The island is a refreshing antidote to the urban sprawl of Cancún and a good place to relax for a few days away from the hurly-burly of package tourism. It is especially pleasant in the evening, when all the Cancún day-trippers have gone. Isla Mujeres town, at the north end of the island, is strictly low-rise, with brightly coloured buildings giving it a Caribbean feel. The island's laws prohibit the construction of any building higher than three floors, and US franchises such as **McDonald's** and **Walmart** are not allowed to open branches here. Restaurants and nightspots are plentiful and good quality, however, and are cheaper than those on the mainland.

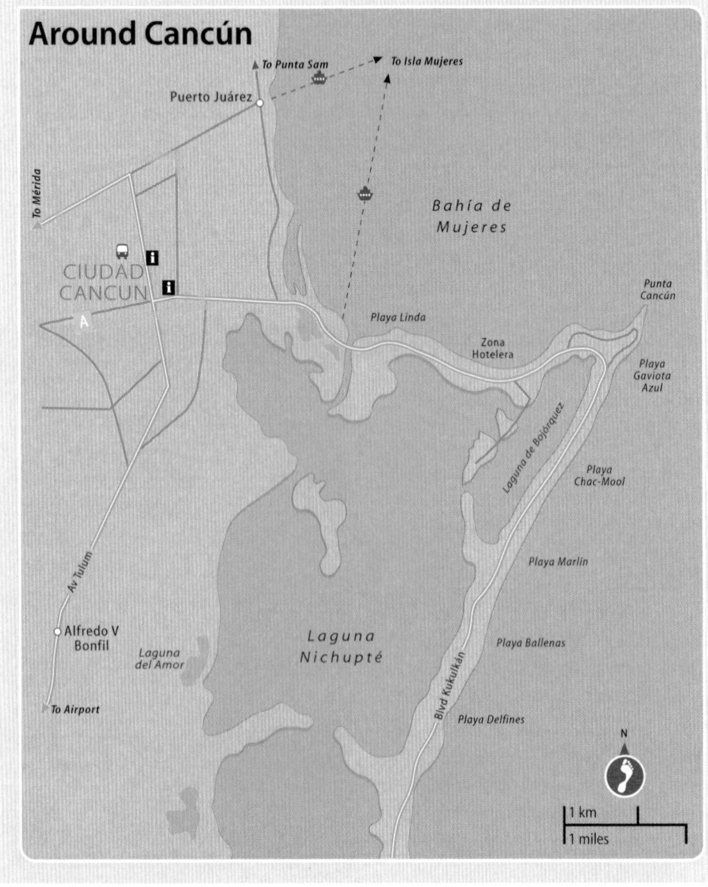

El Garrafón, Isla Mujeres

Ins and outs

Getting there and around Passenger ferries to the island depart from **Puerto Juárez**, 3 km north of Downtown Cancún; regular buses, US$0.50. There are also services from **Playa Linda Pier** in Cancún, between Downtown and the Zona Hotelera, but these are more expensive. Car ferries depart from **Punta Sam**, north of Puerto Juárez. There are several ways to explore the island: you can rent a golf cart, many of which chug around the streets all day, good for families; mopeds and bicycles are cheap and plentiful to rent, and a public bus runs all the way from the town to El Paraíso, towards the south of the island. » *p208.*

Tourist information The **tourist office** ⓘ *Rueda Medina, opposite the ferry dock, Mon-Fri 0900-2100, Sat 0900-1400, www.isla-mujeres.net*, is helpful. Immigration is next door.

Sights

There are several good beaches on Isla Mujeres, the best being **Playa Cocos** on the northwest coast, five minutes' walk from the town. Further south, there are several places to swim, snorkel and observe marine life. Most of the sights south of the town can be seen in a day.

On the east coast, **Playa Paraíso** is an expensive mini-resort for Cancún day-trippers that offers swimming with nurse sharks; a touristy experience not recommended. You have to pay US$1 to **Restaurant Playa Paraíso** for access to the beach. Instead visit the **Turtle Farm** ⓘ *5 km from town, T998-877 0595, daily 0900-1700, US$1, bus to Playa Paraíso, then 5 min walk back along the main road*, where hundreds of sea turtles are kept in humane conditions.

At the centre of the island, marked by a big, new arched gate, are the curious remains of **Casa de Mundaca** ⓘ *Daily 0900-1700, US$1*. Paths have been laid out among the large trees, but there's little to see of the original estate, called Vista Alegre, that the slave-trader and buccaneer, Fermín Mundaca, built for his teenage sweetheart. She rejected him and he died, broken-hearted, in Mérida. To get there, get off the bus at the final stop, and turn the opposite way to the beach; the house is a short walk away.

From the bus stop at Playa Paraíso, a 30-minute walk along the coast will bring you to **El Garrafón** ⓘ *7 km from town, T998-877 1100 snorkelling US$15, lockers US$2 plus deposit, equipment rental available*, a beach and snorkelling centre that is being developed into a luxury resort in the style of Xcaret on the mainland (page 192). The snorkelling is good past the pier, along a reef with some dead coral, where large numbers of different coloured fish can be seen at very close range. You can also take a boat out to snorkel around a 12-m bronze cross submerged offshore (US$13, 1½ hrs, no lunch).

A further 15 minutes' walk from El Garrafón, at the tip of the island, are the ruins of the **Santuario Maya a la Diosa Ixchel**, dedicated to Ixchel the goddess of the moon and fertility. This is the only known Maya shrine to a female deity. Unfortunately, much to the anger of locals, the ruins are no longer free to visit as they are part of the newly developed **El Garrafón 'National Park'** ⓘ *Daily 0900-1730, US$5.50.* A cultural centre has also been built here, with large sculptures by several international artists.

South of Cancún » pp198-213

The fast highway south of Cancún has opened up the Quintana Roo coast to rapid development. Once-deserted beaches and small villages along the so-called 'Riviera Maya' have been transformed into all-inclusive resorts catering for the overspill of tourists from Cancún, often with little regard for social or environmental concerns. However, there are still some places that have held out against the developers, where you can enjoy the stunning coastline in its natural state.

Playa del Carmen

What used to be a pleasant fishing village on the beach has been rapidly developed for tourism but Playa, as it is known locally, has not had the high-rise treatment of Cancún. The beach is dazzling white, with crystal-clear shallow water, ideal for swimming and, further out, there is good scuba diving. There is accommodation for every budget, and plenty of good restaurants and bars of every description. Many travellers choose Playa as their base for trips to Tulum in the south and Cobá in the interior. A new **tourist office** ⓘ *corner of Av Juárez and Av 15, T984-873 0263*, provides useful information and maps. The kiosk on the main plaza will provide a copy of *Destination Playa del Carmen,* a useful guide with maps.

Riviera Maya

Three hours' walk south along the beach from Playa del Carmen is the Maya site of **Xcaret** ⓘ *T987-883 3143, www.xcaret.net, US$49, under 5s free, taxis and tour buses from Playa del Carmen or Cancún.* This was originally an ancient port called Polé, the departure point for voyages to Cozumel, but it has now been turned into an overpriced and very tacky themepark, catering exclusively for day-trippers. The ruins are 1 km from the entrance. Just to the south, **Paamul**, is a fine beach on a bay, with snorkelling and diving on the reef, a few metres off shore. Access to much of the beach is restricted to hotel guests but green and loggerhead turtles also manage to lay their eggs here from June to August. They also venture ashore at **Akumal**, another luxury resort, 20 km north of Tulum, that stretches around a series of sandy bays. Their most important nesting ground, however, is further south at **Xcacel**, a beautiful beach that, for the moment at least, is protected from development.

Now a national park, **Laguna Xel-Há** ⓘ *13 km north of Tulum, daily 0800-1630, US$10, snorkel US$7, locker US$1, bus from Playa del Carmen, 45 mins*, is a beautiful clear lagoon full of fish and surrounded by jungle. The area has been developed with bungalows, first-class hotels and expensive fast-food restaurants and the lagoon is teeming with tourists for much of the day, so arrive as early as possible to see the fish. Xel-Há ruins, known also as **Los Basadres** are located across the road from the beach. There is a beautiful cenote at the end of the ruins where you can swim. Closer to Tulum, at **Tancáh**, are newly discovered bright Post-classical Maya murals, but they are often closed to the public.

Cozumel

Cozumel » pp198-213

Travellers looking for a beach holiday will find the island disappointing compared to Playa del Carmen. There is only one nice beach on the west side and most of the eastern, Atlantic coast is far too rugged and choppy for swimming. Tour groups arrive daily off cruises from Miami and Cancún, and the island's services seem geared towards this type of visitor. But Cozumel is also a mecca for scuba divers, with many beautiful offshore reefs to explore, as well as much interesting marine and birdlife. There are at least 20 major dive sites.

Ins and outs

Getting there and around The **airport** is just north of San Miguel with a minibus shuttle service to the hotels. There are 10-minute flights to and from Playa del Carmen, as well as flights to Mexico City, Cancún, Chichén Itzá and Houston (Texas). The passenger **ferry** from Playa del Carmen runs every two hours, and a car ferry leaves twice daily from **Puerto Morelos**, a quiet little village 34 km south of Cancún. There is no bus service on the island, but taxis are plentiful. The best way to get around, however, is by hired moped or bicycle. San Miguel is small enough to explore on foot. » *p208.*

San Miguel de Cozumel and around

The island's only town is a seedy, overpriced version of Playa del Carmen, with very little character. Passenger ferries dock right next to the main plaza. On the waterfront to the north is the **Museo de la Isla** ⓘ *between Calle 4 and 6, US$3.30,* which provides a well-laid-out history of the island. It has a bookshop, art gallery and rooftop restaurant, which has excellent food and sunset views. North of San Miguel is the **Zona Hotelera Norte**. The beaches here are sandy and wide but the cleanest ones are accessible only through the hotels. Hotels also line the coast south of town, around the cruise ship terminal and car ferry dock.

Exploring the island

Northeast of San Miguel are the restored Maya-Toltec ruins of **San Gervasio** ⓘ *7 km from Cozumel town (take the continuation of Av Juárez), then 6 km to the left up a paved road (toll US$1), daily 0700-1700, US$3.50, guides available, or buy a self-guiding booklet, US$1.* This interesting site is quite spread out, with *sacbés* (sacred roads) between the groups of buildings. There are no large structures, but a nice plaza, an arch, and pigment can be seen in places. It is also a pleasant place to listen to birdsong and spot butterflies, lizards and landcrabs. There are more archaeological sites, such **Castillo Real**, on the island's northeastern coast, heading towards Punta Molas. However, the road to this part of the island is in very bad condition (unsuitable for normal vehicles) and the ruins themselves are small.

On the west coast, **Playa San Francisco**, though not wide, is good, clean and very popular (lockers at **Pancho's**) but other beaches south of San Miguel are generally narrow and rocky. However, there's good (free) snorkelling in front of **Hotel Las Glorias**, 15 minutes' walk south from the ferry; at **Playa Corona**, further south, where's there's a small restaurant and pier; and at **Xul-Ha**, further south still, which has a bar and beach chairs. The Caribbean coast is rockier than the west coast and very picturesque but swimming and diving here can be very dangerous due to hidden currents. The safest spot is at sheltered **Chen Río**, where rocks protect swimmers from the undertow. **Punta Morena** is a surf beach, with good seafood (try the *ceviche*) and accommodation, contact Matt at **Deep Blue**, on Salas 200, for more information and transport. Also visit **Punta Chiqueros** which has a restaurant and bathing, and **El Mirador**, a low viewpoint with sea-worn rocks.

South of the southern hotel zone is **Parque Chankanab** ⓘ *9 km from San Miguel, 0800-1600, US$4, lockers US$2, snorkelling mask and fins US$5, use of underwater camera US$25*, based around an idyllic lagoon behind the beach. The lagoon is crystal clear and offers

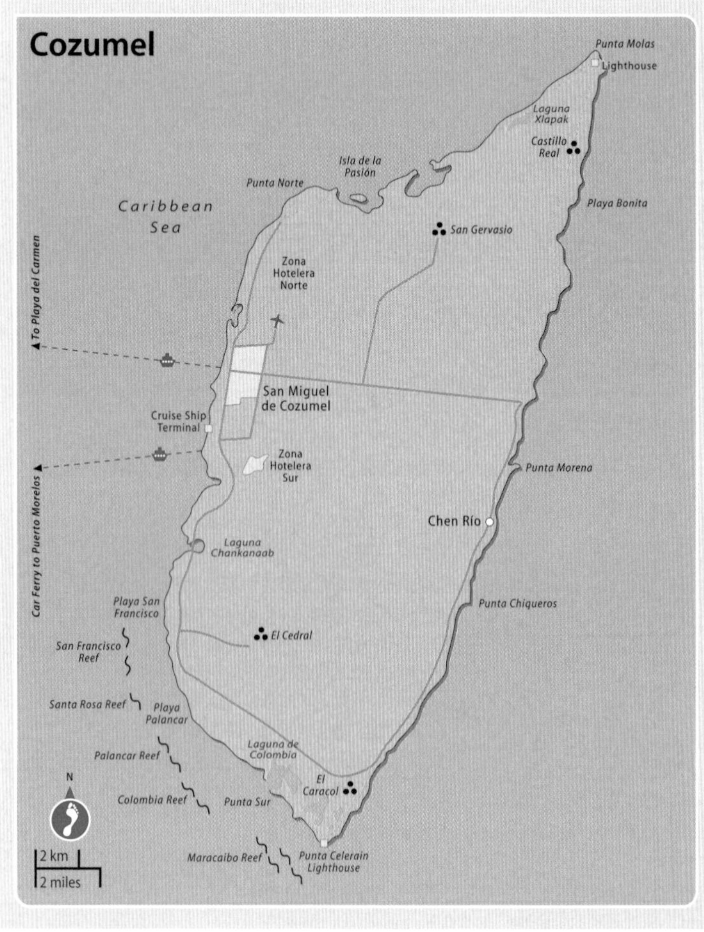

Tulum

swimming, snorkelling, a botanical garden with local and imported plants, a 'Maya Area' (rather artificial), dive shops, souvenirs and expensive but good restaurants. Head 3 km inland from the main road to reach **El Cedral**, a two-room temple, overgrown with trees. It stands in the centre of the village of the same name, which has large, permanent shelters for agricultural shows, rug sellers and locals who pose with *iguanas doradas* (golden iguanas).

Covering the southern end of the island is the **Punta Sur Ecological Reserve** ⓘ *T872-0914, www.cozumelparks.com.mx*, an ecotourism development, with a variety of natural landscapes, lagoons and mangrove jungles. A snorkelling centre has opened here as well as a viewing platform. Also here is **El Caracol**, a Maya site where the sun, in the form of a shell, was worshipped. The lighthouse at **Punta Celarain** is 1 km further on.

Tulum and around » *pp198-213*

Tulum

ⓘ *500 m east of Highway 307. Daily 0800-1800 (allow 2 hrs to view at leisure). US$3.50. Guide books can be bought in the shops at the entrance (*Panorama *guide is recommended); local tour guides can also be hired. Buses drop passengers at El Crucero, 500 m north of the car park (US$1.50); a small train runs from the car park to the ruins, US$1, or it is an easy 500 m walk.*

The Maya-Toltec ruins of Tulum are perched on coastal cliffs in a beautiful setting above the azure sea, with city walls of white stone. The ruins are 12th century and were dedicated to the worship of the Falling God, or the Setting Sun, represented on nearly all the west-facing doors (Cozumel was the home of the Rising Sun). The same idea is reflected in the buildings, which are wider at the top than at the bottom.

The main structure is the **Castillo**, which commands a view of both the sea and the forested Quintana Roo lowlands to the west. All the Castillo's doorways face west. To the left of the Castillo is the temple of the **Falling God**, which aligns with the pillar and the back door in the **House of the Chultún**. The majority of the main structures are roped off so that you cannot climb the Castillo, nor get close to the surviving frescoes on the **Temple of the Frescoes**. Tulum is usually crowded with tourists, so try to visit between 0800 and 0900 for a more peaceful experience. Take a towel and swimsuit if you wish to scramble down from the ruins to one of the two white-sand beaches for a swim.

Tulum town and the beach

Public buses drop passengers at **El Crucero**, 500 m north of the new access road to the ruins. The village of **Tulum** is 4 km south of El Crucero on the main highway. It is not very large but many new hotels and restaurants have sprung up recently, turning Tulum Avenue into a lively spot. **Tourist information** is next to the police station, two blocks north of the bus terminal but the **Weary Traveller** backpacker centre (page 201) has taken over as the primary source of information for this area. Also try the **Sian Ka'an Information Centre** ⓘ *Av Tulum between Satélite and Géminis, Tulum, T/F871-2363, siankaan_tours@hotmail.com*, which has information about the reserve and other sights.

Just over a kilometre south of El Crucero, a paved road leads west to **Cobá** (see below) or east towards the coast, where it turns south to **Boca Paila**. This stretch of coast, from just south of the ruins to the edge of the Sian Ka'an Biosphere Reserve, is lined with cabañas that make the most of the stunning white sand, warm turquoise sea and laidback beach vibe. Backpackers have flocked here for years but there are now some more upmarket places to stay too. The reef is from 600 m to 1,000 m from the shore, so if you wish to snorkel you will need to take a boat trip.

Cobá

ⓘ *47 km from Tulum towards Valladolid. Daily 0800-1700. US$3.50.*

An important Maya city in the eighth and ninth centuries AD, with a population of around 45,000, Cobá was abandoned for unknown reasons. You will not find the great array of buildings here that can be seen at Chichén Itzá or Uxmal; instead, the delight of this large but little-excavated city is its setting in the jungle, surrounded by birds, butterflies, spiders and lizards. The paved road ends at **Lago Cobá**, with the ruins to the left; a second lake, **Lago Macanxoc**, lies within the site. There are turtles and fish in the lakes and toucans and mot-mots to be seen in the early morning but take insect repellent.

The many uncovered structures at Cobá hint at the vastness of the city in its heyday, when it covered around 70 sq km. An unusual feature is the network of ancient roads, known as *sacbés*, which connect the groups in the site and are known to have extended across the entire Maya Yucatán. Over 40 *sacbés* pass through Cobá, some local, some of great length, including a 100-km route to Yaxuná in Yucatán state. The main cluster of buildings are known as the **Cobá Group**, with views of the surrounding jungle and lakes from the summit of the 'Iglesia', the tallest structure. There are three other groups of buildings to visit: the **Macanxoc Group**, mainly stelae, about 1½ km from the Cobá Group; **Las Pinturas**, 1km northeast of Macanxoc, with a temple and the remains of other buildings that had columns in their construction, and the **Nohoch Mul Group**, at least another kilometre from Las Pinturas. Nohoch Mul includes the tallest pyramid in the northern Yucatán, a magnificent structure, from which the views of the jungle on all sides are superb.

Cobá

Cobá is becoming more popular as a destination for tourist buses, which arrive at 1030, so get to the ruins early to avoid the crowds and the heat. The guards at the site are very strict about opening and closing time so it is hard to get in to see the dawn or sunset.

Sian Ka'an Biosphere Reserve

ⓘ *Daily 0900-1500, 1800-2000. For all information, go to the office of Los Amigos de Sian Ka'an, Plaza América, Av Cobá 5, 3rd floor, suites 48-50, Cancún (Apdo Postal 770, 77500 Cancún, T998-884 9583, sian@cancun.rce.com.mx); very helpful.*

This reserve covers 4,500 sq km of the Quintana Roo coast. About one-third is tropical forest, one-third is savannah and mangrove and one-third coastal and marine habitats, including 110 km of barrier reef. Mammals include jaguar, puma, ocelot and other cats, monkeys, tapir, peccaries, manatee and deer; turtles nest on the beaches; crocodiles occupy the mangroves and there is a wide variety of land and aquatic birds. It is possible to drive into the Reserve from Tulum as far as **Punta Allen** (58 km; the road is not clearly marked and the final section is badly potholed); beyond that you need a launch. From the south it is possible to drive to **Punta Herrero** via Cafetal and Majahual (unmade road). Do not try to get there independently without a car. To see other parts of the reserve, join a tour from either Cancún or Tulum. ▸▸ *p205.*

Chetumal and around ▸▸ *pp198-213*

The state capital of Quintana Roo, Chetumal lies 240 km south of Tulum and is a necessary stopover for travellers en route to Maya sites in the south of the peninsula and across the frontier to Belize and Guatemala (page 198). Although tourist attractions are thin on the ground, Chetumal does have the advantage of being a small Mexican city not devoted to tourism and, therefore, has a more authentic feel than most other towns on the Riviera Maya. The city centre is characterized by broad, busy avenues, lined with huge shops selling cheap imported goods. Its affluent atmosphere can be a culture shock to visitors arriving from the much poorer country of Guatemala.

While you're in town, don't miss the **Museo de la Cultura Maya** ⓘ *Av Héroes de Chapultepec by the market, Tue-Thu and Sun 0900-1900, Fri and Sat 0900-2000, US$5.* Although it has few original Maya pieces, it gives an excellent overview of Maya culture, with good models of sites and touchscreen computers explaining the Maya calendar and glyphs. Guided tours are available, and there's a good bookshop with English magazines. The **tourist office** ⓘ *Av Miguel Hidalgo 22, 1st floor, esq Carmen Ochoa de Merino*, is mainly for trade enquiries; it is usually best to get information from a travel agent such as **Tu-Maya** (page 208).

Kohunlich

ⓘ *61 km from Chetumal, just before Francisco Villa, daily 0800-1700, US$2, colectivos 'Nicolás Bravo' from Chetumal, or bus 'Zoh Laguna' from bus station pass the turning.*

The ruins of Kohunlich, meaning 'Cahoon ridge', were discovered in 1967 by a local Maya. Cahoon is the Belizian name for the type of palm that lines the pathways around the ruins. The site was built during the Early Classic period (AD 250-500) and its most outstanding structure is the Pyramid of the Masks, which is flanked by red-tinged masks carved in stucco. Each mask is over 8 ft tall and its features are unique. They are believed to be a representation of gods or of Kohunlich's ruling elite, yet their true identification still eludes archaeologists and historians. This peaceful site makes a welcome change from the over-touristed sites further north.

Sleeping

Cancún *p189, maps p190 & p199*

Some hotels have special offers during Jul and Aug, listed in *Riviera Maya Hotels Guide*, available free at the airport.

Hotel Zone

Accommodation in the Hotel Zone costs around US$50 or more per night, and is best arranged as part of a package holiday. However, discounts can be considerable in the quiet season (Apr-Nov) and outside the northern hemisphere's summer holidays. Many hotels have all-inclusive activities and do not target the independent traveller but if you fancy being a tourist for a while, head along the strip and find one that takes your fancy. The best of the bunch are the sumptuous **Le Meridien**, Retorno del Rey Km 14, T998-881 2200 (**LL**) and the **Presidente Inter-Continental**, Av Kukulcán Km 7.5, T883-0200 (**L**).

Downtown

There are many cheaper options here, but prices are still higher than other parts of the Yucatán Peninsula. Many hotels tend to be full during Jul. Get to them as early as possible or reserve in advance. El

Chetumal-Santa Elena

The border is 11 km west of Chetumal, where a bridge crosses the Río Hondo. Over the bridge is the Belize village of Santa Elena and Belizean passport control. From here the Northern Highway continues south to Corozal (13 km), Orange Walk and Belize City (driving time 3 hrs). The border is open 24 hours a day and formalities are relatively relaxed. However it can be very busy, and therefore slow, especially at holiday times, when coaches bring Belizean shoppers to Mexico.

Leaving Mexico Leaving Mexico by car, go to the Mexican immigration office to register your exit and surrender your vehicle permit and tourist card; very straightforward, no charges. Third party car insurance (obligatory in Belize) can be purchased from the building opposite the immigration post (also money changing facilities here). Entering Belize, your car will be registered in your passport. Note that fresh fruit cannot be imported into Belize. Money is checked on entering Belize. » *p208.*

Leaving Belize Exit tax, US$13.75 (including PACT, p54). Tourist cards for Mexico are available at the border. Sometimes only 15 days are given but you can get an additional 30 days at the Servicios Migratorios in Chetumal or Cancún. If you need a Mexican visa, apply to the Mexican Embassy in Belize City beforehand. All northbound buses from Belize City go to Chetumal.

Exchange There are money changers on the Belize side of the border, but they are not there to meet the early bus from Mexico. Try to exchange Mexican pesos at the border as changing them in Belize can be difficult. Also bear in mind that the US dollar/Belize dollar rate is fixed at 1:2. You can buy pesos at good rates with either US and Belizean currency at the border; once inside Mexico, rates for Belizean dollars will be lower.

Crucero can be unsafe at night.

AL **Margaritas**, Yaxchilán y Jasmines, T/F998-884 9333. Modern, efficient service, restaurant, bar, pool, travel agent and care hire.

B **Cancún Rosa**, Margaritas 2, local 10, T998-884 2873. Close to bus terminal. A/c, TV, phone, comfortable rooms.

C **El Alux**, Av Uxmal 21, T998-884 0662. Clean rooms with a/c, bath, TV, some rooms cheaper, good value.

C **Villa Rossana**, Av Yaxchilán opposite Mexhotel, Lotes 67, 68, 69, T998-884 1943. Popular, central and spacious.

D **Piña Hermanos**, Calle 7 No 35, SM64, M6, L14, near El Crucero, T998-884 2150. Very clean, nice decor, restaurant, friendly staff. Highly recommended.

E **Mexico Hostel**, Palmera 30, T998-887 0191, www.mexicohostels.com The best budget deal in Cancún, very clean dorms, breakfast included, TV, lockers, kitchen.

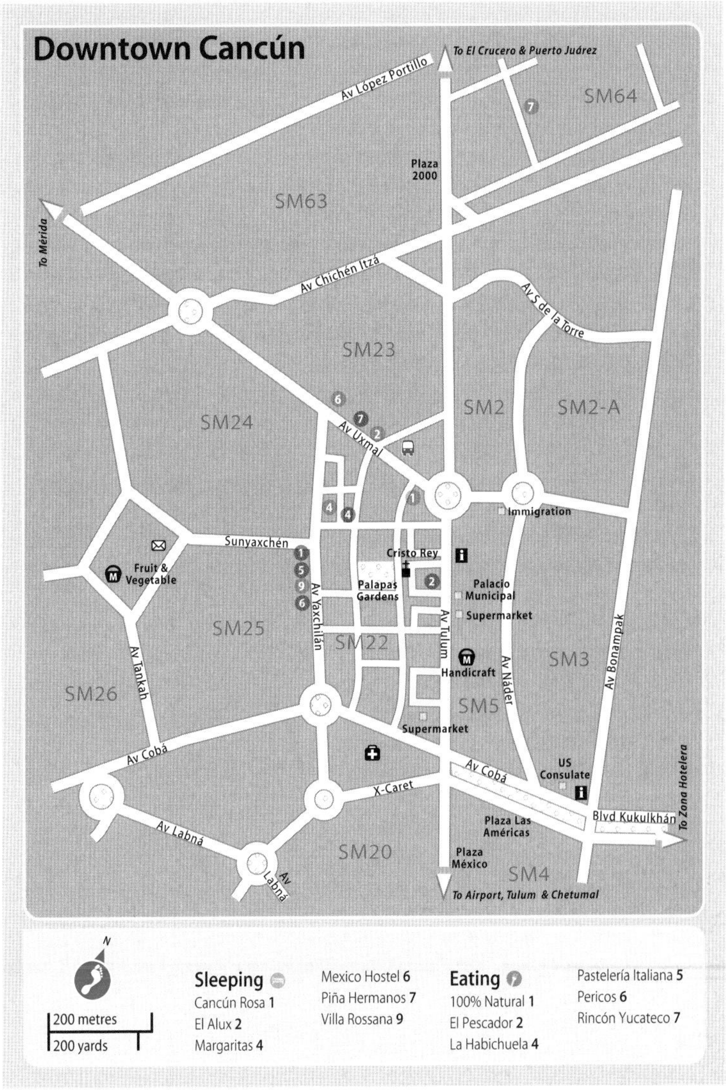

Downtown Cancún

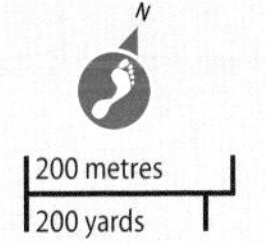

Sleeping
Cancún Rosa **1**
El Alux **2**
Margaritas **4**
Mexico Hostel **6**
Piña Hermanos **7**
Villa Rossana **9**

Eating
100% Natural **1**
El Pescador **2**
La Habichuela **4**
Pastelería Italiana **5**
Pericos **6**
Rincón Yucateco **7**

Isla Mujeres p190

AL **María del Mar**, Av Carlos Larzo 1, T998-877 0179. Close to the nicest stretch of beach, chilled-out cabañas and new rooms, fully equipped with a/c, cable TV, mini bar and sitting area. Relaxed and sociable Caribbean vibe, with hammocks, rocking chairs, pool and very popular bar.

A **Na Balam**, Zazil-Há 118, Playa Norte, T998-877 0279, www.nabalam.com Combines Caribbean atmosphere and Oriental spirituality. Beautiful thatched bungalows with hammocks (some with private pools) surrounded by palms on the island's best beach. Excellent bar /restaurant, with dazzling ocean views. Yoga daily at 0900.

C **Hotel Perla del Caribe**, Av Francisco Madero, 2, T998-877 0444. Looks like a hurricane has hit it but has an enviable location near a sliver of beach. Simple rooms, light, airy and very clean; most have ocean views. Friendly staff will offer discounts the longer you stay.

C **Vistalmar**, 300 m left of ferry dock, T998-877 0209. Ask for rooms on top floor, with bath, balcony, a/c, fan, TV and insect screens. Good value.

C-D **El Caracol**, Matamoros 5, T998-877 0150. Cheaper with fan, hot water, terrace, stoves for guests' use, bar, coffee shop, laundry, central, clean, good value.

Playa del Carmen p192, map p200

Prices are for the high season – Jul-Aug and Dec; during the low season prices drop by about 25%. Prices are much lower a few blocks back from the beach.

AL-B **Blue Parrot**, north end of town between Calle 12 y 14, T984-873 0083. Sociable, upbeat hotel, with beachside *palapas*, studios and deluxe rooms. Fantastic, if pricey, beachside bar, daily yoga classes, massages, dive school on site. Music and revelry until 0400.

B-C **Casa de Gopala**, Calle 2 Nte and Av 10 Nte (PO Box 154), T/F984-873 0054. Concealed among lush vegetation, 5 min walk from the beach and Av 5. Spacious rooms with large windows and colourful Mexican furnishings, fridge, fan and a/c, basic bathrooms. Some rooms need upgrading so ask to see several.

C **Cabañas Tuxatah**, 2 blocks south of Av Juárez, T984-873 0025). Comfortable, clean rooms with bath, hot water, laundry service, beautiful gardens, breakfast US$4.

C **Hul-Kú**, Avenida 20, entre Calle 4 y 6, T984-873 0021, www.hotelhulku.com

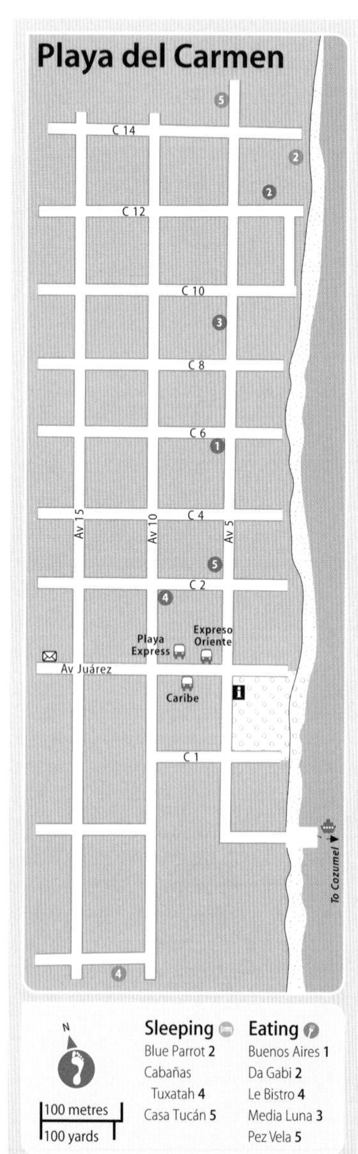

Excellent value. Spotless rooms with cable TV and fans, bamboo furniture and Mexican ceramics. Calming, leafy pool area, with hammocks, birdwatching, sun loungers. Helpful, good security.

D **Casa Tucán**, Calle 4 Nte, between 10 and 15 Av Nte, T/F984-873 0283. Nice patio, small but clean rooms. Pool and good restaurant.

Cozumel *p193, map p194*

Prices may rise by up to 50% around Christmas. Most accommodation focuses on the luxury end of the market.

A-B **Amaranto**, Calle 5 Sur, between 15 and 20, T987-872 3219, amaranto @cozumel.com.mx. New bungalows, with fridge and microwave. English spoken, childcare on request.

B **Tamarindo**, Calle 4 Nte 421, between 20 and 25, T/F987-872 3614. Bed and breakfast, 3 rooms, shared kitchen, hammocks, dive gear storage and rinse tank, purified drinking water, laundry, safe deposit box, TV, run by same couple as Amaranto (above), English spoken, childcare on request.

C **Al Marestal**, Calle 10 y 25 Av Nte, T987-872 0822. Spacious, clean rooms, with fan or a/c, cool showers, swimming pool, very good.

C **Pepita**, Av 15 Sur y Calle 1 Sur, T/F987-872 0098. Very pleasant rooms around a plant-filled courtyard, modern fittings, a/c, fridge in all rooms, free coffee and cookies in the morning.

C **Posada Zuanayoli**, Calle 6 Nte between Av 10 and Av 15 Nte, T987-872 0690. Tall, old building in quiet street, TV, modern facilities, fridge, fan, free coffee and drinking water.

D **Blanquita**, 10 Nte, T987-872 1190. Comfortable, clean, friendly owner speaks English, rents snorkelling gear and motor-scooters.

D **Posada Edem**, Calle 2 Nte 124, T987-872 1166. Kitchen, a/c, fan, also apartments (B), clean, very good value.

Tulum *p195*

Tulum village

Most visitors choose to stay at the beach cabañas (see below), however, new cheap accommodation makes the village a good choice for budget travellers.

F **Weary Traveller Hostel**, 1 block south of ADO bus terminal, T984-871 2461. Backpackers' hostel, good meeting place, price includes basic breakfast and dinner, bunk rooms with comfy beds, book exchange, internet (US$2.5/hr). Also friendly information centre.

Tulum beach

A **Ana y José**, 7 km south of ruins, T984-887 5470. Cabañas and rooms, some are right on the beach, with restaurant and pool, very clean, comfortable and hospitable. Trips to the Sian Ka'an Biosphere Reserve (p197), US$50, daily except Sun.

A **Cabañas Copal**, 3 km from the ruins, www.cabanascopal.com Eco-tourism complex and holistic spa on a spectacular stretch of beach. Daily yoga classes, excellent restaurant/bar and internet café. Casetas and cabañas with mosi nets and tiled bathrooms. No electricity or phone, a blissful escape. Rustic chic at its finest.

D-E **La Perla**, 5 km south of Tulum, T984-871 2382, www.hotelstulum.com /la-perla.htm Cabañas, camping and restaurant, comfortable, good food, family atmosphere, near beach.

E **Mar Caribe**, near the ruins. Small complex, but friendly, peaceful atmosphere, cheaper if you bring own hammock.

E **Santa Fe**, near the ruins, T984-880 5854. Basic cabañas, new but limited shower facilities, US$1extra for mosi net, hammocks or tents, good breakfasts and fish dinners, reggae music, laidback atmosphere, cheaper cabins are badly constructed so watch your belongings.

E-F **El Mirador**, nearest to the ruins (10 mins' walk). Small, quiet cabañas (won't rent to singles), hammocks available, camping, 2 showers, bar and restaurant with excellent views.

Cobá *p196*

B **Villas Arqueológicas** (Club Méditerranée), Lago Cobá, 1 km from ruins, T984-858 1527, www.clubmedvillas.com Blissful location in landscaped gardens on the lakeshore. Peaceful, well-designed villas with a/c. Family-oriented, pool, library, TV room, boutique and very good restaurant. A great base if you want to explore the ruins early in the morning before the tour groups arrive.

Chetumal *p197, map p202*

Decent, good-value accommodation is quite hard to come by.

C **Caribe Princess**, Av Obregón 168, T983-832 0520. About the best of the mid-range options. Unprepossessing 1970s building, en suite rooms have cable TV and a/c. Quiet location, 10 mins from the Malécon.

C **Ucum**, Gandhi 4, T983-832 0711. A/c, fan, bath, pleasant, quiet (rooms away from street), expensive laundry, parking included, good value, restaurant next door recommended for *ceviche*.

Eating

Cancún *p189, maps p190 & 199*

The **Hotel Zone** is lined with expensive restaurants, serving every type of international cuisine imaginable. There are cheaper restaurants in the centre, with the accent on local food. **Av Yaxchilán** has many restaurants in the mid-price range, as well as a few budget *loncherías*; **Av Uxmal** is slightly cheaper, with more street stalls.

El Pescador, Tulipanes 28. Good seafood, well established with excellent reputation but expensive.

La Habichuela, Margaritas 25, T884-3158. One of the oldest and most popular restaurants in Cancún. Lush tropical setting with Maya sculptures, fairy lights, candle-lit tables and live jazz. Award-winning Caribbean cuisine. The house special is *cocobichuela*, lobster and shrimp curry served in a coconut shell (US$32).

100% Natural, Av Yaxchilán y Sunyaxchén. Good choice for vegetarians with another branch in Playa del Carmen, big portions of seafood, salads, healthy breakfasts, juices and shakes, great prices.

Pericos, Av Yaxchilán 71. Archetypal Cancún cantina-style eating house, totally tacky but hugely popular. Jovial staff in bandit costume serve huge shrimp platters, filet mignon and pitchers of frozen margaritas. Live mariachi music.

Rincón Yucateco, Av Uxmal 24, opposite Hotel Cotty. Good Mexican breakfasts, popular.

Mercado 28, near the post office, best budget option for breakfast/lunch, cheap

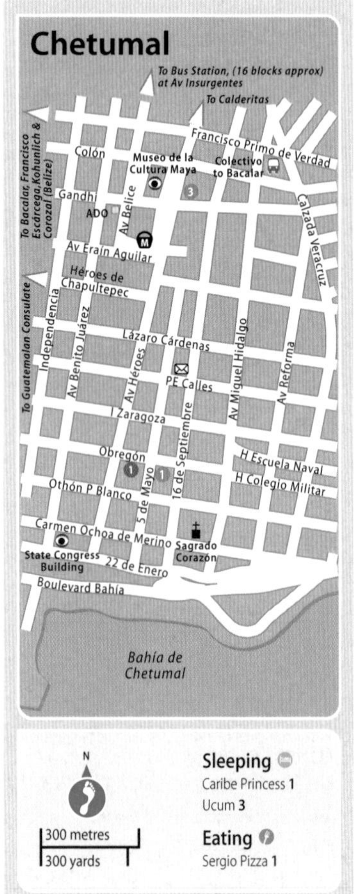

loncherías serving *comida corrida*, very popular with locals, quick service.
¥ **SM64**, opposite Plaza 2000. Small family-run restaurants serve local dishes, including *comida corrida* for as little as US$2. Popular with locals, especially on Sun when it is hard to get a table.

Cafés

Pastelería Italiana, Yaxchilán, just before Sunyaxchén turning. Excellent coffee and pastries, friendly.

Isla Mujeres *p190*

¥¥ **Bistro Francés**, Matamoros 29, Juárez e Hidalgo. Packed by 0830 for the best breakfast in town, including crêpes, eggs, french toast, *huevos rancheros* and *mollitos*. French-inspired cuisine and intimate ambience in the evening.
¥¥ **All Natural**, Plaza Karlita on Hidalgo. Speciality grilled fish and some vegetarian dishes.
¥¥ **El Balcón de Arriba**, Hidalgo 12 towards Playa Norte, above souvenir shop. Tasty fresh fish, seafood and vegetarian options. Large portions, friendly staff. Good for people watching.
¥¥ **Isla Tequila**, Hidalgo 19a. Popular for steak and seafood. Good bar, with live music. Friendly owners have a bookshop next door.
¥ **Lonchería La Lomita**, Juárez 25B. Known as the house on the hill, bargain home-style cooking in a kitsch canteen setting. Delicious *chile rellenos*, served with rice and beans.
¥ **La Susanita**, Juárez y Madero. Excellent home cooking in a friendly locals' place.
¥ **Poc-Chuc**, next door to La Susanita. Very good local food and big portions.

Cafés

Aluxes Café, Av Matamoros, centre of town. Very popular closet-sized coffee shop. Plenty of reading material, Latin music, great cappuccinos, bagels, muffins, cookies, granola and cheesecake.

Playa del Carmen *p192, map p200*

¥¥ **Buenos Aires**, Calle 6 Nte between Av 5 and Av 10, on Plaza Playa. Speciality Argentine meats, good for a change from Mexican food.
¥¥ **Da Gabi**, just up Calle 12 from Blue Parrot. Good pasta, Mexican dishes, breakfast (also has rooms in **C** range).
¥¥ **La Choza**, Av 5 between Av Juárez and Calle 2. Great food, set menus, good breakfasts, Tex-Mex dinners.
¥¥ **Le Bistro**, Calle 2. Caribbean chicken plus French cheese and wine.
¥¥ **Los Almendros**, Calle 6 and Av 10. Excellent Mexican food, friendly.
¥¥ **Media Luna**, Av 5 between Calle 8 and Calle 10. Mediterranean cuisine, nouvelle Mexican setting, hip lounge bar vibe. Great cocktails and breakfast specials.
¥¥ **Pez Vela**, Av 5 y Calle 2. Good atmosphere, with food, drinks and music (closed 1500-1700).
¥ **Argentino Bar Restaurant**, Calle 12, between Av 5 and the **Blue Parrot**. Great BBQs and good, cheap breakfasts, also a sports bar.
¥ **Lonchería Maquech**, Calle 1 between Av 5 and 10. Daily set lunch, cheap and friendly. Recommended.
¥ **Tacos Senjansen**, Av Juárez between Calle 10 and 15. Nice, open-air café under **Posada Marinelly**, breakfast and snacks.

Cafés and bakeries

Coffee Press, Calle 2 between Av 5 and the beach. Espresso, cappuccino, latte and breakfasts.
Java Joe's, Av 5 between Calle 10 and 12. Italian and gourmet coffees, sandwiches and pastries.

Cozumel *p193, map p194*

¥¥¥ **Lobster's Cove**, Av Rafael Melgar 790. Seafood, live music and happy hour 1200-1400.
¥¥¥ **Pancho's Backyard**, Rafael Melgar 27, in **Los Cinco Soles** shopping complex. Mexican food and wine elegantly served.
¥¥¥ **Prima**, Salas 109. Popular Italian. Fresh organic ingredients from the owner's

garden, pastas, seafood and wood-oven pizzas, followed by key lime pie. Outdoor seating and a no-smoking area.
🍴 **Las Palmeras**, just across from the ferry dock. Popular restaurant with street-side tables for people watching. Lively atmosphere, friendly service but food can be hit and miss. Big breakfasts and industrial strength margaritas.
🍴 **Mac y Cía**, off the main road, opposite the turn-off to El Cedral. Excellent fish restaurant on a lovely beach, popular with dive groups for lunch.
🍴 **Museo de la Isla**. Rooftop restaurant, good for breakfast from 0700.

Cafés and bakeries

Coffee Bean, Calle 3 Sur 9 near waterfront. Good coffee, plus great pies, cakes and brownies.

Tulum *p195*

Most of the cabañas have restaurants.
🍴 **Bistro Nocturne**, Av Tulum. Tex-Mex food, very good-value, nice decor (check out the bones above the bar).
🍴 **Charles**, Av Tulum. Beautiful shell decor, nachos, good fish. Patio out back.
🍴 **París de Noche**, Av Tulum. Excellent French-Mexican food, including lobster, outside garden setting, open for breakfast, good value.

Cobá *p196*

There are plenty of restaurants in the village and on the road to the ruins. **Pirámides**, near the Villas Arqueológicas, is especially recommended and moderately priced.

Chetumal *p197, map p202*

🍴🍴 **Chicho's Lobster House**, Blvd Bahía esq Vicente Guerrero, T832-7249. Expensive but good seafood, friendly.
🍴 **Sergio Pizza**, Obregón 182, 2 blocks from Av Héroes. Best value in town. Relaxing, dimly lit setting, with wooden tables and large windows. Delicious pizzas and salads, plus bland pasta dishes.

Entertainment

Cancún *p189, maps p190 & 199*

Bars and clubs

A night out in the Hotel Zone will set you back anywhere between US$20 and US$50. There are many nightclubs, most of them branches of US-run chains, which attract 16-21 year-old Americans for underage drinking. The clubs try to outdo each other by offering wild and wacky entertainment, drinking and dancing competitions. **Señor Frogs**, Hotel Zone, is one of the most popular, while **La Boom**, Hotel Zone, is said to be the craziest.

Downtown nightclubs are cheaper and more down-to-earth; you might even hear a bit of local music. Av Yaxchilán has several, the most popular being **Bum-Bum**, which has a dress code, and is open till late, and **Blue Bar**, next to Restaurant Villa Rica, which fills up about 2200. Many of the restaurants along Av Yaxchilán will serve a beer without making you order any food.

Cinemas

Cine Royal, Av Tulum near the bus terminal. Multiplex showing Hollywood blockbusters with Spanish subtitles, US$2.30. There are a couple of smaller cinemas near El Crucero; 1 of them, Calle 10, SM64, shows vintage Mexican gangster films. Also a multiplex cinema in the Zona Hotelera at Plaza Kukulcán.

Isla Mujeres *p190*

Bar and clubs

Most of the bars have a permanent happy hour, with 2 drinks for the price of 1. This is not particularly good value, since the prices are already double the usual.
Chile Locos, on Hidalgo towards the beach. More sedate than some, with live marimba music.
Daniel's, Hidalgo between Madero and Morelos. Very popular (and loudest) in the early evening, live music every night.
Kokonuts, Hidalgo 65, towards beach from centre. Most popular in town, fills up

after 2200, dance floor, happy hour, young crowd.
La Palapa, Playa Los Cocos. Daytime cocktails and snacks, fills up again after midnight.
La Taverna, on the harbour near the ferry dock. Occasional live music. Pleasant place on wooden stilts in the sea.
Mr Papas, Hildago below Matamoros. Lively bar and nightclub with DJ music.

Playa del Carmen *p192, map p200*

Bars and clubs

The Blue Parrot Inn, Calle 12 y Av 1, next to beach. Live music every night, happy hour 1700-2000 and 2200-2400.
Bourbon Street, Av 5 between Calle 6 and 8. Live Louisiana blues and jazz, Cajun food, relaxed atmosphere early on, draught beer. Friendly.
Buena Onda, Av 5 between Calle 26 and Calle 28. Live music, salsa, funk, reggae.
Crocodillos, Juárez, disco, small cover, popular with the locals, good at weekend.
Fiesta Latina, Calle 8 y Av 25. Live Latin music and ballet show.
Tequila Barrel, Calle 5 between Av 10 and 12. Live blues daily 2000-2400, Tex-Mex Bar and grill, friendly owner and staff.

Cozumel

Bars and clubs

Café Salsa, Av 10 between Juárez and 2 Nte. Salsa Bar, popular alternative and slightly more authentic.
Havana Club, Av Rafael Melgar, north of the ferry. Cigar and jazz bar, live music Wed and Fri 1330-1800.
Scaramouche, Av Rafael Melgar y A R Salas. Hotel nightclub with the best state-of-the-art disco on the island.
The Stadium, Calle 2 Nte y Av 4. US-style bar and grill, with satellite TV.

Festivals and events

Isla Mujeres *p190*

Oct A festival of music, with groups from Mexico and the US performing in the main square
1-12 Dec Fireworks and dances in the plaza until 0400 during the fiesta for the Virgin of Guadalupe.

Shopping

Cancún *p189, maps p190 & 199*

There are several expensive US-style **shopping malls** in the Zona Hotelera. The main one, Plaza Kukulcán, has over 200 shops, restaurants, a bowling alley and video games. The main **craft market** is on Av Tulum near Plaza Las Américas; it is a huge network of stalls, all selling exactly the same merchandise: silver jewellery from Taxco, ceramic Maya figurines, hammocks, jade chess sets. Prices are hiked, so bargain hard. Mercado 23, end of Calle Cedro, off Av Tulum, has cheaper souvenirs of poor quality, but less aggressive salesmen.

Isla Mujeres *p190*

Av Hidalgo is lined with souvenir shops, most of them selling the same things: ceramic Maya figurines and masks; hammocks; blankets; and silver jewellery from Taxco. Bargaining is obligatory. There are more souvenir shops along the harbour front, where the salesmen are more pushy, and more shops along Av Morelos. For new and used books and CDs head to Cosmic Cosas, Matamoros 82, T998-876 3495, it's also an internet café and a good meeting place.

Playa del Carmen *p192, map p200*

There are lots of souvenir shops clustered around the plaza. Cheaper shops, for everyday items are on Av Juárez.

Activities and tours

Cancún *p189, maps p190 & p199*

Boat trips

Atlantis, contact Robert Theofel, T998-883 4963. Submarine trips in a 48-passenger vessel to explore natural and man-made reefs.

M/V Aqua II, T998-887 1909, has all-inclusive day cruises to Isla Mujeres from US$44.

Nautibus, Playa Linda dock, T998-883 3552. A vessel with seats below the waterline, trips to the reefs, 1½ hrs, a good way to see fish. There are a number of other cruises on offer.

Tour operators

Colors Travel, Av Yaxchilán 7C, SM24, T998-887 7929, colors@correoweb.com Very friendly and helpful. Many trips including all-inclusive deals to Río Lagartos and Ek-Balam with guides in various languages; overnight plane trip to Tikal, Guatemala; flights to Cuba. Reliable.

Ecocolors, Cancún, T/F998-884 9580. Tours to the Sian Ka'an reserve, in collaboration with Los Amigos, US$115 for a full day, pick up at hotel 0700, everything included; in winter the tour goes through a canal, in summer it goes birdwatching, in both cases a visit to a Maya ruin, a cenote, snorkelling, all equipment, breakfast and evening meal are included. Also 2-day camping trips. Boat trips through the Biosphere, US$50.

Watersports

Watersports can be organized on the beaches along the hotel zone, including parasailing, water-skiing, windsurfing and jet-skiing.

Isla Mujeres *p190*

Birdwatching

A small island north of Isla Mujeres, **Isla Contoy** has been designated as a bird and wildlife sanctuary. Trips can be arranged through agencies; the specialist is **Ricardo Gaitán**, Av Madero 16, T998-877 0434. His trips include fishing, snorkelling and lunch. Many touts around the main dock will offer trips to Isla Contoy for around US$50 for a full day.

Playa del Carmen

Scuba diving and snorkelling

Bahía, Av Rueda Medina 166, opposite the ferry dock, T998-877 0340. Snorkelling trips depart from the ferry dock daily from 1000 and 1100. They include 2 hrs' snorkelling in various spots and lunch, returning at 1430. US$150 per person.

Coral, Av Matamoros 13A, T998-877 0763, coral@coralscubadivecenter.com PADI-affiliated dive centre with over 20 years' experience, bilingual staff, 50 local dive sites, including reef, adventure or Ultrafreeze options.

Sea Hawk, Zazil-Ha (behind Hotel Na-Balam) T/F998-877 0296. Certified PADI instructors, 2-tank dive US$50, introductory course including shallow dive US$75. Also snorkelling trips and fishing trips.

Tour operators

Prisma Tours, Av Juárez 22, T/F998-877 0938. Tours to Tulum, Cobá, Chichén Itzá, Uxmal, Sian Ka'an in a/c vans. Also cheap and reliable airport transfer from Cancún Airport-Puerto Juárez.

Tercer Milenio, Abasolo 46, between Juárez and Hidalgo, T998-877 0795. Tours to archaeological sites, airport transfer, high-class van rental, reservations for cruises, golf cart, moped and car rental, scuba diving, flights to Cuba, Belize, Guatemala.

Top tips

Cenote diving

There are over 50 cenote dive sites in this area, accessible from Ruta 307 and often well signposted. Cave diving has become very popular. However, it is a specialized sport and, unless you have a cave diving qualification, you must be accompanied by a qualified dive master.

A cave diving course involves over 12 hours of lectures and a minimum of 14 cave dives using double tanks, costing around US$600. Accompanied dives start at around US$60. A word of warning: cenote diving has a higher level of risk than open water diving – do not take risks and only dive with recognized operators. Specialist dive centres offering courses are listed under Activities and tours, below.

Some of the best cenotes are 'Carwash', on the Cobá road, good even for beginners, with excellent visibility, and 'Dos Ojos', just off Ruta 307 south of Aventuras. This is the most famous cenote in the area and links up with Nohoch Nah Chich, the second largest underground cave system in the world, with over 50 km of surveyed passageways connected to the sea. The stunning underwater caverns at Dos Ojos, decorated with stalactites and stalagmites, are accessible to snorkellers as well as divers.

Playa del Carmen *p192, maps p200*

Kitesurfing

IKARUS, Av 5, Calle 16, T984-803 2068, www.ikaruskiteboarding.com Good kit and instruction for US$150.

Scuba diving

Abyss, Calle 12 and the beach, near the Blue Parrot, T984-873 2164, www.abyssdiveshop.com Said to be the best in town. Run by fully certified American instructor David Tomlinson, PADI courses US$324; 1-tank dive US$40, 1-day introductory course US$69, also cavern and night dives.

Adventures Underwater, on plaza, T984-873 2647. Diving courses in English, French or Spanish, 3 certified instructors, 1-day beginner course US$60, open water PADI US$350, advanced refresher course US$250, cavern diving in 2 cenotes US$100.

Tour operators

Classique Travel, Calle 6 between Av 5 and Av 10, T/F984- 873 2598. Long-standing and reliable agency, tours to Chichén Itzá US$72, including transport from hotel, guide, entry, food, also bookings for national and international flights, helpful staff.

Euro Latino, Av 5 No 165B, between Calle 6 and 8, T984-873 0549, eurolatino@grupasesores.net.mx. Efficient agency with young European staff. Tours include **Dawn in Tikal** (Guatemala) US$278, including flight, overnight stay in hotel, all meals, all transfers, and **Weekend on Cozumel**, including dive (all levels) plus 2 nights and the ferry, US$72.

Riviera Maya *p192*

Cenote diving

Aquatech, Villas de Rosa Resort, PO Box 25, Aventuras-Akumal No 35, T984-875 9020, from the US (toll free) T1-866-619-9050, www.cenotes.com. Specialist dive centre.

Hidden World's Cenotes, just south of Xel Ha, Highway 307, T984-877 8535, www.hiddenworlds.com.mx. Cenote diving (from US$50) and snorkelling (US$40) includes Cenotes Dos Ojos and Dreamwater. Only technical fill station in the area.

Mike Madden's CEDAM Dive Centres, PO Box 1, Puerto Aventuras, T/F984-873 5129. Specialist dive centre.

Cozumel *p193, map p194*

Scuba diving

The best reef for scuba diving is **Palancar**, reached only by boat. Also highly recommended are **Santa Rosa** and **Colombia**. For more experienced divers the reefs at **Punta Sur**, **Maracaibo** and **Baracuda** should not to be missed. Almost all Cozumel diving is drift diving, so if you are not used to a current, choose an operator you feel comfortable with: larger centres take divers out to sea in big boats with many passengers; smaller, more personalized dive shops usually have a maximum of 8 people per boat.

Deep Blue, A R Salas 200, esq Av 10 Sur, T/F987-872 5653, www.deepbluecozumel.com Reputed to be the best of the smaller centres, run by an English/Colombian couple. All PADI and NAUI certifications. Open Water Diver US$360; 3-5-day dive packages US$165-250; cavern and cenote diving US$130.

Decompression centres Buceo Médico Mexicano, Calle 5 Sur No 21B, T987-872 2387, immediate localization (24-hr) VHF 16 and 21. Supported by US$1 per day donations from divers with affiliated operators. Cozumel Hyperbarics, Clínica San Miguel, Calle 6 Nte No 135 between Av 5 and Av 10, T987-872 3070, VHF channel 65. Nachicocom, on the seafront and Calle 5 Sur, T987-872 1430. A new one.

Tour operators

Ferinco Travel Tours, T987-872 1781. Tourist flights to all major Maya sites.

Tulum *p195*

Scuba diving

There are several dive shops along the Tulum corridor but also many untrained snorkelling and diving outfits, so take care. See Cenote diving, p207 for details of cavern diving in the area – highly recommended.

Aktun, Ruta 307, 1 km out of Tulum, PO Box 119, T984-871 2311, www.aktundive.comGerman /Mexican-run, experienced NACD and IANTD instructor, cenote and open water diving, very friendly, speaks English.

Cenote Dive Center, Tulum, T984-871 2232, www.cenotedive.com. Norwegian-owned specialist dive centre.

Chetumal *p197, map p202*

Tour operators

Explora Premier, Av Juárez 83, esq Zaragoza, T832-3096, otocarybe@mpsnet.com.mx Eco and adventure tours, car rental.

San Juan Travel Agency, Chetumal bus station, T983-832 5110. Leaves 1500 for Flores, arriving 2100, returns 0500 connecting to 1400 bus to Cancún. US$35 1 way plus US$3 at the Belize-Guatemala border.

Tu-Maya, Av Héroes 165A, T983-832 0555. Tours to Guatemala, Belize and Calakmul.

Transport

Cancún *p189, maps p190 & 199*

Air

For flight details, see p17 and p21. For airport details, see p189.

Airline offices Aerocozumel, Av Cobá 5, Plaza América SM4, T998-884 2000. **AeroMéxico**, Av Cobá 80, SM3, T998-884 3571. **American Airlines**, Aeropuerto, T998-883 4460. **Aviacsa**, Av Cobá 37, SM4, T998-887 4211. **Aviateca**, Av Cobá 5, Plaza América SM4, T998-887 4110. **Continental**, Aeropuerto, T998-886 0006. **Iberia**, Aeropuerto, T998-886 0243. **Mexicana**, Av Tulum, T998-887 4444.

Bus

Local Regular buses to/from the ferry dock at **Puerto Juárez**, US$0.50.

Long distance Cancún bus terminal has plentiful services along the Riviera Maya (highway 307). **Inter Playa Express**, every 30 mins to **Puerto Morelos**, US$1, **Playa del Carmen**, US$2.25 and **Xcaret**, US$2.25. Also 3 daily to **Puerto Aventuras**, US$2.50, and **Xel-Há**, US$3.30, and every 10 mins to **Tulum**, 2 hrs, US$4.60. Other services to Playa del Carmen and Tulum (en route to Chetumal) are marginally more expensive. To **Chetumal**, every 2 hrs, 0500-0030, 5½ hrs, US$16; the 0800 departure arrives in Chetumal in time for the connection to Flores and will get you to Belize City by around 2000. Several other services to Chetumal include **Caribe Express**, deluxe service with a/c.

Heading west, there are many services to **Mérida**, 6 hrs, *Plus* with TV, a/c, etc US$28, 1st class US$19, 2nd class US$11; all call at **Valladolid**, 3hrs, 1st class US$7.50, 2nd class US$5.50. To **Chichén Itzá**, many daily from 0630, 3-4 hrs, US$7-10. To **Palenque**, US$44, and **San Cristóbal**, 7 daily, 1415-2030, 17 hrs, US$42-51. To **Villahermosa**, 1000, 1300 and 1845, 12 hrs, US$49-63.

Car hire

Beware of overcharging and read any documents carefully before you sign. Rates vary enormously, from US$40 to US$80 a day for a VW Golf (VW Beetles are cheaper), larger cars and jeeps available. **Avis**, Plaza Caracol, cheapest but still expensive. **Budget Rent-a-Car**, at the airport, has been recommended.

Car parking Do not leave cars parked in side streets; there is a high risk of theft. Use the parking lot on Av Uxmal.

Isla Mujeres *p190*

Air

The small airstrip in the middle of the island is mainly used for private planes. Flights to/from **Cancún** and **Chichén Itzá** can be booked through **Mundaca Travel**, Hidalgo, T998-877 0025. Charters are available with **Island Airtours**, T998-877 0331, or directly with **Capt Joaquín Ricalde**, T9845-3038 (mob), for sightseeing trips to Isla Mujeres, Holbox, Cozumel, Tulum, Chichén Itzá.

Bike and moped

Many touts along Hidalgo offer mopeds and bikes at similar rates: US$8 per hr, US$20 full day. Golf carts are generally US$40-50 per day with a credit card as deposit. **Sport Bike**, Av Juárez y Morelos, has good bikes. **Cárdenas**, Av Guerrero 105, T/F998-877 0079, has mopeds and golf carts.

Bus

A public bus runs from the ferry dock to Playa Paraíso every ½ hr, US$0.25.

Ferry

Passenger ferries depart from **Puerto Juárez**, every 30 mins 0600-2330, US$3.80, journey time 30 mins. There's also a slightly slower service every 45-60 mins 0600-1800 in an open-decked boat with cool breezes, much nicer, US$1.80. Ferries from **Playa Linda** in Cancún (opposite the **Calinda Quality Cancún Beach**) depart 9 times daily 0900-1645, US$12.50 return, journey time 20 mins; last return 1700. Car ferries leave from **Punta Sam**, 5 daily from 0800, US$7-8 per car, US$1.20 passengers, 45 mins. There is a luggage store, 0800-1800, and a tourist information desk at the jetty.

Taxi

From town to **El Garrafón,** US$3.40. From El Garrafón to the bus stop at **Playa Paraíso**, US$1. Taxis charge an additional US$1 at night.

Playa del Carmen *p192, map p200*

Air

Flights to **Cozumel**, US12.50 single, 10 mins; touts will mingle with the queues for the ferry to get passengers.

Bus

All buses depart from the ADO bus terminal, Av Juárez between Av 5 and 10. The following prices and times are for ADO buses (1st class, a/c, usually showing a video on longer journeys); other 1st-class companies include **Premier** and **Cristóbal Colón**; buses run by **Maya de Oro** tend to be of poorer quality. To **Cancún**, 8 daily, 1 hr 15 mins, US$2.40. To **Chetumal**, 8 daily, 5 hrs, US$10. To **Chichén Itzá**, 6 daily, 4 hrs, US$7. To **Mérida**, 4 daily, 7 hrs, US$10. To **Mexico City**, 3 daily, 24 hrs, US$54. To **San Cristóbal de las Casas**, 3 daily, 16 hrs, US$37. To **Tulum**, 5 daily, 1 hr, US$2; 2nd-class buses to Valladolid also go via Tulum, US$6.50. To **Valladolid**, at 0730 and 1115, 3½ hrs, US$8; most buses to Mérida also stop at Valladolid. To **Xcaret**, frequent service, 10 mins, US$1. To **Xel Há**, 2 daily, 1 hr, US$2.

Car hire

Budget, T984-873 0100. **Caribetur**, Av 10 No 128 between Calle 2 and 4 Nte, T984-873 2292. **Freedom**, Av 5, T984-873 1459. **Happy**, Plaza Tucán, Local 6, T984-873 1739. **Hertz**, T984-873 0703.

Ferry

Ferries to **Cozumel** depart from the main dock, just off the plaza, every hr on the hr, 0400-2200, ½ hr, US$81-way, buy ticket 1 hr before journey.

Taxi

Cancún airport US$25. Drivers who charge only US$5 are likely to charge an extra US$20 for luggage. Tours to **Tulum** and **Xel-Há** from kiosk by boat dock, US$30; tours to Tulum, Xel-Há and **Xcaret**, 5-6 hrs, US$60; taxi to Xcaret US$6.65. Taxis congregate on the Av Juárez side of the square (**Sindicato Lázaro Cárdenas del Río**, T984-873 0032).

Cozumel *p193, map p194*

Air

Most airline offices are based at the airport, 2 km north of the town. **Aerocaribe/ Aerocozumel** (T987-872 3456), have almost hourly flights to **Cancún** as well as flights to **Chichén Itzá**. There are also services to **Mexico City** direct with **Mexicana** (P Joaquin between Salas and Calle 3 Sur, next to Pemex, T987-872 0263), and to **Houston** (USA) with **Continental** (T987-872 0847).

Bike, car and moped

Mopeds cost US$25-30 per day, credit card needed as deposit; bicycles are around US$8 per day, US$20 cash or TC deposit; try **Rentadora Cozumel**, Av 10 Sur No 172 between Salas y Calle 1 Sur, T987-872 1120, or **Splash**, Calle 6 Nte, T987-872 3977. There are also many car hire agencies, including **Budget Jeep and Auto**, Av 5 y Calle 2, T987-872 0903.

Ferry

There are passenger ferries from Playa del Carmen (see above) and car ferries from Puerto Morelos at 0600 and 1500 daily.

Tulum *p195*

Bike

Bikes can be hired in the village for US$1 per hr and are a good way to get around.

Bus

Regular buses go up and down the coastal road travelling from Cancún to Tulum en route to Chetumal, stopping at most places in between, including El Crucero for the ruins. However, some buses may be full when they reach Tulum and very few buses begin their journeys here. It may be better to go to **Playa del Carmen** (US$1.40) for more connections to nearby destinations and if travelling far, take a bus to **Felipe Carrillo Puerto** and transfer to ADO there. Note that there are no buses to Tulum beach; to reach the cabañas, get off the bus in town and take a taxi (US$3-5 depending on season)

To **Felipe Carrillo Puerto**, several 0600-1200 and 1600-2200, 1 hr, US$4.70, continuing to **Chetumal**, 4 hrs, 2nd class, US$10, 1st class US$12. To **Cobá**, take the

Playa del Carmen-Valladolid bus, which passes El Crucero at 0600, 1100 and 1800, 45 mins, US$1.35, returning to El Crucero at 0715 and 1545 (all times approximate, may leave 15 mins early). To **Mérida**, several daily, 6 hrs, US$10, 2nd class. To **Palenque**, via Escárcega, 0800, US$34. To **San Cristóbal**, 1845, often late, US$45. To **Villahermosa**, 1630, 2100, US$35. To **Mexico City**, 0815, 1315, 2100, US$85.

Taxi

Tulum town to ruins US$3.50; to the cabañas US$3.50; to Cobá about US$25.

Cobá *p196*

Buses into the village turn round at the road end. There are 3 daily from Playa del Carmen and Tulum to **Valladolid**, 2 hrs, US$2.50, passing through Cobá at 0630, 1130 and 1830. To **Tulum**, US$1, and **Playa del Carmen**, 2 daily, at 0630 and 1500. If you miss the bus there is usually a taxi at El Bocadito.

Chetumal *p197, map p202*

Air

Airport (CTM) 2½ km from town. Flights to **Cancún**, **Mérida**, **Belize City** (Aerocaribe, Plaza Varudi, Av Héroes 125), **Mexico City**, **Monterrey** and **Tijuana** (Aviacsa, T983-832 7765).

Bus

Bus information T983-832 5110. The main bus terminal is 3 km out of town at the intersection of Insurgentes y Belice. Taxi into town US$1.20 or by bus from Av Belice. Left luggage lockers cost US$0.20 per hr. If buying tickets in advance, go to the ADO office on Av Belice esq Ghandi, 0800-1600. There are often more buses than those marked on the display in the bus station, so always ask at the information desk. There are no city buses.

Long distance Buses are often all booked a day ahead, so avoid unreserved connections. Expect passport checks on buses for Mexican destinations. To **Cancún**, almost hourly, 6 hrs, 2nd class, US$16, luxury at midnight, US$20. To **Tulum**, 8 a day, 4 hrs, US$10. To **Playa del Carmen**, every couple of hrs, 5 hrs, US$10. To **Mexico City**, Autobuses del Caribe, 2100, 20 hrs, US$70. To **Campeche**, 1200, 6 hrs, US$18. To **Xpujil**, 5 a day, 2½ hrs, US$5. To **Mérida**, 0730, 1330, 1730, luxury US$18, and 2330, sleeper, US$31. To **Palenque**, 2215, 14 hrs, US$21, or take bus to **San Cristóbal**, 0130 and 1845, US$27, and 2115, 13 hrs, US$30 calling at **Escárcega** (US$12), **Emiliano Zapata** (11½ hrs, US$19), **Palenque** (US$21) and **Ocosingo** (13½ hrs, US$26). To **Tuxtla Gutiérrez**, 2115, US$34. To **Villahermosa**, 5 between 1830 and 2230, 9 hrs, US$25; the road is bad so the journey sometimes takes longer.

To Belize Many buses go to the **border**, US$0.30. Also *colectivos* from in front of the hospital (1 block from the bus station) marked 'Chetumal-Santa Elena', US$1. Novelo's, 1045, 1400 and 1700 (schedules change frequently) departs from the bus station to **Corozal**, **Orange Walk**, 2½ hrs, US$4.50, and **Belize City**, 3½-5 hrs, US$7. If intending to stay in Belize City, do not take a bus that arrives at night as it is not recommended to look for a hotel in the dark.

To Guatemala Direct daily buses to **Flores**, at 0620, 0700, 1400 and 1430, 8 hrs, US$17-22.

Taxi/colectivo

Taxis run on fixed-price routes, US$0.50 on average. Cars with light-green licence plates are a form of taxi. Taxi from Chetumal to **border**, 20 mins, US$6 for 2. Colectivos to Bacalar and Francisco Villa (for **Kohunlich** and **Xpujil**) depart from the junction of Av Miguel Hidalgo and Francisco Primo de Verdad.

Directory

Cancún *p189, maps p190 & 199*

Banks There are 11 Mexican banks along Av Tulum, all in SM 4 and SM5. To change American Express traveller's cheques, visit the office on Av Tulum, just south of Av Cobá, for the best rates. Many *casas de cambio* in the centre, mainly around the bus terminal and along Av Tulum; *casas de cambio* in the Hotel Zone give slightly lower rates for TCs than those in the centre. **Embassies and consulates** Canada, Plaza Caracol, 3rd floor, Zona Hotelera, T998-883 3360. US, Plaza Caracol, 3rd floor, Zona Hotelera, T998-883 0272. **Hospitals and clinics** American Hospital (24-hr), Viento 15, Centre, T998-884 6133. **Immigration office** On the corner of Av Náder and Av Uxmal. There is also an office in the airport, T998-886 0492, where the staff are better trained and speak English. **Internet** Numerous cafés charging US$1-1.50 per hr. Generally good servers, open until around 2300. **Post office** At the end of Av Sunyaxchén, near Mercado 28, Mon-Fri 0800-1900, Sat 0900-1300. Fax service. **Telephones** Public phones everywhere, phone cards available from general stores and pharmacies. Collect calls can be made without a card. Also many public phones designed for international calls, which take coins and credit cards.

Isla Mujeres *p190*

Banks Banco del Atlántico, Av Juárez 5. Banca Serfín, Av Juárez 3. Both can get very busy. Good rates, varying daily, are offered by several *casas de cambio* on Av Hidalgo. **Doctors** Dr Antonio Salas, Hidalgo, next to *Farmacia*, T998-877 0477. 24 hrs, house calls, English spoken, air ambulance. Dr Antonio Torres, Av Matamoros esq Guerrero, T998-877 0050. 24 hrs, English spoken. **Internet** Several new internet cafés operate on the island US$2-2.50 per hr, but can be a little slow. **Language school** Ixchel Language Institute, Matamoros 82, 1-wk survival courses, US$10 per hr, individual, US$5.50 group lessons. **Laundry** Tim Pho, Juárez y Abasolo. **Post office** At the end of Guerrero towards the beach. **Telephone** Phone cards can be bought at some of the souvenir shops along Hidalgo. International calls and faxes at Gold & Silver, Av Hidalgo 58.

Playa del Carmen *p192, map p200*

Banks Bancomer, Av Juárez between Calle 25 and 30. Banamex, Av Juárez between Calle 20 and 25. Banorte, Av 5 between Av Juárez and the beach. HSBC, Av Juárez between Calle 10 and 15. There are several *casas de cambio* along Av 5, which change TCs with no commission. Short changing is not uncommon. **Dentist** Perla de Rocha Torres, Av 20 Nte between 4 and 6, T984-873 0021, speaks English. Recommended. **Hospitals and clinics** International Medical Services, Dr Victor Macías Orosco, Av 35 between Calle 2 and 4, T984-873 0493. 24-hr emergency service, land and air ambulance, ultrasound, most major insurance accepted. Tourist Divers Medical Centre, Dr Mario Abarca, Av 10 between Av Juárez and Calle 2, T984-873 0512. Air and land ambulance service, hyperbaric and diving medicine, affiliated with South Miami Hospital, all insurance accepted. **Immigration office** Centro Comercial, Plaza Antigua, Av 10 Sur, T984-873 1884. **Internet** Cybercafés in town charge between US$1.50-2 per hr. **Language schools** Playalingua, Calle 20 between 5 and 10, T984-873 3876, cidi@playalingua.com, US$150 per wk (20 hrs). Solexico Language and Cultural Center, Av 35 between 6 and 6 bis, T984-873 0755, www.solexico.com Variable programme with workshops. **Laundry** Av Juárez, 2 blocks from bus station; another on Av 5. **Police** Av Juárez, next to the post office, T984-873 0291. **Post office** Av Juárez y Av 15, Mon-Fri 0800-1700, Sat 0900- 1300. Telegraph office is around the corner on Av 15.

Cozumel *p193, map p194*

Banks 4 banks on the main square, all exchange money in morning only, but not at same hours. *Casas de cambio* on

Av 5 Nte and around square, 3.5% commission, open longer hours. **Dentist** Dr Hernández, T987-872 0656. **Hospitals and clinics** Centro Médico de Cozumel, Calle 1 Sur No 101, esq Av 50, T987-872 3545. English spoken, international air ambulance, 24-hr emergency service. **Internet** Several internet cafés charging around US$1.50 per hr. **Laundry** Express, Salas between Av 5 and Av 10, T987-872 3655. **Pharmacy** Salas between Av 12 and Av 20, 0700-2400. **Post office** Av Rafael Melgar y Calle 7 Sur, Mon-Fri 0900-1800, Sat 0900-1200. **Telephone** Ladatel phones (if working) on main square at corner of Av Juárez and Av 5. For calls to the US, go to The Stadium. Telmex phone offices on the main square, 0800-2300, and on Salas between Av 10 and 15. There are also expensive Computel offices in town, eg at the cruise ship dock. Telephone centre for long distance on corner of Rafael Melgar and Calle 3 Sur.

Tulum *p195*

Banks 4 money exchange booths near bus station in Tulum village. TCs can be changed at the offices of the GOPI Construction Company, although not at a very good rate. **Hospitals and clinics** Malaria prophylaxis available from Centro de Salud, opposite hospital (request tablets for *paludismo*). **Telephone** Long-distance phones in ADO terminal in town.

Chetumal *p197, map p202*

Banks Banks close at 1430. There are several ATMs. For exchange, Banamex, Obregón y Juárez, changes TCs. Banks do not change quetzales into pesos. Good rates at Bodegas Blanco supermarket beside bus terminal; will change US dollars and Belize dollars if you spend at least 15 of the total on their groceries! Pemex stations will accept US and Belizean dollars, but at poor rates for the latter. Money-changers in Chetumal bus terminal offer marginally poorer rates than those at the border (see p198). San Francisco de Assisi supermarket changes TCs, next to bus station. **Embassies and consulates** Belize, Consulate General, Armada de Mexico 91, T983-832 1803; visas, US$25, can take up to 3 weeks, many only issued in Mexico City. Guatemala, Av Héroes de Chapultepec 354, T983-832 6565, open for visas Mon-Fri 0900-1700. It is advisable to organize visas, if required, in your home country before travel. **Hospitals and clinics** Malaria prophylaxis available from Centro de Salud, opposite hospital (request tablets for *paludismo*). **Internet** Eclipse, 5 de Mayo 83 between PE Calles and Zaragoza. 0930-1500, 1800-2100, US$3 per hr. **Laundry** Lavandería Automática 'Lava facil', corner of Héroes and Confederación Nacional Campesina. **Post office** 16 de Septiembre y PE Calles. Mon-Fri 0800-1730, Sat 0900-1300. Packets to be sent abroad must be taken unwrapped to the bus terminal for customs before taking them to the post office. Parcel service not available Sat. Western Union office attached to post office, same hrs.

Belize

Red-eyed tree frog

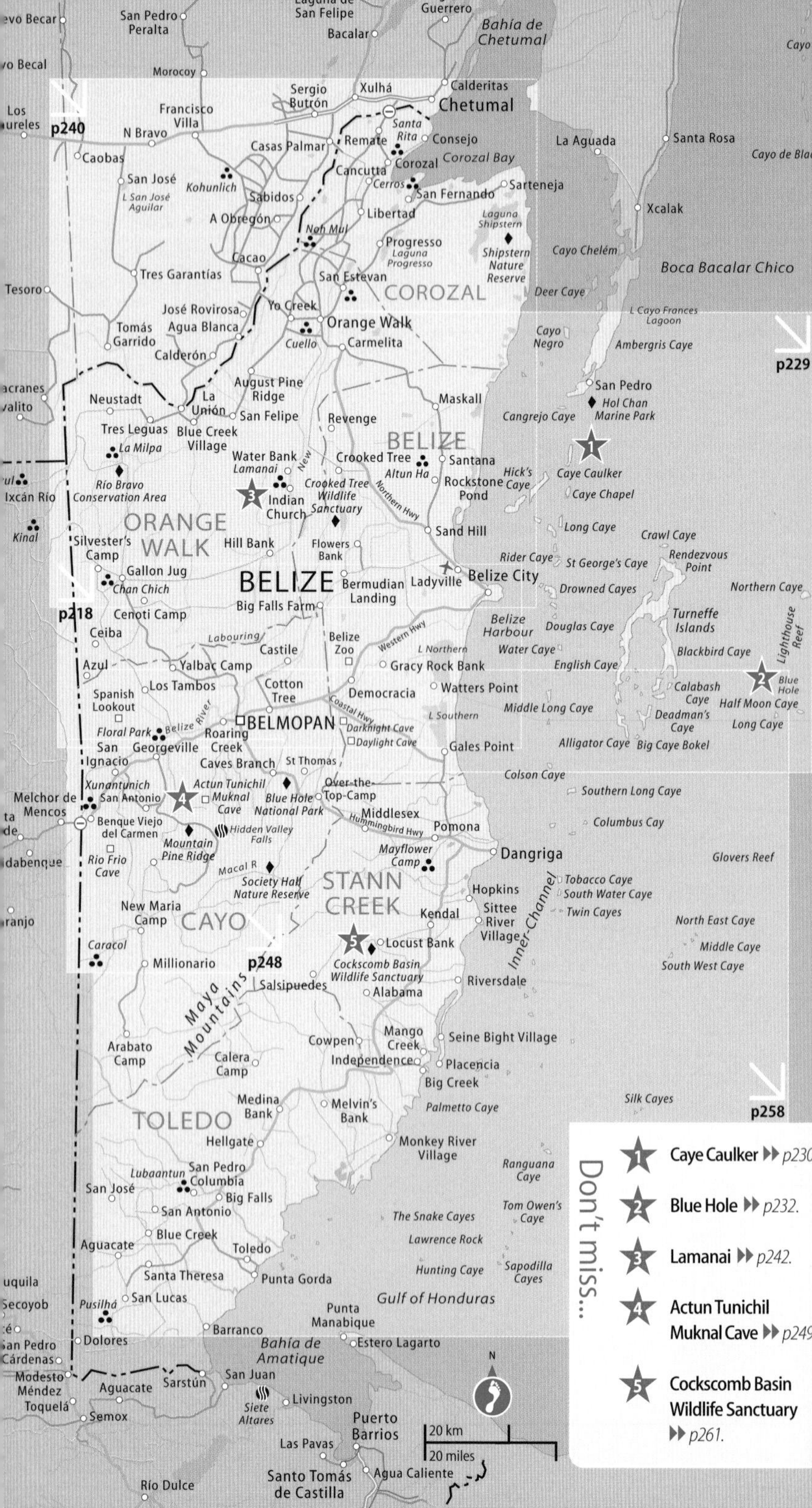

Laguna de San Felipe
Guerrero
San Pedro Peralta
Bacalar
Bahía de Chetumal
Cayo
Morocoy
Sergio Butrón
Xulhá
Calderitas
Chetumal
Francisco Villa
p240
N Bravo
Santa Rita
Consejo
Casas Palmar
Remate
La Aguada
Santa Rosa
Caobas
Corozal
Corozal Bay
Cayo de Blac
San José
Kohunlich
Cancutta
L San José Aguilar
Cerros
San Fernando
Sarteneja
Sabidos
Xcalak
A Obregón
Libertad
Noh Mul
Laguna Shipstern
Progresso
Laguna Progresso
Shipstern Nature Reserve
Cayo Chelém
Cacao
Boca Bacalar Chico
Tres Garantías
San Estevan
Tesoro
COROZAL
Deer Caye
José Rovirosa
Yo Creek
L Cayo Frances Lagoon
Tomás Garrido
Agua Blanca
Orange Walk
Cayo Negro
Cuello
Carmelita
Ambergris Caye
Calderón
p229
August Pine Ridge
Neustadt
La Unión
Maskall
San Pedro
Hol Chan Marine Park
San Felipe
Revenge
Cangrejo Caye
Tres Leguas
Blue Creek Village
BELIZE
La Milpa
Water Bank
Crooked Tree
Santana
Lamanai
New
Altun Ha
Hick's Caye
Caye Caulker
Río Bravo Conservation Area
Crooked Tree Wildlife Sanctuary
Rockstone Pond
Caye Chapel
Ixcán Río
Indian Church
Northern Hwy
ORANGE WALK
Sand Hill
Long Caye
Crawl Caye
Kinal
Silvester's Camp
Hill Bank
Flowers Bank
Rider Caye
St George's Caye
Rendezvous Point
Gallon Jug
Belize City
Chan Chich
BELIZE
Bermudian Landing
Ladyville
Drowned Cayes
Northern Caye
p218
Big Falls Farm
Turneffe Islands
Cenoti Camp
Belize Harbour
Douglas Caye
Lighthouse Reef
Ceiba
Labouring
Belize Zoo
Western Hwy
Castile
L Northern
Water Caye
Blackbird Caye
Azul
Yalbac Camp
Gracy Rock Bank
English Caye
Los Tambos
Cotton Tree
Democracia
Watters Point
Blue Hole
Calabash Caye
Half Moon Caye
Spanish Lookout
Coastal Hwy
L Southern
Middle Long Caye
Deadman's Caye
Long Caye
Floral Park
Belize River
BELMOPAN
Darknight Cave
Daylight Cave
Roaring Creek
San Ignacio
Georgeville
Gales Point
Alligator Caye
Big Caye Bokel
Caves Branch
St Thomas
Colson Caye
Xunantunich
Actun Tunichil Muknal Cave
Over-the-Top-Camp
Southern Long Caye
Melchor de Mencos
San Antonio
Blue Hole National Park
Middlesex
Benque Viejo del Carmen
Hummingbird Hwy
Pomona
Columbus Cay
Hidden Valley Falls
Mountain Pine Ridge
Mayflower Camp
Dangriga
Glovers Reef
Rio Frio Cave
Macal R
Society Hall Nature Reserve
STANN CREEK
Tobacco Caye
South Water Caye
Hopkins
Sittee River Village
Twin Cayes
New Maria Camp
Kendal
North East Caye
CAYO
Inner Channel
Middle Caye
Caracol
Locust Bank
Millionario
p248
Cockscomb Basin Wildlife Sanctuary
South West Caye
Maya Mountains
Salsipuedes
Riversdale
Alabama
Arabato Camp
Cowpen
Mango Creek
Seine Bight Village
Calera Camp
Independence
Placencia
Big Creek
Medina Bank
Melvin's Bank
Palmetto Caye
Silk Cayes
p258
TOLEDO
Hellgate
Monkey River Village
Ranguana Caye
Lubaantun
San Pedro Columbia
San José
Big Falls
San Antonio
The Snake Cayes
Tom Owen's Caye
Blue Creek
Aguacate
Toledo
Lawrence Rock
Santa Theresa
Punta Gorda
Hunting Caye
Sapodilla Cayes
Pusilhá
San Lucas
Gulf of Honduras
Punta Manabique
Barranco
Dolores
Bahía de Amatique
Estero Lagarto
Modesto Méndez
Aguacate
Sarstún
San Juan
Toquelá
Semox
Siete Altares
Livingston
Puerto Barrios
20 km
20 miles
Las Pavas
Santo Tomás de Castilla
Agua Caliente
Río Dulce
N
Don't miss...
1 Caye Caulker ▸▸ p230
2 Blue Hole ▸▸ p232.
3 Lamanai ▸▸ p242.
4 Actun Tunichil Muknal Cave ▸▸ p249
5 Cockscomb Basin Wildlife Sanctuary ▸▸ p261.

Introduction

Belize gained English as a mother tongue from illegal loggers back in the 1700s and independence from Britain in 1971. This difference in parenting sets it apart from its Spanish-speaking neighbours and gives the country a distinctive Caribbean flavour. Measuring 174 miles north to south and just 80 miles across, Belize nestles on the coast between Mexico and Guatemala, with a land area of only 8,860 sq miles. Yet within its borders are myriad landscapes, from remote mountains and tropical rainforests to bird-filled wetlands and fertile foothills. Off the coast small sandy islands, known as cayes, and a 184-mile barrier reef, with crystal clear water, attract visitors in search of world-class diving, snorkelling and sport fishing. Inland, there are jungle rivers to explore and protected nature reserves, where jaguars, monkeys and other wildlife thrive. Discover Maya ruins above ground or venture into the spiritual underworld on a caving expedition. Poor but improving roads can make it an adventure to get around but, as the beaten-up school bus works its way down the old Hummingbird Highway, you'll be won over by some of the region's most impressive scenery and by the friendly, laid-back attitude of the country's small but ethnically diverse population.

Ratings

Landscape
★★★★★

Chillin'
★★★★★

Activities
★★★★★

Culture
★★

Wildlife
★★★★★

Costs
$$$$$

Belize City and the Western Highway

In any other country Belize City would be a dusty backwater, but in Belize it is the centre of the country, a blend of Latin American and Caribbean influences. Clapboard houses line dusty streets while people huddle in groups as the world drifts idly by. Born of the Belize River, when the logs used to float downstream, it is still the main hub for maritime transport, with boat services to the cayes. Nearby Belize Zoo is a model for zoos throughout the world.

Inland, the capital Belmopan, enjoys the cursed pleasure of being a planned city. Founded after a devastating hurricane struck Belize City, it has survived as the country's political centre, and has recently grown as a response to several hurricanes that hit the country.

Getting there Good US and international air connections. Buses to all towns. Boats to Caye Caulker and Ambergris Caye.
Getting around By foot or taxi around town, and bus along the highway.
Time required 2 days.
Weather Good all year, wettest in Jun/Jul, overcast until Nov.
Sleeping Good range of options, most stylish near Fort George Lighthouse area.
Eating Great variety, but no obvious quality options.
Activities and tours Golf, tours to all parts of Belize.
★ **Don't miss...** meeting the local wildlife at Belize Zoo ▸▸*p221*.

Belize City and around ▸▸ *pp 223-228*

Belize City is the old capital and the largest town in Belize. Most of the houses are wooden, often of charming design, with galvanized iron roofs. Most stand on seven-ft-high piles – signs of a bygone age when the city used to experience regular flooding.

Hurricane Hattie swept a 10-ft tidal wave into the town on 31 October

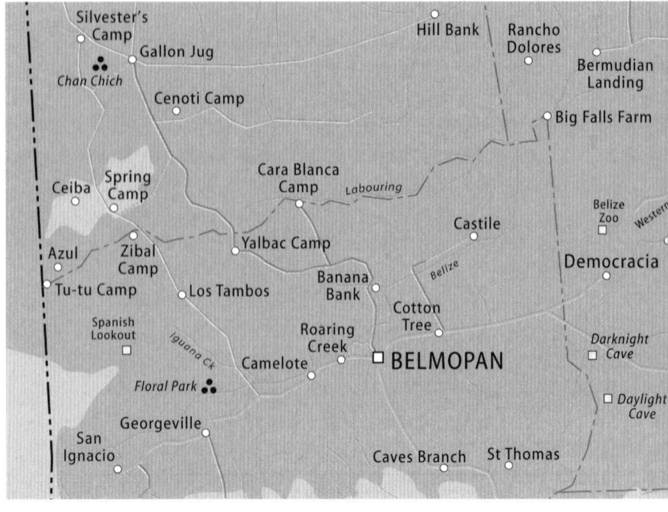

1961, causing devastation and loss of life and, in 1978, Hurricane Greta caused further extensive damage. Belize City and the country escaped Mitch, however, in 1998 as the hurricane literally 'walked round Belize', turning south offshore to hit Honduras and the Bay Islands, before working its way through Guatemala. Hurricane Keith hit Ambergris Caye in October 2000, followed by Hurricane Iris in 2002; both were reminders of the inherent risks of Belize City's location.

The city has improved greatly in recent years with the cleaning of the canals, the reclamation of land and a spate of building around the Eyre Street area. A new Museum of Belize has opened and the Bliss Institute and the House of Culture have both been renovated. Just under a quarter of the total population live here, with the African strain predominant. Humidity is high, but the summer heat is tempered by the northeast trade winds.

Ins and outs

Getting there and around International flights arrive at **Phillip Goldson International Airport (BZE)**, 10 miles from Belize City along the northern highway. Facilities in the check-in area include toilets, a restaurant, bank (daily 0830-1100 and 1330-1630), viewing deck and duty-free shop. No facilities on arrivals side but you can just walk round to the check-in area. Taxi fare to town is US$20, 30 minutes, taxi drivers strongly discourage sharing so team up, if need be, before getting outside. Make sure your taxi is legitimate by checking for the green licence plates. Taxis all operate on a fixed rate, so you should get the same price quoted by every driver. Ask to see a rate sheet if you have doubts about the price. Any bus going up the Northern Highway passes the airport junction (US$1), from where it's a 1½ mile walk. The **municipal airstrip** is 15 mins' drive from the centre on the northern side of town; taxi, US$7.50, no bus service.

Buses run to/from Belize City to all areas of the country; there are also international services to Chetumal in Mexico and to Melchor de Mencos and Flores/Tikal in Guatemala. The bus station is on West Collette Canal Street to the west of town (left luggage, US$0.50), an area that requires some caution. If arriving or leaving at night or in the early morning, arrange for a taxi (US$3 to/from the centre) as walking through this part of town in darkness with luggage can be dangerous.

Speedboats to Caye Caulker and Ambergris Caye (San Pedro) depart from either the **Marine Terminal** southeast of the swing bridge or from the **Thunderbolt** terminal northwest of the swing bridge. ›› *p226*.

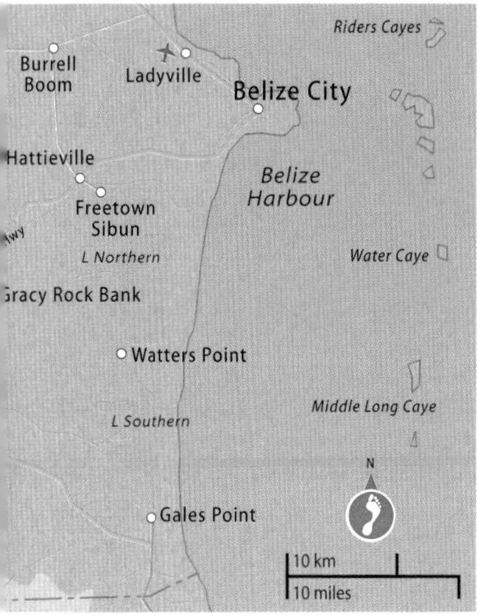

Riders Cayes
Burrell Boom
Ladyville
Belize City
Hattieville
Belize Harbour
Freetown Sibun
L Northern
Water Caye
Gracy Rock Bank
Watters Point
Middle Long Caye
L Southern
N
Gales Point
10 km
10 miles

Tourist offices Belize Tourist Board *ⓘ New Central Bank Building, Level 2, Gabourel Lane, PO Box 325, T223-1913, freephone from USA and Canada T1-800-6240686, www.travelbelize.org, Mon-Thu 0800-1200, 1300-1700, Fri 1630*, provides complete bus schedule (although it may be out of date) with a map of Belize City, as well as a list of hotels and their prices. BTB also has an office on the main floor of the Central Bank and occupies a desk in the Tourism Village as well. The **Belize Tourism Industry Association** *ⓘ 10 North Park St, T227-5717, www.btia.org*, is a private sector body for hotels, tour companies etc, with brochures and information on members throughout Belize.

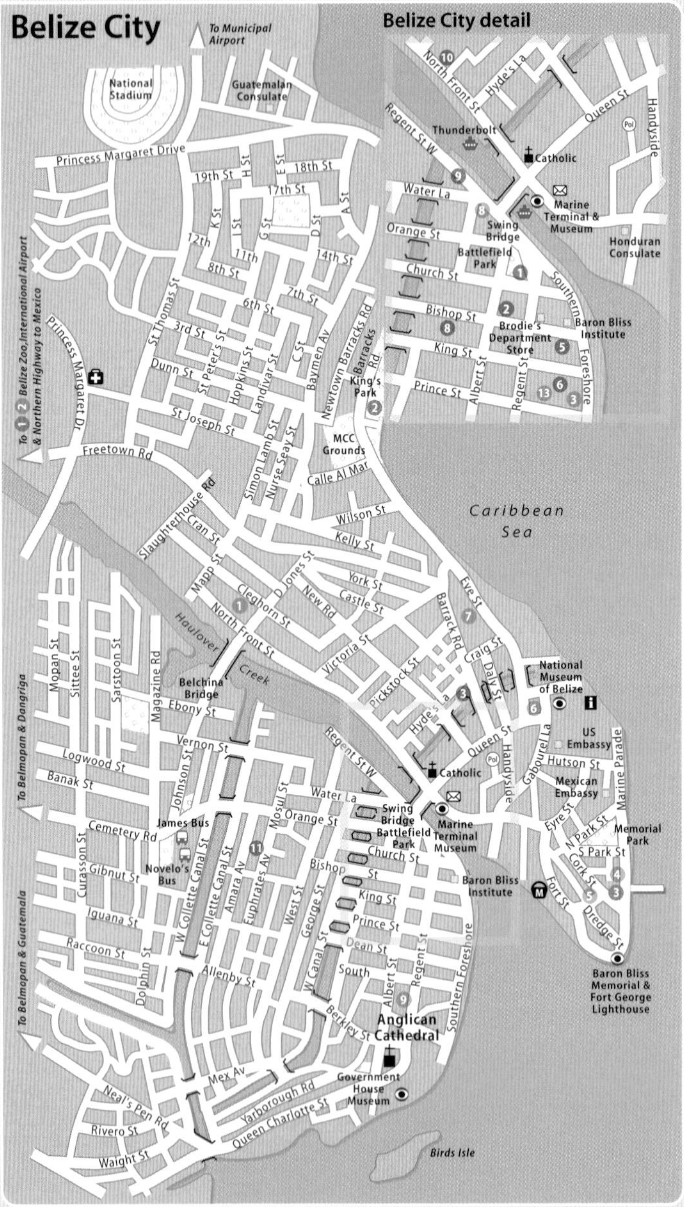

Belize City

Belize City detail

Sleeping

Bakadeer Inn **1**
Belize River Lodge **2**
Bellevue **3**
Chateau Caribbean **4**
Colton House **5**
Downtown Guest House **6**
Freddie's **7**
Isabel Guest House **8**
Mopan **9**
Seaside Guest House **13**

Eating

Big Daddy's **1**
Blue Bird Café **2**
Dario's **3**
El Centro Pizza **5**
Jambel's Jerk Pit **6**
Macy's **8**
Marlin **9**
Mar's **10**
New Chon Saan **11**

Bars & clubs

Paradise 21 **1**
Princess Hotel **2**
Radisson Fort George **3**

Safety The introduction of **tourist police** (dark green uniforms) to patrol the city centre and give advice to visitors has greatly reduced crime in the city; the situation now requires sensible caution rather than paranoia. Nevertheless, you should keep a close eye on your possessions at all times. It is also wise to avoid small, narrow side streets and stick to major thoroughfares, although even on main streets you can be the victim of unprovoked threats and racial abuse. Travel by taxi is advisable, particularly at night and in the rain. Street money changers are not to be trusted. Guides have to be licensed and should carry a photo ID. Watch out for conmen. Cars should only be left in guarded car parks; in return for a tip, hotel security officers will look after cars for a few days while you go to the Cayes.

Sights

Haulover Creek divides the city and is crossed by the antiquated **swing-bridge** which opens to let large vessels pass, if required, usually between 1730 and 1800. Three canals further divide the city. The main commercial area is either side of the swing-bridge: most shops are on the south side along Regent and Albert Streets, with offices and embassies generally on the northern side.

At the top of Regent Street is overgrown **Battlefield Park** (formerly Central Park), surrounded by administration and court buildings. At the southern end of the street is the **Anglican Cathedral** (St John's; not always open, but with regular services), built in the early 19th century with bricks brought from England as ships' ballast. In the days before the foundation of the Crown Colony, the kings of the Mosquito Coast were crowned in the cathedral. Inside, note the 19th-century memorial plaques which give a harrowing account of early deaths from 'country fever' (yellow fever) and other tropical diseases.

Nearby is **Government House Museum** ⓘ *Mon-Fri 0830-1200, 1300-1630, US$2.50*, another Victorian building that draws on the romantic and grand memories of colonialism. It contains some interesting pictures of colonial times, displays of furniture and silver and glassware, as well as a display showing fishing techniques and model boats. Pleasant gardens surround the museum. The wood sculpture of Charles Gabb, who introduced Zericote carving into Belize, can be seen at the **Art Centre**, near Government House.

On the north side of the swing-bridge, turn left up North Front Street for some of the cheaper hotels and the **Thunderbolt** services to Caye Caulker (see page 238) or turn right for the **Marine Terminal Museum** ⓘ *erratic opening hours, US$3*. Housed in a former fire station, the museum features a somewhat tired mangrove exhibition, reef exhibition and aquarium. Further north, the jail building (1857) in front of the Central Bank on Gabourel Lane has been beautifully renovated and is now the **National Museum of Belize** ⓘ *T223-4524, www.museumofbelize.org, Tue-Sat 1000-1800, US$5*, with exhibits on the history of Belize City, and a permanent display about the country's Maya sites. Some exhibits originate from the University of Belize's Department of Archaeology in Belmopan.

Continuing to the right from the swing-bridge on North Front Street, pop into the **Image Factory Art Foundation** ⓘ *91 Front St, Mon-Fri 0900-1800*, which has exhibitions of contemporary local arts – more grassroots than the other galleries. Heading east is the new **Tourism Village**, which caters for cruise ship tourists with an array of souvenir shops, handicraft outlets and snack bars. A little further on, at the tip of the peninsula on Marine Parade, is **Memorial Park**, marked by a small obelisk, two cannon and concrete benches dotted with the holes of land crabs. The views across the bay can be spectacular in the early morning. The small park by the **Fort George Lighthouse** has a children's play area and is a popular meeting place.

West of Belize City

The Western Highway from Belize City heads inland towards Belmopan (a one-hour drive), and San Ignacio. The small but excellent **Belize Zoo** ⓘ *28 miles from Belize City,*

Belize City

www.belizezoo.org, daily 0900-1700, US$7.50, take any bus from Belize City along the Western Highway (1 hr), is definitely worth a visit, even for those who usually hate zoos but get there early to miss the coach party arrivals. The trip is very easy, with buses from Belize City passing the entrance every half hour. The zoo has a wonderful collection of local species (originally gathered for a wildlife film), lovingly cared for and displayed in wire-mesh enclosures amid native trees and shady vegetation, including jaguar and smaller cats, pacas (called gibnuts in Belize), snakes, monkeys, parrots, crocodile, tapir (mountain cow), peccary (wari) and many more. There are tours by enthusiastic guides, as well as T-shirts and postcards sold for fundraising. Apparently Cameron Diaz enjoyed it when she popped in!

At Mile 31½, the **Monkey Bay Wildlife Sanctuary** protects 1,070 acres of tropical forest and savannah between the highway and the Sibun River (great swimming and canoeing). Birds are abundant and guided tours of the trails are available. Some 48 miles from Belize City is the junction for the Hummingbird Highway south to Dangriga (Stann Creek Town).

Belmopan and further west » pp 223-228

As capital of Belize, Belmopan has been the seat of government since August 1970. Its location, 50 miles inland near the junction of the Western and Hummingbird highways, though curious, is easily explained. Following the devastation caused in Belize City by Hurricane Hattie in 1961, it was decided to plan a town which could be a centre for government, business and study away from the coast: Belmopan is the result. Other hurricanes in recent years have renewed interest in developing the capital; several government organizations have relocated to the city, injecting a desperately needed 'heart' to this most eerie of capitals, but of the planned population of 40,000 still only a fraction have materialized. The city can be seen in less than an hour – almost between bus journeys.

From Belmopan to San Ignacio

At the confluence of the Belize River and Roaring Creek is the 50-acre **Guanacaste National Park** ⓘ *US$2.50*, protecting a parcel of 'neotropical rainforest' and a huge 100-year-old *guanacaste* (tubroos) tree, which shelters a wide collection of epiphytes including orchids. Many mammals (jaguarundi, kinkajou, agouti etc) and up to 100 species of bird may be seen from the three miles of nature trails cut along the river. This is a particularly attractive swimming and picnicking spot at which to stop or break the journey if travelling on to Guatemala. It has a visitors' centre, where luggage can be left. To get there, take an early morning bus from Belize City, see the park in a couple of hours, then pick up a bus going to San Ignacio or Dangriga.

Soon after the junction to Belmopan is **Roaring Creek**, once a thriving town but now rather overshadowed by the barely illuminated capital nearby. At Camelote, a dirt road southwards takes you to **Roaring River** » *223*.

The important but unimpressive **Floral Park** archaeological site is just beyond the bridge over **Barton Creek** (Mile 64). Two miles further is **Georgeville**, from where a gravel road runs south into the Mountain Pine Ridge Forest Reserve (see page 252). The highway passes the turn-off at Norland for **Spanish Lookout**, a Mennonite settlement area six miles north (*B & F Restaurant*, Centre Road, by Farmers' Trading Centre, clean, excellent value).

Small settlements provide interest along the way until the highway reaches **Santa Elena**, from where two bridges cross the Macal river to **San Ignacio**. The substantial Hawkesworth suspension bridge is only used by traffic travelling east; to continue west you must use the small, one-lane 'Diversion Bridge': watch for the sign, turn right in front of the Social Security building, then left at the end of the block. The next right turn leads you to the bridge.

Sleeping

Belize City *p218, map p220*

AL **Chateau Caribbean**, 6 Marine Parade, by Fort George, T223-0800, www.chateaucaribbean.com Main building is beautiful, colonial, well maintained with a/c, good bar, restaurant (excellent Chinese and seafood), sea view, good service, disco, parking.

A **Bakadeer Inn**, 74 Cleghorn St, T223-1286, F223-6506, mcfield@btl.net Private bath, breakfast US$4, a/c, TV, fridge, friendly. Recommended.

A **Colton House**, 9 Cork St, T203-4666, www.coltonhouse.com Named after the owners, a delightful 1928 colonial-style home, private bath, some a/c, overhead fans, large rooms, friendly, helpful, quiet. Recommended.

B **Belize River Lodge**, Ladyville, PO Box 459 Belize City, T225-2002, F225-2298, www.belizeriverlodge.com Out of town, 10 mins from the airport on the Belize River, excellent accommodation and food popular for fishing (from lodge or cruises), also scuba facilities, numerous packages, call in advance.

B **Mopan**, 55 Regent St, T227-7351, F227-5383, www.hotelmopan.com 16 rooms with bath, breakfast, a/c, in historic house, has restaurant and bar, nice but pricey, new management very keen to help.

C **Freddie's**, 86 Eve St, T223-3851. With shower and toilet, fan, hot water, clean, very nice, secure, very small.

C **Isabel Guest House**, 3 Albert St, above Matus Store, PO Box 362, T227-3139. 3 double rooms, 1 huge triple room, quiet except when nearby disco operating at weekends, private shower, clean, friendly, safe, Spanish spoken. Isabel is very friendly. Highly recommended.

C-E **Seaside Guest House**, 3 Prince St, T227-8339, seasidebelize@btl.net Private and shared baths, very clean, pleasant verandah with view out to the bay, a great place to stay. Breakfast, drinks, book swap, credit cards accepted, internet access on site. Recommended. E per person in bunk room.

C-F **Downtown Guest House**, 5 Eve St, T223-2057. Mixed rooms, some doubles, some dormitories, hot shower in shared bath, secure, clean and friendly. Good information board if a little rundown.

West of Belize City *p221*

A **Caesar's Place**, Mile 60, PO Box 48, San Ignacio, T824-2341, www.blackrock lodge.com, under same ownership as Black Rock Lodge (see p253). 4 rooms with bath, 4 full hook-ups for RVs, with showers and bathroom facilities, restaurant and bar, gift shop, swimming.

A-D **Roaring River**, Roaring Creek, T820-2037, www.roaringriverbelize.com. New owners, run by a friendly Belgian couple. Nice lodge along the river, cabañas, quiet, swimming pool, bar and tours. D for camping or lodgeroom.

E **Monkey Bay Wildlife Sanctuary**, PO Box 187, Mile 31 Western Highway, Belmopan, T820-3032, www.watershedbelize.org Dormitory accommodation US$7.50 per person, or you can camp on wooden platform with thatched roof for US$5, swim in the river, showers available, take meals with family for US$4 (there are plans to provide cooking facilities in the future).

Belmopan *p222*

A **Bull Frog**, 25 Half Moon Av, a 15-min walk east of the market through the Parliament complex or a short taxi ride from the bus station, T822-3425, www.bullfroginn.com A/c, good, reasonably priced, laundry, karaoke nights on Thu (popular with locals).

C **El Rey Inn**, 23 Moho St, T822-3438, hibiscus@btl.net Big room with fan, hot and cold water, basic, clean, friendly, laundry on request, central. Also restaurant.

Eating

Belize City *p218, map p220*

It can be difficult to find places to eat 1500-1800.

TTT **Jambel's Jerk Pit**, 2 King St, T227-6080. Excellent variety of Belizean and Jamaican dishes, including fresh seafood and vegetarian dishes. Patio.

TT **El Centro Pizza**, 4 Bishop St, T227-2413. Good pizza and local dishes. A/c dining room and delivery available.

TT **Macy's**, 18 Bishop St, T227-3419. Recommended for well-prepared local game, Creole cooking, different fixed menu daily, charming host.

TT **Marlin**, 11 Regent St West, overlooking Belize River, T227-3913. Varied menu, good seafood.

TT **Mar's**, 118 North Front St. Clean, pleasant, family cooking, reasonable prices, good.

TT **Sumathi**, 190 Newtown Barracks, T223-1172. Good Indian food.

T **Big Daddy's** on 2nd floor of market building, Church St, opposite BTL office. Good food, with pleasant view over the harbour. Closes when the food runs out.

T **Blue Bird Café**, Albert St. Cheap fruit juices, specialities, basic, clean.

T **Dario's**, 33 Hyde's Lane. Classic Belizean hot meat pies, try 1 and then buy in bulk if you like them.

T **New Chon Saan**, 55 Euphrates Av, T227- 2709. Best Chinese in town, pleasant atmosphere, takeaway. A thriving Chinese community means most Chinese food in Belize City is authentic.

Belmopan *p222*

Eating options are limited: try El Rey Inn (see Sleeping) or one of several cheap *comedores* at the back of the market. There are a few bakeries near Constitution Drive. Cafés are closed on Sun.

TT **Caladium**, next to market, limited fare, moderately priced, small portions.

T **Aloha Café**, next to Scotiabank, friendly staff, good for breakfast or lunch, coffee, snacks, ice cream. Local newspapers.

Entertainment

Belize City *p218, map p220*

Lots of bars, some with jukeboxes, poolrooms and karaoke nights. Try the local drink, anise and peppermint, known as 'A and P'; also the powerful 'Old Belizeno' rum. The local beer, Belikin, is good, as is the 'stout', strong and free of gas. Guinness is also served, but is expensive. Clubs often have a cover charge of US$5, and drinks are expensive once inside.

The best and safest bars are found at major hotels, Fort George, 2 Marine Parade, T2223-333; Biltmore Plaza, 3 ½ miles on Northern Highway, T223-2302; Bellevue and Princess, which has a wide range of entertainment on offer. Fri night is the most popular for going out. Happy hour on Fri starts at 1600 at Fort George and continues at Biltmore, Princess and elsewhere.

Bellevue Hotel Bar, 5 Southern Foreshore, T227-7051, has multiple entertainment for Fri nights, including 1 or 2 live bands and karaoke.

Eden Nightclub, Newtown Barracks, DJs or live music from 2200 Thu-Sat nights.

MJ's Grand, Newtown Barracks,

Belizean airwaves

Listening to the radio when travelling is a great insight to a country, and the importance of tourism to Belize is clear when you tune into Love FM. Whether in your hotel, on the beach or bouncing along on a bus, you've got to laugh when the big voice booms "Be kind to tourists." How's that for public service broadcasting? Tune in on 88.9 or 95.1FM when travelling around and take a little piece of Belize home by listening to www.lovefm.com on the internet.

multi-story new nightclub, from 2200, lots of live acts and DJ dancing.

Paradise 21, 1 mile out of town on Northern Highway in a former lumber yard at a nice location on the river, recommended.

Princess Hotel, Kings Park, T223-2670. Top bands at weekends in Club Calypso. Bowling lanes Tue-Sun and large games room. Casino, with free drinks while you're gambling, a floor show with Russian dancers and a free buffet at 2330. There's also a 2-theatre modern cinema, showing recent movies for US$7.50.

The Wet Lizard, Colton House, near the Tourism Village. Good American/Creole fare, reasonable prices, great view. From US$8-30, better value for lunch.

Shopping

Belize City *p218, map p220*

The whole city closes down on Sun except for a few shops open in the morning. Banks and many shops and offices are also closed on Sat afternoons.

Brodies Department Store, Central Park end of Regent St. Central one-stop shop for wide selection of groceries (prices are slightly higher than at other stores), books, postcards and Xericote carvings. Open Sun am.

Books

Angelus Press, 10 Queen St. Excellent selection of stationery supplies.

Book Center, 4 Church St, T227-7457, books@btl.net, above **Thrift Center**. Very good selection including second-hand and back issues of some US magazines.

The Book Shop, 126 Freetown Rd. New and second-hand books, book exchange.

Food and drink

The **market** is by the junction of North Front St and Fort St.

Ro-Macs, 27 Albert St. Excellent supermarket includes wide selection of imported foods and wines.

Thrift Center, 2 Church St. Good food store, especially for dry goods at competitive prices.

Crafts and souvenirs

Handicrafts, woodcarvings and straw items are all good buys.

Zericote (or Xericote) wood carvings can be bought at **Brodies**, the **Fort George Hotel**, 2 Marine Parade, T223-3333, or **Egbert Peyrefitte**, 11a Cemetery Rd. To find a carver rather than buy the tourist fare in shops, ask a taxi driver. Some wood carvers sell their work in front of the main hotels.

Belize Audubon Society, across from the Tourist Village near the lighthouse, has a small but good selection of posters, T-shirts, gifts, and jewellery, all locally made in villages, and all at very reasonable prices.

National Handicraft Center, South Park St. The Belize Chamber of Commerce's showcase promotes craftspeople from all over Belize; come here first for an

overview of Belizean art and crafts. Also good books about Belize culture.
Tourist Village. Many vendors are setting up around this area (although only open when a ship is in town).

Activities and tours

Belize City *p218, map p220*

Tour operators

Maya Travel Services, 42 Cleghorn St, T223-1623, www.mayatravelservices.com Positive reports.
S&L Guided Tours, 91 North Front St, T227-7593, www.sltravelbelize.com Recommended group travel (minimum 4 people for most tours, 2 people to Tikal).
Sunrise Travel, T227-2051 or T223-2670, helps arrange diving trips to Lighthouse Reef and the Blue Hole, advance book.

From Belmopan to San Ignacio

Golf

Roaring River Golf, south of Camelote, T614-6525. 9-hole golf course, green fee US$12, clubs US$5-8.

Transport

Belize City *p218, map p220*

Air

Flights to the islands are available from both the international airport and municipal airport. Flights to and from the international airport cost about US$20 more each way but companies link their flights to international arrivals and departures (see p17 and p21). There are hourly flights from the international airport to **San Pedro** and **Caye Caulker** from 0740 to 1640 with Tropic Air and Maya Island Air; less frequent from the municipal airport. Services also to **Corozal** (Tropic Air), **Big Creek**, **San Ignacio**, **Placencia**, **Dangriga**, **Punta Gorda**, with Maya Island Air and Tropic Air. Maya and Tropic also have services to **Flores**, Guatemala.

Airline offices American Airlines, New Rd and Queen St, T223-2168. **British Airways**, T227-7363, airport T225-2060. **Continental Airlines**, 80 Regent St, T227-8223, airport T225-2263. **Belize Global Travel Services**, 41 Albert St, T227-7363, www.belizeglobal.com, provides services for Grupo Taca and US Airways. **Maya Island Air**, 6 Fort St, T233-1140, www.mayaislandair.com **Tropic Air**, Albert Street, T224-5671, www.tropicair.com.

Sea

Boats to **Caye Caulker** (45 mins, US$15 return) and **San Pedro** (Ambergris Caye; US$25 return) leave from the **Marine Terminal**, North Front St, at 0900, 1030, 1200, 1330, 1500 and 1700 (Caye Caulker only). The trip can be 'exciting' if it's rough. There are also services from the **Thunderbolt Terminal**, North Front St, T226-2904, www.ambergriscaye.com/thunderbolt, at 0800, 1300 and 1600, to **Caye Caulker** (US$7.50 single) and **San Pedro** (US$12.50).

Bus

Within the city the fare is US$0.50. There are bus services to all the main towns.

North towards **Chetumal** (Mexico, p197), about 15 daily each way, roughly every 30 mins, 0500-1800, 3 hrs, US$5; also express buses from 0600 stopping at **Orange Walk** and **Corozal** only, US$6.50, 2½ hrs.

West towards **Guatemala**, via **Belmopan** and **San Ignacio**, express bus 0900, US$3, with a/c and refreshments; ordinary bus every 30 mins, Mon-Sat frequent 0600-1900, Sun 0630-1700, US$1 to Belmopan, US$4 to **Benque Viejo**. If heading to Guatemala, the 0600, 0630 and 1015 buses connect at the border with services to **Flores**, Guatemala. The last possible bus connection to Flores leaves the border at 1600, but it is better to get an earlier bus to arrive in daylight. Service provided by Novelo's, T228-2025.

To Flores, Guatemala, minibuses leave the A & R Station on Front St at 0500, make reservation the previous day. Also 1st-class express buses from Belize City to **Flores/Tikal** with Mundo Maya/Línea Dorada 1000 and 1700, with buses connecting to Guatemala City and beyond. Check the Mundo Maya counter in the Marine Terminal on North Front St.

Heading south to **Dangriga**, via Belmopan and the Hummingbird Highway, Southern Transport, T227-3937, from Novelo's bus station, several daily on the hour 0800-1600, plus Mon 0600, US$5. James, to **Punta Gorda** via Dangriga, Cockscomb Basin Wildlife Sanctuary and Mango Creek, daily 0530, 1000 and 1500, 8-12 hrs, US$11.

Car

Car hire Cars start at US$60 plus insurance of around US$15 a day. Most rental firms have offices in Belize City and opposite the international airport terminal building. Avis, Poinsetta Rd, Ladyville, T205-2629, avisbelize@btl.net, largest fleet, well- maintained, Daihatsus and Isuzu Troopers. Budget, 771 Bella Vista, T223-2435, www.budget.com, good service, well-maintained vehicles, good deals (Suzukis and Isuzu Troopers). Crystal Auto Rental, Mile 4¾ Northern Highway, T223-1600, www.crystal-belize.com, helpful, cheapest deals in town, but not always most reliable, wide selection of vehicles including 30-seater bus, will release insurance papers for car entry to Guatemala and Mexico, also buys second-hand cars but at a poor price. Pancho's, 5747 Lizarraga Av, T224-5554, www.panchosrentalbelize, locally owned rental company. Safari/Hertz, 11a Cork St, beside Radisson Fort George Hotel, T223-0268, F223-5395, safari@btl.net, Isuzu Troopers.

Taxis

Official cabs have green licence plates (drivers must also have identification card). There is a taxi stand on Central Park, opposite Barclays, another on the corner of Collet Canal St and Cemetery Rd, and a number of taxis on Albert St, Queen St and around town. Within Belize City, US$3 for 1 or 2 people.

Outside Belize City, US$1.75 per mile, regardless of number of passengers. Best to ask price of the ride before setting off. No meters, so beware of overcharging and make sure fare is quoted in Bz$. Belize City to the resorts in Cayo District approximately US$100-125, 1-4 people (ask for Edgar August or Martin at Radisson Fort George desk, reliable and can do guided tours around Belize).

Belmopan *p222*

Bus

All leave from Novelo's bus station, in the market area. To **San Ignacio**, Mon-Sat, every 30 mins, 0600-2200, Sun hourly, 0700-2000, 1 hr, US$2.50. To **Belize City**, Mon-Sat, every 30 mins, 0600-1900, hourly on Sun, 1 hr, US$3.50. Heading south hourly buses Mon-Sat 0830-1630 (fewer on Sun) to **Dangriga** (1 hr, US$3), **Mango Creek** (3 hrs, US$8) and **Punta Gorda** (4½ hrs, US$9). James Bus leave for Belize City and Punta Gorda from opposite the Novelo bus station (next to the market vendors). To **Orange Walk** and **Corozal** take an early bus to Belize City and change.

Directory

Belize City *p218, map p220*

Banks

All banks have facilities to arrange cash advance on Visa. It is easy to have money wired to Belize City. Guatemalan quetzales and Mexican pesos are best bought at the border. There are several ATMs in Belize City – few are found elsewhere at present – only Barclays (Visa) accept foreign bankcards. Atlantic Bank, 6 Albert St, or 16 New Rd (the latter in a safe area), quick efficient service, small charge for Visa/MasterCard, smaller queues than

Belize Bank or Barclays. Belize Bank is particularly efficient and modern, US$0.50 commission on Amex cheques but a big charge for cash against Visa and MasterCard. Barclays Bank International, slightly better rates, 2% commission, no charge for Visa/MasterCard.

Embassies and consulates

See also Belmopan Directory, below. **Canada**, 80 Princess Margaret Drive, T223-1060. **Guatemala**, 8A St, T223-3150 (consulate),T223-3314 (embassy) 0900-1300, will not issue visas or tourist cards here; will tell you to leave it till you reach your exit point. **Honduras**, 114 Bella Vista, T224-5889. **Mexico**, 18 N Park St, T223-0194. **USA**, 29 Gabourel Lane, T227-7161; consulate is round the corner on Hutson St, office hrs, Mon-Fri 0800-1200, 1300-1700.

Internet

Service at **BTL** and in some hotels, prices around US$6 per hr. Keep an eye out for cheaper options, such as **Mailbox**, on Front St and **KSG@**, King St.

Laundry

Northside Laundromat, North Front St, 0900-2000, US$4 for 6 kg wash and dry. **Belize Dry Cleaners and Laundermat**, 3 Dolphin St, or **Stan's Laundry**, 22 Dean St, Mon-Sat 0800-1800, Sun 0800-1300, full service laundry, US$4 per load.

Medical services

Myo' On Clinic Ltd, 40 Eve St, T224-5616, has been recommended. Nearby is the **Pathology Lab**, 17 Eve St. Also recommended are **Belize Medical Associates**, next to the city hospital, and **Dr Lizama**, Handyside Street, consultation US$17.50.

Post office

The main post office is at Queen St and North Front St, 0800-1700 (1630 Fri). Poste restante letters held for a month.

Telephone

Belizean Telecommunications Ltd (BTL), 1 Church St, just off Central Park, Mon-Sat, 0800-1800, Sun 0800-1200. Also fax and booths for credit card and charge calls.

Useful contacts

Baron Bliss Institute, on the Southern Foreshore, is undergoing major renovation. When it's open there will be a public library, temporary exhibitions, 1 Stela and 2 large discs from Caracol on display. **Programme for Belize**, 1 Eyre St, T227-5616, www.pfbelize.org is a conservation organization which manages land reserves including Río Bravo. **Society for the Promotion of Education and Research (SPEAR)**, 5638 Gentle Av, T223-1668, www.spear.org.bz, with a great reference library for everything Belizean.

Belmopan *p222*

Banks

Barclays Bank International (Mon-Thu 0800- 1300, Fri 0800-1300, 1500-1800). Visa ATM, Visa and MasterCard cash advances, no commission (but see Belize City, above). **Scotia Bank** and **Belize Bank** also provide cash advances.

Embassies and consulates

UK High Commission, North Ring Rd, next to the Governor's residence, PO Box 91, T822-2146, www.britishhighbze.com, Mon-Thu 0800-1200, 1300-1600, Fri 0800-1400. Has a list of recommended doctors and dentists.

Internet

Progress.com, Help for Progress, Constitution Drive, Mon-Sat 0800-2000, Sun 1300-1900, US$3 per hr, satellite connection, all profits to local community projects. Also **Techno Hub** at Novelo bus station, US$4.5 per hr.

Post office

The post office is next to the market (opposite the immigration office).

Northern cayes

The 212 sq miles of cayes off the coast of Belize are attractive, relaxing, slow and very 'Caribbean' – an excellent place for all forms of diving, sea fishing or just lazing about. Palm trees fringe the shore, providing day-long shade for resting in your hammock. They are popular destinations, especially in August and between December and May.

The cayes and atolls – small low islands of coral, rock or sand – were formerly used by fishermen as resting points to clean the catch or grow coconuts. St George's Caye, nine miles northeast of Belize City, was once the capital and the scene of the battle in 1798 that established British possession. The Maya built the site of Marco Gonzales on the southwestern tip of Ambergris Caye, the largest and most populated of the islands. Nearby Caye Caulker is a popular destination for the more budget-minded visitor, while serious divers head for the Turneffe Islands to the east. Other, smaller cayes are home to exclusive resorts or remain uninhabited, many being little more than mangrove swamps. Twelve miles off Belize City, English Caye is beautiful, but has no facilities; take a day trip.

Getting there Frequent daily boats from Belize City and Corozal. Flights from Belize City.
Getting around Hire a bicycle or a golf cart.
Time required As long as you need to relax.
Weather Best mid-November to May.
Sleeping Good range from romantic luxury to backpacker bunkhouse.
Eating Seafood and rice, seafood and beans etc.
Activities and tours Scuba diving, swimming, snorkelling, sailing, fishing, windsurfing.
★ **Don't miss...** Snorkelling or diving at the Blue Hole ›› *p232*.

Ambergris Caye

» pp 232-238

Development on this island (pronounced Am-*ber*-gris) has increased rapidly over the last couple of years, with over 50 hotels and guesthouses now registered on the island. Buildings are still restricted to no more than three storeys in height and the many wooden structures maintain an authentic village atmosphere. Hurricane Keith battered the western shore in late 2000, but repairs are now complete and new hotels are opening all the time.

The main centre on the island is the town of **San Pedro**, in the southeast. The **tourist information** office is in the new **Ambergris Museum** ⓘ *T226-2298, opposite Fido's*, which has excellent displays on the history of the town and the caye.

Although there's sand in abundance, there are few beach areas around San Pedro town. The emphasis instead is on snorkelling and scuba diving on the nearby barrier reef and at Hol Chan Marine Park offshore. There's also fine sailing, fishing and board sailing. It can be dangerous to swim near San Pedro and there have been serious accidents with boats. The main jetties are on the east (Caribbean Sea) side of San Pedro but although boats are restricted to about 5 mph within the red buoys (about 25 yds offshore), this rule is not always adhered to. There is a 'safe' beach in front of the park, just south of the Government dock.

A short distance to the north and south of San Pedro lie miles of deserted beaches, where picnic barbecues are popular for day-tripping snorkellers and birders who have visited the nearby small cayes hoping to glimpse rosets, spoonbills or white ibis. If you go north you have to cross a small inlet with hand-pulled ferry, US$0.50 for foreigners. **Note** Only very experienced snorkellers should attempt to swim in the cutting between the reef and the open sea; seek advice on the tides.

Hol Chan Marine Park

ⓘ *Park office (with reef displays and information on Bacalar Chico National Park to the north), Caribeña St, T226-2247. Park entry fee US$5. Snorkelling trips about US$25 (not including entry fee) for 2 hrs. Contact the Reserve Manager in San Pedro for further information.*

Just south of Ambergris Caye, and not far from Caye Caulker, is the Hol Chan Marine Park, one of the most popular destinations for diving and snorkelling trips. This underwater natural park is divided into three zones: Zone A is the reef, where fishing is prohibited; Zone B is the seagrass beds, where fishing can only be done with a special licence (the **Boca Ciega** blue hole is here, not to be confused with the one in Lighthouse Reef, see page 232); Zone C is mangroves where fishing also requires a licence. Fish feeding, although prohibited, takes place at **Shark-Ray Alley**, where about 15 sharks and rays are fed for the entertainment of tourists. It's not the most natural of experiences but fascinating to see these creatures close up. Only certified scuba divers may dive in the reserve.

Bacalar Chico National Park

Formed in 1996, Bacalar Chico National Park protects almost 27,000 acres at the northern section of Ambergris Caye. The region's corals are a breeding ground for the queen conch and a seasonal spawning bank for the nassau and yellowfin grouper. Green and loggerhead turtles also nest in the area. Access is still limited, with a few dive sites in the area.

Caye Caulker

» pp 232-238

Caye Caulker was a quiet lobster-fishing island until recently but its relaxing, laid-back vibe and its gentle climate now entice increasing numbers of tourists. A thin line of white sandy beach falls to a sea of blue and green, with the reef visible a mile and a half from the shore. By day, there's diving and snorkelling, sea and sand; by night there's eating, drinking and dancing.

Ambergris Caye

Tour operators and hotels on the island have worked hard to improve services for visitors, especially since Hurricane Keith, which gave the island quite a battering in late 2000. The wooden beach houses on stilts remain but there are also a growing number of small restaurants and bars. Apart from walking around barefoot, hired golf buggies are the only means of transportation on the island. The atmosphere is friendly and easy-going – especially out of season. Drugs are readily available, but they are illegal and you shouldn't expect any sympathy should you get into difficulties. Sandflies are ferocious in season (Dec-Feb); take long trousers and a good repellent.

The caye is actually two islands separated by a small channel known as the **Cut**, where everyone congregates at dusk to watch the sunset. All the services are on the southern island, while the north is given over to a **marine reserve** ⓘ *US$2 donation*. The arrival pier is in the centre of town, with all the accommodation on or within a 15-min walk of the main street. The southern end of town is slightly quieter, but it's quite a walk from the 'Cut' for swimming or snorkelling. A map, which can be bought on arrival, lists virtually everything on the island.

A walk south along the shore takes you to the new airstrip and to mangroves where the rare black catbird can be seen and heard. There are loads of mosquitoes in this area, so use plenty of repellent. A campaign is underway to make the black catbird's habitat and the associated reef a nature reserve (called Siwa-Ban, after the catbird's Maya name). Details are available from **Galería Hicaco** (Ellen McCrea, near **Tropical Paradise**).

South of Caye Caulker, **Caye Chapel** was once a small, quiet caye dotted with palms and devoid of sandflies, where you could escape to a bit of quiet and solitude. That has all changed, as it is now exclusively expensive, as well as secluded.

Lighthouse Reef and the smaller cayes ▸▸ *pp 232-238*

Lighthouse Reef

Lighthouse Reef is the outermost of the three north-south reef systems off Belize and is some 45 miles to the east of Belize City. Trips out here are not cheap, but if you like diving and have the money, this is one of the best dive sites in the world. There are two cayes of interest: Half Moon Caye (on which the lighthouse stands) and, 12 miles to the north, the atoll in which the diving shrine of the Blue Hole (see below) is found.

On arrival at **Half Moon Caye**, you must register with the warden near the lighthouse, who will provide maps and tell you where you can camp (US$5 per person). The lighthouse, built in 1820 and now solar-powered, gives fine views of the reef. The caye is the site of the **Red-Footed Booby Sanctuary**, a national reserve. The **Belize Audubon Society** (see page 54) maintains the sanctuary, providing a lookout tower and a trail. Around sunset you can watch the boobies from the lookout as they return from fishing, seemingly totally unperturbed by humans. Besides the booby, magnificent frigate birds also nest on the western side of the island, which has denser vegetation (the eastern side is covered mainly in coconut palms). Of the 98 other bird species recorded on Half Moon Caye, 77 are migrants. The iguana, the wish willy (smaller than the iguana) and the Anolis allisoni lizard inhabit the caye, and hawksbill and loggerhead turtles lay their eggs on the beaches.

The **Blue Hole** ⓘ *US$5 entry, priceincluded in any boat trip*, a circular sinkhole, 1,000 ft across and with depths exceeding 400 ft, was recently declared a National Monument and is rated as one of the best dives in the world. It was probably formed by the collapsed roof of a subterranean cave and was studied by Jacques Cousteau in 1984. Stalagmites and stalactites can be found in the underwater cave. The main dive in the Blue Hole is at least 130 ft; check you are properly qualified and experienced enough to dive here; it is advisable to have at least the Advance Open Water PADI course.

Turneffe Islands

The **Turneffe Islands** are 30 miles off the Belizean mainland. There are a few exclusive resorts around the three atolls, focussing on diving, fishing and top-notch relaxation. **Goff Caye**, 5 miles west of Turneffe Islands, is a paradise - a perfect, circular island, with good snorkelling. During the full moon each January, thousands of Nassau groupers gather to spawn at **Glory Caye** on Turneffe Reef.

Sleeping

Ambergris Caye *p230*

San Pedro

See also Budget buster, p.

AL **San Pedro Holiday Hotel**, T226-2014, holiday@btl.net 16 rooms, central location, fun atmosphere with good facilities.

AL **Sun Breeze**, T226-2191, www.sunbreeze.net Near airport, Mexican-style building, a/c, comfortable, all facilities, good dive shop. Recommended.

AL-A **Spindrift**, T226-2018, www.ambergriscaye.com/spindrift 24 rooms, 4 apartments, unattractive block

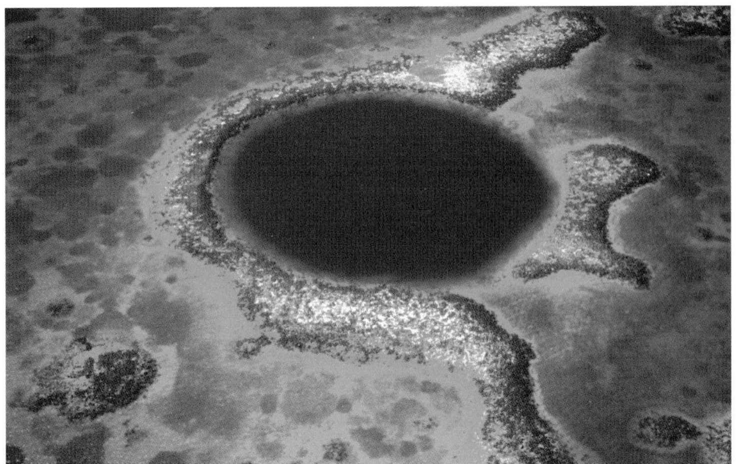

Blue Hole on Lighthouse Reef

but central location, good bar and restaurant, popular meeting place, trips up the Belize River, a/c, comfortable.
AL-B **Coral Beach**, T226-2013, www.coral beachhotel.com Central location, slightly rundown but good local feel and excellent watersports facilities including dive boat charter, tours for fishing and scuba available.
A **Lily's**, T226-2059, www.ambergriscaye.com/lilys Rooms with sea view, some with a/c, others with fan, clean.
C **Tomas**, 12 Barrier Reef Drive, T226-2061. Airy rooms, fan, bath, drinking water, clean, friendly.
C-D **Ruby's**, San Pedro Town on the beach, T226-2063, www.ambergriscaye.com/rubys Fan, private bath, good views, beach cabañas, central. Recommended as best value in town.
D **Milo's Hotel**, T226-2033, F226-2198. 9 rooms, one of the cheapest hotels, bit run down but popular with budget travellers.

Caye Caulker *p230*

In all accommodation, take precautions against theft. Camping on the beach is forbidden. See also Budget buster, p.
AL-C **Tropical Paradise Resort**, PO Box 1206, Belize City, T226-0124, F226-0225. Cabins with hot showers, clean, restaurant, good excursions.
AL-E **Vega Inn**, T226-0142, www.vega.com.bz Suites, private and budget rooms, camping and credit cards accepted. All doubles, with ceiling fan, fresh linen and showers, shared with campsite, which is guarded, drinking water, hot water, clean toilets, barbecue, camping gear (US$6 per person).
A **Anchorage**, near **Ignacio's**, T226-0304, www.anchorageresort.com New 2-storey building, comfortable, tiled rooms with private bathrooms, pleasant atmosphere, friendly family, breakfast and drinks served under shade on the beach.
B **Rainbow Hotel**, on the beach heading north, T226-0123, rainbowhotel@btl.net 17 rooms and 1 apartment, with shower, rooms also, **C** , hot water, good. Beach houses rented for US$50-150 a month.
B **Seaside Cabañas**, first place you reach off the boat, T226-0498, www.seaside cabanas.com 12 comfortable rooms and cabins. Excellent tours and very helpful.
C **Shirley's Guest House**, T226-0145, shirley@btl.net, south end of village. Very relaxing, no kids. Recommended.
C **Tree Tops**, T226-0240, www.treetops belize.com Spotless, spacious rooms, comfortable beds with beach views, German spoken, powerful fan, cable TV, friendly, good value. Recommended.
C-D **Edith's**, T226-0161. Rooms with bath or

private chalet. Recommended.

C-D **Marin's**, T 226-0110, good-sized rooms, shared facilities, internet and coffee available.

D **Daisy's**, T226-0150. With shower, toilet and fan, reductions for longer stays, will store valuables, clean, friendly, safe, cheaper rooms downstairs, cashes TCs, rooms with communal bathroom not good value, hot water.

D **Ignacio Beach Cabins**, T614-9012. Double rooms, small huts or hammocks just outside town, C for a hut for 3-4, quiet, clean. Toilet and shower facilities in private cabins only, cheap lobster and free coconuts. Reef trips. Recommended.

D-E **Lorraine's Guest House**, south end, T206-0162. A handful of simple cabins, basic but friendly and quiet

E **Sandy Lane**, T226-0217, 1 block back from main street. Bungalow-type accommodation, clean, private and cheaper shared bathrooms, hot showers, run by Rico and Elma Novelo. Also have rooms with kitchen and TV for longer stays. Recommended.

E **Tina's Backpacker Hostel**, cheapest on the caye, with rooms, camping or sling a hammock. Very popular and noisy – great for meeting people, but not the place if you want peace and quiet. Dirty at times.

Lighthouse Reef and the smaller cayes *p231*

See also Budget buster, p.

AL **Cottage Colony**, St George's Caye. Contact PO Box 428, Belize City, T227-7051, fins@btl.net Colonial-style cabañas with dive facilities, price varies according to season.

AL-A **Ricardo's Beach Huts**, Middle Long Caye, contact PO Box 55, Belize City, T224-4970. Charming and knowledgeable host, rustic, authentic fish, camp feel, overnight camps to Rendez-vous Caye, English Caye and Sargeants Caye can be arranged, excellent food, snorkelling.

A **Moonlight Shadows Lodge**, Middle Long Caye, T822-3665, still being developed but offers complete isolation.

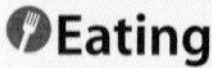

Eating

Ambergris Caye *p230*

For those staying in villas, contact Denny 'The Bun Man', T226-3490, for fresh coffee, orange juice, and excellent cinnamon buns. He will deliver in time for breakfast. See also **Mata Chica** and **Capricorn** resorts, p.

ΨΨΨ **Celi's**, behind **Holiday Hotel**. Good seafood. Recommended.

ΨΨ **Alijua**, San Pedro. Croatian owned, good food, also rents suites with kitchen, US$100 for 4 people.

ΨΨ **Ambergris Delight**, pleasant, inexpensive, clean.

ΨΨ **El Patio**, south of town, beyond Belize Yacht Club. Good, Mexican-style food, live music in evenings.

ΨΨ **Elvi's Kitchen**, popular, upmarket, live music and roof built around flamboyant tree, can be very busy.

ΨΨ **Estel's** on the beach. Good food and 1940s/'50s music.

ΨΨ **Fido's Courtyard**, towards north end of Front St. Lively bar-restaurant often with live music, good lunch and dinner.

ΨΨ **Rasta Pasta**, at **Sunbreeze Hotel**, south end of Front St. Great spicy food and barbecues.

Ψ **Lily's Restaurant**, best seafood in town, friendly, good breakfast, excellent value but quite basic.

Caye Caulker *p230*

All the island's ground-floor restaurants are carpeted in sand which makes it even easier to wander around bare-footed for days on end. Menus don't vary much from restaurant to restaurant – fish, chicken, beans, burgers and burritos are the staple diet. Some places do not open for lunch. Cakes and pastries can be bought at houses displaying signs; recommended are **Daisy's** and **Jessie's**, open 0830-1300, 1500-1700. Buy lobster or fish from the cooperative and cook it at the barbecue on the beach; beer is sold by the crate at the wholesaler on the dock

Budget busters

Several caye resorts offer seclusion and an ambience that borders on paradise. Splash out and enjoy the beach idyll for a few days or a week.

LL **Mata Chica Resort**, 4 miles north of San Pedro, Ambergris Caye, T226-5010, www.matachica.com European owned and managed, beautiful and stylish stucco and thatched cabañas on a lovely beach, fantastic Mambo restaurant.
LL **Lighthouse Reef Resort**, 12 km from the Blue Hole; contact Latin American Reservation Centre, PO Box 1435, Dundee, Fla, US, T1-800-423-3114. Stay for 1 week on a private island on the Lighthouse Reef. Choose between a suite, mini-suite, villa or small cabaña. The restaurant is on a pier looking out to the sunset. All-inclusive price with small airstrip for direct flights.
LL **Caye Chapel Golf Resort**, Caye Chapel. Contact PO Box 192, Belize City, T226-8250, www.cayechapel.com 12 deluxe villas with tennis courts, private airstrip and 18-hole golf course – the ultimate place to get out your clubs.
LL **St George's Island Lodge**, St George's Caye, T220-4444, www.gooddiving.com Contact PO Box 625, Belize City. 8 rooms and half a dozen thatched cottages right on the shore, prices include 2 dives, all meals, transfer from international airport. Specialist diving resort. Boat fare is US$15, day trips are possible.
LL **Turneffe Flats**, Turneffe Islands, 56 Eve St, Belize City, T224-5634, in the US on T1-800-8151304, www.tflats.com Idyllic island living in a divine location. Bleach white sand beaches ideal for simple r'n'r, and with week-long packages for fishing and scuba. Space for 12 guests, soon to be expanded.
LL-AL **Victoria House**, PO Box 22, San Pedro, Ambergris Caye, T226-2067, www.victoria-house.com 3 types of room, a/c, excellent facilities, good dive shop and watersports. Serene comfort and absolute luxury. Perfect for romantics and water lovers. Full board.
LL-AL **Iguana Reef Inn**, Caye Caulker, T226-0213, www.iguanareefinn.com Quiet, relaxing spot, but close enough to walk to the main strip and the split. Probably the best place on the island, relaxing and quiet.
L **Capricorn Resort**, 3 miles north of town, Ambergris Caye, T226-2809, www.ambergris- caye.com/capricorn Lovely wooden cabins on the beach with a truly great restaurant.

by the generator; ice at Tropical Paradise.
TTT **Coco Plum Gardens**, at the southern end of the island. Pricey for Caye Caulker but worth it. Open for breakfast and dinner, Sun-Thu.
TTT **Habanero's**. Excellent food, the best in Belize according to some.
TTT **Marin's**, good seafood everyday, cable TV, expensive but worth it.
TTT **Cindy's Café**, on the main street. Sooner or later you will have to join in the squeeze for one of the most relaxing breakfasts on the island.
TT **Glenda's**, old island favourite, good breakfast and lunches, closed evenings.
TT **Swing Bar**, because the seats are swings. Excellent reggae bar, with Bob Marley paraphernalia everywhere.

Mellow, laid-back, good views from upper deck. Highly recommended, open 1700.

🍴 **Lighthouse**, cantina on the main street. Serving coffee, cake and hot dogs, chairs on the street, always popular.

🍴 **Little Kitchen**, fish and chips, occasionally lobster, good burritos and top milk shakes.

🍴 **Oceanside**, most popular bar on the island. Food OK, music and dancing.

🍴 **Rainbow Bar and Restaurant**, with the restaurant on its own jetty. Delicious burritos good value, beautiful view.

🍴 **Sandbox**, T226-0200, sandbox@btl.net One of the Caye's social centres with a good atmosphere and sandy floors for that complete beach experience. Very popular.

🍴 **Sobre Las Olas**, cool restaurant right on the beach with coloured lights, on main street near **Chocolate's**. Excellent food.

🍴 **Tropical Paradise**. Excellent seafood, varied menu, slightly more expensive than others (also ice-cream).

🍴 **Wishwilly Bar and Grill**, up a side street, virtually opposite the **Hurricane Bar**. The fish is great and barbecued in front of you.

Entertainment

Ambergris Caye *p230*

Big Daddy's Disco, open evenings but cranks up at midnight.

Pier Lounge, Spindthrift Hotel. Try 'Chicken Drop' on a Wed night: bet US$1 on which square the chicken will leave its droppings on.

Tarzan Disco, nearby on Front St, has a good atmosphere.

Caye Caulker *p230*

Many of the restaurants become bars in the evenings. Try the **Swing Bar**, **Oceanside** or **Sandbox**.

Shopping

Ambergris Caye *p230*

Island Supermarket, across from Ramon's, has a good range of supplies. There are many gift shops in the centre of town. Try **Fidos** which has Belizean arts (paintings and prints by local artists), amber jewellery and Realty Café. Wave runners (US$50 per hr) and hobie cats (US$25 per hr) can also be hired here.

Caye Caulker *p230*

There are at least 4 small 'markets' on the island where a variety of food can be bought; prices are 20-50% higher than the mainland. Bookstore on opposite side of island to ferries sells many different magazines, including *Time* and *Newsweek*.

Activities and tours

Ambergris Caye *p230*

Diving

San Pedro is well known for its diving. Long canyons containing plenty of soft and hard coral formations start at around 50-60 ft going down to 120 ft. Often these have grown into hollow tubes which make for interesting diving. **Tackle Box**, **Esmeralda**, **Cypress**, **M & Ms** and **Tres Cocos** are only some of the dive sites in the area. The visibility in this area is usually over 100 ft. There is a recompression chamber in San Pedro and a US$1 tax on each tank fill insures treatment throughout the island.

Instruction to PADI open water level available, US$350-400. Local 2-tank dive US$60, Turneffe US$140-160, Blue Hole US$190. Always check diving shop's recent safety record before diving.

Amigos del Mar, T226-2706, www.amigosdive.com, opposite Lily's. Lots of return customers. Repeatedly recommended.

Blue Hole, T226-2982, www.bluehole.com. Run by Kent and Laurie Gardner, good for advice, information and trips. Repeatedly recommended.

Sea kayaking

Elito Arceo, office just north of airport, T226-3221/T614-6043 (mob). Expert guide.

Reef trips

Tour operators can arrange day cruises to Caye Caulker and the barrier reef on the island trader **MV Winnie Estelle**, a 40-ft motor cruiser with large deck area, US$55, including open bar and snacks. Other day snorkelling trips from US$25 to Caye Caulker with stops at Sting Ray Alley and coral gardens. Snorkel rental US$5. Sailing vessels to the Lighthouse Reef, US$150-250 per day; speedboats US$150 per person, including lunch and 3 dives, recommended. A 2-day overnight trip including 5 dives, US$250.

Bill Hinkis, beside the lagoon off Back Street, just north of the football field. 3-day sailing cruises to Lighthouse Reef on board *Yanira*, US$150 (you provide food, ice and fuel).

Daniel Núñez, T226-3214, snorkelling trips to the Maya sites on the north of the caye in the Bacalar Chico National Park.

Tour operators

Ambergris Caye airport makes it easy to arrange tours to places on the mainland (Altún Ha US$60 per person; Lamanai US$125 per person), while still making the most of the watersports (catamaran sailing US$40 per person, deep-sea fishing US$150-400, manatee trips US$75).

Hustler Tours, T226-2538. Experienced and very helpful.

Out Island Divers, San Pedro. Various 2- or 3-day trips to Lighthouse Reef and the smaller cayes.

Travel and Tour Belize, San Pedro, T226-2031. Helpful. All travel services, can arrange flights, with a request stop at Sarteneja (for Shipstern Nature Reserve).

Caye Caulker *p230*

Equipment available at several spots throughout the island. Make sure you fix prices before going on trips or hiring equipment, and, if you pay the night before, get a receipt. Reef trips are the same as those found on Ambergris Caye (see above): Manatee trips, US$40; San Pedro, Hol Chan and Shark Alley, US$35 for a full day. Generally trips are offered at the same price by all tour operators, who share clients if numbers are insufficient. Don't take valuables. Protect against sunburn on reef and snorkelling trips.

Diving

Belize Diving Services, PO Box 20, Caye Caulker, T226-0143, bzdiveserv@btl.net. Dive shop with similar prices to *Frenchie's*, below. Day trips to the manatee reserve in the south of Belize.

Frenchie's Diving Service, T226-0234, frenchies@btl.net. Friendly and effective. US$250 for a 4-day PADI course; 2-tank dive US$90; also advanced PADI instruction. Day excursion to Half Moon Caye and the Blue Hole, US$157.

Fishing

Rolly Rosardo, 4 hrs, US$45, up to 5 people, equipment, fresh bait and instruction provided.

Sailing

Several full- and half-day and sunset sailing trips from US$20. **Raffamuffin tours** offer a 3-day all-inclusive sailing tour to Placencia leaving Tue and Fri. Beats travelling by bus!

Reef trips and snorkelling

Prices are consistent across all operators. The simplest option is hiring mask, snorkel and fins for US$2.50. The main excursion is to **Hol Chan Marine Park**, visiting **Shark-Ray Alley**, US$30, equipment included. Manatees and Goff Caye, US$45. Snorkelling trips to the Turneffe Islands, Half Moon Caye, Bird Sanctuary and Blue Hole available on request. Sunset snorkelling trips are also popular, US$20.

Dolphin Bay Dive Travel, PO Box 374, Belize City, T/F226-0214, is very helpful and can arrange domestic and international flights as well as local excursions. Highly recommended.

Island Sun, near the Cut. Local husband and American wife, very conscientious.

They offer day tours to reef, plus snorkel hire (1000-1400); day tour to San Pedro and Hol Chan, plus snorkel hire, plus entry fee for reserve, recommended.

Other local operators include: **Neno Rosado**, T226-0302, approved by the association, reliable and knowledgeable; **Ras Creek**, boat trips US$12.50 including lunch; **Alfonso Rosarsdo**, reef trips, 5-6 hrs, sometimes offers meals at his house after; **Obdulio Lulu** at Tom's Hotel, day trips to Hol Chan and San Pedro (if he catches a barracuda on the return, he will barbecue it at the hotel for US$0.75).

Transport

Travel by boat to and around the islands is increasingly regulated and licensing requirements will probably drive the cheaper boats out of business. It is generally easier to arrange travel between the islands once you arrive. Most boats to Caye Caulker and Ambergris Caye leave from the Marine Terminal in Belize City; **Thunderbolt** leaves from the North Front Street gas station. Timetables change so check at your hotel before travelling.

Ambergris Caye *p230*

Air

Tropic Air, T226-2012, and **Maya Island Air**, T226-2345, www.mayaislandair.com, have flights to/from both **Belize City** airports, many hourly, not appealing as travelling by sea. **Maya Island Air** also flies to **Caye Caulker**; both airlines fly to **Corozal**, several daily.

Bicycles/golf carts

Golf carts give quick access to the southern, quieter end of the caye, US$10 per hr, make sure battery is fully charged. Bicycles are also a good way to get around, US$5 per hr.

Sea

Boats to/from **Belize City**, every 1½ hrs until 1500, US$7.50 1-way, US$15 return. All call at Caye Caulker (Caye Chapel and St George's Caye on request). Also boats to/from **Caye Caulker**, US$7.50. **Thunderbolt**, T226-2904, www.ambergriscaye.com/thunderbolt, departs 1500 for **Corozal** in the north, US$20 (return ferry departs Corozal 0700).

Caye Caulker *p230*

Air

Maya Island Air flies to/from **Belize City**, **Corozal** and **San Pedro**, several daily. Flying is recommended if you have a connection to make.

Sea

Boats to/from **Belize City**, daily 0900-1700, US$15 return, journey time 45 mins. There are also regular boats to **San Pedro** with connecting services to Corozal.

Lighthouse Reef *p231*

To charter a motor boat to the **Lighthouse Reef** from Belize City costs about US$50 per person if 10 people are going (6 hrs' journey). Organized trips can also be booked through any dive shop in San Pedro (see Tour operators, above).

Directory

Ambergris Caye *p230*

Banks Atlantic Bank and **Bank of Belize**, Mon-Thu 0800-1300, Fri 0800-1630. Small denominations of $US in regular use.

Caye Caulker *p230*

Banks Atlantic Bank (0800-1400, Visa advances; US$5 commission) and many other places for exchange. Rates for cash and TCs are reasonable. **Internet** Caye Caulker Cyber Café, 0700-2200, US$4 per hr. **Laundry** Several locals will do washing – look out for signs. **Marie's Laundry**, 1 block off main street, operates self service or you can leave your stuff, US$5 for 4 kg. **Post office** West side of the island. **Telephone** International telephone and fax available. Exchange, F501-2260239, open 0900-1230, 1400-1630; international cardphone.

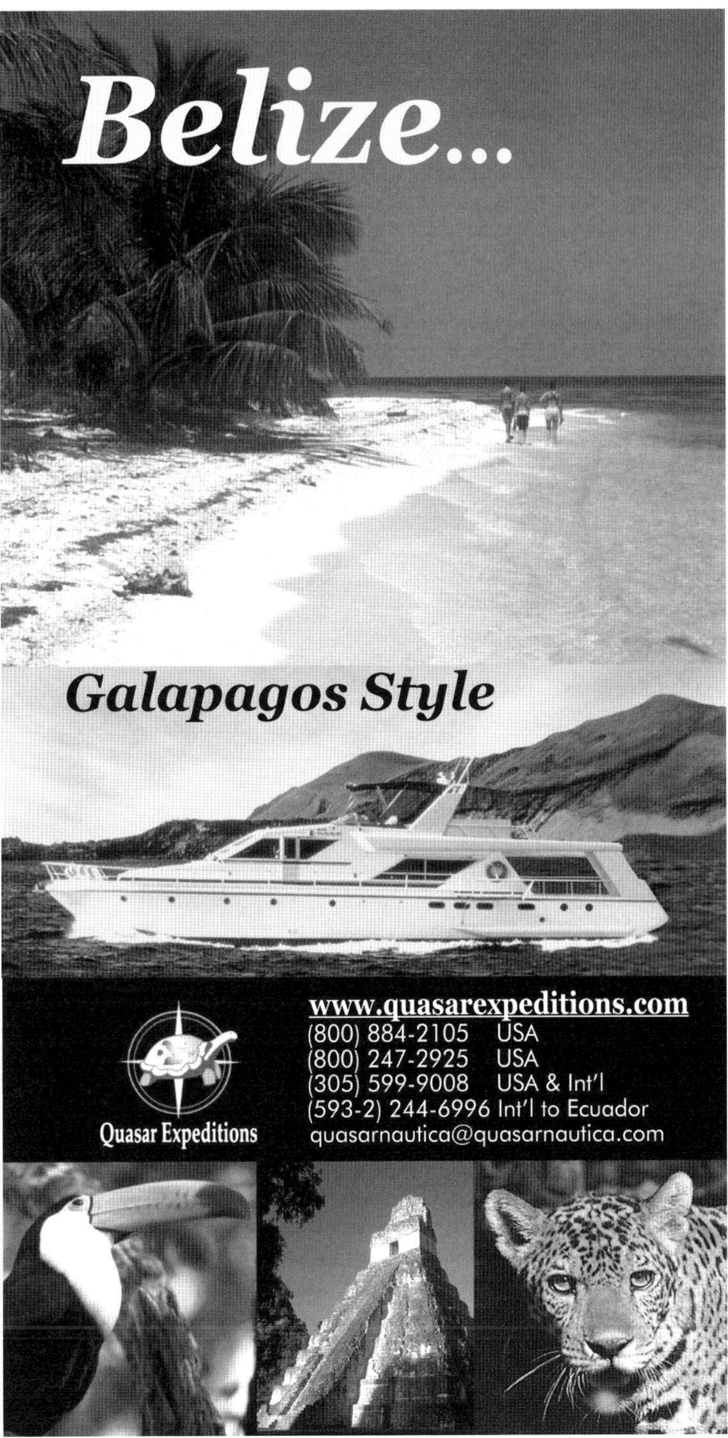
Belize...
Galapagos Style
www.quasarexpeditions.com
(800) 884-2105 USA
(800) 247-2925 USA
(305) 599-9008 USA & Int'l
(593-2) 244-6996 Int'l to Ecuador
quasarnautica@quasarnautica.com
Quasar Expeditions

Northern Belize

Northern Belize is notable for the agricultural production of sugar, fruit and vegetables and for providing much of the country's food. But among the fields of produce are also some well-hidden sights and wildlife magnets. The Maya ruins of Lamanai are just about visible in the spectacular setting of the dense jungle. Wildlife can easily be seen at the Community Baboon Sanctuary, the Crooked Tree Wildlife Sanctuary – home to thousands of beautiful birds – and the wildlife reserves of Shipstern near Sarteneja. The vast Río Bravo Conservation Area nudges up to the Guatemalan border, leading to the truly isolated ruins and lodge of Chan Chich.

Heading north out of Belize City, the Northern Highway leads to the Mexican border. You can do the journey in just a few hours, passing through Orange Walk and Corozal, but you won't see a thing. It's definitely worth stopping off if you have time.

Getting there Regular buses from Belize City, daily speedboat to Corozal from Ambergris Caye.

Getting around Bus or taxi.

Time required Up to a week.

Weather Anytime okay. Dry season mid-November to May.

Sleeping High-class options at Lamanai and Chan Chich, limited elsewhere.

Eating Rice 'n' beans, more choice at hotels.

Activities and tours Visiting the ruins, wildlife watching.

★ **Don't miss...** a day trip from Orange Walk to Lamanai up the New River, but watch out for crocs ▸▸ *p242*.

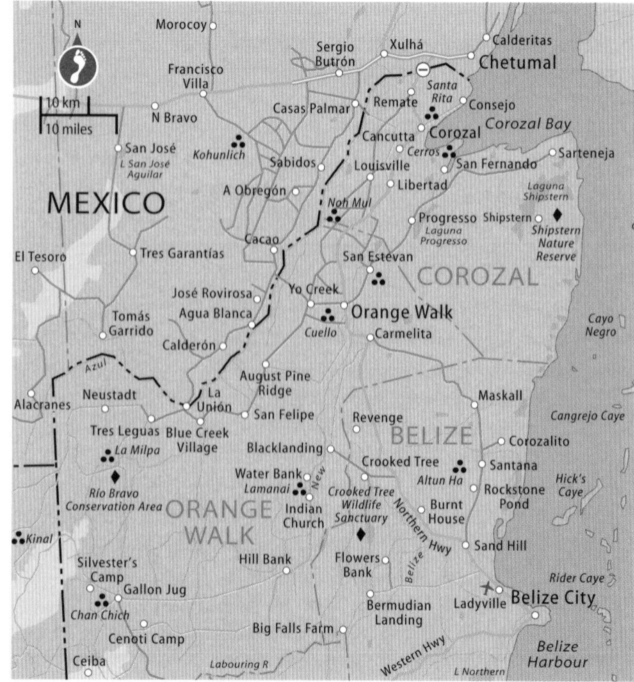

Along the Northern Highway » pp244-247

Bermudian Landing

About 15 miles out of Belize City a road heads west to the small settlement of Bermudian Landing (12 miles on a rough road from the turn-off), which has been thrust into the global conservation spotlight. The small Creole village was once a transfer point for the timber that floated down the Belize River, but now there's a local wildlife museum, sponsored by the WWF, and the **Community Baboon Sanctuary** ⓘ *T220-2181, baboon@btl.net*, set up to protect the endangered black howler monkey (known locally as baboon); the centre has walking trails and offers a variety of activities including canoeing and horse riding.

Crooked Tree Wildlife Sanctuary

ⓘ *Signposted intersection, 33 miles from Belize City (ignore the first sign further south, which just leads to the park boundary). Register at the visitors' centre on arrival. US$4 (Belizeans US$1); drinks on sale, but take food. Buses from Belize City towards Corozal, then hitch; someone is usually willing to take visitors back to the main road for a small charge.*

The Northern Highway continues to **Sand Hill**, and a further 12 miles to the turn-off for the Crooked Tree Wildlife Sanctuary was set up in 1984 in a rich area for birds. The network of lagoons and swamps attracts many migrating birds and the dry season, October-May, is a good time to visit. You may see the jabiru stork, the largest flying bird in the Western Hemisphere at a height of 5 ft and a wingspan of 11-12 ft, which nests here, as well as herons, ducks, vultures, kites, ospreys, hawks, sand pipers, kingfishers, gulls, terns, egrets and swallows. Birdwatching is best in the early morning. In the forest you can also see and hear howler monkeys. Other animals include coatimundi, crocodiles, iguanas and turtles. There is a helpful, friendly warden, Steve, at the visitors' centre. The Creole village is tiny and quaint, with ancient mango and cashew trees. Boats and guides (Glenn Crawford and Sam Tillet are both recommended) can be hired for approximately US$70 per boat (maximum four people); trips include a visit to an unexcavated Maya site.

Altún Ha

ⓘ *2 miles from the Old Northern Highway, 31 miles north of Belize City. Daily 0900-1700. US$1.50. Insect repellent necessary.*

Altún Ha was a major ceremonial centre in the Classic Maya period (AD 250-900) and also a trading station linking the Caribbean coast with Maya centres in the interior. The site consists of two central plazas surrounded by 13 partially excavated pyramids and temples dating from various periods in the Maya past. The largest piece of worked Maya jade ever found, a head of the Sun God Kinich Ahau, weighing 9½ lb (4.3 kg), was found here in the main temple (B-4) in 1968. It is now in a bank vault in Belize City. Nearby is a large reservoir called **Rockstone Pond**.

Howler monkey

Orangе Walk and around » pp244-247

The Northern Highway runs to the country's second city, Orange Walk (66 miles), the multicultural centre of an agricultural district where Creoles, Mennonites (originally from Canada) and Maya earn their living from timber, sugar planting and farming. During the Yucatecan Caste Wars (1840-70s), the only battle fought on Belizean soil took place here, resulting in the shooting of the Maya leader, Marcus Canul, in 1872.

A few pleasant wooden buildings remain on quiet side streets but most are worn out and in bad need of repair, while others have been pulled down and replaced by standard concrete box affairs. The market, which overlooks New River, is well organized, however, with good food stalls and interesting architecture. Buses plying the route from Belize City to the Mexican border stop on Queen Victoria Avenue, the main street, where you'll find the town hall and a recently opened House of Culture, which shows a history of the town's development. Although there is little to keep the visitor in Orange Walk for an extended stay, the impressive ruins of Lamanai make a good day trip. The town is also the departure point for Sarteneja and the Shipstern Peninsula and for the long overland trip to Río Bravo Conservation Area, Chan Chich and Gallon Jug.

Lamanai

ⓘ *near Indian Church, 35 miles drive from Orange Walk via Yo Creek and San Felipe (1 hr); 4WD needed when wet. 22 miles by river; recommended trips with Jungle River Tours in Orange Walk.*

One of Belize's largest archaeological sites, **Lamanai** is on the west side of New River Lagoon, 22 miles by river south of Orange Walk. Difficult to get to and hidden in the jungle, it is a perfect setting to hide the mysteries of the Maya and definitely worth a visit, particularly by river. While the earliest buildings were erected about 700 BC, culminating in the completion of the 112-ft major temple (N10-43) dedicated to Chac about 100 BC, there is evidence the site was occupied as long ago as 1500 BC. It is believed to have the longest history of continuous occupation of any Maya site.

The site has been partially cleared, but covers a large area so a guide is recommended. Visitors can wander freely along narrow trails and climb the stairways. Ascend temple N10-43, the tallest known Pre-classic Maya structure, for superb views. Also look out for the Yin-Yang-like symbol below the throne on one of the other main temples, which also has a 12-ft-tall mask overlooking its plaza. There are many birds in the jungle around the site, best seen on an early-morning boat trip from Orange Walk. Mosquitoes are vicious in the wet season, so wear trousers and plenty of repellent.

At nearby **Indian Church**, a Spanish mission was built over one of the Maya temples in 1580, and the British established a sugar mill here last century. The remains of both buildings can still be seen; note the huge flywheel engulfed by a strangler fig. The community phone for information on Indian Church, including buses, is T309-3015.

Blue Creek and around

West of San Felipe is Blue Creek (10 miles), the largest of the Mennonite settlements. Many of the inhabitants of these close-knit villages arrived in 1959, members of a Canadian colony which had migrated to Chihuahua, Mexico, to escape encroaching modernity. They preserve their Low German dialect, are exempt from military service and their industry now supplies the country with most of its poultry, eggs, vegetables and furniture. In 1998 Belize and Mexico signed an agreement to build an international bridge from Blue Creek across the river to La Unión, together with a river port close to the bridge. However, work has not yet begun and as things stand it is unknown when building will start; at present there is a canoe-service for foot passengers across the Blue Creek.

Lamanai

A good road can be followed 35 miles south to **Gallon Jug**, where a jungle tourism lodge has been built in the **Chan Chich** Maya ruin. The journey to Chan Chich passes through the **Río Bravo Conservation Area** (see page 16), a vast region of agricultural land and untouched forest, along the Río Bravo. This route is rarely travelled and offers excellent chances to see wildlife. Chan Chich has some of the highest number of jaguar sightings in Belize and is also a birdwatchers' paradise. There's a study and accommodation centre near the Maya site of **La Milpa**, which is currently being excavated by a team from the universities of Texas and Boston, USA (» *p245*). To reach La Milpa, go six miles west from Blue Creek to Tres Leguas, then follow the signs south towards the Río Bravo Escarpment. The reserve is privately owned and you will need proof of booking to pass the various checkpoints. Another road has recently been cut south through Tambos to the main road between Belmopan and San Ignacio, but travel in this region is strictly a dry-weather affair.

North of Orange Walk » *pp244-247*

Sarteneja and the northeast

From Orange Walk a complex network of roads and tracks converge on **San Estevan**, which has some missable Maya ruins, and continues northeast to **Progresso**, a village picturesquely located on the lagoon of the same name. A right turn, a couple of kilometres north of San Estevan and signposted, runs off to the Mennonite village of Little Belize and continues (in poor condition) to **Chunox**, a village with Maya houses of pole construction. In the dry season it is possible to drive on from Chunox to the Maya site of Cerros (page 244).

Beyond Progresso is the visitors' centre for **Shipstern Nature Reserve**, which covers 22,000 acres of the northeastern tip of Belize. Hardwood forests, saline lagoon systems and wide belts of savannah shelter a wide range of mammals (coatis and foxes, and all the fauna found elsewhere in Belize, except monkeys), reptiles and 200 species of bird. You'll also see the mounds of Maya houses. At the visitors' centre is the **Butterfly Breeding Centre** ⓘ *daily 0900-1200, 1300-1600, except Christmas and Easter, US$5 including excellent guided tour*, and there's a botanical trail leading into the forest from the visitors' centre, with trees labelled with Latin and local Yucatec Maya names; mosquito repellent is essential.

At the end of the road is **Sarteneja**, a small fishing and former boat-building settlement founded by Yucatán refugees in the 19th century. The main catch is lobster and conch. On Easter Sunday a popular regatta is held here, with all types of boat racing, dancing and music. The remains of an extensive Maya city are scattered throughout the village; archaeological exploration is continuing to the south, around the area of Shipstern Lagoon.

Corozal and around

North of Orange Walk, the Northern Highway passes the archaeological site of **Nohmul**, at San José and San Pablo, a ceremonial centre whose main acropolis dominates the surrounding cane fields (the name means 'Great Mound'). The highway continues to **Corozal**, 96 miles from Belize City, formerly the centre of the sugar industry. Although it is equally depressed economically, Corozal is much safer than Orange Walk. Much of the old town was destroyed by Hurricane Janet in 1955 and it is now a mixture of modern concrete commercial buildings and Caribbean clapboard houses on stilts. It is open to the sea with a pleasant waterfront where the market is held. There is no beach but you can swim in the sea and lie on the grass. Check out the local website at www.corozal.com.

There's better swimming and cleaner water six miles northeast of Corozal at **Four Mile Lagoon**. The lagoon is about a quarter of a mile off the road to Chetumal (buses will drop you there) and has some food and drinks available; it is often crowded at weekends. From Corozal, another road leads seven miles northeast to **Consejo**, a quiet, seaside fishing village on Chetumal Bay.

Across the bay to the south of Corozal stand the mounds of **Cerros**, once an active Maya trading port whose central area was reached by canal. Some of the site is flooded but one pyramid, 69-ft high with stucco masks on its walls, has been partially excavated. To get there take a boat from Corozal, walk around the bay (crossing the mouth of the New River by boat) or do the dry-season vehicular trail from Progresso and Chunox (see above). More easily accessible are the free ruins of **Santa Rita**, a mile out on the Northern Highway, opposite the Coca Cola plant; once a powerful and cosmopolitan city, and still occupied when the Spaniards arrived in Belize, the site's Post-classic murals and buildings were destroyed long ago, leaving only the 50-ft-tall Structure Seven still standing.

Sleeping

Bermudian Landing *p241*

A-C **Howler Monkey Lodge**, 400 m from museum, T/F220-2158, www.howlermonkeylodge.bz; PO Box 694, Belize City. Screened windows, fans, cheaper with shared bath. Also camping, US$5 per person, bring tent. Transport from Belize City in pick-up add US$40, 1-4 people, on request. Breakfast, lunch and dinner, US$5-9. Good tours including river tours, US$25, and night-time crocodile adventures, US$40. Canoe rentals in Burrell Boom for trips on Belize River to see birds, howler monkeys, manatee, hicatee.

C **Community Baboon Sanctuary**. Cabañas alongside the visitors' centre, bath, hot water. Basic lodging also available with families in the village, arranged through the sanctuary office.

Crooked Tree Wildlife Sanctuary *p241*

AL-B **Bird's Eye View Lodge**, T203-2040, T/F570-588 0843 (in USA), www.birdseyeviewlodge.com. Single and double rooms, shower, fan, meals available, boat trips, horse riding, canoe rental, nature tours with licensed guide, ask for information at the **Belize Audubon Society** (see p54).

A **Paradise Inn**, T225-7044. Cabins with hot showers, restaurant, well maintained and friendly, boat trips, fishing, riding.

B-C **Sam Tillet's Hotel**, T220-7026, samhotel@btl.net, in centre of village. Wood and thatch cabin, tiny restaurant, great trips. Cabins may be rented at

Budget buster

Jungle retreats

LL **Maruba Resort Jungle Spa**, Altún Ha, T322-2199, in USA T1-713-799-2031, www.maruba-spa.com A hotel, restaurant and spa with a wide range of new age treatments including mud-therapy. All rooms different with traditional colonial, through to ethnic charm, some with a/c, German spoken, good birdwatching, including storks in the nearby swamp.
LL **Chan Chich**, PO Box 37, Belize City, T/F223-4419, or in the USA and Canada 1-800-343-8009, www.chanchich.com Set among the ruins of Chan Chich, the 12 comfortable, thatched roof and screened cabanas immerse you in the jungle, while protecting you from the bad stuff. Packages with or without meals. Plenty of trails to explore, and a pool for relaxing. Incredible place, recommended. Phone before setting out for Chan Chich for reservations and information on the roads.

US$33 for a night, up to 4 people. Cheap rooms and camping (**F**) can also be arranged, if requested.

Orange Walk *p242*
AL-A **Mi Amor**, 19 Belize-Corozal Rd, T302-2031. Choice of rooms with shared bath, with bath and fan, or with bath and a/c, nice, clean. Also restaurant.
C **St Christopher's**, 10 Main St, T/F302-1064. Beautiful clean rooms and bathrooms, highly recommended.
C-D **Akihito Japanese Hotel**, 22 Belize Corozal Rd, T302-0185, akihitolee@hotmail.com. Affordable place in the centre of town.
D-E **Lucia's Guest House**, 68 San Antonio Rd, 5-mins west of town, T322-2244, www.luciasbelize.com. A new budget place that's getting recommendations.

At **August Pine Ridge**, between Yo Creek and San Felipe, you can camp at the house of Narciso Novelo or 'Chicho' (T323-3019). It's a relaxing place to stay set among bananas, pine trees, bushes and flowers. No fixed cost, just pay what you think. Daily bus to Orange Walk at 1000; Chicho will meet you off the bus.

Lamanai *p242*
AL **Lamanai Outpost Lodge**, Indian Church, T223-3578, www.lamanai.com Run by the incredibly friendly Howells, this beautiful lodge is a short walk from Lamanai ruins, overlooking New River Lagoon, package deals available, day tours, thatched wooden cabins with bath and fan, hot water, electricity, restaurant. A resident archaeologist and a naturalist run field study courses here. In addition, **Nazario Ku**, the site caretaker, permits camping or hammocks at his house, good value.

Blue Creek and around *p242*
AL **La Milpa Field Station**, La Milpa, T323-0011, contact the Programme for Belize (T227-5616, www.pfbelize.org). 4 double cabañas, spacious, comfortable, with a thatched roof overhanging a large wooden deck, or a dormitory for up to 30.
C **Hill Bank Field Station**, on the banks of the New River Lagoon, T323-0011, or contact the Programme for Belize (T227-5616, www.pfbelize.org). Dorm sleeping up to 30. A good base for exploring trails and birdwatching.

Sarteneja and the northeast *p243*
B **Krisami's Bay View**, Sarteneja, T423-2283, krisamis@msn.com Rooms with private bath, a/c and TV.
B-C **Fernando's Guest House**, seafront, Sarteneja, T423-2085, sartenejabelize@hotmail.com Four simple, clean, fan-

cooled rooms with views out to sea.

E **Shipstern Nature Reserve**. Dormitory accommodation at the visitors' centre, rather poor, US$10 per person.

Corozal and around *p244*

AL-B **Tony's**, South End, T422-2055, www.tonysinn.com With a/c, clean, comfortable units in landscaped grounds. Recommended, restaurant is overpriced.

A **The Copa Banana**, PO Box 226, 409 Corozal Bay Rd, T422-0284, www.copabanana.bz US-owned hotel, newest place in town, 5 suites all with private bathrooms. Complimentary coffee. Ask the bus driver to drop you off.

B-C **Hok'Ol K'in Guest House**, 4th Av and 4th St South, T422-3329, www.corozal.net Immaculate rooms. Runs tours to Cerros.

C-D **Nestor's**, 123, 5th Av South, T422-0196, www.nestorshotel.com With bath and fan, OK, *refrescos* available, good food, lively bar downstairs. Big renovation underway.

D **Caribbean Village Resort**, South End, PO Box 55, T422-2045. Hot water, US$5 camping, US$12 trailer park, restaurant, recommended.

D **Central Guest House**, 22 6th Av, T422-2358, www.corozal.bz/cgh Basic, clean rooms, shared area with TV, lots of information about Belize and the area. Close to the bus terminal.

Eating

Orange Walk *p242*

ŸŸ **King Fu**, Baker's St. Chinese, excellent and filling.

ŸŸ-Ÿ **Juanita's**, 8 Santa Ana St, open 0600 for breakfast and all meals. Good, inexpensive Creole cooking.

Ÿ **Central Plaza Restaurant**, behind the main bus terminal. A popular choice, with typical Belizean food, in a handy location.

Ÿ **The Diner**, Clarke St, behind the hospital. Good meals, friendly, taxi US$4 or walk.

Corozal and around *p244*

Nestor's, **Tony's** and **The Copa Banana** all have hotel restaurants. There are many Chinese restaurants in town.

ŸŸŸ **Café Kela**, in a beachfront palapa on the shore. Best restaurant in town, intimate setting, fine food, good value, just sit back and enjoy.

ŸŸ **Cactus Plaza**, 5th Av South. A loud bar with lots of fluorescent lighting and great a/c. Worth trying if you're stuck in town for the night.

ŸŸ **Club Campesino**, decent bar, good fried chicken after 1800.

ŸŸ **Purple Toucan**, #52, 4th Av North, good restaurant and lively bar with pool table and good music. Opposite is **Marcelo's** which serves good pizza.

Ÿ **Border**, 6th Av South, friendly Chinese, good food.

Ÿ **Corozal Garden**, on 4th Av, 1 block south, has good, quick local food.

Activities and tours

Orange Walk *p242*

Tour operators

Jungle River Tours, in **Lovers' Café** on the southeastern corner of the park, PO Box 95, 20 Lovers Lane, T302-2293, lamanaimayatour@btl.net. *The* specialists on the region. Organize and run fantastic boat trips to Lamanai, departing 0900, returning 1600, 5 passengers per boat, US$40 (including lunch), plus entrance fee, US$2.50. The brothers are excellent and knowledgeable tour guides, consistently recommended. Also regular trips to Altún Ha and New River area. Will run a tour to any destination in Belize for a minimum of 4 people.

Transport

Bermudian Landing *p241*

Buses from **Belize City**, with **Mcfadzean Bus** from corner of Amara Av and Cemetery Rd Mon-Fri 1215 and; Sat 1200 and 1400. **Rancho Bus** (**Pook's Bus**) from Mosul St, Mon-Fri 1700, Sat 1300, check details, US$1.50-2, 1 hr. Alternatively, any bus travelling the Northern Highway can drop you off at the turn-off to Bermudian Landing where you can wait for a bus, or hitch a ride. A day trip is difficult by public transport, so it is best to stay the night.

Crooked Tree Wildlife Sanctuary *p241*

Buses from **Belize City** with JEX depart 1035, return from Crooked Tree at 0600-0700 or later.

Altún Ha *p241*

Little transport on this road, so it's best to go in a private vehicle or a tour group. Overnight parking permitted free, with warden's permission. Vehicles leave **Belize City** for the village of Maskall, 8 miles north of Altún Ha, several days a week, but same-day return is not possible.

Orange Walk *p242*

Bus

Bus station beside the fire station, on the main road. All buses from Belize City to Corozal stop in Orange Walk. To **Belize City**, US$3; to **Corozal**, US$1.50, 50 mins; to **Indian Church** (for Lamanai), Mon, Wed, Fri 1600; to **Sarteneja**, 5 daily, 1300-1900, from Zeta's Store on Main St, US$2.50; to **Progresso**, 1100 and 1130.

Blue Creek and around *p242*

Charter flights to Chan Chich from **Belize City**, US$215 for 3, US$337 for 5. Road travel possible, 4 hrs on a dirt road.

Sarteneja and the northeast *p243*

Air

Private charter flights from **Corozal** cost about US$75 for the 30-min journey (compared with 3 hrs by road).

Boat

Thunderbolt, T226-2904, thunderbolttravels@yahoo.com, will stop at Sarteneja on request at no extra charge. Departs **Corozal** at 0700 and **San Pedro** at 1500, full trip US$20.

Bus

From **Belize City**, departs from the corner of Victoria and North Front St, 1200, US$4.50. Also from **Corozal**, 1400, via Orange Walk, 1530.

Corozal and around *p244*

Air

Maya Island Air, 3 daily from Belize City via Caye Caulker and San Pedro; Tropic Air daily from San Pedro. Airstrip 3 miles south, taxi US$1.50.

Bus

Heading south to **Belize City**, every 30 mins, 0400-1830. Regular service 3 hrs, US$5, express service, 2½ hrs, US$6.50, at 0600, 0700, 1200, 1500 and 1800. Buses from Belize City stop at Corozal before continuing north to **Chetumal** (p197), Mexico, with time for immigration procedures, every 30 mins, 0500-1800.

Taxi

Leslie's Taxi Service, T422-2377. Transfers from Corozol to the **Mexican border** (p198), US$22 for a 4-person taxi. Reliable.

Boat

Thunderbolt, T226-2904, fast ferry to **San Pedro** (Ambergris Caye) 0700; departs San Pedro at 1500, US$20 1 way.

Directory

Orange Walk *p242*

Banks Belize Bank on Main St (down Park St from Park, turn left). Scotia Bank on Park, US$0.50 commission. Shell Station will change TCs. **Internet** K&M, on Main St, US$3 per hr, Mon-Sat 0800-1300, 1400-1700 and 1900-2100.

Corozal and around *p244*

Banks Atlantic Bank (US$2.50 for Visa cash advances), Bank of Nova Scotia, and Belize Bank. Also ask at the bus station. **Internet** Charlotte's Web, 5th Av between 5th and 6th St South, cyber café and book exchange, US$7 an hr.

West Belize

The bustling town of San Ignacio is the capital of Cayo District, a highland area in the west of the country that is characterized by impressive limestone scenery and and abundant wildlife. The Macal River weaves its way through this landscape, creating the ideal opportunity for canoe trips, while remote forest hideaways provide the perfect base for jungle adventures. Explore dramatic cave systems and waterfalls in the Mountain Pine Ridge Forest Reserve or visit the spectacular Maya ruins at Caracol, Xunantunich and Cahal Pech. From San Ignacio, there's also easy access west to Guatemala for a quick visit to Tikal and El Petén.

Getting there Bus from Belize City, connections to Guatemala.
Getting around Hire a bike or take a taxi.
Time required 3-4 days, but enough for up to 2 weeks.
Weather Any time of year.
Sleeping Good range of lodges and cabañas in hills and forests around San Ignacio.
Eating Rice 'n' beans and the occasional curry.
Activities and tours Mountain biking, caving, canoeing, as well as trips to waterfalls and Maya ruins.
★ **Don't miss...** Actun Tunichil Muknal Cave. ▸▸ *p249*.

San Ignacio and around *pp253-257*

Sixty-eight miles from Belize City and 10 miles from the Guatemala border, San Ignacio (locally called **Cayo**) is Western Belize's largest town. It's an agricultural centre serving the citrus, cattle and peanut farms of the area, and a good base

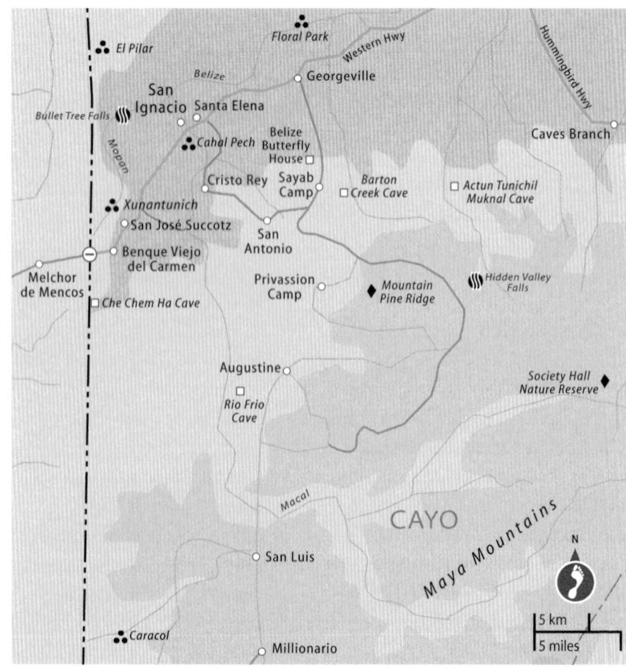

Background

Paddling the Great Macal River

Time it right and you can paddle down the length of the Belize River taking part in La Ruta Maya canoe race. It's a gruelling 3-day open canoe race, starting in San Ignacio covering 170 miles along the river before ending in Belize City on Baron Bliss Day (early March). All food and water is provided for the trip, but you'll need to be fit and healthy. You'll struggle to compete at the racing end of the field unless you're a top athlete and have a canoe of modern design, but plenty of people enter the race for the challenge and it's possible to turn up, talk with people around town and find yourself a place on a boat. For information visit www.bighjuices.com

for excursions into the Mountain Pine Ridge and Western Belize. It's also a good place to rest on arrival from Guatemala. The town stands amid attractive wooded hills at 200-500 ft, on the eastern branch of the Old, or Belize River, which is known as the **Macal**. An 185-mile canoe race down the river to Belize City is held every year around the 9 March (see box above).

The recently opened **tourist information office** ⓘ *next to the Savannah Taxi stand on the market square, Mon-Sat 0900-1700*, offers information on tours, hotels and lodges in Cayo. Brochures and maps available. Also try the **Community and Tourist Resource Center** ⓘ *90 Burns Av, T824-2373*, which has a small café.

A short walk from **Hotel San Ignacio** (see page 253) is **Cahal Pech** ⓘ *daily, US$2.50*, an impressive Maya site and nature reserve on a wooded hill overlooking the town, with a visitor centre and small museum. The man who sells tickets will lend you a guidebook written by the archaeologists who worked on the site, but it must be returned.

Four miles west of San Ignacio on a good road is **Bullet Tree Falls**, a pleasant cascade amid relaxing surroundings on the western branch of the Belize River (known here in its upper course as the Mopan River). Seven miles north of here is **El Pilar** – one of Belize's largest ruins from the Classic period, with several buildings reaching 50-70 ft in height. There are also several nature trails in the area.

Caves

A popular trip from San Ignacio is the 1½-hour drive followed by a 1½-hour canoe trip (US$30 per person, minimum 3 people) through **Barton Creek Cave**. The cave vault system is vast, with beautiful rock formations and an eery silence. Tours can be arranged at almost every place in San Ignacio. For a more adventurous caving tour, visit **Actun Tunichil Muknal Cave** (the Cave of the Stone Sepulchre), a one-hour drive from San Ignacio to the Tapir Mountain Nature reserve, followed by a 45-minute jungle hike and 3½ hours of adventurous caving. In addition to the beautiful rock formations, this cave is full of Maya artefacts and only two companies are allowed to guide tours. Maya artefacts can also be seen in **Che Chem Ha Cave** ⓘ *south of Benque Viejo, T820-4063, tours at 0900 and 1300, US$25 for 2 people, US$10 for every additional person*, on the private property of the Moralez family on the Vaca Plateau. In contrast to Barton Creek and Actun Tunichil Muknal, this is a so-called 'dry' cave. Tours include a 30-minute hike to the entrance, followed by a 1-1½ hour cave walk. The view from the property is stunning and the family serves lunch. If you go by private transport, call the family in advance and make sure you arrive on time. Or book a tour with an agency in San Ignacio. ▲ ▸▸ *p256.*

Xunantunich

Xunantunich

ⓘ *12 km west of San Ignacio. Daily 0800-1700. US$2.50; leaflet available from the Archaeological Dept, US$0.15; helpful guides at the site. Bus from San Ignacio to San José Succotz (7 miles), free ferry (0800-1600) across the Mopan River, then 2 km walk; government employees accompany visitors due to threat of robbery. Little or no shade, so start early.*

The Classic Maya remains of Xunantunich ('Maiden of the Rock') are located in beautiful surroundings above the Mopan River. The heart of the city consisted of three plazas aligned on a north-south axis, lined with temples and the remains of a ball court, and surmounted by the Castillo. At 130 ft this was thought to be the highest man-made structure in Belize until recent measurement of the Sky Palace at Caracol. The impressive view takes in the jungle, the lowlands of Petén and the blue flanks of the Maya Mountains. Friezes on the Castillo, some restored in modern plaster, represent astronomical symbols. Maya graffiti can still be seen on the wall of Structure A-16. Extensive excavations took place in 1959-60 but only limited restoration work has been undertaken since then. Apart from a small refreshment stand, there are no facilities for visitors at Xunantunich, but a new museum has been built and a couple of stelae have been put on display. About 1½ miles further north are the ruins of **Actuncan**, probably a satellite of Xunantunich. Both sites show evidence of earthquake damage.

The ferry to Xunantunich departs from **San José Succotz**, a large Yucatec Maya village, where Spanish is the first language and a few inhabitants preserve the old Maya customs of their ancestral village (San José in the Petén). The colourful fiestas of St Joseph and the Holy Cross are celebrated on 19 March and on a variable date in early May each year. Just east of the ferry, on a street off the highway, **Magaña's Art Centre** and the **Xunantunich Women's Group** sell locally made crafts and clothing.

Chial Road

Southwest of San Ignacio towards the Guatemalan border, a left turn head east along the Chial Road. Half a mile down the road, a sharp right turn takes you through Negroman, the modern site of the ancient Maya city of **Tipu**, which has the remains of a Spanish Mission from the 1500s. Across the river from here is **Guacamallo Camp**, the starting point for canoe trips on the Macal River. Two miles further up, also across the river, is **Ek Tun** (see Budget buster, page 254).

The renowned 'Rainforest Medicine Trail' at **Ix Chel** has now closed but the founder, Dr Arvigo, still sells selections of herbs (the jungle salve, US$5, has been found effective against mosquito bites) and a book on medicinal plants used by the Maya (US$8, US$2 postage and packing, from General Delivery, San Ignacio, Cayo District). The herbs are also sold in most local gift shops. Towards the eastern end of Chial Road are the **New Belize Botanic Gardens** ⓘ *T824-3101, www.belizebotanic.org, daily 0700-1700, US$2.50, guided walks 0730-1500, US$7.50*. Fifty acres of rolling hills are planted with hundreds of orchids, dozens of named tree species, ponds and lots of birds.

Benque Viejo-Melchor de Mencos

The border, open 0600-2100, lies 12 miles west of San Ignacio, near the small town of Benque Viejo del Carmen. On the Guatemalan side is the town of Melchor de Mencos. All cross-border buses stop at the border itself (contrary to what taxi drivers might tell you). The road into Guatemala is only semi paved but is the main route to/from Santa Elena/Flores.

Leaving Belize Belizean entry and exit formalities take place in Benque Viejo del Carmen, 2 km east of the border, 0800-1200 and 1400-1700. Everyone leaving Belize has to pay the PACT exit tax (see p54) plus additional exit taxes of US$10. Most nationalities can obtain a tourist card for Guatemala (sometimes a visa) at the border. There is also a Guatemalan consulate opposite the ferry in San José Succotz, Mon-Fri 0900-1300, which can arrange visas for those who need them. Guatemalan border officials charge US$4.50 to enter Guatemala; ask for receipts. Not all buses to Benque Viejo continue through the border to Melchor de Mencos; you may have to get off the bus and walk to the border post or take a taxi (US$1.50); on the Guatemalan side someone will carry the luggage to Melchor de Mencos. » *p257*.

Leaving Guatemala Officials charge US$1.30 to leave Guatemala; ask for receipts. If you need a visa for either Belize or Mexico obtain it in advance at the consulates in Guatemala City. As a back-up, 72-hr transit visas are available at the border, which will cover you through Belize as far as the Mexican border at Santa Elena-Chetumal (see p198), but not into Mexico itself. If you intend to stay in Belize, you may be able to get a visa at the border but there could be extra charges when you leave the country.

Exchange You will get better rates purchasing quetzales at the border than anywhere before Puerto Barrios or Guatemala City. Compare rates at the Banco de Guatemala with the money changers. Check what you receive and do not accept damaged notes. Belizean dollars are difficult to change beyond Santa Elena/Flores so try to use up your local currency before you get to the border.

Mountain Pine Ridge *pp253-257*

Mountain Pine Ridge is a Forest Reserve (146,000 acres) that covers the northwest section of the Maya Mountains, an undulating landscape of largely undisturbed pine and gallery forest, and valleys of lush hardwoods, filled with orchids, bromeliads and butterflies. There's river scenery to enjoy, high waterfalls, numerous limestone caves and shady picnic sites. The easiest way of visiting is on a trip from San Ignacio (from US$40); it's a popular excursion despite the rough access roads. The four forest reserves which cover the Maya Mountains are the responsibility of the Forestry Department, who have only about 20 rangers to patrol over a million acres of heavily forested land. A hunting ban prohibits the carrying of firearms. Legislation, however, allows for controlled logging; all attempts to have some areas declared national parks or biosphere reserves have so far been unsuccessful. The area Forestry Office is in San Antonio.

Towards the reserve

From the Western Highway, two roads lead into the reserve (4WD recommended, especially in the wet season). From Georgeville the road to the reserve passes the **Belize Butterfly House** ⓘ *Green Hills, 1 mile before the reserve entrance, daily 0900-1600 Christmas-Easter, US$2.50; outside this period, contact Belize Tropical Forest Studies, PO Box 208, Belmopan, T822-3310.* Opened by Jan Meerman and Tineke Boomsma, it houses a fine collection of butterflies in a natural environment, with an associated botanical collection that provides foodstuff for the butterflies. A fascinating place for the enthusiast.

The alternative route from Santa Elena goes via Cristo Rey to **San Antonio**, a Mopan Maya village with many thatched-roof houses. Stelae and musical instruments have been unearthed at the nearby Pacbitun archaeological site. In San Antonio, the García sisters run a workshop, museum, shop (where they sell carvings in local slate) and guesthouse (**D**). You can sample Maya food and learn about the use of medicinal plants. This is a regular stop on tours to the Mountain Pine Ridge; a donation of US$0.50 is requested and US$12.50 is charged to take photos of the sisters at work. If you're interested in traditional Maya medicine, also ask at **Green Dragon** (see Tour operators, page 257), about the Bol family, who live close to San Antonio and have a 'museum' cave and a medicine trail on their private property.

Exploring the reserve

The main forest road meanders along rocky spurs, from which unexpected and often breathtaking views emerge of jungle far below and streams plunging hundreds of feet over red-rock canyons. A lookout point, with a picnic area and some small shops, has been provided to view the impressive **Hidden Valley Falls**, said to be over 1,000 ft high. On a clear day it is said that you can see Belmopan from this viewpoint but the falls are often shrouded in fog from October to January. The viewpoint is quite a long way from the main road and is probably not worth the detour if time is short, particularly in the dry season when the water flow is restricted.

Eighteen miles into the reserve the road crosses the **Río On**, where the river tumbles into inviting pools over huge granite boulders; this is one of Belize's most beautiful picnic and swimming spots. The rocks form little water slides and are good for children. However, bathing is not possible in the wet season. Five miles further on is the tiny village of **Augustine** (also called Douglas D'Silva or Douglas Forest Station), where there is a shop, accommodation in two houses (book through the Forestry Department in Belmopan) and a camping ground. Ask rangers for all information on the area. A mile away, in rich rainforest, is the **Río Frío Cave** (in fact a tunnel). The entrance is over 65 ft high, with many spectacular rock formations and sandy beaches where the river flows out. The Cuevas Gemelas nature trail starts one hour from the Río Frío cave. Trees in the area are labelled. It's a beautiful excursion and highly recommended.

Caracol ▲ *pp253-257*

ⓘ *24 miles south-southwest of Augustine (about 1 hr by 4WD). Very knowledgeable guides escort groups around the site twice daily. US$10.*

Caracol is a rediscovered Maya city and a National Monument Reservation. Caracol was established about 300 BC and continued well into the Late Classic period (glyphs record a victorious war against Tikal). Why Caracol was built in such a poorly watered region is not known, but Maya engineers showed great ingenuity in constructing reservoirs and terracing the fields. The **Sky Palace** (*Caana*) pyramid, which climbs 138 ft above the site, is being excavated by members of the University of Central Florida from February to May but there are year-round caretakers who will show you around and a new information centre has been built. Take your own food as there is none at the site; otherwise Five Sisters Lodge (page 255) or Blancaneaux Lodge (page 254) are open for lunch.

The road to Caracol has been improved and is passable for much of the year with normal vehicles and year-round with 4WD. It is an interesting journey as you pass through the Mountain Pine Ridge, then cross the Macal River and enter a broadleaf tropical forest.

Sleeping

San Ignacio and around *p248, map p255*

Some hotels in town and on Cahal Pech Hill may be noisy at weekends but the area around San Ignacio has many jungle hideaways, ranging from secluded and exclusive cottages to full activity resorts. Before booking, make sure you know what's included in the price; food is often extra. See also Budget buster p254.

AL-B **Black Rock Lodge**, Mile 60, south of San Ignacio, T824-2341, www.blackrocklodge.com A spectacular setting, despite the barbed wire fences. 6 cabañas, with solar-powered electricity and hot water. Hiking, riding, canoeing, birdwatching, excursions on offer. Breakfast US$7, lunch US$8, dinner US$15. Access road may require 4WD depending on weather.

AL-B **Maya Mountain Lodge**, ¾ mile east of San Ignacio at 9 Cristo Rey Rd, Santa Elena, PO Box 46, San Ignacio, T824-2164, www.mayamountain.com Welcoming, special weekly rates. Excursions more expensive than in town, 10% service charge. Restaurant, laundry, postal service, self-guided nature trail, swimming, hiking, riding, canoeing, fishing can be arranged.

AL-B **San Ignacio**, 18 Buena Vista Rd, T824-2034, www.sanignaciobelize.com Southern end of town, on the road to Benque Viejo, with bath, a/c or fan, hot water, clean, helpful staff, swimming pool, excellent restaurant. Recommended.

A **Martha's Guest House**, 10 West St, T824-3647, www.marthasbelize.com Comfortable rooms with balcony and lounge area, , friendly, clean. Good restaurant and kitchen facilities. Also runs **August Laundromat** (US$5 per bag).

B **Cahal Pech Village**, south of San Ignacio, near Cahal Pech, T824-3740, www.cahalpech.com Thatched cabins or a/c rooms, with restaurant, bar and meeting facilities.

B **Chiclero Camp**, south of San Ignacio, near Cahal Pech, T824-4119. Small rustic cabins in lush jungle setting, good restaurant, inconsistent management, so call first.

B **Rose's Guesthouse**, south of town, near Cahal Pech, T824-2282 5 rooms in a private house, Rose is a charming hostess, lovely garden restaurant, closest to entrance to Cahal Pech ruins.

C **Aguada Hotel**, Santa Elena, across the river, T824-3609, www.aguadahotel.com Full-service hotel, 12 rooms, private baths, a/c US$5 more, fresh water pond and heart-shaped swimming pool, quiet part of town, excellent restaurant and bar.

Budget busters

LL **The Lodge at Chaa Creek**, off the Chial Rd, after the turn to Ix Chel Farm, T824-2037, www.chaacreek.com; hotel office at 56 Burns Av, San Ignacio. This place has evolved from a working farm with jungle cottages to an upscale lodge, with a spa, conference centre, morpho butterfly breeding centre, natural history movement and an adventure centre. Strong supporter of environmental projects and sponsor of La Ruta Maya River Challenge. Chaa Creek Inland Expeditions, offers tours and excursions to all local attractions.
LL-AL **Blancaneaux Lodge**, Mountain Pine Ridge Rd, southeast of San Ignacio, Central Farm, PO Box B, Cayo District, T/F824-3878, www.blancaneauxlodge.com. Once the mountain retreat of Francis Ford Coppola, now luxurious villas and cabañas, with full amenities and legendary pizza. Overlooking a small stream, complete with private air strip for the Hollywood crowd that head this way.
L **Ek Tun**, southwest of San Ignacio, T820-3002, in USA T303-4426150, www.ektunbelize.com. A 500-acre private jungle retreat on the Macal River, access by boat only. Two very private deluxe guest cottages, excellent food, spectacular garden setting, secluded sandy river beaches, birdwatching, caving, mineral pool for swimming, miles of hiking trails, canoeing and tubing down the river. Ideal for couples. 3-night minimum.
AL **Mopan River Resort**, Benque Viejo, T823-2047, www.mopanriverresort.com Belize's first all-inclusive, luxury resort on the Mopan River, opposite Benque Viejo, accessible only by boat, 12 thatched cabañas with verandas nestled in a lush coconut grove, swimming pool, water garden, minimum stay 7 nights.

C **Backpackers Inn**, Bullet Tree Rd (10-min walk from bus station or take a taxi), T601-2299. Spacious wooden rooms (**E** for bunkbeds), swimming pool, relaxed atmosphere, friendly Canadian owners.
C **Casa Blanca Guesthouse**, 10 Burns Av, T824-2080. Clean rooms, private shower, fan or a/c, TV, use of kitchenette, friendly.
C **Parrot Nest**, near Bullet Tree Falls, 3 miles north of San Ignacio (taxi US$5), T820-4058, www.parrot-nest.com. Small comfortable tree houses in beautiful grounds by the river, breakfast and dinner included, canoeing, birdwatching, riding.
C-D **Clarissa's Falls**, down a signed track from the Benque road at Mile 70, T824-3916, www.clarissafalls.com. Thatched cottages on the bank of the Mopan River beside a set of rapids. Also bunkhouse with hammocks or beds (US$7.50 per person) and camping space with hook-ups for RVs. Rafting, kayaking and tubing available. Wonderful food in the restaurants.
D **New Belmoral**, 17 Burns Av, T824-2024, attorney@btl.net With shower, cable TV, hot water, fan or a/c. A bit noisy but clean and friendly.
D **Pacz Guest House**, 4 Far West St, T824-4538, paczghouse@btl.net Good, clean, tidy. Near the centre but quiet.
E **Central**, 24 Burns Av, T824-2253, easyrider@btl.net Clean, secure, fans, shared hot showers, book exchange, friendly, veranda with hammocks, uncomfortable beds but recommended, no restaurant but **Eva's Bar** next door.
E **Hi-Et**, 12 West St, T822-2828. Noisy, fans, low partition walls, nice balcony, friendly, helpful, family-run, clothes washing permitted, no meals, use of kitchen possible.

Camping

D-E Inglewood Camping Grounds, west of San Ignacio at Mile 68¼, T824-3555, www.ingelwoodcampingground.com Palapas, tent camping, RV hook-ups, hot and cold showers, maintained grounds, some highway noise.

F Mida's, ½ mile from town on Branch Mouth Rd via Burns Av, T824-3172, www.midas belize.com. Hot showers, electricity, water, restaurant, very helpful, good value, cabins available (**B-C**) and they also organize trips to Tikal.

Mountain Pine Ridge *p252*

AL Five Sisters Lodge, southeast of San Ignacio, 2½ miles beyond **Blancaneaux Lodge** (see above), T820-4005, www.fivesisterslodge.com Rustic cottages lit by oil lamps, great views, good-value restaurant. Recommended.

AL Mountain Equestrian Trails, Mile 8, Mountain Pine Ridge Rd, south of Georgeville, Central Farm PO, Cayo District, T820-4041, in USA T1-800 838-3913, www.metbelize.com Double cabañas with bath, no electricity, hot water, mosquito nets, good food in *cantina*, ½-day, full-day and 4-day adventure tours on horseback, 'Turf 'n' Surf' packages, excellent guides, bird-watching tours in and around the reserve.

Camping

The campground at Augustine charges US$1 per night, no mattresses; keep your receipt, as a guard checks it on the way out of Mountain Pine Ridge.

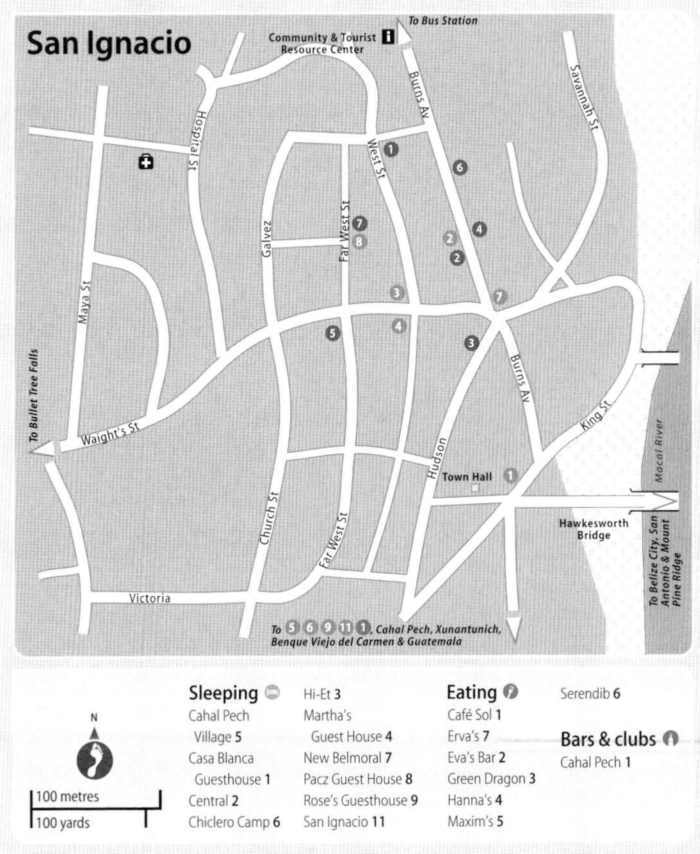

Eating

San Ignacio and around *p248, map p255*

₸₸₸ **Running W**, in the **San Ignacio Hotel**. One of the best restaurants in town. Also live music in the bar, 2nd Sat each month.

₸₸ **Café Sol**, between Burns Av and West St. Coffee and pastries, with vegetarian, chicken and seafood dishes for lunch and dinner. Also has bookstore and gift shop.

₸₸ **Erva's**, 6 Far West St, T824-2556. Vegetarian available, reasonable prices.

₸₸ **Eva's Bar**, 22 Burns Av, T804-2267. Good diner-style restaurant, local dishes, helpful with good local information, bike rental, Internet facilities, tours.

₸₸ **The Green Dragon**, 8 Hudson St, T824-4782. Great for coffee, espresso, tea and smoothies. Also internet, books, tours and healthfood store. Sells different herbal remedies made in Belize, like **Ix Chel Farm's**, **Harry Guy** and **Rubby Dub**.

₸₸ **Hanna's**, 5 Burns Av. Very good Indian-Belizean curry, vegetarian and excellent fish. Ingredients fresh from their farm, good value. Friendly, highly recommended.

₸₸ **Martha's Kitchen**, below **Martha's Guest House**. Very good breakfasts and Belizean dishes, good information.

₸₸ **Sanny's Grill**, several blocks down the hill off the Western Highway. Serves the 'world's best conch ceviche', full dinner menu, charming setting.

₸₸ **Serendib**, 27 Burns Av. Good food and good value, Sri Lankan owners, Indian-style food, Mon-Sat 1030-1500, 1830-1100.

₸₸ **The Wildside Café**, 34 Burns Av. Belizean and international vegetarian food, breakfast available, cheap, specialize in medicinal teas made from Belizean herbs. Friendly owners form an art cooperative.

₸ **Hode's Place**, Branch Mouth Rd, just outside town. Popular with locals and good value. Belizean food in huge portions, open daily, pleasant yard outside.

₸ **Maxim's**, Bullet Tree Rd and Far West St. Chinese, good service, cheap, very good food, popular with locals, noisy TV.

Entertainment

San Ignacio and around *p248, map p255*

Bars and clubs

Cahal Pech, on a hill opposite Cahal Pech ruins, beside the road to Benque Viejo before the edge of town. Music and dancing at weekends, *the* place to be, live bands are broadcast on TV and radio all over Belize, good views.

Coconuts, right turn off King St to river. The open-air bar is at the back of the building, popular spot, open daily.

Culture Club, same building as Coconuts, upstairs, live reggae Thu-Sat night, popular with foreigners and local Rastas.

Legends 200, Bullet Tree Rd. Disco, popular with locals.

Starbucks, Santa Elena, along the river, bar, nice view, open daily for drinks, more lively during the weekends.

Activities and tours

San Ignacio and around *p248, map p255*

Local tour operators offer similar tours at similar prices. Many of the resorts and lodges in this area also organize tours and expeditions (see Sleeping, above). **Canoe trips** up the Macal River are worthwhile, 3 hrs upstream, 1½ hrs return. Hiring a canoe to go upstream without a guide is not recommended as there are Class II rapids 1 hr from San Ignacio. Tours of **Mountain Pine Ridge** available, but shop around carefully. Also day trips to **Caracol**, US$60-75 per person in a group, or US$200 for a private tour, or **Tikal** in Guatemala, about US$70 per person.

Tour operators

David's Adventure Tours, near main bus stop, T804-3674. Recommended for visits to Barton's Creek Cave or guided canoe trips along the Macal River. Good reports.

Easy Rider, Bullet Tree Rd, T824-3734, for horse riding. Full-day tours for US$40.

Eva's Bar, T804-2267. Bob from the UK is the best starting point for information on trips in the area. Canoe trips with bird- and wildlife watching, US$12.50 per person or jungle canoe trips, US$30 for 2 for full-day tour, highly recommended. Trips to Caracol from around US$75 per person including Río Frío Cave, Río On pools and García sisters' gift shop, 12 hrs.
The Green Dragon, 8 Hudson St, T824-4782, www.greendragonbelize.com. Very helpful, will arrange hotel bookings all over Belize as well as tours around San Ignacio.
International Archaeological Tours (**IAT**), West St, next to Martha's Guest House, T824-3991, www.belizeweb.com/iat. Tours throughout Belize and El Petén, very helpful advice about the area. Ramón Silva is a recommended guide.
Mayawalk Tours, 19 Burns Av, T824-3070, www.mayawalk.com. Offers the standard tours plus a few innovative ones, including Actun Tunichil Muknal Cave. Good recommendations.
Pacz Tours, Burns Av, T824-2477 /T610-3638.Great trips to Actun Tunichil Muknal Cave, US$65 including lunch. Excellent guides, highly recommended.

Transport

San Ignacio and around *p248, map p255*

Bus

Novelo bus station is on Burns Av (in front of the church). To **Belize City**, every 30 mins Mon-Sat 0400-1800, every hr Sun 0530-1800, 2-3 hrs, US$3.50. To **Belmopan**, same schedule as Belize City, 1 hr, US$1.50. To **Benque Viejo** (p251), every 30 mins, Mon-Sat 0730-2300 (fewer on Sun), 15 min, US$0.50 (some continue to Melchor de Mencos); also *colectivo* from central square, US$2.50. To **Chetumal**, Mexico, 1 daily at 0415. To **San Antonio**, daily 1000 and 1430, from the market area; check times of return buses before leaving San Ignacio.

To Guatemala Buses to **Flores** depart from the border at 1330, US$2.65; also several daily from Melchor de Mencos, 3½ hrs, US$2.65; last bus 1600 but get an earlier service to arrive in Flores in daylight. There are also minibuses from Melchor to **Santa Elena**. Minibus from San Ignacio to **Tikal**, US$20 per person return; otherwise catch the border-Flores bus and change at El Cruce.

Taxi

To **Belize City** US$75.To **Xunantunich** US$20. To **Benque Viejo**, about US$5; taxis in Benque Viejo will take you to **Melchor de Mencos** (US$1.50, colectivo US$0.50) but rip offs are common – so bargain hard. To **Tikal** US$100.

Mountain Pine Ridge *p252*

Mountain Pine Ridge has no public transport and the private pick-ups between San Ignacio and Augustine are usually packed, so hitching is impossible. Apart from tours, the only alternatives are to take a taxi (US$88 for 5 people), or hire a vehicle or a mountain bike (available from Eva's Bar or somewhere in San Ignacio). Everything is well signposted. Roads are passable but rough Jan-May, marginal after Jun and are impossibly wet Sep-Nov; essential to seek local advice.

Directory

San Ignacio *p248*

Banks Mon-Fri 0830-1400, Sat 0830-1200, most at southern end of Burns Av. Belize Bank offers full service, TCs, Visa and MasterCard cash advances. Western Union, in Celina's (supermarket), Burns Av, open later. Eva's Bar and Martha's change TCs. **Internet** About US$3 per hr at CayoCom, Hudson St; Green Dragon, next to CayoCom, and Eva's Bar. **Laundry** August Laundromat at Martha's and Mike's, and Laundromat at Burns Av, US$5. **Post office** Hudson St, reliable parcel service. **Telephone** BTL office, far end of Burns Av, opposite Venus Hotel, long-distance calls and fax service.

South Belize and the Southern cayes

Southern Belize is the remotest part of the country and has poor roads, but it is well worth exploring. Dangriga is the largest of several Garífuna settlements that burst into life every year on Settlement Day in November and the paradise beaches of Hopkins and Placencia are relaxing destinations that are perfect for watersports. Cockscomb Basin Wildlife (Jaguar) Sanctuary offers one of the best chances of seeing a big cat in the wild, while the sparsely populated far south around Punta Gorda is dotted with impressive Maya ruins and indigenous settlements .

Getting there Flights or slow buses from Belize City to Dangriga, Placencia and Punta Gorda. Boats from Honduras and Guatemala.
Getting around Bus and taxi; rough roads in many places.
Time required 4-10 days.
Weather Gets wetter as you go south, May-Nov.
Sleeping Exceptional around Placencia, good range elsewhere.
Eating Seafood in Placencia, rice 'n' beans elsewhere.
Activities and tours Scuba diving, watersports, caving, fishing.
★ Don't miss... Cockscomb Basin Wildlife Sanctuary » *p261*.

South to Dangriga *pp265-273*

The Coastal Highway

From the Western Highway two routes head southeast to Dangriga: the first is the Coastal Highway (a good dirt road), which branches off about two miles beyond Belize Zoo and runs southeast to **Gales Point**, 15 miles north of Dangriga. This is a charming fishing village on a peninsula at the south end of Manatee Lagoon. The villagers are keen to preserve natural resources and there are still significant numbers of the endangered manatee and hawksbill turtles.

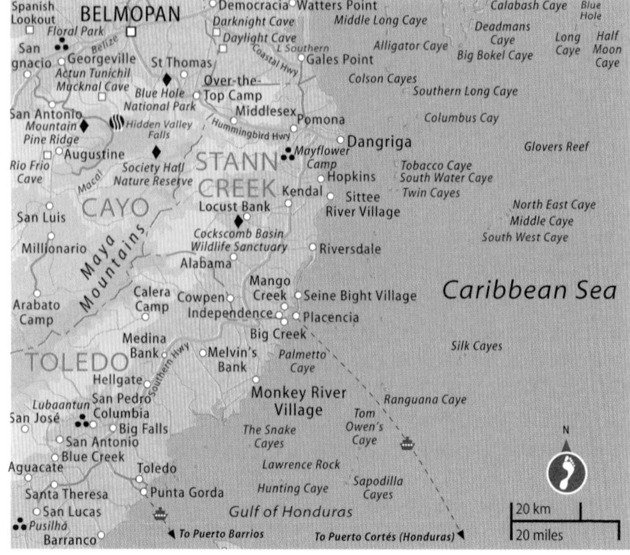

Background

The Garífuna

The Garífuna have had a long and rough ride to what is now their tropical home on the Caribbean coast of Belize, Guatemala and Honduras. Their unusual history began back in the 17th century, when a slave ship carrying Nigerian slaves was shipwrecked off the island of St Vincent in the Caribbean. After initial conflicts, the surviving slaves intermarried with the Arawak and Kalipuna inhabitants of St Vincent. The Spanish called their descendants 'Black Caribs'. According to some anthropologists, the name Garífuna comes from 'Kalipuna', meaning 'cassava-eating people'.

In the 18th century war broke out between French colonists who wanted a slice of St Vincent and the British, who had already colonized the island but were greedy for the land now occupied by the Garífuna. The French sided with the Caribs but, after much bloodshed and starvation, were forced to surrender to the British. In 1796 the British deported all the Caribs to Roatán, one of the Bay Islands, off Honduras, and when Spain took Roatán from the British a year later, some 5,000 were moved on to Trujillo on the Honduran coast. From Trujillo they fanned out along the Caribbean coastline of Central America.

The Garífuna flag is three fat stripes of black, white and yellow. Black remembers the Garífuna lives lost in the trip from St Vincent; white represents the hope for a new life in Central America; and yellow represents money.

In May 2001 UNESCO officially recognized the culture of the Garífuna. Their language is a blend of Arawak, French and African tongues, with some English and Spanish influences. The Garífuna believe that God is the principal being and that ancestors guide the living and help to make decisions. The Bible, translated into Garinagu, is used and the sea is worshipped for its continued importance to the Garífuna people. *Dugu*, a sacred healing ceremony is one of the principal rituals of the religion. The most compelling element of Garífuna culture for the visitor, however, is likely to be the music and dance, including the *punta*, an exhausting fertility dance involving some serious leg, bum and hip work, accompanied by a drum (*garaón*), made from a hollow trunk and animal skin, maracas, a conch shell and a turtle shell. Feel the rhythym on Garífuna Day, celebrated annually on 19 November in southern Belize (see page 270) and on 26 November in eastern Guatemala (see page 352).

The Hummingbird Highway

The narrow Hummingbird Highway heads south at Belmopan, 48 miles west of Belize City. Skirting the eastern edge of Mountain Pine Ridge, the newly surfaced road meanders through a lush landscape of cohune palms and across vast flood plains filled with citrus trees. The road first climbs through rich tropical hardwood forest to Mile 13, where a visitor centre marks the entrance to the **Blue Hole National Park** ⓘ *Mile 13, daily 0800-1600, US$6*. This is typical karst limestone country with sinkholes, caves and underground streams. Two paths, with good birdwatching, lead through shady ferns from the centre to **St Herman's Cave**, which has a unique microclimate. You can walk for more than a mile underground but it can be slippery if wet; torch and spare batteries essential. A rough 2½-mile trail (good hiking boots required) heads from the cave through low secondary forest to the **Blue Hole** itself, an azure blue swimming hole fringed with vines and ferns, fed by a stream from St Herman's Cave. After its long journey underground, the water here is deliciously cool until it disappears again into the top of a large underwater cavern. Eventually this joins the Sibun River which enters the sea just south of Belize City. The Blue Hole is also accessible from a car park at about Mile 14; a sign on the roadway warns visitors against thieves. An armed guard and wardens have been hired to prevent further theft and assaults.

The peaks of the Maya Mountains dominate the south side of the highway until about Mile 30, when the valley of **Stann Creek** begins to widen out into Belize's most productive agricultural area, where large citrus groves stretch along the highway. At **Over-the-Top Camp**, canoeing or tubing trips can be organized down **Indian Creek** to visit numerous caves; vehicle support is brought to meet you on the Coastal Highway near Democracia. Follow the track opposite **Over-the-Top Camp**, turn right and cross the stream, continuing for four miles along a gravel road to reach **Tamandua**, a wildlife sanctuary in **Five Blue Lakes National Park** ⓘ *Friends of 5 Blues, PO Box 111, Belmopan, T809-2005.* There's camping 1½ miles beyond Tamandua; follow signs for the National Park.

Dangriga and around *pp265-273*

North Stann Creek meets the sea at Dangriga ('standing waters' or 'sweet water' in Garífuna), the chief town of the Stann Creek District. Populated largely by Black Caribs (Garífuna; see page 259), it is a cheerful and busily commercial place, alive with flotillas of boats and fishermen. The town has the usual Belizean wooden clap-board houses elevated on piles, several gas stations, a good hospital and an airfield with regular flights. The beach has been considerably cleaned up and extended; it is particularly nice at the far north of town near the **Pelican Beach Hotel**, where it is raked and cleaned daily and by **Pal's Guest House**, where palm trees have been planted and the beach has been enlarged.

Cayes near Dangriga

From Dangrigia, speedboats ferry visitors to **Tobacco Caye**, a tiny and quite heavily populated island, with lots of local flavour and charm. Although it is becoming a little commercialized, it still has an authentic feel. There is no electricity on the island, but it has a good atmosphere and is great fun. The caye sits right on the reef and you can snorkel from the sandfly-free beach, although there are no large schools of fish to see. Book in advance if you want to stay overnight. South of Tobacco Caye, **South Water Caye** is the focus of a new marine reserve. It is a lovely palm-fringed tropical island with beautiful sandy beaches, particularly at the south end.

Glover's Reef, part of North East Caye, lies about 45 miles offshore. It is an atoll with beautiful diving and has been a Marine Reserve since 1993. The reef here is pristine and the cayes are generally unspoilt. However, yellow blight has killed most of the existing palm trees on **Long Caye**, and the combination of Hurricane Mitch and high water temperatures in recent years has damaged the coral, so snorkelling is not as good as it once was.

South of Dangriga

Six miles inland from Dangriga, the Southern Highway (now completely paved except for a stretch of a mile or so) branches off the Hummingbird Highway and heads south through mixed tropical forests, palmettos and pines along the fringes of the Maya Mountains towards

Cockscomb Basin Wildlife Sanctuary

Punta Gorda. West of the road, about five miles from the Hummingbird junction, a track leads to **Mayflower**, a Maya ruin. Some experts say it will eventually be the biggest archaeological site in southern Belize. Fifteen miles from Dangriga, a minor road forks off four miles east to the Garífuna fishing village of **Hopkins**. Watch out for sandflies when the weather is calm. Some 20 miles south of Dangriga, the Southern Highway crosses the Sittee River at the small village of **Kendal** (ruins nearby). Turning east towards the Caribbean, a road follows the river to the coast at **Sittee River Village** and **Possum Point Biological Station**.

Cockscomb Basin Wildlife Sanctuary and around

ⓘ *Visitors' centre at Quam Bank, 7 miles west of Maya Centre. Note that sanctuary guards leave for the day at 1600. US$5, Belizeans US$1.25; donations very welcome.*

One mile beyond Kendal is the village of **Maya Centre** (or Center), founded by the former milpa-farming inhabitants of Quam Bank. From Maya Centre, a poor seven-mile track winds west through Cabbage Haul Gap to the **Cockscomb Basin Wildlife Sanctuary** (51,800 ha). This is the world's first jaguar sanctuary and is definitely worth an extended visit if you have two or three days.

The sanctuary is sponsored by the Belizean government, the **Audubon Society**, the **Worldwide Fund For Nature** and various private firms. It was created out of the Cockscomb Basin Forest Reserve in 1986 to protect the country's highest recorded density of jaguars (*Panthera onca*) and their smaller cousins: the puma or red tiger, the endangered ocelot, the diurnal jaguarundi and that feline cutey, the margay. Many other mammals share the heavily forested reserve, including coatis, collared peccaries, agoutis, anteaters, Baird's tapirs and tayras (a small weasel-like animal). There are red-eyed tree frogs, boas, iguanas and fer-de-lances, as well as over 290 species of bird, including king vultures, great curassows, several types of toucan, hummingbirds and scarlet macaws, if you get up early enough.

As well as watching the wildlife, you can shower under waterfalls, tube down the river, and explore the 18-mile network of jungle trails that spreads out from the informative visitors' centre at Quam Bank. The paths range in distance from a few hundred yards to 2½ miles. Walkers probably won't see any of the big cats as they are nocturnal (if you fancy a walk in the dark you may be lucky; see Jaguar spotting, 262); you are, however, likely to see birds, frogs, lizards, snakes and spiders. Longer hikes can also be planned with the staff. Nearby is one of

Travellers' tales

Jaguar spotting

I really wanted to see a jaguar so I decided to stay overnight at the Cockscomb Basin Wildlife Sanctuary. Walking the paths by day I'd got a feel for the trail system, I'd cooled off in the waterfalls and floated downstream on an inner tube but I hadn't yet seen a big cat. As dusk fell, word quickly got round the communal kitchen that we were heading out into the night for some jaguar-spotting. Adrenaline-fuelled anticipation steadily built up. We couldn't get a guide to help us out but, one by one, the interested, intrigued and the curious joined the group.

Stepping out into the quiet darkness of the early morning, we killed the torch and let our eyes adjust their night vision with just the faintest of clear moons illuminating the trails. Stalking the unseen wildlife was exhilarating; the flutter of a potoo's wings was enought to send the pulse rate through the roof: what was that in the bush? Should we move closer? We didn't see a jaguar that night but, never mind; the thrill was in the chase. *Peter Hutchison*

Belize's highest summits, **Victoria Peak** (3,675 ft), which is an arduous four- or five-day return climb and should not be undertaken lightly; February to May are the best months to attempt it. There is virtually no path so a guide is essential. ▲▸▸ *p271*.

Placencia and around *pp265-273*

Continuing down the Southern Highway beyond Riversdale, the road (now very rough, 4WD advisable) turns south to follow a spit of land to **Maya Beach** and, eventually, **Placencia**. This small, former Creole fishing village, 30 miles south of Dangriga, was hit hard by Hurricane Iris in October 2001 but most hotels, restaurants, bars, dive shops and guide services opened again as soon as the basic infrastructure was repaired. Placencia continues to attract visitors looking for an 'end of the road' adventure. It's a relaxing spot that combines palm trees, beaches, fishing, snorkelling and diving, with lots of Jamaican music, particularly around Easter and Christmas. If you visit from March to May, you may witness the migration of the whale shark – the largest fish in the world at up to 55 ft . It's also worth being around for the **Lobster Fest**, with two days of music, dancing and lobster, during the last week of June.

Amenities, such as electricity, good water, telephones and internet services can be found along the village's single dirt road. The local **Placencia Tourism Center** ⓘ *T523-4045, www.placencia.com*, is next to the petrol station and produces the local monthly news sheet *Placencia Breeze*, available online at www.placenciabreeze.com.

Around Placencia

From Placencia, trips can be made to local cayes and to the Barrier Reef, approximately 18 miles offshore. Several hotels and guide services have kayaks that can be rented to explore the nearer islands or the quieter waters of the Placencia Lagoon. Day tours by boat south along the coast from Placencia visit **Monkey River**, with a good chance of seeing howler monkeys, toucans, manatees and iguanas en route. **Monkey River Village** can also reached by a rough road (not recommended in wet weather), which ends on the north side of the river; call over for river transport.

Snorkelling around the cayes, off Placencia

Fifteen miles after the Riversdale turn-off, another road branches off the Southern Highway to the mangrove coast opposite Placencia on the mainland. This road runs four miles east through the **Savannah Forest Reserve** to **Mango Creek**, a banana-exporting port, **Independence** and **Big Creek**. Mango Creek is significant for its bus and boat connections to Guatemala and elsewhere; the easiest way to get here from Placencia is by water taxi across the lagoon. *p271*.

Cayes near Placencia

Ranguana Caye is a private caye reached by regular boats and day trips from Placencia. It's great for snorkelling or just relaxing but divers must bring their own scuba equipment. The **Silk Cayes**, also known as the **Queen Cayes**, are a small group of tiny, picture-perfect islands that sit on the outer barrier reef. Together with Gladdens Spit, they now form the core zone of the country's newest marine reserve. The Silk Cayes boast superb diving, especially on the North Wall. Coral in the deeper areas is in good condition, with many tube and barrel sponges, and sharks, turtles and rays often seen cruising the reef wall. The Silk Cayes are a popular destination for Placencia-based dive operators, however, it's not possible to dive in this area during periods of rough weather.

At the southernmost end of the Mesoamerican Barrier Reef are the **Sapodilla Cayes**, reach by tour from Placencia or from Río Dulce and Lívingston in Guatemala. There are settlements on a few of the Cayes including **Hunting Caye**.

The far south *pp265-273*

In the far south of Belize, **Toledo District** is well off the beaten path and yet it has some of the most spectacular views, rivers, waterfalls, rainforest and cayes and some of the friendliest people in the country. Countless species of birds make their homes along the rivers, as do troops of howler monkeys and other wildlife; kayaking is a good way to view them. There are also plenty of logging trails and hunters' tracks penetrating the southern flanks of the Maya Mountains but, if hiking in the forest, do not go alone. White-sand beaches line the cayes off Punta Gorda, where fly fishing, snorkelling and scuba diving are popular.

Towards Punta Gorda

About 35 miles beyond the Mango Creek junction half a mile west of the road, is the **Nim Li Punit** ('The Big Hat') archaeological site – look for the sign on the highway. It was discovered in 1974, when a score of stelae, 15-20 ft tall and dating from AD 700-800, were unearthed, as well as a ball court and several groups of buildings. Day trips are offered from Placencia. A short distance beyond, the highway passes **Big Falls Village**, which was almost completely destroyed by Hurricane Iris. Take a short hike back to the hot springs for a swim, to camp or to sling a hammock, but first seek permission from the landowner, Mr Peter Aleman. Four miles from Big Falls, the highway reaches a T-junction, know locally as the '**Dump**', where the paved road turns sharp left and runs down through a forest reserve for 13 miles to Punta Gorda.

Punta Gorda

Punta Gorda is the southernmost town of any size in Belize, a marketing centre and fishing port with a varied ethnic makeup of Creoles, Q'eqchi', Mopan, Chinese, East Indians and other descendants of labourers brought over in ill-fated settlement attempts. A few miles north, near **Toledo**, are the remains of the sugar cane plantation founded by Confederate refugees after the American Civil War. The coast at Punta Gorda is about 10 ft above sea level and is fringed with coconut palms. It is clean and enjoyable – once you get away from Front Street, where the lively and colourful market comes with the associated smells of fish and rotting vegetables. The *Voice of America* has an incongruous antenna complex to the south of town.

Toledo Visitors' Information Center, also called '**Dem Dats Doin**' ⓘ *in booth by pier, PO Box 73, T722-2470, demdatsdoin@btl.net*, can provide information on travel, tours, guiding and accommodation with indigenous families in the whole of Toledo district. The **Tourist Information Centre** ⓘ *Front Street, T722-2531, Mon-Sat 0800-1200 and 1300-1700*, also provides a wealth of information, including bus schedules to local Maya villages. The **Toledo Ecotourism Association** (see page 268), in the same building, can offer information on the Village Guesthouse and Ecotrail programme, as well as booking transport to the villages.

Punta Gorda-Puerto Barrios and Lívingston

The southern border with Guatemala runs along the Sarstún River. There are no roads to this border; instead boats go from Punta Gorda to either Puerto Barrios or Lívingston. *p271.*

Leaving Belize PACT exit tax payable, see p54. If you need a visa for Guatemala, it must be obtained in advance in Belize City. Exit stamps for people and vehicles can be obtained at the Customs House next to the pier on Front Street in Punta Gorda. Be there at least one hour before departure, or two hours if loading a motorcycle. Bike and motorbike transportation may be difficult as officials in Lívingston do not have the authority to issue vehicle permits to anything other than water craft. On arrival in Guatemala, you must go straight to the Puerto Barrios or Lívingston immigration offices, both open 24 hours, where tourist cards are issued.

Leaving Guatemala Guatemalan immigration is in Puerto Barrios and Lívingston. There are exit fees to leave Guatemala by boat, but the official fee varies according to the time of departure. You must have your exit stamp from immigration before you can buy a ticket. Anyone who takes you to Belize by boat must have a manifest with passengers' names, stamped and signed at the immigration office.

Exchange There are money changers on both sides (ask for Emilio from **Grace** restaurant in Punta Gorda) but it is better to get rid of Bz$ in Belize and then buy quetzales with US$ in Guatemala. Neither side changes traveller's cheques.

San Antonio and around

Inland from Punta Gorda are several interesting villages in the foothills of the Maya Mountains. Take the main road to the 'Dump' road junction and then continue west to **San Antonio**, which was founded by refugees from San Luis in Guatemala in the late 19th century. There's a community phone, T702-2144, for checking buses and other information, or you can contact **Dem Dat's Doin** in Punta Gorda (see above). On the way to San Antonio, a branch road leads to **San Pedro Columbia**, a Maya village, where the inhabitants still speak the Q'eqchi' language and women wear colourful costumes, including Guatemalan-style *huípiles*. There are many religious celebrations here, the most intense of which is San Luis Rey Day on 5 Aug. **Blue Creek** is another attractive indigenous village, south of San Antonio; turn off at **Roy's Cool Spot** (good restaurant; daily truck and all buses pass here). From the village a marked trail leads through the forest and along rock-strewn creeks to **Blue Creek Caves**, where there are Maya drawings. There's good swimming nearby but choose a spot away from the strong current. Blue Creek participates in the **TEA guesthouse** programme, see page 268.

Lubaantun

ⓘ *1 mile northwest of San Pedro. Daily 0800-1600.* Lubaantun ('Fallen Stones') was the major ceremonial site of southern Belize and consists of a series of terraced plazas surrounded by temples and palaces, which ascend along a ridge from south to north. Extensive work has been undertaken to restore a large part of this unique site, which dates from AD 800-900, late in the Maya culture. The buildings were constructed with unusual precision and some of the original lime-mortar facings can still be discerned. Excavations at Lubaantun have revealed whistle figurines, iron pyrite mirrors, obsidian knives and conch shells from Wild Cane Caye. One of the great controversies of the site was the 'discovery' in 1927 of the Crystal Skull by the daughter of the explorer FA Mitchell-Hedges. The light-reflecting, translucent skull is the size of a small watermelon and weighs just over 5 kg. It is one of only two ever found in Central America and its date of manufacture is unknown; some experts claim it is over 3,600 years old. Today the skull is reported to still be an ornament in the house of the ageing Anna who has promised, one day, to reveal the truth about how she found it. The site now has new visitor centre and a caretaker is on hand to point out areas of particular interest. However, you should take your own refreshments and watch out for the vicious mosquitoes.

Pusilhá

Pusilhá is one of the most interesting Maya cities, only accessible by boat. Many stelae have been found here dating from AD 573-731, and carvings are similar to those at Quiriguá, Guatemala. Rare features are a walled-in ball court and the abutments remaining from a bridge, which once spanned the Moho River. Swimming in the rivers is safe.

Sleeping

The Coastal Highway *p258*

A **Manatee Lodge**, Gales Point, T220-8040, in the US T1-877-462-6283, www.manateelodge.com Resort on the shores of the Southern Lagoon, with trips to all local areas.

E **Gales Point Bed and Breakfast Association**, contact Hortence Welch on arrival or call T220-9031. Basic rooms, no indoor plumbing, meals available.

The Hummingbird Highway *p259*

AL-A **Caves Branch Jungle Lodge**, PO Box 356, Belmopan, ½ mile past St Herman's Cave, T822-2800, www.cavesbranch.com Secluded spot on banks of river, cabañas with private bath or **E** per person in the bunkhouse, camping US$5 per person, clean, shared bathrooms, great 'jungle showers', delicious buffet meals. Great trips through caves, 7-mile underground floats, guided jungle trips, tubing, kayaking, mountain

Budget busters

LL Turtle Inn, on beach just north of the airstrip, Placencia, T523-3244, www.turtleinn.com Francis Ford Coppola rebuilt this impressive resort after Hurricane Iris. Hardwood, thatched roof villas and cottages right on the beach blending Balinese and Belizean themes. Huge palapa restaurant and beach bar looking out to the pool.

LL-AL Manta Reef Resort, Glover's Reef Atoll, PO Box 215, 3 Eyre St, Belize City, T223-1895. 9 individual cabins with full facilities, in perfect desert island setting, 1-week packages available only, reservations essential, excellent diving and fishing, good food. Highly recommended.

biking and rappelling. Excellent guides from US$60, highly recommended.
E **Palacios Mountain Retreat**, Mile 31, Augustus Palacio, St Martha, T822-3683, www.palaciosretreat.com Good for relaxing, cabañas, friendly, helpful, family atmosphere, safe, good local food, swimming in river, tours to waterfall in forest, caves and lagoon, Five Blue Lakes National Park, beware of sandflies.

Dangriga *p260*

AL-A **Bonefish**, Mahogany St, seafront near post office, T522-2243, www.bluemarlinlodge.com A/c, cable TV, hot water, accepts Visa. Restaurant, diving and fishing.
C-D **Bluefield Lodge**, 6 Bluefield Rd, T522-2742. Bright hotel, owner very nice, spotless, comfortable beds, very helpful, secure. Highly recommended.
D-E **Pal's Guest House**, 868A Magoon St, T522-2365, www.palsbelize.com 10 units on beach, all with balconies, sea views, bath, fan, cable TV, cheaper rooms in main building, shared bath downstairs, private upstairs. Dangriga Dive Centre runs from next door (see Activities and tours, below).

Cayes near Dangriga *p260*

Contact Slick Rock Adventures, T800-3905715 (US Toll-free), PO Box 1400, Moab, UT 84532, www.slickrock.com, in advance for all-inclusive itineraries on Glover's Reef.
AL **Blue Marlin Lodge**, South Water Caye, T522-2243, marlin@btl.net An excellent dive lodge offering various packages, snorkelling off the beach, good accommodation and food, tours.
AL **Ocean's Edge Fishing Lodge**, Tobacco Caye, T614-9633, USA T281-8940548, www2.symet.net/beltex Full board, 6 cabins on stilts joined by elevated walk-ways, run by Raymond and Brenda Lee, excellent food, diving and fishing.
C **Hotel Larnas**, Tobacco Caye, T522-2571/2, USA T909-9434556. Own fishing pier, snorkelling equipment hire US$10 per day, good Caribbean-style food, mosquito net, shared shower. Recommended.
C **Island Camps**, Tobacco Caye, PO Box 174 (51 Regent St, Belize City, T227-2109). Owner Mark Bradley will pick up guests in Dangriga, A-frame huts and campground US$5 per person per night, meals on request, reef excursions, friendly, good value. Recommended.
C-D **Glover's Atoll Resort**, North East Caye, PO Box 563, Belize City, T614-7177 or T520-5016, www.glovers.com.bz Facilities are simple, don't expect luxury. Phone for a full breakdown of services and costs. 8 cabins with wood-burning stoves and camping. Rates include round-trip transportation from Sittee River, p271. Occasional meals provided,

groceries and drinking water (US$1.50 a gallon) available, but bring everything you need, including food, drinks, torch, soap, candles, sun screen, toilet paper, in case supplies are short or bad weather stops boats running. Boats for hire, with or without guide, also canoes, windsurfing, fly fishing, snorkelling and full PADI/NAUI dive centre.

South of Dangriga *p260*

A **Hopkins Inn**, Hopkins, T523-7013, hopkinsinn@btl.net. White cabins on the beach, with private bathroom, very clean and friendly. Rates include breakfast.
B-F **Toucan Sittee**, Sittee River, 400 yd down river from **Glover's** (see below), T523-7039. Lovely setting, rooms with screens, fans and hot water, or fully-equipped riverside apartments, meals around US$6, grow fruit and veg and over 50 medicinal plants.
C-D **Sandy Beach Lodge**, Hopkins, T522-2023, T523-7006, 20-min walk south of village. Run by 14 women who work in shifts, arrive before 1900 or they will have gone home, 6 beachside cabañas, quiet, safe, friendly, clean.
E **Swinging Armadillos Bunk House**, on the pier, Hopkins, T522-2016. 5 rooms, outdoor shower, seafood restaurant, bar, usually the best in the village.
E-F **Glover's Guest House**, on river bank, Sittee River, T802-2505. 5 rooms, restaurant, camping, jungle river trips. Start point for the boat to the Glover's Atoll Resort (see above and p271). Price per person.

Cockscomb Basin Wildlife Sanctuary and around *p261*

There is usually space on arrival, but to guarantee accommodation, contact the **Belize Audubon Society**, see p54.
B-E **Park HQ** New purpose-built cabins, and cheaper dormitories. Earth toilets, drinking water available, but bring your own food, other drinks, matches, torch, sheet sleeping bag, eating utensils and mosquito repellent. There is a picnic area, but the nearest shop is at Maya Centre.
C-E **Mejen Tz'il's Lodge**, T520-3032; lsaqui@btl.net Screened rooms with double beds or bunk beds, veranda, private hot water showers and toilets in a separate building, restaurant on premises.
D **Nu'uk Che'il Cottages**, Maya Centre, T520-3021. Simple thatched rooms in a garden next to the forest, take the botanical trail and learn about Maya medicine from Aurora Saqui; her husband can arrange transport to the Park HQ.

Placencia and around *p262*

Rooms may be hard to find in the afternoon after arrival of the bus from Dangriga. The bus stop outside **Kingfisher** office is a good place to start looking for rooms, lots of budget accommodation nearby. Contact the **Placencia Tourist Centre**, T523-4045, placencia@btl.net, for details of accommodation in the surrounding area. See also Budget busters, p266.
AL-L **Ranguana Caye**, reservations through **Robert's Grove**,T523-3565, www.robertsgrove.com 3 charmingly simple cabañas, each with a double and single bed and gas stove. Private hot showers and toilet in separate building. BBQ pits provided so bring food, but meals also available at US$35 per person.
A **Trade Winds Cottages**, South Point, T523-3122, trdewndpla@btl.net Cabins in a spacious plot on the south beach.
A-B **Serenade Guest House**, T523-3380, hotelserande@btl.net Spacious and airy rooms, all with a/c and private bath. Upstairs rooms more expensive. The owners also operate the **Serenade Island Resort** (**L**) on the Sapodilla Cayes.
A-D **Seaspray**, T/F523-3148, www.seasprayhotel.com Very nice, comfortable and friendly. Good-value rooms, ranging from beachside cabañas to small doubles in original building. De Tatch restaurant.
B **Cozy Corner**, T523-3450, cozycorner@btl.net On the beach, just behind **Advance Dive Shop**. With fridge, TV, some cheaper rooms without a/c and good restaurant in front.

Time for TEA - the Guesthouse Programme

An interesting alternative to staying in Punta Gorda is to stay in an indigenous village. The Guesthouse Programme is run by villagers as a non-competitive cooperative, called the Toledo Ecotourism Association (TEA), with gross profits ploughed back into the villages' infrastructure, schools and other community projects. One night for two people, with a forest tour and two meals, costs nearly US$50 but all profits go directly to the villages. Dormitory accommodation is US$9 per person. The scheme is co-ordinated by the TEA Office at the Tourist Information Center (BTB Building) in Punta Gorda, T722-2096, ttea@btl.net. Staff provide information about the participating villages, the key attractions, tours and courses, take bookings and help arrange transport.

Participating villages San Miguel, San José (Hawaii), Laguna, Blue Creek, Santa Elena and Pueblo Viejo are all isolated villages beyond the 'Dump'. Medina Bank is more accessible as it is just off the southern highway. Barranco is a Garífuna village south of Punta Gorda, accessible by boat or poor road. Each has built a well-appointed guesthouse, simple, but clean, with sheets, towels, mosquito nets, oil lamps, ablutions block, and two four-bunk rooms. Visitors stay here, but eat in the villagers' houses on strict rotation, so each household gains equal income and the workload is shared. Many village men and children speak English. The villagers have been relearning old dances and are trying to rescue the art of making and playing the harp, violin and guitar for evening entertainment. Excursions are also arranged, varying from a four-hour trek looking at medicinal plants, to visits to out-of-the-way sights like caves and creeks (take boots, even in dry season). The village tour can be skipped, although you deprive the 'guides' of income.

Homestay Programme This a similar scheme that involves actually staying with a family in their house. Several villages in the area participate. As you are living with the family, privacy is generally limited and the experience is more intense. Details can be discussed with Dem Dat's Doin in Punta Gorda (see page 264), who will also help to arrange transport if required.

Both programmes are a unique way to explore the Maya villages; you are unlikely to find such an experience elsewhere.

B **Dianni's Guest House**, T/F523-3159, diannisbelize@yahoo.com Spacious rooms with a/c, most with 1 double and single bed. Fridge, coffee and tea provided, nice balcony with hammocks, internet.

C **Deb and Dave's Last Resort**, T523-3207, www.toadaladventure.com 4 very good budget rooms with shared bathroom, hot water, kayak and bike rental. Walk-ins only, no advance reservations. Also runs tours in local area.

D **Lydia's Rooms**, T523-3117, lydias@btl.net 8 double rooms, shared toilet and shower, situated across the sidewalk on a quiet part of the beach. Kitchen facilities. Simple, but very chilled. Recommended.

D **The Yellow House**, T523-3481, ctbze@btl.net Between the road and sidewalk, about halfway down – bright yellow. 4 very comfortable rooms with communicating doors, so excellent for a family or group of friends. Front rooms have microwave and coffee machine. Excellent value.

Punta Gorda and around *p263*

Contact **Dem Dats Doin'** (see p264) and **TEA** (see p268) for details of accommodation in the villages around Punta Gorda.

B **Sea Front Inn**, PO Box 20, Front St, T722-2300, www.seafrontinn.com 14 rooms with private bath, hot water, a/c and TV, restaurant with great views and international menu. **Maya Island Air** and **Tropic Air** agents.

C **Tate's Guest House**, 34 José María Nuñez St, T722-2196. A/c, cheaper without, clean, hot water, bathroom, TV, parking, friendly, breakfast before 0730 only, laundry.

C-D **Punta Caliente**, 108 José María Nuñez St, T722-2561, puntacal@btl.net Private bath, hot water, fan and cable TV, good value, restaurant.

D **Mahung's Hotel**, corner North and Main St, T722-2044. Reasonable, private bath, cable TV, also rents mountain bikes, US$5 per day.

D **Nature's Way Guest House**, 65 Front St, T702-2119. Clean, friendly, good breakfast, camping gear for rent. Recommended.

D **St Charles Inn**, 23 King St, T722-2149. With or without bath, spacious rooms, fan, cable TV, good.

E **Wahima**, on waterfront, T722-2542. Clean and safe, all rooms with private bath, owner Max is local school teacher, friendly and informative. Also rents kitchenettes for US$50 per week.

Eating

Dangriga *p260*

ǂ **Ritchie's Dinette**, on main street north of police station. Creole and Spanish food, simple, large portions, popular breakfasts.

ǂ **Riverside Café**, south bank of river, just east of main road. Nicer inside than it looks, good breakfast, good service and food, best place to get information on boats to Tobacco Caye.

ǂ **Ruby's Rainforest Café**, past the Riverside Café, on the beach. Open sporadically but good food. Ruby is quite a character, very friendly, and you'll get the full family history. No good if in a rush!

South of Dangriga *p260*

ǂǂ **Ronnie's Kitchen**, turquoise house on stilts north of the police station in Hopkins (follow the road left from the bus stop). Excellent food, friendly service, open 0630-2100, lunch includes burritos and chicken, Ronnie also runs a library and gives good local advice.

Placencia *p262,*

ǂǂǂ **Merlene's**, in the Bakeder area south of Placencia Village dock. One of the best, opens early for good breakfast, also has an apartment for rent.

ǂǂǂ **Trattoria**, directly on the beach just north of **Tipsy Tuna Sports Bar**. The only Italian restaurant in the village.

ǂǂ **BJ's Restaurant**. Good fried chicken and traditional Creole food. Also stir-fries and pizza – inexpensive and popular.

ǂǂ **Cozy Corner**, very nice beachside bar and restaurant. Good, mid-priced barbecue and grilled seafood.

ǂǂ **De Tatch Café**, just before the north end of the sidewalk. Legend says it's the best coffee in town, certainly hugely popular with excellent seafood specials at night and snappy service.

ǂǂ **Jake's Purple Space Monkey Internet Café**, on main road just west of the Placencia docks. Very good US-style breakfasts and burgers for lunch, excellent coffee, dinner menu features local seafood. Internet on site.

ǂǂ **J-Byrd's Bar**, owned by Janice Leslie, owner and operator of **Tradewinds Hotel**. Bar looks out to sea, great place to chill.

𝖄 **John the Bakerman**, freshly baked bread and cinnamon buns each afternoon (takeaway only).
𝖄 **Miss Lilly's**, lunch only, authentic Creole food cooked by Miss Lilly, a village elder and local comedienne.
𝖄 **Omar's Diner**, on the sidewalk, fish, meat, burgers, burritos, good cheap breakfasts. Also has some rooms.

Punta Gorda *p263*
Several cafés around the market area with good views over the bay.
𝖄𝖄 **Bobby's** Main St. Excellent fish dishes, Bobby is a fishing guide and arranges trips.
𝖄𝖄 **Earth Runnings Café and Bukut Bar**, Main Middle St, also with tourist info. Good for breakfast and dinner. Reggae music and internet café.
𝖄𝖄 **Emery Restaurant**, Main St, local dishes and seafood, popular with locals, reasonable prices, friendly.
𝖄𝖄 **Gomier's**, behind the Sea Front Inn. For vegan meals and soya products.

Festivals and events

Dangriga *p260*
18-19 Nov, Garífuna, or Settlement Day, celebrates the landing of the Black Caribs in Belize in 1823 with dancing all night and next day; very popular. Private homes rent rooms but booking is advisable for accommodation. At this time, boats from Puerto Barrios to Punta Gorda (see below) tend to be full, but launches take passengers for US$10 per person.

Activities and tours

The Coastal Highway *p258*
There's a wide variety of day and overnight excursions available from Gales Point, from US$30 per boat for 6-8 people. Contact Kevin Andrewin of Manatee Tour Guides Association on arrival. Community phone, T02-12031, minimum 48 hrs notice is advisable, ask for Alice or Josephine.

Dangriga and around *p260*

Diving

Dangriga Dive Centre, T522-3262, runs from next door to Pal's Guesthouse. Derek Jones arranges fabulous trips to the cayes.
Off The Wall Dive Center, Long Caye, PO Box 195, Dangriga, Belize, T614-6348, www.offthewallbelize.com. Dive courses for guests from Slick Rock (see Sleeping, above) and private guests. Friendly owners. Packages include transport, accommodation, meals and diving.
Second Nature Divers, Hopkins, T523-7038, divers@btl.net, or enquire at Hamanasi. English owned, good guides and equipment, recommended spot to visit is Sharks' Cave.

Tour operators

Rosado's Tours, T522-2119, 35 Lemon St, Government Services, can provide advice and information.
Treasured Travels, 64 Commerce St, T522-2578, very helpful, run by Diane.

Placencia *p262*
Day trips to the Barrier Reef include snorkelling and a beach BBQ, from US$45 per person, plus 8% sales tax. To Ranguana Caye, US$35 including lunch, great for snorkelling; divers must bring their own equipment. Monkey River tours, US$40 per person, plus 8% sales tax.

Diving

Full PADI scuba diving courses are available at most local dive shops and from high-end resorts. Of the in-town operators Seahorse, Advance and Splash/Natural Mystic enjoy solid reputations. However, environmental standards and genuine concern for the reef is somewhat lacking – something that could be improved with a little 'customer encouragement'. Prices are from about US$75, plus 8% sales tax, for 2-tank dives to Laughing Bird Caye, US$105 to outer reef (gear extra).
Advance Dive Centre, T523-74037, advancdive@btl.net, owned by Vance

Cabral, good solid operation.
Splash/Natural Mystic Dive Shop, T/F 523-3151, mysticdiversbz@yahoo.com. Partnership between 2 companies who share some facilities. Owners helpful – specialize in dive training and courses.
Seahorse Dive Shop, T523-3166, www.belizescuba.com, ask for Brian Young. Good selection of gear.
Naudi Dive Shop, T523-3595, www.nauticalinbelize.com, **Robert's Grove Dive Shop**, T523-3565, www.robertsgrove.com, and **Ocean Motion Guide Services**, are all reputable snorkelling tour operators.

Fishing

Fishing, especially saltwater fly-fishing, is excellent in the Placencia area, with recognized world-class permit fishing. Flats are hard-bottomed and good for wade fishing. Rates for a full day of light tackle and fly fishing, including lunch, average US$275 per day, plus 8% sales tax, maximum 2 anglers per boat for fly fishing. Reputable licensed guides and tour operators include **Daniel Wyatt** and **Egbert Cabral**, T523-3132; **Kurt**, T523-3277, and **Earl Godfrey**, T523-3433, lgodfrey@btl.net. **Destinations Belize** (formerly **Kevin Modera Guide Services**), T523-4018, www.destinationsbelize.com, offers combination cayes camping and fishing/snorkelling trips, plus whale shark interaction tours.

Kayaking

Toadal Adventures, T523-3207, www.toadaladventure.com, is a reputable tour operator for multi-day kayaking trips to cayes and Monkey River.

Cockscomb Basin Wildlife Sanctuary and around *p261*

The most knowledgeable guides to the reserve live in Maya Centre; contact Julio Saqui, of **Julio's Cultural Tours**, T05-12020, who runs the village shop and looks after luggage, or Greg Sho, at **Greg's Bar**, on the main road in the middle of the village. Greg also arranges kayak trips. Full-day Mopan Maya cultural tours of Maya Centre Village are also available; contact Liberato or Araceli Saqui.

Punta Gorda *p263*

Tour operators

Green Iguana Eco Adventures, T722-2475, a wide range of tours and services.
Tide Tours, Main St, T722-2124, eco-tours.

Transport

Coastal Highway *p258*

Gales Point can be reached by inland waterways from Belize City, but buses have largely superseded boat services. **Southern Transport** run at least 2 daily between Belize City and Dangriga along the coastal road.

Dangriga and around *p260*

Air

Maya Island Air and **Tropic Air** to/from **Belize City**, several daily, US$33-51 single, also to **Punta Gorda**, US$61, and **Placencia**, US$37 . Tickets from the airstrip, T522-2129, or the **Pelican Beach Hotel**.

Boat

To **Tobacco Caye**, 35 mins by speedboat, US$15; ask at **Riverside Café** on the south bank of the river. To **North East Caye**, catch a bus to **Glover's Guest House** in Sittee River (see Sleeping) to connect with the sailing boat, which leaves Sittee River 0800 Sun, 5 hrs, US$20 per person 1-way (price included in accommodation package), returns Sat. At other times, charter a boat (skiff or sailing boat, US$200 1-way, up to 8 people; diesel sloop US$350, up to 30 people). You can also hire a boat for around US$25 per person in a party to **Belize City**, enquire locally. See also Going further, p273.

Bus

The **Southern Transport**, T522-2160, bus terminal at the south end of town. To

Belize City, via Hummingbird Highway, several daily from 0530, US$5, 3½-4 hrs; the bus passes entrance to the Blue Hole National Park; also via Coastal Highway, 2 hrs. To **Belmopan**, 2½ hrs, US$4.50. To **Sittee River**, 4 daily; alternatively, take any bus south to the Sittee junction and hitch a ride. To **Placencia**, daily at 1215, 1530 and 1715, 3 hrs, US$5, via Hopkins and Sittee River, US$4.

Cockscomb Basin Wildlife Sanctuary and around *p261*

All buses going south from Dangriga go through **Maya Centre**, 40 mins, US$4; there are return buses north from 0700 onwards. A taxi from Dangriga will cost about US$50. Locals will drive you from Maya Centre to the reserve, otherwise it is a 6-mile, uphill walk – allow 2 hrs and leave all unwanted gear in Dangriga or at Julio's store in Maya Centre for a daily fee.

Placencia and around *p262*

Air

Placencia has its own airstrip. Maya Island Air and Tropic Air (T523-3410) have several daily flights to **Belize City** (international, US$75, and municipal, US$64), also **Dangriga**, US$37, and **Punta Gorda**, US$37.

Boat

The Hokey Pokey Water Taxi crosses the lagoon to **Mango Creek** at 1000 and 1600, US$5. To **Ranguana Caye**, free if it fits in with one of the regular trips, otherwise US$150 each way for up to 4 people. See also Going further, p273.

Bus

Southern Transport buses to **Dangriga** at 0530, 0600, 0700 (Sun only) and 1330, 3 hrs, US$5. Also 3 daily buses to **Sittee River**. For **Punta Gorda**, take the Hokey Pokey Water Taxi (see below) and then catch the 1130 or 1750 bus from Independence Village. Times, fares and operators change constantly. There are also services to **Belize City**, US$8.50, and **Belmopan**, US$10.50, from Mango Creek, with Southern Transport, or the less regular James Bus.

Punta Gorda *p263*

Air

The airstrip is 5 mins' walk east of town. Daily flights with Maya Island Air and Tropic Air to **Dangriga**, **Placencia** and **Belize City** (both airports). Tickets from Alistair King's (at Texaco station), Bob Pennell's hardware store on Main St, the Sea Front Inn on Front St or the offices alongside the airstrip. Advance reservations recommended.

Boat

To **Puerto Barrios** in Guatemala, Requena Water Taxi, 12 Front St, T722-2070, fast skiffs daily 0900 from the main dock in front of immigration, US$15, 1 hr, returning at 1400; Pichilingo, daily at 1600, returning at 1000, US$17.50. Pichilingo also provides a service to **Lívingston**, Tue and Fri, 1000, US$10, returning from Lívingston at 0700. Both companies provide additional charter services to Puerto Barrios and Lívingston on request, see p264. Requena also offers charters and trips to the **cayes**.

Bus

Southern Transport terminal is at south end of José María Núñez St; Traveller's Inn serves as ticket office. To **Belize City**, Mon-Sat 0300, 0400, 0500 and 1000, Sun 0400, 0500 and 1000, stopping at **Mango Creek**, **Dangriga** and **Belmopan**, beautiful but rough ride, 8 hrs (longer in heavy rain), US$11. Also James bus to **Belize City**, daily 0600, 0800, 1100 and 1200, from government buildings near ferry dock.

The 'market' buses to the **villages** leave Punta Gorda, from the west side of the central park, every Mon, Wed, Fri and Sat at 1130 or 1200 depending on the village, US$1.50; return the same day, departing at 0400, 0500 or 0600. For the latest information on schedules, contact Dem Dat's Doin', see p264. Hitching is not recommended. To **San Antonio**, 1-1½

Going further

Honduras

Check procedures for exit formalities in advance. Nationals of the UK, USA, Canada, Australia and New Zealand should not require a tourist card or visa for Honduras. A fast skiff, T522- 3227 (ask for Carlos), leaves Dangriga 0900 Sat (be there at 0800) for Puerto Cortés, Honduras, US$50. It's an irregular service.

The *Gulf Cruza*, T202-4506 or T603-7787, provides a regular weekly service from Placencia to Puerto Cortés, US$50. The journey can be quite choppy so take motion sickness pills if required. The boat leaves the dock near the petrol station in Placencia at 0930 every Fri, arriving in Mango Creek at 0940 to complete immigration formalities. Departure from Mango Creek is around 1100 (ask Antonio Zabaneh at his store, T503-2428, to check times), arriving Puerto Cortés at 1330. The return service leaves Puerto Cortés on Mon at 1100.

hrs, continuing to **Santa Cruz**, **Santa Elena** and **Pueblo Viejo** (1 hr from San Antonio); alternatively, get a ride in a truck from the market.

Directory

Dangriga p260
Banks Bank of Nova Scotia, Barclays Bank International, MasterCard and Visa, and ATM. Belize Bank (Visa cash advances). **Hospital** New Southern Regional Hospital, T522-2078, dannhis @btl.net **Immigration office** South end of Commerce St. **Internet** Val's laundry and Pelican Beach Hotel. **Laundry** Val's, Mahogany Rd near Bonefish, also has internet access. **Post office** Mahogany Rd. **Telephone** BTL office is on the main street.

Placencia p262
Banks Atlantic Bank near the gas station at the south point, Mon-Fri 0800-1400, US$1 per TC, no cash. Belize Bank in Mango Creek/Independence, is open Fri only 0900-1200. **Hospital** Basic medical care available at the clinic behind St John's Memorial School on the sidewalk. **Internet** On the main road is Jake's Purple Space Monkey Internet Café; nearer the centre is Placencia Office Supplies. Some hotels also offer access. **Post office** by the docks, Mon-Fri 0800-1200, 1330-1600. **Telephone** BTL office in the centre for international calls and fax messages. Payphones here, at the gas station and the ballfield.

Punta Gorda p263
Banks Belize Bank, at end of the park, changes excess Bz$ for US$ on production of passport and ticket out of the country. Also changes Tcs but not quetzales. US$5 charge for advancing cash against Visa and MasterCard. Open Mon-Thu 0800-1300, Fri till 1630. Western Union, run by Mahung's, corner North and Main St, Mon-Sat 0800-1200, 1330-1700. **Internet** Punta Graphics, acapps@btl.net, round the back of the Texaco station. Also next door to Sea Front Inn. Carisha's, by clock tower, US$6 per hr. **Laundry** Sony's Laundry Service near airstrip. **Telephone** The BTL office is on Main St and King St.

Antigua & around

BAJA VERAPAZ
Chichicastenango
Granados
Mixco Viejo
Los Encuentros
El Cuchillo
Las Trampas
Pan-American Hwy
Chuarrancho
CHIMALTENANGO
Sololá
Tecpán
San Antonio Las Flores
Panajachel
Iximiché
Las Canoas
Comalapa
San Juan Sacatepéquez
Godínez
San Antonio Palopó
Patzún
Lake Atitlán (1,558m)
San Pedro Sacatepéquez
Chimaltenango
Zaragoza
San Lucas Tolimán
Patzicía
CA1
Santiago Sacatepéquez
GUATEMALA CITY
San Andrés Itzapa
SACATEPEQUEZ
Volcán Atitlán
Jocotenango
San Antonio Aguas Calientes
Antigua
Santa Catarina Pinula
Volcán Acatenango
San Miguel de las Dueñas
Ciudad Vieja
Amatitlán
Volcán Fuego
Alotenango
Santa María de Jesús
Volcán de Agua
Lago de Amatitlán
Patalul
San Vicente Pacaya
Palín
El Baúl
Volcán Pacaya
GUATEMALA
Santa Lucía Cotzumalguapa
Bilbao
Siquinalá
Escuintla
CA2
San Sebastian
La Democracia
Pueblo Nuevo Viñas
Masagua
ESCUINTLA
Pacific Hwy
CA2
Taxisco
María Linda
Acomé
Obrero
Otacingo
Finca Maria Laura
Puerto San José
La Avellana
Chulamar
Puerto Quetzal
Iztapa
Monterrico
Pacific Ocean
Don't miss...
1 Antigua ▸▸ p278.
2 Semana Santa in Antigua ▸▸ p280.
3 Volcán Pacaya ▸▸ p286.
4 Monterrico ▸▸ p289.
5 All Saints Day in Santiago Sacatepéquez ▸▸ p297.
N
10 km
10 miles

Introduction

Antigua is the colonial crème de la crème of the New World. Trapped in a time warp following a cataclysmic 18th-century earthquake, it lies gracefully ruined with toppled church arches, cloistered courtyards and pretty patios. Its one-storey homes, dusted in terracotta shades, line cobbled streets garlanded with bougainvillea. Guatemala City is an ugly place by comparison, with few treasures, but appearances can be deceptive – some of its bars, unusual buildings and the artefacts it houses in its major museums – are worth getting to know.

The red-hot crater lip of the active Volcán Pacaya, south of the capital, invites a hike to its mouth, stained with burnt-orange and brilliant turquoise. Scree-surf down its cone after peering into the fiery, stinking, bowels of the earth. South from Antigua, the highway heads straight between the perfect cones of Agua and Fuego, a passage through Guatemala's giant cleavage, to laid-back Monterrico. Fringed with palms on the Pacific Coast, it is an escape from city life where tiny turtles waddle to their freedom over its baking sands every winter.

Ratings

Culture
★★★★

Landscape
★★★★

Chillin'
★★★★

Activities
★★★

Wildlife
★

Costs
$$$-$$

Antigua and around

Antigua is one of Guatemala's most popular destinations, overflowing as it is with colonial architecture and fine churches. In the late-afternoon light, buildings such as Las Capuchinas are very attractive and, in the evening, the cathedral is beautifully illuminated as if by candlelight. Shops are overflowing with arts and crafts, restaurants serve varied international cuisine and a steady stream of students and visitors buoys up the atmosphere. What's more, the city's Easter processions are some of the most fascinating and flamboyant in Christendom. If the city itself were not treasure enough, its setting is truly memorable. Agua volcano (3,766 m) is due south, while to the west are the imposing peaks of Volcán Acatenango (3,976 m) and Volcán Fuego (3,763 m), which still emits the occasional column of ash.

Getting there Flights to Guatemala City airport. Shuttles between Guatemala City and Antigua.
Getting around Explore Antigua on foot. Regular regional buses to other destinations.
Time required At least 3 days.
Weather Hot in the day, cold after sunset. Humid on the coast, rainfall heaviest Jun and Sep.
Sleeping Sumptuous colonial hotels and serviceable hostels in Antigua. Don't bother staying in Guatemala City.
Eating Full international spread in Antigua, more limited elsewhere.
Activities and tours Biking, volcano climbing, turtle watching
★ **Don't miss...** Climbing Volcán Pacaya ▸▸ *p285.*

Ins and outs

Getting there La Aurora airport (page 283) lies south of Guatemala City, 45 km from Antigua. A taxi costs around US$25 and takes usually 45 minutes outside rush hour. A pre-arranged shuttle by an Antigua tour operator costs around US$10 in the daytime and about the same price as a taxi at night. Buses between Guatemala City and Antigua are not recommended. *Flight information ▸▸ p17 and p21.*

Getting around You can walk from one end of the town to another in less than 15 minutes. Avenidas are numbered upwards running from east (Oriente, Ote) to west (Poniente, Pte), and Calles upwards from Norte to Sur, in relation to where 5 Calle and 4 Avenida cross on the corner of the Parque Central; house numbers do not give any clue as to how far from the Parque Central a particular place is. Taxis park close to the cathedral and outside the bus terminal on Alameda Santa Lucía. Horse-drawn carriages are available on fiesta weekends around the plaza, US$1.30. ▸▸ *p300.*

Tourist information INGUAT ⓘ *corner of 5 C Ote and 4 Av Sur, T7832-0763, Mon-Fri 0800-1300, 1400-1700, Sat and Sun 0800- 1600,* is very helpful, with lots of maps and information. English spoken. The free monthly magazine *The Revue* is also a useful source of information.

Safety Antigua is generally safe but it's best to keep to the well-lit area near the centre at night and to take advice on areas to avoid from the tourist office and tourist police (green uniforms), based at 4 Avenida Norte at the side of the Municipal Palace. Report incidents to police and the tourist office.

La Merced

History

Until it was heavily damaged by an earthquake in 1773, Antigua was Guatemala's capital city. Founded in 1543, after the destruction of an even earlier capital, Ciudad Vieja (page 282), it grew to be the finest city in Central America, with numerous great churches, a University (1676), a printing press (founded 1660), and a population of around 50,000, including many famous sculptors, painters, writers and craftsmen. Buildings in Antigua were frequently destroyed by earthquakes and then rebuilt, usually in a grander style.

Following the final cataclysm in 1773, the city lay abandoned for many years and most of the accumulated treasures were moved to Guatemala City. It was slowly repopulated in the 19th century but little was done to prevent further collapse of the main buildings until late in the 20th century, when the inestimable value of the remaining monuments was finally appreciated. A major earthquake in 1976 was a further setback but now you will see many sites that are busy with restoration, preservation or simple clearing.

Sights » *pp291-303*

In the centre of the city is the **Parque Central**, the old Plaza Real, where bullfights and markets were held in the early days. The present park was constructed in the 20th century though the fountain dates back to the 18th century. The **catedral** ⓘ *US$0.40*, to the east, dates from 1680 (the first cathedral was demolished in 1669). Much has been destroyed since then and only two of the many original chapels are now in use. The remainder can be visited. The **Palacio de los Capitanes Generales** is to the south. The original building, from 1558, was virtually destroyed in 1773 but was partly restored in the 20th century and now houses police and government offices. The **Cabildo**, or Municipal Palace, is to the north and an arcade of shops to the west. The **Museo de Santiago** ⓘ *Tue-Fri 0900-1600*, is in the municipal offices to the north of the Plaza, as is the **Museo del Libro Antiguo** ⓘ *Sat-Sun 0900-1200, 1400-1600, US$1.30*, which contains a replica of a 1660 printing press (the original is in Guatemala City), old documents and a collection of 16th-18th century books (1,500 volumes in library). The **Museo de Arte Colonial** ⓘ *hours as Museo de Santiago, US$3.25*, is half a block from Parque Central at Calle 5 Oriente, in the building where the San Carlos University was first housed. It now has mostly 17th-18th century religious art, well laid out in

Semana Santa

This week-long event is the biggest Easter celebration in Latin America, a spectacular display of religious ritual and floral design. Through billowing clouds of incense, processions of floats carried by purple-robed men make their way through the town. The cobbled street are covered in carpets of flowers and coloured sawdust, known as *alfombras*. The largest processions with some of the finest carpets are on Palm Sunday and Good Friday.

Floats (*andas*) are topped by colonial sculptures of the cross-carrying Christ, wearing velvet robes of deep blue or green, embroidered with gold and silver threads. The float is carried on the shoulders of 80 men (*cucuruchos*), who heave and sway their way through the streets for as long as 12 hours. The processions, arranged by a religious brotherhood (*cofradía*), are accompanied by banner and incense carriers, centurions, and a loud brass band.

- Don't miss the procession from **La Merced** on **Palm Sunday** at 12-1300; the procession from **San Francisco** on **Maundy Thursday**; the 0200 sentencing of Jesus and 0600 processions from **La Merced** on **Good Friday**; the crucifixion of Christ in front of the **cathedral** at noon on **Good Friday**; and the candlelit procession of the crucified Christ, passing the **central park** at 2300 on **Good Friday**.
- Accommodation is booked way ahead. If you haven't reserved a room, arrive a few days before Palm Sunday.
- Semana Santa is a fantastic photo opportunity; for a decent picture, remember the Christ figure always faces right.
- Walk the route before the procession to see all the carpets.
- Don't rush: each procession lasts up to 12 hours.

large airy rooms around a colonial patio. The **Casa Popenoe**, ⓘ *1 Av Sur, on the corner of 5a Calle, Mon-Sat 1400-1600, US$1.30*, is a restored colonial house (1632) containing many old objects from Spain and Guatemala.

Casa Santo Domingo is one of Antigua's most beautiful sights – a converted Dominican church and monastery. During the excavation of a burial vault under the chapel of Nuestra Señora del Socorro in September 1996, one of the greatest archaeological finds in Antigua's history was unearthed. The vault had been filled with rubble but care had been taken to place the stones a few feet away from the walls. The removal of the rubble revealed a mural in pristine colours of natural red and blue, dating from 1683 and depicting Christ, the Virgin Mary, Mary Magdalene and John the Apostle.

Within the monastery grounds is the **Colonial Art Museum**, with displays of Guatemalan baroque imagery and silverware. The **Archaeological Museum** ⓘ *3 C Ote 28, 0900-1600, US$2.20, free for hotel guests*, is situated in the original meeting room of the monastery and includes some Maya ceramics and pots. There is also a workshop where candles and glass are made by hand. Human remains are displayed in the crypt.

There is a fabulous panorama from the **Cerro de la Cruz**, which is 15 minutes' walk from the northern end of town along 1 Avenida Norte. The tourist police will escort you there, leaving 1000 and 1500 daily.

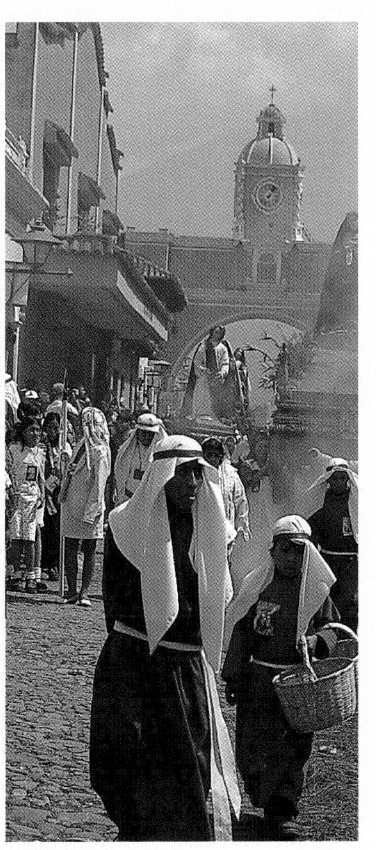

Churches, convents and monasteries

There are many fine colonial religious buildings in Antigua: 22 churches, 14 convents and 11 monasteries, most ruined by earthquakes and in various stages of restoration. Top of the list are the cloisters of the convent of **Las Capuchinas** ⓘ *2 Av Nte y 2 C Ote, 0900-1700, US$3.90*, which have immensely thick round pillars (1736) adorned with bougainvillea.

The church and monastery of **San Francisco** ⓘ *Av 1 Sur y 7 C Ote*, has been restored, with a small museum in the south transept. It is much revered by local communities for the tomb of Pedro de Betancourt (Hermano Pedro), who was canonized in 2002. Hermano Pedro worked as a gardener and planted an *esquisuchil* tree at **El Calvario** church, reached by an interesting set of the Stations of the Cross from San Francisco. He also founded the **Belén Hospital** in 1661, which was destroyed in 1773. Some years later, his name was given to the **San Pedro Hospital** one block south of the Parque Central.

The convent of **Santa Clara** ⓘ*US$3.90, 6 C Ote y 2 Av Sur*, was founded in about 1700 and became one of the biggest in Antigua, until the nuns were forced to move to Guatemala City. The adjoining garden is an oasis of peace.

El Carmen ⓘ*3 C Ote y 3 Av Nte*, has a beautiful façade with strikingly ornate columns, tastefully illuminated at night, but the rest of the complex is in ruins. Likewise **San Agustín** ⓘ*5 C Pte y 7 Av Nte*, once a fine building that only survived intact from 1761 to 1773; earthquake destruction caused the final portion of the vault to collapse in 1976, leaving an impressive ruin. **La Compañía de Jesús** ⓘ *3 C Pte y 6 Av Nte*, at one time covered the whole block. The church is closed for restoration but you can access the rest of the ruins from 6 Av Norte. (There is a craft market in front of the church.) The church and cloisters of **Escuela de Cristo** ⓘ *C de los Pasos y de la Cruz*, a small independent monastery (1720-30), have survived and were restored between 1940 and 1960. The church is refreshingly simple and has some interesting original artwork. **La Recolección** ⓘ *C de la Recolección,0900-1700, US$3.90*, despite being a late starter (1700), became one of the biggest and finest of Antigua's religious institutions. It is now the city's most awe-inspiring ruin. **San Jerónimo** ⓘ, *C de la Recolección, 0900-1700,US$3.90*, was at first a school (early 1600s) for La Merced, three blocks away, but later became the local customs house. There is an impressive fountain in the courtyard.

La Merced ⓘ *1 C Pte y 6 Av Nte, US$0.26*, with its white and yellow façade dominates the surrounding plaza. The church (1767) and cloisters were built with earthquakes in mind and survived better than most. The church remains in use and the cloisters are being further restored. Antigua's finest fountain is in the courtyard.

Travellers' tales

Pedal power

After a few days idling in Antigua, I decided that a 20-km bicycle ride up and through the hills to the house of Maximón at San Andrés Itzapa would be an ideal way to combine exercise and sightseeing. I signed up for a 20-km guided ride at (US$25 for intermediates) and set off on arguably the best off-road bike I've ever ridden.

We rode through the outskirts of Antigua, past some stunningly grand premises and, although I began to feel some interesting sensations creeping through the athlete's saddle, I was fairly convinced that I could handle the route ahead. The ride passed through some fantastic countryside, offering a chance to see the secret ruins of Ciudad Viejo and to experience the rural traffic on Guatemala's mountain tracks. The hilly terrain was planted with asparagus, tomatoes, broccoli and, sometimes, even blackberries; we saw horses bearing all manner of crops and local farmers, who greeted us cheerfully as we cycled past.

The route turned out to be more demanding than I'd expected, even in relatively mild temperatures (around mid 20s Celsius), with a number of vigorous uphill climbs. My guide, however, had little consideration for the dangers of heat exhaustion and flew along the steep tracks, resulting in a couple of spectacular and stylish falls. I chose, instead, to take it easy and go at my own pace. Even so, I got through roughly two litres of water during the four-hour round-trip and, when I woke up the next day, my muscles were complaining bitterly. *John Bell*

Santa Teresa, 4 Avenida Norte, was a modest convent, but the church walls and the lovely west front have survived. It is now the city's men's prison. Other ruins, including **Santa Isabel**, **Santa Cruz**, **La Candelaria**, **San José El Viejo** and **San Sebastián** are to be found round the edges of the city.

Ciudad Vieja

Ciudad Vieja – the former capital – is 5½ km southwest of Antigua at the foot of Volcán Agua (page 286). In 1527, Alvarado moved his capital, known then as Santiago de Los Caballeros, from Iximché to San Miguel Escobar, now a suburb of Ciudad Vieja. On 11 September 1541, after days of torrential rain, an immense mudslide came down the mountain and swallowed up the city. Alvarado's widow, Doña Beatriz de la Cueva, newly elected Governor after his death, was among those drowned. Today Ciudad Vieja is itself a suburb of Antigua, but with a handsome church, founded in 1534 that is one of the oldest in Central America.

North of Antigua

It's worth catching the free shuttle from Antigua's central park north to **Jocotenango** in order to visit the music museum, **Casa K'ojom** ⓘ *Mon-Fri 0830-1630, Sat 0830-1400, US$3.25*. The museum is housed in the Centro Cultural La Azotea and has displays of traditional Maya and colonial-era instruments. Beyond Jocotenango, the road heads north through mountains to Pastores, Parramos and **Chimaltenango**, a town busy with traffic on the Pan-American Highway. At **San Andrés Itzapa** , 6 km south of Chimaltenango, is a very interesting chapel to Maximón (page 312), open till 1800 daily. Shops by the chapel sell prayer pamphlets and pre-packaged offerings. *Pedal power ›› p282.*

Guatemala City ›› *pp291-303*

Smog-bound and crowded, Guatemala City is the commercial and administrative centre of the country: a sprawl of industrial activity lightly sprinkled with architectural treasures, engaging museums and out-of-place tributes to urban sculpture. Rarely rated by visitors, this is the beating heart of Guatemala and worth a couple of days of exploration if time permits – and if you can bear the noise and pollution in Zona 1. The city was founded by decree of Charles III of Spain in 1776 to serve as the capital after earthquake damage to Antigua in 1773. It was almost completely destroyed by earthquakes itself in 1917-18 and rebuilt in mock colonial style, only to be further damaged by an earthquake in 1976. Most of the affected buildings have been restored.

The old centre of the city is Zona 1, a busy commercial area, with several good hotels and restaurants, and many of the cheaper places to stay. However, the main commercial activity of the city, including the best hotels and restaurants, has been moving south for some years, first to Zona 4, now to Zonas 9, 10 and 14. Guatemala City is surrounded by active and dormant volcanoes easily visited on day trips.

Ins and outs

Getting there **La Aurora** airport lies 4km south of Guatemala City's central park. Official taxis (unmetered) wait across the road from the arrivals hall (Zona 1 US$9, Zonas 9 and 10 US$7, Zona 13, US$6). There are Visa ATMs on the second floor and just before you leave the arrivals hall. Banks in the arrival and departure areas offer reasonable rates: **Banco del Quetzal**, Mon-Fri 0600-2000, Sat and Sun 0600-1800, with MasterCard ATM, and **Banrural**, just past customs 0500-2400. There are no left luggage facilities in the airport. Airport services close at 2100.

The Zona 4 chicken bus terminal between 1-4 Av and 7-9 C is the dirtiest and grimmest public area in the whole of the city. It serves the Occidente (west), the Costa Sur (Pacific coastal plain) and El Salvador. The area of 19 C, 8-9 Av, Zona 1, next to the Plaza Barrios market, contains many bus offices and is the departure point for the Oriente (east), the Caribbean zone, Pacific coast area towards the Mexican border and the north, to Flores and Tikal. First-class buses often depart from company offices in Zona 1 (see map). ›› *p303.*

Getting around Any address not in Zona 1 is probably some way from the centre. Addresses themselves, being purely numerical, are usually easy to find. For example, 19 C, 4-83 is on 19 Calle between 4 Av and 5 Av at number 83. Walking is the best way to explore Zona 1; take a taxi to get to the other zones. Exercise caution if travelling alone and watch your bags everywhere, especially in the Zona 4 bus terminal.

Tourist information INGUAT ⓘ *7 Av, 1-17, Zona 4 (Centro Cívico), T1801-INGUAT-1 (24 hrs), T2421-2800, www.inguat.gob.gt Mon-Fri 0800-1600.* English is spoken. They are very friendly and provide a hotel list, a map of the city, and general information on buses, market days, museums, etc. There's also a helpful office in the arrivals hall of the international airport ⓘ *T2331-4256, Mon-Fri 0600-2100, Sat and Sun 0800-2000.*

Around Zona 1

At the city's heart lies the **Parque Central**, intersected by 6 Avenida, the main shopping street. The Parque Central is popular on Sunday with many *indígenas* selling textiles. To the east of the plaza is the classical **catedral**, completed in 1815 with notable blue cupolas and dome. Inside are paintings and statues from ruined Antigua as well as solid silver and sacramental reliquary in the east side chapel. Aside from the cathedral, the most notable public buildings constructed after the 1917 earthquake are the **Palacio Nacional**, built of light green stone, the Police Headquarters, the Chamber of Deputies and the post office.

A few blocks southeast of the cathedral, **Museo Nacional de Historia** ⓘ *9 C, 9-70, T2253-6149, Mon-Fri 0800-1700, free*, has historical documents and objects from Independence until the present day. Nearby is the **Museo de la Universidad de San Carlos de Guatemala (MUSAC)** ⓘ *9 Av, 9-79, T2232-0721, musac@intelnet.net.gt, Mon, Wed-Fri 0930-1730, Sat 0930-1300, 1400-1730, guided tours 1100 and 1500, US$1.05*, which charts the history of the university. The Salon Mayor is where Guatemala signed its independence from Mexico in 1823, and where the Central American Federation abolished slavery in the union in 1826. The country's president 1831-38, Doctor Mariano Gálvez, is buried here.

South again is **Casa MIMA** ⓘ *8 Av, 14-12, T2253-6657, casamima@hotmail.com, Mon-Sat 0900-1230, 1400-1700, US$2 adults, US$1.30 students, US$0.65 children, no photography*, the only authentic turn-of-the-19th-century family home open to the public. It was once owned by the family Ricardo Escobar Vega and Mercedes Fernandez Padilla y Abella and is furnished in European-influenced style with 15th- to mid 20th-century furniture and ornaments.

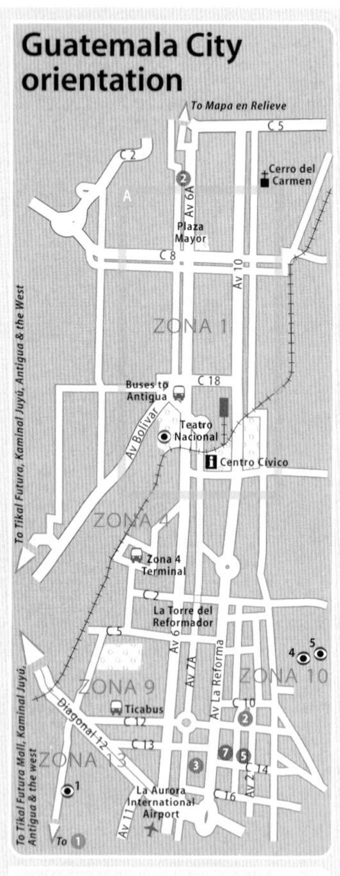

South of the centre

The modern **Centro Cívico**, which links Zona 1 with Zona 4, incorporates several commercial and government buildings, including the tourist board. The **Teatro Nacional** ⓘ *Mon-Fri 0800-1630 for tours, free, but tips appreciated*, dominates the hilltop to the west. It's an unusual building, covered in mosaics, with an excellent view of the city and mountains from the roof. An old Spanish fortress provides a backdrop to the adjoining open-air theatre. To the southwest at 26 Calle and Avenida Bolívar is the **Santuario Expiatorio Nacional**, a vast, colourful church in the shape of a fish. The entrance is a giant arch of multi-coloured stained glass; a mosaic mural stretches the length of one of the walls, and there are almighty doll-like figures of women inside and outside the building.

Cuatro Grados Norte, located on Vía 5 between Ruta 1 and Ruta 2, in Zona 4, is a

Parque Central

pedestrianized area that surrounds the IGA theatre. The **Centro Cultural de España** is located here with live music, films, exhibitions and an excellent bookshop. At weekends, there is a street market with craft and jewellery stalls, cultural events and children's entertainment. Sit back and enjoy watching the strange sight of wealthy Guatemalans with their poodles mixing with alternative street market types.

Museo Ixchel del Traje Indígena ⓘ *University campus, 6 C Final, Zona 10, T2331-3622, Mon-Fri 0900-1700, Sat 0900-1300, US$2.60, students US$1.05*, has a collection of Indian costumes as well as early 20th-century photos, paintings and interesting videos. A shop sells fixed-price textiles that aren't usually available on the tourist market. Nearby is **Museo Popol Vuh de Arqueología**, ⓘ *6 C Final, T2361-2301, Mon-Fri 0900-1700, Sat 0900-1300, US$2.60, students US$1.05, photography US$2*, which has an extensive collection of pre-Columbian and colonial artefacts, as well as a replica of the Dresden Codex, one of the only Maya parchment manuscripts in existence. The **Museo Nacional de Antropolgía y Etnología** ⓘ *Salón 5, Parque Aurora, Zona 13, T2472-0489, Tue-Fri 0900-1600, Sat-Sun 0900-1200, 1330-1600, US$3.90, no photos*, contains outstanding Maya pieces including stelae from Piedras Negras and typical Guatemalan costumes, as well as good models of Tikal, Quiriguá and Zaculeu. There are sculptures, murals, ceramics, textiles, a collection of masks and an excellent jade collection.

Volcanoes

The three volcanoes around Antigua give incomparable views of the countryside and are best climbed at full moon, or after a very early morning start. Altitude takes its toll so plenty of time should be allowed for ascending. The descent takes from a third to a half of the ascent time. Take a flashlight, refreshments, lots of water and a fleece, as the summits are cold. Climbing boots are also recommended, especially on Fuego and Pacaya. There have been a few incidents of robbery and assault on Agua in recent times, including climbers being robbed of all their clothes and having to descend stark naked. No such incidents have occurred on Pacaya, since security was tightened a few years ago, but consult the tourist office in Antigua before setting out. A list of authorized independent guides is also available here.

Volcán Pacaya

ⓘ *Official entrance at San Francisco de Sales. Entrance fee US$3.25; do not go with a guide who tries to avoid paying. Tours from Antigua usually depart 1300 and return at 2100, USS$5 (plus entrance fee). Security officers go with the trips and police escorts ensure everyone leaves the area after dark. Check the situation in advance for camping below the crater lip.*

Volcán Pacaya (2,552 m) has erupted about 20 times since 1565, but since the mid-1960s it has been erupting continuously. If you're in Antigua at the right time, you may see some spectacular lava flows but always check its alert status before signing up for a tour to the summit. It is about 1½ hours to the base of the crater, then a further 30 to 45 minutes scrambling up warm and lethally sharp black basaltic rock – depending on how good you are at tackling the 'one step forward, two steps back' syndrome. The sulphurous gases that are belched out are chokingly disgusting but the yellow, green and red colours blotched on the crater lip are striking and the roaring magma-filled mouth can be seen on the far side of the crater once the gases disperse. Try to avoid going on a mid-morning tour, which usually arrives at the summit just as it is covered in cloud. One of the highlights of the tour is the descent, surfing down the scree at high speed as the sun sets. You'll see Volcán Agua silhouetted in the distance, with a weak orange line streaked behind it on the horizon. Sunrise comes with awesome views over the desolate black lava field to the distant Pacific (airborne dust permitting) and the peaks of Fuego, Acatenango and Agua.

Volcán Agua

ⓘ *Ascent begins at Santa María de Jesús; ask for directions in the village or speak to Aurelio Cuy Chávez at the Posada El Oasis, who offers a guide service. The early bus to Santa María will allow you to climb the volcano and return to Antigua in one day. Otherwise, tours leave Antigua at 0500, US$20 per person with guide and security.*

Volcán Agua (3,760 m) is the easiest of the three volcanoes to climb but solo ascents are not recommended by INGUAT, as there are several old avalanches you have to cross before regaining the trail. If you're fit, it's a three- to five-hour ascent from **Santa María de Jesús**, a charming village with a beautiful view of the city. The descent takes at least two hours. To get the best views of Volcán Fuego before the clouds cover the summit, it is best to stay at the radio station at the top, where there is a small shelter (none too clean). Climbing at night (particularly Saturday-Sunday) is recommended, either by torchlight or by the light of the moon. Agua can also be climbed from **Alotenango**, 9 km from Antigua.

Volcán Pacaya

Background

Volatile Guatemala

There are more than 30 volcanoes dotted across Guatemala. Most are not active but those that are have caused havoc and misery. According to official statistics one of the largest eruptions in the last 10,000 years was that of **Santa María** in Quetzaltenango in 1902, which left 1,500 dead. Out of its side has grown **Santiaguito**, considered one of the most dangerous volcanoes in the world by vulcanologists. It has left one Highland village a ghost town (see page 336). Near Antigua is **Volcán Fuego** which has erupted more than 60 times since 1524. In 1974 an ash cloud from Fuego soared over four miles into the sky and hot rocks swept down its slopes at 35 mph. This eruption affected the local microclimate for months.

South of Guatemala City is **Volcán Pacaya**, which has erupted at least 23 times since 1565. It lay dormant from 1860 to 1961, but in March of that year, it erupted continuously for a month. In the following year, part of the cone collapsed forming a crater, inside which a new cone is now growing.

It's not only volcanoes that make Guatemala a highly volatile land; it's also susceptible to earthquakes and is in the line of destruction when hurricanes hit the Caribbean. In October 1949 monumental floods killed 40,000. The last major quake to strike was on 4 February 1976, destroying 23,000 lives, injuring 76,000 and causing US$1,100 million in property damage. In 1998, **Hurricane Mitch** left its legacy in the Izabal region.

Volcán Acatenango

ⓘ *Ascent begins at La Soledad (2,300 m), 15 km west of Ciudad Vieja; ask for a guide in La Soledad or take a tour from Antigua.*

Classified as a dormant volcano, Acatenango is the third-tallest in the country (3,975 m) with two peaks. Its first recorded eruption was in 1924, with two other eruptions reported in 1924-27 and 1972. The best trail (west of the one shown on the 1:50,000 topographic map) heads south at **La Soledad**, 300 m before Route 5 turns right to Acatenango. A small plateau, La Meseta on maps but known locally as El Conejón, provides a good campsite two-thirds of the way up (three or four hours). From here it is a further three or four hours' harder going to the summit. There is a shelter, holding up to 15 people, on the lower of the two peaks; although it's dirty and in poor condition, this is the best place to sleep. The views of Fuego from the higher peak are excellent and you can also watch the activity of Pacaya at night.

Volcán Fuego

Fuego (3,763 m) has had frequent dangerous eruptions in recent years, although generally not without warning. Its last major eruption was in 1974. Check in Antigua before attempting the ascent – for experienced hikers only. It can be climbed via Volcán de Acatenango, sleeping on the col between the two volcanoes where there is a primitive shelter, then climbing for a further four hours over tiring loose ash to the crater. More difficult is the long climb from Alotenango. This is a very hard seven-hour ascent with an elevation gain of 2,400 m. Take a guide and do not underestimate the amount of water you will need. It is possible to camp about three-quarters of the way up.

South of Antigua ›› pp291-303

The southern coastal plain of Guatemala supports plantations of coffee, sugar and tropical fruit trees, which thrive in its hot and humid climate. Amid the fincas are some of curious archaeological finds that display a mixture of Mesoamerican influences. On the coast are black-sand beaches, nature reserves and laid-back resorts at Sipacate and Monterrico, where nesting turtles burrow in the sand. Casting a shadow over the coast, the Central Highland volcanoes of Lake Atitlán, and the Antigua trio of Fuego, Acatenango and Agua, look spectacular, looming on the horizon above the lowlands.

Santa Lucía Cotzumalguapa

West of Siquinalá, amid the sugar-cane fields and fincas of Santa Lucía Cotzumalguapa, lie an extraordinary range of carved stones and images with influences from pre-Maya civilizations, including the Izapa civilization from the Pacific coast area of Mexico near the Guatemalan border. All sights can be visited on foot from Santa Lucía. Alternatively, take a taxi from the town (next to the plaza) and negotiate a trip to all four areas, around US$16-19.

Confusion rages about who carved the monuments and stelae in a blend of pre-Columbian styles. Some say, that the prominent influence is Toltec, a civilization from Mexico, who are believed to have been the ancestors of the Maya K'iche', Kqchikel, Tz'utujil and Pipiles. The principal tribe was the Nahualt-speaking Tolteca-Pipil, who had, in turn, been influenced by the culture of Teotihuacán near Mexico City (page 79). Others argue that there is no concrete evidence to suggest that the Pipiles migrated to this area as early as AD 400 or that they were influenced by Teotihuacán. All in all, the cultural make-up of this corner of Guatemala may never be known.

Four large boulders – known locally as 'Las Piedras' – are located in cane fields at **Bilbao**, just outside town (don't wander around here alone as there have been numerous assaults). It is thought that the city was inhabited between 1200 BC and AD 800. The remnants were first re-discovered in 1860, buried deep in the sugar cane, and show pre-Maya influences. A copy of Bilbao Monument 21 is now housed in the **Museo de Cultura Cotzumalguapa** ⓘ *Finca Las Ilusiones, 1 km east of town, Mon-Fri 0800-1600, Sat 0800-1200, US$1.30, ask the person in charge for the key*. It also displays numerous artefacts collected from the *finca*. To get to the museum, walk east along the Pacific Highway and take a left turn.

Six kilometres north of Santa Lucía, along a tarmacked road, is **El Baúl**, a Late Classic ceremonial centre, dating from between AD 600 and AD 900 (there is no shade, so take lots of water). The left fork on the main road heading out of town leads to the **Finca El Baúl** refinery,

Ciudad Tecún Umán-Ciudad Hidalgo

The Pacific Highway goes west from Escuintla to the Mexican border at Ciudad Tecún Umán, some 200 km away, passing Siquinalá, where there is a brand new bypass that emerges the other side of Santa Lucía Cotzumalguapa (buses run through the centre of these places), and on to Mazatenango and Retalhuleu. The border is marked by a 1 km bridge over the Río Suchiate to the Mexican town of Ciudad Hidalgo. From here, buses head north to Tapachula, 30 mins.

Leaving Guatemala Guatemalan immigration is at Ciudad Tecún Umán, normally open 24 hrs. For a fee, boys will help you with your luggage to Mexican immigration at the foot of the bridge. This is located a few blocks from the town plaza in Ciudad Hidalgo. Cycle taxis cross the bridge for about US$1, pedestrians pay US$0.15.

Exchange There are numerous banks and plenty of money changers in Tucún Umán. Traveller's cheques cannot be changed in Ciudad Hidalgo.

where there is a collection of sculptures and stelae gathered from finca grounds. The centrepiece of the stone collection is a well-preserved jaguar sitting up on its haunches.

La Democracia

At Siquinalá a road heads south to La Democracia (10 km), where large sculptures found on the nearby Monte Alto and Costa Brava *fincas,* are displayed in the main plaza. These **stones**, carved from basaltic boulders, are believed to date from 400 BC or earlier and show clear Olmec influence. Many of them are vast Buddha-like figures, with fat eyelids and flattened noses and foreheads. There is an associated **museum** ⓘ *Daily 0800-1200, 1400-1600, US$1.30.*

Monterrico

Monterrico is a small, black-sand resort where the sunsets are a rich orange and the waves crash spectacularly on to the shore. However, the real stars here are the olive ridely turtle (*Parlama blanca* and *Parlama negra*), which lays its eggs between July and October, and the Baule turtle, which lays between October and February. The town has a **turtle hatchery** ⓘ *daily 0800-1200, 1400-1700, US$1*, and if you are in the area between September and January, you can sponsor a baby turtle's waddle to freedom every Saturday at 1700, when they are lined up on the beach for a race to the sea.

The landing stage is 10 minutes' walk from the ocean, clustered with restaurants and places to stay. Leaving the dock, the main beach hotels, mostly rustic and laid-back, are to your left on Calle del Proyecto or Calle del Muelle; walking straight on from the dock takes you to the main drag in town, where there are a few shops and *comedores*. Female travellers should take care after dark. You should also not underestimate the power ocean – people have died here. The sand is blisteringly hot and there is no shade on the beach. Take insect repellent for dusk.

Monterrico is surrounded by canals carpeted in aquatic plants and by mangrove swamps with bird and turtle reserves in their midst. These make up the **Monterrico Nature Reserve**. Just behind the turtle hatchery (see above) are 300 breeding crocodiles, 150 turtles and iguanas. Anteater, armadillo, racoon and weasel also live in the area. Take a boat trip at sunrise or sunset, to see migratory North and South American birds, including flamingo.

Olive ridely turtle, Monterrico

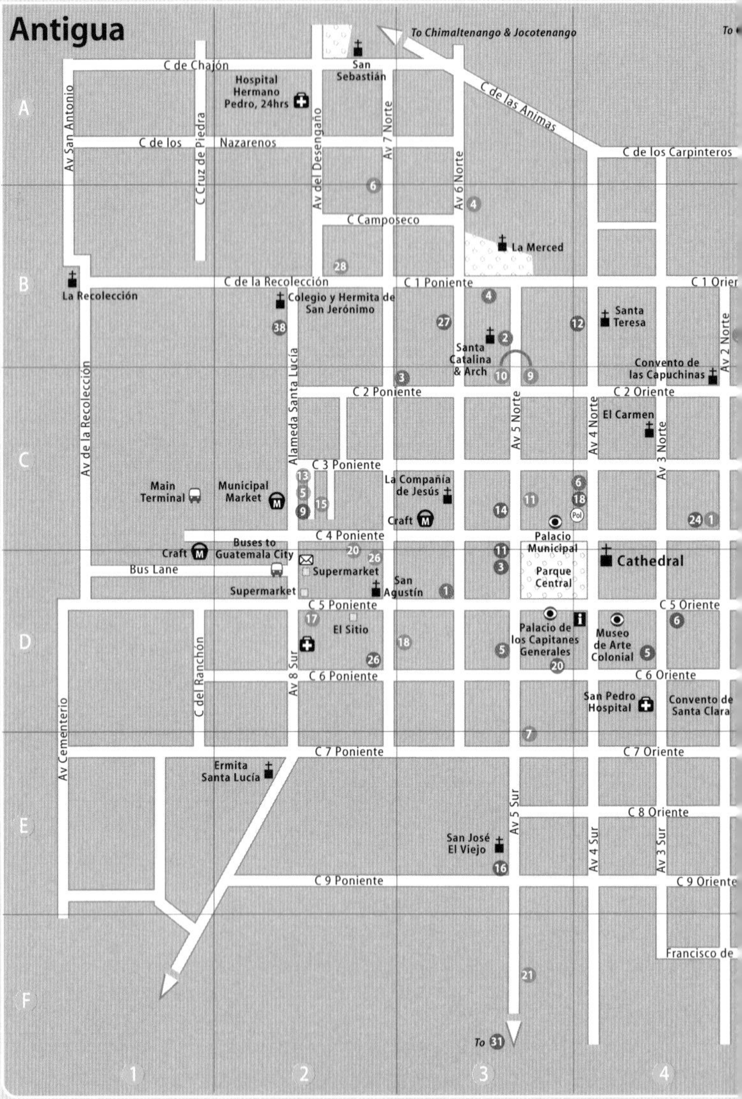

Antigua

To Chimaltenango & Jocotenango
C de Chajón
Hospital Hermano Pedro, 24hrs
San Sebastián
C de las Animas
Av San Antonio
C de los Nazarenos
C Cruz de Piedra
Av del Desengaño
Av 7 Norte
Av 6 Norte
C de los Carpinteros
C Camposeco
La Merced
C de la Recolección
C 1 Poniente
C 1 Oriente
La Recolección
Colegio y Hermita de San Jerónimo
Santa Teresa
Santa Catalina & Arch
Convento de las Capuchinas
Av 2 Norte
Av de la Recolección
Alameda Santa Lucía
C 2 Poniente
C 2 Oriente
Av 5 Norte
Av 4 Norte
El Carmen
Av 3 Norte
C 3 Poniente
Main Terminal
Municipal Market
La Compañía de Jesús
Craft
Pol
C 4 Poniente
Buses to Guatemala City
Palacio Municipal
Cathedral
Parque Central
Bus Lane
Supermarket
San Agustín
C 5 Poniente
C 5 Oriente
El Sitio
Palacio de los Capitanes Generales
Museo de Arte Colonial
C del Ranchón
Av 8 Sur
C 6 Poniente
C 6 Oriente
Av Cementerio
San Pedro Hospital
Convento de Santa Clara
C 7 Poniente
C 7 Oriente
Ermita Santa Lucía
Av 5 Sur
C 8 Oriente
Av 4 Sur
Av 3 Sur
San José El Viejo
C 9 Poniente
C 9 Oriente
Francisco de
To 31

100 metres
100 yards

Sleeping

Aurora **1** *C4*
Casa Capuchinas **3** *B4*
Casa de Santa Lucía 3 **4** *B3*
Casa de Santa Lucía 4 **5** *C2*
Casa Florencia **6** *B2*
Casa los Cántaros **7** *E3*
Casa Santo Domingo **8** *C6*
Cloister **9** *C3*
Convento Santa Catalina Mártir **10** *C3*
El Descanso **11** *C3*
Juma Ocag **13** *C2*
La Casa de Don Ismael & Casa de los Mixtas **15** *C2*
Landivar **17** *D2*
La Tatuana **18** *D3*
Mesón Panza Verde **21** *F3*
Mochilero's Place **20** *D2*
Posada Doña Luisa & Café Luna **26** *D2*
Yellow House **28** *B2*

Eating

Café Barroco **2** *C5*
Café Condesa **3** *D3*
Café Condesa Express **4** *C6*
Café Flor **5** *D4*
Café Flor (original) **6** *D4*
Café Sky **33** *D5*
Comedor Antigueño **9** *C2*
El Portal **11** *D3*
El Sereno **12** *B4*

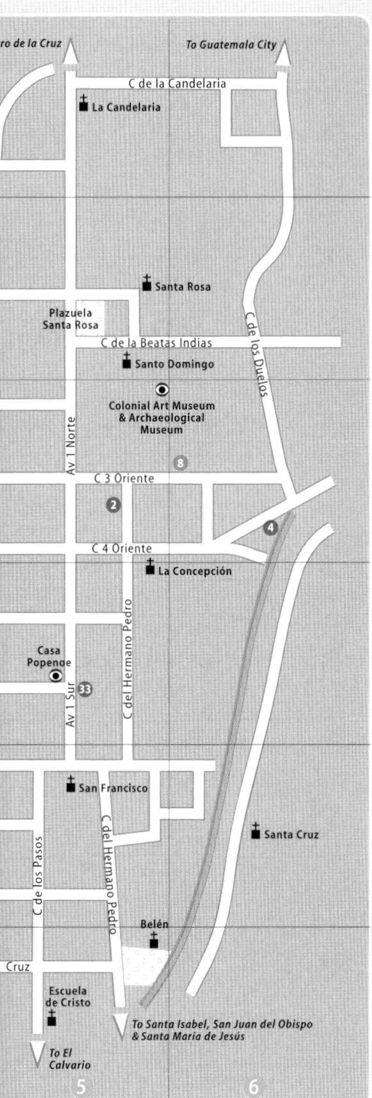

Fonda de la Calle Real **14** *C3*
La Antigua Vineria **16** *E3*
La Escudilla **18** *C4*
La Fuente **24** *C4*
Mediterraneo **20** *D3*
Peroleto **38** *B2*
Rainbow Café **26** *D2*
Rocio **27** *B3*
Vivero y Café de la Escalonia **31** *F3*

Bars & clubs

Café 2000 **1** *D3*
Casbah **2** *B3*
La Chiminea **3** *C3*
Los Arcos Reds **4** *B3*
Monoloco **5** *D3*
Rikki's **6** *C4*

Sleeping

Antigua *p278, map p290*

In the better hotels, advance reservations are advised for weekends and Dec-Apr. During Holy Week hotel prices are much higher. In Jul-Aug period, find your accommodation early in the day.

A **Casa Florencia**, 7 Av Nte 100, T7832-0261, www.casaflorencia.visitanuestrohotel.com. Sweet little hotel, with welcoming staff and views towards Volcán Agua. One room has a balcony with access to the 7 Av Nte. 11 rooms and a kitchen for guests. The balcony has *cola de quetzal* plants lining it. No credit cards.

B **Posada Landivar**, 5 C Pte 23, T7832-2962, www.merced-landivar.com Close to the bus station. Rooms with private bathroom and a/c. It's safe and in a good position. Discounts for longer stays. Parking US$3. Recommended.

C **El Descanso**, 5 Av Nte 9, T7832-0142. Rents 4 clean rooms on the 2nd floor, with private bath. Family atmosphere, extremely friendly and welcoming. Owners run a small bar service as well.

C **La Tatuana**, 7 Av Sur 3, T7832-1223. Colourful, with a beautiful leafy courtyard. Friendly, clean and safe; discounts are available off-season. Some rooms are a little dark; choose carefully. (Allegedly Tatuana was a witch condemned to death by the Spanish Inquisition and burnt in the central plaza in the capital.)

C-D **Bugambilia**, 3 C Ote 19, T/F832-5780. 24 rooms, some with bath. Rooms have table, bedside lamp and candles. Small restaurant/pizzeria attached to the hotel and a small patio and balconies to hang out on. Parking US$3.25 a night. Also an apartment with 4 beds and a small kitchen, US$55 per night.

D **Casa de Santa Lucía No 3**, 6 Av Nte 43A, T832-1386. 20 standard clean rooms, all with private bathrooms, towels, soap, hot water and free drinking water. Beautiful views of La Merced and Volcán de Fuego. Parking US$1.25.

Budget busters

Many of Antigua's grandiose colonial homes have been converted into luxurious hotels. Some are smart, some shabby chic but the attention to design detail – furniture, tiles, lighting, paintings and warm colours – is consistently high. Many also have beautiful gardens, with tropical plants and flowers.

LL-AL **Casa Santo Domingo**, 3 C Ote 28, T7832-0140, www.casasantodomingo.com.gt A beautifully designed hotel with 107 rooms in the ruins of a 17th-century convent (p280). Attentive service, beautiful gardens, a magical pool and a good restaurant with breakfast included.
L **Casa los Cántaros**, 5 Av Sur 5, T7832-5525, www.travellog.com/guatemala/casa/cantaros.html 5 rooms set around a gorgeous patio with flourishing orange and lemon trees, genuine colonial house. Very peaceful and intimate, breakfast included.
L-AL **Mesón Panza Verde**, 5 Av Sur 19, T7832-2925, www.panzaverde.com This is colonial indulgence at its height: 3 doubles, 9 suites, breakfast included. The bathrooms are pamper palaces in their own right, with cupolas and arresting design features. There's also a slither of a swimming pool.
AL **Casa Capuchinas**, 2 Av Nte 7, T7832-7941, www.casacapuchinas.com Fine, large rooms, with colonial furnishings, fireplaces, massive beds and beautiful tiled bathrooms. A continental breakfast is included. Highly recommended.

D **Casa de Sta Lucía No 4**, Alameda Sta Lucía Sur 4, T7832-3302. Modern, colonial- style house, with dark wood columns and large clay bowls on the patio. Parking US$2.50.
D **Mochilero's Place**, 4 C Pte 27, above **La Bodegona** supermarket, T7832-7743. Warm welcome and 10 rooms, some with bath. Shared bathrooms are ultra clean, with good showers. Free coffee, cable TV in reception. Some street noise. Stores luggage, US$0.60 for non-residents.
D **Posada Doña Luisa**, T7832-3414, 7 Av Nte 4. www.guatemalaenvivo.com Near the San Agustín church, good view of ruins at night. Clean, friendly, family atmosphere. 8 rooms with private bath and a small cafeteria. US$5 for an extra bed, parking.
D **Posada Juma Ocag**, Calzada Santa Lucía Nte 13, T7832-3109. Small, clean and nicely decorated, using local textiles as bedspreads. Enclosed roof terrace, shared bathrooms. Quiet and friendly.
D **La Casa de Don Ismael**, 3 C Pte 6, lotificación 2a callejón, T7832-1932, www.casadonismael.com Fabulous terrace with ringside views of Volcán Agua. 7 rooms, 3 shared bathrooms, guests get free coffee and water.
D-E **Yellow House**, 1 C Pte 24, T7832-6646. Welcoming colonial-style hostel with 8 clean rooms, 3 with bath, breakfast included. Laundry service, free internet use, kitchen, patio, parking, travel agent. Recommended.

Guatemala City *p283, map p294*

Don't bother staying here, unless it is absolutely necessary. Thefts have occurred in many hotels and single rooms are not always available. There are cheap *pensiones* near bus and railway stations and markets but they are not very salubrious.
B **Posada Belén**, 13 C "A", 10-30, Zona 1, T2232-9226, www.posadabelen.com, www.guatemalaweb.com Colonial-style

house, with friendly English-speaking owners. Laundry, email, luggage store and dining-room. Parking US$5. Tours.

C Chalet Suizo, 14 C, 6-82, Zona 1, T2251-3786. Good central position. Secure rooms with hotwater showers (cheaper with shared bathroom). Popular, so often crowded. Locked luggage store and safety box. Rooms on the main street are noisy; some have thin walls. Free parking.

C-D Dos Lunas Guest House, 21 C, 10-92, Aurora II, Zona 13, T2334-5264, lorena@intelnet.net.gt Comfy B&B close to the airport with free transfer. Internet, US$3 per hr, storage service, free coffee and water, tourist information. Shuttles, taxis and tours arranged. English spoken. Reservations highly advisable.

D CentroAmérica, 9 Av, 16-38, Zona 1, T2220-6371. 58 rooms with or without bath or TV. Safe deposit and internet (US$4/hr). Peaceful, with helpful staff. An excellent deal for single travellers. Cheap restaurant next door.

D Spring, 8 Av, 12-65, Zona 1, T2230-2858. Bright rooms with TV (costs extra). Quiet haven of tranquillity and flowers. Patio garden, good breakfasts, nearby parking. Free coffee, email US$1.30/hr, luggage store US$1 daily. Recommended.

Monterrico *p289*

All telephone numbers are mobiles or are in Guatemala City. Most hotels are fully booked by Sat midday so book ahead.

B Hotel Pez de Oro, T2368-3684, pezdeoro@intelnett.com 11 spacious bungalows set around a swimming pool. Private bathrooms, mosquito lamps, bedside lights and fan. Some have a/c.

C San Gregorio, behind El Kaiman, C del Proyecto, T/F2238-4690. 22 modern rooms with bath, fan and mosquito nets. Large, part-shaded pool (non-guests US$3.90) and restaurant.

D Eco Beach Place, T5611-6637, ecobeachplace@hotmail.com Cosy rooms with bath, fan and mosquito net. Pool and restaurant. Breakfast included. Discount for longer stays.

D El Delfín, T5702-6701, eldelfin99@yahoo.com Rooms and bungalows on the beach, with mosquito nets, fans and private bathroom. Courtyard and pool at the back. Restaurant. Organizes shuttles.

D Kaiman, T5507-9285. Big bar and restaurant on the beach, open 1000 till late Sat and Sun. Rooms are very clean, with bath, fan, and mosquito nets. 2 pools for adults and children, but they are not in top shape. Discounts for longer stays.

Eating

Antigua *p278, map p290*

ΨΨΨ El Sereno, 4 Av Nte 16, T/F7832-0501. A grand entrance with massive heliconia plants in the courtyard. Lovely terrace bar and a cave for romantic dining; popular at weekends. International/Italian cuisine.

ΨΨΨ Casa Santo Domingo, 3 C Ote 28, T7832-0140. Sun-Thu 0600-2200, Fri and Sat 0600-2400. International and national food (mixed reports) in a superb setting. Very good service and music.

ΨΨΨ Mesón Panza Verde, 5 Av Sur 19, T7832-2925. Tue-Sat 1200-1500, 1900-2200, Sun 1200-1600. One of the best restaurants in town, beautiful patios, a great staircase and a long swimming pool. Very popular with wealthy Guatemalans for Sun lunch.

ΨΨΨ-ΨΨ Caffé Mediterráneo, 6 C Pte 6A, T7832-7180, 1 block south of the plaza. Absolutely mouth-watering Italian cuisine with great candlelit ambience. Wed-Mon 1200-1500, 1830-2200.

ΨΨΨ-ΨΨ Fonda de la Calle Real, 5 Av Nte 5 and No 12, also at 3 C Pte 7. Fantastic setting. Speciality is *queso fundido* and local dishes including *pepián* and *Kak-ik*.

ΨΨ La Antigua Vineria, 5 Av Sur 34A T/F7832-7370. Next door to San José ruins. Excellent selection of wines and grappa, plus very good food. Feel free to write your comments on the walls. Mon-Thu 1800-0100, Fri-Sun 1300-0100.

ΨΨ-Ψ Café Flor, 4 Av Sur 1. Daily 1100-1500, 1800-2400. Delicious Thai/Guatemalan and Tandoori food.

Discounts available. Friendly staff. Now also at 3 Av Sur 4.

🍴-🍴 **Café Rocio**, 6 Av Nte 34. Mouthwatering Asian food. Don't miss *mora crisp*: hot blackberry sauce sandwiched between vanilla ice cream.

🍴-🍴 **La Escudilla**, 4 Av Nte 4, in the same building as the **Rikki's Bar**. Extremely good value tasty food. Plant-filled courtyard. Good place to meet and mingle.

🍴-🍴 **Rainbow Café**, 7 Av Sur, on the corner of 6 C Pte. Vegetarian food in a plant-filled

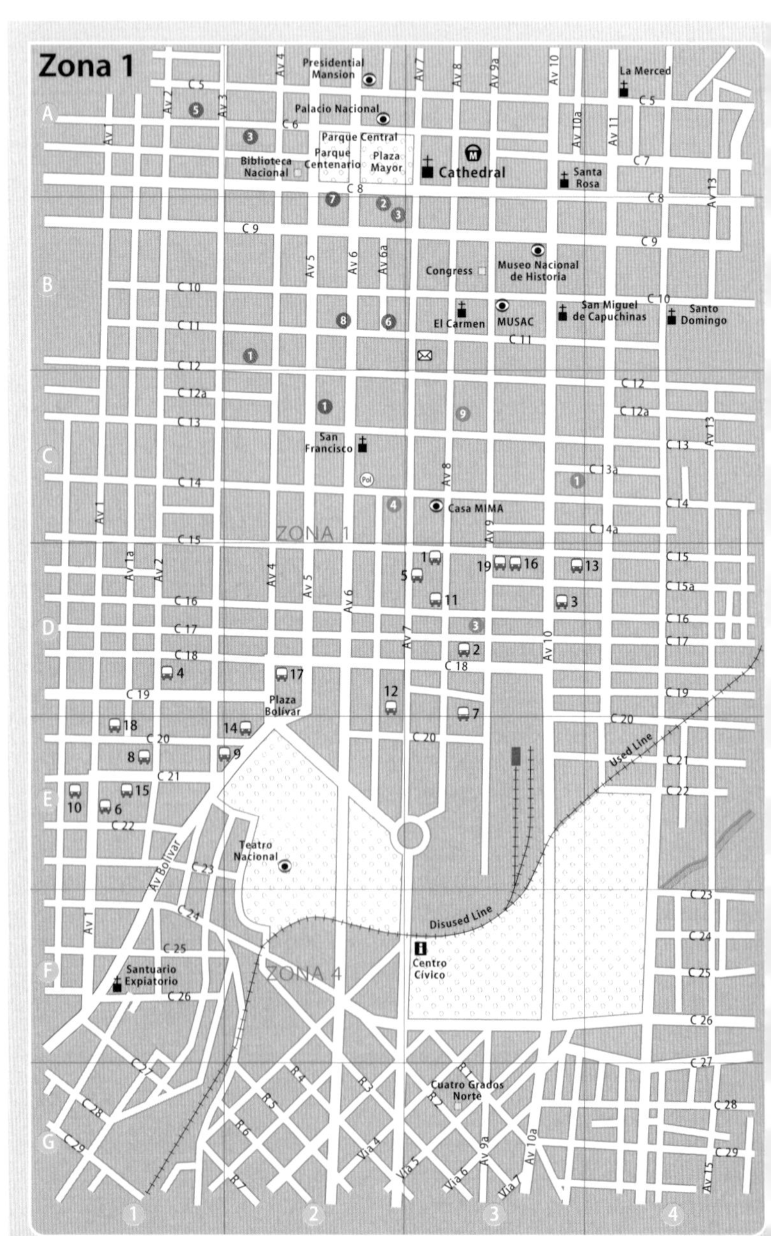

courtyard. Filling breakfasts, indulgent crepes, live music, book exchange, internet and **Bar Pacific** at night.

Comedor Antigüeño, Alameda Sta Lucía 4, near the PO. Locally run. *Menú del día* is a bargain. Very popular, so arrive before 1300.

Sleeping
Belén **1** *C3*
CentroAmérica **3** *D3*
Chalet Suizo **4** *C2*
Spring **9** *C3*

Eating
Altuna **1** *C2*
Café de Imeri **3** *A2*
Helados Marylena **5** *A1*
Los Canalones **6** *B2*
Rey Sol 1 **7** *B2*
Rey Sol 2 **8** *B2*

Bars & clubs
Bodeguita del Centro **1** *B2*
El Portal **2** *B2*
El Tiempo **3** *B2*
Las Cien Puertas **3** *B2*

Transport
Autobuses del Norte (ADN) **19** *D3*
Escobar-Monja Blanca to Cobán **1** *D3*
Fuente del Norte to Río Dulce & Santa Elena/Flores **2** *D3*
Línea Dorada to Río Dulce & Flores **3** *D3*
Líneas Américas to Quetzaltenango **4** *D1*
Los Halcones to Huehuetenango **5** *D3*
Marquensita to Quetzaltenango **6** *E1*
Rutas Orientales to Chiquimula & Esquipulas & Transportes Fortaleza to Tecún Umán **7** *D3*
Tacana to Quetzaltenango **8** *E1*
Terminal for buses to Chimaltenango, Panajachel & Santa Cruz del Quiché **9** *E1*
Transportes Alamo to Quetzaltenango **10** *E1*
Transportes Centro América to San Salvador **11** *D3*
Transportes Galgos to Mexico **12** *D2*
Transportes Litegua to Puerto Barrios & Río Dulce **13** *D3*
Transportes Poaquileña to Tecpán **14** *E2*
Transportes Rebuli to Panajachel **15** *E1*
Transportes Rosita to Santa Elena/Flores & Melchor de Mencos **16** *D3*
Transportes Unidos to Antigua **17** *D2*
Transportes Velásquez to Huehuetenango & La Mesilla (Mexican border) **18** *E1*

La Casa de los Mixtas, 3C Pte 3 Cjón 2A Cheap Guatemalan fodder with tables on the pavement, good breakfasts, excellent set lunch, US$1.50, friendly. Mon-Sat 0900-1900. For *elote, tortillas, tostadas* and *enchiladas*, go to the stalls on the corner of 4 C Pte and 7 Av Nte, and those at the corner of 5 C Pte and 4 Av Sur

Cafés and delis

Café Barroco, Cjón de la Concepción 2, T7832-0781. Peaceful garden, delicious cakes, coffees and huge selection of English tea for the deprived.

Café Condesa, 5 Av Nte 4, west side of the main plaza. Set in a pretty courtyard. Breakfast with free coffee re-fills. Popular Sun brunch US$7.

Café Sky, above **Guatemala Ventures**, 1 Av Sur 15. Daily 0900-2100 . Rooftop café-cum-bar with panoramic views over town, happy hour.

El Portal, 5 Av Nte 6. Hang out for the young and beautiful, coffee from their own Finca Philadelphia, homemade cakes, pies, pasties, cappuccinos, espressos and *licuados* to take away, daily 0700-2100.

La Fuente, 4 C Pte 14 next to **Doña Luisa**, sandwiches, light meals and cakes at tables around fountain, popular, excellent service. *Huípiles* and *cortes* for sale Sat. From 1900 this becomes **Dali Tapas Lounge**.

Vivero y Café de La Escalonia, 5 Av Sur Final 36c. Delightful place, well worth the walk – a café amidst a garden centre with luscious flowers everywhere, pergola, classical music. Daily 0900-1800.

Guatemala City *p283, map p294*

There are all kinds of food available in the capital, from simple national cuisine to French, Chinese and Italian. A reasonable set meal will cost no more than US$2.50.

Altuna, 5 Av, 12-31, Zona 1. Huge tasty portions of Spanish food. Delicious coffee. Beautiful Spanish interior, with great ambience. Also in Zona 10 at 10 C, 0-45.

Kacao, 2 Av, 13-44, Zona 10. Ample portions of delicious local and national dishes. Giant, thatched room, with *huípiles*

for tablecloths and beautiful candle decorations. Highly recommended.

🍴🍴 **Café de Imeri**, 6 C, 3-34, Zona 1. Closed Sun. Sandwiches, salads, soups, cakes and pastries in a patio garden. Set lunch. Popular with yuppie Guatemalans.

🍴🍴 **Arrin Cuan**, 5 Av, 3-27, Zona 1. A local institution. Traditional food from Cobán (*subanik*, *gallo en chicha*, and *kak ik*). Small courtyard, with lunchtime marimba music. Also on the 16 C, 4-32, Zona 10.

🍴🍴 **Los Canalones – Parrillada Argentina**, 6 Av A, 10-39, Zona 1. Barbecue on the street, 1200-1600: tasty chunks of meat and chorizo, with salad, soup, endless tortillas and *refresco*, US$5.60, wine and beer available.

🍴 **Helados Marylena**, 6 C, 2-49, Zona 1. Serving up the weirdest ice-cream flavours for 90 years: fish, chile, yucca, cauliflower, maize and beer. Cones start from US$1.30. Daily 1000-2200.

🍴 **Rey Sol**, 8 C, 5-36, Zona 1. Canteen-style vegetarian eaterie with wholesome food and ambience, popular with the locals. Closed Sun. Also at 11 C, 5-51.

🍴 **Sophos**, Av La Reforma, 13-89, El Portal 1, Zona 10, T2332-3242, sophos@gold.guate.net. Attractive café with the best bookshop in town. Literary events Thu eve.

Monterrico p289

Be careful eating *ceviche* here. Lots of local *comedores* along C Principal, which leads to the beach. The majority of the hotels have restaurants. **Restaurant Italiano**, at **Hotel Pez de Oro**, T2368-3684, is popular and consistently good.

Entertainment

Antigua p278, map p290

Bars and clubs

Café 2000, 6 Av Nte 8, between 4 and 5 C Pte. Indie music, free films and sports events on a giant screen. Cool decor. Daily 0800-0100. Happy hour Tue-Sat 1930-2300.

Casbah, 5 Av Nte 30. The closest thing to a nightclub in Antigua, with good dance and Latin music. Thu-Sat 1800-0100, US$4 includes a drink. Gay night Thu.

La Chiminea, 7 Av Nte 18. Seriously cheap, relaxed atmosphere, mixed young crowd, dance floor, salsa, rock. Mon-Sat 1700-2430.

Los Arcos Reds, 1 C Pte 3. Red decor, pool table, satellite TV, patio with hammocks, free films, long menu, good frozen licuados. Happy hour 1900-2400.

MonoLoco, 5 Av Sur 6. Rooftop veranda, heaving at weekends, happy hour 1700-2000, good *nachos*, burritos and burgers, Wed ladies' night. Daily 1100-2400.

Rikki's Bar, 4 Av Nte 4, inside **La Escudilla**. Packed with international and local students, visitors and the gay fraternity. Good mix of music, including jazz.

Cinemas

Numerous 'lounge' cinemas show films or videos either in English or with subtitles. Try **Café 2000**, 6 Av Sur; **Cinema Bistro**, 5 Av Sur 14, or **Maya Moon**, Maya Moon Hotel, 6 Av Nte 1A. The only real cinema is **Cine Sin Ventura**, 5 Av Sur 8, US$1.30.

Cultural centres

El Sitio, 5 C Pte 15, T7832-3037. Plays, workshops, movies, exhibitions, concerts, very good library with books in English, quiet coffee shop, Tue-Sun 1100-1900.

Guatemala City p283, map p294

Bars and clubs

Colloquia, inside La Cúpula at 7 Av 13-01, Zona 9. Tue-Sat 0900-2400. One of Guate's hotspots. Poetry meetings on Tue; techno, trance and house on Thur.

El Portal, Portal del Comercio, 8 C, 6-30, Zona 1. A favourite of Che Guevara's; imagine him sitting at the long wooden bar. *Comida típica* and marimba music, beer from the barrel. Mon-Sat 1000-2200.

El Tiempo, Pasaje Aycinea, 7 Av, 8-44, just south of Plaza Mayor, Zona 1. Bohemian atmosphere, political satire on the walls and alternative films. **Las Cien Puertas**, opposite, offers the same plus food.

La Bodeguita del Centro, 12 C, 3-55, Zona 1, T2239-2976. Hip and atmospheric, pics of

All Saints Day, Santiago Sacatepéquez

Che Guevara, Bob Marley and Archbishop Romero. Live music Thu-Sat 2100, talks, plays, films upstairs. Free popcorn with drinks, cheap menu. Daily 0900-0100.
Shakespeare's Pub, 13 C, 1-51, Zona 10, English-style basement bar with a good atmosphere, safe for women. Mon-Fri 1100-0100, Sat and Sun 1400-0100.

Monterrico *p289*
La Jaula, Funky giant cage-cum-bar, serving the most potent daiquiris in Guatemala. Also food and a book exchange, mosquito-free. Closed Mon.

Festivals and events

Antigua *p278, map p290*
Easter Semana Santa, p 280.
21-26 Jul for the feast of San Santiago
31 Oct-2 Nov All Saints and All Souls, in and around Antigua. The celebrations at **Santiago Sacatepéquez**, north of Antigua, are particularly recommended, with giant kites in the town cemetery to carry souls to heaven.
7 Dec, the citizens celebrate the Quema del Diablo (burning of the Devil) by lighting fires in front of their houses and burning an effigy of the Devil in the

Market days in Guatemala

Monday Antigua; Chimaltenango; Lanquín; Zunil.
Tuesday San Lucas Tolimán; Sololá Totonicapán.
Wednesday Momostenango; San Juan Cotzal.
Thursday Aguacatán; Antigua; Chichicastenango; Esquipulas; Lanquín; Nebaj; Panajachel; Rabinal; Santa Cruz Verapaz; Uspantán.
Friday San Andrés Itzapa; San Francisco El Alto; San Lucas Tolimán.
Saturday San Juan Cotzal; Todos Santos Cuchumatán.
Sunday Aguacatán; Cantel; Chichicastenango; Esquipulas; Momostenango; Nebaj; Nahualá; Panajachel; Rabinal; San Lucas Toliman; Santa Cruz Verapaz; Santa Lucía Cotzumalguapa; Santiago Atitlán; Santiago Sacatepéquez; Uspantán.

Plazuela de La Concepción at night, thereby starting the Christmas festivities. **15 Dec** the start of the **Posadas**, where a group of people leave from each church, dressed as Mary and Joseph, and seek refuge in hotels. They are symbolically refused lodging several times, but are eventually allowed in.

Shopping

Antigua *p278, map p290*
Antigua is a shopper's paradise, with textiles, furniture, candles, fabrics, clothes, sculpture, candies, glass, jade and ceramics on sale everywhere. The **main municipal market** is on Alameda Santa Lucía next to the bus station, where you can buy fruit, clothes and shoes. There are *artesanía* stalls inside.

Art and crafts

Stores selling textiles, handicrafts, antiques, silver and jade are found on 5 Av Nte between 1 and 4 C Pte and 4 C Ote. A *huipil* market is held in the courtyard of **La Fuente** (see Eating) every Sat 0900-1400. A number of jade-carving factories may be visited, including **Jades, SA**, 4 C Ote 34 (also at Nos 1 and 12), and **La Casa del Jade**, 4 C Ote 10.
Angelina, 4 C Ote 22. Wild furniture carved from gigantic slabs of wood.
Casa Chicob, Callejón de la Concepción 2, www.casachicob.com. Beautiful textiles, candles and ceramics.
Casa de los Gigantes, 7 C Ote 18. Textiles and handicrafts.
Colibrí, 4 C Ote 3B. Quality weavings.
Mercado de Artesanías, next to the main market at the end of 4 C Pte.
Nim P'ot, 5 Av Nte 29, T7832-2681, www.nimpot.com A mega-warehouse of traditional textiles and crafts from around the country.
Wer Art Gallery, 4 C Ote 27 y 1Av, T7832-7161, www.guiantigua.com/wer.htm. Large gallery displaying everything from Cuban ceramics to oil paintings.

Bookshops

Numerous shops sell books in English and Spanish, postcards, posters, maps and guides, including *Footprint Guatemala* and *Central America & Mexico*. Check out **Casa del Conde**, 5 Av Nte 4, for a full range, and the **Rainbow Café**, 7 Av Sur 18, for secondhand titles.

Food

Doña María Gordillo, 4 C Ote 11. Famous throughout the country for *dulces*. It is impossible to get in the door most days.
Tienda de Doña Gavi, 3 Av Nte 2. All sorts of potions and herbs, candles and homemade biscuits. Doña Gaviota also owns **Helados Marylena**, p296.

Activities and tours

Antigua *p278, map p290*

Mountain biking

Mayan Bike Tours, 3 Calle Poniente y 7 Avenida Norte, T7832-3743, guided tours from US$15 per person.

Old Town Outfitters, 5 Av Sur, 12 "C", T5399-0440, www.bikeguatemala.com Mountain bike tours (half-day tour, US$25), also kayak tours (5 days, US$350), equipment on sale, maps, very helpful.

Spa

Mayan Spa, Alameda Sta Lucía Nte 20, T7832-0381. Massage US$12 per hr. Pampering package, including sauna, steam bath and jacuzzi, Mon-Sat 0900-1900.

Tour operators

Antigua Tours, Casa Santo Domingo, 3 C Ote 22, T7832-5821, www.antigua tours.net. Walking tours of the city (US$18 per person), book in advance, Mon 1400-1630, Tue-Wed, Fri-Sat 0930-1230. Extra tours during Lent and Holy Week. Highly recommended.

Aventuras Vacacionales, 1a Av Sur #19 B, T7832-9036, www.sailing-diving-guatemala.com. Organizes sailing trips from Río Dulce (see p 356).

Eco-Tour Chejo's, 3 C Pte 24, T7832-5464. Well-guarded volcano treks: Agua US$20 for 2, Pacaya US$10. Also tours to coffee *fincas* and plantations, shuttle service, horse riding, very helpful.

Gran Jaguar, 4 C Pte 30, T7832-2712, www.guacalling.com/jaguar/ Volcano tours with official security, great fun; highly recommended for the Pacaya trip. Also shuttles and trips to Tikal.

Guatemala Ventures, 1 Av Sur 15, T7832-3383, www.guatemala ventures.com. Mountain biking, hiking, volcano climbing, rafting and combined trips. Tikal packages and cell phone rental. **ViaVenture**, T291-4344, www.viaventure.com, and **Mayan Bike Tours** (see above) are also here.

Monarcas Travel, Alameda Sta Lucía, T7832-4305, monarcas@conexion.com.gt Reliable airport shuttle and trips to Copán (0400, US$25), Semuc Champey and the kite festival at Santiago Sacatepéquez.

Rainbow Travel Center, 7 Av Sur 8, T7832-4202. Full travel service, specialists in bargain flights. Sells ISIC, Go25 and teachers' cards. Manager, Phillipa Myers, is the warden for the British Embassy. Co-owner runs **www.guatemalareservations.com**, T5212-3943.

Sin Fronteras, 5 Av Nte 15 "A", T7832-1017, www.sinfront.com Local tours, horse riding, bicycle tours, national and international air tickets including discounts with ISIC and Go25 cards. Also travel insurance. Agents for rafting experts **Maya Expeditions**.

Vision Travel, 3 Av Nte 3, T7832-3293, www.guatemalainfo.com. Shuttles and tours. Recommended. Guidebooks for reference or to buy, water bottle filling service to encourage recycling. Cheap phone call service. Closed Sun.

Guatemala City *p283, map p294*

Tour operators

Anfañona,11 Av, 5-59, Zona 1, T2238-1751. Walking tours of the centre, Mon-Fri, 2 hrs, US$10 per person, including hotel pick-up. Reserve in advance.

Clark Tours, 7 Av 14-76, Zona 9, T2470-4700, www.clarktours.com.gt. Long established, very helpful, tours to Copán.

Maya Expeditions, 15 C 'A', 14-07, Zona 10, T2363-4955, www.mayaexpeditions.com Very experienced and helpful, river/hiking tours, whitewater rafting, bungee jumping, cultural tours, tours to Piedras Negras.

Mayapan, 6 Av, 7-10, Zona 2, T2254-1428, www.infovia.com.gt/mayapan Maya cultural tour packages.

Monterrico *p289*

Fishing

The Pacific coast provides rich pickings – tuna, dolphin fish, roosterfish and mackerel. Contact **Artmarina**, at Iztapa, www.artmarina.com, for details.

Tour operators

Horses can be hired for a jaunt on the beach, also *lancha* trips and turtle tours. **El Arco de Noé**, C del Proyecto, T5703-3781. Noé Orantes is an INGUAT-registered guide. Tours along the canals 0600 and 1800 daily, US$5 per person. **Iguana Tours**, 1 block from the dock on C Principal, T/F7885-0688, with a rep at the sanctuary. Office hours 0800-1900 daily.

Transport

Antigua *p278, map p290*

Bus

INGUAT recommends that visitors take shuttles to and from **Guatemala City** (see below); public buses depart when full 0530-1900, US$0.65, 1-1½ hrs, from Alameda Santa Lucía near the market.

All other buses leave from behind the market. To **Ciudad Vieja**, US$0.10, every 30 mins, 15 mins. To **San Miguel de las Dueñas**, take a bus marked 'Dueñas', every 30 mins, 15 mins, US$0.20. To **Alotenango**, 0700-1800, 40 mins. To **La Soledad** (for the ascent of Acatenango), take a bus heading for Yepocapa or Acatenango village. To **Chimaltenango**, on the Pan-American Highway, 0700-1800, every 30 mins, US$0.32, for connections to **Los Encuentros** (for **Lake Atitlán** and **Chichicastenango**) and **Cuatro Caminos** (for **Quetzaltenango**). It is possible to get to Chichi and back by bus in a day for the market on Thu and Sun. To **Panajachel**, Popeye, 0700, from 4 C Pte, in front of La Bodegona, US$4.50, 2½ hrs, returning 1100. To **Escuintla**, at 0645, 0730, 0745, 0830, 1000, and 1600, 1½-2 hrs, US$0.65.

International To **Copán**, direct with **El Condor**, 4 C Pte 34, T498-9812, 0400, returns 1430, US$30 return.

Shuttles

Hotels and travel agents run frequent shuttles to and from **Guatemala City** and the **airport** (1 hr) 0400-2000 daily, US$7-10 depending on the time of day; details from any agency in town. Private shuttle to Guatemala City US$10-30, depending on the number of people. Also shuttles to **Chichicastenango**, US$12, **Panajachel**, US$10-12, **Quetzaltenango**, US$25, and other destinations; check prices and days of travel. To **Monterrico**, via Iztapa, US$10-12, 2 hrs, tickets from **Don Quijote**, ALM School, C del Proyecto, T5611-5670, donquijotetravel@yahoo.com

Taxi

Servicio de Taxi 'Antigua'. Manuel Enrique Gómez, T417-2180, recommended.

Guatemala City *p283, map p294*

Air

For international flights, see p17. For domestic and regional flights, see p21.

Airline offices **American Airlines**, Hotel Marriott, 7 Av, 15-45, Zona 9, T2337-1177. **British Airways**, 1 Av, 10-81, Zona 10, Edif Inexsa, 6th floor, T2332-7402/4. **Continental Airlines**, 18 C, 5-56, Zona 10, Edif Unicentro, T2366-9985. **Delta Air Lines**, 15 C, 3-20, Zona 10, Edif Centro Ejecutivo, T2337-0642. **Grupo Taca** at the airport and Hotel Intercontinental, Zona 10, T2331-8222, for reservations, T2334-7722, www.taca.com. **Iberia**, Av La Reforma, 8-60, Zona 9, Edif Galerías Reforma, T2332-0911. **KLM**, 6 Av, 20-25, Zona 10, T2367-6179. **Lufthansa**, Diagonal 6, 10-01, Zona 10, T2336-5526. **Mexicana**,13 C, 8-44, Zona 10, Edif Plaza Edjma, T2333-6001/5. **Tikal Jets**, 11 Av 7-15, Zona 13, T2360-9797, www.tikaljets.com. **United**, Av La Reforma, 1-50, Zona 9, Edif La Reformador, 2nd floor, T2332-1994.

Bus

Local City buses operate 0600-2000, US$0.15 per journey on regular buses, US$0.20 on red buses known as *gusanos* ('worms') and other standard red city buses (US$0.19 on Sun and public holidays). One of the most useful services is the **101**, which travels through Zona 1, Zona 4 and then all the way down the Av La Reforma, Zona 10. You can pick it up at 6 Av and 20

C near the Antigua bus terminal. Keep an eye on your possessions.

Hundreds of 'chicken' buses for the south and west of Guatemala, as well as local city buses, leave from the horrible Zona 4 terminal. To **Chichicastenango**, and **Santa Cruz del Quiché**, hourly 0500-1800, with Veloz Quichelense and Esperanza. Chicken buses for **Los Encuentros**, **Chimaltenango** and **Santa Cruz del Quiché** leave from 20 C and Av Bolívar, Zona 1, opposite Transportes Poaquileña. Walk under the underpass (safe) and bear to the right.

Long distance For shuttles to Antigua, see above. The majority of first-class and international buses have their own offices and departure points around Zona 1. Any bus heading west from Guatemala City stops at **Chimaltenango**. To **Quetzaltenango** (Xela), 4hrs, US$1.90, and **San Marcos**, 5 hrs, US$2.90, with Tacana, 2 Av, 20-42, Zona 1, T2251-8039, every 30 mins 0400-1630; also Pulman 0900, 1400, 1500, US$3.15 /US$3.75; Líneas Américas, 2 Av, 18-47, Zona 1, T2232-1432, 0430-1800, 7 daily, US$4; Galgos, 7 Av, 19-44, Zona 1, T2253-4868, 0530-1700, 5 daily to Xela, 4 hrs, US$4.30; Marquensita, 1 Av, 21-31, Zona 1, T2253-5871, hourly 0600-1700, US$3.75, on to San Marcos US$4.40.

To **Biotopo del Quetzal** and **Cobán**, 3½ hrs and 4½ hrs respectively, hourly from 0400-1700, US$3.90, with Escobar-Monja Blanca, 8 Av, 15-16, Zona 1, T2238-1409. To **Chiquimula** (for **El Florido**, Honduran border, p347), 3½ hrs, US$2.75, and **Esquipulas**, 4½ hrs, US$3.80, with Rutas Orientales, 19 C, 8-18, Zona 1, T2253-7282, every 30 mins 0430-1830. To **Zacapa**, 3¼ hrs, US$2.50.

To **Panajachel**, with Figeroa, every 2 hrs from 20C Av Bolívar, Zona 1, 0600-1530, 3 hrs, US$1.75; with Transportes Rebuli, 21 C, 1-34, Zona 1, T2474-1539, hourly from 0600-1600, 3 hrs, US$1.75, also to **San Lucas Tolimán** 0500-1500, 3 hrs US$1.75.

To **Puerto Barrios**, with Transportes Litegua, 15 C, 10-40, Zona 1, T2220-8840, www.litegua.com, 0430-1700, 21 a day, 5 hrs, US$5.20, and **Río Dulce**, 0600, 0900, 1130, 1300, 5 hrs, US$5.20. To **Río Dulce**, 5 hrs, US$5.20, and **Santa Elena**, 9-10 hrs, US$10.40, with Fuente del Norte (same company as Líneas Máxima de Petén), 17 C, 8-46, Zona 1, T2251-3817, frequent, midnight-2130; buses vary in quality and price. Also luxury service (fewer stops) at 1000 and 2130, with Maya del Oro, US$16.25. Línea Dorada, 16 C, 10-03, Zona 1, T2220-7990, iclic.com at 1000 and 2000, 2200 normal service, US$14.00; 1000, 2100, luxury service to **Flores**, US$22.50, 8 hrs and on to **Melchor de Mencos** (Belize border, p251), 10 hrs, US$25. Autobuses del Norte (AND), 15 Calle 9-18, Zona 1, T2221-2515, 1000 and 2100, US$27 one way to **Santa Elena**. Transportes Rosita, 15 C, 9-58, Zona 1, T2253-0609, departs 1500, 1700, 2000 to **Santa Elena**, 10 hrs, *especial* US$10, and on to **Melchor de Mencos**, 12 hrs; also normal service 1900, US$6.50/US$8.45. To **Santa Elena**, AND, 15 C 9-18A Zona 1, T2414-2666, 1000 and 2100, new luxury service, toilets, TV and snacks US$26.90; also Rápidos de Sur, 20C 8-55, Zona 1 T2232-7025. 0600 and 2200, 7hrs, fast service US$12.50; María Elena, 19C 10Av Zona 1, 0600, 2200, Pulman, US$12.50.

International Trans Galgos Inter, 7 Av, 19-44, Zona 1, T2220-6905, 2 daily to **Tapachula** via El Carmen (p336), 0730, 1330, 7 hrs, US$20. Línea Dorada to **Tapachula**, 0800 and 1500, US$32.50. Transportes Velásquez, 20 C, 1-37, Zona 1, 0800-1600, hourly to **La Mesilla** (p130), 7 hrs, US$3.90. Transportes Fortaleza, 19 C, 8-70, Zona 1, T2232-3643 to **Tecún Umán** (p288), 0130, 0300, 0330, 0530 via Retalhuleu, 5 hrs, US$5.20; frequent slower buses via Reu and Mazatenango. To **Chetumal** (p198) via Flores and **Belize City** with Línea Dorada, 2100 and 0500, arrives Chetumal 1500 (or later due to border crossings.)

Taxi

Call a taxi from your hotel or get someone to recommend a reliable driver; there are more than 300 illegal taxis in the city which should be avoided. **Taxis rotativos** are unmetered; they have numbers (and often a logo) on the side and the letters 'TR', followed by 4 numbers, on the back windscreen; they operate in all zones: airport to Zona 1 about US$7.50; Zona 1 to Zona 4 about US$3; beware overcharging. **Taxis estacionarios** have numbers on the side (no logo) and the letters 'TE', followed by 4 numbers on the back windscreen; they are found at fixed locations, including bus terminals and hotels; unmetered but cheaper than *rotativos*. Do not get in a taxi that does not match these descriptions. **Taxis amarillos** are metered telephone taxis; single zone US$3.25-4.50; Zona 1 to the airport US$7.50, depending on traffic. **Amarillo Express**, T2332-1515, run 24 hrs.

South of Antigua *p288*

Bus and boat

The transport hub of **Escuintla** is served by buses from Guatemala City, Antigua and by buses along the CA2 Pacific Highway. Change in Escuintla for **Santa Lucía**, 35 mins, US$0.50; an occasional bus marked 'Río Santiago', goes from Santa Lucía to **Colonia Maya**, close to El Baúl. Also from Escuintla to **Monterrico**, via Iztapa and Pueblo Viejo, frequent until 2030. The alternative route to Monterrico is bus to **Taxisco** from Escuintla, every 30 mins, 0700-1700, 40 mins, US$1.05, then bus to **La Avellana**, hourly until 1800, US$0.40, then boat through mangroves, 20-30 mins, US$0.40, every hr 0630-1800 to **Monterrrico**. Return boats to **La Avellana** leave Monterrico at 0330-1600. For shuttles from Antigua, see above.

Directory

Antigua *p278, map p290*

Banks Bancafé, 4 C Pte on the edge of the plaza, 24 hr ATM for Visa, Plus. **Banco de América Central**, on the plaza, Visa and MasterCard ATM (Cirrus and Plus), bank hours only. **Banco Industrial**, 5 Av Sur 4, near plaza, Visa ATM (24 hr) and accepts Visa credit card for cash at normal rates, no commission. **Banquetzal** on plaza, good rates, no commission, MasterCard (Cirrus) ATM.

Hospitals and clinics Casa de Salud Santa Lucía, Alameda Sta Lucía Sur 7, T7832-3122. Open 24 hrs, good and efficient. Prices vary. **Hospital Privado Hermano Pedro**, Av El Desengaño 12A, T7832-6419. **Dr Julio Castillo Vivar**, Alameda Sta Lucía 52 esq 6 C Pte, next to Farmacia El Pilar. Helpful, speaks English, recommended, open late. **Hospital San Pedro**, emergencies, T7832-0301. **Optica Santa Lucía**, 5 C Pte 28, T7832-0384.

Internet Enlaces, 6 Av Nte 1, discount cards available. Mon-Sat 0800-2000, Sun 0800-1300. **FunkyMonkeyNet**, Paseo de los Corregidores, 5 Av Sur 6. Daily 0800-2230.

Language schools Antigua is one of the most popular places in Central America to learn Spanish. **Footprint** has received favourable reports for the following: **Amerispan**, 6 Av Nte 40, T7832-0164, www.amerispan.com. **Centro Lingüístico Maya**, 5 C Pte 20, T/F7832- 1342, www.clmmaya.com. **Don Pedro de Alvarado**, 6 Av Nte 39, T7832-4180, www.guacalling.com /donpedroschool. 20 years' experience. **Latinoamérica Spanish Academy**, 3 C Pte 19A, Lotificación Cofiño, T7832-1484. **Proyecto Bibliotecas Guatemala** (PROBIGUA), 6 Av Nte 41B, T/F7832-2998, www.probigua.conexion.com. Gives a percentage of profits to14 public libraries in rural towns; frequently recommended. **Quiché**, 3 Av Sur 15A, T7832-0780. **Sevilla Spanish Academy**, 1 Av Sur 8, T/F7832-5101, www.sevillantigua.com. **Spanish School Antigüeño**, 1 Pte 10, T/F7832-7241, www.granjaguar.com /antiguena

Police National Police Palacio de los Capitanes General, south side of the plaza, T7832-266. **Tourist police**, 4 Av Nte, between 3 and 4 C Ote, T7832-7290, 0700-2200 daily, with night cover for emergencies, Jun-Oct.

Post office Alameda Sta Lucía and 4 C Pte, near the market. Mon-Fri 0800-1830, Sat 0830-1400.

Guatemala City *p283, map p294*

Banks Rates and commission charges vary; shop around. Bancafé, 18 C, 8-75, near the Zona 1 bus terminals, has a Visa ATM. Bancared, near Parque Centenario on 6 C and 4 Av has 24-hr ATM for Visa/Cirrus. Quetzales may be bought with MasterCard at Credomatic, beneath the Bar Europa, at 11 C, 5-6 Av, Zona 1. Mon-Sat 0800-1900. MasterCard ATM also at Banco Internacional, Av La Reforma and 16 C, Zona 10. Western Union, T2360-1737, collect 1-800-360-1737.

Embassies & consulates Addresses change frequently. Belize, Europlaza, Torre 2, 5 Av 5-55, Zona 14, apt 1502, T2367-3883. Mon-Fri 0900-1200, 1400-1600. Canada, 13 C, 8-44, Zona 10, T2333-6104. Mon-Fri Mon, Thu, Fri 0800-1630. Honduras, 12 C, 1-25, Zona 10, T2335-3281. Mon-Fri 0900-1300 (takes 24 hrs to get a visa, quicker in Esquipulas, T943-1143, Mon-Fri 0900-1800). Mexico, 15 C, 3-20, Zona 10, T2333-7254/8. Mon-Fri 0900-1300, 1500-1800; Mexican Consulate, Av La Reforma, 6-64, Zona 9, T2339-1007. Mon-Fri 0800-1200, for tourist card applications. UK, Av La Reforma, 16-00, Zona 10, Edif Torre Internacional, 11th floor, T2367-5425; embassy Mon-Thu 0800-1230, Fri 0800-1200; consulate Mon-Thu 0830-1200, Fri 0830-1100. Also for UK citizens in El Salvador, Honduras and Nicaragua. Australian/New Zealand citizens should report loss of passports here. USA, Av La Reforma, 7-01, Zona 10, T2331-1541, usembassy.state.gov /guatemala Mon-Fri 0800-1700.

Immigration Immigration office, 7a Av 1-17, Zona 4, 2nd floor of INGUAT building. For visa extensions. If you need new entry stamps in a replacement passport (eg if one was stolen), you will need a police report and photocopy, plus a photocopy of your passport. The will also ask for your date and port of entry.

Medical services Good hospitals are: Bella Aurora, 10 Calle A Zona 14; Centro Médico, 6 Av 3-47, Zona 10, T2332-3555, and Herrera Llerandi, 6 Av/9 C, Zona 10, T2334-5959. English spoken, you'll need full medical insurance or sufficient funds. Immunization centre at Centro de Salud No 1, 9 C, 2-64, Zona 1, Guatemala City (no yellow fever vaccinations). Dr Boris Castillo Camino, 6 Av, 7-55, Zona 10, Of 17, T2334-5932. 0900-1230, 1430-1800. Optico Popular, 11 Av, 13-75, Zona 1, T2238-3143, excellent for glasses repairs.

Post office Main post office, 7 Av and 12 C, Zona 1, Mon-Fri 0830-1700. This the only post office in the country from which parcels over 2 kg can be sent abroad.

Telephone Telgua, 7 Av, 12-39, Zona 1.

Lake Atitlán & the Western Highlands

Nebaj, Ixil Triangle

Don't miss...
1 Lake Atitlán ▸▸ p308.
2 Chichicastenango on market day ▸▸ p314.
3 Todos Santos Cuchumatán ▸▸ p326.
4 Nebaj ▸▸ p328.
5 Zunil and Fuentes Georginas ▸▸ p335.
MEXICO
CHIAPAS
GUATEMALA
HUEHUETENANGO
QUICHE
SAN MARCOS
TOTONICAPAN
QUETZALTENANGO
SOLOLA
CHIMALTENANGO
BAJA VERAPAZ
GUATEMALA CITY
p325
p332
p308
La Pinta
Chicomucelo
Paso Hondo
Laguna del Cofre
La Mesilla
La Democracia
Jalcatenango
San Miguel Acatán
Coatán
Eulalia
Soloma
Xexán
Guadalupe Victoria
Siltepec
La Grandeza
San Juan Ixcoy
Sierra de los Cuchumatanes
Area de Protección Especial Sierra de los Cuchumatanes
La Libertad
Ajal
Todos Santos Cuchumatán
La Torre
Chajul
Cotzal
Nebaj
El Porvenir
Motozintla
Ixahuacán
Cuilco
Colotenango
San Rafael Petzal
San Sebastián Huehuetenango
Chiantla
Aguacatán
Cunén
Uspantán
El Triunfo
Zaculeu
Huehuetenango
San Miguel Ixtahuacán
Sacapulas
Los Trapichitos
Rancho de Tela
Guadalupe
Comaltitlán
211
Concepción Tutuapa
Tacaná
Tojoj
Sipacapa
Malacatancito
La Estanzuela
Tzujil
Chimul
Ixchiguán
San Andrés Sajcabaja
Huixtla
Zaragoza
Volcán Tacaná
Chiquibal
Pan-American Hwy
Parque Nacional Riscos de Momostenango
Cubulco
Tajumulco
Comitancillo
San Pedro
Rabinal
CA1
Momostenango
Santa María Chiquimula
Sta Cruz Del Quiché
Zacualpa
Teincal
Huehuetán
Unión Juárez
Volcán Tajumulco
Sierra de Chuacúas
San Pedro Sacatepéquez
San Marcos
San Francisco El Alto
Cacahoatán
El Carmen
Chichicastenango
Tapachula
Tuxtla Chico
San Pablo
San Cristóbal Totonicapán
Totonicapán
Granados
San Andrés Xecul
Salcajá
Malacatán
El Tumbador
San Martín Sacatepéquez
Quetzaltenango (Xela)
Nahualá
Los Encuentros
Mixco Viejo
Mazatán
Nica
Catarina
Vol Lacandón
El Cuchillo
Chuarrancho
El Bejucal
Chicabal
Zunil
Cantel
El Carmen
Pueblo Viejo
Zanjón San Lorenzo
Vol Sta María
Pico Zunil
Santa Cruz La Laguna
Sololá
San Antonio Las Flores
San Juan Sacatepéquez
Vol Santiaguito
Panajachel
Iximiché
Comalapa
Puerto Madero
La Unión
Colomba
Sta María de Jesús
San Marcos La Laguna
Ciudad Hidalgo
Pacific Hwy
San Pedro La Laguna
Lake Atitlán (1,558m)
San Antonio Palopó
Patzún
Chimaltenango
San Pedro Sacatepéquez
CA9
Ciudad Tecún Umán
Coatepeque
El Viejo Palmar
Xojola
Volcán San Pedro
San Lucas Tolimán
Patzisia
San Andrés Itzapa
CA1
Los Ocotes
Abaj Takalik
Chocolá
Santiago Atitlán
Volcán Tolimán
Río Naranjo
CA2
San Antonio Suchitepéquez
Volcán Atitlán
Santa Catarina P
10 km
M Alemán
Cuyotenango
Chicacao
Ciudad Vieja
Antigua
N
Sibicté
Cobán
Tactic
Salam
190

Introduction

A ribbon of volcanoes, like conical buttons on a coat, stretch out to form the backbone of the Highlands, the Maya heartland. Its axis is Lake Atitlán. Formed by a mega explosion that blew the lid off a super volcanic mountain, the sparkling blue lake is truly stunning. Over time, three volcanoes were born around its edges. To the Tz'utujil Maya who live on the lakeshore, Lake Atitlán is the birthplace of creation and the world was delivered from its deep primordial waters.

At highland markets – San Francisco El Alto, Chichicastenango and Sololá – pigs rub shoulders with clothes pegs and colour, craft and culture combine. To the west around Quetzaltenango, thermal baths, the dawn rise over Volcán Santa Maria and the daily eruption of Santiaguito draw visitors. Further north is the Sierra de los Cuchumatanes, where the remote villages of the Ixil Triangle offer trekking opportunities. Maya dressed in primary colours are welcoming despite the decimation of the area during the Civil War.

High up in a sky-hugging valley is the Maya village and weaving centre of Todos Santos Cuchumatán. The pink and purple sartorial style of the villagers and their gorgeous woven bags make it worth a visit, especially for the annual horse race spectacle in November.

Ratings

Culture
★★★★★

Landscape
★★★★★

Chillin'
★★★★★

Activities
★★★★★

Wildlife
★★

Costs
$$$-$$

Lake Atitlán and around

Beautiful scenery stretches west of the capital, through the Central Highlands. Volcanic landscapes are dotted with colourful markets and the Maya wear traditional clothes in the towns and villages. Aldous Huxley called Lake Atitlán 'the most beautiful lake in the world'. Walking, eating, drinking, horse riding, meditating, relaxing and Spanish learning are the pleasures of this area. The cult of Maximón should also not be missed – a Maya tradition that stretches back centuries and whose devotional rites during Easter are fused with Roman Catholicism in the village of Santiago Atitlán. Further north, Chichicastenango fills with hawkers, vendors, tourists and locals at the vibrant weekly markets.

Getting there Shuttle or bus from Antigua or Quetzaltenango.
Getting around Boat, foot and bus.
Time required At least 3 days.
Weather Hot, but can be windy. Dry season Nov-Apr.
Sleeping Beautiful lakeside hotels and serviceable hostels.
Eating Full range of international cuisine with plenty at the cheap end.
Activities and tours Diving, boating, waterskiing, alternative therapies.
★ **Don't miss**... Chichicastenango on market day ▸▸ *p314*.

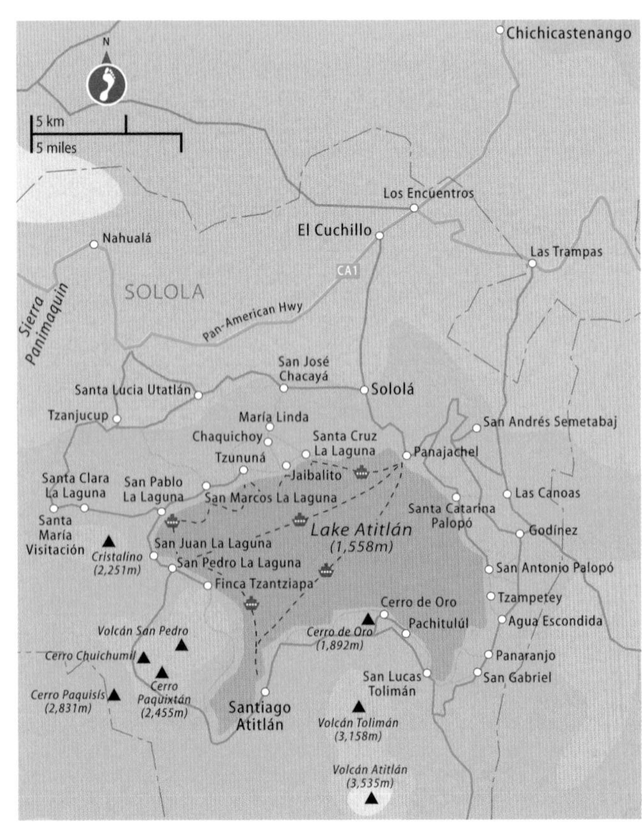

Ins and outs

Getting there The easiest way to get to this area is on one of the numerous buses along the Pan-American Highway west from Guatemala City to **Los Encuentros**, where a paved road heads 18 km northeast to **Chichicastenango**, page 314. Chichi is served by numerous chicken buses from Los Encuentros and Santa Cruz del Quiché, as well as by direct buses from Xela and Guatemala City and shuttles from Antigua and Panajachel. About 2 km beyond the Chichi turnoff at **El Cuchillo**, a road heads south to **Sololá** (page 321), from where it weaves and twists through a 550 m drop in 8 km to **Panajachel**. The views are impressive at all times of day, but particularly in the morning. Time allowing, you can walk down the road (two hours) to miss the unnerving bus ride. Many shuttle buses go direct to Panajachel from Antigua and other tourist centres.

Getting around From Panajachel there is a scheduled ferry service to Santiago Atitlán and *lanchas* to all other villages. The tourist office has the latest schedule information. Bad weather can, of course, affect the boat services. Crossings are generally rougher in the afternoons. Some villages are also served by buses. » *p323.*

Tourist information INGUAT ⓘ *C Santander 1-87, Centro Comercial San Rafael, Zona 2, Panajachel, T7762-11106, www.atitlan.com, www.atitlantimes.com, daily 0900-1700.*

Safety There have been a number of reports from travellers who have suffered or been threatened with armed robbery when attempting to climb the volcanoes around the lake, with and without guides. Seek local advice from INGUAT before planning an ascent.

Panajachel » *pp 316-324*

The old town of Panajachel (pronounced Pana ha' chel but often simply called Pana) is charming and quiet but the newer development, strung along a main road, is a tucker and trinket emporium, brash, loud and busy. This area is a gringo magnet, so if you want to fill up on international food and drink for a few days, then it's a good place to stay. Tourism began here in the early 20th century with several hotels on the waterfront. In the 1970s came an influx of young travellers, quite a few of whom stayed on to enjoy the climate and the easy life. Drugs and the hippy element eventually gave Panajachel a bad name, but rising prices and other pressures have encouraged this group to move on – some to San Pedro across the lake (page 312); others joined the commercial scene and still run services today.

The town centre is the junction of Calle Principal and Calle (or Avenida) Santander. The main bus stop is here, stretching south back down Calle Real, and marks the junction between the old and the modern towns. Tuc tucs will take you anywhere within town for US$1.25. It takes about 10 minutes to walk from the junction to the lake shore.

Sights

The original settlement was tucked up against the steep cliffs to the north of the present town, about 1 km from the lake. Virtually all traces of the original Kaqchikel village have disappeared but early Spanish impact is evident in the narrow streets, public buildings, plaza and the restored Franciscan **church**, which dominates the old town. The church was founded in 1567 and was used as the base for the Christianization of the area. It has a fine decorated wooden roof and a mixture of Catholic statues and Maya paintings in the nave. A block up the hill is the daily **market**, worth a visit on Sunday mornings especially for embroideries. The fertile area of the river delta was used for coffee production, orchards and many other crops, some of which are still grown today.

View of San Pedro La Laguna

The modern town, almost entirely devoted to tourism, spreads out towards the lake. Calle Santander is the principal street, leading directly to the short but attractive **promenade** and boat docks. The section between Calle Santander and Calle Rancho Grande has been turned into a park, which delightfully frames the traditional view across the lake to the volcanoes. Near the promenade, at the **Hotel Posada de Don Rodrigo**, is the **Museo Lacustre Atitlán** ⓘ *open 0900-1200, 1400-1800, except Tue, US$4.60*, created by a prominent local diver and archaeologist to house some of the many items found in the lake. The geological history is explained and there is a fine display of Maya Classical pottery and ceremonial artefacts classified by period. A submerged village is currently being investigated at a depth of 20 m. For those interested in local art, visit **La Galería** (near **Rancho Grande Hotel**), where Nan Cuz sells her painting evoking the spirit of traditional village life. She has been painting since 1958 with international recognition.

Around Lake Atitlán » *pp 316-324*

Travelling slowly round the lake is the best way to enjoy its stunning scenery and the effect of changing light and wind on the mood of the area. You can walk on or near the shore for most of the 50 km circumference, although, here and there, the cliffs are too steep for easy walking and some private properties will force you to move inland. With accommodation at towns and villages on the way, there is no problem finding somewhere to bed down for the night if you want to make a complete circuit. Otherwise, *lanchas* serve all the lakeside communities. At almost any time of year, but especially between January-March, strong winds (*El Xocomil*) occasionally blow up quickly across the lake. This can be dangerous for small boats.

The eastern shore

Within easy walking distance (4 km) of Panajachel is **Santa Catarina Palopó**, which has an attractive adobe church. Reed mats are made here, and you can buy *huípiles* (beautiful, green, blue and yellow) and men's shirts. Watch weaving at **Artesanías Carolina** on the way out towards San Antonio. There are hot springs close to the town and an art gallery. Six kilometres beyond Santa Catarina, **San Antonio Palopó** has a fine 16th-century church which lies in an amphitheatre created by the mountains behind. Up above there are hot springs and a cave in the rocks used for local ceremonies. The village is noted for the men's costumes and headdresses; *huípiles* and shirts are cheaper here than in Santa Catarina.

Collecting weed from the lake at dawn.

San Lucas Tolimán and around

San Lucas, at the southeastern tip of the lake, is known for its fiestas, especially Holy Week and 15-20 October, and for its markets, held on Tuesday, Friday and Sunday (the best). **Comité Campesino del Altiplano** ⓘ *Quixaya, 10 mins from San Lucas, T5804-9451, www.ccda.galeon.com*, produces fair trade organic coffee with beans bought from small farmers. From mid 2005 you will be able to visit their organic processing plant on a small coffee finca and learn about its *café justicia* and political work.

From San Lucas the cones of **Volcán Atitlán** (3,535 m) and **Volcán Tolimán** (3,158 m) can be climbed. Cloud on the volcano tops is common, but is least likely November-March. The route leaves from the south end of town and makes for the saddle (known as Los Planes, or Chanán) between the two volcanoes. From there it is south to Atitlán and north to the double cone and crater of Tolimán. Neither climb is difficult but they are complicated by many paths and thick cover above 2,600 m. If you are fit, either can be climbed in seven hours, five hours down. Ask Father Gregorio at the Parroquia church, two blocks from the Central Plaza, or at the Municipalidad for information and for recommended guides; **Carlos Huberto Alinan Chicoj** charges US$28 for the day trip, leaving at 2400 with torches to arrive at the summit by 0630 to avoid early cloud cover.

Santiago Atitlán

Santiago is a fascinating town, as much for the stunningly beautiful clothing of the locals, as for its mix of Roman Catholic, evangelical and Maximón worship. The men wear striped, half-length magnificently embroidered trousers (the most stunning in Guatemala). There are 35 evangelical temples in town as well as the house of the revered idol Maximón. The Easter celebrations here rival Antigua's for interest and colour and are some of the most curious and reverential ceremonies in the world, page 312.

The house of **Maximón** is open to visitors for a small fee. Wherever he is stationed in Santiago Atitlán he is accompanied by his father – Padre Santa Cruz and his mother María (although some sources say María is his wife). His room is decked out in bunting, gourds, maize cobs, toys, balloons, inflatables, fruit and herbs. Jesus lies in a neon-lit coffin nearby, which plays Rudolf the Red Nosed Reindeer and Santa Claus is Coming to Town. Candles are lit and burning copal incense clouds the room. Maximón wears a hat and a bib of scarves, into which quetzal notes have been tucked. There is normally an entrance fee for foreigners and a charge for photographs; exercise discretion and don't take a snap, while an offering is being made.

Background

Welcome to the world of Maximón

Few things are stranger than the sight of the Maya worshipping a wooden image decked in scarves, smoking a cigar and drinking fire water – the room enveloped in incense and filled with the sound of Christmas jingles and candle-light. In the corner lies a Christ figure in a glass coffin, studded with light bulbs that flash in time to the tunes.

Maximón is "basically, a flat piece of wood about 2½ feet high and 6-8 inches thick" (Dr E Michael Henderson, 1959), yet he has been fervently worshipped by the Maya for centuries. He is petitioned by his believers to bring luck, good harvests, rain, a fair price for maize and success. Offerings of cigarettes, alcohol, flowers and scarves are brought and laid before the image so that the prayer will be heard and answered.

Dr Henderson is referring to the Maximón of **Santiago Atitlán** but Maximón appears in similar guises elsewhere, notably in **San Lucas Tolimán** on Lake Atitlán, and in **Zunil** and **San Andrés Itzapa**, near Antigua. In Zunil, Maximón is given aguardiente to drink. As soon as the firewater is poured down his throat he pees into a bowl beneath the wooden chair he is sitting on.

Maximón's cult history, a mixture of Roman Catholic and Maya ritual, is even more intriguing than his bizarre physical appearance. The name is believed to have come from 'Mam-Shimon', meaning 'grandfather Simon'. He is also known as San Pedro, San Andrés, San Miguel, Pedro de Alvarado (Guatemala's conqueror) and Judas. This last name comes from an early confusion of Saint Simon and Saint Jude Thaddeus in Biblical history, whose feast days both fall on the 28 October; the date on which Maximón first appeared to locals in the mountains around Lake Atitlán. Further complexity arises from the fact that Jude, the patron of hopeless causes, shares his name with Judas Iscariot who betrayed Jesus. Some experts argue that during the procession of the crucified Christ on Good Friday (see below), Maximón represents Judas Iscariot.

Elsewhere, the fine **church**, has a wide nave decorated with colourful statues. It was founded in 1547 but the original roof was lost to earthquakes. There is a daily market, best on Friday, where all sorts of art work and crafts can be bought. Also visit the weaving centre at **Asociación Cojol ya** ⓘ *T7721-7268, Mon-Sat 0900-1600, free, weaving tours, US$6.50.*

San Pedro La Laguna and around

San Pedro is a small Tz'utujil Maya town set on a tiny promontory. The lakeside fringes are planted with coffee bushes and threaded with tracks lined with hostels and restaurants. From the dock facing Panajachel (known as the *muelle*), a cobbled road climbs up a very steep hill to the centre, while another goes down, more or less at right angles, to another dock (known as the *playa* – beach), which faces Santiago. Market days are Thursday and Sunday (better).

San Pedro is a favoured spot to hang out for a while after the rigours of travelling. Some of the transient gringo inhabitants now run bars and cafés or sell jewellery and the like. Both

The elaborate rituals of Easter week in Santiago Atitlán are performed to prepare Maximón for another year of office. On Holy Monday, he is stripped of his clothing and laid in a box in the rafters of his current abode. The clothes are then carried ceremoniously through the streets to the lake, led by rattle carriers and incense bearers. During a candle-lit ceremony, Maximón's followers ask the lake's permission to wash the clothes. The washing ritual takes place by moonlight to the accompaniment of hypnotic music, with onlookers standing by on the lake shore.

On Holy Tuesday, Maximón's clothes and hat are carried back to the house and dried. He is dressed and attended to behind locked doors in an all-night vigil, before being paraded through the streets the next morning to the Mayor's office where he is laid out with fruit. He is later taken to a chapel to wait for the Crucified Christ. On Maundy Thursday the Roman Catholic priest re-enacts the Last Supper and washes the feet of 12 young boys in the garden by the chapel. On Good Friday, Christ is taken off the cross, surrounded by dead animals and fruit and carried in a red neon-lit coffin. When Christ passes the chapel where Maximón has been resting, Maximón is 'brought back to life'.

soft and hard drugs can be found, although police have now been drafted in for greater law enforcement. For general local information ask at **Bigfoot**, who will advise on horse riding to neighbouring villages, guides for climbing Volcán San Pedro and whatever else you have in mind. A visit to the solar-heated **thermal baths** ⓘ *Mon-Sat 0800-1900, about US$3.20 a session*, is a relaxing experience, with massage also available.

The town lies at the foot of the **Volcán San Pedro** (3,020 m), which can be climbed in four to five hours, three hours down. Go early (0530) for the view, because after 1000 the top is usually smothered in cloud; an early start also means you will be walking in the shade all the way up and part of the way down. The route starts 1.5 km along the road to Santiago. Where the road takes a sharp turn to the right, go left through coffee plantations to the west flank of the volcano; after one hour there is only one path and you cannot get lost. A guide is advisable, particularly given a spate of recent attacks (page 309). A recommended guide is **Ventura Matzar González** ⓘ *C Principal, Cantón Chuacante, San Pedro, T7762-1140.*

Good Friday, Santiago Atitlán

The north shore

Two and a half kilometres northeast of San Pedro is **San Marcos La Laguna**, a village that has grown rapidly in recent years with the development of massage, yoga and therapy centres; it is now the ideal place to be pampered. The main part of the community is 'hidden' up a gentle slope, reached by two paved walkways that run 300 m through coffee and fruit trees from the lake. Beyond the centre, a cobbled road leads 300 m east to the main dock of the village; some waterfront hotels also have their own moorings.

From the road to the dock, a rough track leads east through coffee plantations to **Tzununá** (passable for small trucks and 4WD vehicles), with views across the lake all the way. There is a dock on the lakeside but no facilities. The bridge over the intermittent stream is the end of the road, from where a path continues through steep stretches of forest and maize fields, with spectacular views of the lake and the southern volcanoes. **Jaibalito** is even smaller than Tzununá and is hemmed in by the mountains.

Santa Cruz La Laguna is set in the most dramatic scenery on the lake. Three deep ravines come down to the bay separating two spurs. A stone roadway climbs up the left-hand spur, picks up the main walking route from Jaibalito and crosses over a deep ravine (unfortunately used as a garbage tip) to the plaza, 120 m above the lake. Behind the village are steep, rocky forested peaks, many too steep even for the locals to cultivate. Communal village life centres on the plaza but hotels are located on the lake shore.

Chichicastenango » *pp 316-324*

Chichicastenango is a curious blend of mysticism and commercialism. It is famous for its market where hundreds come for bargains but, with its mixture of Catholic and indigenous religion readily visible, it is more than just a shopping trolley stop. On a hilltop peppered with pine, villagers worship at a Maya shrine, while in town, brotherhoods venerate saints in a time-honoured tradition. The air of intrigue is almost as palpable as the mist that encircles the valley late in the afternoon.

'Chichi', also known as Santo Tomás, is the hub of the Maya-K'iche' highlands. The name means 'place of the *chichicaste*', a prickly purple plant like a nettle, which grows profusely in the area. Today the locals call the town 'Siguan Tinamit' meaning 'place surrounded by ravines'. About 1,000 *ladinos* live in the town, but 20,000 Maya live in the hills nearby and flock to the town for the Thursday and Sunday markets. The men's traditional outfit is a short-waisted embroidered jacket and knee breeches of black cloth, a woven sash and an embroidered kerchief round the head. The cost of this outfit, now over US$200, means that fewer and fewer men are wearing it. Women wear *huípiles* with red embroidery against black or brown and their *cortes* have dark blue stripes. **Tourist information** is provided by the local tourism committee ⓘ *7 C 5-43, half a block east of the main square, T/F7756-2022, Mon-Fri 0800-1700.*

Santo Tomás and flower sellers in Chichicastenango

Sights

The town lies on a little knoll in the centre of a cup-shaped valley, surrounded by high mountains. Winding streets of white houses, with bright red tiled roofs, converge on a large plaza that is the focus of the town. Two white churches, Santo Tómas and **Calvario**, face one another across the plaza. **Santo Tomás**, the parish church, was founded in 1540. It is open to visitors, although photography is not allowed and visitors are asked to enter discreetly through a side door. Next to Santo Tomás are the cloisters of a Dominican monastery (1542), where the famous *Popol Vuh* manuscript of the Maya creation story was found. A human skull wedged behind a carved stone face, found in Sacapulas, can be seen at the **Museo Arqueológico Regional** ⓘ *Tue, Wed, Fri, Sat 0800-1200, 1400-1600, Thu 0800-1600, Sun 0800-1400, closed Mon, US$0.25, photography and video not permitted*, on the main plaza. Also here is a jade collection once owned by 1926-1944 parish priest Father Rossbach.

On Sunday and Thursday mornings, the steps of Santo Tómas are blanketed in flowers as the women, in traditional dress, fluff up their skirts to sell baskets of lilies, roses and blackberries. The **markets** are very touristy and bargains are harder to come by once the shuttle loads of people arrive mid-morning but articles from all over the Highlands are available; you will find things here that you don't see in Antigua or Panajachel.

On a pine-covered hilltop behind the town is a shrine for the idol, **Pascual Abaj**, a god of fertility, represented by a large black stone with faintly visible human features. The shrine is covered by flowers, sugar and the wax of a thousand candles, and surrounded by crosses in the ground, where believers pray for the health of men, women and children, and for the dead. If you wish to undergo a ceremony, either to plead for a partner, or to secure safety from robbery or misfortune, ask the *curandero* (US$7 including photographs). It's a 30-minute walk to reach the deity from town; it can easily be visited independently or with an INGUAT-approved guide who will explain the history and significance (US$6.50).

Sleeping

Panajachel *p309, map p318*

A **Rancho Grande**, C Rancho Grande, T7762-1554, www.ranchograndeinn.com Cottages in charming setting, 4 blocks from beach, popular for long stays, breakfast with pancakes included. Pool with café in spacious gardens. Staff are helpful. Recommended.

A-B **Primavera**, C Santander, T7762-2052. www.primaveratitlan.com. Clean, bright rooms, with TV, cypress wood furniture, gorgeous showers, washing machine available, friendly. Expensive restaurant **Chez Alex** serves French food, lovely patio at the back. Avoid rooms over the street.

B **Cacique Inn**, C del Embarcadero, T/F7762-1205, large, comfortable rooms some with fireplace, credit cards accepted, swimming pool, magnificent house and spacious gardens, English spoken, good food. Recommended.

B **Müllers Guest House**, C Rancho Grande, 1-81, T7762-2442. Comfortable, quiet, good breakfast included.

C **Las Casitas**, C Real 1-90, T7762-1224/1069, neat bungalows in the old town, buses stop outside but it's quiet at night. Breakfast available, with bath, hot shower, attractive gardens, friendly. Medical Lab at entrance.

C **Posada de los Volcanes**, C Santander, 5-51, T7762-0244, www.posadadelos-volcanes.com. 12 rooms with bath, hot water, clean, comfortable, quiet, friendly.

D **La Zanahoria Chic**, I Av.0-46, Av de los Arboles, T7762-1249, restaurant with rooms in the old town, clean, TV, hot water, colonial style, friendly, coffee, luggage store.

D-E **Mario's Rooms**, C Santander esquina C 14 Febrero, T7762-1313, cheaper without bath, garden, clean, bright rooms, hot showers, good breakfast extra, popular and friendly.

E **Casa de Huéspedes y Cafetería Las Hermanas**, Barrio Santa Elena 4-02, 10m from the bus stops, T7762-0673, pretty garden, 5 rooms, one with bath, family atmosphere, meals available, good value. Several other cheap hotels along this passage.

E **Hospedaje Villa Lupita**, Cjón Don Tino, T7762-1201, pretty courtyard in the old town, hot showers, clean, friendly, parking, good value, recommended.

Eastern shore *p310*

A **Villa Santa Catarina**, Santa Catarina Palopó, T7762-1291/2827, www.villasdeguatemala.com Comfortable rooms with balconies around the pool, good restaurant.

B **San Tomas Bella Vista**, 3 km south of Santa Catarina Palopó, T7762-1566. Bungalows for 5 overlooking lake, 2 private beaches, children's playground, pool, ecological gardens, trails for birdwatching, bar, restaurant, camping.

B **Terrazas del Lago**, San Antonio Palopó, T7762-0157. On the lake with view, bath, clean, restaurant, a unique hotel built up over the past 28 years.

San Lucas Tolimán *p311*

B **Pak'ok**, Av 6, one block from the lake, T7722-0033, rooms and suites, colonial style, good but expensive restaurant (reservations), gardens.

D **Casa Cruz Inn**, Av 5 4-78, a couple of blocks from the park, clean, comfortable

Background

The Cofradías of Chichicastenango

There are 14 Cofradías (brotherhoods) (known as Chaq P'tan in Maya K'iche') in Chichicastenango, made up of six or eight members, with different ranks and responsibilities. Each Cofradía guards a saint's image, which is kept in the house of the first mayor. The saint is only taken out for processions and its own feast days, after which the image is moved to a new home and two pine fronds are hung either side of his door.

The chief saint is Santo Tomás, whose feast (the town's principal *fiesta*) is celebrated 13-21 December. Santo Tomás is a life-size sculpture encased in a glass box. He wears a crown and a sparkling silver *traje* and has dollar bills tucked into his hands at chest height. At his feet are scattered white petals. Opposite him is a table on which sit two large wooden snakes, dried cobs of corn, an offertory bowl, vases of white petals and white candles. Next to the saint are crates of the firewater *Quetzalteca*. The floor of the house is covered in a carpet of pine needles and the ceiling is laden with bunting and Christmas decorations. Candles remain lit at all times.

beds, run by an elderly couple, garden, quiet, good value.

Santiago Atitlán *p311*

Book ahead for Holy Week.

A-E **Posada de Santiago**, 1½ km south, T/F7721-7167, www.posadade-santiago.com Comfy stone cottages and cheaper rooms, restaurant serving home-grown food, plus tours, massage and language classes. Friendly and amusing management. Highly recommended. Has its own dock or walk from town.

B **Bambú**, on the lakeside, 500 m by road towards San Lucas, T7721-7332, www.ecobambu.com Cabins in attractive setting, restaurant, a few mins by *lancha* from the dock (US$3).

E **Chi-Nim-Ya**, first left up from the dock, T7721-7131, good, clean, comfortable and friendly, cheaper without bath, good-value café with large helpings.

E **Tzutuhil**, above **Ferretería La Esquina**, on left up the road from the dock, T7721-7174, with bath, cheaper without, restaurant, great views, good.

San Pedro La Laguna *p312*

Accommodation is mostly cheap and laid back: your own sleeping bag will be useful but take care of belongings. There are few private telephones but you can try to make contact through the **Telgua** office, T7762-2486.

E **Mansión del Lago**, T5811-8172, www.hotelmansiondellago.com. Up a hill with good views, bath, hot water, TV costs more, very good value.

E **Sak' Cari**, T7721-8096, T5812-1113. Lovely rooms with bath and hot water. Great garden and fabulous lake views. Extremely good value. Recommended.

North shore *p314*

Many of the hotels in San Marcos La Laguna are in Zona 3 below the centre towards the lake. There are 3 docks; if you land at the *muelle principal* from Pana, you a short, steep climb into the village.

A **Villa Sumaya**, Paxanax, 15 mins beyond the dock, Santa Cruz La Laguna, T5810-7199, www.villasumaya.com Including breakfast, with its own dock, sauna, massage and healing therapies, comfortable, peaceful.

B **La Casa del Mundo**, east of San Marcos at Jaibalito, T5218-5332, www.lacasadelmundo.com Enjoys one of the most spectacular positions on the entire lake.

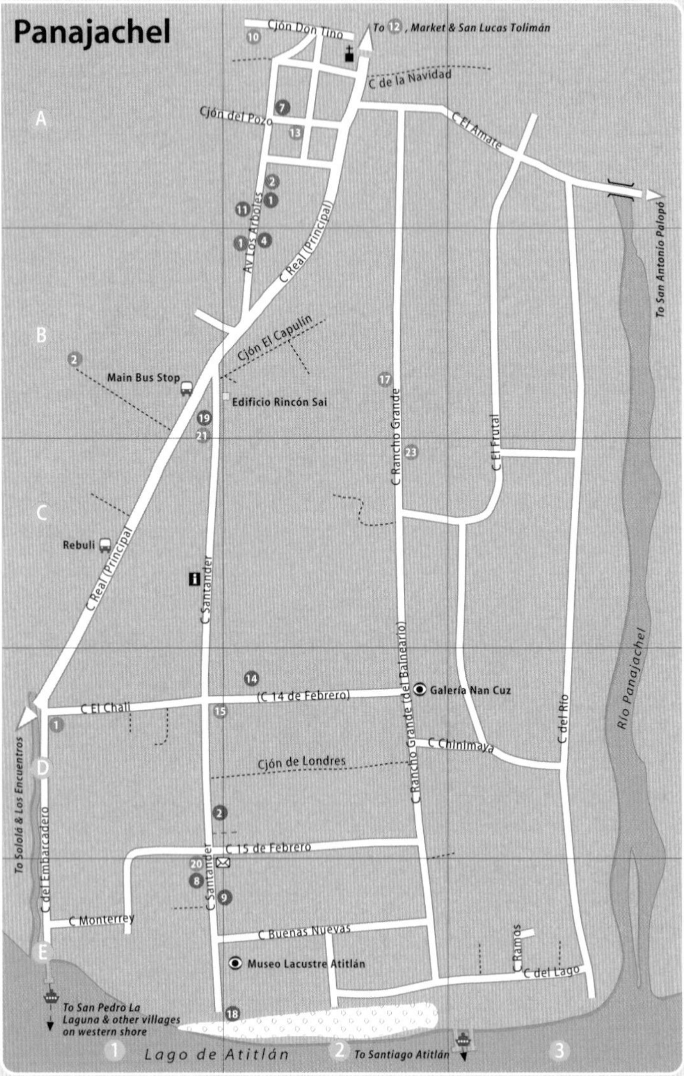

Panajachel

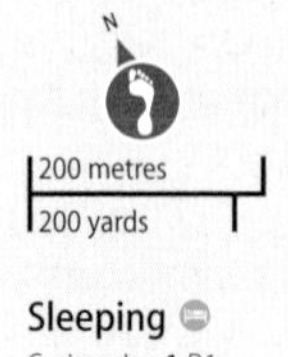

Sleeping

Cacique Inn **1** *D1*
Casa de Huéspedes y Cafetería Las Hermanas **2** *B1*
Hospedaje Villa Lupita **10** *A2*
Las Casitas **12** *A2*
La Zanahoria Chic **13** *A2*
Mario's Rooms **15** *D1*
Müllers Guest House **17** *B2*
Posada de los Volcanes **20** *E1*
Primavera **21** *B1*
Rancho Grande **23** *C2*

Eating

Al Chisme **1** *A2*
Bombay **2** *D1*
Circus Bar **4** *B2*
Delipan **7** *A2*
El Bistro **8** *E1*
El Pájaro Azul **9** *E2*
Fly'n Mayan **11** *A2*
Last Resort **14** *D2*
Pana Pan **19** *B1*
Sunset Café **18** *E2*

Bars & clubs

Chapiteau **1** *B2*
El Aleph **2** *A2*

Budget busters

LL **Casa Palopó**, less than 1 km beyond Santa Catarina Palopó, T7762-2270, www.casapalopo.com On the left up a steep hill is one of the finest hotels in the country, opened in 2001. Six 6 beautiful rooms, flowers on arrival, excellent service, heated pool, top class restaurant – reservations necessary.

L-AL **Santo Tomás**, 7 Av, 5-32, Chichicastenango, T7756-1061. A very attractive building, with beautiful colonial furnishings, pool, sauna and good restaurant and bar. Buffet lunch (US$12) is served on market days in the stylish dining room. Attendants wear traditional costume. Often full at weekends.

Many facilities, standard family-style dinner US$9, lakeside hot tub, a memorable place with fantastic views. Cheaper rooms available.

B-C **Posada Schumann**, 2nd dock, San Marcos La Laguna, T5202-2216, www.posadaschumann.com. Bungalows in attractive gardens on the waterfront, with dock. Some have kitchenettes, also sauna and restaurant.

D **Arca de Noé**, left of the dock, Santa Cruz La Laguna, T5515-3712, thearca @yahoo.com Bungalows, cheaper in dormitory with shared bath, good restaurant, BBQ, lake activities arranged, nice atmosphere, veranda overlooking really beautiful flower-filled gardens and the lake, low voltage solar power.

D **Jinava**, 2nd dock, left at the top of first pathway, San Marcos La Laguna, T5299-3311. Heaven on a hill. 5 lovely rooms, plus restaurants, terraces and a patio with fabulous views. Books, games or solitude. Close to the lakeshore with its own dock. Breakfast included.

D-E **Aaculaax**, Las Pirámides dock, San Marcos La Laguna, niecolass @hotmail.com A German-run artistic hangout on the lakeshore. Each room is filled with unique quirky decor. Run on an eco-basis, which means compost loos. Also a restaurant, bar and bakery.

D-F **La Iguana Perdida**, opposite dock, Santa Cruz La Laguna, T5706-4117, www.laiguanaperdida.com. Rooms and dorm with shared bath (some new rooms ensuite), delicious vegetarian food, BBQ, popular, lively, friendly, **ATI Divers** centre (see p322), waterskiing; kayaks US$0.65 per hr. Electricity only for hot showers and fridges, so bring a torch.

F **Casa Azul**, 1st dock, paulinitafeliz @yahoo.com Gorgeous little place offering yoga classes, reiki and massages. Also workshops in shamanism. Vegetarian food every night. Hammock space, lockers, some rooms. Eco philosophy, so bathrooms are organic.

Chichicastenango *p314*

You won't find accommodation easily on Sat evening, when prices are increased. As soon as you get off the bus, persistent boys will swamp you and insist on accompanying to certain hotels. The **Posada Belén** and the **Salvador** charge you Q3-10 as the boys' commision; insist that you have walked there yourself and refuse to pay extra.

C **Posada El Arco**, 4 C, 4-36, T7756-1255. Clean, small, friendly and very pretty, with garden, good view, parking and washing facilities. Negotiate lower rates for staying more than one night. English spoken.

D **Chalet House**, 3 C, 7-44, T/F7756-1360. Dingy street but a clean, guesthouse, with family atmosphere and hot water.

 D-E El Salvador, 10 C, 4-47, 50 large rooms with bath, a few with fireplace, good views, parking. Cheaper, smaller rooms without bath available.
E **Posada Belén**, 12 C, 5-55, T7756-1244. Rooms with bath, cheaper without, hot water, clean, will do laundry, fine views from balconies and hummingbirds in attractive garden, good value.

Eating

Panajachel *p309, map p318*

ΨΨΨ **Al Chisme**, Av Los Arboles 0-42, old town, T7762-2063, good food, try eggs 'McChisme' for breakfast, fresh pasta, excellent banana cake, popular, a bit pricey, 0700-2300 daily. Live piano music at weekends, friendly service.
ΨΨΨ **Circus Bar**, Av Los Arboles 0-62, old town, T7762-2056. Italian dishes including good pizzas and coffee, popular. Live bands at weekends, excellent atmosphere. Daily 1200-2400.
ΨΨΨ **El Bistro**, at end of C Santander near the lake, T7762-2585. Daily 0700-2200. Homemade Italian and international food, great salads, breakfasts and chocolate mousse, good value, live music weekends.
ΨΨΨ **El Pájaro Azul**, C Santander 2-75 local 5, T7762-2596. Café, bar and creperie serving sweet or savoury crepes, cakes and pies. Vegetarian options. Reasonable prices, good for late breakfast. Daily 1000-2200. Recommended.
ΨΨΨ **Sunset Café**, lakeside. Daily 1100-2400. Excellent for drinks, light meals and main dishes, live music, superb location but you pay for the view.
ΨΨ **Bombay**, C Santander near C 14 Febrero, T7762-0611. Vegetarian recipes, German beer, Mexican food, set lunch popular, good service. Very highly recommended. Daily 1100-2130.
ΨΨ **Fly'n Mayan**, Av Los Arboles, old town. Pastas, black pepper steaks, breakfasts and double-chocolate layered cake. Live jazz music at weekends.
ΨΨ **The Last Resort**, C 14 de Febrero 2-88, T7762-2016. Classic gringo bar, all-you-can-eat breakfasts, friendly, huge portions and reasonable prices, table tennis, good information, open fire.

Bakeries

Don´t miss the stall a block down from **Orale** on Santander, which sells cakes, pies, *tostadas, atoles*, hot chocolate and other treats for the seriously deprived.
Pana Pan, C Santander 1-61. Excellent wholemeal breads and pastries, banana bread comes out of the oven at 0930, cinnamon rolls also recommended.

Santiago Atitlán *p311*

Cheap *comedores* near the centre; the best restaurants are at the hotels.
ΨΨΨ **Posada de Santiago**, 1.5 km south of town, T/F721-7167. Delicious food and excellent service in lovely surroundings.
Ψ **Restaurant Wach'alal**, close to **Gran Sol**, a small yellow-painted café serving breakfasts, snacks and cakes. Airy and pleasant. Daily 0800-2000.

San Pedro La Laguna *p314*

Be careful of drinking water in San Pedro; both cholera and dysentery exist here.
ΨΨ **Arte Libre**. Little café in a garden with basketwork chairs.100% pure veg and fruit juices and breakfasts. Closed Mon.
ΨΨ **Rosalinda**, near centre of village. Friendly, serves breakfast, local fish and good banana and chocolate cakes.
ΨΨ **Thermal Baths** along shore from *playa*. Good vegetarian food and coffee, pricey.
ΨΨ-Ψ **Luna Azul**, along shore. Popular for breakfast and lunch, good omelettes.
ΨΨ-Ψ **Pachanay**, opposite **Hotel San Pedro**. Cheap rice dishes for lunch and dinner, reggae music, chilled, art gallery.
ΨΨ-Ψ **Tin Tin**. Good value Thai food, delightful garden. Recommended.
ΨΨ-Ψ **La Ultima Cena**, opposite Municipalidad. Good pizzas, pancakes, very popular.

Chichicastenango *p314*

On market days there are plenty of good food stalls and *comedores* in the centre of the plaza, offering chicken in different guises or a set lunch for US$1.50. There are also several good restaurants in the **Centro Comercial Santo Tomás** on the north side of the plaza (market).

ΨΨ **Caffé Tuttos**, near **Posada Belén**. Good breakfast deals, pizzas and *menú del día*, reasonable prices but some bad smells.

ΨΨ **La Fonda de Tzijolaj**. Great view of the market below, good meals, pizza, prompt service, reasonable prices.

ΨΨ **Tziguan Tinamit**, 5 Av, esquina 6C. Some local dishes, steaks, tasty pizzas, breakfasts, good pies.

ΨΨ-Ψ **La Villa de los Cofrades**, on the plaza. Café downstairs, good for breakfasts and coffee. More expensive restaurant up the street, great for people-watching and to escape the market hubbub, popular for breakfast.

Entertainment

Panajachel *p309, map p318*

Bars and clubs

Circus Bar. Good live music at weekends, daily 1700-0100.

Discoteca Chapiteau, Av los Arboles 0-69. Nightclub Thu-Sat 1900-2400.

El Aleph, Av los Arboles. Popular bar, Thu-Sat 1900-0300.

San Pedro La Laguna *p312*

Bars

Nick's Place is popular in the evening. Nearby are **Bar Alegre**, a sports bar and **D'noz**. **Bar Jorji's** is another popular spot as is **Ti Kaaj**. **El Otro Lado**, has food, nightly movies and a rooftop bar.

Festivals and events

Around Lake Atitlán *p310*

In addition to the major celebrations noted below, the lake communities have their own fiestas that are well worth attending: **Santa Cruz**, 7-11 May; **San Antonio Palopó**, 12-14 Jun; **San Pedro**, 27-30 Jun; **Panajachel**, 1-7 Oct; **San Lucas Tolimán**, 15-20 Oct; **Santa Catarina Palopó**, 25 Nov. Also visit **Sololá** for a great fiesta on 11-17 Aug.

Easter **Semana Santa** Processions, arches and carpets at San Lucas Tolimán on Maundy Thu and Good Fri. Intriguing rituals at Santiago Atitlán, featuring images of Christ and Maximón (p312) in the Good Friday processions.

28 Oct Maximón feast day in Santiago Atitlán.

Chichicastenango *p314*

Festivals of the 14 *cofradías* take place on **1 Jan** Padre Eterno; **Jan** San Sebastián; **19 Mar** San José; **Fri** in **Lent** Jesús Nazareno and María de Dolores; **29 Apr** and **29 Jun** San Pedro Mártir; Corpus Christi; El Sacramento; **3 May** and **14 Sep** Santa Cruz; **18 Aug** Virgen de la Coronación; **29 Sep** and **1 Nov** San Miguel; **30 Sep** San Jerónimo Doctor; **1st Sun in Oct** Virgen del Rosario; **2nd Sun in Oct** Virgen de Concepción; **13-21 Dec** Santo Tomás (p317), with **21 Dec** being the main day: processions, dances, *Palo Volador*, marimba music, well worth a visit but very crowded. During **Semana Santa**, there are processions to the church led by Jesus, the Virgin and all 14 *cofradía* saints.

Shopping

Sololá *p309*

Sololá's bustling market brings the town to life every Tue and Fri morning, when Maya gather from surrounding communities to buy and sell local produce. Women and particularly men wear traditional dress. It is primarily a produce market but there is also a good selection of used *huípiles*.

Panajachel *p309, map p318*

The main tourist shops are on C Santander, with the most upmarket places in the centre, including **El Güipíl**, which has the best quality items in town. The **Tinamit Maya Shopping Centre** has several stalls selling typical items; barter for good prices. Sometimes there are better bargains here than in Chichi, although textiles are better bought from the weavers themselves. Maya sell their varied wares cheaply on the lakeside; the market on Sun in the old town is also worth a look. Bartering is the norm.

Around Lake Atitlán *p310*

Visit the markets of **San Lucas Tolimán** and **San Pedro** on Sun; **Santiago Atitlán** on Fri.

Chichicastenango *p314*

Locals and tourists flock to Chichi for the twice weekly market (Thu and Sun). Wooden masks, textiles, crafts and food are displayed in hundreds of stalls crammed between the town's two churches. One highlight is the flower sellers that pile up on the steps of Santo Tomás church. The market is regarded as the best in the country.

Activities and tours

Panajachel *p309, map p318*

Boat trips

Day trips, 0830-1530, to San Pedro, Santiago and possibly San Antonio Palopó, with stops of 1 hr or so at each, US$6-7 per person but go early to the lakefront and bargain; be careful not to miss the boat at each stage or you'll have to pay again. Boats (*lanchas*) can also be hired US$26 one way, US$30 round trip, max 10 passengers.

Diving

ATI Divers, El Patio, C Santander, T7762-2621, www.laiguanaperdida.com, Mon-Sat 0930-1300. PADI Advanced Course (4 days) US$140, beginners US$175, fun dive US$25, 2 for US$45. PADI Rescue and Dive Master also available. Altitude speciality, US$65. Altitude dives are made off Santa Cruz La Laguna, where there are spectacular walls, rock formations, underwater trees and hot spots. Take advice on visibility before you opt for a dive.

Fishing

Black bass (*mojarra*) up to 4 kg can be caught in the lake. Boats for up to 5 people can be hired for about US$15. Check with **INGUAT** for latest information.

Tour operators

Several agencies on C Santander offer shuttles to Chichicastenango, Antigua, etc, as well as activities on and around the lake; try **Centroamericana Tourist Service**, T/F7762-2496.

Adrenalina Tours, Atitrans office (T7762-2336, www.atitrans.com), Edif Rincón Sai, T7762-0146, www.adrenalinatours.com Good, fun tours and a shuttle service.

Watersports

ATI Divers at Iguana Perdida in Santa Cruz, offer water-skiing US$7.50 for 15 mins. Kayak hire is around US$3 per hr; ask at the hotels, **INGUAT** and the lakeshore. Beware strong winds on the lake, especially Jan-Mar.

Around Lake Atitlán *p310*

Alternative therapies

Aum Rak Mayan Science Centre, opposite **Quetzal**, San Marcos La Laguna, T5305-2070, www.aumrak.com. Workshops in Maya science.

Las Pirámides, San Marcos La Laguna, T5205-7151, www.laspiramides.com.gt Residential meditation centre. US$10 per person per day for 1 month, including accommodation. Shorter courses also available. In the grounds are a sauna, a vegetarian restaurant with freshly baked bread and a library. Relaxing, peaceful.

San Marcos Centro Holistico, beyond Unicornio, San Marcos La Laguna, www.sanmholisticcentre.com. Iridology, acupuncture, kinesiology, Indian head massage, reflexology, massage classes.

Horse riding

Aventura en Atitlán, Finca San Santiago, 10 km outside Santiago, T5515-3712, wildwest@amigo.net.gt. Riding and hiking tours (US$30-50).

Tour operators and guides

Bigfoot, San Pedro La Laguna, T7721-8203. Daily 0800-1700, until 2000 in high season. Super-helpful tour agency and information service.

Francisco Tizná from the **Asociación de Guías de Turismo**, Santiago Atitlán, T7721-7558, is an extremely informative guide; ask for him at the dock or at any of the hotels; payment by donation.

Transport

Panajachel *p309, map p318*

Bicycle

Alquiler de Bicicletas Emanuel, on C 14 de Febrero. US$0.65 up per hr or US$5 for 8 hrs, US$7 per 24 hrs. Different machines available. Also several rental places on C Santander, try **Maco Cycle Rental** and **Tono Cycle Rental**.

Boat

To **Santiago Atitlán**, from the end of C Rancho Grande, 0545, 0830, 0930, 1030, 1130, 1300, 1500, 1630, US$1.30 each way, 1¼ hrs in the **Naviera** ferry or 20-35 mins by fast *lancha*. Some *lanchas* to the other villages also leave from here but will always call at the C Embarcadero dock, where most *lanchas* depart. *Lanchas* leave C Embarcadero when full, 0700-1700, calling at **Santa Cruz**, **Jaibalito**, **Tzununa**, all US$1.30, then **San Marcos**, **San Pablo**, **San Juan** and **San Pedro**, US$4.90 (negotiable). Also up to 10 *lanchas* daily until 1400 direct to **San Pedro**, US$2. See also boat trips, above.

Bus and pick-ups

There are pick-ups and buses to **Santa Catarina**, **San Antonio** and **San Lucas** and buses to **San Lucas** and **Santiago**.

Transportes Rebuli leaves from opposite **Hotel Fonda del Sol** on C Real, otherwise, the main stop is where C Santander meets C Real.

Rebuli to **Guatemala City**, 3½ hrs, US$2.50, crowded, hourly, 0500-1500. To **Quetzaltenango**, direct 7 a day, 0530-1415, US$2.10, 2½ hrs. To **Chichicastenango**, direct Thu and Sun, 0645, 0700, 0730 and then hourly to 1530; other days 0700-1500, US$1.40, 1½ hrs. To **Cuatro Caminos**, direct, US$1.30 from 0530, for connections to Quetzaltenango, etc. To **Chimaltenango** US$1.40, for connections to Antigua, 45 mins, US$0.32; also direct to **Antigua**, with **Transpopeye**, 1030-1100, daily, US$4.60, from opposite the bank. To **Sololá**, US$0.20, 20 mins, every 30 mins.

Shuttles

Services run jointly by travel agencies, including **Atitrans**, Edif Rincón Sai, T7762- 2336. Guatemala City-Antigua-Panajachel, 4 daily, normally collecting /delivering at hotels, US$10 per stage. Also services to/from **Chichicastenango** US$10, **Quetzaltenango** US$15 and the **Mexican border** US$35.

Around the lake *p310*

Boat

Each of the lakeside communities has a dock; buy tickets on the boat as touts on the dockside overcharge. There is a scheduled ferry between **Panajachel** and **Santiago** (see above), as well as reliable *lancha* services between **Panajachel**, **Santiago**, **San Pedro** and **San Marcos**, US$1.30 per journey, until 1600; if you wait at the smaller docks on the western side up to this time, you can flag down a ride; if you leave it any later you're likely to get stuck.

San Lucas Tolimán *p311*

Buses to **Santiago Atitlán**, hourly and to **Guatemala City** via **Panajachel**. For boat services, see above.

Santiago Atitlán *p311*

Buses to **Guatemala City**, 5 daily from 0300, US$2.15, also 2 **Pullmans**, US$2.80. To **Panajachel**, 0600, 2 hrs, or take any bus to the main road south of San Lucas and change. For boat services, see above.

San Pedro La Laguna *p312*

Buses to **Guatemala City**, several in the early morning and early afternoon, 4 hrs, US$2.50; to **Quetzaltenango**, in morning, 3½ hrs, US$2. Frequent pick-ups along the main road to **San Marcos**, US$0.40. Also occasional pick-ups to **Tzununá**. For boat services, see above.

Chichicastenango *p314*

Bus

To **Guatemala City**, every 15 mins, 0200-1730, 3 hrs, US$2. To **Panajachel**, 1 hr, US$1.50, 0700, 0900, 1200, 1400, or any bus heading south and change at **Los Encuentros**, US$0.40. To **Antigua**, any bus heading south and change at Chimaltenango. To **Quetzaltenango**, 5 daily 0430-0830, 2½ hrs. To **Mexico**, and all points west, any bus to Los Encuentros and change. To **Santa Cruz del Quiché**, for **Nebaj**, at least every ½ hr 0600-2000, US$0.40, 30 mins.

Shuttles

Chichi Turkaj Tours, 5 Av, 4-42, T5215-0731, daily 0800-2000. Shuttles to the capital, Xela, Panajachel, Huehuetenango and Mexican border. Maya Chichi Van, 6 Av, 6-45, T7756-2187. Shuttles and tours US$10-650.

Directory

Panajachel *p309, map p318*

Banks Banco Industrial, C Santander (TCs and Visa ATM), Banco de Comercio, C Real, US$TCs and cash, Visa ATM opposite. **Doctors** Dr Hernández Soto, office near the Texaco station, US$5 for a short consultation. **Hospitals and clinics** Centro de Salud on C Real, just downhill from the road to San Antonio Palopó. **Internet** Many in centre, shop around for best prices: standard is US$2 per hr. **Language schools** Jardín de America, C 14 de Febrero, T7762-2637, www.atitlan.com/jardin.htm, US$75 for 20 hrs tuition per week, US$95 for 30 hrs per week, lodging with family US$60 per week. Jabel Tinamit, behind Edif Rincón Sai, T7762-0238, www.jabeltinamit.com Similar tariff. **Pharmacies** Farmacia Santander, top end of C Santander, very helpful. **Post office** C Santander. Possible to send parcels of up to 1 kg abroad here as long as packing requirements are met. Get Guated Out, Centro Comercial, Av Los Arboles, T/F7762-2015, good but more expensive service. DHL, Edif Rincón Sai, C Santander. **Telephone** Telgua, on C Santander.

San Pedro La Laguna *p314*

Banks Banrural changes cash and TCs only. **Hospitals and clinics** Good doctor at Centro Médico opposite Educación Básica school. **Internet** Several internet and phone offices in town. **Language schools** This is a popular place for learning Spanish. Tuition is about US$50/week, homestay plus tuition US$90/week. Try Casa Rosario, www.casarosario.com; Corazón Maya, T7721-8160, www.corazonmaya.com, also Tz'utujil classes; San Pedro, T5694-9271, www.sanpedrospanish-school.org. An attractive alternative is La Escuela, in San Marcos, run by a Québécois couple from their dream home. Teaching in *palapas* on the terraces, US$50 a week.

Chichicastenango *p314*

Banks Bancafé, corner 5 Av/6 C, accepts Visa and MC and has 24 hr Visa ATM. Mayan Inn will exchange cash. **Internet** Occasional connection at Aces, inside Hotel Girón, 6 C, 4-52, expensive. **Post office** 7 Av, 8-47. Cropa Panalpina, 7 Av opposite post office, T7756-1028, cropachi@amigo.net.gt Will pack and ship purchases home by air cargo. **Telephone** Telgua, 6 C between 5 y 6.

Sierra de los Cuchumatanes

La Sierra de los Cuchumatanes stretches from Jacaltenango in the east to just beyond Uspantán in the west, making it the largest area over 3,000 m in Central America. The mountains dominate the skyline north of Huehuetenango and help to preserve the isolation and culture of many remote highland villages.

Some of the best weaving is done in the Mam-speaking village of Todos Santos, where the men wear brightly striped costumes with embroidered collars and cuffs, but the town is even more famous for its annual horse race, a riot of colour, energy and drunkenness.

Further east, in the Ixil Triangle, the traditional costume of the Nebaj women is an explosion of primary colours. The forested mountainous scenery of this area provides great opportunities for walking, despite widespread deforestation.

Getting there Buses from Cuatro Caminos/Huehuetenango to Todos Santos; buses from Los Encuentros/Chichi/Santa Cruz del Quiché to the Ixil Triangle.

Getting around Bus, horse, truck, by foot, minibus tours.

Time required Minimum 3 days in the Ixil Triangle and 3 days in Todos Santos due to long journey times.

Weather Sunny but can be very cold. Dry season Nov-Apr.

Sleeping A few very basic guesthouses and hostels.

Eating Basic restaurants and cafés serving local food or simple international dishes.

Activities and tours Horse riding, trekking, saunas.

★ **Don't miss...** Todos Santos Cuchumatán »*p326*

Ins and outs

Getting there and around Huehuetenango is the main transport hub for this area, with buses serving the Cuchumatanes Mountains and the Mexican border (see page 130). Todos Santos Cuchumatán is a two- or three-hour bus ride from Huehuetenango. Santa Cruz del Quiché is a useful hub for buses north from Chichicastenango. Nebaj is the principal village of the Ixil Triangle and is reached by bus from Santa Cruz del Quiché, passing through Sacapulas, or from Huehuetenango, via Aguacatán and Sacapulas; with good connections, this journey should take three hours. It is not so easy to get to Chajul and San Juan Cotzal, but buses arriving in Nebaj sometimes continue to both. » *p340*

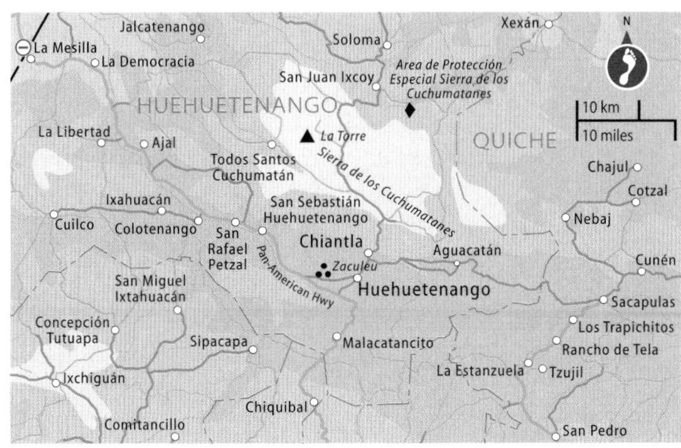

Huehuetenango and around » pp 329-331

Huehuetenango, colloquially known as Huehue, is a quiet, pleasant, large town with little to detain the visitor. However, its bus terminal, 2 km from town, is one of the busiest in the country so you're likely to spend at least some time here to change buses.

Aguacatán

A semi-paved road with good views runs east from Huehuetenango, towards Sacapulas (for connections to Nebaj) and on to Santa Cruz. After 26 km the road reaches the village of Aguacatán, where women wear the most stunning headdresses in the country, made from a long, slim textile belt of muliticoloured woven threads, on sale in *tiendas* in town. The women also wear beautiful dark *cortes* with horizontal stripes of yellow, pink, blue and green. The town fiesta, celebrating the Virgen de la Encarnación, is 40 days after Holy Week.

Todos Santos Cuchumatán

Hemmed in by 3,800-m high mountains that squeeze the town into one long, 2-km street, Todos Santos is a Mam-speaking village that maintains its traditional way of life and its adherence to the 260-day Tzolkin calendar. The town is famous for its stunning textiles and for the horse race that takes place here on 1 November each year (see page 327) but it also has a sober recent history; the early 1980s saw many people flee the region at the height of Civil War atrocities.

The men of the village wear famous red-and-white striped trousers and striped jackets in white, pink, purple and red, with intricately embroidered collars and cuffs in beautiful colours. Their straw hat is wrapped with a blue band. The women wear navy blue *cortes* with thin, light blue, vertical stripes. You can buy the embroidered cuffs and collars, the red trousers, fine *huípiles* and gorgeous crocheted bags in the co-operative on the main street and direct from the makers. » p330.

There are walking and hiking opportunities in the area. At **Las Letras** the words 'Todos Santos' are spelt out in white stone on a hillside above the town. The walk takes an hour; take the path down the side of Restaurant Cuchumatlan.

The highest point of the Cuchumatanes, and the highest non-volcanic peak in the country, **La Torre** (3,837 m), is to the northeast of Todos Santos and can be reached from the village of Tzichem on the road to Concepción Huista.

Harvest maize at Chajul

Traditional dress in Todos Santos

Background

La Corrida

The horse race in Todos Santos is one of the most celebrated and spectacular in Central America. It is also a frenzied day that usually degenerates into a drunken mass. Quite simply the riders race between two points, having a drink at each turn until they fall off. The aim is to consume as much alcohol as possible and still remain on top of your horse and in the race at the end of the day.

The origins of the event date back to the arrival of the *conquistadores* in Todos Santos, who came on horseback in colourful clothes with bright scarves flowing down their backs and feathers in their hats. The locals imitated them and thus the tradition was born. Until the practice was stopped by the Roman Catholic Church in the 1970s, cockerels were strung up along the route and the men had to wring their necks as they raced by. At least one cockerel, a symbol of male power and fertility, is still used in the race as a horsewhip.

The local men make a promise a year beforehand that they will ride in the *corrida*; if they don't fulfil this promise, they believe they will die. A rider will also agree with his wife not to have sex for nine days before the race to ensure that he will not fall off!

When the race begins at 0800, the men are already pretty tipsy (having indulged in the festivities for days beforehand) but as the day wears on and gallons of beer are guzzled, they become increasingly drunk and dishevelled. There are about 15 riders on the course at any one time and they ride with arms outstretched – whip in one hand and beer bottle in the other. Their faces are mud spattered and they moan and groan from near-lethal alcohol consumption. At times a rider will fall apparently lifeless on the track, at which point he is dragged unceremoniously by the scruff of the neck to the edge of the fence to avoid being trampled. A fall means instant dismissal from the race. Wardens with batons stand on the sideline, exchanging tired horses when they see fit and dealing with fallen riders, who try to get back onto their horses.

By the end of the day the spectacle is pretty grotesque: the horses are drenched with sweat and wild-eyed with fear; the men are completely paralytic from alcohol, and the edge of the course is littered with semi-comatose bodies.

Over the years people have died in this race. It used to be believed that a death was good luck; it meant that there would be a plentiful harvest the following year.

Ixil Triangle » pp 329-331

The Ixil Triangle is made of up of the highland communities of Nebaj, Chajul and Cotzal. Much of this area was decimated during the Civil War and then repopulated with the introduction of 'model villages' established by the government. Evidence of wartime activities can still be seen but more remote Maya Ixil-speaking villages are gradually opening up to visitors with the introduction of hostel and trekking facilities. The bus ride from Santa Cruz del Quiché (unpaved beyond Sacapulas) is full of fabulous views and hair -raising bends.

Nebaj

The town of Nebaj is high in the Cuchumatanes Mountains and its green slopes are often layered with mist. However, the town is infused with colour by the beautiful costume of its local women: an extravaganza of predominantly green, with red, yellow, orange, white and purple. The *corte* is usually maroon, with vertical stripes of black and yellow, although some are bright red, and the *huipil* is of a geometric design. The women also wear a headdress adorned with colourful bushy pom-poms. The men's traditional costume is a red jacket, embroidered in black designs but this is hardly ever worn.

The main plaza is dominated by a large, simple white church around which are weaving co-operatives selling *cortes, huípiles* and handicrafts from the town and the surrounding area – bargaining is possible. Nebaj also has Sunday and Thursday markets. For information on the area, visit the office of **PRODONT-IXIL** (Proyecto de Promoción de Infraestructuras y Ecoturismo), Av 15 de Septiembre, in a grey building on the right 1 block after the **Gasolinera El Triángulo** on the road to Chajul. The director, Pascual, is very helpful. Also here is Solidaridad Internacional, which runs tours and has an excellent website (www.nebaj.org), with useful phrases in Ixil and your daily horoscope.

Around Nebaj

There is good walking west of Nebaj and a number of 'model villages' resettled by the government following the widespread destruction of this region. **La tumba de la Indígena Maya** is a shrine just outside Nebaj (15 minutes) where some of those massacred during the Civil War are buried. The village of **Acul** was founded on 22 December 1983. To get there, follow 5 Calle out of town (the road to the right if you are facing the church at the bottom of the plaza), downhill, then over the bridge. Another 50 m further on the main path veers left, but go straight on; from here the route is self-evident, any forks come back together, approximately two hours. By road leave town on Avenida 4, the Shell station road; at the first fork after the 'tower', follow the main road left and at the next fork take the small, unsigned track to the left. One kilometre west of the village is **Finca San Antonio**, where they make the best cheese in Guatemala. The Italian Azzari family has owned the finca for decades and sells all sorts of cow, goat and cream cheeses at reasonable prices. B&B accommodation is also sometimes available, T439-3352.

Chajul and Cotzal

It is a six-hour walk from Nebaj to **Chajul**, the second-largest village in the Ixil Triangle. This is where the brother of the Nobel Peace Prize-winner, Rigoberta Menchú, was killed in the plaza during the Civil War. According to her book, *I, Rigoberta Menchú*, her 16-year-old brother Petrocinio was kidnapped on 9 September 1979, after being turned in for 15 quetzales. He was tortured in the plaza by the army along with numerous others. Villagers were forced to watch the torture under threat of being branded communists. People were set on fire but the onlookers had weapons and looked ready to fight so the army eventually withdrew.

Children walk to school in the Ixil Triangle.

It is possible to walk from Chajul to **Cotzal**, a village spread over a large area on a number of steep hills. Market days are Wednesday and Saturday. You can hire bikes from **Maya Tour** on the Plaza. Nebaj to Cotzal is a pleasant four-hour walk.

Sleeping

Todos Santos Cuchumatán *p326*
Reservations necessary in the week before the Nov horse race, but even if you turn up and the town is full, locals offer their homes.
F Casa Familiar, up the hill, close to central park, myearth@c.net.gt. Run by the friendly family of Santiaga Mendoza Pablo. Hot shower, traditional sauna, breakfast, dinner US$2.50, but slow service (chase them up), delicious banana bread, spectacular view, popular. The Mendoza family make and sell *típicas* and give weaving lessons, US$1 per hr.
F Hotel Mam, next to Hotelito Todos Santos. Friendly, clean, hot water, but needs 1 hr to warm up, not too cold in the rooms as an open fire warms the building, good value.
F Hotelito Todos Santos, above the central park, hot water, clean, small café.

Nebaj *p328*
Boys will meet you from incoming buses and will guide you to a *hospedaje* – they expect a tip.

Beyond Nebaj, near Acul, **Finca Mil Amores** has attractive chalets with tiled rooves and fireplaces where you can stay the night; for more information and alternatives, ask at the **PRODINT** office. There are also a couple of very basic *hospedajes* in Chajul.
E Hotel Turanza, 1 block from plaza down 5 C, T7775-8219, formerly **Posada Don Pablo**, tiny rooms, but very clean, soap, towels, second floor rooms are nicer, TV and parking, little shop in entrance, phone service.
E Ixil, 2 Av, 9 C, 1 block back up the slope from the bus terminal and one block to the left, T7756-0036. Cream and maroon building with no sign, rooms with private bath and TV, cheaper without, quiet.
F Hostal Don Juan, 0 Av A, 1 C B, Canton Simocol. Take Av 15 de Septiembre and turn left at **Comedor Sarita**, opposite PRODONT-IXIL, then it's 100 m to the right, T7755-4014/1529. Part of **Programa Quiché**, run with the support of the EU. 6 beds in 2 rooms, each bed with a locked strongbox, and

hot showers. The colonial building has a traditional sauna, *chuj*, US$2, plus a *boxbol*.

F **Solidaridad Internacional** supports 6 hostels in the villages of Xexocom, Chortiz, Xeo, Cocop, Cotzol and Parramos Grande where there is room for 5 people.

Eating

Todos Santos Cuchumatán *p326*

There are *comedores* on the 2nd floor of the market selling very cheap meals.

Comedor Katy, vegetarian meals on request, good value *menú del día*.

Cuchumatlán, sandwiches, pizza and pancakes, popular at night.

Mountain Muse. Run by American Rebecca who serves up vegetable curry, pasta and breakfasts. Books to swap also.

Patz Xaq, signposted 100 m down a track just before **Hotel La Paz** on the right, serving *comida típica* from 0700-2100, great view.

Tzolkin, good food, the most popular gringo hangout, also arranges local tours.

Nebaj *p328*

Boxboles are squash leaves rolled tightly with masa and chopped meat or chicken, boiled and served with salsa and fresh orange juice.

Cafetería y Restaurante Naabá, Calzada 15 de Septiembre. 0700-2200. Traditional food and snacks.

El Descanso, popular volunteer hang out, good food and useful information about their other community based projects (see www.nebaj.com) and **La Red Internet Café**.

Pizza del César, opposite **Bancafé**, breakfasts and mouth-watering strawberry cake, daily 0730-2100.

Shopping

Todos Santos Cuchumatán *p326*

The following shops all sell bags, trousers, shirts, *huípiles*, jackets and clothes. Prices have more or less stabilized at the expensive end, but the best bargains can be had at the **Tienda Maribel**, further up the hill from Casa Familiar and at the **Cooperativa Estrella de Occidente**, on the main street. **Casa Mendoza**, just beyond **Tienda Maribel**, is where Telésforo Mendoza makes clothes to measure; a pair of trousers including material costs US$19.50. **Domingo Calmo** also makes clothes to measure, 4-5 hrs; a pair of trousers will cost US$3.90 plus material. His large, brown house with tin roof is on main road up from Casa Familiar to the Ruinas (5 mins); ask for the **Casa de Domingo**. There is also a colourful Sat market and a smaller one on Wed.

Festivals

Todos Santos Cuchumatán *p326*

The festival begins on **21 Oct** but **La Corrida** takes place on **1 Nov** (see p327). 0800-noon and then 1400-1700. In the afternoon, the **Baile de Conquistadores** takes place in front of the church; locals in large masks, representing the Spanish conquerors, bulls and maidens, take it in turns to dance.

2 Nov Day of the Dead. Locals visit the cemetery and leave flowers and food.

Ixil Triangle *p328*

Lent The main festival in **Chajul** takes place on the Fri of the 2nd week. A pilgrimage to Christ of Golgotha also takes place Wed-Fri; the image is escorted by 'Romans' in blue police uniforms.

21-24 Jun fiesta in **Cotzal**, culminating in the day of St John the Baptist on 24 Jun.

12-15 Aug fiesta in **Nebaj**, with traditional dancing.

Activities and tours

Todos Santos Cuchumatán *p326*

Horses can be hired from **Casa Mendoza** for US$2.60 per hr.

Nebaj p328

Gaspar Terraza Ramos guides tourists to all the local places. He usually waits near the bus station or in the plaza and will probably find you. He lost both his parents during the war and fled to Chiapas for 5 years. He can also arrange horse hire.
Guias Ixiles, Felipe and Miguel Brito, El Descanso Restaurant, T5311-9100, contactus@nebaj.com Half- to 3-day hikes, bike rental, new trek to Todos Santos.
Solidaridad Internacional, PRODONT-IXIL office, Av 15 de Septiembre, www.nebaj.org. 2-, 3-and 4-day hikes, horses also available.
Trekking Ixil, T5418-3940, trekkingixil@hotmail.com 1- to 4-day treks, mountain bike rental, horse riding.

Transport

Huehuetenango p, map p

Bus

To **Guatemala City**, 5 hrs, US$3.75, with Los Halcones, 7 Av, 3-62, Zona 1 (not from the terminal) at 0430, 0700, 1400, reliable. Also 12 daily from the bus terminal 0215-1600 via **Chimaltenango**, 5 hrs, US$3.70. To **Todos Santos Cuchumatán**, 0300, 0500, 1200, 1400, 1500, 1600, 2-3 hrs, US$1.25. To **Quetzaltenango**, 13 daily, 0600-1600, US$1.05, 2-2¼ hrs. To **Cuatro Caminos**, US$1, 2 hrs. To **Los Encuentros**, for Lake Atitlán and Chichicastenango, 3 hrs, US$2.60. To **Aguacatán**, for connections to **Sacapulas** and **Nebaj**, 12 daily, 0600-1900, 1 hr 10 mins, US$0.52. To **Sacapulas**, direct 1130 and 1245; note that, although it is still advertised, the 1130 service to Sacapulas no longer runs as far as Nebaj. To **Cobán**, take the earliest bus to Aguacatán, then Sacapulas and continue to Uspantán. To **La Mesilla** for Mexico (see p130), frequent buses 0330-1700, US$1.05, 2½ hrs; last bus returns to Huehue at 1800.

Aguacatán p326

Bus

To **Huehue**, 0445-1600,1 hr 10 mins, US$0.52. Buses to **Sacapulas**, for onward connections to **Nebaj** and **Cobán**, depart 1030-1400, 1½ hrs, US$0.65; after 1400 you will have to rely on pick-ups; all transport to Sacapulas leaves from the main street going out of town; wait anywhere along it to catch your ride. Also buses to **Guatemala City** at 0300, 1100.

Todos Santos Cuchumatán p326

Bus

To **Huehuetenango**, Mon and Fri, 0400, 0500, 0600, 0615-30, 1145, 1230, 1300, 2-3 hrs, crowded. Possible changes on Sat so ask beforehand.

Nebaj p328

Bus

To **Sacapulas**, 9 daily, US$0.80, 1¾ hrs, and on to **Santa Cruz del Quiché**, US$1.30, 3 hrs from Nebaj. Or change in Sacapulas for **Aguacatán** and **Huehuetenango**, US$1.20, 2¼ hrs from Sacapulas. Buses to/from **Chajul** have no schedule; ask at the bus station the day before you want to travel.

Directory

Todos Santos Cuchumatán p326

Bank Banrural no credit cards; TCs and dollars cash only. **Language schools** Hispano Maya, opposite Hotelito Todos Santos, www.personal.umich.edu/~kakenned/ with homestay. Nuevo Amanecer, T308-7416, mitierra @c.net.gt, US$115 with homestay. Proyecto Lingüístico de Español, US$115 with homestay, food reported as basic.

Quetzaltenango and around

Quetzaltenango (known as Xela – pronounced 'shayla') is the most important urban centre in western Guatemala and the country's second city. It is set among a group of high mountains and volcanoes, one of which, Santa María, caused widespread destruction in the area after an eruption in 1902. The city centre has 19th-century buildings and narrow streets surrounding a pleasant park, overlooked by the façade of the colonial cathedral. Xela is an excellent base from which to visit visit nearby hot springs, religious idols, volcanoes and market towns.

Getting there Shuttle/bus from Panajachel and Antigua.
Getting around Bus or minibus tours.
Time required At least 2 days.
Weather Sunny, cold at night.
Sleeping Limited range of standard hotels.
Eating National and international cuisine.
Activities and tours Volcano climbing, thermal baths, markets.
★ **Don't miss...** A trip to Zunil and Fuentes Georginas » *p335*.

Ins and outs

Getting there and around Long distances buses pull into the Zona 3 Minerva Terminal; taxi to the city centre, US$2.60. Leaving Xela, it's often quicker to catch a bus from the *rotonda* rather than making you're way back to the terminal. City buses for the terminal leave from 4 Calle and 13 Avenida, Zona 1; those straight for the *rotonda* leave from 11 Avenida and 10 Calle, Zona 1. A taxi within Zona 1 or from Zona 1 to a closer part of Zona 3 costs US$1.30-2. » *p340* .

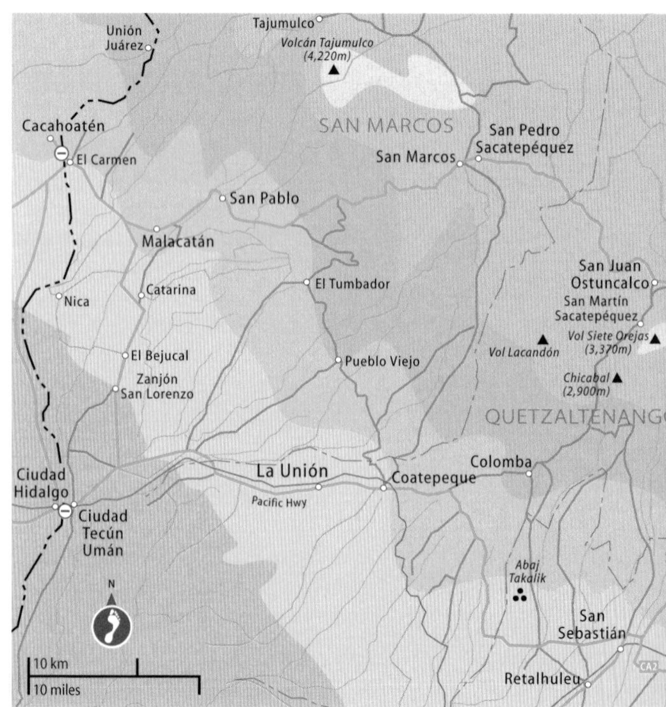

Tourist information INGUAT ⓘ *7 C, 11-35, on the park, T7761-4931, Mon-Fri, 0900-1800, Sat 0900-1300*. General information can also be found at www.xelapages.com.

Background

The most important battle of the Spanish conquest took place near Quetzaltenango, when the great K'iche' warrior Tecún Umán was slain by Pedro de Alvarado on 18 February 1524. In October 1902 Volcán Santa María erupted, showering the city with half a metre of dust. An ash cloud soared 8.6 km into the air and some 1,500 people were killed by volcanic fallout and gas. A new volcano, Santiaguito (page 337), was born from the 1902 eruption and first became dangerously active some 20 years later. Xela's prosperity, evident in the city's grand neoclassical architecture, was built on the back of the success of the coffee *fincas* on the nearby coastal plain.

Sights

The **Parque Centro América**, is the focus of the city. It is surrounded by a number of elegant neoclassical buildings, constructed during the late 19th and early 20th century. The surviving façade of the 1535 **Catedral del Espíritu Santo** is also visible after undergoing restoration since 1996. It is beautiful, intricately carved and has portions of restored murals on its right side. The modern cathedral, **Catedral de la Diócesis de los Altos**, constructed in 1899, is set back behind the original. On the park's south side is the **Museo de Historia Natural** ⓘ *Mon-Fri 0800-1200, 1400-1800, US$0.90*, which houses a morbidly curious collection of deformed stuffed animals, pre-Columbian pottery, sports memorabilia and dinosaur remains. Look out for the sea creature that looks like an alien, known as *Diabillo del Mar* (little sea devil). The neoclassical columns of the **Municipalidad**, built between 1881 and 1897, straddle the eastern edge of the park. Other buildings worth seeing are the stately **Teatro Municipal** (1892-96) on 14 Avenida y 1 Calle, which can be visited outside performance hours and the **Teatro Roma**, to its left, on Avenida 14 "A", which opened in 1931 as the country's first cinema. It was restored in 2000. ⏵⏵ *p339*.

Inside the sickly green, modern church of **Sagrado Corazón**, on Parque Benito Juárez, is a gigantic, free-standing painting, with swooping angels and Christ in a glass box built into the picture. The church of **La Transfiguración**, near the corner of 11 C and 5 Av, Zona 1, contains Central America's largest crucified Christ figure (San Salvador del Mundo) at almost 3 m in height. The city's **cemetery** ⓘ *20 Av y 4 Calle, 0700-1900*, houses the remains of the Quetzalteco President, Estrada Cabrera (1898-1920) in a small cream neoclassical temple. Behind his tomb are the unmarked graves of 19th-century cholera victims. Manuel Lisandra Barillas (Guatemalan President 1885-1892) is also entombed here. There's also a large area for those that died as martyrs in the Civil War and a memorial to those that perished in the September Revolution of 1897.

San Andrés Xecul

North of Quetzaltenango » pp 337-341

Cuatro Caminos is one of the largest transport junctions in the country. All buses stop here for points south to Xela, north to Huehuetenango and Todos Santos, west to the Mexican border and east to Guatemala City. Two kilometres along the highway north of Cuatro Caminos is a paved road to San Francisco El Alto (3 km), continuing to Momostenango (19 km).

Salcajá

The small *ladino* town of Salcajá revolves around textiles; jaspé skirt material has been woven here since 1861. Yarn is tied, dyed and untied, and then wraps are stretched around telephone poles along the road or the riverside. It's also worth a visit for its famous church, built in 1524. **San Jacinto**, 6 Avenida y 2 Calle, is the oldest church in Central America founded by conquering Spaniards; it's a small building, currently undergoing restoration, so it may not always be open. You can see textiles being produced outside the church and there's a workshop that can be visited nearby. *Caldo de frutas*, a highly alcoholic drink is also made in the town and drunk on festive occasions, although it is illegal to sell and drink it in public places. Also look out for *rompope*, a drink made with eggs. Market day is Tuesday.

San Andrés Xecul

Some 8 km north of Xela, San Andrés Xecul is a small village in stunning surroundings with an extraordinarily lurid church. Painted a deep-mustard yellow in 1900, its figurines include angels with blue wings and pastel-pink skirts, and the apostles, sporting blue crowns and blue musical instruments. Columns are entwined in evergreen vines, oodles of plant material sprout out of red vases and, at its peak, jaguars clutch a white pole. Climb the hill above the town to catch a glimpse of the fantastic multi-coloured dome. With your back to the church a cobbled street leads up the right hand side of the plaza to a yellow and maroon chapel peering out across the valley; the view from here is spectacular. There is a small but attractive market on Thursdays opposite the church.

San Francisco El Alto

San Francisco stands high (2,640 m) in the cold mountains above the great valley in which lie Totonicapán, San Cristóbal and Quetzaltenango. It is famous for its bustling Friday market, where locals buy all sorts, including woollen blankets for resale throughout the country. It's an excellent place to purchase woven and embroidered textiles of good quality (beware of pickpockets). Climb up through the town for 10 minutes to see the animal market (ask for directions), where creatures from piglets and calves to kittens and budgies are sold on a small dusty plain. On market days, the magnificent **church** on the main square is often full of locals lighting candles. The white west front of the church complements the bright colours of the rest of the plaza, especially the vivid green and pink of the **Municipalidad**. You can get a good view of the stall-covered plaza on market day by climbing the bandstand in the centre.

Momostenango

Momostenango (2,220 m) represents *Shol Mumus* in K'iche', meaning 'among the hills'. It is set in a valley with ribbons of houses climbing higgledy-piggledy up the hillsides. On the outlying hills are numerous altars and the hilltop image of a Maya god. Stone peaks known as *riscos* (eroded columns of sandstone with embedded quartz particles) can be seen on the outskirts of town. The town is the centre for the weaving of wool blankets in Guatemala, known as *chamarras*. **Artesanía Paclom** at the corner of 1 Calle and 3 Avenida, Zona 2, has weaving looms in the back yard and will give demonstrations. ▸▸ *p340.*

Momostenango still follows the traditional Maya calendar. The feast of **Wajshakib Batz' Oj**, pronounced 'washakip', is celebrated in the town by hundreds of *Aj Kij* (Maya priests), who are initiated for the start of the ritual new year. This event is not open to visitors but you can learn more about Maya culture and cosmology at **Takilibén Maya Misión** ⓘ *3 Avenida, 6-85, Zona 3, T7736-5051, Mon-Fri 0800-1200, 1400-1700*. The Chuch Kajaw (day keeper), Rigoberto Itzep, offers courses and does Maya horoscope readings (US$2.60). He also has a Maya sauna (*tuj*) ⓘ *Tue and Thu 1400-1700, US$6.50*. Some 300 medicine men are said to practise in the town; their insignia of office is a little bag containing beans and quartz crystals.

South of Quetzaltenango ▸▸ *pp 337-341*

Zunil

Some 9 km from Quetzaltenango, pinned in by a steep-sided valley, the town of Zunil is famous for its worship of the well-dressed idol San Simón (**Maximón**; page 312). As well as wearing an array of different costumes – an entire skiing outfit, maybe, or a black suit and wide-brimmed hat, complete with cigar – the Zunil idol also has firewater poured down his throat causing him to 'pee' into a basin below. Enquire locally for his present location.

The **church** is striking, with a large decorated altarpiece and a small shrine to murdered Bishop Gerardi at the altar. The façade is white with serpentine columns wrapped in carved ivy and decorated with large, dangling coloured bulbs. To the left of the church, the **Santa Ana Co-operative** sells beautiful *huípiles*, shirt and skirt materials, as well as bags and bookmarks. A **market** is held on Mondays.

The extinct **Volcán Pico Zunil**, rises to 3,542 m to the southeast of the town. On its slopes are the thermal pools of **Fuentes Georginas** ⓘ *8 km south of Zunil, Mon-Sat 0800-1700, Sun 0800-1600, US$1.30, children US$0.65, pick up truck from village US$9.10 return with 1 hr wait*. Several different-sized pools are set into the mountainside surrounded by thick, luscious vegetation and enveloped in steam. There are spectacular views en route. You can walk to the pools from Zunil in two hours (300 m ascent; take the right fork after 4 km) but take care, as robberies have been reported. If you come by bus to Zunil, get off before town at the Pepsi stand on the main road and walk to the entrance road, 100 m away on the left.

Zunil market

El Viejo Palmar

This is Guatemala's Pompeii. The small town of 10,000 was evacuated following a series of serious lahars (flows of mud, water and volcanic material) from the active **Santiaguito** volcano in the 1990s. Then, in August 1998, the whole south end of the ghost town was destroyed by a massive lahar that crushed the church and shifted the course of the Río Nimá I directly through the centre of the ruins. Very heavy erosion since has left the church's west front and its altar separated by a 30-m deep ravine – an unbelievable sight.

The town is some 4 km from the road. The beginning of the urban zone is marked by a pale green building on the right. Everywhere is overgrown, with homes looking more like greenhouses, although you can still see the school building on one of the streets. Walk further

El Carmen–Talismán

The Mexican border, open 24 hrs, is 18 km west of Malacatán at **El Carmen**, where an international bridge crosses the Río Suchiate to **Talismán** in Mexico. Beyond the bridge the road continues 8 km to Tapachula where it joins Highway 200 west along the Pacific coast. There is a *hospedaje* at the border.

Leaving Guatemala Most long-distance traffic uses the border at Tecún Umán (p288). However there are services to Talismán from Xela and crowded *colectivos* will get you there from Malacatán. It is a 200-m walk between the two border posts. If entering Mexico by car, especially a rented car, be prepared for red tape, miscellaneous charges, vehicle fumigation and frustration. Car papers are issued at the Garita de Aduana on Route 200 out of Tapachula. Photocopies of documents must be made in town; no facilities at the Garita.

Leaving Mexico Exit tax US$0.45. Lots of pushy children offer to help you through border formalities; pay US$2-3 for one, which keeps the others away. The toilet at Mexican immigration is dangerous, with hold-ups reported day and night. Crossing into Guatemala by car can take several hours. If you don't want your car sprayed inside it may cost you a couple of dollars. Do not park in the car park at the control post, as it is very expensive. The nearest **Guatemalan consulate** is in Tapachula, Calle 2 Ote 33 and Av 7 Sur, T626-1252, Mon-Fri 0800-1600.

Exchange Change money in Tapachula rather than with men standing around customs on the Guatemalan side; always check rates before dealing with them, and haggle; there is no bank on the Guatemalan side.

in as far as you can, then bear to the right and you will see the ravine; be very careful at the edge. To cross the ravine, return to the green abandoned building and turn right to reach an Indiana Jones-type wooden bridge, with a scary view of the gorge below.

Volcán Santa María and Santiaguito

Santiaguito (2,488 m), formed after the eruption of Santa María in 1902 (page 333) spews clouds of dust and ash on a daily basis and is considered one of the most dangerous volcanoes in the world. To see it erupting you need to climb Santa María (3,772 m). This is a rough 5½-hour climb (1,500 m) starting from **Llano del Pinal**, 7 km from Xela. Get off the bus at the crossroads and follow the dirt road towards the right side of the volcano; when the road sweeps right (after about 40 mins) take the footpath to the left; bear right at the saddle where another path comes in from the left, but look carefully as it is easily missed. From Santa María you can look down at ash blasts and occasional lava flows from the smaller volcano. It is possible to camp at the summit of Santa María, or on the saddle to the west, but it is cold and windy. The dawn, however, provides views of the country's entire volcanic chain and the almighty shadow cast across the area by Santa Maria's form.

Abaj Takalik

ⓘ *4 km from El Asintal, near Retalhuleu. T614-0606. Daily 0700-1700. US$3.25; volunteer guides welcome tips. Taxi from Reu, US$13 including waiting time or pick-up from El Asintal, US$6.50-7.50 including waiting time.*

One of Guatemala's best ancient sites outside El Petén is Abaj Takalik, a ruined city that lies in sweltering conditions on the southern plain. Its name means 'standing stone' in K'iche'. The site was discovered in 1888 by botanist Doctor Gustav Brühl and is believed to have flourished in the Late Pre-classic period 300 BC to AD 250, when it controlled commerce between the Highlands and the Pacific coast. However, the presence of Olmec-style monuments is evidence that it was first occupied much earlier than this. There are some 239 monuments, including 68 stelae, 32 altars and 71 buildings, all set in peaceful surroundings. The main buildings are only up to 12 m high, suggesting a date before techniques were available to build Tikal-sized structures. Human and animal figures abound: frogs facing east for fertility and birth; jaguar and crocodile facing west towards darkness and the afterlife. The environment is loved by birds and butterflies and by orchids, which flower magnificently between January and March.

Laguna Chicabal

ⓘ *40 min walk from the car park to the lake. Daily 0700-1800. US$1.30. Parking US$1.30; last bus to Quetzaltenango at 1900, 1 hr.* This jelly-green lake lies at 2,712 m in the crater of an eponymous extinct volcano (2,900 m), with wild white lilies, known as *cartucho*, growing at its edges. The Maya believe the waters are sacred and it is thought that if you swim in the lake you will become ill. Ceremonies of Maya initiation, known as **Jueves de la Ascensión**, are held at the lake on rotating annual dates in early May. The two-hour climb to the lake starts at **San Martín Sacatepéquez**, west of Xela. It's possible to camp at the lake and walk around it but start early; the mist rolls down very quickly, obscuring the views. The highlight of a trip is the sight of the clouds tumbling down over the circle of trees that surround the lake and appearing to bounce on the surface of the water before dispersing.

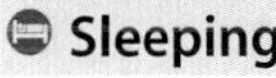

Sleeping

Quetzaltenango *p332, map p339*
At Easter, 12-18 Sep and Christmas, book rooms well in advance.

A **Casa Mañen**, 9a Av, 4-11, Zona 1, T7765-0786, www.comeseeit.com
Consistently good, great breakfasts, friendly, welcoming staff. Room 2 has a bed on a mezzanine. Some rooms have

microwave, fridge and TV. All are comfortable and attractive. Small, pretty courtyard and secure parking.

B **Modelo**, 14 Av "A", 2-31, Zona 1, T7761-2529, www.xelapages.com/ Friendly hotel, 20 rooms with TV, some set around a garden patio. Hot showers, restaurant and bargain breakfasts from 0715. Safe parking. Annexe also available.

B **Villa Real Plaza**, 4 C, 12-22, Zona 1, T7761-4045. Dignified colonial building, 58 rooms with TV. Good-value restaurant serves vegetarian food. Parking available.

D **Casa Kaehler**, 13 Av, 3-33, Zona 1, T761-2091. 6 very nice old rooms, clean, hot water all day in private bathrooms, some rooms are very cold though. Breakfast included.

D **Altense**, 9 C, 8-48, Zona 1, T7765-4648. 16 rooms with bath, hot water, parking, secure and friendly. A good deal for single travellers. Rooms on the 9 Av side are noisy during rush hour.

D **Kiktem-Ja**, 13 Av, 7-18, Zona 1, T7761-4304. Central, 16 colonial-style rooms, nicely furnished, local blankets on the beds, wooden floors, all with bath, hot water, open fires, parking inside gates.

D **Los Olivos**, 13 Av, 3-22, T761-0215, Zona 1. 26 pleasant rooms with private bathroom, TV, and a restaurant with cheap breakfasts and meals for around US$4.

E **Hostal Don Diego**, 7 C, 15-20, Zona 1, T7761-6497, dondiegoxela@hotmail.com Sweet hostel, with an interior courtyard, rooms with shared bathroom. Hot water and breakfast included. Bright and clean. Weekly and monthly rents available.

E-F **Casa Argentina**, Diagonal 12, 8-37, Zona 1, T761-0010, lemovi@yahoo.com 25 clean rooms, hot water, 10 shared bathrooms, cheaper 18-bed dorm, cooking facilities with purified water, friendly, laundry service.

Zunil *p335*

B **Las Cumbres Eco Saunas y Gastronomía**, Km 210 towards the coast, T5399-0029/7767-1746. Daily 0700-1800. Just the place for R&R with saunas emitting natural steam from the geothermal activity nearby. 11 rooms, with sauna (cheaper without), plus separate saunas (US$3.25) and jacuzzis for day visitors. Restaurant serves wholesome regional food and natural juices.

Eating

Quetzaltenango *p332, map p339*

TTT-TT **Cardinali**, 14 Av, 3-25, Zona 1, T7761-0924. Owned by a NY Italian, large pizzas with 31 varieties (2-for-1 Tue and Thu); tasty pastas, extensive wine list. Also delivery in 30 mins.

TTT-TT **Las Calas**, 14 Av "A", 3-21, Zona 1. Breakfasts, salads, soups, paella and pastas served around a courtyard with art on the walls. Tasty but small portions. Breakfast service is very slow. Bar. Closed Sun.

TTT-TT **Restaurante Royal París**, 14 Av "A", 3-06, Zona 1. Delicious food including vegetarian choices. Also cheap options. Live music from 2000 Fri.

TT **Salón Tecún**, Pasaje Enríquez, 12 Av y 4 C, Zona 1. Bar, with local food, breakfasts, TV, popular with gringos and locals.

TT **Ut'z Hua**, Av 12, 3-02, Zona 1. Pretty restaurant with purple tablecloths, typical food, always very good and filling. Don't miss the *pollo con mole*.

Cafés and bakeries

Bakeshop at 18 Av, 1-40, Zona 3. Mennonite bakery. Cookies, muffins, breads and cakes, plus fresh yoghurt and cheeses. Tue and Fri 0900-1800, get there early as all the goodies go really fast.

Café Baviera, 5 C, 13-14, Zona 1. Good cheap meals and excellent pies, huge cakes and coffee, walls lined with old photos and posters. Good for breakfast.

Café y Chocolate La Luna, 8 Av, 4-11, Zona 1. Delicious hot chocolate, good cheap snacks, chocolates and *pasteles*, pleasant atmosphere in a colonial house decorated with moon symbols, fairy lights, and old photos.

Entertainment

Quetzaltenango *p332, map p339*

See also **Salón Tecún**, above.

Casa Verde, 12 Av, 1-40, Zona 1, T7763-0271. The place to be on a Thu night when townsfolk and gringos flock to shake a bit of salsa leg. Plenty of partners to go around. Music, drinking and dancing 2000-0030.

Cinema Paraíso Café, 1 C, 12-20, art house films, some in Spanish only, US$1.30, students US$1.05, café.

Latin Dance School, Casa Verde, (see, above), Mon-Fri 1700-1800 merengue, 1800-1900, salsa, US$3.25 per hr.

Teatro Municipal, 14 Av y 1 C. Theatre, opera, etc May-Nov, tickets US$7.

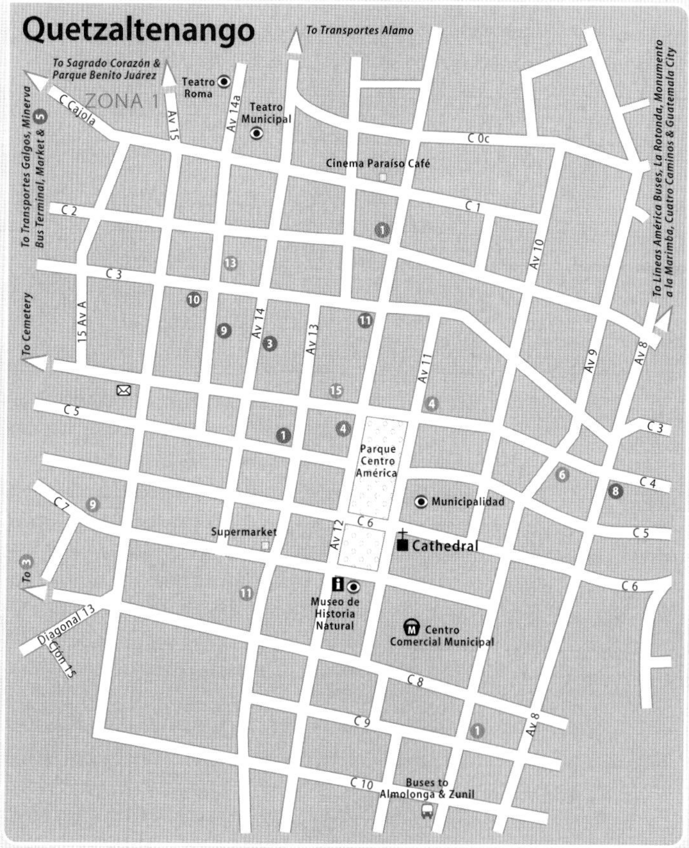

Quetzaltenango

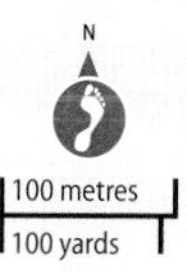

Sleeping

Altense **1**
Bonifaz **4**
Casa Argentina **3**
Casa Mañen **6**
Hostal Don Diego **9**
Kiktem-Ja **11**
Modelo **13**
Villa Real Plaza **15**

Eating

Bakeshop **5**
Baviera **1**
Cardinali **3**
La Luna **8**
Las Calas **9**
Royal Paris **10**
Ut'z Hua **11**

Bars & clubs

Casa Verde **1**
Salón Tecún **4**

Festivals

Quetzaltenango *p332, map p339*
Fiestas are held during Semana Santa, **9-17 Sep** and **Oct** for the Virgen del Rosario.

North of Quetzaltenango *p334*
Fiestas are held in San Andrés Xecul on **21 Nov**, **30 Nov** and **1 Dec**. Also in San Francisco El Alto on **1-6 Oct** in honour of St Francis of Assisi. Momostenango's popular fiesta takes place **21 Jul- 4 Aug**, with the town's patron saint, Santiago Apóstol, celebrated on 25 Jul. The town's elaborate Baile de Convites is held in Dec, with traditional dances on 8, 12 and 31 Dec and 1 Jan.

South of Quetzaltenango *p335*
Zunil fiesta is **22-26 Nov** (main day 25) and there is a very colourful Holy Week.

Shopping

Quetzaltenango *p332, map p339*
At the southeast corner of Parque Centro América is the Centro Comercial Municipal, with craft and textile shops on the upper levels, food, clothes, etc below. Vrisa, 15 Av, 3-64, T7761-3237, has a good range of English language second-hand books and also hires out bikes. The main **market** is at Templo de Minerva at the western edge of town (local bus, US$0.10). There is another at 2 C y 16 Av, Zona 3, south of Parque Benito Juárez, and an *artesanía* market in the central park, with a marimba band on the 1st Sun of each month.

Momostenango *p335*
Markets on Wed and Sun, the latter is good for weaving, especially blankets. On non-market days try Tienda Manuel de Jesús Agancel, 1 Av, 1-50, Zona 4, for good bargains.

Activities and tours

Quetzaltenango *p332, map p339*

Tour operators

Make sure your guides stay with you at all times when ascending the volcanoes.

Adrenalina Tours, Pasaje Enríquez, T7761-4509, www.adrenalinatours.com Numerous tours including bike trips and volcano treks. Also bike hire.

Quetzaltrekkers, Casa Argentina, Diagonal 12, 8-37, T7761-5865, www.quetzaltrekkers.com, www.quetzalventures.com. Non-profit agency, recommended for 3-day hike (Sat-Mon pm) to Lake Atitlán, US$65. Proceeds to the Escuela de la Calle for kids at risk and to a dorm for homeless children. Also 5-day trek from Nebaj to Todos Santos, US$100, and a full-moon hike up Santa María. Also day hikes.

Mayaexplor, 1 Av "A", 6-69, Zona 1, T7761-5057, www.mayaexplor.com. Day trips, longer tours and treks with advance notice.

Transport

Quetzaltenango *p332, map p339*

Bus

Local City buses run 0630-1900. Between the town centre and Minerva terminal, bus No 6, Santa Fe, from the corner of 4 C and 13 Av by Pasaje Enríquez, US$0.10, 15-30 mins, depending on traffic. Buses to the Rotonda leave from the corner of 11 Av and 10 C, US$0.10, or catch bus No 6, 10 or 13, from Av 12 y 3 C. To **San Francisco El Alto**, **Momostenango**, **Zunil** (US$0.20) and the **south coast**, get off the local bus at the Rotonda, then walk a few steps into a feeder road where all the buses line up.

All buses to Cuatro Caminos go through **Salcajá**, 10 mins, and pass the turning to **San Andrés Xecul**, from where there are pick-ups to the village, US$0.65. Also direct to **San Andrés Xecul**, US$0.22, 30 mins. To **San Francisco El Alto**, 50 mins, US$0.33; last bus back 1800.

Long distance To **Guatemala City**, Galgos, C Rodolfo Robles, 17-43, Zona 1,

T7761-2248, 1st-class buses, 5-7 a day from 0300-1615, US$3.90, 4 hrs, will carry bicycles (mixed reports); **Marquensita** several a day, from the Minerva Terminal, US$3.90, comfortable, 4 hrs. **Transportes Alamo** from 4 C, 14-04, Zona 3, T7767-7117, 0430-1430, 5 daily, US$3.90, 4 hrs. For **Antigua**, change at **Chimaltenango** (Galgos, US$2 to Chimaltenango, **Marquensita**, US$2.90).

The following destinations are served by buses from the Minerva Terminal, Zona 3 and the Rotonda. To **Chichicastenango**, **Transportes Veloz Quichelense de Hilda Esperanza**, at 0500, 0600, 0930, 1045, 1100, 1300, 1400, 1530, US$1.05, 2½ hrs. To **Cuatro Caminos**, US$0.20, 30 mins. To **La Mesilla** (p130) 0500, 0600, 0700, 0800, 1300, 1400, with **Transportes Unión Fronteriza**, US$1.60, 4 hrs. To **Llano del Pinal** (for Volcán Santa María), every 30 mins; last bus back 1800. To **Momostenango**, every 30 mins, US$0.52, 1½ hrs. To **Panajachel**, with **Transportes Morales**, 0500, 0600, 0800, 1100, 1200, 1500, US$1.40, 2½-3 hrs. To **Retalhuleu** (for Abaj Takalik, the Pacific Highway and the Mexican border), every hr, 1½ hours, US$0.78. To **San Marcos**, every 30 mins, US$0.78, 1 hr. To **San Martín Sacatepéquez** (San Martín Chile Verde), US$0.40, 1 hr. To **Santiago Atitlán**, with **Ninfa de Atitlán**, 0800, 1100, 1230, 1430, 4½ hrs. To **Zunil**, every 30 mins, US$0.26, 20-30 mins.

To Mexico From Quetzaltenango, there are frequent buses to **Talismán** (p336) via either San Marcos (slow highland route with spectacular scenery) or Coatepeque on the Pacific Highway, usually with a change in **Malacatán**, 40 mins from the border. Or, take a frequent bus to **Retalhuleu** (see above), from where there are regular connections to **Tecún Umán** (p288) and Talismán.

Taxi

Taxis can be found all over town, US$2.60. Round trip to **El Viejo Palmar**, US$20. **Taxis Xelaju**, T7761-4456.

Momostenango *p335*

Bus

To **Cuatro Caminos**, US$0.40, and **Quetzaltenango**, US$0.52, 1½ hrs, every 30 mins, 0430-1600.

Directory

Quetzaltenango *p332, map p339*

Banks Many on Parque Centro América. **Bancared**, 24 hr Visa ATM on the park next to **Banrural**. **Banco Industrial**, corner of 5 C y 11 Av, 24 hr Visa ATM, Visa accepted. **G&T Continental**, 14 Av, 3-17, up to US$65 on MasterCard. **Emergencies** Police T7761-5805; **Fire** T7761-2002; **Red Cross** T7761-2746. **Hospitals** Hospital Rodolfo Robles, private hospital on Diagonal 11, Zona 1, T7761-4229. **Internet** Internet, 15 Av, 3-51, international phone calls also. **Maya Communications**, inside Bar Salón Tecún, phone service. **Language schools** In addition to Spanish tuition, many schools offer homestays, activities, Maya languages and community projects, US$100-150 per week. Refer to **www.xelapages.com/schools.htm** and enquire carefully about non-profit status. **Centro de Estudios de Español Pop Wuj**, 1 C, 17-72, T7761-8286, www.pop-wuj.org; **INEPAS**, 15 Av, 4-59, T7765-1308, www.inepas.org, emphasis on social projects, extremely welcoming; **International Language School English Club**, Diagonal 4, 9-71, Zona 9, T7767-3506, Harry Danvers is an expert on indigenous culture, you can also learn K'iche' and Mam; **Kie-Balam**, Diagonal 12, 4-46, Zona 1, T7761-1636, www.xelapages.com/kiebalam; **Proyecto Lingüístico Quetzalteco de Español**, 5 C, 2-40, Zona 1, T/F7763-1061, www.hermandad.com; **Sakribal**, 6 C, 7-42, Zona 1, T7763-0717, www.sakribal.com, community projects available. **Laundry** Minimax, 14 Av, C-47, US$2.60. **Post office** 15 Av y 4 C. **Telephone** Telgua, 15 Av "A" y 4 C. **Voluntary work** Entre mundos, T7761-2179, www.entremundos.org puts people in touch with opportunities.

Eastern Guatemala & El Petén

Ocellated turkey, Tikal

MEXICO
GUATEMALA
BELIZE
HONDURAS
EL SALVADOR
Pacific Ocean
p366
p359
p346
Polboxal
Mamantel
Libertad
Dzinapara
Conhuas
Becán
Xpujil
Los Laureles
Caobas
Sergio Butrón
Xulhá
Desecho
San Agustín del Palmar
Haro
Hormiguero
Casas Palmar
Kohunlich
Luna
Selva Negra
Narciso Mendoza
Candelaria
Concepción
Esperanza
Calakmul
Reserva de la Biosfera Calakmol
El Tesoro
Tres Garantías
Cacao
Noh Mul
Orange
Cuello
Carmelita
Cuauhtémoc
San Juan
El Naranjo
Nuevo Coahuila
Playa Bonita
Alacranes
El Piche
San Miguel
El Gallinero
La Unión
La Milpa
Lamanai
Altun Ha
Paxbán
Dos Lagunas
ORANGE WALK
El Coco
Reserva de la Biosfera Maya
La Florida
Carmelita
Los Cuyos
Tenosique
Cenoti Camp
Ceiba
Uaxactún
Yalbac Camp
Benito Juárez
El Zotz
BELMOPAN
El Naranjo
San Pedro
El Perú
Paso Caballos
Tikal
Nakum
Georgeville
Blue Hole National Park
Gales Point
Piedras Negras
Cruce dos Aguadas
Parque Nacional Tikal
Yaxhá & Topoxte
San Ignacio
Middlesex
PETÉN
Motul
Biotopo Cerro Cahuí
Laguna Yaxhá
San Antonio
Usumacinta
Lago Petén Itzá
El Remate
Melchor de Mencos
Augustine
Cintalapa
San José
San Andrés
Flores
San Benito
Santa Elena
CAYO
STANN CREEK
Yaxchilán
San Javier
Bethel
Las Cruces
Frontera Echeverría
La Libertad
Santa Ana Vieja
Caracol
Riverside
Lacanjá
Bonampak
Cockscomb Basin Wildlife Sanctuary
La Puente
Maya Mountains
El Subín
Boca Locantún
Altar de los Sacrificios
Sayaxché
Benemérito
Dos Pilas
El Ceibal
Dolores
Medina Bank
Independence
Amador Hernadez
Pipiles
Laguna Petexbatún
Chiringuicharo
Aguateca
TOLEDO
Poptún
Lubaantun
Big Falls
Pico de Oro
San Luis
Santa Theresa
Toledo
Punta Gorda
Río Salinas
Monte Flor
Chajul
Flor de Cacao
Pusilhá
Barranco
Gulf of Honduras
Agua Negra
Chalcaté
Dolores
Bahía de Amatique
Santa Rosa
Yalchactí
ALTA VERAPAZ
Livingston
Barillas
Biotopo Chocón Machacas
Puerto Barrios
Xexán
Parque Nacional Grutas de Lanquín
Sierra de Chamá
Sierra de Santa Cruz
Río Dulce
Santo Tomás de Castilla
El Cinchado
El Golfete
QUICHÉ
Castillo San Felipe
Lanquín
Finca El Paraíso
Cobán
San Juan Chamelco
El Estor
Lago de Izabal
Santa Cruz Verapaz
Monumento Natural Semuc Champey
Senahú
Mariscos
Bananera/ Morales
Nebaj
Cotzal
Cunén
Refugio de Vida Silvestre Bocas del Polochic
Tucurú
San Cristóbal Verapaz
Tactic
Quiriguá
Sacapulas
Chimul
La Estanzuela
Reserva de la Biosfera Sierra de las Minas
Biotopo del Quetzal
Atlantic Hwy
Momostenango
Cubulco
ZACAPA
Rabinal
Salamá
San Agustín Acasaguastlán
Chichicastenango
BAJA VERAPAZ
Zacapa
El Rancho Junction
Copán Ruinas
El Cuchillo
Mixco Viejo
EL PROGRESO
El Florido
Copán
Sololá
Chiquimula
Iximiché
GUATEMALA CITY
CHIQUIMULA
Lake Atitlán
Jalapa
Los Mixcos
JALAPA
San Lucas Tolimán
Chimaltenango
Esquipulas
Volcán Acatenango
Antigua
San José Pinula
Monjas
Amatillo
El Baúl
Santa María de Jesús
Santa Lucía Cotzumalguapa
Bilbao
Carrizal
Asunción Mita
Escuintla
Pan-American Hwy
Jutiapa
Siquinalá
ESCUINTLA
Pacific Hwy
Cuilapa
El Amate
Jalpatagua
Chiquimulilla
Texcuaco
La Democracia
Nancinta
Taxisco
La Laguna
Otacingo
Papaturro
El Obraje
Puerto San José
Monterrico
Garita Chapina
CA1
CA2
CA9
N
30 km
30 miles
Don't miss...
1 A boat trip up the Río Dulce ▶▶ p351.
2 Semuc Champey ▶▶ p362
3 El Remate on Lago Petén Itzá ▶▶ p268.
4 Tikal ▶▶ p369.
5 Caving at Finca Ixobel ▶▶ p3

Introduction

On Guatemala's eastern coast, coconut palms, waterfalls and leaning wooden buildings provide a border to the warm waters of the Caribbean. This is the home of the Garífuna, originally ship-wrecked slaves, whose rich culture of language, music and dance is quite different from that found in the rest of the country.

Inland, water has carved its way through the landscape, inviting spelunking, swimming and sailing. Along the Río Dulce, plants plunge down a gorge into the glassy waters below; at Semuc Champey nature has created a limestone and liquid wonder of spa-like pools and throughout the Verapaces caves are riddled with stalactites and stalagmites.

Deep in the tropical jungles of El Petén, lost cities of the Maya were buried, smothered by centuries of vine and vegetation. Early explorers stumbled upon temples, stelae, pyramids and plazas. Later evidence of human sacrifice, self-mutilation, and astronomical genius was found. At first there was little clue as to the nature of the original inhabitants or why they had left their grandiose homes, but with the passing of time the jungle's fingerprints have been read, revealing the dynastic history and traditions of the mysterious Maya.

Ratings

Landscape
★★★★★

Chillin'
★★★★★

Activities
★★★★★

Culture
★★★★★

Wildlife
★★★★★

Costs
$$$-$$

Towards the Caribbean

From the capital to the Caribbean the Atlantic Highway passes through the Río Motagua Valley, punctuated by cacti, with the Sierra de Las Minas mountains rising abruptly in the west. The Black Christ of Esquipulas and the Maya ruins of Quiriguá can be found on or close to the highway. Copán in Honduras is also accessible from here. On the coast, the banana port of Puerto Barrios, is the jumping off point for the Garífuna town of Lívingston and for trips down the lush gorge of the Río Dulce. There are some great places to see and stay along the banks of the river and on the shores of Lago de Izabal.

Getting there Bus and boat.
Getting around Bus and boat.
Time required 3-4 days.
Weather Hot and humid with rainfall possible Sep-Jun, close to the Caribbean.
Sleeping Top Caribbean hotels and budget hangouts.
Eating Range of cuisine, much of it infused with Caribbean flavours.
Activities and tours River trips, sailing.
★ **Don't miss...** Boat trip up the Río Dulce ›› *p351*.

Ins and outs

Getting there The Carretera al Atlántico (Atlantic Highway), stretches from Guatemala City all the way to Puerto Barrios on the Caribbean Coast. Most of the worthwhile places to visit are off this fast main road, which is served by numerous buses. From Puerto Barrios, regular fast *lanchas* depart for Livingston, 23 km away by sea (35 minutes). ›› *p356*.

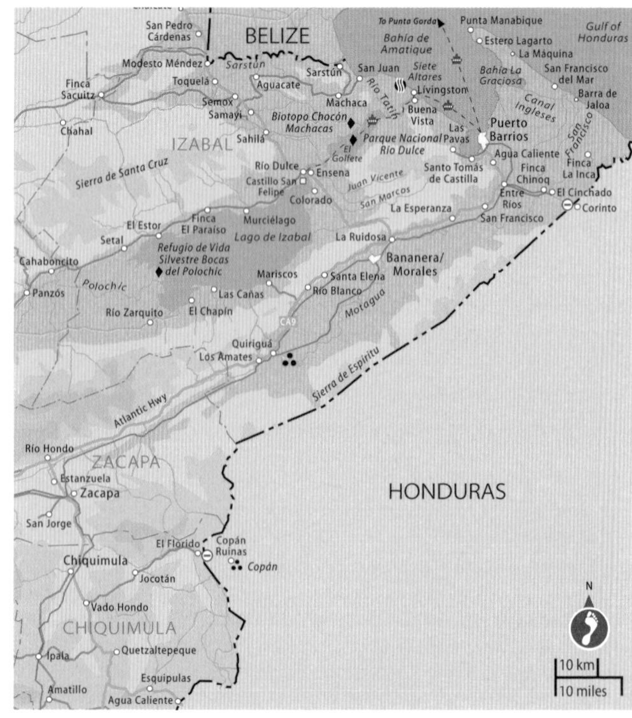

South to Honduras » pp353-358

Chiquimula

Just before Río Hondo (Km 138), a paved road turns south off the Atlantic Highway via Estanzuela and Zacapa to **Chiquimula**. This pleasant town is a popular stop-off point to or from Copán Ruinas, for those travellers who can't make the connection in one day.

Esquipulas

Southeast of Chiquimula, near the Honduras border at Agua Caliente, is the pilgrimage town of Esquipulas. It is dominated by a large, white basilica, which houses an image of a Black Christ (*Cristo Negro*) on a gold cross, elaborately engraved with vines and grapes. The image was carved by Quirio Cataño in dark balsam wood in 1595 and attracts over one million pilgrims per year from all over Central America; some crawl on their hands and knees to pay homage. The main pilgrimage times are 1-15 January (with 15 January being the busiest day), during Lent, Holy Week and 21-27 July.

The history of the famous Black Christ records that in 1735 Father Pedro Pardo de Figueroa, suffering from an incurable chronic illness, stood in front of the image to pray, and was cured. A few years later, after becoming Archbishop of Guatemala, he ordered a new church to be built to house the sculpture. The basilica was completed in 1758 and the *Cristo Negro* was transferred from the parish church shortly after that.

The town has pulled out the stops for visitors, who, as well as a religious fill, will lack nothing in the way of food, drink, candles, relics, mementoes, not to mention some of the best kitsch souvenirs on the market. A mirador 1 km from the town affords a spectacular view of the basilica, which sits at the end of the main avenue.

El Florido-Copán

At Vado Hondo, 10 km south of Chiquimula, a smooth dirt road branches east to the Honduran border at El Florido, passing through an impressive landscape of green hills and rivers. Copán Ruínas village and the Maya site are 11 km beyond the border. The border is open 0700-1900.

Leaving Guatemala If you are going to Copán for a short visit, the Guatemalan official will give you a 72-hour pass, stapled into your passport. Guatemalan exit fee, US$1.30. Honduran immigration is at El Florido on the border. Honduran entry fee, US$1.50. Nationals of the UK, USA and many other countries do not require a visa for Honduras; if in doubt ask at the consulate office at Hotel Payaquí, Esquipulas. Travel agents in Antigua do a 1-day trip in minibuses for about US$35 per person to US$125 including an overnight stop. » p356.

Leaving Honduras Exit fee of US$0.75. Ask for a receipt for any 'extra' charges. Pick-up trucks run every day when full until 1700 between Copán Ruinas and the border, connecting with buses to Guatemalan destinations, 30 mins, about US$2.50 but bargain for a fair price. They leave from one block west of the park, near the police station. From the border there are buses to Chiquimula at 0530, 0630 and then hourly 0700-1700, and also to Guatemala City and Antigua. There's also a direct minibus to Antigua, run by **Monarcas Travel**, next to Posada del Annie, in Copán, US$29 one way, 1500 daily, pick-up from hotels.

Exchange Many money changers at the border but you'll get better rates for US$ or TCs in Copán itself.

Copán archaeological site

ⓘ *1 km from Copán Ruinas village, www.copanhonduras.org. Site and museum daily 0800-1600; sendero natural daily 0800-1700; get to the ruins early or stay late so you have a chance to be there without hordes of people. US$10 site, US$5 museum, US$12 tunnels. Copán Guide Association tours (kiosk in the car park), US$20, 2 hrs, recommended. Spanish/English guide book for the ruins, which is rather generalized. Luggage can be left for no charge.* p347.

The magnificent ruins at Copán are one of Central America's major Maya sites and mark the southeastern limit of Maya dominance. Copán flourished as a city state from the fifth century AD onwards, with much of the building work taking place in the eighth century under the ruler, Smoke Shell. The last stela was put up in Copán between AD 800 and 820, after less than five centuries of civilized existence. When the British explorers Stephens and Catherwood discovered the ruins in 1839, they were engulfed in jungle. In the 1930s the Carnegie Institute cleared the ground and, since then, the ruins have been maintained by the government. The nearby river has been diverted to prevent it encroaching on the site.

Museo de Escultura Maya and Sendero Natural

At the entrance is a visitors' centre and an impressive two-storey museum, which houses the excavated carvings and stelae, with good explanations in Spanish and English. In the middle of the museum is an open-air courtyard with a full-size reproduction of the Rosalila temple, found buried under Temple 16 (see below). A reproduction of the doorway to Temple 16 is on the upper floor. Over 2,000 other objects found at Copán are also in the museum, making it an essential stop before you tackle the ruins. A *sendero natural* (nature trail) leads south of the museum through the jungle to a minor ball court. The trail takes 30 minutes and has a few signposts explaining the plants, animals and spirituality of the forest to the Maya. Visit after 1600 to see animals on the trail; take mosquito repellent.

The site

Some of the most complex carvings at Copán are found on the 21 stelae, 3-m columns of stones, in the main plaza. The stelae are believed to record the passage of time and are deeply incised with carved faces, figures and animals; there are royal portraits and inscriptions recording deeds and lineage, as well as dates of birth, marriage and death.

South of the main plaza is a ball court and a pyramid scaled on one side by the **Hieroglyphic Stairway**, the highlight of the site. The stairway is decorated with thousands of glyphs telling the story of the royal dynasty of Copán. It is covered for protection, but a good view can be gained from the foot of the pyramid and there is access to the top via the adjacent plaza.

Excavations at the site have revealed layers of earlier buildings underneath the surface of the site, including the **Rosalila Temple** under Temple 16, which was discovered with its original paint and carvings intact. The Rosalila excavation tunnel and the much longer **Jaguar** tunnel can be explored for an extra fee; worth it as long as you're not claustrophobic.

The ruins at Copán extend far beyond the main site. One kilometre away is the beautifully excavated residential area of **Las Sepulturas**, where ceramics dating back to 1000 BC have been found, while 4 km from the principle ruins is **Los Sapos**, a Pre-classic site with stone carvings.

Copán Ruínas

Although this town thrives and survives on visitors passing through to visit the ruins, it is arguably the best preserved and most charming town in Honduras. If you have enough time, stay the night here rather than visiting the ruins in a day.

B **Camino Maya**, T+504 651-4646, hcmaya@david.intertel.hn. With bath, good restaurant, rooms bright and airy, fans, rooms on courtyard quieter than street, English spoken, patio garden.

B **Hacienda San Lucas**, south out of town, T+504 651-4106, www.haciendasanlucas.com No electricity and much better for it! Great spot for calm and tranquillity. 2 rooms with private hot water bath, restaurant, lovely views of Copán River and hiking trails.

B **La Casa de Café**, T+504 651-4620, www.casadecafecopan.com, casacafe@hondutel.hn Renovated colonial home, with beautifully designed garden and lovely views, breakfast, coffee all day, library, good information, friendly and interesting hosts, English spoken, very popular so best to reserve in advance, protected parking.

D-E **Café ViaVia Copán**, T+504 651-4652, www.viaviacafe.com Great rooms, special price for students with card and discounts for more than one night, hot water, good beds, bar and great vegetarian food.

Towards the coast » pp353-358

Quiriguá

ⓘ Reached by a dirt road from the Atlantic Highway, 3 km from Quiriguá village. Daily 0730-1630, US$3.25. Take insect repellent. Toilets and café on site; store your luggage with the guards. No accommodation at the site, but you can camp.

The remarkable Late Classic ruins of Quiriguá cover a small area but include the tallest stelae found in the Maya world. The UNESCO World Heritage Site includes an excavated acropolis but the highlights are the ornately carved stelae and the zoomorphic altars.

It is believed that Quiriguá was inhabited from the second century AD as a ceremonial centre and an important trading post between Tikal and Copán. The earliest recorded monument dates from AD 480. The rulers of Quiriguá were involved in the rivalries, wars and changing alliances between Tikal, Copán and Calakmul. The most important Quiriguá ruler was Cauac Sky, who ascended to the throne in AD 724 having been appointed by 18 Rabbit, the powerful ruler of Copán. In AD 738 Quiriguá attacked Copán and captured 18 Rabbit, beheading the Copán King in the plaza at Quiriguá as a sacrifice (the scene is depicted on one of the stelae here). Following this victory, Quiriguá became an independent kingdom and gained control of the Motagua Valley. From AD 751 to 806, the time of greatest prosperity, a monument was carved and erected at Quiriguá every five years.

The tallest stelae at the site is Stelae E, which is 10.66 m high with another 2.5 m or so buried beneath. It is 1.52 m wide and weighs 65 tonnes. One of its dates corresponds with the enthronement of Cauac Sky but it is thought to date from AD 771. Some monuments are carved in the shape of animals, some mythical and all of symbolic importance to the Maya.

Puerto Barrios

Puerto Barrios, on the Caribbean coast, is a hot and dusty port town, still an important banana exporter, but now largely superceded as a port by Santo Tomás around the bay. Although it's not an unpleasant town, Puerto Barrios is not a destination in itself, but rather a launch pad to more beautiful spots, including the Garífuna town of Lívingston, up the coast. Boats to Lívingston leave from the municipal dock. Note that the sea can get rough in the afternoons.

Entre Ríos-Corinto

The Honduras border is southeast of Puerto Barrios, near Entre Ríos, marked by a new bridge over the Río Motagua. Guatemalan immigration is just before the bridge in El Cinchado. Honduran immigration is in Corinto, 30 minutes beyond the border, via a rough track. For most travellers, the direct boat services from Puerto Barrios to Puerto Cortes are more convenient than this land crossing. » p357.

Leaving Guatemala If you need a visa for Honduras, you must obtain it in Guatemala City or Esquipulas. There is no entry tax at this border. From the border there are pick ups to Tegucigalpita. From Corinto there are regular buses to Tegucigalpita and connections to Omoa (US$0.40, 1¼ hrs) and Puerto Cortes (US$0.80, 2 hrs). Do not leave Puerto Barrios later than 0800 for this crossing in order to pick up connections; in the rainy season, start even earlier.

Leaving Honduras Get your exit stamp at immigration in Corinto. The nearest Guatemalan consulate is in San Pedro Sula.

Exchange There is a handful of moneychangers at the border. More extensive banking and exchange services are available in Puerto Barrios and Puerto Cortes.

Laid-back Lívingston

Lívingston and around ›› pp353-358

Located 23 km by sea from Puerto Barrios, Lívingston (or La Buga) is populated mostly by Garífuna (page 259), who bring a colourful flavour to this corner of the country. With its tropical sounds and smells, it is quite unlike the rest of Guatemala and is a good place to hang out for a few days, sitting on the dock of the bay, or larging it up with the locals, punta-style.

The town is the centre of fishing and shrimping in the Bay of Amatique and is only accessible by boat. From the dock at the mouth of the Río Dulce estuary, the town spreads northeast up a small steep slope and east along the river estuary; everything is within walking distance. Food and locally made jewellery are sold in the streets. To gain a better understanding of Garífuna culture, visit the town's **Centro Cultural Garífuna-Q'eqchi'**, perched on a hillock with the best views in the whole of Lívingston. At the other side of town is the **Asociación Garífuna Guatemalteca Büdürü-Ogagua**, ⓘ *T7947-0105, 0800-1200, 1400-2000*, which focuses on dance, music, *artesanía*, food and ecotourism.

The Caribbean beach is pretty dirty nearer the river estuary but a little further up the coast, it is cleaner, with palm trees, accommodation, plus a couple of bars and weekend beach discos. Six kilometres north along the coast is **Siete Altares**, a set of small waterfalls and pools hidden in the greenery that are great for alfresco bathing.

Up the Río Dulce

For one of the best trips in Guatemala take a boat up the **Río Dulce** through the sheer-sided canyon towards Lago de Izabel. Trees and vegetation cling to the canyon walls, their roots plunging into the waters for a long drink below. The scenery here is gorgeous, especially in the mornings, when the waters are unshaken. Tours can be arranged from Lívingston for US$9, see under Tour operators below, or from the dock at Río Dulce. You can also paddle up the Río Dulce gorge on *cayucos*, which can be hired from some of the hotels in Lívingston.

Travellers' tales

Garífuna Day

The boat from Puerto Barrios scudded across the water, as pelicans dive-bombed into the sea all around and cormorants hung their out wings to to dry on the mangrove-lined shore. The dock at Lívingston was busy with offers of boat trips and accommodation but we struck up the hill to Hotel Río Dulce, a clapboard building with a large balcony sweeping around the upper storey, where we chilled out on hammocks and watched the world go by. The street was lively with gaggles of small children, old men on bicycles and huge women in vivid dresses and large hats laughing and scolding at everyone in sight. We'd arrived on Garífuna Day so there was a party atmosphere in the air. Under a large orange tent, advertising 'Crush', everyone shimmied and jived to the *punta* beat: old ladies with enormous bottoms wiggled unashamedly, girls and boys gyrated with unnerving assurance, while a handful of embarrassed gringos tried their best to feel the rhythm. Gallo bottles were strewn everywhere and drunkenness had already got the better of several people but the atmosphere was good natured and thoroughly infectious. *Sophie Jones*

On the northern shore of **El Golfete**, where the river broadens out, is the **Biotopo Chocón Machacas** ⓘ *half way between Río Dulce town and Lívingston, 0700-1600, US$2.60*, a mangrove zone administered by CECON, where the elusive **manatee** (sea cow) hangs out. The adult manatee can measure up to 4 m long and can weigh over 450 kg. It eats for six to eight hours daily and can consume more than 10% of its body weight in 24-hours. However, you are unlikely to see one munching his way across the lake bottom, as they are very shy and retreat at the sound of a boat motor. Within the 6,245 ha reserve are carpets of water lilies, dragonflies, blue morpho butterflies, pelicans and cormorants. On land spot army ants, crabs, mahogany trees and the *labios rojos* ('hot lips') flower. Four Q'eqchi' communities of 400 people also live here.

Proyecto Ak' Tenamit ⓘ *T5908-3392, www.aktenamit.org* (meaning 'new village' in Q'eqchi'), is 15 minutes upriver from Lívingston in a lovely spot. It was set up to help 7,000 Q'eqchi' Maya displaced by the civil war. There is a shop selling hand-made crafts.

Lago de Izabal ▸▸ pp353-358

This lake is the largest in Guatemala at 717 sq km. At its eastern end is the town of Río Dulce and the Castillo de San Felipe; on the northern shore is the town of El Estor, and on the southern shore the smaller town of Mariscos. This area can be wet in the rainy season, but there's usually a lull in the weather in July, known as the *canícula*.

Río Dulce and around

The town of Fronteras, better known as **Río Dulce**, sits at the narrow neck of Lago de Izabal, 23 km upstream from Lívingston. It is easily accessible from Puerto Barrios by road and is the last major stop before travelling north into El Petén. It's also a good place to collect information about the area stretching from El Estor to Lívingston, www.mayaparadise.com. Before you hurry on, however, allow yourself to relax here for a few days: laze on a boat for the afternoon, walk in the nearby jungle, or eat and drink at one of several dockside restaurants.

Castillo de San Felipe

Two kilometres upstream (or a 5-km walk) is the old Spanish fort of **Castillo de San Felipe** ⓘ *0800-1700, US$1.30, boat or camioneta from Río Dulce*. The fortification was first built in 1643 to defend the coast against attacks from pirates.

El Estor and around

El Estor enjoys one of the most beautiful vistas in Guatemala. It is strung along the northwest shore of Lago de Izabal, backed by the Santa Cruz mountain range, and facing the Sierra de las Minas. It is so relaxed that young guys bicycle right through the doors of some restaurants screeching to a halt at the bar, and local men sell freshly plucked strawberries. The town dates back to the 19th century, when a Briton and a Dutchman used to run 'a store' at this spot (hence 'el estor'), supply Europeans living in the region with their provisions. The shop is now the **Hotel Vista al Lago**.

You can hire a boat from Río Dulce to El Estor for about US$60, passing near the hot waterfall, inland at **Finca El Paraíso**, which can be reached by a good trail in about 40 minutes. It is a delightful place to swim, and the hot water has eroded the rock behind it into an interesting sculpture. Beyond, the Sauce River cuts through the impressive **Cañon El Boquerón**, where you can enjoy an exhilarating swim with the current all the way down the canyon. There's lots of *barba de viejo* (old man's beard) hanging down, strange rock formations, and otters and troops of howler monkeys whooping about. One of the locals will paddle you upstream for about 800 m, US$0.65. Exploring the **Río Zarco**, closer to El Estor, also makes for a good trip, with cold swimming.

South of El Estor on the western shores of the lake is the **Refugio de Vida Silvestre Bocas del Polochic**. This 23,000-ha protected area shelters howler monkeys, over 350 bird species, iguanas and turtles; there's also the chance of sighting crocodiles and manatees.

Sleeping

Esquipulas *p347*

There are plenty of hotels, *hospedajes* and *comedores* all over town, especially in and around 11 C, also known as Doble Vía Quirio Cataño. Prices tend to rise for the Jan feast day, Easter and at weekends.

A Hotel Chortí, on the outskirts of town at Km 222, T7943-1148. 20 rooms with a/c, TV, phone and *frigobar*. There are 2 pools, a restaurant and bar.

D Los Angeles, 2 Av, 11-94, T7943-1254, spotless rooms with bath, TV and fans, parking, friendly service.

D Payaquí, 2 Av, 11-26, T7943-1143. The 40 pleasant rooms, with *frigobars* full of beer, hot showers, swimming pool, parking, restaurant, bar; credit cards, Honduran lempiras and US$ accepted.

Quiriguá p350

D-E **Hotel y Cafetería Edén**, Quiriguá village, T7947-3281. Helpful, clean, cheaper without bath, basement rooms are dark.
E **Hotel Restaurante Santa Mónica**, Los Amates, 2 km south of Quiriguá village on the highway, T7946-3602. 25 rooms, all with bath, TV and fan, restaurant, pool, internet. Convenient if you don't want to walk the 10-15 mins into Quiriguá village for the 2 hotels there. There are a couple of shops, banks, and *comedores* here.

Lívingston p351

C-E **Hospedaje Doña Alida**, 150 m to the right of the main street, T7947-0027. Guesthouse and restaurant in a quiet location with direct access to the beach. Best rooms have sea views and balconies.
D **Casa Rosada**, on the waterfront, 600 m from the dock, T7947-0303, info@hotelcasarosada.com. 10 bungalows with attractive hand-painted furniture. Also a large, uncrowded dorm, overlooking the bay. Daily set meals. Often full, so reservations are advisable.
D-E **Ríos Tropicales**, T7947-0158. 8 rooms, with fans, funky mirror frames and terracotta-tiled floors, 2 with private bath, plus a laundry, book exchange and an 8% discount on meals at McTropic.
E **Garífuna**, T7947-0183. 10 comfortable, ultra-clean rooms with private bath, laundry.
E **Hotel Río Dulce**, T7947-0764. 19th-century wooden building on the main street, with a seriously sloping balcony on the first floor – a good place to watch the world pass by. Try to get a room upstairs. Also a restaurant on the ground floor with tables on the street.
E **Waba**, barrio Pueblo Nuevo, T7947-0193. Run by a friendly family, upstairs rooms with private bath, balcony and sea views. Clean and cool, with fan. *Comida típica* served at the wooden restaurant (0700-2130) on site. Good value and recommended.

Up the Río Dulce p351

E-F **Finca Tatin**, Río Tatin tributary, *lancha* from Lívingston US$5.20, T5902-0831, www.fincatatin.centroamerica.com. B&B, rooms with private bath or dorm beds. Spanish classes (20 hrs) plus lodging US$120 a week. Great dock space to hang out on.

Fronteras/Río Dulce p352

A **Catamaran Island Hotel**, 10 mins by *lancha* from Río Dulce (US$6.50) or call for a pick up, T7930-5494, www.catamaranisland.com Finely decorated cabañas set on the lake edge, an inviting pool, large restaurant with good food. Recommended.
A-F **Hacienda Tijax**, 2 mins by *lancha* from the dock, T7930-5505, www.tijax.com. Tranquil and beautiful site with jungle lodges, other simpler accommodation and camping facilities. Also jungle trail, rubber plantation, bird sanctuary, pool with whirlpool and jacuzzi, natural pools to swim in, horse riding, rowboat hire. Afternoon sailing until sunset, US$25, and water skiing. Excellent food in the riverside restaurant. The Lívingston *lancha* will pass by here if you pre-arrange at reception. Highly recommended.
C-F **Bruno's**, on the lake, near where the buses stop, T7930-5174, www.mayaparadise.com/brunoe.htm. Best rooms overlook the lake, also dorms, camping, campervan parking, pool, restaurant. Service is consistently not up to scratch.
D-E **Tortugal Marina**, T5514-3316, www.tortugal.com 5 beautiful bungalows with soft rugs on the floor. Shared bathrooms with plentiful hot water. Also cheaper *ranchito*. Riverside restaurant and bar, pool table in a cool upstairs attic with books, satellite TV, internet, phone and fax service. Super friendly and relaxed.
D-F **Hotel Backpacker's**, by the bridge south bank of the river, T7930-5169, www.hotelbackpackers.com. Restaurant and bar, dorms with lockers, internet and telephone service, profits go to Casa Guatemala. Recommended.

El Estor p353

C **Marisabella**, 8 Av and 1 C on the waterfront, T7949-7215, urlich@internet detelgua.com.gt Large rooms with tiled private bathrooms, some with TV, internet service, US$11.70/hr.

D **Hotel Vista al Lago**, 6 Av, 1-13, T7949-7205. 21 clean rooms with private bath and fan. Ask for rooms with the pleasant wooden balcony. Friendly owner will take you fishing, and runs ecological and cultural tours.

E **Hotel Central**, T7949-7244, faces the park with lake views from the 2nd floor. Family run, extremely good value, 12 rooms with private bath and fan, communal TV.

Eating

Esquipulas p347

There are plenty of restaurants, but prices are high for Guatemala.

¥¥¥ **La Hacienda**, 2 Av, 10-20. Delicious barbecued chicken and steaks. Kids' menu available, breakfasts available, one of smartest restaurants in town.

¥¥ **Restaurante Payaquí**, 2 Av, 11-26, inside the hotel of the same name. Specialties include turkey in *pipián*, also lunches and breakfasts. A poolside restaurant makes a pleasant change.

Lívingston p351

Fresh fish is available everywhere, ask for *tapado* in restaurants – a rich soup with various types of seafood, banana and coconut. *Coco pan* and *cocado* (a coconut, sugar and ginger *dulce*) are sold in the streets. You can also buy cold, whole coconuts, split with a machete, US$0.20.

¥¥ **Bahía Azul**, excellent breakfasts, but dreadful coffee. Tables on the street as well as a dining-room. Specializes in salsas, *camarones* and *langosta*. Tourist service and Exotic Travel Agency.

¥¥ **Happy Fish**, near Hotel Río Dulce. Popular restaurant with internet café. Serves a truckload of fish with good coffee. Live music at weekends.

¥¥ **Río Dulce** (see Sleeping). Delicious Italian food prepared with panache by the hospitable chef, Fernando Capelli.

¥ **El Malecón**, 50 m from the dock on the left. Serves *Chapín* and western-style breakfasts, seafood and chicken *fajitas* in a large, airy wooden dining area.

¥ **Ubouhu**, near the Ubafu. Garífuna-run place, meaning world, has *pollo* (chicken), *bistec* (steak) and shrimps, as well as drinks. Popular for local gossip, has street tables.

Fronteras/Río Dulce & around p352

See also Sleeping for hotel restaurants.

¥¥ **Restaurante y Pizzería Río Bravo**, friendly management, dockside location serving breakfasts, seafood, chicken, pastas and pizzas up to US$8.

El Estor p353

¥¥-¥ **Restaurante Típico Chaabil** Thatched restaurant right on the lakeside, with plenty of fish. Cheap breakfasts.

¥ **Dorita**, a *comedor* serving seafood, excellent value and popular.

¥ **Restaurant Elsita**, 2 blocks north of the market on 8 Av. A great people-watching place. Large menu and tasty food.

Entertainment

Lívingston p351

Bars and clubs

Beluba Ñuruba and **Cocobongo** are happening bars down on the beach.

Black Sheep Cinema & Bar, a popular Bob Marley shrine with happy hour. Also shows afternoon movies. Daily 1400-dawn.

Happy Fisherman's Place, on the beach north of town. Popular and mellow.

Tropicool, around the corner from Bahía Azul. One of the most popular hang-outs open 0800-0100; happy hour until 2100.

Ubafu, on the road to African Place. Unmissable large, wooden bar, decked out in Bob Marley posters and Rastafarian symbols. Heaving most nights. Live *punta* band, with drums, a conch shell and turtle shells. Try *coco loco*, rum and coco milk served in a coconut. Worth a visit.

Festivals

Lívingston p351

24-31 Dec Virgen del Rosario, with traditional dancing, including the *punta*.
26 Nov Garífuna Day (p352).

Activities and tours

Lívingston p351

Tour operators

Exotic Travel Agency, Bahía Azul restaurant (see Eating), T7947-0049, exotictravel agency@hotmail.com
Happy Fish, (see Eating) T7947-0661, www.happyfishresort.com. You can also contract any of the *lancheros* at the dock to take you to Río Dulce, US$9.10 (US$15.60 round trip); to Playa Blanca, US$9.75; to Siete Altares, US$26.

Fronteras/Río Dulce p352

The lake is full of *robalo, mojarra* and *tilapia* ; consult tour operators for sport fishing trips.

Sailing

Captain John Clark's sailing trips on his 46-ft Polynesian catamaran, *Las Sirenas*, are highly recommended. Food, taxes, snorkelling, fishing gear, and windsurf boards included. Contact **Aventuras Vacacionales SA**, 1a Av Sur 19 B, T7832-9036, in Antigua, or consult the website, www.sailing-diving-guatemala.com

Tour operators

Atitrans Tours, on the little road heading to the dockside. To Finca Paraíso, US$20.
Otiturs, opposite Atitrans, T5219-4520. Friendly and helpful. Minibus service as well as tours to local sites, internal flights and boat trips.
Tijax Express, next to Otiturs, T7930-5505, info@tijax.com, also has internet.
Lancheros offer trips on the river and the lake from the *muelle principal*, under the bridge. Ask for César Mendez, T5819-7436, or ask at **Atitrans** (above).

El Estor p353

Tour operators

Aventuras Ecoturísticas y Café Internet Planeta Tierra, 5 Av, 2-65, T5913-5598 Tours to El Boquerón, the source of the Río Sauce, the former nickel plant, Finca El Paraíso and the Bocas del Polochic. Bicycle rent, horse rental, *lancha* tours and sport fishing also arranged.

Transport

Chiquimula p347

Bus

There are 3 small terminals in Chiquimula, all within 50 m of each other.

To **Guatemala City**, Transportes Guerra and **Rutas Orientales**, hourly, US$3, 3¼-3½ hrs, leave from 11 Av between 1 and 2 C, as do buses for **Puerto Barrios**, several companies, every 30 mins, between 0300-1500, 4 hrs, US$2.60. To **Quiriguá**, US$1.55, 1 hr 50 mins. Take any Puerto Barrios-bound bus. To **Río Dulce**, take the Barrios bus and get off at La Ruidosa junction and change, or change at Bananera/Morales.

From the terminal inside the market at 10 Av between 1 and 2 C, to **Esquipulas**, every 10 mins, US$1.05, until 1900. To **Cobán** via El Rancho (where a change must be made), US$1.65.

Transportes Vilma to the border at **El Florido** (p347) from inside the market at 1 C, between 10 and 11 Av, T7942-2253, on the hour 0530-1230 and then 1320, 1345, 1430, 1500, 1530, 1630, US$1.05, 1½ hrs.

Taxi

Chiquimula-border US$16. Chiquimula-Copán and back in a day, US$32.

Esquipulas p347

Bus

To **Guatemala City**, every 30 mins, 0200-1700, 4½ hrs, US$3.60, with **Rutas Orientales**, from 1 Av "A" and 11 C, T7943-1366. To **Chiquimula**, by minibus, every 30 mins, 0430-1830, US$1.05. To

Santa Elena, Petén, at 0400, 0900,1300, 11 hrs, US$7.80, with **Transportes María Elena**, 12 C, between 5 and 6 Av.

Quiriguá *p350*

Bus

Take any bus along the highway and get off at the crossroads for the *ruinas*. From here, take a pick-up (very regular), 10 mins, US$0.40, or bus (much slower and less regular) to the ruins, 4 km away; last bus back, 1700. To get to the village of Quiriguá, 3 km south of the crossroads, take a local bus from the highway, US$0.13 and emphasize to the bus driver you want Quiriguá *pueblo*, not the *ruinas*. Otherwise it's an easy walk. A frequent daily bus service runs a circular route between Los Amates, Quiriguá village and the entrance road to the ruins, US$0.13.

Puerto Barrios *p350*

Boat

From the **Litegua** bus station, it's a 10-min walk to the municipal dock at the end of C 12; taxi, US$0.65 per person. The ferry *(barca)* for **Lívingston** leaves at 1000, 1½ hrs, US$1.30. There are also *lanchas*, which leave with a minimum of 12 people, 35 mins, US$3.25. The only scheduled *lanchas* depart at 0630 and 0730; the last departure, if there are enough people, is at 1800.

To Belize Transportes El Chato, 1 Av, between 10 and 11 C, T7948-5525, pichilingo2000@ yahoo.com, runs *lanchas* to **Punta Gorda** at 1000, returning at 1600, 1 hr, US$13. There are also Belizean-operated services at 1000 and 1400.

To Honduras To **Puerto Cortés**, *lancha*, US$300 for min 6 people. Get your exit stamp at Guatemalan immigration in Puerto Barrios. If you need a visa, obtain it in Guatemala City or Esquipulas.

Bus

To **Guatemala City**, with **Litegua**, 6 Av between 9 and 10 C, T7948-1002, www.litegua.com, 18 a day, 5 hrs, US$5.20; these buses will stop at **La Ruidosa** (for **Río Dulce**), 15 mins, **Quiriguá**, 2 hrs, US$2, and **El Rancho** (for Biotopo del Quetzal and Cobán), 4 hrs.

To **Chiquimula**, with **Carmencita**, 4 hrs, US$3; alternatively, catch a Guatemala City bus to **Río Hondo**, and then a *colectivo* or bus to Chiquimula.

Minibuses to **Entre Ríos** (the Honduras border, p350), leave the market on 8 C every 15 mins 0630-1800, US$0.40; they stop for immigration at El Cinchado and then continue (15 mins) over the Río Motagua, where a pick-up will take you to Honduran immigration in Corinto. From here there are connections to Omoa, Puerto Cortés and La Ceiba. Leave Puerto Barrios no later than 0800 if you want to make this crossing.

Lívingston *p351*

Boat

Ferry to **Puerto Barrios**, 0500 and 1400 daily (theoretically to connect with the last bus to Guatemala City), also private launches for 16-25 people, from 0600, 35 mins, US$3.25. To **Río Dulce**, with short stops at Aguas Calientes and the Biotopo Chacón Machacas, US$9.10 one way, US$15.60 round trip; also direct *lanchas* at 0900 and 1300 (no stops). **Happy Fish**, runs boat/shuttle service to **Antigua**, **Quirigúa**, and **San Pedro Sula**.

To Belize There is no regular ferry from Lívingston but fast *lanchas* make the trip to **Punta Gorda** most days (see also p264); enquire at the dock and negotiate a fare with the *lanchero* association, US$13 per person, min 8 people; also to the **cayes**, US$39 per person round trip, max 8 people. **Bahía Azul** runs boats to **Placencia**, US$50 per person, min 4 people, and to Zapotilla caye, US$35 per person, min 6 people. Anyone who takes you to Belize must have a manifest with passengers' names, stamped and signed at immigration.

To Honduras *Lanchas* can be organized at the dock, to **Omoa**, US$32.50 per person, min 7 people, also with **Bahía Azul**, US$35 per person including exit tax, min 6 people. With Bahía Azul to **Utila**, US$90, 2 days.

Río Dulce and around *p352*

Boat

Colectivo lanchas leave for **Lívingston** from 0900 and 1300, US$10. Private *lanchas* to any of the river or lakeside hotels can be arranged at the dock .

Bus

To **El Estor**, 0500-1600, hourly, US$1.30, 1½ hrs on a partially paved road, via **Finca El Paraíso**, 45 mins, US$0.90. These buses leave north of the bridge, from the corner of the first road to the left, where there is a Pollandia restaurant. To **Puerto Barrios**, take any bus to **La Ruidosa**, 35 mins, US$0.65 and change; from the junction it's a further 35 mins and US$0.65. To **Guatemala City**, with Litegua, T7930-5251, www.litegua.com, 0300, 0545, 0745 and 1200, US$3.90, 6 hrs; with Fuente del Norte, T5692-1988, 23 daily, 0700-0230, US$5, luxury service 1300, 2400, US$13; with Línea Dorada, at 2400 and 1300, luxury service, 5 hrs, US$30. To **Flores** 20 daily, 0630-0300, 4½ hrs with Fuente del Norte, US$6.40, luxury service, 1430, US$13. This bus also stops at **Finca Ixobel** and **Poptún**, US$3.90. Línea Dorada, to Flores, 2400, 1430, 3½ hrs, luxury service with a/c, TV and snacks, US$30, and on to **Melchor de Mencos** for Belize (p251). Fuente del Norte to **Melchor de Mencos**, US$11, at 1230, 2030, 2230-0300; also to **Sayaxché** at 2200 and **Naranjo** at 2100.

Shuttles

Atitrans, T7930-5111, www.atitrans.com runs a shuttle service at 1500 to **Antigua**, min 2 people, US$40, 4½ hrs. Also express minibus to **Flores**, US$115.

El Estor and around *p353*

Bus

To **Río Dulce**, 0500-1600, hourly, 1¼ hrs, US$1.30, passing via **Finca El Paraíso**, at 40 and 50 mins past the hour. For **Cañon El Boquerón**, take the Río Dulce bus and ask to be dropped at the entrance.

To **Cobán**, with Transportes Valenciana, 1200, 0200, 0400 and 0800, 8 hrs, long and dusty with no proper stop, US$2.60; the 0800 service does a massive tour of the town before finally departing, packed to the rafters. To **Guatemala City**, 0100 direct, via Río Dulce, 7½ hrs or at 2400 and 0300 via Río Polochic Valley; more frequent services from Río Dulce. To **Santa Elena** (Petén) 0500.

Directory

Esquipulas *p347*

Banks There are a number of banks and ATMs in town close to the park, Visa and MasterCard accepted. Also money changers in the centre for Honduran *lempiras*. Better rates than at the border.

Lívingston *p351, map p*

Banks Bancafé, cash advance on Visa and MasterCard, TCs and cash changed, 24-hr Visa-only ATM. Banco de Comercio will change Amex and MasterCard TCs and cash. Some hotels will change cash, including Casa Rosada. **Immigration** on C Principal, opposite Hotel Tucán Dugú, 24 hrs daily, T947-0240, just knock if the door is shut. **Internet** Happy Fish, US$4.20/hr, also at Black Sheep Cinema and Bar. **Post office** Next to Telgua, behind the Municipalidad. **Telephone** Telgua, 0800-1800.

Río Dulce *p352*

Banks 2 banks: Visa, TCs and cash only. Two ATMS. **Internet** Captain Nemo's Communications, behind Bruno's US$2.50/ hr and phone call service. Tijax Express, US$2.30/hr.

El Estor *p353*

Banks Corpobanco and Banrural accept TCs and cash. **Internet** Café Internet Planeta Tierra, US$5.45/hr.

The Verapaces

Propped up on a massive limestone plateau eroded over thousands of years, the Verapaz region is riddled with caves, underground tunnels, stalactites and stalagmites. Once worshipped by the Maya as entrances to the underworld, these subterranean spaces are now visited by travellers, who marvel at the natural interior design. Nature has worked its magic above ground too. In the lowlands, a reserve provides a rare chance to glimpse the red or green feather flash of the elusive quetzal. And at Semuc Champey, pools of tranquil, turquoise-green water span a monumental limestone bridge, while a river thunders violently beneath. The imperial city of Cobán, provides respite for the traveller with a clutch of museums honouring the Maya, the coffee bean and the orchid. It also puts on a fantastic spectacle at the end of July with a whirlwind of traditional dances and a Maya beauty contest.

Getting there Bus.
Getting around Bus.
Time required At least 3 days.
Weather Hot.
Sleeping Some attractive hotels, others standard.
Eating Small range of restaurants serving international and national cuisine.
Activities and tours Trekking, river tubing.
★ **Don't miss...** Languishing in the hot pools of Semuc Champey ▸▸ *p362.*

Ins and outs

The main road into the Verapaces leaves the Atlantic Highway at El Rancho (one hour, US$1.30 east of Guatemala City). Some buses also head due north of the capital to Baja Verapaz, a beautiful, occasionally heart-stopping ride. ▸▸ *p364.*

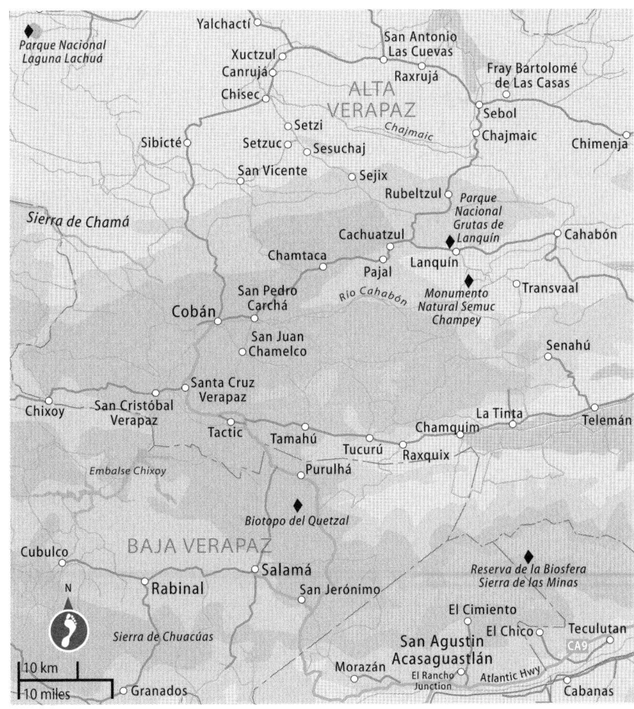

Background

Before the Spanish conquest, Las Verapaces had a notorious reputation as Tezulutlán (land of war). Its aggressive residents fought repeated battles with their neighbours, the K'iche' Maya and strongly resisted the Spanish *conquistadores*, eventually forcing the invaders to replace theirs weapons with the power of the cross. The Dominican friar, Bartolomé de las Casas arrived in 1537 and succeeded in converting the local population to Christianity and Carlos V of Spain gave the area the title 'Verdadera Paz' (true peace) in 1548. During the 19th century, Germans were invited into this area by the Guatemalan government to set up coffee fincas. The incomers also introduced cardamom to the Verapaces, when a *finquero* requested some seeds for use in biscuits. Although many of the German-owned farms were expropriated during World War II, Guatemala is now the world's largest producer of cardamom and this area produces some of the country's finest coffee – served up with some of its finest cakes!

Baja Verapaz » *pp362-365*

Salamá and around

Northwest of El Rancho is **San Jerónimo**, where there is a Dominican church and convent, from where friars tended vineyards, exported wine and cultivated sugar. An old sugar mill (*trapiche*) is on display at the *finca* and there's a huge aqueduct of some 124 arches that was used to transport water to the sugar cane fields and the town. Further west, **Salamá** sits in a valley, with a colonial cathedral, containing carved gilt altarpieces, at its heart. The town has one of the few remaining Templos de Minerva in the country, built in 1916. Behind the Calvario church is a hill – Cerro de la Santa Cruz – that affords a good view of the valley. Market day is Monday and is worth a visit.

The village of **Rabinal** was founded in 1537 by Bartolomé de Las Casas. It has a handsome 16th-century church, and a busy Sunday market, where brightly lacquered gourds, beautiful *huípiles* and embroidered napkins are sold. The glossy lacquer is made from the body oil of a scaly insect called the *niij*, which is boiled in water then mixed with soot powder. The **Museo Rabinal Achí** ⓘ *2 C y 4 Av, Zona 3, T5311-1536, museoachi@hotmail.com*, has historical exhibits and bilingual books about the Achi culture.

West of Rabinal, set amid maize fields and peach trees, **Cubulco** is known for its pole dance, *Palo Volador,* which is performed every 20-25 July. Men, attached to a rope, leap out from the top of a pole and spiral down, accompanied by marimba music.

Biotopo del Quetzal

ⓘ *4 km south of Purulhá, Km 160.5; run by CECON, Av Reforma, 0-63, Zona 10, Guatemala City, T2331-0904. Daily 0700-1600, US$2.60. Parking. Buses from Guatemala City, with Escobar-Monja Blanca, 3½ hrs, US$3.90; also buses from El Rancho and Cobán.*

The Biotopo del Quetzal, or **Biosphere Mario Dary Rivera**, lies 53 km south of Cobán. Increasing numbers of quetzals have been reported in the Biotopo, but they are still very elusive. Ask for advice from the rangers before tackling the two trails.

Quetzal, Guatemala's national bird

Cobán and Alta Verapaz » pp362-365

The region of Alta Verapaz is based around a gigantic mountain, Sierra de Chamá. Dinosaurs roamed the area more than 65 million years ago before it was engulfed by sea. It later emerged, covered with limestone rock, which over millions of years has left the area pockmarked with caves, and dotted with small hills. The year-round soft rainfall in this area, known as *chipi-chipi*, is a godsend to the coffee and cardamom plants growing around the Imperial City of Cobán. In the far northwest of the department are the mystical, emerald-green waters of Laguna Lachuá.

Santa Cruz Verapaz and around

On the main Guatemala City-Cobán road, **Tactic** is famous for beautiful *huípiles*, silverwork, and for its 'living well', in which the water becomes agitated as people approach. From here a dusty road heads east through good hiking country in the **Polochic valley** to El Estor on the shores of Lago de Izabal (page 353). West of Tactic are the Poqomchi' Maya villages of **Santa Cruz Verapaz** and **San Cristóbal Verapaz**; each has a fine, white, colonial church. From the church in San Cristóbal, the long, straight Calle del Calvario heads up to a hill-top **calvary church**. At Easter, the entire road is carpeted in flowers that rival those on display in Antigua. Also in town is the **Museo Katinamit** ⓘ *T7950-4039, cecep@intelnet.net.gt Mon-Fri 0900-1200, 1500-1700*, run by the Centro Communitario Educativo Poqomchi', which is dedicated to the preservation and learning of the Poqomchi' culture. There are approximately 260,000 Poqomchi' Maya speakers today.

Cobán

Cobán was founded by Bartolomé de Las Casas in 1538 and was made an Imperial City by Carlos V of Spain. The centre is perched on a long, thin plateau, with a 16th century **cathedral** at its heart. Exceptionally steep roads wind down from the central plaza, where there's an unofficial, but informative **tourist office**, www.cobanav.net. To the south are some well-preserved colonial buildings and the coffee-producing **Finca Santa Margarita** ⓘ *3 C, 4-12, Zona 2, gustavg@intelnet.net.gt, Mon-Fri 0800-1230, 1330-1700, Sat 0800-1200, US$2.50*. This coffee plantation supplies the multinational **Starbucks** chain and is a must for coffee fans, with tours in English and Spanish. The restored chapel of **El Calvario**, in the northwest of town, has its original façade still intact. It's worth climbing the 142 steps to get a birds-eye view of Cobán; on the way up are altars used by worshippers, who freely blend Maya and Roman Catholic beliefs. The **Museo El Príncipe Maya** ⓘ *Mon-Sat 0900-1300, 1400-1800, US$1.30, 6 Av, 4-26, Zona 3*, is an excellent private museum of pre-Columbian artefacts.

Don't miss a visit to the flower-filled world of **Vivero Verapaz** ⓘ *2½ km southwest of town, Mon-Sat 0700-1800, US$1.30, 40-min walk, or taxi ride, US$1.30*, an orchid farm with more than 23,000 specimens, mostly flowering from December to February.

East of Cobán

San Pedro Carchá is 5 km east of Cobán on the main road. It is famous for the production of pottery and silver, and for *kaq Ik*, a turkey broth. To the south, 8 km from Cobán, is **San Juan Chamelco**, with an old colonial church. Beyond the village, towards Chamil, is **Aldea Chajaneb** (see Sleeping), the **Grutas Rey Marcos** and **Balneario Cecilinda** ⓘ *Sat and Sun 0800-1700*. Southeast of Chamil are cloud forests up to heights of 2,650 m.

Lanquín and Semuc Champey

Lanquín lies 56 km east of Cobán, 10 km from the Pajal junction. It is surrounded by mountainous scenery, reminiscent of an Alpine landscape, and nestles in the bottom of a

Semuc Champey

river valley. It is a good place to kick back for a few days and inhale the high altitude air. Just outside the town are the **Grutas de Lanquín** ⓘ *0800-1600, US$2.60, 30-min walk from town*. The caves are lit for 200 m, but it's worth taking a torch to see the thousands of stalactites hanging from the cave ceiling; some have been given names. Hold on to the handrails, as it's dangerously slippery underfoot. At dusk, watch the swarms of bats flying out of the cave to feed. You can swim in the river outside the cave and camp for free.

From Lanquín, visit the natural limestone bridge of **Semuc Champey** ⓘ *10 km south of Lanquín, 0600-1800, US$2.60, parking US$0.65*, a liquid paradise stretching 60 m across the Cahabón Gorge. The bridge is spanned by clear blue and green water pools, where you can swim; some have natural hot water pouring into them. Upstream, watch the river being channelled under the bridge and, at its voluminous exit, climb down from the bridge and see it cascading past. It's a three-hour walk to Semuc Champey from Lanquín, quite tough for the first hour as the road climbs very steeply out of Lanquín. If planning to return to Lanquín the same day, start very early to avoid the midday heat. Transport is very irregular along this road so arrange any lifts in advance, about US$13 return.

Sleeping

Baja Verapaz *p360*

B **Posada Montaña del Quetzal**, Km 156, Biotopo del Quetzal, T2331-0929. Bungalows or rooms with private bathrooms, hot water, café, bar, swimming pool and gardens.

D **Tezulutlán**, Ruta 4, 4-99, Zona 1, Salamá, T7940-1643. Just off the plaza, clean and quiet rooms with bath (some have hot water), cheaper without, also a restaurant on site.

Cobán *p361, map p365*

Accommodation is extremely hard to find on the Fri and Sat of Rabin Ajau and in Aug. Reserve in advance.

A **La Posada**, 1 C, 4-12, Zone 2, T7952-1495. Colonial hotel with well-kept flourishing gardens and 14 attractive rooms with private tiled bathrooms and fireplaces, credit cards accepted. Also stylish restaurant with terrace and fireplace, café open afternoons.

B-C **Posada de Don Juan Matalbatz**, 3 C, 1-46, Zona 1, T/F7952-1599. Colonial-style hotel with rooms around a courtyard. Despite the nearby bus terminal it is very quiet and safe. All rooms have TV. Restaurant, pool table, parking, tours.

C **Hotel de Posada Carlos V**, 1 Av 3-44, Zona1, T7951-1133, victormoino @hotmail.com. Lantern-lined entrance,

Going further

Parque Nacional Laguna Lachuá

ⓘ *4.2 km from Playa Grande (1-hr walk), northwest of Cobán. UICN Lachuá, T7704-1509, www.visitchisec.com, US$5.20. Buses from Cobán.*

This deep velvet-green lake at 170 m above sea level was formed by a meteor impact that created a 4-sq-km crater. The lake is 220 m deep in places and is surrounded by dense jungle, which is virtually unspoilt. There is a guided nature trail through the park and the chances of seeing wildlife at dawn and dusk are high. Camping is available but you'll need to bring all food and water with you. Otherwise stay at **Finca Chipantun** (E-G), on the borders of the national park, T7951-3423. It has rooms, hammocks or camping space on the bank of the Río Chixoy. Meals are extra but excellent value – the most expensive is dinner at US$3.

Also in the area is the **Río Ikbolay**, a green river that runs underground through caves, before emerging as a blue river on the other side. The river has changed its course over time leaving some of its run-through caves empty, making it possible to walk through them. The **Proyecto**, page 364, runs jungle hikes in this area.

Swiss chalet style, Italian family, fireplace in lounge, restaurant, bar, cosy. The modern annexe is not as nice.

C-F **Hostal de Doña Victoria**, 3 C, 2-38, Zona 3, T7951-4213. A 400-year-old former Dominican convent with colonnaded gallery, attractive gardens, and a good restaurant (see below). Also cheap dorm beds. Excursions arranged.

D **Central**, 1 C, 1-79, T7952-1158, T/F7952-1442, has no sign, but is next to **Café San Jorge**, near the cathedral. 15 very clean large rooms around a patio, with hot showers. TV extra.

E-F **Casa D'Acuña**, 4 C, 3-11, Zona 2, T7951-0482, casadeacuna@yahoo.com 2 bunk beds in each room, ultra clean bathrooms with hot water, laundry service, internet, excellent meals, tempting goodies and coffee in El Bistro courtyard restaurant (see Eating). Also a tourist office, shop and tours.

East of Cobán *p361*

B **Don Jerónimo's**, Km 5.3, carretera a Chamil, Aldea Chajaneb, T/F5301-3191, www.dearbrutus.com/donjeronimo All inclusive bungalows, with 3 vegetarian meals a day, hiking, swimming, tubing, massage, great for relaxation. Taxi from Cobán, 30 mins, US$6. Or bus to Chamelco, then bus or pick-up to Chamil.

Lanquín and Semuc Champey *p361*

C **El Recreo**, village entrance, T7952-2160. Clean, good meals, friendly. The swimming pool is not always full.

F **El Retiro**, campsite, *cabañas*, dorm beds and restaurant, gorgeous riverside location. Open fire for cooking, hammocks, tubes for floating on the river. To get there, continue on the road to Cahabón for 5 mins and ask to be dropped off. Highly recommended.

Eating

Cobán *p361, map p365*

ŤŤŤ **El Bistro**, in Casa D'Acuña. Excellent menu with massive portions. Try the blueberry pancakes and check out the tempting cake cabinet.

ŤŤ **El Refugio**, 2 Av, 2-28 , Zona 4, T7952-1338. Very good service and substantial portions at good-value prices

– steaks but also fish, chicken and snacks, set lunch, cocktails, big screen TV, bar.

🍴🍴 **Hostal de Doña Victoria**, 3 C, 2-38, Zona 3. Breakfast, lunch and supper in a semi-open area with a pleasant ambience. Good Italian food, including vegetarian options. Also a romantic cellar bar, El Estable.

🍴 **Cafetería San Jorge**, next to Hotel Central. Tacos, tostadas and *pie de queso*, plus cheap breakfasts, set lunch and snacks, friendly service, shut Sun.

🍴 **Tropikuba**, 2C 8-24, Zona1, daily 1830-2230, family atmosphere, bamboo and salsa music, excellent meat options, good value beer and food.

Cafés

Café El Tirol, 1 C, 3-13, on the main park. 52 coffees, 17 teas and 9 hot chocolates, homemade bread, good cakes. Daily 0700-2200.

Café La Posada, part of **La Posada** (see Sleeping). Divine brownies and ice-cream, sofas with a view of the central park and of some very ugly satellite dishes.

Lanquín and Semuc Champey *p361*

Tiendas in Lanquín sell good fruit and veg, also a couple of bakeries, all open early, so stock up for a trip to Semuc Champey.

🍴 **Comedor Shalom**, excellent value, basic food, drink included.

🍴 **Rancho Alegre**, relaxing hammock bar ideal for a chilled beer.

Entertainment

Cobán *p361, map p365*

Bars

Milenio, 3 Av 1-11, Zona 4. Dance floor, live music weekends, beer by the jug, pool table, big screen TV, weekends minimum US$3, popular.

Festivals and events

Santa Cruz Verapaz *p361*

1-4 May Town fiesta, at which the wonderful **Danza de los Guacamayos** (scarlet macaws) is performed.

Cobán *p361, map p365*

Easter Semana Santa.

Jul Rabin Ajau, in the last week, is a major celebration for the election of the Maya Beauty Queen. Around this time the Paa banc is also performed, electing the chiefs of brotherhoods for the year.

1-6 Aug is the town's own fiesta in honour of its patron, **Santo Domingo**, with various activities.

Activities and tours

Cobán *p361, map p365*

Proyecto Ecológico Quetzal, 2 C, 14-36, Zona 1, T/F7952-1047, www.ecoquetzal.org. Trips to the Río Ikbolay, northwest of Cobán, p363, and to the mountain community of Chicacnab. Contact David Unger.

Transport

Salamá and around *p360*

Bus

To **Rabinal**, US$0.50, 1-1½ hrs, for connections to **Cubulco**, supplemented by pick-up rides. To **Guatemala City** via El Progreso, US$1.60, also slower direct service from Rabinal, 5½ hrs.

Cobán *p361, map p365*

Bus

Local To **San Juan Chamelco**, every 15 mins 0530-1900, US$0.13 from 5 Av and 3 C. To **San Pedro Carchá**, every 10 mins, US$0.13, 0600-1820. All capital-bound buses run through **Tactic**, or take a local bus 0645-2000, returning 0500-1730, 40 mins, US$0.32. To **Santa Cruz Verapaz**, 0600-1915, every 15 mins, US$0.26, 40 mins. To **Lanquín**, El Cahabonero minibuses from 2 Av 2-25, Zona 4, 6 daily from 0900, US$3.15, 3hrs; services at 1015 and 1500 go direct to **Semuc Champey**; a further 9 minibuses go as far as **Cahabón**, US$2.50, 2hrs. To **Purulhá**, for **Biotopo del Quetzal**, 0645-2000, last return 1730, US$0.52, 1hr 20 mins, or take any capital-bound bus, 1 hr, US$1.05.

Long-distance To **Guatemala City**, with **Transportes Escobar-Monja Blanca**, hourly 0130-1730, 4 hrs, US$4, from its own offices near the terminal. From the main Cobán terminal to **El Estor**, 10 daily, first at 0400, 8 hrs, US$2. To **Salamá**, minibus, US$1.75, 2¼ hrs. To **Fray Bartolomé de las Casas**, for connections to Poptún, 0600-1600 by bus, pick-up and trucks, every 30 mins, uncomfortable journey. To **Flores**, via Raxruha and Sayaxché, minibuses with **Microbuses del Norte** from 1 Av 3C, T7952-1086, 0630-1730 (buses direct to Sayaxché leave at 1100 and 1400), 4 hrs, US$3.15; in Sayaxché take a passenger canoe or ferry across the river to catch minibuses to Flores, 45 mins. To **Uspantán**, for connections to Sacapulas and Santa Cruz del Quiche, 1000 and 1200, 5 hrs, US$1.40. To **Playa Grande** (Ixcan Grande) for Parque Nacional Laguna Lachuá, 0500, 1000 and 1230, the first 2 via Chisec, 4½ hrs, US$3.90; also minibuses, US$5.20.

Directory

Cobán *p361, map p365*
Banks Banks around Parque Central will change money. MasterCard accepted at **G&T Continental**, 1 C and 2 Av. **Hospitals** Policlínica y Hospital Galen, private institution on 3 Av, 1-47, Zona 3, T7951-2913. **Internet and telephone** Access Computación, US$3.90 per hr, fax and collect call phone service. **Infocel**, 3 Av, between 1-2 C, Zona 4. US$2.60/hr.

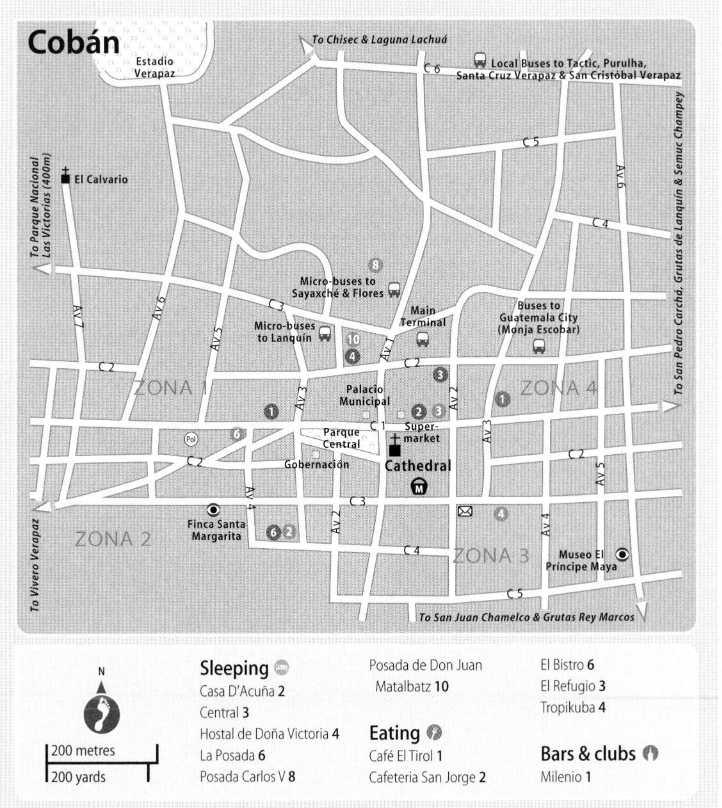

Deep in the lush lowland jungles of the Petén lie lost Maya cities, pyramids and ceremonial centres. At Tikal, temples push through the tree canopy and battles and burials are recorded in intricately carved stone. Although human activity has ceased in these once powerful centres, the forest is humming with the latter-day lords of the jungle, howler monkeys who roar day and night. There are also toucans, hummingbirds, spider monkeys, wild pig and coatimundi. Jaguar, god of the underworld in Maya religion, stalks the jungle but remains elusive. Away from the well beaten track to Tikal, the adventurous traveller can explore the more remote sites of El Zotz, El Perú, El Ceibal and Uaxactún by river, by foot or on horseback.

Getting there Plane, bus.
Getting around Bus, organized tour and on foot.
Time required 3 days for Lago Petén Itzá' and Tikal; longer for more remote Maya sites.
Weather Very hot and humid. Wet season May-Oct.
Sleeping Top-class hotels and basic hostels.
Eating Range of cuisine.
Activities and tours Trekking, wildlife spotting.
★ Don't miss... Tikal in the morning ›› *p369*.

Ins and outs

Getting there The main hub for this region are the twin towns of Flores and Santa Elena separated by a causeway on Lago Petén Itzá'. Daily flights from Guatemala City (US$90-120 return, shop around) arrive at **Santa Elena airport** (FRS), 2 km south of Flores. There are also flights to/from Belize City and Cancún. The airport departures hall has **Banquetzal**, cash or TCs only. A taxi from the airport into Santa Elena or Flores, US$1.30, 5 minutes, bargain hard, or take a local yellow school bus, US$0.13. If you arrive by long-distance bus from Guatemala City, Mexico or Belize you will be dropped in the heart of Santa Elena. There are hotels within walking distance or you can walk to Flores across the causeway (10 to 15 minutes) or take a taxi. ›› *p379*.

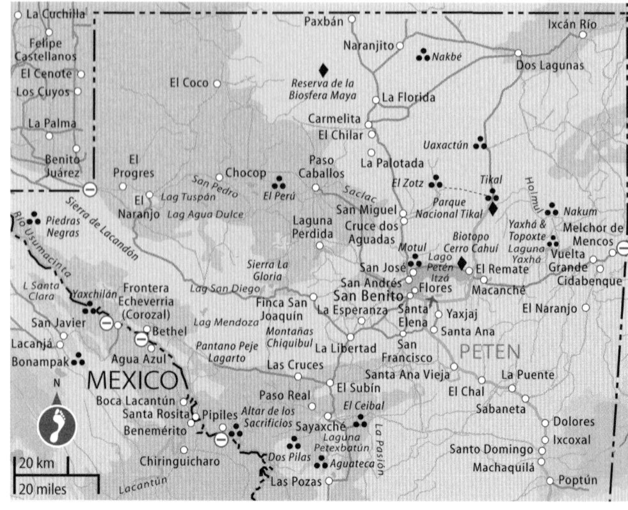

Visiting El Petén

In the summer months (November to early May), access to all sites is possible as all the tracks are bone-dry. There are also fewer mosquitoes and plenty of birdwatching opportunities but the ruins at Tikal are busiest with tourists at this time. In the rainy winter months (May-early November), tracks become quagmires and are often impassable, the humidity is greater and the pesky mosquitoes are out in force; take plenty of repellent and reapply frequently. From April to December it rains everyday for a while. However, there is a far better chance of hearing frog choruses and seeing wild animals, large and small, at this time of year. Note that there's another flurry of tourists to Tikal during the northern hemisphere's summer holidays in August. There are some climactic variations within the Petén – ask before visiting. It is, however, fiercely hot and humid at all times in these parts so lots of sunscreen and drinking water are essential.

Tourist information INGUAT has an office in the airport ⓘ *daily 0700-1200, 1500-1800*, and on the plaza in Flores ⓘ *0800-1200, 1230-1630*. Also on the plaza is **CINCAP** ⓘ *Centro de Información sobre la Naturaleza, Cultura y Artesanía de Petén, T7926-0718, www.alianzaverde.org*, which has free maps of Tikal and publishes a free magazine *Destination Petén*. Housed in the same building is the **Alianza Verde**, which promotes eco-tourism. **ProPetén** ⓘ *C Central, T7926-1370, www.propeten.org*, is associated with **Conservation International**, and tries to involve local communities in tourism projects.

Safety Armed minibus hold ups have occurred on the road between Flores and the Parque Nacional Tikal. The situation appears to have improved recently but get independent, up-to-date advice before visiting and leave all valuables at your hotel.

Background

Predominantly covered in jungle, the Petén is the largest department of Guatemala and has the smallest number of inhabitants. The region around La Isla de Tah Itza' (Tayasal in Spanish), now modern-day Flores, was settled by the Maya Itzá' Kanek in about AD 600 and remained untouched by the Spanish until Hernán Cortés and chronicler Bernal Díaz del Castillo dropped by in 1525 on their way to Honduras. The area was not conquered, however, until 1697, when Martín Urzua y Arismendi, the governor of the Yucatán, crossed Lago Petén Itzá'. His soldiers killed 100 indigenous people, captured King Kanek and ransacked the temples and palaces of Tayasal, thus destroying the last independent Maya state.

In 1990, **CONAP**, the National Council for Protected Areas, set aside 21,487 sq km of northern Petén, as the **Reserva de la Biosfera Maya** (Maya Biosphere Reserve). It is now the largest protected tropical forest area in Central America and encompasses the Parque Nacional Tikal, Parque Nacional Mirador-Río Azul and Parque Nacional Laguna del Tigre.

Poptún

Poptún is best known for its association with **Finca Ixobel**. Otherwise, it is just a staging-post between Río Dulce and Flores, or where to switch buses for the ride to Cobán. *p374.*

Lago Petén Itzá' » pp374-380

Flores and Santa Elena

Flores is perched on a tiny island in Lake Petén Itzá'. Red roofs and palm trees jostle for position as they spread up the small hill, which is topped by the white twin-towered **cathedral**, Nuestra Señora de los Remedios y San Pablo del Itzá'. It's plain inside but houses a Black Christ (*Cristo Negro*), part of a chain of Black Christs that stretches across Central America, with the focus of worship at Esquipulas (page 347). Many houses and restaurants in Flores have been daubed with lashings of colourful paint, giving the town a Caribbean flavour. *Lanchas* drift among lilies and dragonflies at the lake edges.

On the mainland, **Santa Elena** is the dustier, less elegant and noisier twin town, where the cheapest hotels, banking services and buses can be found. Three kilometres south of Santa Elena are the **Actún Kan caves** ⓘ *0800-1700, US$1.30*, a fascinating labyrinth of tunnels, where legend has it, a large serpent once lived (30 to 45 minutes' walk).

Around the lake

Tours of the whole lake cost about US$10 per boat, calling at the **zoo** ⓘ *Paraíso Escondido, US$0.25*, and the Maya ruin of **Tayasal**, the last place of occupation of the Maya Itza' Kanek. On the lake's western edge, 16 km by road from Santa Elena, is the village of **San Andrés**, with sweeping views across the water. The attractive village of **San José**, a traditional Maya Itzá community, is 2 km further northeast, with painted and thatched homes huddled on the steep shoreline. Efforts are being made here to preserve the Itza' language and revive old traditions. It takes 20 minutes to walk between the two villages.

At the eastern side of Lake Petén Itzá is **El Remate**, where there are many lovely places to stay. The sunsets are superb here and the lake is flecked with turquoise blue in the mornings. You can swim from the shore in certain places, away from the local women washing their clothes and the horses taking a bath. West of El Remate is the **Biotopo Cerro Cahuí** ⓘ *administered by CECON, daily 0700-1600, US$2.60*, a lowland jungle area where three species of monkeys, deer, jaguar, peccary, ocellated wild turkey and some 450 species of bird can be seen. If you do not wish to walk alone, hire a guide; ask at your *posada*.

Flores

Temple 1, Tikal

Parque Nacional Tikal » pp374-380

ⓘ Park administration, T2361-1399. Daily 0600-1800; it is no longer possible to get extended passes to see the ruins at sunrise/sunset. Entry fee S$7 (Q50) payable at the national park entrance, 18 km from the ruins; if you enter after 1500 your ticket is valid the following day. Tourist Guide Association tours from 0800, 3-4 hrs, min US$10 per person (min 4 people) - highly recommended. It is best to visit the ruins after 1400 or before 0900 as there are fewer visitors.

With its Maya skyscrapers pushing up through the jungle canopy, Tikal will have you transfixed. Steep-sided temples for the mighty dead, stelae commemorating powerful rulers, inscriptions recording noble deeds and the passing of time, and burials stuffed with jade and bone funerary offerings, all contribute to the fascination of this great Maya city.

The low-lying hill site was first occupied around 600 BC but the first buildings date from 300 BC. Tikal became an important Maya centre from AD 300 onwards, in line with the decline of El Mirador to the north, and was governed by a powerful dynasty of 30-plus rulers between about the first century AD until about AD 869. At its height, the total 'urban' area of Tikal was more than 100 sq km, with a population somewhere between 50,000 and 100,000. Tikal's main structures, which cover 2½ sq km, were constructed from AD 550 to AD 900 during the Late Classic period. These include the towering temples, whose roof combs were decorated with coloured stucco figures of Tikal lords and whose lintels were intricately carved with figures and symbols. Tikal's stelae tell of kings and accessions, war and death. The imagery and decorative technique suggest the city was heavily influenced by forces from Teotihuacán (page 79).

After the collapse of Teotihuacán in AD 600, a renaissance at Tikal was achieved by the ruler Ah Cacao (aka Lord Cocoa, Ruler A, Moon Double Comb, Hasaw Chan K'awil I, Sky Rain), who succeeded to the throne in AD 682 and died sometime in the 720s. However, in the latter part of the eighth century the fortunes of Tikal declined – the last date recorded on a stela is AD 889 – and the site was finally abandoned in the 10th century. Most archaeologists now agree the collapse was due to drought, warfare and overpopulation.

Wildlife

Tikal is a fantastic place for seeing wildlife, including spider monkeys, howler monkeys, three species of toucan (most prominent being the keel-billed toucan – 'Banana Bill'), deer, foxes and many other birds and insects. Pumas have been seen on quieter paths and coatimundis (*pizotes*) are sometimes seen rummaging through the bins in large family groups. The ocellated turkeys, with their sky-blue heads and orange baubles, are seen in abundance at the entrance and at **El Mundo Perdido**. December to April is the best time for birdwatching.

Museums and visitor centre

Located on the entrance road are the visitor centre and the **Museo Lítico** ⓘ *T2361-1399, free*, which has some great photographs of the temples as they were originally found, and of their reconstruction, including the 1968 rebuild of the Temple II steps. There are also some stelae on display. The visitor centre has a post office, which stores luggage, exchange facilities,

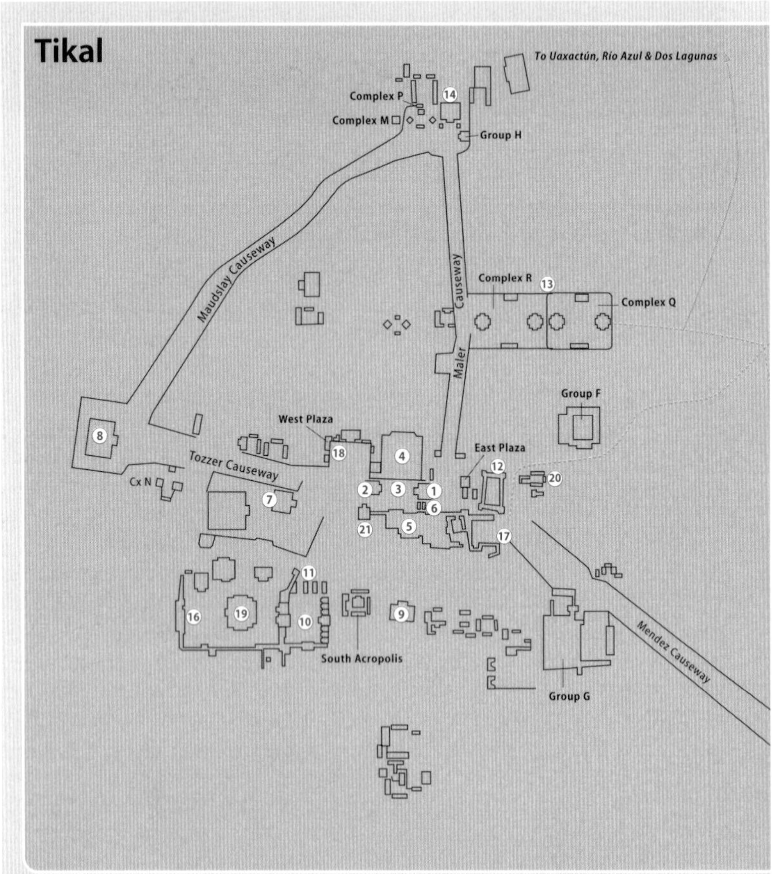

Tikal

To Uaxactún, Río Azul & Dos Lagunas
Complex P
Complex M
Group H
Maudslay Causeway
Maler Causeway
Complex R
Complex Q
Group F
West Plaza
East Plaza
Tozzer Causeway
Cx N
South Acropolis
Mendez Causeway
Group G

Sights ○

Temple I (Temple of the Great Jaguar) **1**
Temple II (Temple of the Masks) **2**
The Great Plaza **3**
North Acropolis **4**
Palace Complex (Central Acropolis) **5**
Ball Court **6**
Temple III (Temple of the Jaguar Priest) **7**
Temple IV (Temple of the Headed Serpent) **8**
Temple V **9**
Plaza of the Seven Temples Group **10**
Triple Ball Court **11**
Market **12**
Twin Pyramid Plazas **13**
North Group **14**
Temple VI (Temple of Inscriptions) **15**
El Mundo Perdido (Lost World) **16**
Structure 5D 38 **17**
Structure 5D II **18**

toilets, a restaurant and a few shops that sell relevant guidebooks, including *Tikal*, by W R Coe (US$6.50), which has an excellent map. Near the minibus park is the **Museo Cerámico (Museo Tikal)** ⓘ *Mon-Fri 0900-1700, Sat and Sun, 0900-1600, US$2.60*, which has a collection of Maya ceramics, but its prize exhibits are Stela 31, with its still clear carvings, and the reconstruction of the tomb of Tikal's great ruler, Ah Cacao, who was laid to rest under Temple 1, with 16½ lbs of jade, seashells, human and animal bones and ceramics. Photography is no longer allowed in either of the museums

Exploring the site

A guide is highly recommended as outlying structures can otherwise easily be missed. Take a hat, repellent, water and snacks with you.

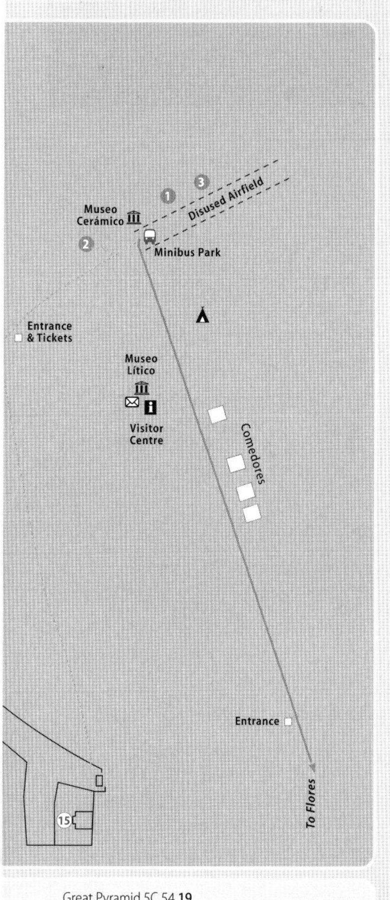

At the heart of the site, the **Great Plaza (3)**, dwarfed by its two principal temples – Temples I and II. The earliest foundations of the plaza were laid around 150 BC and the latest around AD 700. On the north side are two rows of monuments. **Stela 29**, erected in AD 292, depicts Tikal's emblem glyph – a Maya city – and the third century AD ruler Scroll Ahau Jaguar bearing a two-headed ceremonial bar.

Temple I (Temple of the Great Jaguar) (1) on the east side of the plaza rises to 44 m, with nine stepped terraces. It was built by Ah Cacao, whose tomb, the magnificent Burial 116, was discovered beneath the temple in 1962. The **East Plaza** behind Temple I marks the junction of the Maler Causeway, heading north, and the Méndez causeway, heading southeast. **Temple II (Temple of the Masks) (2)** faces Temple I on the Great Plaza and rises to 38 m, although, with its roof comb, it would have been higher. The lintel on the doorway depicts a woman wearing a cape, who may be Ah Cacao's wife.

The **North Acropolis (4)** contains some 100 buildings piled on top of earlier structures over a one-hectare area and was the burial ground of all Tikal's rulers up toAh Cacao. Yax Moch Xok (Great Scaffold Shark) is thought to be entombed in the first century AD grave, Burial 85. Surrounding the headless male body were burial objects and a mask bearing the royal head band. The tombs of Great Jaguar Paw, who died around AD 379, and of Curl Nose (Nun Yax Ayin I), who succeeded Great Jaguar Paw to the throne, were also found in this acropolis. Curl Nose;s remains were found with nine sacrificed servants as well as turtle and

View from the Great Pyramid in El Mundo Perdído

crocodile remains and a plethora of pottery, showing Teotihuacán influence. In 1960, the prized Stelae 31, now in the Museo Cerámico/Tikal, was found under the Acropolis. It was dedicated in AD 445 and is thought to depict the ruler Stormy Sky (Siyah Chan K'awil), Curl Nose's son, who died around AD 457. The base of the stela was deliberately burnt by succeeding Maya and buried under the Acropolis in the eighth century.

On the south side of the Great Plaza, the **Central Acropolis (5)** is made up of a complex of courts connected by passages and stairways, which were expanded over the centuries to cover 1.6 ha. Most of the building work carried out took place between AD 550-900 in the Late Classic era.

Temple III (Temple of the Jaguar Priest) (7) is named after a figure in a glamorous jaguar pelt on a lintel found on the temple. Some experts believe this figure is Ah Chitam (Nun Yax Ayin II, Ruler C), son of Yax Kin, and grandson of the great Ah Cacao. Temple III was constructed around AD 810 and is 55 m tall.

At the western end of the Tozzer Causeway, **Temple IV (Temple of the Double-Headed Serpent) (8)** is the highest building in Tikal at 70 m. It was built in the Late Classic period around AD 741, probably to honour Yax Kin, the son of Ah Cacao, who became ruler in AD 734. Lots of tourists climb Temple IV, although, most mornings, the temple is surrounded by mist and those sun rays will be just a figment of your imagination.

At the centre of **El Mundo Perdido (The Lost World) (16)** is the flat-topped Great Pyramid, with stairways flanked by masks. It is a Pre- and Early Classic structure and, together with other buildings to the west, formed part of an astronomical complex. At 30 m high, this is the largest pyramid at the site and, from the summit, you can enjoy a great view of Tikal's temple roofcombs pushing up through the jungle canopy. The Mundo Perdido complex is unbeatable in the early morning, when the ocellated turkeys meet for their morning gossip and toucans and parrots squawk for attention in the trees nearby. In addition to the Great Pyramid, there are several twin pyramid complexes at Tikal, built to mark the passing of the *katun* – a Maya 20-year period, including **Complexes Q** and **R (13)**.

East of el Mundo Perdido is the Plaza of the **Seven Temples (10)**, constructed during the Late Classic period (AD 600-800). There is a triple court ball court at its northern edge. **Temple V (9)** constructed between AD 700-750 during the reign of Yax Kin, is 58 m high. It is the mortuary temple of an unknown ruler.

Temple VI (Temple of the Inscriptions) (15) was discovered in 1951. The 12 m-high roof comb is covered on both sides in hieroglyphic text and is the longest hieroglyphic recording to date. At the base of the temple are Altar 9 and Stela 21, said to depict the sculptured foot of the ruler Yax Kin to mark his accession in AD 734. Unfortunately because of the location of this temple away from the rest of the main structures it has become a hideout for robbers and worse. Some guides no longer take people, so take advice before venturing there alone.

Other Maya ruins

There are literally hundreds of Maya sites in the Petén. Below are a handful whose ruins have been explored and whose histories have been, at least partly, uncovered.

Uaxactún

ⓘ *24 km north of Tikal. Buses from Santa Elena. Foreigners have to pay US$2 to pass through Parque Nacional Tikal on their way to Uaxactún.*

The village of Uaxactún (pronounced Waash-ak-tún) is little more than a row of houses and a disused airstrip, with the main groups of ruins (**A** and **B**) to the northwest, and a smaller group (**E**) 400 m to the southwest. Uaxactún was one of the longest-occupied Maya sites. Its origins lie in the Middle Pre-classic period (1000-300 BC) and its decline, like many of its neighbours, came in the Early Post-classic period (AD 925-1200). The name, Uaxactún ('eight stone), is taken from the final stelae, dated AD 889, which corresponds to Baktun 8 (8 x 400) Maya years. In **Group B**, Stela 5 marks the takeover of the city, launched from Tikal. Next door, under Temple B-VIII, the remains of two adults, including a pregnant woman, a girl of about 15 and a baby, were found. It is believed they may have been the governor and his family, who were sacrificed in AD 378. In **Group A** is Palace A-XVIII, the highest structure in the complex, with red paint still visible on the walls. The highlight of the site, however, is **Group E**, the oldest complete Maya astronomical complex ever found. The main observatory (E-VII-sub) faces structures in which the equinoxes and solstices were observed. When the pyramid (E-VII) covering this sub-structure was removed, stucco masks of jaguar and serpent heads were found flanking the stairways.

El Zotz

El Zotz, meaning bat in Q'eqchi', is so called because of the nightly flight of thousands of bats from a nearby cave, streaking the dark blue sky with columns of black. One of the best trips you can do in the Petén is the three-day hike from Cruce dos Aguadas (one hour by truck from Flores) to El Zotz (24 km, five hours) and on through the jungle to Tikal (30 km, eight hours). The journey, although long, is not arduous, and is accompanied by birds, blue morpho butterflies and spider monkeys chucking branches at you all the way. The excellent campsite at El Zotz has covered buildings for hammocks and tents. The El Zotz ruins are 3 km from the camp; many buildings have been tragically damaged by looters. The highest temple in the complex is Temple IV, at 75 m; incredibly, from the top, it is possible to see Temple IV at Tikal, some 30 km away. The route to Tikal should not be attempted without a local guide as the path is not always visible. Tours are offered by **EcoMaya**.

Laguna Yaxhá and around

On the Belize road, about 65 km from Flores, is a left turning along a dry weather road to **Laguna Yaxhá**. On the northern shore and accessible by causeway is **Yaxhá** (Green Water), the third-largest known Classic Maya site in the country. This untouristy site is good for birdwatching and the views of the milky green lake from the temples are outstanding. From Yaxhá take a boat (15 minutes) across the lake to the island of **Topoxte**, an unusual Late Post-classic site (AD 1200-1530). About 20 km further north of Yaxhá lies **Nakum**, which is thought to have been both a trading and ceremonial centre. You will need a guide and your own transport to get here if you are not on an organized tour.

Laguna Yaxhá

Around Sayaxché

The major ceremonial site of **El Ceibal** is reached by a 45-minute *lancha* ride up the Río de la Pasión from Sayaxché or on a day tour from Flores (around US$50). The site is hidden in vegetation about 1.5 km from the left bank and extends for 1.5 sq km. Archaeologists agree that El Ceibal was abandoned between about AD 500 and AD 690 and then later repopulated, with an era of stelae production between AD 771 and AD 889. It was finally was abandoned for good during the early decades of the 10th century.

From Sayaxché the ruins of the **Altar de los Sacrificios** at the confluence of the Ríos de la Pasión and Usumacinta can also be reached. This was one of the earliest sites in the Péten, with a founding date earlier than that of Tikal. More ruins are clustered around **Laguna Petexbatún**, 16 km south of Sayaxché and reached by outboard canoe. These unexcavated ruins are generally grouped together under the title **Petexbatún**, and include Arroyo de la Piedra, Dos Pilas and Aguateca. Again, a tour is advisable.

Piedras Negras

Still further down the Río Usumacinta in the west of Petén is Piedras Negras, a huge Classic period site. It was here that Tatiana Proskouriakoff first recognized that periods of time inscribed on stelae coincided with human life spans or reigns and so began the task of deciphering the meaning of Maya glyphs. Advance arrangements are necessary with a rafting company to reach Piedras Negras. **Maya Expeditions** (page 12), run expeditions, taking in Piedras Negras, Bonampak, Yaxchilán and Palenque. This trip is a real adventure. The riverbanks are covered in the best remaining tropical forest in Guatemala, inhabited by elusive wildlife and hiding more ruins. Although most of the river is fairly placid, there are the 30-m Busilhá Falls to negotiate, where a crystal clear tributary cascades over limestone terraces, and two deep canyons; you reach the take-out two days later. For information on crossing the border into Mexico here, see page 149.

Sleeping

Poptún *p367*

C-G **Finca Ixobel**, 3 km south of Poptún, T5410-4307, www.fincaixobel.com, buses will drop you nearby, then it's a 15-20 min walk, or taxi from Poptún, US$2.60. Finca Ixobel is a working farm and a highly acclaimed travellers' 'paradise' that has become the victim of its own reputation and is frequently crowded especially at weekends. However, you can still camp

Background

Stunning in scarlet

There are fewer than 1,000 scarlet macaws in the wild – just 38 in the Petén jungle – and they are destined to disappear altogether unless something radical is done to halt their demise. A number of factors threaten their survival, primarily, their loss of habitat through changing land use, the fragmentation of the land from road building, and oil exploration in northwestern Petén. Scientists have also discovered evidence of reduced reproduction rates among scarlet macaws and a fall in migration, possibly due to changes in the countryside.

Another problem is the illegal wildlife trade. Scarlet macaws are famed for their stunningly beautiful plumage – a feathered rainbow of red, yellow, blue and green. They are relatively easy prey, too, being curious creatures and nesting within reach of poachers. A baby macaw, *guacamayo* in Spanish, is worth US$130 on the local market, US$650 in the capital, and US$5,000 on the foreign market.

The **Estación Biológica Guacamayo** ⓘ *Río San Pedro, near Paso Caballos, contact Propeten, T7926-1370, www.propeten.org, US$1.30*, in the Parque Nacional Laguna del Tigre, is trying to conserve the life of this beautiful species. The national park is the bird's main breeding area and the chances of seeing the birds here during the mating season (March, April and May) are high. Visits to the national park also take in the remote Maya ruins at El Perú. There's little to see at the site but the surrounding jungle is full of wildlife, including howler monkeys, spider monkeys, white-lipped peccaries, white turtles, eagles, fox and kingfishers. Note that this area may be completely inaccessible during the rainy season.

peacefully and there are great treehouses, dorm beds and private rooms. It also serves delicious food and offers a range of activities that could keep you there for days: swimming, riding, inner tubing, short and longer jungle treks and the unmissable River Cave Trip (US$8). The *finca* also runs transport to Tikal at 0800.

Flores *p368, map p377*

B **Casazul**, T7926-0692, www.corpetur.com 9 blue rooms, most with lakeside view. All with cable TV, a/c and fan. Staff friendliness has improved.

B **Casona de la Isla**, T7926-0523, www.corpetur.com On the lake with elegant rooms, fans, TV, clean, friendly, good restaurant (0600-2200), nice breakfasts, bar, garden, pool.

B **Sabana**, T/F7926-1248, http://hotelsabana.com. Huge, spartan rooms, good service, clean, pleasant, good view, caters for European package tours, lakeside pool (US$2 for non-guests) Restaurant 0600-2200 daily.

D **Villa del Lago**, on the lakeside, T7926-0629. Very clean, cheaper with shared bath. Terrace with lake view where breakfast (open to non-guests) is served, service is very slow.

D-E **Doña Goya**, C Unión, T7926-3538. 6 clean rooms, 3 with private bath, 3 with balcony, terrace with superb views, friendly family run the place.

E **Mirador del Lago**, C 15 de Septiembre, T7926-3276. Beautiful view of the lake and a jetty to swim from. All rooms with fan and private bathrooms with hot water, but this is irregular. New quiet annexe opposite.

E **Tayasal**, T7926-0568. Rooms of various sizes, fan, showers downstairs, some with private bath, roof terrace, very helpful, Tikal trips. Travel agency in reception.

E **Doña Martas**. For a different experience find **La Unión** restaurant and call Marta and Oscar who live across the water behind Flores T7926-1452, they will pick you up and take you to their house on the water's edge where a cool breeze blows away the mosquitoes.

Santa Elena *p368*

A **Casa de Elena**, Av 6y C2, just before the causeway, T7926-2238, reservaciones @casaelena.com A beautiful tiled staircase, rooms with cable TV, pool, restaurant 0630-2100.

A **Hotel del Patio Tikal**, Av 8y C2, T7926-0104. Clean, modern rooms with a/c, TV, expensive restaurant, beautiful pool and gym. Best booked as part of a package for cheaper rates.

D-F **San Juan**, close to the Catholic church, Av 6 towards Flores, T7926-0562, sanjuant@itelgua.com.gt Some newer rooms with a/c and TV, also older rooms, cheaper with shared bath, usually full of budget travellers. Credit cards accepted, also cash advances, exchanges US dollars and Mexican pesos and buys Belizean dollars. Public phone and parking.

Around Lake Petén Itzá *p368*

C-D **La Casa de Don David**, 20 m from the main road, El Remate, T7928-8469, www.lacasadedondavid.com. Clean and comfortable, but a little overpriced, all rooms with private bath, hot water costs more, great view from the terrace restaurant, cheap food, bike hire free. Transport to Tikal.

D-G **Hotel y Restaurante Mon Ami**, El Remate, T7928-8413, demonsb @hotmail.com Conservation-minded tours to Yaxhá and Nakum. Lovely new bungalows and hammocks for sleeping. English spoken. Restaurant 0700-2130, with wines and seriously cheap chicken, pastas and other dishes served.

E-G **La Casa Roja**, El Remate, T5909-6999. A red house with a tranquil, oriental feel. Rooms are under thatched roofs, with separate bathrooms in attractive stone and wood design. The rooms don't have doors but there are locked trunks. Hammock space and camping possible. Kayaks for rent and trips arranged.

F **La Casa Doña Tonita**, El Remate, T5701-7114, one of the most chilled out places along the shore, run by a friendly family. Shared bathroom, rooms and a dorm. Enormous portions of good food.

F **Sun Brezze Hotel**, on the corner, El Remate, T5209-6091. Little wooden rooms with views over the lake. Fans and *mosquiteros* in each room. Daily service to Tikal and other trips. Friendly.

Parque Nacional Tikal *p369*

In high season, book accommodation in advance. Take a torch: 24-hr electricity is not normally available.

AL-C **Jungle Lodge**, T2361-4098, junglelodge@junglelodge.guate.com. Not recommended, except for guided tours of the ruins (US$5).

A-B **Tikal Inn**, T/F7926-0065, hoteltikalinn @itelgua.com. Bungalows and rooms, hot water 1800-1900, electricity 0900-1600, 1800-2200, beautiful pool for guests' use only. Natural history tours at 0930, US$10, minimum 2 people, helpful.

A-E **Jaguar Inn**, T7926-0002, www.jaguartikal.com Full board or room only. Dormitory with 6 beds, US$10 per person, hammocks with nets and lockers, US$2.60, picnic lunch, US$1.30. Electricity 1800-2200, hot water in the morning or on request Mar-Oct and 0600-2100 Nov-Feb. Will store luggage.

Uaxactún *p373*

E **El Chiclero**, T7926-1095, chiclerocamp @ecotourism-adventure.com. Neat and clean, hammocks and rooms in a garden, also good food by arrangement (dinner US$5, breakfast US$3).

F **Posada Aldana**, T5801-2588, edeniaa@yahoo.com Clean white *casitas*, plus tent and hammock space behind **El Chiclero**. Run by a friendly family.

Laguna Yaxhá and around *p*

B **El Sombrero**, Laguna Yaxhá, T7926-5229, www.ecosombrero.com. Comfortable cabins and restaurant. The owner organizes riding trips. You can also camp for US$10.

D **Río Mopan Lodge**, Río Mopan, near Melchor de Mencos, T7926-5067, www.tikaltravel.com. Cool, clean rooms in flourishing gardens, with river views, restaurant (0700-2000 daily). Jungle and archaeological trips arranged.

Around Sayaxché *p374*

B **Posada Caribe**, T/F7928-6114, Comfortable cabañas with bathroom, shower and full board. Excursions to Aguateca by launch. Guide available.

Eating

Flores *p368, map p377*

ŦŦ-Ŧ **La Luna**. Serves refreshing natural lemonade and a range of fish, meat and vegetarian dishes. The restaurant has a beautiful courtyard with blue paintwork set under lush pink bouganvillaea, recommended. Closed Sun.

ŦŦ **La Unión**. Deceptive from the outside, this restaurant has a gorgeous thatched

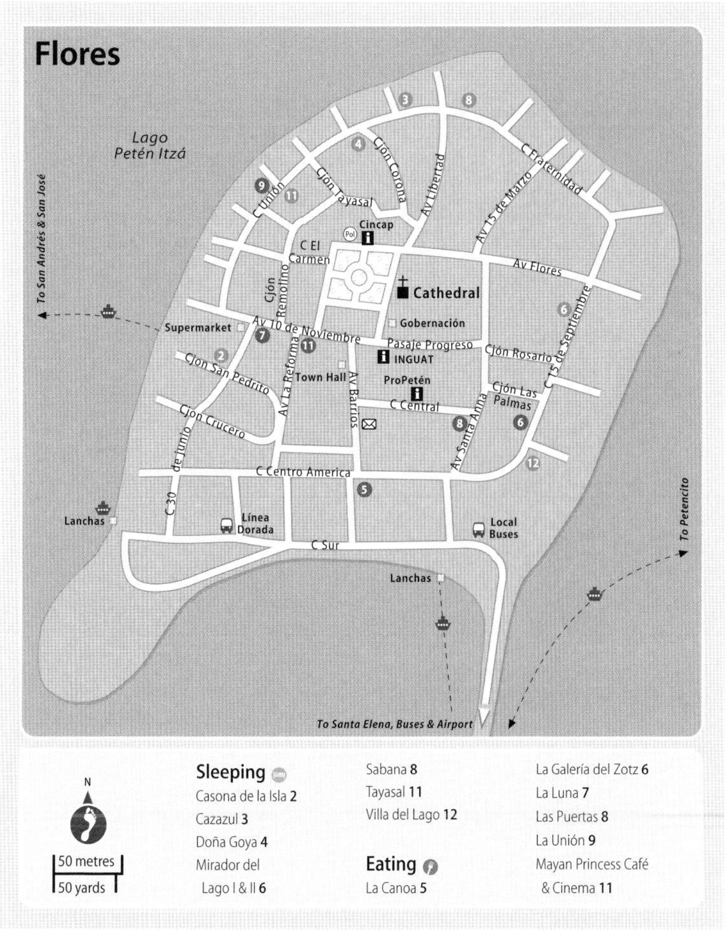

Flores

Lago Petén Itzá
To San Andrés & San José
C Unión
Cjón Tayasal
Cjón Corona
Av Libertad
C Fraternidad
Av 15 de Marzo
Cincap
C El Carmen
Cjón Remolino
Cathedral
Av Flores
Supermarket
Av 10 de Noviembre
Gobernación
Pasaje Progreso
Cjón Rosario
C 15 de Septiembre
INGUAT
Cjón San Pedrito
Town Hall
Av La Reforma
Av Barrios
ProPetén
C Central
Cjón Las Palmas
Cjón Crucero
Av Santa Anna
C 30 de Junio
C Centro America
Lanchas
Línea Dorada
Local Buses
C Sur
To Petencito
Lanchas
To Santa Elena, Buses & Airport

Sleeping
Casona de la Isla **2**
Cazazul **3**
Doña Goya **4**
Mirador del Lago I & II **6**
Sabana **8**
Tayasal **11**
Villa del Lago **12**

Eating
La Canoa **5**
La Galería del Zotz **6**
La Luna **7**
Las Puertas **8**
La Unión **9**
Mayan Princess Café & Cinema **11**

wooden terrace on the lake with great views. Try the fish. Recommended more for the setting than the food.

¶¶ **Mayan Princess Café and Cinema**. The most adventurous menu on the island including daily specials with an Asian flavour, relaxed atmosphere, bright coloured cloths on the tables. Internet and free films. Closed Sun.

¶ **La Canoa**. Good breakfasts (try the pancakes), dinners start at US$1.50, with good *comida típica*, very friendly owners.

¶ **La Galería del Zotz**. A wide range of food, delicious pizzas, good service and presentation, popular with the locals.

¶ **Las Puertas Café Bar**. Huge menu, with seriously cheap breakfasts and large pasta portions. Popular with travellers. Jackson Pollock paint effect on the walls, chilled atmosphere, games available. No food after 2300, closes at 2400. Cine Las Puertas opposite shows videos at 1930.

Santa Elena *p368*

¶ **El Petenchel**, C2 e/ Av 4 y 5. Vegetarian and meat dishes. Excellent breakfasts. Good value *menú del día*. Music and prompt service.

¶ **Restaurante Mijaro**, Av 6 e/ C 3y 4. Great filling breakfasts and a bargain *menú del día* at US$1.70, all under a thatched roofed in a roadside location.

Parque Nacional Tikal *p369*

¶ There are good-value *comedores* in the park: Comedor Tikal, Imperio Maya (opens 0530), La Jungla; the chicken is best at Imperio Maya. Also a restaurant in an annexe of the visitor centre.

Festivals and events

Lago Petén Itzá *p368, map p377*

12-15 Jan Petén *feria* in Flores.

1 Nov Holy Skull Procession in San José.

11-12 Dec Virgen de Guadalupe celebrations in Flores.

Activities and tours

Flores and Santa Elena *p368, map p377*

Dugouts or fibreglass canoes can be hired for about US$2 per hr to paddle yourself around Lake Petén Itza (ask at hotels). Check the dugouts for lake-worthiness. Swimming in the lake is not advised.

Tour operators

Backabush, Av Barrios, T5612-8678. Bicycle tours in the area.

Conservation Tours Tikal, C 15 de Septiembre, opposite Of Contable Tayasal, T7926-0670, lprinz@rarecenter.org. This organization, funded by UNESCO, employs people from Petén communities to take visitors to local sites. English spoken. Also jungle tours, birdwatching, horse treks and kayaking. 5% of profits go to conservation.

EcoMaya, C Centroamérica, T7926-0718, www.ecomaya.com Agency created by ProPetén to involve and benefit the local community, with tours to El Perú, El Mirador, Nakbé, El Zotz, Yaxhá, Dos Lagunas and Uaxactún. Also runs shuttles and sells bus and air tickets.

El Tigre, C Centroamérica, T7926-0527, rafaelandrade45@hotmail.com Very helpful, good flight deals.

Martsam Travel, C Centroamérica, T7926-0346, www.martsam.com Tours to El Zotz, El Mirador, Yaxhá and Nakum. Specialists in wildlife, ornithology and archaeology. Highly recommended. Also runs Ixchel Spanish school.

San Juan Travel Agency, Av 6, Sta Elena, T/F7926-2011, sanjuan@internetdetel gua.com.gt. Reliable tours to Tikal, US$50. Excursions to Ceibal, US$50, and Uaxactún, US$50, with Spanish-speaking guide. Also excellent service to Belize, US$20, and Chetumal, US$25. Don't buy public bus tickets here (see Transport, below).

Uaxactún *p373*

Tour operators

For guided walks around the ruins ask for any of the 13 trained guides, US$9.

Recommended is **Angela Fajardo**. For expeditions further afield, contact Elfido Aldana at **Posada Aldana** (see Sleeping). All tours include food, transport and guide. Neria Baldizón at **El Chiclero**, has high clearance pick-ups and plenty of experience in organizing trips to any site, US$195 per person to Río Azul.

Around Sayaxché *p374*

Tour operators

Viajes Don Pedro, on the river front, Sayaxché, T7928-6109. Launches to El Ceibal (US$32 for up to 3), Petexbatún and Aguateca (US$52 for up to 5), Dos Pilas (US$45 for small group). Trip possible by jeep in the dry season, Altar de los Sacrificios (US$97 min 2) and round trips to Yaxchilán for 3 days (US$390). Mon-Sat 0700-1800, Sun 0700-1200.

Transport

Flores and Santa Elena *p368, map p377*

Air

Be early for flights, as overbooking is common. **Tikal Jets** closes its check-in 45 mins before departure from Santa Elena. **Grupo Taca**, T7926-1238, leaves Guatemala City daily at 0640, 50 mins, returns 1620. **Tikal Jets**, T7926-0386, www.tikaljets.com, leaves the capital 0900 and 0630 Mon, Fri, Sat, returning 0730 and 1630; and at 0630 and 1730 on Sun, returning 1030 and 1630, journey time 30 mins. Also flights with **Tag**, T7926-0653, T2360-3038.

To **Cancún**, **Grupo Taca**, 0740. To **Belize City**, **Tropic Air/Maya Island Air**, T7926-0348, departs 0930 and 1530.

Boat

Lanchas leave from the corner of **Hotel Petén Esplendido** in Santa Elena; from C Sur in Flores; from behind **Hotel Santana**; and from the dock behind **Hotel Casona de Isla**.

Bus

Local Buses to Santa Elena, the airport or San Benito, all US$0.13, departing from the end of the causeway in Flores. For transport to **Tikal**, see p380. Any bus/minibus heading for Tikal can stop at **El Remate**, US$2-2.50, or take a bus for the Belize border and get off at El Cruce. Returning to **Flores**, there is a bus from El Remate at 0700, 0800, 0930, 1300 and 1400, US$0.80, or pick up any minibus heading south (a lot easier after 1300 when tourists are returning).

Transportes Pinita, at Hotel San Juan, Santa Elena, 0800-1700, T7926-0726, runs daily buses within Petén, including around the lake to **San Andrés**; the 1200 service continues to **Cruce dos Aguadas** and **Carmelita**, US$3, 3 hrs, for access to El Mirador, returning the following day at 0700. To **Uaxactún**, from Santa Elena 1300, via Tikal and El Remate, arriving 1600-1700, US$2.60, returning 0600. To **Sayaxché** from the market area with **Pinita** and **Rosío** 0500, 0700, 0800, 1000, 1300, 1500, US$1.95, 2 hrs. There are also *colectivos* from the new *colectivo* station, which leave when full. To **Melchor de Mencos** (Belize border, p251), 0500, 0800, 1000, US$2, 2 hrs, returning 1100, 1300, 1400, 1430. Also *colectivos*, 1½ hrs, US$2.

Long distance All long-distance buses leave from Santa Elena unless otherwise stated. Bus stops are on or just off Calle 4. Do not buy bus tickets to Guatemala City from the **San Juan Travel Agency**, which charges commission; buy direct from the bus companies.

To **Guatemala City**, **Autobuses del Norte (AND)**, T7926-3827, 1000 and 2100, US$27 one way, seniors and children 50% discount; **Línea Dorada**, office at C Sur, Flores, T7926-0528, www.lineadorada.com, daily 0500-2200, services depart from Santa Elena on the main drag, T7926-1788, at 1000 and 2100, 1st class, US$28, also at 2000, 2200, 2nd class, US$14, 8 hrs; **Fuente del Norte**, 18 buses 0630-1930, most US$8-10, 12 hrs, services at 2000, 2015, 2030, US$10.40, 8 hrs, service at 2100, US$17, 8 hrs; **Transportes Rosita** departs 1900, US$6.50, and 2000, US$9.75; **Rápidos** del Sur departs 2200, 2300, US$13 (take your own toilet paper).

If you are going only to **Poptún**, 2 hrs, US$2.60, or **Río Dulce**, US$7, 3½-4 hrs, make sure you do not pay the full fare to Guatemala City; you will probably have to take a 2nd-class bus, such as Fuente del Norte. To **Chiquimula**, with Transportes María Elena,1400, US$6.50, continuing to **Esquipulas**, 8 hrs, US$7.80; change at Chiquimula for services to El Florido (p347) and **Copán**; alternatively, take any bus to the capital and change at Río Hondo.

To **Belize City**, take a bus to Melchor de Mencos (see above) and wait for connecting services (if you catch the 0500 bus from Santa Elena you can be in Belize City by 1200). Also Línea Dorada at 0500, 0730, US$15, 4 hrs. In addition, there is a non-stop minibus service, with San Juan Travel Agency (see Activities and tours), at 0500 and 0730, from Santa Elena, US$20, 5 hrs, wake up call if you stay at San Juan Hotel, otherwise will collect from your hotel; this service terminates at the A&R Station in Belize for boats to the cayes; return service to Santa Elena departs Belize City at 1000 and 1600.

To Mexico Transportes Pinita to **Bethel**, 0500, 0900, 3½-4 hours, US$3.25, via La Libertad, for connections to La Tecnica and 20-min ferry, US$6.50, to the border at **Frontera Echeverría** (p149). From the border it is 4 hrs by bus to Palenque, US$5.50. To get to Palenque in 1 day, take the 0500 bus from Santa Elena. San Juan Travel Agency run a daily shuttle service to Palenque, 0500, US$30. Línea Dorada also ply this route for US$30, 0600, 7 hrs.

The alternative route to Mexico (Yucatán) is via Belize, with San Juan Travel Agency, 0500 to **Chetumal**, arriving 1300 (Mexican time), US$30, plus US$3.50 to leave Belize. Also Línea Dorada to Chetumal, 0500, US$21, 7 hrs.

Taxi

To **El Remate**, US$20; to **Tikal**, US$30 one way. Try Taxi Mayrely, T7926-1600.

Parque Nacional Tikal *p369*

From Santa Elena, San Juan Travel Agency minibuses leave hourly 0500-1000 and again at 1400; return 1230-1800, 1 hr, US$5 one way. Several other companies also run minibuses. Discounted seats are often available on a return bus. Minibuses also meet Guatemala City-Flores flights. You can also visit Tikal with a package tour from Guatemala City or Antigua; 1-day excursions from US$119 return (including flights and transfers), 2 days US$149.

Directory

Flores and Santa Elena *p368, map p377*

Banks Banquetzal, at the airport, cash or TCs only, open until 1700. In Flores, Banrural, next to the church. TCs only. Banco del Café, Santa Elena, best rates for Amex TCs. Banco Industrial, Visa ATM 24 hrs. The major hotels and travel agents change cash and TCs. There are other banks near the bus terminal. **Hospitals and clinics** Hospital Nacional, in San Benito, T7926-1333, open 24 hrs. Centro Médico Maya, Santa Elena, Dra Sonia de Baldizón, T7926-0714, speaks some English. Recommended. **Immigration** at the airport, T2475-1390. **Internet** Tikal Net, Santa Elena, US$3/hr, phone calls also. Flores Net, Flores, US$3/hr.
Post office In Flores and in Santa Elena.
Telephone Telgua in Santa Elena.
Language school Ixchel Spanish Academy, Cjón Central, T7926-3225, spanishacademy@martsam.com, 20 hrs a week plus homestay, US$175.
Laundry Lavandería Petenchel, US$3.20 per load, wash and dry. Open 0800-1900.

Around Lake Petén Itzá *p*

Language schools The Escuela Bio-Itzá, San José, T7928-8142, offers classes, homestay and camping (20 hrs per week with homestay US$175).

Index » *Mexico (M), Guatemala (G), Belize (B), Honduras (H). Entries in red are maps.*

Index

Advertisers' index

Credits

Footprint credits

Authors: Claire Boobbyer (Guatemala), Peter Hutchison (Belize, Mexico), additional Mexico information provided by Caroline Lascom
Editor: Sophie Blacksell
Deputy editor: Nicola Jones
Editorial assistant: Angus Dawson
Map editor: Sarah Sorensen
Picture editor: Claire Benison
Cover design: Robert Lunn

Publisher: Patrick Dawson
Editorial: Alan Murphy, Felicity Laughton, Laura Dixon, Sarah Thorowgood
Cartography: Robert Lunn, Claire Benison, Kevin Feeney, Angus Dawson, Thom Wickes, Esther Monzon
Advertising: Debbie Wylde
Finance and administration: Sharon Hughes, Elizabeth Taylor, Lindsay Dytham

Photography credits

Front cover: Alamy (Weavings, Santiago de Atitlán, Guatemala)
Inside: Alamy, Claire Boobbyer, Corel Professional Photos, David Hoey, Jamie Marshall, Photolibrary, Powerstock, Ron Mader, South American Pictures, James Sturke, Travel Ink, Lisa Young
Back cover: Alamy (Blue Hole, Belize)

Print

Manufactured in Italy by Printer Trento
Pulp from sustainable forests

Every effort has been made to ensure that the facts in this guidebook are accurate. However, travellers should still obtain advice from consulates, airlines etc about travel and visa requirements before travelling. The authors and publishers cannot accept responsibility for any loss, injury or inconvenience however caused.

Publishing information

Footprint Belize, Guatemala & Southern Mexico
1st edition

April 2005
ISBN 1 904777 28 7
CIP DATA: A catalogue record for this book is available from the British Library

Published by Footprint

6 Riverside Court
Lower Bristol Road
Bath BA2 3DZ, UK
T +44 (0)1225 469141
F +44 (0)1225 469461
discover@footprintbooks.com
www.footprintbooks.com

Distributed in the USA by

Publishers Group West

Neither the black and white nor colour maps are intended to have any political significance.